WELLNESS

Concepts and Applications

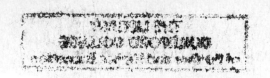

To the memory of our friend and colleague
Elijah Vance "Lige" Turman

WELLNESS

Concepts and Applications

David J. Anspaugh, P.E.D., Ed.D., CHES
Professor, Health, Physical Education, and Recreation
Memphis State University
Memphis, Tennessee

Michael H. Hamrick, Ed.D., CHES
Professor, Health, Physical Education, and Recreation
Memphis State University
Memphis, Tennessee

Frank D. Rosato, Ed.D.
Professor, Health, Physical Education, and Recreation
Memphis State University
Memphis, Tennessee

Second Edition

 Mosby

St. Louis Baltimore Boston Chicago London Madrid Philadelphia Sydney Toronto

Mosby
Dedicated to Publishing Excellence

Editor-in-Chief: James M. Smith
Editor: Vicki Malinee
Developmental Editor: Michelle Turenne
Project Manager: Carol Sullivan Wiseman
Production Editors: Linda McKinley and Catherine Schwent
Design Manager: Betty Schulz
Illustrators: Tandy and Associates and Donald O'Connor Graphic Studios
Design: Rokusek Design

Credits for all materials used by permission appear after the index.

SECOND EDITION
Copyright © 1994 by Mosby–Year Book, Inc.

Previous edition copyrighted 1991

Printed in the United States of America
Composition by The Clarinda Company
Printing/binding by Von Hoffmann Press, Inc.

Mosby–Year Book, Inc.
11830 Westline Industrial Drive
St. Louis, Missouri 63146

Library of Congress Cataloging in Publication Data
Anspaugh, David J.
    Wellness : concepts and applications / David J. Anspaugh, Michael
  H. Hamrick, Frank D. Rosato. — 2nd ed.
      p. cm.
    Includes index.
    ISBN 0-8016-7832-3
    1. Health.   2. Self-care, Health.   3. Medicine, Preventive.
  I. Hamrick, Michael H.   II. Rosato, Frank D.   III. Title.
  RA776.A57   1993
  613—dc20
                                                                  93-38587
                                                                      CIP

94 95 96 97 98 / 9 8 7 6 5 4 3 2

Preface

Wellness: Concepts and Applications is unique because it assumes that health is not a destination but a journey. Wellness is not a static condition but a continual balancing of the different dimensions of human needs—spiritual, social, emotional, intellectual, and physical. Because we are all responsible for our own growth in these areas, this book strives to emphasize the importance of self-responsibility. And because we know that knowledge alone stimulates change for very few people, the reader is challenged to be actively involved in the learning process by constantly assessing how the information presented affects lifestyle from a personal perspective.

Wellness: Concepts and Applications is neither a fitness book nor a personal health text. Instead this text is designed to help students gain knowledge and understanding in a variety of areas, with the goal being to take that information and use it to make behavioral changes that will have a positive impact on their lives. In many cases these changes are necessary if people are to develop the skills, attitudes, beliefs, and habits that will ultimately result in the highest possible level of health and wellness.

Audience

When the fitness/wellness concept appears in university courses and programs, it is usually a scaled-down model of the traditional personal health course or an upscale version of physical fitness courses. In some cases it is a hybrid of both personal health and fitness courses, with emphasis on self-participation in the medical marketplace. In terms of content, *Wellness: Concepts and Applications* is a hybrid because the physical components of wellness are blended with its many other components. However, caution will be exercised to avoid covering topics commonly found in personal health texts. The primary objectives of this text are to present cognitive health and wellness information appropriate for today's college students and to offer suggestions for their application. These suggestions consist of lifestyle behaviors over which people can exert some control. The emphasis is on self-responsibility, and this theme is implemented through a strong self-analysis and assessment component.

New Highlights to This Edition

Every chapter of *Wellness: Concepts and Applications* has been carefully updated. New chapters, features, and issues found in this edition are highlighted below.

Increased Coverage of Fitness

Each of the health-related components of fitness, including cardiorespiratory endurance, muscular strength and endurance, flexibility, and body composition, is now covered in its own separate chapter. Additional fitness laboratories and tests have also been added and are located in the Assessment Activities at the end of each chapter.

Chapter 3, "Cardiorespiratory Endurance," presents the guidelines for developing cardiorespiratory or aerobic fitness. The principles of aerobic fitness are identified and examined, and basic physiological changes that occur from training are discussed. Temperature regulation and mechanisms of heat loss are discussed with tips on how to safely exercise in different environmental conditions. Chapter 4, "Muscular Strength and Endurance," examines selected methods for developing muscular strength and endurance. The principles for developing these components are discussed and various exercises are illustrated using machine weights and free weights. A rationale for resistance training is presented, as are the health implications. Chapter 5, "Flexibility," discusses the components of flexibility, the types of stretching, and how to stretch safely. The chapter also provides information on how to lift properly to prevent injury. Chapter 7, "Body Composition" differentiates between obesity and overweight while presenting the health implications of obesity and regionally distributed fat. The chapter presents the different ways of measuring body composition as well as the principles and methods for achieving desirable body weight.

Updated Coverage of Nutrition

Chapter 6, "Forming a Plan for Good Nutrition," has been extensively revised to include the latest information on the dietary guidelines for Americans, the new food pyramid, suggestions to lower the risk of cancer, and the new food labeling laws that include reference daily intakes for essential vitamins and the daily reference values for fat, saturated fat, cholesterol, sodium, carbohydrates, potassium, and fiber. A discussion on vitamin supplements and antioxidants is also included.

Updated coverage of weight control

Chapter 8, "Overcoming the Diet and Weight Obsession," discusses current theories associated with the development of fat cells, weight gain, and obesity. Hazards associated with dieting in general and with popular fad diets are pointed out. The eating disorders bulimia and anorexia nervosa are also discussed. The chapter stresses that the positive effects of exercise on body composition and weight management is the most healthful solution for weight control. The chapter concludes with a detailed plan for lifetime management of weight control.

Updated Coverage of Additional Topics

Chapter 1, "Wellness and Fitness: Managing Lifestyle Change," presents the basic wellness model including the concepts of self-responsibility for enhancing quality of life. The benefits of high-level wellness are identified, and opportunities are provided to determine positive and negative behaviors in the quest for a higher quality of health. Steps to initiate lifestyle change are discussed. Chapter 2, "Cardiovascular Health and Wellness," has been completely revised to reflect the latest aspects of cardiovascular health, including prevention and treatment. For example, physical activity and longevity and the benefits of antioxidants are presented. The emphasis of the chapter is on those lifestyles that reduce the risk for cardiovascular disease. Chapter 9, "Coping With and Managing Stress," examines the factors that cause stress and the psychological effects of stress on the body. Activities are provided to help students identify their personal stressors and determine effective means for dealing with stress. This includes expanded coverage of relaxation techniques. Chapter 10, "Assuming Responsibility for Substance Abuse," provides information on tobacco products, cocaine, marijuana, and other drugs, including the potential negative effects of each. New discussions of the addictive personality and the nicotine patch are also included. Activities are provided to emphasize the importance of taking individual responsibility for substance use. Chapter 11, "Preventing Sexually Transmitted Diseases," provides the latest information on HIV, AIDS, chlamydia, herpes, and other diseases, with an emphasis on following safer sex practices. Chapter 12, "Impact of Lifestyle on Common Conditions," has been updated to include the timely topic of osteoporosis. Coverage of cancer has been expanded to include the health effects of tanning devices. New findings regarding the advantages of exercise as a preventive strategy are emphasized. The chapter continues to emphasize the role of lifestyle in the prevention of these conditions. Chapter 13, "Self-Responsibility in the Health-Care Market," discusses the importance of making wise decisions in the health-care market. New and expanded topics include self-care home medical test kits, sources of information, health insurance, and diagnostic tests. The chapter also provides guidelines for determining when, where, and how to choose health care wisely and includes suggestions for identifying information that can be trusted.

Revised Appendixes

Appendix A, "Lifestyle Assessment Inventory," should be completed at both the beginning and the end of the course. It will provide a picture of how current lifestyle patterns are shaping students' lives and provide a comparison to determine lifestyle improvements. Keep in mind that there are no right or wrong answers. The only useful answer is one that best reflects current practices. Appendix B, "Assessment Activity Scoresheet," is completed by filling in the first scores obtained from the Assessment Activities. The Assessment Activities can be retaken at the end of the course or at a later time to help form a comprehensive picture of how well the individual student is doing and the personal progress toward a higher quality of life. Appendix C, "Food Composition Tables," has been expanded to include more cereals, combination foods, and fast foods and also includes skim milk.

Content Highlights

Important features unique to *Wellness: Concepts and Applications* make it distinct from other texts.

Balanced approach: Unlike other approaches that emphasize only physical fitness as a major route to wellness, *Wellness: Concepts and Applications* provides a balanced presentation of the health benefits of exercise, diet, and cardiovascular wellness, along with the management of lifestyle change and consumer responsibility to achieve lifetime wellness.

Complete lifestyle decision-making information: Along with Assessment Activities that help apply the content, coverage of substance use, sexually transmitted diseases, and chronic health conditions is provided to enable and encourage responsible student decision-making.

Consumer-oriented: Chapter 13, "Self-Responsibility in the Health-Care Market," offers information to help students become wise consumers.

Interdisciplinary author team: Two health educators and a fitness educator presently teaching wellness courses have combined their expertise to provide the most balanced presentation possible.

Full-Color: A full-color format is used throughout the photographs, line drawings, and design of the text to increase visual impact and to enhance the teaching-learning process.

Pedagogical Highlights

Wellness: Concepts and Applications uses a variety of learning aids to enhance student comprehension.

Key Terms: The most important terms for student retention have been boldfaced in the text for easy identification.

Chapter Objectives: These are introduced at the beginning of each chapter. They assist the student in identifying the chapter's key topics. Accomplishing the objectives indicates fulfillment of the chapter's intent.

Chapter Summaries: These identify the major parts of the chapter and reinforce the chapter objectives.

Action Plan for Personal Wellness: These are provided at the end of the chapters to help students identify plans to implement change based on knowledge gained from the chapter.

Review Questions: Questions are provided to help students review and analyze material for overall understanding.

References: Accurate and current documentation is provided at the end of the chapters.

Annotated Readings: Additional current resources are provided for students to obtain further information.

Assessment Activities: Each chapter concludes with at least two Assessment Activities to help students apply the content learned in the chapter to their own personal decision-making. The text is perforated for easy removal of the Assessment Activities.

Appendixes:

▶ Lifestyle Assessment Inventory—Students complete the inventory at the beginning and end of the course to determine their lifestyle improvements.

▶ Assessment Activity Scoresheet—Students enter their scores from the Assessment Activities. The Assessment Activities can then be retaken at a later time to determine how well they are doing in moving toward a higher quality of life.

▶ Food Composition Tables—The nutritive values of common food items are provided. These values assist students in completing Assessment Activities in Chapter 6.

Glossary: A comprehensive glossary is provided at the end of the text that includes all key terms as well as additional terms used in the text. In addition, cross-references to the text are provided after each definition.

Supplements

An extensive package is available to the adopters of *Wellness: Concepts and Applications.* The package has been developed to assist the instructor in obtaining maximum benefit from the text. Each ancillary has been thoroughly reviewed to provide the highest quality possible. These features, which will enhance the appeal of the text, are the following:

Instructor's Manual and Test Bank: Each chapter begins with a brief overview of the content followed by a list of the objectives for that chapter. A detailed lecture outline and additional class activities have been developed for each chapter. Each chapter concludes with a resource section, including relevant media, software, and organization sources, and additional annotated readings. The Test Bank includes more than 1400 multiple choice, true-false, matching, and essay questions. All test items have been thoroughly checked for accuracy, clarity, and range of difficulty by instructors who also served as reviewers for the text. A special note of thanks must also be given to Beverly Zeakes of Radford University for her attention to detail in reviewing the Test Bank. The manual concludes with 65 full-page transparency masters of helpful illustrations and charts.

Computerized Test Bank

This software provides a unique combination of user-friendly aids that enable the instructor to select, edit, delete, or add questions as well as construct and print tests and answer keys. The computerized Test Bank package is available to qualified adopters of the text for the IBM and Macintosh microcomputers.

Overhead Transparency Acetates: A total of 54 of the text's most important illustrations, diagrams, tables, and charts are available as acetate transparencies. Attractively designed in full-color, these useful tools facilitate learning and classroom discussion and were chosen specifically to help explain difficult concepts. This package is also available to qualified adopters of the text.

Laboratory Activity Software

For an additional charge, your students can also receive laboratory activities on disk. Please consult your Mosby sales representative for further details.

Acknowledgments

The authors with to express their heartfelt thanks to Susan Bingham and Susan Hunter for their support, research, and typing of the manuscript. Although unstated at times, their patience and perseverance have always been appreciated.

We also wish to thank the reviewers, whose contributions have added significantly to the text. To the following, a grateful acknowledgment of their expertise and assistance:

For the Second Edition:

Joel Barton III
Lamar University

Mary Eagan
University of Illinois at Chicago

Mimi Frank
California State University
  at Dominguez Hills

Rick Guyton
University of Arkansas
  at Fayetteville

Vicki Kloosterhouse
Oakland Community College

Rebecca Rutt Leas
Clarion University

John McIntosh
Shoals Community College

Kenneth Sparks
Cleveland State University

Laurel Talabere
Capital University

For the First Edition:

Pat Barrett
Radford University

Wilson Campbell
Northeast Louisiana University

Arlene Crosman
Linn-Benton Community College

Betty Edgley
Oklahoma State University

Mary Mahan
Miami-Dade Community College

Eva W. McGahee
North Georgia College

Brenda Obert
University of Maine-Farmington

Glen J. Peterson
Lakewood Community College

Russell F. Smiley
Normandale Community College

John G. Smith
Long Beach City College

Rod Smith
Clark College

James A. Streater, Jr.
Armstrong State College

Michael L. Teague
University of Iowa

Luke E. Thomas
Northeast Louisiana University

Gary L. Wilson
The Citadel

A sincere word of thanks to Jim Smith and Vicki Malinee for their help in ensuring that the conceptualization of this project became a reality. Sincere appreciation must also be expressed to the excellent production staff at Mosby: Linda McKinley, Catherine Schwent, Carol Wiseman, and Betty Schulz. Finally, a special tribute is due to Michelle Turenne for caring so much that the ultimate product be the best product possible. Her judgment, creativity, and refining of the text have added immeasurably to the project.

David J. Anspaugh
Michael H. Hamrick
Frank D. Rosato

Contents in Brief

Contents

Wellness and Fitness: Managing Lifestyle Change

Key terms

behavioral contract

health

health promotion

health-behavior gap

health-promoting
behaviors

locus of control

preventive health
behaviors

self-efficacy

self-help

wellness

Objectives

After completing this chapter you will be able to:

▷ Define health and wellness.

▷ Describe the components of wellness.

▷ Describe the concepts associated with making wellness decisions.

▷ Discuss some of the underlying assumptions of lifestyle change.

▷ Explain the advantages and disadvantages of various approaches to lifestyle change.

▷ Describe basic principles of lifestyle management.

▷ Formulate a self-help plan for lifestyle change.

Today, the five leading causes of death in the United States are cardiovascular disease, cancer, cerebrovascular disease, accidents, and chronic obstructive pulmonary disease. These conditions accounted for 76% of the number of deaths in the United States in 1990[1] and show the dangers of negative lifestyle choices.

Traditionally, if an individual displayed no disease symptoms, that individual was considered "healthy." This concept changed in the 1940s, when the World Health Organization (WHO) proposed that health was "a state of physical, mental, and social well-being and not merely the absence of disease or infirmity."[2] Although this definition was an expansion of previous concepts, it still viewed health as primarily a static condition and limited the human potential to affect health. A better current definition of **health** is "a continuous balancing of the physical, emotional, social, intellectual, and spiritual components of an individual to produce happiness and a higher quality of existence." This definition indicates that health is not static and that the potential for change is always present. Figure 1-1 depicts the way health moves along a continuum from optimal health to premature death. An individual's position on this continuum is always subject to change and is affected by many factors, including physical health, activity level, nutritional patterns, personal demands, career goals, time of year, and effectiveness in managing stress.

The direction you move on the continuum is largely determined by the activities you pursue and your attitudes toward these activities. These activities and attitudes can prevent illness and promote health or can destroy peace of mind and physical well-being. Because your behaviors are intrinsic to health, you must learn to assume responsibility for your health by developing the skills necessary to improve it.

Wellness means engaging in attitudes and behaviors that enhance quality of life and maximize personal potential. Although wellness implies working toward a highly developed level of health, it does not mean that an individual will make the best choice in every situation or that "perfect wellness" is achievable. Wellness emphasizes the need to take responsibility for engaging in behaviors that develop optimal health. The ongoing process of wellness requires daily decision making in nutrition, stress management, physical fitness, preventive health care, emotional health, and other aspects of health.

In the past, medicine approached health from a different perspective. It neither encouraged participation in activities that educated people about chronic conditions and diseases nor reduced the incidence of these diseases. Instead, it attempted to repair the consequences of disease without eliminating the causes. **Health promotion** efforts help people change their lifestyles and thereby move toward a higher state of wellness.[3] Wellness requires individuals seek ways to prevent, delay, or diminish the effects of chronic or disabling conditions. People choose to develop a sound diet, a sufficient exercise program, methods of managing stress, and a regular schedule of medical check-ups. They can also choose to reduce or eliminate the use of drugs, tobacco, and alcohol. The rest of this text provides information and suggests health-promoting activities to help people accept the personal challenge of wellness.

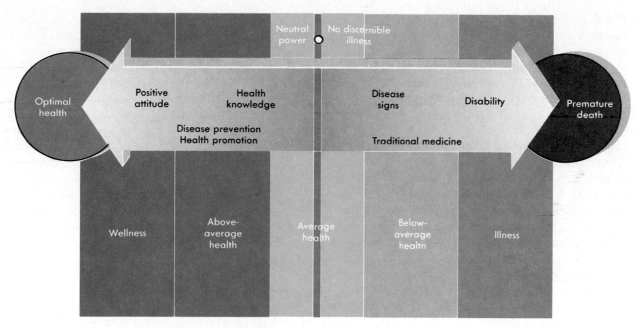

FIGURE 1-1 The health continuum.

Components of Wellness

Achieving a high level of wellness requires constant balance and maintenance of certain components (Figure 1-2):

▶ Spiritual—the belief in some force that unites human beings: This force can include nature, science, religion, or a higher power. It also includes your morals, values, and ethics. Everyone has a personal perception of spirituality. The spiritual component provides meaning and direction in life and enables you to grow, learn, and meet new challenges. Optimal spirituality is your ability to discover, articulate, and act on your basic purpose in life.[4] The spiritual dimension of wellness is different from religion. Spirituality is related to religious precepts but does not adhere to any religious structure. Religious affiliation may enhance the personal spiritual dimension.[5] Spirituality has been defined as that "which is involved in contracting the divine within the Self or self."[6] From the wellness perspective, spirituality is the quest for a higher quality of life.

▶ Social—the ability to interact successfully with people and the environment: Social health is the ability to develop and maintain intimacy with others and to have respect and tolerance for those with different opinions and beliefs.

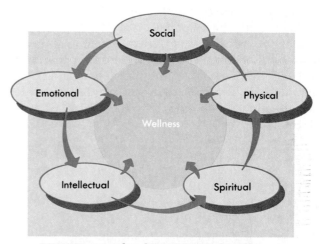

FIGURE 1-2 The dimensions of wellness.

▶ Emotional—the ability to control stress and to express emotions appropriately and comfortably: Emotional health is the ability to recognize and accept feelings and to not be defeated by setbacks and failures.

▶ Intellectual—the ability to learn and use information effectively for personal, family, and career development: Intellectual wellness means striving for continued growth and learning to deal with new challenges effectively.

▶ Physical—the ability to carry out daily tasks, develop cardiovascular fitness, maintain adequate nutrition and proper body fat level, and avoid abusing drugs and alcohol or using tobacco products: In general, physical health is an investment in positive lifestyle habits.

Personal environment is not a direct component of wellness but does influence quality of life. The five primary components of wellness can be enhanced or diminished according to your immediate environment. For example, people who are subject to physical or verbal abuse at home need energy to protect themselves; this energy could be used to develop a wellness lifestyle. In contrast, people who feel loved at home can direct this energy into developing themselves to their highest potential. For people to achieve their highest potential, they must feel safe. Personal environment includes everything that you learn and perceive. Only genetic factors are excluded.

These five components of wellness overlap, and factors in one component often directly affect the factors in another. Some factors are under the individual's direct control, and some are not. About 53% of the factors influencing quality of life can be affected by the lifestyle of the individual (Figure 1-3). Of the factors affecting quality of life, 21% are environmental, meaning they involve relationships and interaction with family, friends, and the community, and 10% are affected by the physicians and healthcare facilities available.[7] Altogether, 84% of the factors affecting health are within the control of the individual.

Hypothetically, 16% of the factors affecting health are beyond the individual's control. This 16% consists of the genes and hereditary tendencies received from the parents. However, if medical history indicates a family predisposition toward a particular disease such as heart disease, the health decisions that an individual makes can delay the onset, minimize the effects, or possibly prevent the disease from developing.

For example, the effects of a genetic predisposition to heart disease can be minimized significantly if the individual chooses to exercise, to follow proper nutrition guidelines, and to not smoke. Preventing disease is not always possible, but the choices you make do affect your health and quality of life.

Wellness involves working on all aspects of the model, not emphasizing just one or two areas. If obvious issues are handled in a positive manner, less overt issues will be handled in a healthier manner. For example, learning to control daily stress levels from a physiological perspective helps to maintain the emotional stamina needed to handle a crisis situation.

Breslow identified the following lifestyle habits that seemed to be associated with good health and longevity[8]:

▶ Sleeping 7 to 8 hours a night
▶ Eating breakfast regularly
▶ Never or rarely eating between meals
▶ Staying at or near the ideal weight for an individual's height
▶ Never smoking
▶ Drinking alcohol moderately or not at all
▶ Exercising regularly

In a 9 year follow-up of the above study, five of the seven health habits were found to contribute to lower mortality (the incidence of death), morbidity (the incidence of disease), and higher quality of life:

▶ Maintaining normal weight
▶ Having never smoked cigarettes
▶ Drinking alcohol in moderation
▶ Exercising regularly
▶ Sleeping up to 8 hours

This list is far from inclusive; for example, medical services, physical environment, and social interactions include factors that also affect quality of life, but everyday activities form the basis for the other decisions an individual makes. The results show that you can change your quality of life with positive health choices.[9,10] The more wellness activities an individual engages in (unless obsessive behaviors begin to occur), the more positive the results.

The chance of premature death can be reduced

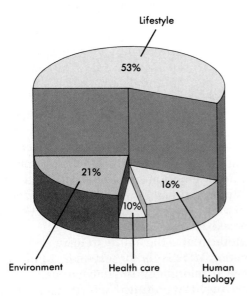

Lifestyle

53%

21%

10%

16%

Environment   Health care   Human biology

FIGURE 1-3 Influences on determining quality of life.

significantly by following a wellness lifestyle. Deaths associated with heart disease have been reduced by 30% in the last 15 years. This decline has been attributed directly to the reduction of smoking among men, decreased intake of dietary fat, increased exercise, and control of body weight. These adjustments incorporated healthy lifestyle changes.[11]

Why Wellness?

Assuming responsibility for a person's own health requires forethought and effort. *Why* should a person undertake this effort? First, many of the 10 leading causes of death are lifestyle-related diseases (Table 1-1). People in the United States have become victims of high-fat, high-salt, high-sugar, and low-fiber diets. This situation has been complicated by stress, lack of exercise, smoking, and the use of alcohol and drugs. Among younger Americans, accidents remain the leading killer. Particularly disturbing is that many of the accidents are alcohol and drug related.

The number one killer for men and women is heart disease. The American Heart Association (AHA) reports that more than 69 million Americans have some form of cardiovascular disease and that 1.5 million of these people will experience a heart attack: One half of these will be fatal.

The second leading cause of death in the United States is cancer, a disease with no age limits. Cancer is responsible for the death of more children ages 3 to 14 than any other disease. In 1992 more than 91,130,000 people were diagnosed as having cancer, and approximately 520,000 people died from the disease. This is a death rate of about 1400 deaths a day from cancer or one out of every five deaths in the United States. Medical costs for cancer were estimated to be $710.4 billion in 1990.[12]

Aside from the risk of disease, an estimated 15% of the gross national product (GNP) will be spent on health care in the early 1990s.[13] These costs reflect lost productivity and an increase in business costs, which are passed to the consumer. The overall annual cost of health care in the United States has skyrocketed from $50 billion to $500 billion in the last 20 years. In some states the cost of insurance for a family of four has risen by 400% since 1980.[14]

To contain costs, some businesses have stopped hiring smokers or overweight individuals. Some businesses and corporations offer health-promotion programs in nutrition education, weight management, stress reduction, and exercise.[15] These measures help employees reach their potential while cutting health-care costs for the company.

Enhancing the quality of life for Americans is a priority for the United States. Since 1987, the Public Health Service of the Department of Health and Human Services has led an effort to formulate the national disease-prevention and health-promotion objectives for the year 2000. These objectives are intended to increase the quality of life of the nation's people. Figure 1-4 contains a list of these proposed objectives.[15]

Benefits of High-Level Wellness

Because wellness is a daily striving toward being the best that a person can be, it demands commitment and involves regular exercise, proper nutrition, maintenance of optimal body composition, awareness of personal needs and efforts to fulfill these needs in a positive manner, and overall healthy behavior. Although a wellness lifestyle appears difficult, the alternative is more difficult because it results in more illness, depression, premature death, decreased quality of life, diminished sense of fulfillment, and diminished satisfaction with life. People also improve the way they look and feel while on the journey toward wellness. Figure 1-5 lists the benefits of wellness.

The biggest benefit of wellness is the attitude that helps each person to see life's possibilities and to work toward the ones that are the most personally fulfilling.

TABLE 1-1 Estimated Number of Deaths From the 10 Leading Causes

1. Heart disease	767,400
2. Cancer	488,240
3. Cerebrovascular diseases	150,300
4. Accidents	97,500
5. Chronic obstructive pulmonary disease	81,960
6. Pneumonia and influenza	77,330
7. Diabetes mellitus	39,610
8. Suicide	30,260
9. Chronic liver disease, such as cirrhosis	26,080
10. Atherosclerosis	23,700

Figure 1-4   Health Objectives for the United States for the Year 2000

▶ Increase to at least 60% the proportion of people age 6 and older who participate in moderate physical activities three or more days per week for 20 or more minutes per session

▶ Increase to at least 30% the proportion of people age 6 and older who participate in vigorous physical activities that promote the development and maintenance of cardiorespiratory fitness three or more days per week for 20 or more minutes per session

▶ Increase to at least 50% the proportion of people age 6 and older who regularly perform physical activities that maintain muscular strength, muscular endurance, and flexibility

▶ Reduce the number of overweight people (ages 20 to 74 years) to a prevalence of less than 20%

▶ Reduce the number of overweight adolescents (ages 12 to 17 years) to a prevalence of less than 15%

▶ Increase to at least 75% the proportion of overweight people age 12 and older who have adopted sound dietary practices combined with physical activity to achieve weight reduction

▶ Increase to at least 80% the proportion of people age 6 and older who know that regular exercise reduces the risk of heart disease, helps maintain appropriate body weight, reduces the symptoms of depression and anxiety, and enhances self-esteem

▶ Increase to at least 25% the proportion of people age 6 and older who can correctly identify the frequency and duration of exercise thought to promote cardiorespiratory fitness most effectively

▶ Increase to at least 65% the proportion of primary-care providers who assess and counsel their patients on the frequency, duration, type, and intensity of each patient's physical activity as part of a thorough evaluation and treatment program

▶ Increase to at least 50% the proportion of children and adolescents in grades 1 through 12 who participate in daily school physical education

▶ Increase to at least 70% the proportion of physical education teachers who spend 30% or more of class time on skills and activities that promote lifetime participation in physical activity

▶ Increase the proportion of companies offering employer-sponsored fitness programs as follows:
Companies with 50 to 99 employees: 20%
Companies with 100 to 249 employees: 35%
Companies with 250 to 749 employees: 45%
Companies with 750 or more employees: 80%

▶ Increase to at least 40% the proportion of people age 6 and older who participated in the physical-activity programs of at least one community organization within the past year

▶ Increase the number of community swimming pools; hiking, biking, and fitness-trail miles; and park and recreation open-space acres to at least one pool per 25,000 people, one trail mile per 10,000 people, and four acres of developed open space per 1000 people (or one managed acre per 250 people)

▶ Increase to at least 30% the proportion of life insurers that offer lower individual premiums to people who exercise regularly and maintain a physically active lifestyle

▶ Increase to at least 50% the proportion of school physical education classes that students spent being physically active, preferably engaged in lifetime physical activities

▶ Reduce dietary fat intake to an average of 30% of total calories and average saturated fat intake to less than 10% of total calories among people age 2 and older

▶ Increase complex carbohydrate and high-fiber foods in the diets of adults to five or more daily servings for vegetables and fruits and six or more daily servings for grain products

▶ Increase to at least 50% the proportion of overweight people age 12 and older who have adopted sound dietary practices combined with regular physical activity to attain an appropriate body weight

▶ Reduce deaths among people aged 15 through 24 years caused by alcohol-related motor vehicle crashes to no more than 18 per 100,000 people

▶ Reduce the initiation of cigarette smoking of youth so no more than 15% have become regular cigarette smokers by age 20

▶ Reduce smokeless tobacco use by males age 12 through 24 years to a prevalence of no more than 4%

▶ Increase to at least 90% the proportion of sexually active, unmarried people aged 19 years and younger who use contraception, especially combined-method contraception that effectively prevents pregnancy and provides protection against disease

Figure 1-5   Benefits of Wellness

- Improves cardiovascular system
- Increases muscle tone, strength, flexibility, and endurance, resulting in improved physical appearance
- Decreases risk of developing or dying from chronic diseases and accidents
- Decreases recovery time after injury, illness, and childbirth
- Regulates and improves overall body function
- Helps prevent some forms of diabetes
- Increases the ability to cope with stress and resist depression
- Increases the energy level and job productivity and decreases absenteeism
- Delays the aging process and decreases recovery time after injury or illness
- Improves awareness of personal needs and the ways to meet them
- Increases the ability to communicate emotions to others and to act assertively rather than aggressively or passively
- Supplies the body with proper nutrition
- Expands and develops intellectual abilities from a cognitive base and applies these abilities to their fullest extent in society
- Acts from an internal locus of control
- Learns to view life's difficulties as challenges and opportunities rather than overwhelming threats
- Develops self-confidence and ability to reach out to, understand, and care about others

Aerobics is one of many activities to enhance cardio-respiratory endurance.

Health-Related Fitness

To achieve some protection against the chronic conditions, such as cardiovascular disease, cancer, musculoskeletal conditions, digestive disorders, and stress, people need to strive for a lifestyle conducive to high-level wellness. Primary to living a positive lifestyle are the areas referred to as *health-related fitness*. Health-related fitness is the possession of various physical attributes that reduce the probability of disease and are vital to the quality of life. The components consist of cardiovascular endurance, muscular endurance, muscular strength, flexibility, and body composition.

Cardiovascular endurance refers to the heart and circulatory system's ability to provide adequate amounts of oxygen to the cells to meet the demands of prolonged physical activity. This is the best physiological measure of total body endurance. *Muscular endurance* (see Chapter 3) is the ability to exert repetitive muscular force. *Muscular strength* (see Chapter 4) is the maximal force that a muscle can exert in a single contraction. *Flexibility* (see Chapter 5) is the ability of a given joint to move through its full range of motion. *Body composition* (see Chapter 7) refers to the amount of lean body tissue versus fat tissue.

The Wellness Challenge

The key to striving for high-level wellness is motivation. No single principle or incident can provide the stimulus necessary to institute change and maintain positive lifestyle habits.

To make beneficial changes, you need to understand the many influences that create individual behavior. The *family* initiates health habits and outlooks. Children do not begin to brush their teeth because of a concern for dental care but because their parents insist on it. *Social pressure* becomes increasingly important as children age. All people are influenced by the desire and need to belong or to act like someone they admire. Adolescents and teenagers are especially susceptible to wanting to "fit in," sometimes in a way that harms their health. For example, a friend or family member who smokes may influence a youngster's decision to begin to smoke.

A significant contribution to accepting the challenge of wellness is the knowledge and attitudes assimilated during a lifetime. To change their health habits, people must internalize information and consider it valuable. Unfortunately, knowledge alone is not enough to bring about change. The discrepancy between knowing what is good for health and doing it is the **health-behavior gap.** People know that they should wear their seat belts and that they should not smoke, yet many people do not buckle up and continue to use tobacco products. For change to occur, the person's belief system must be affected.

An *attitude* is a predisposition for action; that is, what people believe and value as having importance is what they are most likely to pursue. To build a sound and accurate knowledge base, people need to consider the following factors:

▶ Based on the information, is the person at risk for negative lifestyle consequences?

▶ How high a risk exists if a decision is made *not* to institute change?

▶ If a lifestyle change is made, what are the benefits or advantages?

People are motivated by what they value. For some people, motivation is in the form of attitudes (values) concerning the desire to look better, feel better, or be more self-reliant. The more highly a health benefit is valued, the greater the chance of making and adhering to the change. Support in the form of compliments from friends and family certainly helps to provide motivation and reinforcement. However, for the challenge of wellness to be accepted for a lifetime, changes must eventually be made based on an internalized desire to make that difference. The ability to achieve any health change must result from a personal, ongoing goal and not from a desire to please or impress another person. If people engage in wellness activities because the activities are important to them, the wellness challenge has been accepted.

Accepting the Wellness Challenge

Understanding the concept of **locus of control** is important to be successful in the quest for improved quality of life. An individual's locus of control may be either internal or external. When people view problems concerning their health or other parts of their lives as generally "out of their control" (that is, they view themselves as being at the mercy of other people, places, and events), they have an *external locus of control.* On the other hand, people who view their own behaviors as having a major effect, who feel that they are at least partially the "masters of their fate," and who recognize that they can change

Figure 1-6   Improvements in Preventive Health Behaviors

According to a survey on preventive health behaviors conducted by Louis Harris and Associates, Americans showed improvement in several important areas:

▶ The proportion of adults who say they smoke cigarettes has fallen to 26%. This is the lowest smoking rate ever registered in a Harris survey measuring this trend and is 15% lower than it was in the 1970s.

▶ Approximately 5% of adults reported using recreational drugs. This rate represents a 4% decrease from 1984. The biggest drop in drug use is among young adults.

▶ The majority of people who have tried to lose weight use measures such as gaining more self-control (77%), cutting down on sugar (75%), and cutting down on red meat (67%).

▶ Many people have made progress in avoiding a high-cholesterol diet. Approximately 48% of adults, up 6% from 1983 and 1987, say they "try a lot" to avoid eating too many high-cholesterol foods.

▶ The proportion of American adults who frequently walk for exercise has increased. Of those surveyed, 52% say they had walked at least several times a week during the month before the survey.

the course of their health have an *internal locus of control.* People with an internal locus of control are more likely to succeed in wellness activities because they assume the necessary responsibility for their actions.

Another vital concept in a wellness lifestyle is **self-efficacy.**[16,17] Self-efficacy refers to peoples' belief in their ability to accomplish a specific task or behavior. Perhaps the most important influence in determining success of a wellness plan is people's perceptions that they can complete it. Although the support of others is encouraging, success is likely to require generating a personal sense of competence. Self-efficacy is not earned, inherited, or acquired; it is something you bestow on yourself.

Self-efficacy suggests that people's beliefs in their ability to perform specific behaviors influences the following[18,19]:

▶ Their choice of behavior and the situations that will be avoided or attempted, such as to reduce use of drugs, alcohol, or cigarettes; to initiate an exercise regimen; or to practice relaxation

▶ The effort they will expend participating in a specific task (Often, more energy is devoted to a task, such as brushing and flossing teeth, when the individual perceives that it will be successful.)

▶ How long a person will persist with a task, such as maintaining an exercise program, even when facing difficulties

▶ Emotional reactions, such as anxiety (Negative emotions may be aroused when an individual is confronted with the threat of failure.)

People define their ability to succeed at various tasks in the following four ways[20,21]:

▶ By actually performing or accomplishing the task

▶ By seeing others perform or accomplish the task without adverse effects

▶ Through verbal persuasion

▶ Through stressful or taxing experiences or circumstances that arouse the emotions

A strong sense of efficacy through healthy behavior is essential for self-regulation.[22] For high-level wellness to be achieved, individuals must see themselves as successful and believe that they can accomplish a task. Self-efficacy establishes behavior leading to high-level wellness. Self-efficacy links knowing what to do and actually accomplishing the task.

Lifestyle Change: A Matter of Choice

Most people believe that they control their lifestyle. According to a survey,[23] almost three fourths of people believe that if they eat right, do not smoke, and get regular checkups, they have a good chance of preventing cancer. An even larger number, more than 80%, believed that they can significantly reduce their chances of having a heart attack. This has motivated many Americans, especially older Americans, to work toward improved health and well-being (see Figure 1-2). Older Americans are also more likely to engage in **preventive health behaviors,** which are health practices that promote wellness and prevent or reduce morbidity and mortality (Figure 1-6). Although the trend toward healthy living is encouraging, improvement is needed among college-age students.

In a recent study, comparisons of health behaviors by age groups led to the following conclusion: "While those aged 65 or more have the best overall records for practicing good health and safety behavior, change for the better is being led by those in the middle years. And we still have not found the way to motivate young adults to start good health behavior."[23]

The ultimate decision on lifestyle depends on the individual.

A Self-Help Plan

A **self-help** approach assumes that individuals can manage their lifestyle changes and can learn to control those features in the environment that are detrimental to health. In other words, expensive, long-term, professional help is not a prerequisite for everyone trying to make a lifestyle change. However, a self-help approach takes time and thought devoted to planning. Successful lifestyle change is almost impossible to achieve without a plan. The self-help plan that follows applies principles of behavior management and should turn your health goals into reality.

First, take an inventory. The first step in any lifestyle-change program is to evaluate personal health habits and practices. A good way to start is simply to make a list of your **health-promoting behaviors,** things you do to maintain or improve your level of wellness (Figure 1-7). Make another list of *health-inhibiting behaviors,* things you do that may

Figure 1-7   Examples of Health-Promoting Behaviors

Specific Behaviors Conducive to Good Health

▶ I avoid the extremes of too much or too little exercise.
▶ I get an adequate amount of sleep.
▶ I avoid adding sugar and salt to my food.
▶ I include 15 to 20 g of fiber in my diet each day.
▶ I plan my diet to ensure consumption of an adequate amount of vitamins and minerals.
▶ I brush and floss my teeth after eating.
▶ I avoid driving under the influence of alcohol or drugs.
▶ I drive within the speed limit.
▶ I wear my seat belt whenever traveling in an automobile.
▶ I avoid the use of tobacco.
▶ I consume fewer than two alcoholic drinks per day.
▶ I know the instructions provided with any drug I take.
▶ I do my part to promote a clean and safe environment.
▶ I feel positive and enthusiastic about my life.
▶ I can express my feelings of anger.
▶ I can say "no" without feeling guilty.
▶ I engage in activities that promote a feeling of relaxation.
▶ I am able to develop close, intimate relationships.
▶ I am interested in the views of others.
▶ I am satisfied with my study habits.
▶ I am satisfied with my spiritual life.
▶ I am tolerant of the values and beliefs of others.

be detrimental to your health (see Assessment Activity 1-1). If your lists are specific and identify behaviors that relate to wellness in its broadest sense (that is, the physical, social, emotional, and psychological aspects of health), comparing the two should give insight and information about your lifestyle.

Detailed, comprehensive lifestyle questionnaires, such as the one that accompanies this text (see Appendix A), can provide even more information about specific health practices and behavioral tendencies that can be targeted for change. Many of these questionnaires are similar to those you might complete for your physician. Regardless of the tool you use, remember that the goal is to learn more about yourself.

Two reasonable questions to ask at this point are "Which behaviors present the greatest threat to my health?" and "Which behaviors should be targeted first for change?" The answer to the second question is strictly individual and depends on the frequency and intensity of various behaviors, genetic predisposition to certain health problems, overall health profile, personal motivation, and perhaps the answer to the first question. The first question can be answered by referring to Figure 1-8, which lists 21 health-promoting behaviors in increasing importance as rated by a panel of public health experts.[23] Each activity has an assigned weighted score based on a 10-point scale indicating its importance in preventing disease and promoting health. Smoking, with a score of 9.78, is viewed as having the greatest effect on health. Getting 7 to 8 hours of sleep each night, with a score of 6.71, has the least effect on health. However, a low score on the prevention index does not minimize the importance of an activity. All activities have a significant influence on health.

Second, start with the right attitude. If you have the right attitude, there are few limits to what you can do. Answering the questions in Assessment Activity 1-2 may help determine whether you are ready to start a lifestyle-change program.

Most people make two serious mistakes when starting a lifestyle change. First, they expect miracles by setting unrealistic goals. Setting goals that are too ambitious often guarantees failure. For many people the fear of failure easily discourages future efforts at a lifestyle change.

Second, people often view lifestyle change as a temporary goal rather than a lifetime change. This is especially true for weight-loss programs. People set a goal, diet until they reach their goal, revert to their original eating habits, and invariably regain the lost weight. The proper way is to change eating habits so that they will endure for a lifetime. When people try to change some aspect of behavior, they have to deny themselves something that feels comfortable or that provides some source of enjoyment or pleasure. Denial often triggers a preoccupation that worsens the health behavior being changed. This is the reason dieters often become more obsessive-compulsive about food during a diet.

Striving for moderation may be more reasonable than setting goals that require abstinence or a complete reversal of behavior. For example, rather than giving up ice cream completely, a dieter can limit it to smaller portions or substitute low-fat ice cream. Rather than starting a fitness program with a 5-mile jog, an individual can start with a 1-mile walk. For

Health-promoting behaviors

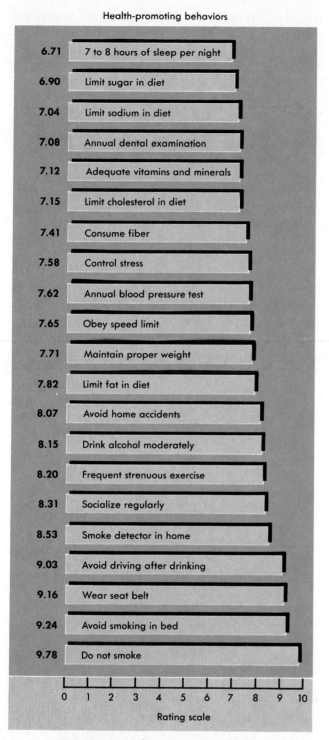

Rating	Behavior
6.71	7 to 8 hours of sleep per night
6.90	Limit sugar in diet
7.04	Limit sodium in diet
7.08	Annual dental examination
7.12	Adequate vitamins and minerals
7.15	Limit cholesterol in diet
7.41	Consume fiber
7.58	Control stress
7.62	Annual blood pressure test
7.65	Obey speed limit
7.71	Maintain proper weight
7.82	Limit fat in diet
8.07	Avoid home accidents
8.15	Drink alcohol moderately
8.20	Frequent strenuous exercise
8.31	Socialize regularly
8.53	Smoke detector in home
9.03	Avoid driving after drinking
9.16	Wear seat belt
9.24	Avoid smoking in bed
9.78	Do not smoke

Rating scale 0 1 2 3 4 5 6 7 8 9 10

FIGURE 1-8 The prevention index.

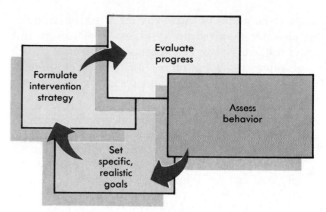

FIGURE 1-9 Steps in planning lifestyle change.

abstinence, success depends on complete avoidance, usually by removing the stimulus, such as a smoker throwing away all cigarettes. A key factor in choosing either moderation or abstinence when changing health inhibiting behaviors is the amount of control a person has over the environment. For example, improving study habits in a college dormitory may be difficult because one person cannot control the noise and distractions of other students. In this case, study habits would be improved in a controlled environment, such as a library.

No single strategy for lifestyle change is right for everyone. The key is to get involved in planning your personal program and to use your imagination to create the most suitable plan. If you start thinking about failure, you can practice a technique called *thought stopping*, in which the negative thought ("I can't improve my study habits; I've always failed in the past") is replaced with a positive one ("I will do better").

Third, develop a plan of action. People should follow basic principles of lifestyle management when structuring a plan of action, including (1) assessing behavior, (2) setting specific and realistic goals, (3) formulating intervention strategies for lifestyle change, and (4) evaluating progress (Figure 1-9).

Assess behavior. Behavior assessment, the collection of data on target behaviors, is the lifeline of any lifestyle-change plan. It involves the process of counting, recording, measuring, observing, and describing. The individual self-assesses any behavior that can be quantified.

Assessment tools are usually daily logs, journals, and diaries. Data should be collected long enough to note behavioral trends, usually a minimum of 1 to 2 weeks.

Sometimes a behavior assessment will prompt a

many people, moderation requires a higher level of learning and adjustment than abstinence. In moderation, success depends on controlling behavior, learning to live with certain stimuli, and still having the discipline to break the behavioral cycle. In

change in behavior without any other action. In most lifestyle-change programs a plan of action is not started until it is clear that assessment alone will not be enough to alter the behavior completely. Bootzin[27] illustrates this point by citing the experience of a friend:

> "A friend of mine discovered that he was interspersing the phrase 'you know' in almost every sentence he spoke. He decided to try to suppress that behavior. The first step he took—as it turned out, the only step that was required—was to record the number of times he said 'you know.' Each day that he recorded, his frequency of emitting that phrase decreased. Recording served as a sufficient intervention to bring that verbal behavior under control."

The assessment phase also provides clues to a person's commitment to making a change in lifestyle. A thorough, detailed log is a good sign that the individual has the motivation to carry out the plan.

When the assessment phase is finished, there should be sufficient information to form a behavioral profile, state specific goals, and customize an intervention program that matches goals and strategies to a person's unique circumstances and personality.

Set specific, realistic goals. Setting specific goals means setting goals that focus on concrete, observable, measurable behaviors. A behavioral goal to overcome shyness is very different from a goal that requires a person to initiate a conversation with a different person each day for the next week. If goals are specific, you know precisely what you are trying to accomplish and where, when, and how often it will occur. By using specific goals, you get instant feedback on your progress. Another way to increase specificity is to establish a timetable for achieving goals. A timetable adds structure to the plan and provides a way to evaluate progress.

Realistic behavioral goals are reasonable and relate to personal circumstances. Setting realistic goals also means forming them in the context of correct information. For example, an informed dieter knows that setting a goal to lose 10 pounds in a week is not reasonable. A more achievable goal is 1 to 2 pounds.

When setting goals, starting off small is best. Setting a modest goal initially facilitates some degree of success, which increases confidence. For complex lifestyle changes, behavioral psychologists recommend breaking down an ambitious, long-range goal into a set of intermediate goals, beginning with the easier ones and then moving gradually to more difficult ones. Goals should be structured in moderation. Extreme goals promote the erroneous attitude that lifestyle change is temporary. They create a strong sense of denial, encourage preoccupation

Figure 1-10   Sample Behavioral Contract for Lifestyle Change

I, _____ pledge that within the next 12 weeks, beginning September 1 and ending November 30, I will accomplish the goals listed below.

_____   _____
Signature   Witness

My health goal is to improve my physical fitness by participating in an activity program 3 days a week for a minimum of 30 minutes a day.

My intermediate goals are the following:
▶ Assess my physical fitness using the Rockport Walking Fitness Test*—September 1
▶ Start a walking program—September 3
▶ Start a walking/jogging program—September 17
▶ Progress to a jogging program—October 15

Intervention strategies:
▶ Work out after classes and before dinner
▶ Involve roommate

Rewards:
▶ Buy a pair of expensive jogging/walking shoes
▶ Buy a jogging suit

Penalty:
▶ Buy jogging shoes and/or jogging suit for my roommate

*See Chapter 3 for information about the Rockport Walking Test.

with target behaviors, and invariably lead to failure. Exceptions include cigarette smoking, alcoholism, and drug dependence, for which abstinence is still the primary treatment.

Formulate intervention strategies. No single strategy is right for all behaviors and all people. An individual must personalize intervention strategies that fit the behavioral profile and goals. Common types of strategies include use of behavioral contracts, stimulus control, positive and negative reinforcers, and behavior substitution.

A **behavioral contract** is a written agreement between people in a lifestyle-change program (Figure 1-10). Although they vary in style and form, most contracts include a statement of long-range and intermediate health goals, target dates for completion of each goal, rewards and punishments, intervention strategies, and signatures of witnesses. They are not legal documents, so simplicity and creativity are encouraged.

After you have drafted a contract, work out a method of graphing your progress (Figure 1-11). Display the contract and graph where you and others can see them. This way, they become tangible affirmations of your commitment to the agreement.

Stimulus control is a behavioral technique that involves elimination or manipulation of the circum-stances associated with the undesirable behavior. One way to change a behavior is to eliminate the stimulus causing it. A smoker cannot smoke if there are no cigarettes, an ice cream binge is not possible if a trip to the ice cream parlor is refused, and loud music cannot interfere with studying if the radio is put away.

Another way to alter a behavior is to modify the stimulus. This is sometimes referred to as *behavior shaping*. Instead of eliminating the stimulus, the situation is modified to prompt, or "shape," desirable behavior. For example, a student who finds it virtually impossible to study in a dormitory may try to study in a different environment, such as the library. Another student may try to improve the quality of studying by setting a study schedule that starts with a 30-minute session and increases over time to several hours a day. When doing so, the student might record the amount of time spent studying. When studying occurs on 3 consecutive days, study time is increased in increments of 30 minutes.

The use of *positive* and *negative reinforcers* is fundamental to stimulus-control strategies (Figure 1-12). Positive reinforcers are rewards earned for achieving lifestyle goals; negative reinforcers are usually penalties. Although the use of positive and/or negative reinforcers is strictly an individual

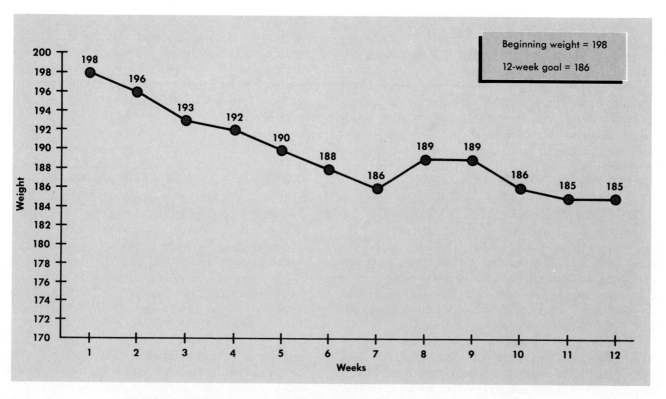

FIGURE 1-11 Example of graph of behavioral contract to lose weight.

Figure 1-12   Examples of Stimulus-Control Strategies for Losing Weight

▶ Eat in a certain place—not all over the house.
▶ Eliminate all food that can be eaten without careful preparation from your immediate environment.
▶ Always sit down to a carefully set place at the table and eat only one helping of planned foods.
▶ Prepare only enough food for one meal.
▶ Eat slowly.
▶ Chew each bite 25 to 50 times.
▶ Put down utensils after every mouthful.
▶ Partway through the meal, stop and relax without eating for 2 to 3 minutes.
▶ Leave some food on your plate at each meal.
▶ Plan to eat some meals alone (there is a tendency to overeat in social situations).
▶ Put your weight record where a friend can see it.
▶ Eat a carefully balanced diet so that you are not deprived of a particular food element.

Involving another person in a lifestyle change program makes is easier to stick to a plan.

matter, most lifestyle-change programs emphasize the positive. Many people like to treat themselves to rewards, which vary according to their financial resources. Rewards can include special treats, the purchase of a desired item, and participation in an enjoyable activity. You may find it helpful to think of a list of rewards for yourself. The actual achievement of a stated lifestyle goal is the strongest positive reinforcement. It provides the best incentive for continuing with a lifestyle-change program.

For many people, negative reinforcers serve as powerful motivators for change. For example, a student who cuts classes and is chronically late for the rest can write a contract that involves depositing $200 with a counselor. The contract may stipulate that the counselor returns $20 each week the student does not miss class or go to class late. For each week the contract is not fulfilled, the student must donate $20 to a charitable organization.

Another good stimulus-control strategy is formation of a *support group*, which may include a roommate, family, friends, classmates, or someone who can identify with the lifestyle goal. Such a group not only provides a source of encouragement but also

holds you accountable for your goals. Involving someone else in the process makes it easier to stick to your plan. Some people enjoy exercise more if they do it with a partner. Others benefit from the discipline of having another person available for reinforcement.

When you join a support group, you are publicly affirming what you plan to do and how and when you plan to do it. The good opinions of others are powerful motivators. In addition, friendships often form in a support group that last a lifetime. Support groups can be the key to success for visible health-change programs.

Behavior substitution, in which a new behavior is substituted for the undesirable one, is the most common technique used by people trying to change some aspect of their lifestyle without professional help. When this technique is applied, the goal is to think of a behavior that is incompatible with the one being altered. Examples include chewing gum to suppress the urge to smoke, substituting diet colas for sweetened colas, and playing a game of racketball instead of watching television.

A person should be careful that the behavior being substituted does not create a new problem while solving the old one. For example, some smokers initiate their cigarette habit as a way to control eating. In other words, they trade compulsive eating for compulsive smoking. The result is a new health habit that is more detrimental. Exercising good judgment and observing sound principles of healthy living are important when choosing substitute behaviors.

Evaluate progress. Constant monitoring is the only way to determine whether a lifestyle-change plan is working. This means assessing each goal according to the conditions and timetable specified at the beginning of the program. Consistent monitoring makes it possible to get immediate feedback about progress. This feedback can then provide a basis for continuing with the program as it is or for adjusting it. However, you should avoid the temptation to overmonitor progress. Plan evaluation checkpoints at time intervals that are short enough to provide sufficient time to achieve goals but not so short that they promote preoccupation with target behaviors. Depending on the nature and complexity of the problem behavior, the timing of evaluations can range from weekly for a weight-loss program to daily for a plan to improve study habits.

Regardless of the results, maintaining the proper perspective about success and failure is important. Many people have the attitude that they either completely succeed or completely fail. This way of thinking can be devastating to a person's motivation. When goals are not fully realized, the proper attitude is to view the shortcoming as justification for making adjustments in the program. The goals may have been too general or unrealistic. The intervention strategies may have lacked relevance. Reshaping goals, setting a more realistic schedule, changing the rewards and penalties, or formulating different intervention strategies may be necessary.

Above all, you should maintain a healthy perspective about yourself and not burden yourself with guilt if you fall short of your goals. What seems important now becomes insignificant when viewed within a broader context. You may consider how significant this event is likely to be to you 2 years from now. Doing this helps establish the right perspective on your progress. More important are the answers to the following questions: "What did you learn from this experience? What did you learn about yourself? What can you do differently?" Lifestyle change is a lifelong project that requires insight, skillful planning, and plenty of practice.

Summary

▶ Health is a constantly changing state of being that moves along a continuum from optimal health to premature death and is affected by an individual's attitudes and activities.

▶ Wellness means to engage in activities and behaviors that enhance quality of life and maximize personal potential by consistent balancing of physical, emotional, spiritual, intellectual, and social health.

▶ Personal motivation is the only way a person can adopt and maintain a wellness lifestyle. This motivation can be affected by family members and social pressure.

▶ For change to occur, knowledge alone is insufficient. Attitudes and beliefs are the catalysts of behavior change because the more highly a health benefit is valued, the greater the chance of making a change and adhering to it.

▶ An external locus of control is a belief that the factors controlling people's lives are outside the people themselves and thus beyond their control. An internal locus of control is a belief in which people view themselves as being in control.

▶ Self-efficacy refers to the beliefs people have in their ability to accomplish a specific task or behavior. These beliefs specifically affect ability to perform and achieve. A strong sense of self-efficacy is central to self-regulation.

▶ Many Americans now believe that it is possible to control many health-promoting and health-inhibiting behaviors.

▶ The discrepancy between health knowledge and health behavior is greatest among young adults.

▶ Lifestyle change is one of the most pervasive human endeavors.

▶ A fundamental belief in lifestyle-change programs is that health behavior is a learned response and therefore can be changed.

▶ Health behavior is influenced by many complex forces, including family, role models, social pressure, advertising, and psychological needs.

▶ The four steps in a lifestyle-change program are assessing behavior, setting specific and realistic goals, formulating intervention strategies, and evaluating progress.

▶ Intervention strategies used in lifestyle change include behavioral contracts, stimulus control, positive and negative reinforcers, support groups, and behavior substitution.

▶ Lifestyle change should be viewed as a learning experience rather than a test of willpower.

Action Plan for Personal Wellness

Use the information presented in this chapter to answer the following questions and to formulate an action plan to enhance your personal wellness.

1 Based on the information presented in this chapter and what I know about my family's health history, the health problems and issues that I need to be concerned about are: _____

_____

_____

2 Of the health concerns listed in number 1, the one I most need to act on is: _____

_____

_____

3 Possible actions that I can take to improve my level of wellness are (be specific): _____

_____

_____

4 Of the actions listed in number 3, the one that I most need to include in an action plan is: _____

_____

_____

5 Factors I need to keep in mind to be successful in my action plan are: _____

_____

_____

Review Questions

1. What are the relationships between the components of wellness and personal health? (Define and explain them.)
2. What are some of the beneficial results of engaging in a wellness lifestyle? What is the key to accepting the challenge of such a lifestyle?
3. When changing behavior, information must be weighed in relation to what factors?
4. What is the difference between internal and external locus of control?
5. What is self-efficacy? What does it influence?
6. What are the five specific health practices that illustrate the generalization that health habits are learned?

7. What are the differences between health-promoting behaviors and health-inhibiting behaviors? Give two examples of each.
8. What are the reasons for the high recidivism rate in many lifestyle-change programs? Discuss all three.
9. What are the similarities and differences among the psychotherapy, cold-turkey, and self-help approaches to lifestyle change?
10. What are five criteria for determining a person's readiness for a lifestyle-change program?
11. If a college student wants to use behavior assessment for study habits, what specific things can be measured, recorded, and/or observed?
12. What is an example of a lifestyle goal that is stated both specifically and realistically?

References

1. National Center for Health Statistics, US Public Health Service, Department of Health and Human Services, Washington, DC, 1990.
2. World Health Organization: Constitution of the World Health Organization, *Chronicle WHO* 1:29-43, 1947.
3. O'Donnell MP: Definition of health promotion, *Am J Health Prom* 1(1):4-5, 1986.
4. Chapman LS: Developing a useful perspective on spiritual health: love, joy, peace, and fulfillment, *Am J Health Prom* 2(22):12-17, 1987.
5. Goodloe NR, Arreola PM: Spiritual health: out of the closet, *J Health Educ* 221(3):26, 1992.
6. Fahlberg LI, Fahlberg LA: Exploring spirituality and consciousness with an expanded science: beyond the ego with empiricism, phenomenology, and contemplation, *Am J Health Prom* 5(4)273-280, 1991.
7. Murphy TA, Murphy D: *The wellness for life workbook*, ed 4, San Diego, 1987, Fitness Publications.
8. Breslow L, Enstrom JE: Persistence of health habits and their relationship to mortality, *Prev Med* 9:469-483, 1980.
9. Wingard DL et al: A multivariate analysis of health-related practices: a 9-year mortality follow-up of the Alameda county study, *Am J Epidemiol* 116:765, 1982.
10. Whelan EM: The truth about America's health, *USA Today*, Society for the Advancement of Education, pp 55-58, May 1987.
11. American Heart Association: *Heart facts: 1992*, Dallas, 1992, The Association.
12. American Cancer Society: *Cancer facts and figures: 1992*, New York, 1992, The Society.
13. Califano JA: *America's health care revolution: who lives? who dies? who pays?* New York, 1986, Random House.
14. Miller A: Can you afford to get sick? *Newsweek*, p 45-46, Jan 30, 1989.
15. US Department of Health and Human Services, Public Health Service: *Promoting health/preventing disease: Healthy People 2000: national health promotion and disease prevention objectives*, Washington, DC, 1990, The Department.
16. Koenig R: HMOs shed socialized image gaining acceptance on Wall Street, *Wall Street Journal*, p 27, Aug 16, 1984.
17. Bandura A: Self-efficacy: toward a unifying theory of behavior change, *Psychol Rev* 84:191-215, 1977.
18. Lyn L, McLeroy KR: Self-efficacy and health education, *J School Health* 56(2):317-321, 1986.
19. Schunck DH, Carbonari JP: Self-efficacy models. In Malarazzo JD and others, editors: *Behavioral health: a handbook of health enhancement and disease prevention*, New York, 1984, John Wiley & Sons, pp 230-247.
20. Noland MP: *The efficacy of a new model to explain leisure exercise behavior*, doctoral dissertation, College Park, 1981, University of Maryland.
21. Greenberg JS: *Comprehensive stress management*, Dubuque, Iowa, 1987, Wm C Brown, pp 232-233.
22. Guerin J, editor: Beating the big ones, *Am Health* 6(3):41, 1987.
23. *Survey highlights: the prevention index '89, summary report, a report card on the nation's health*, Emmaus, Pa, 1989, Rodale Press.
24. Bootzin R: *Behavior modification as therapy: an introduction*, Cambridge, Mass, 1975, Winthrop Publishers.

Annotated Readings

Chapman LS: Developing a useful perspective on spiritual health: well-being, spiritual potential and the search for meaning, *Am J Health Prom* 2:31-39, 1987.
Spiritual health is one component of total wellness. Defines spiritual wellness, reasons for less emphasis on spirituality in today's society, and a spiritual wellness inventory.

Folkenberg J: The mouth as the body's mirror, *FDA Consumer* Dec 1989-Jan 1990.
Surprisingly the mouth offers many clues to both the physical and the mental health of the individual.

Ornstein R, Sobel D: *Healthy pleasures*, Reading, Mass, 1989, Addison-Wesley.
Presents numerous practical suggestions on how to live life in a way that enriches rather than just maintains health, such as ways to mobilize positive beliefs, expectations, and emotions—from cognitive therapy, relaxation training, and successful behavior modification practices.

Podolsky D, Silberner J: 20 medical stories you may have missed, *US News & World Report* 113(5)58-60, 1992.
Medical authorities complain that some stories never draw the attention that they deserve. Other information that does make headlines only causes confusion. This article provides information on obscure, odd, and overlooked stories and what can be learned from them.

Sears C: Jungle potions, *Am Health* 11(8):70-75, 1992.
The world's rain forests may contain lifesaving drugs. If these areas are not destroyed, there is the potential to discover drugs that can help treat cancer, heart disease, hepatitis, and HIV infection. Currently the National Cancer Institute has tested over 33,000 extracts that have yielded five compounds for further research.

Stehlin D: Getting information from the FDA, *FDA Consumer* 24(10):28-30, 1990.
Finding out how to use the information system from the FDA can be bewildering. Article provides strategy on how to prepare for finding what information is desired from the agency. Also provided is information on when it is better to seek help or ask some other agency.

Tierney J: Buying time, *Health* Jan/Feb 1990, pp 35-44.
Various individuals claim that they can keep people young. This article examines the claims that are made.

Willis JL: Keeping time to circadian rhythms, *FDA Consumer* 24(6):18-21, July/Aug 1990.
The human body has rhythmical patterns that repeat themselves daily. Researchers are now starting to seriously consider these rhythms to devise safer, more effective ways to administer some treatments.

ASSESSMENT ACTIVITY 1-1

Barriers to Change

Most people have changes they want to make in their lives or things they want to accomplish, but they have so many "reasons" why they cannot make these desired changes. When they say they are "too busy" or "too tired" or the change is "too difficult," they are making excuses. Excuses are *barriers* to change.

Directions: Below is a rating scale that will help you to recognize the barriers you may find when you try to make a change. Decide on a health or lifestyle change you would like to make, and check it against each of the barriers listed by circling the appropriate rating. For example, you may want to start an exercise program. Is the cost of joining a spa or fitness club a major barrier to you in starting the program? If you circle 5, 6, or 7, you are encountering a major obstacle.

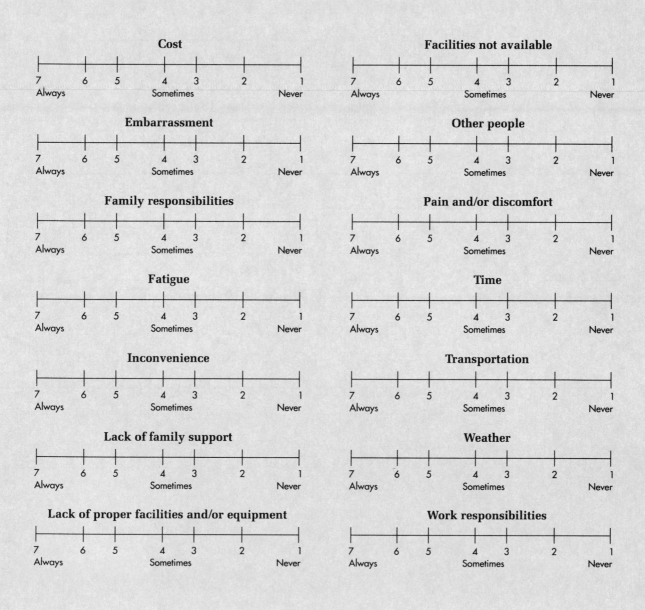

After completing the rating scale, review the barriers to the change or changes desired. What are some possible solutions or strategies for dealing with the barriers you identified?

Barrier   **Solution**

_____   _____

                                                     _____

                                                     _____

                                                     _____

_____   _____

                                                     _____

                                                     _____

                                                     _____

_____   _____

                                                     _____

                                                     _____

                                                     _____

_____   _____

                                                     _____

                                                     _____

                                                     _____

_____   _____

                                                     _____

                                                     _____

                                                     _____

_____   _____

                                                     _____

                                                     _____

                                                     _____

Health Locus of Control

Locus of control is an important component of individual wellness. This activity will assist you in identifying your locus of control and its ability to affect your health. This rating scale is an adaptation of the Multidimensional Health Locus of Control Scales. The test is composed of three subscales:

1. The *Internal Health Locus of Control Scale (I)* measures whether you feel that you have control over your own health.
2. The *Powerful Others Health Locus of Control Scale (P)* measures whether you feel that powerful individuals, such as physicians or other health professionals, control your health.
3. The *Chance Health Locus of Control Scale (C)* measures whether you feel your health is due to luck, fate, or chance.

Directions: For each answer, choose a number from 1 to 5 that best describes your feelings.

5 = Strongly agree	2 = Disagree
4 = Agree	1 = Strongly disagree
3 = Neither agree nor disagree	

Subscale 1: Internal Health Locus of Control

_____ If I get sick, my behavior determines how soon I get well.
_____ I am in control of my health.
_____ When I get sick, I am to blame.
_____ If I take care of myself, I can avoid illness.
_____ If I take the right actions, I can stay healthy.
_____ TOTAL

Subscale 2: Powerful Others Health Locus of Control

_____ Having regular contact with my physician is the best way for me to avoid illness.
_____ Whenever I don't feel well, I should consult a medically trained professional.
_____ My family has a lot to do with my becoming sick or staying healthy.
_____ Health professionals control my health.
_____ When I recover from an illness, it's usually because other people such as doctors, nurses, family, and friends, have been taking good care of me.
_____ Regarding my health, I can only do what my doctor tells me to do.
_____ TOTAL

Subscale 3: Chance Health Locus of Control

_____ No matter what I do, if I am going to get sick, I will get sick.
_____ Most things that affect my health happen to me accidentally.
_____ Luck plays a big part in determining how soon I will recover from an illness.
_____ My good health is largely a matter of good fortune.
_____ No matter what I do, I am likely to get sick.
_____ If it is meant to be, I will stay healthy.
_____ TOTAL

To obtain your score for a subscale, add the numbers you chose.

1. A score of 23 to 30 on any subscale means you have a strong inclination toward that particular subscale. For example, a high C score indicates you hold strong beliefs that your health is a matter of chance.
2. A score of 15 to 22 means you are moderate on that particular subscale. For example, a moderate P score indicates you have moderate belief that your health is due to powerful others.
3. A score of 6 to 14 means you are low on that particular subscale. For example, a low I score means you generally do not believe that you control your own health.

ASSESSMENT ACTIVITY   1 - 3

Assessing Your Health Behavior

Before planning a lifestyle-change program, you should take an inventory of your health behaviors. This reveals important information about your lifestyle and should also help identify areas in need of improvement.

Directions: In this assessment, you are asked to make two lists. In the left column, list the things you do to maintain or improve your level of health. These are your health-promoting behaviors. In the right column, list the things you do that may be detrimental to your health. These are your health-inhibiting behaviors. Try to be specific. Include the things that affect your mental, emotional, social, spiritual, and physical health. If you have a difficult time thinking of specific activities, you can refer to Figure 2-2 or the Lifestyle Inventory in the appendix.

Health-Promoting Behaviors   **Health-Inhibiting Behaviors**

1. _____   1. _____

2. _____   2. _____

3. _____   3. _____

4. _____   4. _____

5. _____   5. _____

6. _____   6. _____

7. _____   7. _____

8. _____   8. _____

9. _____   9. _____

10. _____   10. _____

11. _____   11. _____

12. _____   12. _____

13. _____   13. _____

14. _____   14. _____

15. _____   15. _____

Which health-inhibiting behavior would you be willing to change right now?_____

_____

_____

_____

ASSESSMENT ACTIVITY 1 - 4

Assessment of Readiness For Lifestyle Change

Directions: Indicate "yes" or "no" to each of the following questions by placing a check mark in the appropriate column. If you can answer "yes" to the following questions, you are ready to begin a lifestyle-change program.

Questions	Yes	No
1. Do you view lifestyle change as a lifetime goal rather than a temporary, short-term goal?	_____	_____
2. Are you willing to get personally involved in planning a lifestyle-change program?	_____	_____
3. Are you prepared for some disappointments?	_____	_____
4. Are you willing to experiment with different ideas?	_____	_____
5. Do you have the patience to accept success in small increments stretched over a long period?	_____	_____
6. Are you willing to set modest, realistic goals?	_____	_____
7. Are you willing to make some changes in the way you live?	_____	_____

Cardiovascular Health and Wellness

Key terms

aneurysm

antioxidants

atherosclerosis

cerebral hemorrhage

cholesterol

embolus

hypertension

myocardial infarction

thrombus

Objectives

After completing this chapter, you will be able to:

▷ Describe the gross anatomy and function of the heart.

▷ Trace the development of cardiovascular disease during this century in the United States.

▷ Identify and differentiate between several types of cardiovascular disease.

▷ Identify the risk factors for heart disease and discuss ways to reduce them.

▷ Explain the lifestyle behaviors that contribute to health and longevity.

Cardiovascular disease includes a group of diseases that affect the heart and blood vessels. Cardiovascular disease—the leading cause of death in the United States—accounts for 43.8% of all deaths.[1] About 25% of Americans (approximately 69 million people) have one or more forms of heart or blood vessel disease. Approximately 1.5 million heart attacks have occurred every year in the last few years, and more than 500,000 of these resulted in death each year. A total of 300,000, or 60%, of these deaths occurred before the victim reached a hospital emergency room. However, a significant number of these premature deaths could have been prevented with early treatment.

Of heart attack victims, 50% wait an average of 2 hours before seeking medical attention. Denying the possibility that a heart attack is occurring is the primary reason for the delay. The symptoms of a heart attack are similar to those of other physical ailments, and people are more prone to believe that it is one of the other problems rather than a heart attack.

Although the figures are foreboding, substantial progress has occurred during the last 40 years. The death rate for cardiovascular diseases has declined by approximately 51% since 1950.[1] Although an impressive accomplishment, it is somewhat diminished by the fact that cardiovascular diseases remain by far the leading cause of death in the United States. Two types in particular, coronary heart disease and strokes, are the first and third leading causes of death. The downward trend in the death rate from cardiovascular disease has been attributed primarily to lifestyle changes and more sophisticated medical diagnosis and treatment.

Circulation

The Heart, Blood, and Blood Vessels

Circulation is better understood if you are familiar with the basic anatomy and function of the heart. The heart consists of cardiac muscle and weighs between 8 and 10 ounces. It is about the size of a fist and lies in the center of the chest. The heart is divided into two halves, or pumps, by a wall (the septum), and each half is subdivided into an upper chamber (the atrium) and a lower chamber (the ventricle). The right heart, or pulmonary pump, receives deoxygenated blood from the tissues and transports it to the lungs so that carbon dioxide can be exchanged for a fresh supply of oxygen. From the lungs, the oxygen-rich blood is sent to the left heart, or systemic pump, so that the oxygenated blood can be transported to all the tissues of the body. Both pumps work simultaneously. The systemic pump carries the heavier workload of the two and thus has a more muscular ventricular wall. Figure 2-1 illustrates pulmonary and systemic circulation.

The arteries carry oxygenated blood away from the heart while the veins carry deoxygenated blood to the heart. There are two exceptions. First, the pulmonary artery carries deoxygenated blood from the right heart to the lungs to exchange carbon dioxide for a fresh supply of oxygen. Second, the pulmonary vein carries fully oxygenated blood from the lungs to the left heart for distribution throughout the body.

The primary function of circulation is to provide a constant supply of blood and nutrients to the cells while removing their waste products. Under ordinary circumstances, the interruption of blood flow for as little as 4 minutes can impair the brain and may result in death.

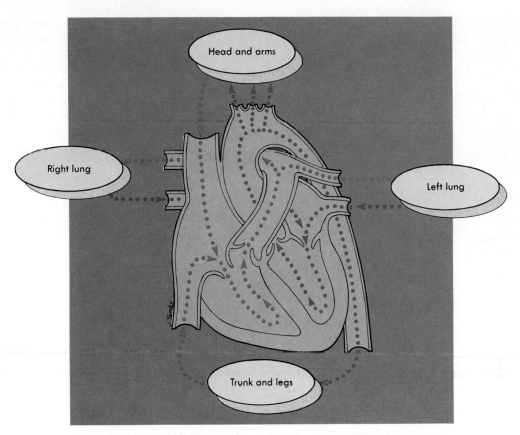

FIGURE 2-1 Circulation of the pulmonary and systemic pumps.

The average heart beats 70 to 80 times per minute at rest. Endurance athletes often have resting heart rates in the 30 and 40 beat range, whereas some overweight and sedentary smokers have resting heart rates in the 90s. The low heart rates of endurance athletes reflect physiological adaptations to training that represent normal values for this group. The Framingham Heart Disease Study showed that a rapid resting heart rate increased the risk of death from heart attack. Mortality increased progressively with higher resting heart rates, especially among males.

The resting heart rate is established by the sinoatrial node (SA node, or pacemaker), which is located in the right atrium as shown in Figure 2-2. The atria contract, forcing blood into the ventricles as the electrical impulse travels from the SA node to the atrioventricular node (AV node), which is located between the right atrium and right ventricle. The electrical impulse pauses for one tenth of a second at the AV node to allow the ventricles to fill with

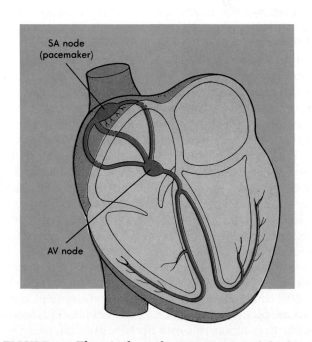

FIGURE 2-2 Electrical conduction system of the heart.

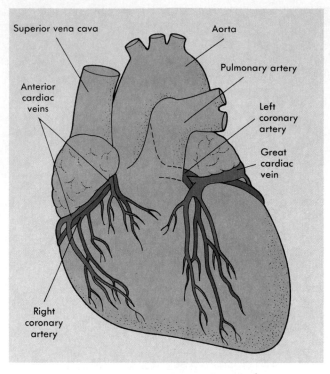

FIGURE 2-3 Coronary circulation.

blood and then resumes down the system and spreads throughout the ventricular walls. The ventricles contract during this time, ejecting blood from these chambers.

Blood that enters the chambers of the heart does not directly nourish the heart muscle. Cardiac muscle receives its nourishment when the heart contracts, sending blood via the aorta (the largest artery in the body) to the coronary arteries that supply it with blood and nutrients. Coronary circulation is illustrated in Figure 2-3. The left coronary artery supplies a major portion of the myocardium (heart muscle) with blood, whereas the right coronary artery serves less of it. Both vessels divide and subdivide downstream and eventually culminate in a dense network of capillaries (the smallest blood vessels in the body). Blood supply to the myocardium is so important that every muscle fiber is supplied by at least one capillary. The coronary veins return deoxygenated blood to the right atrium so that it can enter pulmonary circulation. The veins bring deoxygenated blood from all tissues back to the right atrium.

Blood plasma is a clear, yellowish fluid that carries approximately 100 chemicals. Plasma represents 55% of the blood contents. The remaining 45% consists of blood solids—the erythrocytes (red blood cells), the leukocytes (white blood cells), and the blood platelets. The red blood cells are the most abundant of the blood solids, composing about 98% of the total. Attached to hemoglobin, an iron-containing protein, the red blood cells carry oxygen and carbon dioxide to and from the tissues of the body. The white blood cells are an important part of the body's defense system against invading microorganisms and other foreign substances. The blood platelets are involved in the complex processes that lead to the formation of clots for repairing damaged blood vessels.

Cardiovascular Disease: A Twentieth-Century Phenomenon

Cardiovascular disease, a relatively rare event 100 years ago, reached epidemic proportions during the middle of the twentieth century. The term *angina pectoris* (chest pain) was introduced into the medical literature by William Heberden, a British physician, in the latter part of the eighteenth century. He was unable to offer any treatment for this strange malady. It was not until 1910 that recurrent episodes of angina pectoris began to be connected to heart disease by physicians. Chest pain and other manifestations of a heart attack were not identified with obstructions of the coronary arteries until the early 1900s. The first accurate description of the events associated with a heart attack by an American physician occurred in 1912. The illness he described, which afflicted a 55-year old man with no previous evidence of disease, is now a common occurrence in American life. The man died 3 days after the onset of symptoms. A postmortem examination of the heart revealed the formation of a clot that had occluded, or blocked, one of the major coronary arteries. In 1912, this was a medical rarity.

Coronary heart disease is responsible for the majority of heart attack deaths, but other forms of heart disease contribute to disability and death. *Congenital heart defects* exist at birth and affect approximately 30,000 newborns annually. Approximately 5800 of these infants die from their defects. *Rheumatic heart disease,* caused by a streptococcal infection of the throat or ear, is virtually 100% preventable. Antibiotic treatment during the infection stage will arrest the processes that might lead to rheumatic heart disease. *Congestive heart failure* occurs when the heart muscle is so damaged that it can no longer contract with sufficient force to pump blood throughout the body. The damage is usually caused by long-standing hypertension. Mild to moderate hypertension may be controlled through appropriate lifestyle interventions; severe hypertension requires medication in addition to lifestyle modifications.

Coronary Heart Disease

Coronary heart disease is actually a disease of the arteries that supply the heart with blood and nutrients. A heart attack, or **myocardial infarction** (death of heart muscle tissue), occurs when an obstruction or spasm disrupts or terminates blood flow to a portion of the heart muscle. The amount of heart muscle damage is determined by the location of the obstruction or spasm and the speed with which medical intervention is begun. Heart attacks of any magnitude produce irreversible injury and myocardial tissue death. Dead cardiac tissue usually takes 5 to 6 weeks to form a fibrous scar. This area of dead tissue can no longer contribute to the pumping of blood, resulting in a less-efficient heart. Massive heart attacks that cause extensive muscle damage result in death.

Although most heart attacks occur after the age of 65, the dysfunctions leading to them often begin before adolescence. These processes are insidious and often go undetected until, without warning, a heart attack occurs. The attack is sudden but the circumstances leading to it are long standing. In fact, there is considerable evidence that the silent phase of coronary heart disease has pediatric origins.

The ongoing Framingham Study, which began in 1949, identified the risk factors connected with heart disease.[2] Cigarette smoking, high blood pressure, elevated cholesterol levels, diabetes, obesity, stress, physical inactivity, age, gender, and family history were found to be highly related to heart attack and stroke. As the risks were discovered, the realization evolved that heart disease was not the inevitable consequence of aging or bad luck but an acquired disease that was preventable. After a few years, researchers realized that preventive efforts should be-gin in childhood, and more years passed before they investigated the prevalence of these risks among children and adolescents.

Autopsy studies of 18-year-olds have shown a positive relationship between blood cholesterol levels and the prevalence of fatty streaks on the walls of the coronary arteries and aorta. The evidence indicates that the average cholesterol level in children in overfed, underexercised societies such as the United States is too high.

High blood pressure has been reported in children as young as 3 years of age, and blood pressure levels generally continue into adulthood.[3] Almost 19% of high school seniors smoke cigarettes daily, and the use of smokeless tobacco products has increased substantially among 17- to 19-year-old males.[4] An estimated one in five youngsters between the ages of 5 and 17 years are substantially overweight; that is, a minimum of 20% above their desirable weight.

Autopsy studies of American combat battle casualties, who had an average age of 22 years, in the Korean and Vietnam wars showed obstructions in the coronary arteries.[5,6] Native Korean and Vietnamese soldiers had clean and open arteries. These obstructions are caused by **atherosclerosis,** which is a slow, progressive disease of the arteries that can originate in childhood. It is characterized by the deposition of plaque beneath the lining of the artery (Figure 2-4). Plaque consists of fatty substances, cholesterol, blood platelets, fibrin, calcium, and cellular debris that anchor to a roughened site in the artery. Several theories have been advanced regarding the development of rough spots in arteries, but whatever the trigger, the smooth muscle cells beneath the lin-

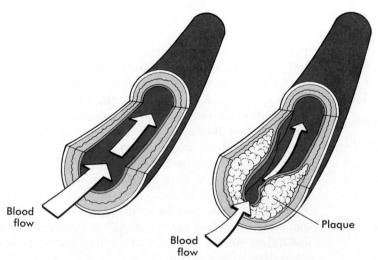

Blood flow

Blood flow

Plaque

FIGURE 2-4 Progressive narrowing of a normal coronary artery (atherosclerosis).

Figure 2-5   Signs of a Heart Attack

The Warning Signs

▶ Uncomfortable pressure, fullness, a squeezing sensation as if a band were being tightened around the chest, pain in the center of the chest lasting longer than 2 minutes

▶ Pain that spreads to the shoulders, arms, or neck

▶ The above warning signs as well as dizziness, fainting, sweating, nausea, and shortness of breath

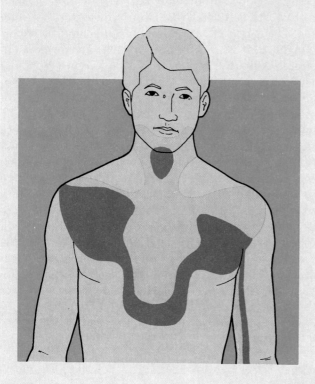

What You Should Do If These Signs Appear

If you have chest discomfort lasting more than 2 minutes:

▶ Do not deny what may be occurring.

▶ Call the emergency service or have a friend or family member drive you to the nearest hospital that has 24-hour emergency cardiac care.

▶ Know in advance which hospitals have such a service.

▶ Prominently display the telephone number of the emergency rescue service and also carry a copy with you.

ing erupt and form a network of connective tissue that eventually becomes plaque. Plaque enlarges over many years, progressively narrowing the arterial channel through which blood must flow. The affected heart muscle becomes *ischemic* (diminished supply of blood). Eventually the channel narrows to the extent that a clot forms and closes the vessel completely. The heart muscle formerly supplied by the occluded artery dies. The atherosclerotic process is responsible for 80% of the coronary heart disease deaths in the United States.

As many as one third of all heart attacks are imperceptible to the victim. These events usually involve small areas of the heart muscle and may go unnoticed unless verified by an electrocardiogram (ECG). The ECG remains abnormal for about 72 hours after a silent heart attack. If the diagnosis is not made during this time, it will probably be missed. The typical heart attack is very noticeable, and the symptoms are overt. Figure 2-5 lists the warning signs of a heart attack.

Atherosclerotic lesions are more likely to form where single arteries branch into two smaller arteries. Vessel diameters reduce where branching occurs. This increases blood turbulence, which produces greater damage at these sites. This combination of events renders these sites more vulnerable to injury and the development of plaque. This phenomenon may occur in the arteries leading to the brain, kidneys, lungs, and legs as well as the heart.

Coronary heart disease may be delayed or prevented by keeping the risk factors associated with heart disease in check. Most can be modified and controlled through appropriate lifestyle behaviors.

Stroke

The majority of strokes (cerebrovascular accidents) follow the same sequence of events that results in coronary heart disease. A stroke is essentially the result of diseased blood vessels that supply the brain. It shares the same risk factors as coronary heart disease, and it takes years to develop.

Strokes are caused by a **thrombus** (a clot that forms and occludes an artery supplying the brain) or an **embolus** (a clot that forms elsewhere in the body and fractures, dislodges, and is transported to one of the cerebral blood vessels that is too small for its passage). **Cerebral hemorrhage** (the bursting of a blood vessel in the brain because of arterial brittleness or aneurysm) is also a cause of stroke. An **aneurysm** is a weak spot in an artery that forms a balloonlike pouch that can rupture. It may be a congenital defect or the result of uncontrolled or poorly controlled hypertension.

Strokes that are caused by hemorrhages result in a 50% mortality rate. These victims die from the pressure imposed by blood leaking into the brain. However, those who survive this type of stroke are likely to recover more of their normal functions than those whose strokes were caused by a blood clot. A clot chokes off blood to a portion of the brain that quickly dies and never regenerates. On the other hand, the blood that spills on the brain during a hemorrhagic stroke produces pressure that gradually abates as the blood is absorbed by the body. Function is regained as the pressure relents.

On many occasions a stroke is preceded by warning signs and signals that may be experienced days, weeks, or months before a major stroke. These must first be recognized and then acted on so that prompt medical and lifestyle interventions may be instituted to prevent or delay a stroke (Figure 2-6).

Preventing a stroke is similar to preventing coronary heart disease. Both include blood pressure and cholesterol control, smoking cessation, weight management, exercise, and proper nutrition. A study of 22,071 middle-aged male physicians showed that those who took one aspirin every other day had 44% fewer first heart attacks than those who took a placebo, but there was an accompanying increase in the incidence of strokes among the aspirin takers.[2] However, the latest analysis showed that the risk of stroke among the aspirin group was quite small, and the benefits of aspirin in reducing heart attacks by far outweighed this risk.

Figure 2-6   Stroke: The Warning Signs

The American Heart Association suggests that people be familiar with the following warning signs:

▶ Temporary loss of speech or difficulty in speaking or understanding speech
▶ Unexplained dizziness, unsteadiness, or sudden falls
▶ Temporary dimness or loss of vision, particularly in one eye
▶ Sudden, temporary weakness or numbness of the face, arm, and leg on one side of the body
▶ Occurrence of a series of minor strokes, or transient ischemic attacks (TIAs),

Management of stroke victims depends on the nature and extent of the damage as determined by diagnostic tests. In addition to a physical examination, cerebral arteriography provides information on the status of the cerebral arteries, computed tomography (CT) scan enables physicians to examine structures within the body that cannot be observed with conventional x-ray procedures, and an electroencephalograph provides radiographic imaging of the brain.

Risk Factors for Heart Disease

The risk factors for cardiovascular disease have been categorized by the American Heart Association (AHA) as the following: (1) major risk factors that cannot be changed (increasing age, male gender, and heredity), (2) major risk factors that can be changed (elevated blood cholesterol levels, high blood pressure, cigarette smoking, and physical inactivity), and (3) other contributing factors (obesity, diabetes, and stress).

Major Risk Factors That Cannot Be Changed

Age. Approximately 55% of all heart attacks occur in people who are 65 years of age or older. This age group accounts for more than 80% of the fatal heart attacks.

Americans 65 years of age and older represent about 12% of the total population, but their health care expenditures are approximately one third of the US total.[7] Cardiovascular diseases, primarily coronary heart disease, are responsible for more than half of the deaths in this age group. "Nonpharmacological approaches, including diet, exercise, and health-promoting lifestyles, are more important than ever to prevent cardiovascular disease."[7]

Male gender. Until recently, the incidence of coronary heart disease among women has been largely unexplored. Men have been the primary subjects in the coronary heart disease and risk factor studies because of the high incidence of both among men. However, coronary heart disease is also the leading cause of death and disability among women, accounting for almost 250,000 deaths annually.[8] Women have less heart disease than men, particularly before menopause. The reasons for the difference include the following: (1) the female hormone estrogen protects the coronary arteries from atherosclerosis and (2) women have higher circulating levels of high density lipoprotein (HDL) cholesterol, which also protects the arteries. After menopause, though, the heart attack rate among women increases significantly until the mid-70s, when women's risk is equal to that of men the same age.

An alarming trend in recent years is the increased incidence of heart attacks in premenopausal women who have been smoking cigarettes long enough for it to affect their health, especially when combined with oral contraceptive use.

Heredity. According to the AHA, "A tendency toward heart disease or atherosclerosis appears to be hereditary, so children of parents with cardiovascular disease are more likely to develop it themselves."[1] A history of first-degree relatives (parents, grandparents, and siblings) who have died of coronary heart disease before the age of 55 years indicates a strong familial tendency. If the family history is positive, the modifiable risk factors must be controlled.

Major Risk Factors That Can Be Changed

Cholesterol. Cholesterol is a steroid that is an essential structural component of neural tissue; it is used in the construction of cell walls and for the manufacture of hormones and bile (for the digestion and absorption of fats). A certain amount of cholesterol is required for good health, but high levels in the blood are associated with heart attacks and strokes.

The AHA suggests that Americans reduce cholesterol consumption to less than 300 milligrams per day (300 mg/day), that fat intake be reduced to a maximum of 30% of the total calories consumed, and that saturated fat be reduced to no more than 10% of the total calories. Many authorities are convinced that limiting total fat and saturated fat is more important than being overly restrictive of cholesterol.

Cholesterol is consumed in the diet (exogenous, or dietary cholesterol), but it is also manufactured by the body from saturated fats (endogenous). A normally functioning adult liver manufactures 1500 to 2500 mg of cholesterol daily.[9] The cells lining the small intestine provide another 500 mg daily, so the body is manufacturing up to 3000 mg/day.

If you add the typical dietary intake of 450 to 750 mg/day to this total, you can see that the body must

TABLE 2-1 Sources of Dietary Cholesterol and Saturated Fat

	Cholesterol (mg)	Saturated fat (mg)		Cholesterol (mg)	Saturated fat (mg)
Meats (3 oz)			**Fish (3 oz)**		
Beef liver	372	2500	Squid	153	400
Veal	86	4000	Oily fish	59	1200
Pork	80	3200	Lean fish	59	300
Lean beef	56	2400	Shrimp (6 large)	48	200
Chicken (dark meat)	82	2700	Clams (6 large)	36	300
Chicken (white meat)	76	1300	Lobster	46.5	75
Egg	274	1700			
			Other Items of Interest		
Dairy Products (1 Cup; Cheese, 1 oz)			Pork brains (3 oz)	169	1800
Ice cream	59	8900	Beef kidney (3 oz)	683	3800
Whole milk	33	5100	Beef hot dog (1)	75	9900
Butter (1 tbsp)	31	7100	Prime ribs of beef (3 oz)	66.5	5300
Yogurt (low fat)	11	1800	Doughnut (1)	36	4000
Cheddar	30	6000	Milk chocolate (3 oz)	18	16,300
American	27	5600	Green or yellow vegetable or fruit	0	Trace
Camembert	20	4300	Peanut butter (1 tbsp)	0	1500
Parmesan	8	2000	Angel food cake	0	1960
			Skim milk (1 cup)	4	300
Oils (1 Tbsp)			Cheese pizza (3 oz)	6	800
Coconut	0	11,800	Buttermilk (1 cup)	9	1300
Palm	0	6700	Ice milk, soft (1 cup)	13	2900
Olive	0	1800	Turkey, white meat (3 oz)	59	900
Corn	0	1700			
Safflower	0	1200			

TABLE 2-2 Risk of Total Cholesterol	
Cholesterol (mg/dl)	**Risk**
<200*	Desirable level
200-239	Borderline
≥240†	High level

Figure 2-7 Strategies for Lowering Cholesterol

▶ Reduce dietary cholesterol to less than 300 mg/day or, ideally, less than 200 mg/day.
▶ Reduce consumption of fat to less than 30% of the total calories.
▶ Reduce saturated fat to less than 10% of the total calories.
▶ Reduce body weight so that it is commensurate with height.
▶ Stop smoking cigarettes.
▶ Increase consumption of fiber, particularly the soluble type such as that found in oats, legumes, fruits, and vegetables (see Figure 2-8).
▶ Exercise at least three to four times per week for at least 30 minutes each time.

process, use, or remove considerable amounts of cholesterol to prevent it from accumulating and clogging the arteries. The liver alone produces enough cholesterol to meet the body's needs. Therefore consuming cholesterol is not necessary to maintain health. Table 2-1 lists some common foods that contain cholesterol and saturated fat.

A number of population studies during the last 20 years have indicated a positive relationship between serum cholesterol (the level of cholesterol circulating in the blood) and the development of coronary heart disease. The National Heart, Lung, and Blood Institutes has reviewed this evidence and concluded that high circulating levels of serum cholesterol will cause heart disease.

Values of serum cholesterol above 200 milligrams per deciliter (mg/dl) of blood are higher than the average risk. The ideal value for adults is between 130 and 190 mg/dl. Table 2-2 categorizes cholesterol and the risks associated with each level.

An important collaborative study involving 12 research centers throughout the United States provided clinical evidence implicating cholesterol as a culprit in coronary heart disease.[10] Half of a group of 3806 subjects was given a cholesterol-lowering drug, and the other half was given a placebo (a substance that looked like the drug but had no medicinal properties). The subjects were followed for approximately 7.4 years, at which time the data indicated that the drug group reduced their cholesterol levels by 13%, suffered 19% fewer heart attacks, and experienced 24% fewer fatal heart attacks. The incidence of coronary bypass surgery and angina were also significantly reduced. The researchers concluded that each 1% reduction in cholesterol level results in a 2% reduction in the risk of coronary heart disease.

A follow-up of this study indicated that the reduction in coronary heart disease is probably closer to 3% for every 1% that cholesterol is lowered.[11,12] The strategies for lowering cholesterol in the blood are presented in Figure 2-7.

The cholesterol carriers. The amount of cholesterol circulating in the blood accounts for only part of the total cholesterol in the body. Unlike sugar and salt, cholesterol does not dissolve in the blood, so it is transported by protein packages, which facilitate its solubility. These transporters are the lipoproteins. They include the chylomicrons, very low-density lipoprotein (VLDL), intermediate-density lipoprotein (IDL), low-density lipoprotein (LDL), and high-density lipoprotein (HDL). Dietary cholesterol enters the body from the digestive system attached to the chylomicrons. The chylomicrons shrink as they give up their cholesterol to the cells of the body. The fragments that remain are removed by the liver and used to manufacture and secrete VLDLs, which are triglyceride-rich lipoproteins. The triglycerides represent 99% of the stored fats in the body. The VLDLs are degraded as their cargo of triglycerides are either used by the cells for energy or stored in adipose cells. The VLDL remnants may be removed by the liver or converted to LDLs.

LDLs are the primary transporters of cholesterol and the most capable of producing atherosclerosis. Michael S. Brown and Joseph L. Goldstein won a 1985 Nobel Prize in medicine and physiology for discovering that the liver and the cells of the body have receptor sites that bind LDLs, removing them from circulation. The liver contains 50% to 75% of these sites; the remainder are in other cells of the body. When LDL concentrations are excessive, the liver sites become saturated, and further removal of them from the blood is significantly impeded. As a result, plasma levels of cholesterol rise, leading to

Figure 2-8   Does Oat Bran Lower Cholesterol?

The results of a study in the *New England Journal of Medicine* raised serious questions about the effectiveness of oat bran in lowering serum cholesterol. In this study, wheat fiber performed almost as well as oat bran in lowering serum cholesterol. The researchers concluded that oat bran functioned indirectly in lowering cholesterol by replacing some of the fatty foods that the subjects would have normally eaten.

This was a small study (20 subjects) of short duration (6 weeks). The subject's average serum cholesterol at the beginning of the study was 186 mg/dl, which was in the desirable range. Furthermore, the subjects were also atypical in that they habitually consumed 23 grams of fiber daily (twice the American average). Many of the earlier studies that reported the beneficial effects of oat bran used subjects that had high cholesterol levels (above 250 mg/dl) who were consuming a less than healthful diet. A change to a high-fiber diet should and actually did significantly help these subjects.

Of course, oat bran is just one of many foods that are high in soluble fiber, and soluble fiber is just one type of fiber. Although increasing daily intake of fiber is important, lowering the intake of total fat, saturated fat, and cholesterol remain the major lifestyle changes in reducing serum cholesterol. At the very least, oat bran and other foods high in complex carbohydrates may lower serum cholesterol by leaving less room for foods high in fat and calories. Oat bran may contain inherent properties that directly lower serum cholesterol, as earlier studies had indicated. More study is needed, but regardless of the effect of fiber on cholesterol, oats and other grains are low in calories and fat and high in vitamins and minerals. Oat bran and other fibers are good food.

Swain JF et al: Comparison of the effects of oat bran and low-fiber wheat on serum lipoprotein levels and blood pressure, *New Engl J Med* 322:147-152, 1990.

the formation or exacerbation of atherosclerotic plaque.

The scientific community hopes that atherosclerosis may then be delayed or prevented by increasing consumption of a class of vitamins known as the **antioxidants.** Vitamins C, E, and beta carotene may deter atherosclerosis.[14] The vitamins appear to be safe even when taken in larger doses than recommended. (Refer to Chapter 6 for more information on vitamin supplements and antioxidants.)

How the antioxidants reduce atherosclerosis is not completely understood, but there is a theory. Each cell uses oxygen to fuel its normal functions. One of the byproducts of cellular metabolism is the formation of free radicals or oxidants. Free radicals are toxic, destructive elements that damage the body's cells. They are implicated in the development of cardiovascular disease, cancer, arthritis, and biological aging.

Free radicals contribute to the development of atherosclerosis by altering LDL cholesterol. In an altered or damaged state, LDLs cause injury to the artery linings. At this point, LDLs are recognized as harmful elements to the body that trigger the body's immune system. The immune system responds by sending specialized cells to encounter and engulf these LDLs. These specialized cells become bloated with the damaged LDLs and eventually infiltrate the artery lining at points of injury. Now they become lipid-laden foam cells and the initial stage of atherosclerosis has begun.

The body has natural defense mechanisms to control the effects of free radicals. Fortunately, most of the oxygen-burning processes are contained in organelles or compartments known as the mitochondria (the cell's powerhouse). The mitochondria are the body's furnaces where oxygen is burned to produce energy in the form of ATP. These organelles are analogous to home furnaces or fireplaces in that combustion occurs in, and is confined to, these areas. When free radicals escape from the mitochondria, other antioxidant systems must mobilize to protect the body. It is here that the antioxidant vitamins play a crucial role. Vitamin E and beta carotene are found within the LDL particle. They protect the body from within the LDL by disarming free radicals and preventing the oxidation of the host LDLs. On the other hand, vitamin C travels through the circulatory system attacking free radicals in the bloodstream. Regardless of the location, when free radicals come in contact with antioxidants they are rendered harmless.

Based on the evidence thus far, should we begin to take daily antioxidant supplements? According to nutritional and medical scientists, supplements are the least preferred way to obtain these substances. The preferred method is to eat foods that are rich in antioxidants. For instance, beta carotene can be obtained in significant quantities in orange vegetables, such as sweet potatoes and carrots. It is also found in dark green vegetables, such as spinach, kale and broccoli. Rich sources of vitamin C can be found in fruits and vegetables. Particularly good are citrus fruits and juices, papaya, and cantaloupe. Vitamin

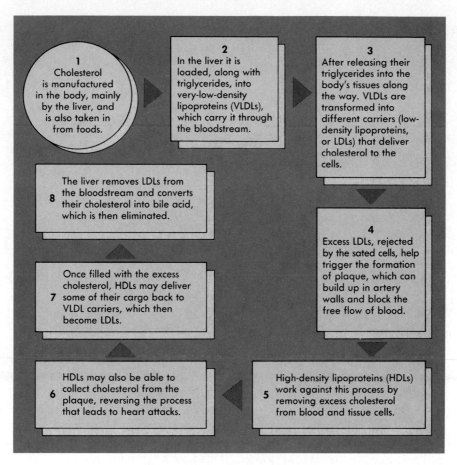

FIGURE 2-9 Cholesterol carriers.

E is found in cereal grains, vegetable oils, and assorted nuts and seeds. Food sources containing antioxidants also contain other nutrients that may be equally important in containing the destructive actions of free radicals. However, if your diet is deficient in foods that supply antioxidants, supplementation would be beneficial. LDL cholesterol is a significant contributor to the development and progression of atherosclerosis but it appears that the only harmful LDLs are those that are oxidized.[13] Figure 2-9 is a schematic drawing of how the lipoproteins are made and what each does.

Heart attacks are rare when LDL values in the blood are below 100 mg/dl. A national panel of experts has developed guidelines for safe and unsafe levels of LDL, and these appear in Table 2-3. A high circulating level of LDL cholesterol is positively related to cardiovascular disease. Weight loss, a diet low in saturated fat and total fat, exercise, and medication (if needed) will lower LDL levels in the blood.

HDLs are involved in reverse transport; that is, they accept cholesterol from the blood and tissues and transfer it to VLDLs and LDLs for transport to the liver, where it can be degraded, disposed of, or recycled. HDLs protect the arteries from atherosclerosis by clearing cholesterol from the blood. Cardiovascular health depends greatly on low levels of total cholesterol and LDLs and a high level of HDLs.

TABLE 2-3 Risk of LDL Cholesterol

LDL Cholesterol (mg/dl)	Risk
<130	Desirable level
130-159	Borderline—high risk
>160	High risk

TABLE 2-4 Ratio of Total Cholesterol to HDL Cholesterol

Risk	Male	Female
Very low (one half of average)	<3.4	<3.3
Low risk	4.0	3.8
Average risk	5.0	4.5
Moderate risk (two times average)	9.5	7.0
High risk (three times average)	>23	>11

Cigarette smoking, diabetes, elevated triglyceride levels, and anabolic steroids lower HDL, whereas physical exercise, weight loss, and moderate alcohol consumption raise it.

Moderate alcohol consumption (two drinks or less per day) increases HDL cholesterol levels. However, alcohol is a depressant that is responsible for nearly 50,000 traffic deaths annually and contributes to one third of all drownings and boating deaths.[14] Alcohol impairs judgment and removes inhibitions so that people under its influence behave in ways they ordinarily would not while sober. Alcohol should not be consumed as an acceptable way to raise HDL cholesterol. (See Chapter 10 for a more complete discussion of the effects of alcohol.)

Assessing cholesterol risk. Assessing cholesterol risk requires the measurement of total cholesterol, HDL, and LDL levels. A person with a desirable total cholesterol level could be at substantial risk if the HDL value is low. Men whose HDL is below 25 mg/dl and women whose HDL is below 40 mg/dl are at three times the risk for heart disease.[12] The ratio between total cholesterol (TC) and HDL (TC/HDL) should also be considered when the risk is interpreted. This ratio is determined by dividing TC by HDL (Table 2-4). The average value for men is 45 mg/dl, and for women it is 55 mg/dl. This biological difference in HDL levels between genders partly explains the lower incidence of heart disease in premenopausal women as compared with men. After menopause, HDL levels in women begin to decrease, as does their protection provided by this subfraction of cholesterol.

Blood pressure. Blood pressure, which is recorded in millimeters of mercury (mm Hg) is the force exerted against the walls of the arteries as blood travels through the circulatory system. Pressure is created when the heart contracts and pumps blood into the arteries. The arterioles (smallest arteries) offer resistance to blood flow, and if the resistance is persistently high, the pressure rises and remains high. The medical term for high blood pressure is **hypertension.**

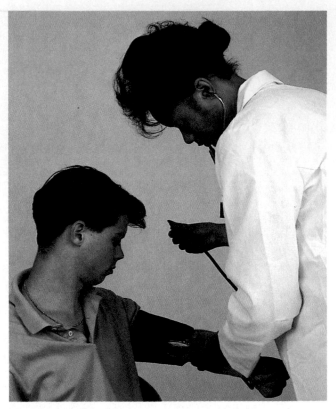

Periodic blood pressure checks can help determine whether dietary or other changes may be needed to control hypertension.

Hypertension is a silent disease that has no characteristic signs or symptoms, so blood pressure should be checked periodically. Blood pressure can be measured quickly with a sphygmomanometer. A rubber cuff is wrapped around the upper arm and inflated with enough air to compress the artery, temporarily stopping blood flow. A stethoscope is placed on the artery below the cuff so that the sound of blood coursing through the artery can be heard when the air is released. The first sound represents the systolic pressure (the maximum pressure of blood flow when the heart contracts), and the last sound heard is the diastolic pressure (the minimum pressure of blood flow between heart beats). A typical pressure for young adults is 120/80. Pressures of 140/90 or greater are considered to be hypertensive.[1] The lower limit of normal is 100/60. From a health perspective, having a low to normal blood pressure

TABLE 2-5 Classification of Blood Pressure for Adults Age 18 Years and Older

Category	Systolic (mm Hg)	Diastolic (mm Hg)
Normal	<130	<85
High Normal	130-139	85-89
Hypertension		
Stage 1 (Mild)	140-159	90-99
Stage 2 (Moderate)	160-179	100-109
Stage 3 (Severe)	180-209	110-119
Stage 4 (Very Severe)	≥210	≥120

and maintaining it as long as possible is advantageous. Standards for classifying blood pressure in adults appear in Table 2-5.

This table represents the latest thinking among medical researchers as they describe the stages of blood pressure values. All hypertensive values in the table represent an increased risk for cardiovascular events and kidney disease. The higher the blood pressure, the greater the risk.

Approximately 62.8 American adults and children have high blood pressure, and 31,630 people die of its complications annually.[15] The cause of high blood pressure is not known in 90% to 95% of the cases. This is referred to as *essential hypertension. Essential* is a medical term that means "of unknown origin or cause." Essential hypertension cannot be cured, but it can be controlled. The other 5% to 10% of the cases of hypertension have a specific cause. If the cause can be determined and eliminated, blood pressure returns to normal.

The heart is adversely affected by uncontrolled or undiagnosed hypertension of long duration. Pumping blood for years against high resistance in the arteries increases the workload of the heart, and it hypertrophies in response to the strain. The heart receives inadequate rest because the resistance to blood flow is consistently high, and this produces muscle fibers that become overly stretched. They progressively lose the ability to rebound. The end result is that they contract less forcefully. At this point the heart loses its efficiency and weakens. If intervention does not occur early, congestive heart failure is inevitable. Hypertension also damages the arteries and accelerates atherosclerosis.

Treatment for hypertension. Treatment for hypertension may include all or some of the following: weight loss, salt and alcohol restriction, calcium and potassium supplementation, voluntary relaxation techniques, exercise, and medication. Excess body weight increases the work of the heart because it must meet the nutrient demands of the extra tissue.

High salt intake increases the blood pressure in those who are salt sensitive. These people must stop adding salt to food and eating salt-laden foods. Salt is an acquired taste, and all people should reduce their intake to the recommended amount. Approximately 10% of Americans are salt sensitive.

Some calcium-deficient hypertensives may normalize their blood pressure by taking calcium supplements. However, calcium supplementation does not work for all calcium-deficient hypertensives, and it does not work for hypertensives who are not calcium deficient.

Yoga, meditation, hypnotherapy, biofeedback, and other relaxation techniques may help alleviate tension and anxiety and lower high blood pressure. Exercise is also an effective relaxation therapy. (Its effects on blood pressure are discussed in Chapter 3.) Many people drink alcohol because it relaxes

Relaxation techniques may help to reduce stress and lower blood pressure.

them, but ingestion of more than 2 ounces of alcohol per day raises blood pressure in some people. The same precautions regarding the use of alcohol and HDL cholesterol apply for hypertension.

Medications that control blood pressure have been developed. However, they have side effects that include weakness, leg cramps, stuffy nose, occasional diarrhea, heartburn, drowsiness, anemia, depression, headaches, joint pain, dizziness, impotence, and skin rash. The side effects are unique to the drug being used to control blood pressure. Despite these side effects, many people find it easier to take the medicine than to make the difficult lifestyle changes that lower blood pressure. The effort to control blood pressure with medication should not negate the importance of controlling lifestyle factors that contribute to hypertension. Medicine and lifestyle efforts are not mutually exclusive—each contributes to blood pressure management.

Cigarette smoking. Many medical authorities consider cigarette smoking the most harmful of the preventable risk factors associated with chronic illness and premature death[16] (Figure 2-10). Approximately 40% of male smokers and 28% of female smokers die prematurely. Smokers have twice the risk of having a heart attack and are two to four times more likely to die suddenly from a heart attack than nonsmokers.[1]

Hypertension results from peripheral resistance to blood flow, and cigarette smoking contributes to peripheral resistance by constricting the arterioles. Smoking significantly exacerbates the effects of high blood pressure. Although the number of people who smoke is declining, 29% of Americans over the age of 20 continue to smoke.[16]

Harmful products in cigarette smoke. Nicotine, carbon monoxide and other poisonous gases, tars, and chemical additives for taste and flavor are the hazardous products in cigarettes. Carbon monoxide and nicotine have a devastating effect on the heart and blood vessels. Carbon monoxide, a noxious gas that is a by-product of the combustion of tobacco products, displaces oxygen in the blood because it has a greater affinity for hemoglobin. The diminished oxygen-carrying capacity of the blood is partly responsible for the shortness of breath that smokers experience with mild physical exertion.

Cigarettes and other tobacco products are not regulated by the Food and Drug Administration because tobacco is not classified as a food or drug. Therefore the tobacco industry is under no mandate to disclose the nature and type of chemicals that are added to tobacco products. These products may be harmful. The public has a right to know, but the tobacco industry has successfully resisted attempts by government agencies and consumer groups to force disclosure.

The harmful effects of cigarette smoking are insidious and take time to appear. The medical profession measures the damage from smoking in pack years. Smoking one pack of cigarettes per day for 15 years is equal to 15 pack years (15 years × 1 pack per day = 15 pack years). Two packs per day for 15 years is equal to 30 pack years (15 × 2 = 30). Medical problems become evident after 25 to 30 pack years.

The challenge of quitting. To quit the tobacco habit, you have to first break the addiction to nicotine and then break the psychological dependence on smoking. This involves a change in behavior as well as effective ways to deal with the social and situational stimuli that promote the desire to smoke. Males have been more successful quitters than females. Since 1964, 21.4% of males have quit compared with 5.8% of females.[17] Today, more young women than young men are smoking, representing a reversal of a long-standing trend.[15] The increasing number of young female smokers, coupled with the number of years that women have been smoking, has reversed another trend: lung cancer has replaced breast cancer as the leading cause of cancer death among women.

Complicating the effort to quit, particularly among young women, is the fear of gaining weight. Approximately 65% of these who quit do gain weight, but the physiological adaptations that occur may only account for a 7- to 8-pound weight gain.

Figure 2-10   Nicotine

Nicotine is a powerful stimulant that does the following:
- ▶ Increases LDL and lowers HDL levels
- ▶ Causes the platelets to aggregate, increasing the probability of arterial spasms
- ▶ Increases the oxygen requirement of cardiac muscle
- ▶ Constricts blood vessels
- ▶ Produces cardiac arrhythmias (irregular heart beat)
- ▶ Is a causative agent in the 30% of coronary heart disease deaths related to smoking

The physiological mechanisms responsible are probably associated with a slowing of metabolism and slower transit time of food in the digestive system so that more is absorbed by the body. Weight gain beyond 8 pounds is probably caused by altered eating patterns rather than physiology. Food smells and tastes better. It may substitute for a cigarette, especially during social activities, it may provide some of the oral gratification previously obtained from smoking, and it may relieve tension. Weight gain can be avoided by eating sensibly and exercising moderately and frequently. Cigarette smoking and caffeine intake is a common combination. (Figure 2-11 gives some information on the caffeine/nicotine connection.)

As a group, smokers are 7% thinner than nonsmokers, but smokers tend to distribute more fat in the abdominal area.[18] The waist-to-hip ratio (WHR) is greater in smokers even though they are thinner. This fat distribution is not only aesthetically unappealing but also predisposes to coronary heart disease, diabetes, stroke, and some forms of cancer.

Figure 2-11   The Caffeine/Nicotine Connection

Stopping smoking is very difficult, and giving up coffee and cola drinks at the same time is even more difficult. Why should smokers attempt to stop both simultaneously? Smokers metabolize caffeine more quickly than nonsmokers, so they experience its stimulating effects for a much shorter time. Four days of nonsmoking normalizes the response to caffeine. The enhanced effect causes former smokers to suffer from caffeine jitters at a time when the tensions associated with withdrawal from smoking are occurring. Two cups of coffee at this time have the same effect of five cups when the individual was a smoker, so it takes less to induce the coffee "buzz."

Coffee- and cola-drinking smokers who are quitting the smoking habit need to be aware of their heightened sensitivity to caffeine and that the jitters and crankiness they are experiencing are the effects of the caffeine plus nicotine. The obvious solution is to reduce or eliminate caffeinated drinks and other caffeine-containing substances. You can substitute caffeine-free coffee and cola drinks to get the same taste without the jitters.

Passive smoking and smokeless tobacco. Involuntary or passive smoking (inhaling the smoke of others) is associated with premature disease and death. Estimates indicate that 53,000 nonsmokers who are regularly exposed to environmental smoke die annually from smoking-related causes.[19] The majority of these 37,000 die from heart disease, 4000 die from lung cancer, and the other 12,000 die from other forms of cancer. There is a dose-response effect. The more the nonsmoker is exposed to environmental smoke, the greater the risk for premature morbidity (illness) and mortality (death).

Children of smoking parents are more likely to experience a higher incidence of influenza, colds, bronchitis, asthma, and pneumonia. The impact of passive smoking on them can last a lifetime and may range from delayed physical and intellectual development to the hazards associated with prolonged exposure to carcinogenic substances.

An alarming trend is the escalating sale of smokeless tobacco products. Chewing tobacco and dipping snuff have become popular among high school and college males. The World Health Organization (WHO) has described the growing use of smokeless tobacco as a new threat to society. Nicotine is an addictive drug regardless of the method of delivery, and its effects are similar whether it is inhaled, as in smoking, or absorbed through the tissues of the oral cavity, as in dipping and chewing. The incidence of oral cancer may be 50 times higher among long-term users of smokeless tobacco products than among nonusers. Smokeless tobacco is addictive and deadly.

Physical inactivity. Physical inactivity is finally being officially recognized as a major risk factor for cardiovascular disease by the American Heart Association.[20] The upgrading of physical inactivity appeared in their latest position statement and reflects the importance of participating in physical activities regularly. The change occurred because the weight of the evidence that has been accumulating in the last 10 years shows that exercise produces many important health benefits. This is good news for those who have been physically active and may motivate some sedentary people to become active.

Physical inactivity (*hypokinesis*) is debilitating to the human body. A couple of weeks of bed rest or chair rest produces muscle atrophy, bone demineralization, and a decreases in aerobic capacity and maximum ventilatory capacity. Your body was constructed for and thrives on physical exertion. The American College of Sports Medicine has established guidelines for the development and maintenance of physical fitness. The amount of physical activity needed to improve and maintain good health and to affect longevity is still undetermined.

The evidence of investigators at the Centers for Disease Control provided the statistical basis for the position change by the American Heart Association.[21] These researchers showed a relationship between physical inactivity and heart disease that was similar in magnitude to that of cigarette smoking, high serum cholesterol levels, and hypertension. Approximately 29% of the population smokes cigarettes, 30% have blood pressures greater than 140/90, and 32% have cholesterol levels greater than 200 mg/dl. Although these numbers are impressive and a significant change in any one would lower the incidence of heart disease, the researchers concluded that regular exercise was the one lifestyle change that could most affect the health of the nation. This is based on the fact that 80% of Americans are sedentary or exercise too infrequently to enhance their health. Regular physical activity also has a modifying effect on many of the risks for cardiovascular disease.

Other major studies have supported the view that people who regularly engage in physical activities of moderate intensity have significantly less heart attacks and experience fewer deaths from all causes than people who exercise little or not at all. Moderate activity was the equivalent of walking 1 to 2 miles per day for a total of 5 to 10 miles per week. The greatest health benefits were gained by those who expended 2000 calories per week (20 to 22 miles of walking) in physical activity.[22] A total of 17,000 men were followed for more than 20 years. Those who regularly walked, climbed stairs, or participated in sports activities decreased their risk from all causes of mortality. Those who expended a minimum of 500 calories per week (5 miles of walking) to a maximum of 3500 calories per week (35 miles of walking) experienced a progressive increase in longevity (Figure 2-12).

Sallis et al[23] found that although moderate physical activity did not produce measurable improvement in cardiorespiratory endurance, it did produce healthful changes in the coronary risk factors.

Investigators at the Dallas Aerobics Center[24] added further validity to the effectiveness of moderate exercise as an attenuating factor in cardiovascular disease. Their epidemiological study showed that physically fit people with cholesterol levels equal to

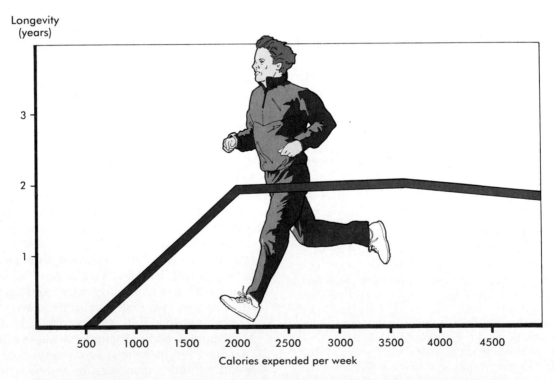

FIGURE 2-12 Physical activity and longevity. Physical activity expending approximately 2000 calories per week produced the greatest benefits for the time and energy invested. Notice that the longevity for those who expended more than 3500 calories decreased.

or greater than 280 mg/dl were three times less likely to die prematurely of heart disease than unfit people whose cholesterol was in the desirable range. In addition, physically fit hypertensives had less chance of dying from coronary heart disease then physically unfit normotensives (people with normal blood pressure). Therefore being fit with elevated cholesterol and high blood pressure is better than having normal levels of both and being unfit. The amount of activity to obtain this protection from cardiovascular disease could be acquired by walking.[23]

Investigators at the Institute for Aerobics Research[25] studied the relationship between physical fitness and mortality from all causes. The uniqueness of this study was twofold: First, the researchers measured the physical fitness level of all subjects by treadmill testing, and second, more than 3000 of the 13,344 subjects were women. Because of their lower risk for cardiovascular disease, women have essentially been neglected as subjects in heart disease studies.

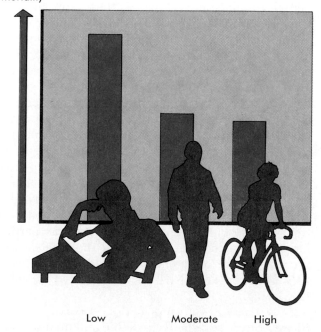

FIGURE 2-13 Physical fitness and all-cause mortality. The moderately fit experienced two thirds of the deaths of the low fit group. There was little difference between the moderately fit and the highly fit in all-cause mortality.

The results of this study indicated that a low physical fitness level increased the risk of death from cardiovascular disease, cancer, and all other forms of disease. The difference in all-cause mortality was greatest between those who were in the moderately fit category and those in the low-fit category (Figure 2-13). The difference between the moderately fit and the highly fit was insignificant. For people who exercise regularly, the risk of dying from a heart attack compared to the risk for sedentary people is 35% to 55% less.[26]

A study completed using only women as subjects investigated the physical fitness benefits versus the health benefits of three levels of walking intensity.[27] One group walked at 5 mph, a second group walked at 4 mph, and a third group walked at 3 mph. The results showed that physical fitness improved on a predictable dose-response basis. The fastest walkers improved the most and the slowest walkers improved the least, but the cardiovascular risk was reduced equally among the three groups. Low-level exercise was as effective as the highest level in promoting cardiovascular health. Exercise for health does not have to be as strenuous as exercise for physical fitness. Ideally, this message will improve and motivate exercise adherence for a lifetime.

A sedentary lifestyle imposes a financial burden on all people. Active people pay a price—a lifetime subsidy of approximately $1900 to support the medical costs of sedentary people.[28] The costs come from collectively financed programs such as health insurance, sick-leave coverage, disability insurance, and group life insurance. Because premiums and payroll taxes that finance these programs are equal for both sedentary and active people, the programs subsidize unhealthy behaviors. If sedentary people became more active, they would live longer and healthier, thus reducing the cost they impose on others.

The health and longevity returns from exercise and a physically active lifestyle are significant. Estimates indicate that longevity is increased by 1 minute for every minute spent walking and by 2 minutes for every minute spent jogging.[29]

For most sedentary people, the thought of exercise conjures up pain and sweating, and neither prospect is appealing. Actually, physical activities selected by the health enthusiast should not be painful. Those who dislike exercise should realize that the health benefits may also be obtained with everyday activities as opposed to fitness activities such as jogging, swimming, and cycling. Activities such as walking, climbing stairs, carrying your packages from the store, mopping and vacuuming floors, mowing the lawn (without a riding or self-propelled mower), and gardening may contribute minimally to physical fitness, but their cumulative effect will positively affect a person's health status. These activities should be viewed as opportunities to exercise and not as chores that have to be done. Developing and cultivating this attitude and the resultant behavioral changes that accompany it will provide many health and cosmetic benefits, perhaps enhancing self-esteem. These activities, however, will not contribute to good health and fitness if participation is sporadic. Activities that develop cardiorespiratory and muscular fitness (such as jogging, swimming, cycling, and cross-country skiing) produce health benefits such as weight loss, lower serum cholesterol levels, higher HDL-cholesterol levels, and lower blood pressure more effectively than everyday activities. Exercise for physical fitness produces fitness benefits such as increasing aerobic capacity, stroke volume, cardiac output and lowering resting heart rate. and health benefits; exercise for health produces health benefits with some improvement in physical fitness.

Other Contributing Risk Factors

Obesity. Obesity is not conducive to increased longevity because it is a strain on the heart and a precursor for many of the modifiable risk factors that promote cardiovascular disease. The National Institutes of Health (NIH) has summarized the data that were collected before 1985 on the relationship between obesity and health. The results indicated that obesity is highly related to increased sickness and death. Studies since 1985 have confirmed the NIH results. This section concentrates on the relationship between obesity and cardiovascular disease. (Other hazards associated with obesity are discussed in Chapter 7.)

The incidence of high blood pressure is three times greater among the obese than among normal-weight people.[30] The same relationship was observed in schoolchildren.[31] Obese children and adults are more likely to have higher levels of blood cholesterol and triglycerides.[25] More of their cholesterol is in the form of LDL and less in the form of HDL. The risk factors for heart disease are more prevalent among the obese, and mortality is higher and occurs earlier.[32] Estimates indicate that there would be 25% less coronary heart disease, 35% less congestive heart failure, and 35% less strokes if all Americans were at their optimum weight.[33] The prevalence of type II diabetes (non-insulin dependent) is three times greater among the obese than among normal-weight people.[34] Poorly controlled diabetes has a devastating effect on the blood vessels. Weight loss by type II diabetics results in predictable improvement in their insulin and blood glucose levels, often normalizing these values. The risks to health associated with obesity are reversible with weight loss. (The strategies for weight loss are discussed in Chapter 8.)

Diabetes mellitus. Diabetes mellitus has numerous long-range complications. These primarily involve degenerative disorders of the blood vessels and nerves. Diabetics who die prematurely are usually the victims of cardiovascular lesions and accelerated atherosclerosis. The incidence of heart attacks and strokes is higher among diabetics than nondiabetics.

The arteries supplying the kidneys, eyes, and legs are particularly susceptible to atherosclerosis. Kidney failure is one of the long-term complications of diabetes. Diabetes is also the second-leading cause of blindness in the United States. Impaired delivery of blood to the legs may lead to gangrene, necessitating amputation of the affected tissues. In addition to circulatory problems, degenerative lesions in the nervous system lead to multiple neuropathies that result in dysfunction of the brain, spinal cord, and peripheral nerves. Unfortunately, medical science has been unable to identify the biological mechanisms responsible for these long-term vascular and neural complications. However, these complications can be mitigated by leading a balanced, well-regulated life, thereby keeping diabetes under control. Control includes dietary manipulation, exercise, weight control, rest, and medication if needed.

The landmark Physician's Health Study was the first major effort to show that exercise reduced the risk of developing type II diabetes.[35] Type II diabetes (non-insulin—dependent diabetes mellitus [NIDDM]) represents 90% of all diabetes cases and usually occurs in middle-aged, overweight people. The physicians who exercised vigorously five or more times per week had a 42% reduction in NIDDM compared with those who exercised less than one time per week. The reduction in risk was particularly pronounced among those at the greatest risk: the obese. The researchers concluded that at least 24% of all cases of NIDDM were related to sedentary living.

Stress. Stress is difficult to define and quantify. Authorities agree that distress or chronic stress produces a complex array of physiological changes in the body (see Chapter 8). Stress probably does not cause disease, but it predisposes a person to illness and may hasten the process of subclinical disease (incipient disease that is not yet detectable).

Figure 2-14 Iron-Rich Blood and Heart Disease?

A study completed in Finland produced evidence that too much stored iron in the body is a risk for heart disease. Ferritin is the major stored form of iron in the body. Finnish men who had high blood levels of iron (more than 200 micrograms per liter of blood) were twice as likely to have a heart attack as men who had lower levels. If correct, this theory provides an explanation for some unknown factors. For example, the low risk for heart disease among premenopausal women may be attributed to the loss of iron in menstrual blood flow. Their ferritin serum levels are typically 25 to 50 micrograms per liter of blood. Aspirin may protect the heart because it provokes intestinal bleeding and consequently iron loss. Exercise training may reduce the incidence of heart disease because it reduces the iron level in the blood. Eating red meat may contribute to heart disease because it is rich in iron.

These examples appear to support the iron connection to heart disease. However, these assumptions may also be used to rebut the iron/heart disease relationship. For example, is it the iron lost in menstruation or is it the production of estrogen that protects the heart? Estrogen's effect on the heart has been proved. Does aspirin use promote enough blood loss to deplete iron to the point that it is protective?

The answer is probably not. Does the moderate amount of exercise needed to protect the heart reduce the serum iron level enough to reduce the risk of heart disease? Again the answer is probably not. Is it the iron in meat that causes heart disease or is it the saturated fat? The saturated fat is the more likely culprit.

Follow-up studies will need to determine the role of iron in heart disease. Meanwhile, people should continue to lower the proved risk factors and defer lowering dietary intake of iron.

The mechanisms through which stress weakens the body are not well understood, but the immune system appears to be involved. Chronic stress may depress the immune system for weeks, months, or years. Under chronic stress, the body secretes above-normal amounts of hormones (catecholamines) that circulate at high levels in the bloodstream. The catecholamines, which ready the body for physical action, are metabolized and efficiently removed from the bloodstream when a physical response is made.

Blood levels remain elevated if no physical action occurs. Circulating catecholamines constrict the arteries and increase the workload of the heart.

The individual's reaction to stress rather than the stressor itself presents the problem. Two people may react differently to the same stressor. One might perceive a stressor as an exciting challenge to overcome, whereas the other views the same stressor as anxiety producing and threatening. A course in stress management and the use of stress-reduction techniques such as exercise and voluntary relaxation should help mitigate the stress response.

Recently, high levels of iron in the blood have been implicated as a risk for heart attack. See Figure 2-14 for a discussion of this relationship.

Now that you have a good foundation of knowledge of the risk factors for cardiovascular disease, refer to Assessment Activities 2-2 and 2-3. Read the case studies and answer the questions.

Lifestyle changes commensurate with positive health behaviors are the cornerstone of health promotion. However, for many reasons—familial, genetic, and environmental—most people will require medical attention at some time in their lives. Great strides have been made in the diagnosis and treatment of disease, including cardiovascular disease.

Diagnostic Techniques

Diagnosing cardiovascular disease is becoming more sophisticated. Diagnosis begins with a medical examination and patient history. This procedure may be supplemented with a variety of tests that may confirm or refute the physician's suspicions of the presence of cardiovascular disease. Exercise stress tests using a motor driven treadmill with the patient hooked to an ECG have gained popularity in the last 10 years or so. It is a noninvasive test using surface electrodes on the chest that are sensitive to the electrical actions of the heart. Mechanical anomalies of the heart produce abnormal electrical impulses that are displayed on the ECG strip. These are read and interpreted by the physicians.

The treadmill "road tests" the heart as it works progressively harder to meet the increasing oxygen requirement as the exercise protocol becomes more physically demanding (Figure 2-15). This test is more accurate for men than women. The gender difference in response to the treadmill test is not completely understood, but it is believed that women's breasts and extra fat tissue interfere with the reception of electrical impulses by the chest electrodes.

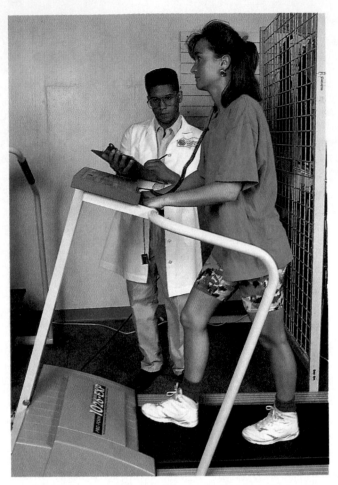

FIGURE 2-15 The treadmill test may be used as a diagnostic tool and to measure aerobic capacity.

In some cases a thallium treadmill test is required because it is more sensitive; however, it is also much more expensive. This involves the injection of radioactive thallium during the final minute of the treadmill test. Thallium is accepted, or taken up, by normal heart muscle but not by ischemic heart muscle. The absorption or nonabsorption of thallium can be seen on a television monitor. The thallium stress test increases diagnostic sensitivity to cardiovascular disease to approximately 90%.

Echocardiography is a safe, noninvasive technique that uses sound waves to determine the size of the heart, the thickness of the walls, and the function of its valves. *Cardiac catheterization* is an invasive technique in which a slender tube is threaded from a blood vessel in an arm or leg into the coronary arteries. Areas of blockage can be seen on a television monitor.

Medical Treatment

A variety of drugs have been developed that lower blood pressure and cholesterol, minimize the likelihood of blood clotting, and dissolve clots during a heart attack. Even aspirin seems to play a significant role in preventing a second heart attack or an initial heart attack. The more aspirin is studied, the better it appears to be. See Figure 2-16 for a more complete update.

Surgical techniques have also affected the treatment of cardiovascular disease. *Coronary artery bypass surgery* is designed to shunt blood around an area of blockage by removing a leg vein and sewing one end of a leg vein into the aorta and the other end into a coronary artery below the blockage, thereby restoring blood flow to the heart muscle (Figure 2-17).

Balloon angioplasty uses a catheter with a doughnut-shaped balloon at the tip. The catheter is positioned at the narrow point in the artery, and the balloon is inflated to compress the fatty deposits against the arterial walls. The channel is opened, and blood flow is enhanced (Figure 2-18). A laser beam (a powerful light beam) precisely directed can dissolve clots in blood vessels. This technique has great potential for treating cardiovascular disease if it can be perfected. *Coronary artherectomy*, one of the newest techniques, uses a specially tipped catheter equipped with a high-speed rotary cutting blade to shave off plaque.

Artificial valves have been developed to replace defective heart valves, and these work quite well. On the other hand, artificial (mechanical) hearts have not performed to expectation because modern technology has not produced a surface smooth enough to simulate the natural interior of the human heart. Blood clotting continues to occur at the valves in these devices. However, mechanical assist devices have been successfully used to aid a failing heart while the patient awaits a heart for transplantation.

Heart transplants have prolonged many lives. The outlook for patients has improved considerably because of the development and use of cyclosporine, an antirejection drug. The 5-year survival rate is up to 72%.

Candidates for transplants are those whose hearts are irreversibly damaged with disease that does not respond to conventional treatment. Without a new heart, these people will die. In 1968, 23 heart transplants were performed; in 1990, 2071 were performed. The major problems associated with heart transplantation involve too few donors, procurement of a compatible donor heart, and the constant battle against organ rejection by the recipient.

Figure 2-16 Aspirin—Better Than We Thought

As a medical remedy, aspirin dates back 2000 years. Traditionally, aspirin's primary function was to relieve pain and reduce fever and inflammation. Recently, investigators have become interested in aspirin's other qualities, namely, its anticlotting properties. The early attention was focused on people who had a previous heart attack or stroke and on those who had angina pectoris (chest pain). Aspirin therapy was found to decrease the risk for a subsequent cardiovascular event. The results from 25 studies indicated that low-dose aspirin (1) lowered the risk for major cardiovascular or cerebrovascular complications by 25%, (2) lowered the total death rate for a vascular event by 15%, (3) reduced the risk of nonfatal heart attack by 32%, and (4) reduced the risk of nonfatal stroke by 27%.

Taking aspirin within a couple of hours after a heart attack has reduced mortality by 23% during the first 5 weeks following the attack. Aspirin plays an important role in preventing a second or third heart attack. Its potential for preventing an initial heart attack was addressed in the Physician's Health Study. One standard aspirin tablet taken every other day lowered the heart attack risk by 44% in a population of male physicians 40 to 84 years of age.

Because the subjects in these studies were males, the effect of aspirin use on females is unclear. However, a study of a large population of nurses is currently underway to determine if females respond similarly to preventive and therapeutic aspirin therapy.

The ideal aspirin dosage required to protect the heart is not known. Available evidence suggests that less than one tablet every other day is sufficient. The best dose may be less than a quarter of a tablet. In the case of aspirin for protection against a first heart attack, more of the drug is definitely not better.

Aspirin reduces the risk and incidence of heart attack because of its anticlotting properties. It prevents the blood platelets from clumping together to form a plug. When a plug develops at the site of a diseased coronary or cerebral artery, a heart attack or stroke will occur.

Even though aspirin appears to be effective in preventing heart attacks and strokes, current medical advice is to consult a physician to determine if it is desirable for you. Regular aspirin usage does have undesirable side effects. It can cause gastrointestinal distress and internal bleeding. The most serious complication of aspirin use occurs in people with uncontrolled hypertension, which is the leading cause of a hemorrhagic stroke. Because aspirin promotes bleeding, the risk of a stroke of this type becomes greater than aspirin's preventive effect against a heart attack.

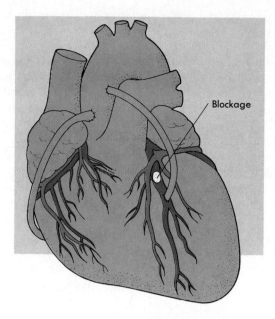

FIGURE 2-17 Coronary bypass graft.

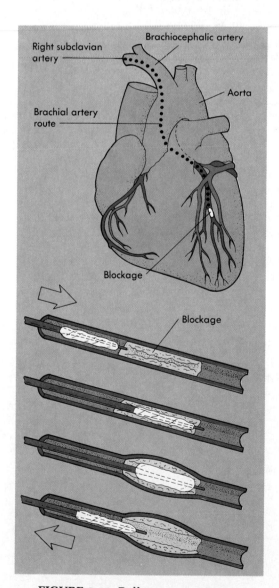

FIGURE 2-18 Balloon angioplasty.

Prevention of Heart Disease

Prevention remains the best method to prevent heart disease. It includes regular exercise, maintenance of optimum body weight, sound nutritional practices, abstinence from tobacco products, nonuse or use of alcohol in moderation, and abstinence from drugs. Dealing with stress in constructive ways, removing oneself as much as possible from destructive and disease-producing environmental conditions, and having periodic medical examinations are other aspects of prevention. It is much better physically, psychologically, and economically to make the effort to enhance health now rather than to reject or ignore health promotion principles and treat disease later. It is never too late to change behavior. Even patients with coronary artery disease can benefit from lifestyle changes. In fact, one study whose subjects were coronary heart disease patients showed that comprehensive lifestyle changes actually reversed their coronary atherosclerosis to some extent in just 1 year.[36] These patients exercised regularly, lost weight, ate a high fiber—low fat diet, stopped smoking, and learned techniques for managing stress.

Refer to Assessment Activity 2-1 at the end of this chapter. Respond to each of the risk factors and determine your risk status.

Summary

▶ Approximately 1.5 million heart attacks occur each year, and 500,000 of these result in death.

▶ From 1976 to 1986, the death rate from coronary heart disease declined by 28%.

▶ The heart is actually two pumps in one: the pulmonary pump, which sends deoxygenated blood to the lungs, and the systemic pump, which sends oxygenated blood to all tissues of the body.

▶ Blood plasma is a clear, yellowish fluid that makes up about 55% of the blood. The remaining 45% consists of blood solids—red blood cells, white blood cells, and blood platelets.

▶ Strokes are caused by a thrombus, an embolus, or a hemorrhage.

▶ Coronary heart disease is actually a disease of the coronary blood vessels that bring nourishment and oxygen to the heart.

▶ Many of the risk factors for heart disease originate in childhood.

▶ The treatment of heart disease includes the development of appropriate lifestyle habits and medical intervention.

▶ The major risk factors that cannot be changed are age, male gender, and heredity.

▶ The major risk factors that can be changed are elevated cholesterol levels, hypertension, cigarette smoking, and physical inactivity.

▶ The other contributing risk factors are obesity, diabetes mellitus, and stress.

▶ Cholesterol is a steroid that is essential for many bodily functions, but too much circulating in the blood is a risk for cardiovascular disease.

▶ Low-density lipoproteins are associated with the development of atherosclerotic plaque.

▶ High-density lipoproteins protect the arteries from the formation of plaque.

▶ Blood pressure is the force exerted against the walls of the arteries as blood is pumped from the heart and travels through the circulatory system.

▶ *Hypertension* is the medical term for high blood pressure.

▶ Cigarette smoking may be the most potent of the risk factors associated with chronic illness and premature death.

▶ Involuntary, or passive, smoking is associated with premature disease and death.

▶ Obesity often co-exists with many of the other risk factors for cardiovascular disease.

▶ Diabetes mellitus must be controlled to reduce the cardiovascular complications that accompany it.

▶ Regular exercise significantly reduces the risk for non-insulin—dependent diabetes mellitus.

▶ Stress predisposes a person to illness and may hasten the process of subclinical disease.

Action Plan for Personal Wellness

Use the information presented in this chapter to answer the following questions and to formulate an action plan to enhance your personal wellness.

1 Based on the information presented in this chapter and what I know about my family's health history, the health problems and issues that I need to be concerned about are:_____

_____

_____

2 Of the health concerns listed in number 1, the one I most need to act on is:_____

_____

_____

3 Possible actions that I can take to improve my level of wellness are (be specific):_____

_____

_____

4 Of the actions listed in number 3, the one that I most need to include in an action plan is:_____

_____

_____

5 Factors I need to keep in mind to be successful in my action plan are:_____

_____

_____

Review Questions

1. Define pulmonary pump and systemic pump and discuss the function of each.
2. Describe the advent of heart disease in the United States.
3. Identify and describe the causes of stroke.
4. What is coronary heart disease? Discuss the treatment options that are available.
5. What are the risk factors for heart disease and how are they categorized by the AHA?
6. What is cholesterol? LDL? HDL?
7. What is the relationship between total cholesterol and HDL?
8. What is essential hypertension?
9. What ingredients in cigarettes increase the risk for cardiovascular disease? Describe their effect on the heart and blood vessels.
10. What is the risk associated with smokeless tobacco products?
11. Defend the proposition that a moderate level of exercise improves health and increases longevity.
12. What are the cardiovascular complications of diabetes mellitus?
13. How does stress contribute to cardiovascular disease?

References

1. American Heart Association: *1992 heart and stroke facts*, Dallas, 1992, The Association.
2. Kannell WB et al: Epidemiology of acute myocardial infarction: the Framingham study, *Med Today* 2:50-57, 1968.
3. Task Force on Blood Pressure Control in Children: Report of the second task force on blood pressure control in children—1987, *Pediatrics* 79:1-25, 1987.
4. US Department of Health and Human Services: *The health consequences of smoking*, Washington, DC, 1988, US Government Printing Office.
5. Enos WF et al: Coronary disease among United States soldiers killed in action in Korea: preliminary report, *JAMA* 152:1090-1093, 1953.
6. McNamara JJ et al: Coronary artery disease in combat casualties in Vietnam, *JAMA* 216:1185-1187, 1971.
7. Van Camp SP, Boyer JL: Cardiovascular aspects of aging, *Physician Sportsmed* 17(4):121-130, 1989.
8. Bush TL: Influence on cholesterol and lipoprotein levels in women, *Cholesterol Coronary Dis—Reducing Risk* 2(6):1-5, 1990.
9. Lamb L: Update on cholesterol and triglycerides, *Health Letter* 39(suppl):1-8, 1992.
10. The lipid research clinics coronary primary prevention trial results: I. Reduction in the incidence of coronary heart disease, *JAMA* 251:351-364, 1984.
11. LaRosa JC et al: The cholesterol facts: a summary of the evidence relating dietary fats, serum cholesterol, and coronary heart disease: a joint statement by the American Heart Association and the National Heart, Lung, and Blood Institute, *Circulation* 81:1721, 1990.
12. Manninen V et al: Lipid alterations and decline in the incidence of coronary heart disease in the Helsinki heart study, *JAMA* 260:641-651, 1988.
13. Steinberg D, Witztum JL: Lipoproteins and atherogenesis—current concepts, *JAMA*, 264:3047-3051, 1990.
14. US Department of Health and Human Services—Public Health Services: *Healthy people 2000*, Washington, DC, 1990, The Department.
15. US Department of Health and Human Services—Public Health Services: *Healthy people 2000*, Washington, DC, 1990, Department of Health and Human Services.
16. American Cancer Society: *Cancer facts and figures—1992*, Atlanta, 1992, The Society.
17. Lamb LL, editor: Cigarettes and women, *Health Letter* 31:4, 1988.
18. *The health consequences of smoking—nicotine addiction, a report of the Surgeon General*, Rockville, Md, 1988, US Department of Health and Human Services.
19. Passive smoking: a threat to health? *Harvard Health Letter*, 3:8, 1991.
20. It's official: inactivity increases coronary risk, *Harvard Health Letter*, 3:8, 1992.
21. Powell KE: Physical activity and the incidence of coronary heart disease, *Annu Rev Pub Health*, 8:253-261, 1987.
22. Paffenbarger RS et al: Physical activity, all cause mortality, and longevity of college alumni, *New Engl J Med* 314:605-613, 1986.
23. Sallis JF et al: Moderate-intensity physical activity and cardiovascular risk factors: the Stanford five-city project, *Prev Med* 15:561-568, 1986.
24. Blair SN: Low physical fitness and increased risk of death and disability, speech delivered at Southern District American Alliance for Health, Physical Education, Recreation, and Dance (SDAAHPERD) Convention, Chattanooga, Tenn, Feb 24, 1989.
25. Blair SN et al: Physical fitness and all-cause mortality—a prospective study of healthy men and women, *JAMA* 262:2395-2401, 1989.
26. Manson JE et al: The primary prevention of myocardial infarction, *New Engl J Med* 326:1406-1416, 1992.
27. Duncan JJ et al: Women walking for health and fitness, *JAMA* 266:3295-3299, 1991.
28. Keeler EB et al: The external costs of a sedentary lifestyle, *Am J Pub Health*, 79:975-980, 1989.
29. Paffenbarger RS, Hyde RT: *New Engl J Med* 315:400-401, 1986 (letter).
30. Hubert HB et al: Life-style correlates of risk factor change in young adults: an 8 year study of coronary heart disease risk factors in the Framingham offspring, *Am J Epidemiol* 125:812-831, 1987.
31. Jequier E: Energy, obesity, and body weight standards, *Am J Clin Nutr* 45:1035-1047, 1987.
32. Hamm P et al: Large fluctuations in body weight during young adulthood and twenty-five year risk of coronary death in men, *Am J Epidemiol* 129:312-318, 1989.
33. Bray GA, Gray DS: Obesity. I. Pathogenesis, *West J Med* 149:429-441, 1988.
34. National Institutes of Health Consensus Development Conference Statement: Health implications of obesity, Feb 11-13, 1985, *Ann Intern Med* 103:981-1077, 1985.
35. Manson JE et al: A prospective study of exercise and incidence of diabetes among U.S. male physicians, *JAMA* 268:63-67, 1992.
36. Ornish D et al: Can lifestyle changes reverse coronary heart disease, *Lancet* 336:129-133, 1990.

Annotated Readings

Low doses of estrogen may protect against heart disease, *Mayo Clin Health Letter* 10:5, 1992.
Presents two ways that estrogen replacement therapy may protect postmenopausal women against atherosclerosis: (1) it lowers blood levels of LDL cholesterol, and (2) it raises blood levels of HDL cholesterol. Low doses of estrogen have proved to be as effective as higher doses with fewer side effects.

Women and heart disease, *University of California at Berkeley Wellness Letter* 8:4-5, 1992.
Advances some of the reasons why women have been neglected as subjects in heart disease studies. Covers the risks for women and the role of prevention and therapy. Suggests ways for lowering a woman's risk for heart disease and stroke.

Simon HB: Can you run away from cancer? *Harvard Health Letter*, 17:5-7, 1992.
Suggests from studies in the United States and other countries that a sedentary life increases the risk for many forms of cancer. Focuses on colon cancer, breast cancer, and cancers of the reproductive system. Also covers theories of how exercise works to prevent cancer.

The nicotine patch, *Harvard Heart Letter* 3:1-3, 1992.
Discusses the pros and cons of using the transdermal nicotine patch as an aid to stop smoking. Addresses the central issue of whether preventing nicotine withdrawal actually helps a smoker to quit.

Daniels SR, Loggie JMH: Hypertension in children and adolescents, *Physician Sportsmed* 20:121-134, 1992.
Discusses how although exercise is clinically useful in treating hypertension, strenuous exercise may not be appropriate for all hypertensive children. Focuses primarily on who may be helped and who may not benefit from strenuous exercise.

ASSESSMENT ACTIVITY

2 - 1

Arizona Heart Institute Cardiovascular Risk Factor Analysis

Directions: Indicate the points in the column on the right for each of the following risk factors. When you finish, total your points and compare that with the results at the end of the activity.

Risk Factors	Score	
▶ Age	Age 56 or over	1
	Age 55 or under	0 _____
▶ Gender	Male	1
	Female	0 _____
▶ Family history	If you have:	
	Blood relatives who have had a heart attack or stroke at or before age 60	12
	Blood relatives who have had a heart attack or stroke after age 60	6
	No blood relatives who have had a heart attack or stroke	0 _____
▶ Personal history	Age 50 or under: if you had a heart attack, a stroke, heart or blood vessel surgery	20
	Age 51 or over: if you had any of the above	10
	None of the above	0 _____
▶ Diabetes	Diabetes before age 40 and now on insulin	10
	Diabetes at or after age 40 and now on insulin or pills	5
	Diabetes controlled by diet or diabetes after age 55	3
	No diabetes	0 _____
▶ Smoking	Two packs per day	10
	Between one and two packs per day or quit smoking less than a year ago	6
	Smoke six or more cigars a day or inhale a pipe regularly	6
	Less than one pack per day or quit smoking more than one year ago	3
	Never smoked	0 _____
▶ Cholesterol (if known)	Cholesterol level—276 or above	10
	Cholesterol level—between 225 and 275	5
	Cholesterol level—224 or below	0 _____
▶ Diet (if cholesterol unknown)	Does your normal eating pattern include:	
	One serving of red meat daily, more than seven eggs a week, and daily consumption of butter, whole milk, and cheese	8
	Red meat 4 to 6 times a week, 4 to 7 eggs a week, margarine, low-fat dairy products, and some cheese	4
	Poultry, fish, little or no red meat, three or fewer eggs a week, some margarine, skim milk, and skim milk products	0 _____
▶ High blood pressure	If either number is:	
	160/100 or higher	10
	140/90 but less than 160/100	5
	If both numbers are less than 140/90	0 _____

▶ Weight Ideal weight formula:
Men = 110 lb plus 5 lb for each inch over 5 feet
Women = 100 lb plus 5 lb for each inch over 5 feet
25 lb overweight   4
10 to 24 lb overweight   2
Less than 10 lb overweight   0 _____

▶ Exercise Do you engage in any aerobic exercise (brisk walking, jog-
ging, bicycling, racketball, swimming) for more than 15
min:
Less than once a week   4
One to two times a week   2
Three or more times a week   0 _____

▶ Stress Are you:
Frustrated when waiting in line, often in a hurry to complete   4
work or keep appointments, easily angered, and irritable
Impatient when waiting, occasionally hurried, or occasionally moody   2
Comfortable when waiting, seldom rushed, and easygoing   0 _____

TOTAL _____

Score Results

PLEASE NOTE: A high score does not mean you will develop heart disease. It is merely a guide to make you aware of a potential risk. Because no two people are alike, an exact prediction is impossible without further individualized testing.

With answer to high blood pressure question		Without answer to high blood pressure question	
High risk	≥40	High risk	≥36
Medium risk	20-39	Medium risk	19-35
Low risk	≤19 and below	Low risk	≤18

A S S E S S M E N T   A C T I V I T Y   2 - 2

A Case Study on Bill M.

Directions: To determine your understanding of cardiovascular health and wellness, read the following case study and answer the accompanying questions.

Bill, a 38-year-old man who is 5′8″ tall and weighs 205 lb, has the following history:

▶ His father died of a heart attack at age 48 years; his grandfather died of a heart attack at age 52 years.

▶ His cholesterol level is 256 mg/dl, LDL is 172 mg/dl, and HDL is 40 mg/dl.

▶ His blood pressure is consistently in the 150/95 range.

▶ He smokes one pack of cigarettes per day.

▶ He drinks six to eight brewed cups of coffee daily.

▶ He eats two eggs with bacon or sausage and buttered toast daily.

▶ Meat is a major part of supper; he skips lunch.

▶ His favorite snacks are ice cream, buttered popcorn, and salted peanuts.

▶ He occasionally plays tennis on Sunday afternoons.

▶ He owns his own business and often works 55 to 60 hours per week.

Answer the following:

What are his risk factors for coronary heart disease?_____

_____

Which of these can he control?_____

_____

What suggestions can you give him regarding his current diet?_____

_____

What effect may a change in diet have on his coronary risk profile?_____

_____

What suggestions can you make regarding his need for exercise and how might a change in his activity level affect his coronary risk profile?_____

_____

What are the risks associated with obesity?_____

_____

ASSESSMENT ACTIVITY   2 - 3

A Case Study on Bill M. Jr.

Directions: Read the following case study and answer the accompanying questions.

Bill M. Jr. is Bill M.'s son. He is a 16-year-old adolescent who is 5'9" tall, weighs 195 lb, and has the following history:

▶ He has a family history of heart disease (see Assessment Activity 2-1).

▶ He is 20 lb overweight.

▶ His total cholesterol level is 220 mg/dl; HDL is 28 mg/dl.

▶ His blood pressure is 140/85.

▶ He regularly uses smokeless tobacco products.

▶ He drinks 5 to 6 Classic Cokes per day.

▶ He eats 3 to 5 meals per week at fast-food restaurants.

▶ He does not like vegetables and eats only potatoes.

▶ He occasionally plays pick-up basketball.

Answer the following:

What are his risks factors for coronary heart disease? _____

_____

What suggestions can you make to him regarding his eating pattern? _____

_____

What suggestions can you give him about regular exercise? _____

_____

Bill Jr. says he is too young to be concerned about future health problems. How would you respond to this? _____

_____

Cardiorespiratory Endurance

Technology has affected American life by increasing productivity while simultaneously reducing and in some cases eliminating the amount of physical work for labor. Therefore physical fitness can no longer be attained on the job, and leisure hours represent the only time for its development. Literally dozens of activities that are sufficiently different are so available, almost anyone can find a physical activity that is enjoyable and challenging. This chapter focuses on the principles and concepts required to develop and maintain a physical fitness program to improve cardiorespiratory endurance.

The Components of Physical Fitness

Authorities do not agree on a definition of physical fitness, but most have endorsed the concept of *performance-related* and *health-related* fitness. **Performance-related fitness,** or sports fitness, consists of the following components: speed, power, balance, coordination, agility, and reaction time. These are essential sports skills, but they may not contribute significantly to those activities performed for health enhancement (Figure 3-1).

Speed is velocity or the ability to move rapidly. Power is the product of force and velocity and the rate at which work is performed. Balance, or equilibrium, is the ability to maintain a desired body position either statically or dynamically. Coordination is the harmonious integration of the body parts to produce smooth fluid motion. Agility is the ability to change direction rapidly. Reaction time is the time required (usually measured in hundredths of a second) to respond to a stimulus.

The components of **health-related fitness** are cardiorespiratory endurance, muscular strength, muscular endurance, flexibility, and body composition. In this text the exercise emphasis is on health-related fitness. Performance-related and health-related fitness, although separate, are not mutually exclusive. For example, competitors may find that the health-related components of their sport or activity are essential for success. Racquetball, tennis, basketball, soccer, and handball require one or more of the health-related components. Conversely, health enthusiasts may engage in physical activities that require some or all of the performance-related components. However, the development and maintenance of health-related fitness does not depend on athletic ability or activities that are high in the performance components. Fitness for health purposes can be achieved with minimal psychomotor ability when activities such as walking, jogging, cycling, hiking, backpacking, orienteering, swimming, rope jumping, and weight training are selected.

Remember the old adage, "no pain, no gain"? Trying to comply with it has done more harm than good to sedentary people attempting to become physically active. The health benefits of exercise occur when exercise is somewhat uncomfortable rather than painful. Only the most dedicated health enthusiasts and competitors can face exercise that constantly produces pain. Although exercise for health enhancement should stress cardiorespiratory development, the other components of fitness should not be neglected. Flexibility exercises should be a part of the warm-up and cool-down procedures. Resistance/strength training plays an important role and should be an integral part of a well-rounded fitness program.

Figure 3-1   What's the Difference?

Components of fitness

Health related
▶ Cardiorespiratory endurance
▶ Muscular strength
▶ Muscular endurance
▶ Flexibility
▶ Body composition

Performance related
▶ Speed
▶ Power
▶ Balance
▶ Coordination
▶ Agility
▶ Reaction time

Activities

Health related
▶ Walking
▶ Running
▶ Jogging
▶ Cycling
▶ Hiking
▶ Swimming
▶ Rope jumping
▶ Weight training
▶ Cross-country skiing

Performance related
▶ Raquetball
▶ Handball
▶ Squash
▶ Tennis
▶ Badminton
▶ Soccer
▶ Softball
▶ Basketball
▶ Football
▶ Water polo

Cardiorespiratory Endurance

Cardiorespiratory endurance is the ability to take in, deliver, and extract oxygen for physical work. It is the ability to persevere at a physical task. Cardiorespiratory endurance improves with regular participation in aerobic activities such as speed walking, jogging, cycling, swimming, and cross-country skiing. The term **aerobic** literally means "with oxygen," but when applied to exercise, it refers to activities in which oxygen demand can be supplied continuously during performance. Aerobic performance depends on a continuous and sufficient supply of oxygen to burn the carbohydrates and fats needed to fuel such activities. In other words, the intensity or the energy requirement is within the capacity of the performer to sustain for longer than a couple of minutes.[1] Figure 3 illustrates aerobic activity in which the oxygen demand of the activity and the body's ability to supply it are balanced.

Cardiorespiratory endurance is also referred to as **aerobic capacity,** or maximum oxygen consumption (VO_2 max). Cardiorespiratory endurance is the most important component of physical fitness and the foundation of total fitness.

The physiological changes that result from car-

diorespiratory training are referred to as the long-term, or *chronic, effects of exercise.* The effects of training are measurable and predictable.

Heart Rate

A few months of aerobic training lowers the resting heart rate by 10 to 25 beats per minute. It also low-

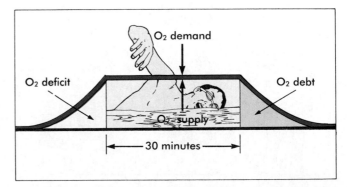

FIGURE 3-2 Aerobic exercise lasting 30 minutes. While performance is in "steady state," the individual's ability to supply oxygen is equal to the oxygen demand of the activity. The condition of steady state is characteristic of aerobic types of activities.

ers the heart rate for a given workload. For example, a slow jog may produce a heart rate of 165 beats per minute before training and 140 beats per minute after a few months of training. The trained heart is a stronger, more efficient pump that is capable of delivering the required oxygen with fewer beats. This is accomplished because the trained heart is capable of ejecting more blood per beat.

Stroke Volume

Stroke volume is the amount of blood that the heart can eject in one beat. Aerobic training increases the stroke volume by (1) increasing the size of the cavity of the ventricles, which results in greater filling of the heart with blood, and (2) increasing the contractile strength of the ventricular wall, so contraction is more forceful and a greater amount of blood is ejected from the ventricles. Figure 3-3 compares a trained and an untrained heart. Training increases the size of the cavity of the left ventricle and the thickness of the ventricular wall. These adaptations result in greater filling and emptying capabilities and therefore an increase in stroke volume. This is one of the major mechanisms responsible for the improvement in aerobic capacity.

Cardiac Output

Cardiac output is the amount of blood ejected by the heart in 1 minute. Cardiac output (Q) is the product of heart rate (HR) and stroke volume (SV) ($Q = HR \times SV$). Cardiac output increases with aerobic training during maximal effort—it does not increase at rest or during submaximal exercise.

The average cardiac output at rest is 4 to 6 liters of blood per minute. During maximal exertion, cardiac output reaches values of 20 to 25 liters of blood per minute for the average person but may reach as much as 40 liters per minute for large, well-conditioned athletes. This amount of blood the heart can pump in 1 minute during exercise of maximal intensity is equivalent to 10 to 20 2-liter bottles filled with liquid. Maximum cardiac output improves with training because of the increase in stroke volume. Maximum heart rate is essentially unaffected by training; therefore its influence on cardiac output is constant and unchanging. Any increase in cardiac output is accounted for by increases in stroke volume.

Blood Volume

Aerobic training increases total blood volume, plasma volume (the liquid portion of the blood), and the blood solids (the red blood cells, white blood cells, and blood platelets). The increase is greatest in plasma volume, so the blood becomes more liquid. The increase in the ratio of plasma volume to red blood cell volume is an adaptation to exercise that lowers the viscosity or thickness and stickiness of the blood. This change decreases the resistance to blood flow, allowing it to circulate more easily through the blood vessels.

Blood is automatically shunted by the body to areas of greatest need. At rest, a significant amount is sent to the digestive system and kidneys. During vigorous exercise as much as 85% of the blood is sent to the working muscles, reducing the amount sent to the digestive and urinary systems.[2]

Heart Volume

The muscles of the body respond to exercise by growing larger and stronger. As a muscular pump, the heart is no exception. The volume and weight of the heart increase with endurance training. Training that lowers the resting heart rate stimulates greater filling of the ventricles, whose muscle fibers respond to the increased pool of blood by stretching. This produces a recoil effect in the muscle fibers that results in a stronger contraction with more blood ejected per beat. Continued training causes the ventricles to enlarge and grow stronger, so the weight as well as the size of the heart increases. The hypertrophied (enlarged) heart is a normal response to endurance training that has no long-term detrimental

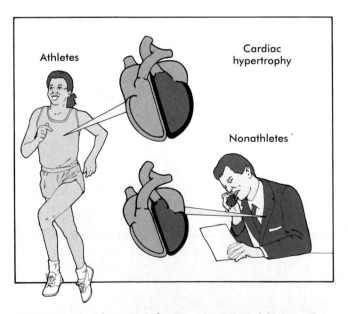

FIGURE 3-3 The trained versus untrained heart. The athlete's heart exemplifies the results of aerobic training. The ventricles are larger than the nonathletic heart and the walls are slightly thicker.

effects. In fact, although maintaining this effect for life is beneficial, several months of inactivity will reduce heart weight and size to pretraining levels. The atrophy (wasting away) associated with physical inactivity is inevitable.

Respiratory Responses

The chest muscles that support breathing improve in both strength and endurance. Vital capacity, which is the amount of air that can be expired maximally following a maximum inspiration, increases slightly. A corresponding decrease occurs in "dead space" air or residual volume, which is the amount of air remaining in the lungs after a maximal expiration.

Training substantially increases maximal pulmonary ventilation (the amount of air moved in and out of the lungs). Before training, the lungs can ventilate approximately 120 liters of air per minute. Pulmonary ventilation increases to about 150 liters of air following a few months of training. Highly trained athletes commonly ventilate 180 to 200 liters of air per minute.

Blood flow to the lungs, particularly to the upper lobes, appears to increase after training. This results in a larger and more efficient surface for the exchange of oxygen and carbon dioxide.

Metabolic Responses

Endurance training improves aerobic capacity by 15% to 30% in previously untrained, healthy adults. The improvement is the result of several physiological adaptations that increase the body's production of energy. First, *ATP* (adenosine triphosphate), the actual unit of energy for muscular contraction, is increased because organelles within the cells that use oxygen to produce ATP increase in number and size. These organelles are the *mitochondria* and are often referred to as the cell's *powerhouse*. Second, an increase in the enzymes located within the mitochondria that accelerate the production of ATP occurs. Third, cardiac output and blood perfusion of the muscles performing the work increase. Finally, training facilitates and increases the extraction of oxygen by the exercising muscles. These are some of the major adaptations that combine to enhance aerobic endurance.

Aerobic capacity is limited by heredity and is finite. Reaching your aerobic potential can only occur through aerobic endurance training. High genetic potential along with diligent and knowledgeable training result in endurance. Many people have participated in marathons, ultramarathons, triathalons, cross-country runs, long-distance swims, and long-distance bike races. Most people are average in aer-

Achieving health-related fitness does not depend on athletic ability.

obic ability and cannot compete with specially endowed athletes, but all individuals can achieve their aerobic potential with endurance training.

Aerobic capacity reaches a peak after 6 months to 2 years of steady endurance training. At this point, it levels off and remains unchanged for a number of years, even if training is intensified. However, aerobic performance continues to improve with harder training, since a higher percentage of the aerobic capacity can be maintained for a longer period. For example, 6 months of appropriate training may allow you to jog 3 miles at 60% of your aerobic capacity. Another year of harder training may allow you to run 3 miles at 85% of your capacity. Capacity has not changed during this time, but physiological adaptations have occurred that enable the body to function at progressively higher percentages of maximum capacity.

Aerobic capacity does decrease with age, but an excellent longitudinal study indicates that it declines more slowly in physically active subjects as compared with sedentary subjects.[3] The subjects were middle-aged men whose average age at the inception of the study was 45 years. They were involved in consistent physical training for the next 23 years, and at the end of that time, they experienced only one third of the aerobic decline that was measured in a nonexercising control group. In addition, their body weights decreased by an average of 8 pounds, and blood pressure did not increase with age, which often occurs among sedentary people.

The effects of training persist as long as training continues. Fitness developed with years of continuous training can be lost in months if training is interrupted or discontinued. Subjects who suspended training for 84 days after 10 years of active participation experienced a significant decline in aerobic capacity after 3 weeks of inactivity and returned to pretraining levels in most fitness parameters by the end of the study.[4] The exceptions to complete reversal were muscle capillary density and mitochondrial enzymes, which remained 50% higher than levels measured in sedentary control subjects.[5] This study indicated that the results of inactivity are variable and affect some systems more quickly than others. Physical decline cannot be prevented with physical inactivity.

Four different methods for assessing your cardiorespiratory endurance are presented in the activity assessments. These include the Rockport Fitness Walking Test, the 3-mile walking test, the 1.5 mile run/walk test, and a 3-minute bench stepping test. Each is accompanied by norms, so you can compare your performance against the standards.

Cardiorespiratory Endurance and Wellness

Most Americans believe that exercise is good for them, but the majority cannot explain how or why. This section provides some of the answers.

Consistent participation in exercise is necessary to improve health status. Sporadic exercise does not promote physical fitness or contribute to health enhancement. In fact, infrequent participation increases the risk of sudden death during the time of exercise.[6] Those who exercise regularly and vigorously have a slightly elevated chance of dying suddenly during exercise, but the long-term compensatory health advantages gained from training clearly outweigh this minimal risk. Some selected health benefits of regular exercise are listed in Table 3-1.

Cholesterol

Regular participation in aerobic exercise reduces many of the risks associated with cardiovascular disease. The risk imposed by cholesterol can be reduced through exercise. The primary effect of exercise is on the high-density lipoprotein (HDL) fraction. HDL is the only lipoprotein that is involved in reverse transport; that is, it acts as a scavenger by picking up cholesterol from the blood and tissues and transferring

TABLE 3-1 Health-Related Benefits Associated With Regular Aerobic Exercise

Reduces the risk of cardiovascular disease
▶ Increases HDL cholesterol
▶ Decreases LDL cholesterol
▶ Favorably changes the ratios between total cholesterol and HDL-C and between LDL-C and HDL-cholesterol
▶ Decreases triglyceride levels
▶ Promotes relaxation; relieves stress and tension
▶ Decreases body fat and favorably changes body composition
▶ Reduces blood pressure, especially if it is high
▶ Makes blood platelets less sticky
▶ Decreases the incidence of cardiac arrhythmias
▶ Increases myocardial efficiency
  1. Lowers resting heart rate
  2. Increases stroke volume
▶ Increases oxygen-carrying capacity of the blood

Helps control diabetes
▶ Makes cells less resistant to insulin
▶ Reduces body fat

Develops stronger bones that are less susceptible to injury

Promotes joint stability
▶ Increases muscular strength
▶ Increases strength of the ligaments, tendons cartilage, and connective tissue

Contributes to fewer lower back problems

Acts as a stimulus for other lifestyle changes

Improves self-concept

it to other lipoproteins for delivery to the liver. The liver degrades and recycles or removes cholesterol from the body. The higher the level of HDL, the better. Exercise, particularly of the aerobic type, is the primary way to increase HDL.

Total cholesterol (TC) and low-density lipoproteins (LDL) are affected indirectly by exercise. LDLs that are oxidized are primary factors in the development and growth of plaque that, if unchecked, narrows and eventually closes arterial vessels, leading to heart attacks and strokes. Exercise effectively promotes weight loss that results in a reduction in both TC and LDL levels.

Triglyceride Levels

Evidence continues to mount implicating blood triglyceride levels in the development of atherosclerosis.[7] The role of triglycerides is complex, but it becomes significant when an abnormal cholesterol profile coexists. When serum triglyceride is high and the LDL/HDL cholesterol ratio is also high (a value greater than 5), the incidence of cardiac events is four times higher. If the ratio between LDL and HDL levels is high but the triglyceride level is low, the risk is not increased. Another elevation in risk occurs when the triglyceride level is high and HDL cholesterol level is low. Triglycerides alone appear to be less important than other risk factors, but when combined with high cholesterol, they tend to compound the risk of disease.

Triglyceride levels in the blood may be reduced by lifestyle changes. Intervention programs include smoking cessation, alcohol restriction, a diet low in fat and cholesterol, weight loss, and exercise. Aerobic exercise suppresses triglycerides for 48 to 72 hours, so you must exercise at least every other day to maintain lower levels in the blood.

Hypertension

Hypertension, the medical term for high blood pressure, is another major risk factor that can be changed. Aerobic exercise is one of several nonmedical approaches effective in lowering blood pressure. Exercise reduces the blood level of circulating epinephrine and norepinephrine. These two hormones are vasoconstrictors; that is, they constrict the arterioles (the smallest arteries) and decrease their diameters. In one study, 16 weeks of aerobic exercise decreased the blood levels of both hormones and reduced blood pressure.[8] Other investigators examined the effect of aerobic exercise on plasma norepinephrine levels and peripheral resistance.[9] Peripheral resistance, which is the resistance to blood flow, is one of the major contributors to high blood pressure.

Aerobic exercise reduced peripheral resistance, plasma norepinephrine levels, and blood pressure.

Smoking

Cigarette smoking is possibly the most important of the major risk factors that can be changed. There are many methods, suggestions, and support systems for quitting the cigarette and tobacco habit, but the majority of users find it difficult. Exercise is one alternative that has had some degree of success. Cigarette smoking seriously limits the ability to perform in endurance events, so exercisers who smoke learn early that they must quit to maximize the results of training. Moreover, those who move from a sedentary to an active lifestyle may be more amenable to quitting because participation in physical activity shows an inclination toward making healthful changes.

Diabetes Mellitus

Diabetes mellitus is a risk factor for cardiovascular disease. Diabetics who are particularly at risk are those whose condition is either not controlled or poorly controlled. Aerobic exercise contributes to the control of diabetes in the following ways: (1) it reduces the insulin requirement; (2) the lower the insulin dosage, the more normal the body's physiology, resulting in less of a "roller coaster" effect and more effective control; (3) it reduces blood platelet adhesiveness for about 24 hours; (4) it has a mitigating effect on most of the risk factors associated with coronary artery disease; and (5) it increases the cells' sensitivity to insulin.

Stress

Stress is another risk factor that can be managed. Researchers[10] examined the relationship between aerobic or cardiorespiratory fitness and psychosocial stress by reviewing 34 relevant studies. This study indicated that fit subjects were less negatively affected by any of the stressors and recovered more quickly from stress than unfit subjects. The effects of anaerobic activities (such as weight training and sprinting) on stress reduction are inconclusive because some studies found these to be stress reducing and others show no such benefit. However, the longitudinal study of Howard et al.[11] has shown that any exercise, aerobic or anaerobic, is beneficial to the mind and body. Exercise is a readily identifiable, concrete stressor that replaces ambiguous or nonspecific stress. In addition, it is an excellent release for excess energy and stifled emotions. Exercise is an important coping mechanism because it reduces the severity of the stress response, shortens recovery time, reduces stress-related vulnerability to disease, and gives a sense of control.

Principles of Conditioning

Becoming familiar with the principles of exercise is necessary to maximize the results of a physical fitness program. Your objectives can be met through the appropriate manipulation of intensity, frequency, duration, overload, progression, and specificity. Setting of objectives, warm-up, cool-down, and type of activity are important elements that add to the enjoyment and effectiveness of exercise.

Intensity

Intensity refers to the degree of vigorousness of a single session of exercise. The intensity level recommended by the American College of Sports Medicine (ACSM) is 60% to 90% of the maximum heart rate (HR_{max}).[12] HR_{max} can be measured by a physical work capacity test on a treadmill or cycle ergometer. Because most people do not have access to such tests, HR_{max} can be estimated by subtracting age from 220. A 20-year-old person has an estimated HR_{max} of 200 beats per minute ($220 - 20 = 200$). This formula predicts rather than measures HR_{max}; therefore a measurement error of approximately plus or minus 10 beats per minute is associated with its use.

After the HR_{max} has been determined, the target for exercise may be calculated. The target zone for exercise provides the desirable heart rate for the development of physical fitness. For the 20-year-old individual whose HR_{max} is 200 beats per minute, the target zone for exercise is calculated as follows:

$$
\begin{array}{r}
200 \text{ (estimated } HR_{max}) \\
\times 0.60 \text{ (60\% of } HR_{max}) \\
\hline
120 \text{ (lower limit target)} \\
200 \text{ (estimated } HR_{max}) \\
\times 0.90 \text{ (90\% of } HR_{max}) \\
\hline
180 \text{ (upper limit target)}
\end{array}
$$

This 20-year-old person should exercise at a heart rate between 120 and 180 beats per minute, depending on objectives and level of fitness. The target for a person whose level of fitness is average is 150 to 160 beats per minute for exercise. The training effect occurs at heart rate levels below the maximum.

Another method for calculating exercise heart rate, the Karvonen formula, considers fitness level and resting heart rate.[13] The training heart rate is calculated with this formula by using a percentage of the *heart rate reserve*, which is the difference between the HR_{max} and the resting heart rate. The best way to determine the resting heart rate for this method is to count the pulse rate for 15 seconds while in the sitting position immediately after waking in the morning. You should repeat this for 4 to 5 consecutive days and average the readings for a relatively accurate representation of resting heart rate. Next, you should estimate your level of fitness based on your exercise habits and select a category from Table 3-2 to determine the appropriate exercise intensity level. If you cannot decide which category is the most appropriate, take one of the three fitness tests at the end of this chapter. Your performance on these should place you in a category that reflects your physical fitness level.

As an example, the Karvonen calculations for a 25-year-old person with a resting heart rate of 75 beats per minute and an average fitness level is as follows:

▶ Calculate HR_{max}:

$$
\begin{array}{r}
220 \\
- 25 \\
\hline
195 \text{ } (HR_{max})
\end{array}
$$

▶ The Karvonen formula is the following:

$$THR = (MHR - RHR) \times T1\% + RHR$$

where *THR* is the training heart rate, *MHR* is the maximum HR, *RHR* is the resting heart rate, and T1% is the training intensity (see Table 3-2). Therefore the exercise heart rate is calculated as follows:

$$
\begin{aligned}
THR &= (195 - 75) \times 0.70 + 75 \\
&= 120 \times 0.70 + 75 \\
&= 84 + 75 \\
&= 159
\end{aligned}
$$

The training heart rate for this 25-year-old subject is 159 beats per minute. Assessment Activity 3-5 is provided at the end of the chapter for you to determine your target heart rate for exercise.

TABLE 3-2 Guidelines for Selecting Exercise Intensity Level

Fitness Level	Intensity Level (%)
Low	60
Fair	65
Average	70
Good	75
Excellent	80-90

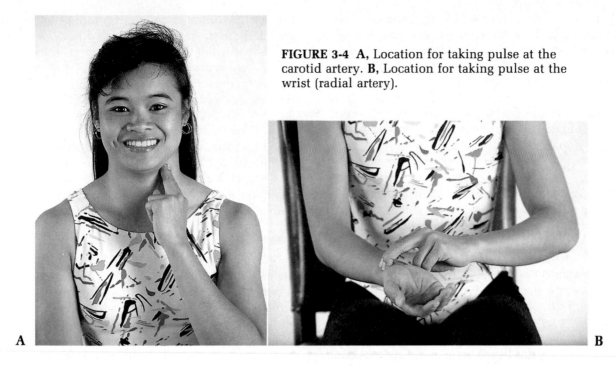

FIGURE 3-4 A, Location for taking pulse at the carotid artery. **B,** Location for taking pulse at the wrist (radial artery).

A   B

Learning to take the pulse rate quickly and accurately is necessary to monitor exercise intensity by heart rate. Two of the most commonly used sites for taking the pulse rate are the radial artery at the thumb side of the wrist and the carotid artery at the side of the neck (Figure 3-4). You use the first two fingers of the preferred hand to palpate the pulse. At the wrist, the pulse is located at the base of the thumb with the hand held palm up. For the carotid pulse, you should slide your fingers downward at the angle of the jaw below the earlobe to the side of the neck. You apply only enough pressure to feel the pulse, particularly at the carotid artery. Excessive pressure at this point stimulates specialized receptors that automatically slow the heart rate, leading to an underestimation of the rate actually achieved during exercise. The wrist is the preferred site for the *palpation* (examination by touch or feel) of the pulse rate. You should use the carotid pulse if you cannot feel your pulse at the wrist.

You should locate and count the pulse rate immediately after exercise stops. You count the beats for 10 seconds and multiply by 6 to get beats per minute. You may start the count by assigning a zero to the first beat that is felt, or you may, as nurses do, start the count by assigning the first beat felt a value of "one." Regardless of which technique you use, you should be consistent in its application. Some practice is required to locate the pulse quickly and to count it accurately.

Another method for monitoring the intensity of exercise is by rating your subjective perception of the effort. On some days, exercise seems easier than normal, and other days, it may seem more difficult. The "perceived exertion scale" in Figure 3-5 can be used to quantify the effort. The intensity level of exercise for most people should fall in the categories of 11 to 15, and this should correspond approxi-

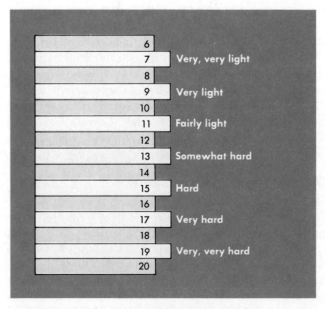

6	
7	Very, very light
8	
9	Very light
10	
11	Fairly light
12	
13	Somewhat hard
14	
15	Hard
16	
17	Very hard
18	
19	Very, very hard
20	

FIGURE 3-5 The perceived exertion scale.

mately to the target heart rate. In other words, if you are in the appropriate target heart rate zone, the perceived exertion will probably be between 11 and 15.

Frequency

The *frequency* of exercise refers to the number of days of participation each week. The ACSM recommends that exercise be pursued 3 to 5 days per week for optimal results. Less than 3 days is an inadequate stimulus for developing fitness, and conversely, more than 5 days per week represents a point of diminishing returns from exercise and increases the likelihood of injury.[12] These guidelines can be used with some flexibility. For example, exercise may be pursued more than 5 days per week if (1) low-intensity exercises of moderate duration (20 to 40 minutes) such as walking are the preferred forms of activity, (2) you use cross-training (participating in different activities each day or per each exercise session), and (3) weight loss is the objective.

You can overdo exercise—too much results in staleness or overtraining. The signs of overtraining include the following:

▶ A feeling of chronic fatigue and listlessness
▶ Inability to make further fitness gains or regression of the level of fitness
▶ Sudden loss of weight.
▶ An increase of 5 beats per minute in the resting heart rate
▶ Loss of enthusiasm for working out
▶ An increase in the risk for injury
▶ The occurence of irritability, anger, and depression

Treatment requires that the individual cut back on training or stop completely for 1 to 2 weeks. When exercise is resumed, it must be of lower intensity, frequency, and duration. The exerciser must rebuild and regain fitness gradually. Prevention is the best treatment for overtraining, since people for whom exercise is a way of life are reluctant to discontinue training, even temporarily, for fear that they will lose their fitness edge. Convincing them that continuing exercise is the worst possible action is extremely difficult.

Duration

Duration refers to the length of each exercise session. Intensity and duration are inversely related—the more intense the exercise, the shorter its duration. Intensity is always an important consideration for the development of physical fitness. Reducing the intensity somewhat while increasing the frequency and duration is the most beneficial method for health enhancement. The ACSM recommends 20 to 60 minutes of continuous or noncontinuous aerobic activity.[12] Another way to monitor duration is by the number of calories expended per exercise session. The ACSM recommends that if you expend 300 calories per exercise session, you can exercise three times per week; if you expend only 200 calories per exercise session, you can exercise four times per week. These guidelines are sufficient for health benefits to accrue, but for fitness purposes, they should be viewed as a minimum level of exercise. (Table 8-5 in Chapter 8 discusses the way to determine how long you need to exercise in the activities of your choice to achieve these goals.)

Progression, Overload, and Specificity

As people attain a level of fitness that meets their needs and further improvement is not desired, the program switches from developing fitness to maintaining it. At this point the principles of overload and progression may be mistakenly set aside, but both are necessary for the improvement phase of fitness. *Overload* involves subjecting the body to unaccustomed stress. Challenging the body to periodically accept a slightly increased level of work forces it to adapt by attaining a higher level of fitness. When to impose each new challenge involves the principle of progression. The workload is increased only when the exerciser is ready to accept a new challenge. For aerobic exercise, target heart rate and/or perceived exertion may be used to establish criteria for scheduling the progression of exercise. For example, if you jog, swim, or cycle a certain distance, the exercise heart rate will decrease over time as your body adapts to training. When the exercise heart rate drops to a predetermined level, you should adjust the pace and/or distance to return to the original target zone.

The principle of *specificity* of training suggests that the body adapts according to the specific type of stress placed on it. The muscles involved in any activity are the ones that adapt, and they do so in the specific way in which they are used. For example, jogging prepares you for jogging but is poor preparation for cycling. Cycling does not prepare you for swimming. Although all these activities stress the cardiorespiratory system, they are sufficiently different that there is little fitness carry-over among them.

The principle of specificity is particularly important for competitive athletes. Competitors attempt to maximize the returns from their training effort; therefore runners must train by running, swimmers must swim, and cyclists must cycle. The focus is on maximal improvement in one activity so that the body is trained in a specific manner. This locks athletes into regimented training programs, but people who exercise for health reasons are not under such constraints. They can vary activities and prevent the boredom of participating in the same activity week after week. Cycling, jogging, swimming, racquetball, cross-country skiing, and weight training may be used in any combination or order for the development of physical fitness. This is the essence of **cross-training.** Not only does cross-training relieve boredom, it may reduce the incidence of injury because the same muscles are not being stressed in the same way during every workout.

Cross-training has many advantages and is an excellent technique for attaining the health benefits of exercise. Variety, the major attraction of cross-training, is also a disadvantage. By participating in many different activities, you seldom become proficient in any one. However, if the objective is health enhancement, proficiency is incidental.

Setting Objectives

Identifying goals provides some direction for the activities selected and the way the principles of exercise are to be manipulated to increase the probability of success. Only one or two major goals should be selected, and these should be as specific as possible so that an effective exercise program may be devised. Activities, objectives, and principles must match.

When you have identified the objectives and know what you wish to achieve from the exercise program, the means for sustaining the program must next be identified. The resolve to exercise is shakiest during the early stages of the program, usually because people push untrained bodies beyond their limits. This results in sore muscles, stiffness, and possible injury. The drop-out rate is highest in the beginning of any exercise program. The irony is that the greatest return for the effort is attained during this phase. Some tips for sustaining that effort are presented in Figure 3-6.

Warming Up For Exercise

Warming up prepares the body for physical action. The process involves stretching exercises and physical activities that gradually heat the muscles and elevate the heart rate. (Figures 5-1 to 5-8 illustrate some typical stretches that are appropriate to use during the warm-up.) A brisk walk, slow jog, jogging or hopping in place, rope jumping, and selected calisthenics will raise the heart rate and increase muscle temperature. Participants should break out in a

Figure 3-6   Motivational Tips

▶ Exercise with a friend. Make sure both of you have compatible goals and are similar in fitness level. Friends can help each other to sustain the program, particularly during busy times when the temptation to push exercise out of an already crowded schedule is quite high.
▶ Exercise with a group. Exchange ideas and literature about exercise with group members.
▶ Gain the support of friends and family. Their support is a powerful source of reinforcement.
▶ Associate with other exercisers. They represent an enthusiastic, positive, and informative group—and these values are contagious.
▶ Join an exercise class or a fitness club. This gives you a place to go and meet people who want to exercise.
▶ Keep a progress chart. Figure 3-7 gives an example of the types of information to include. A progress chart will give you an objective account of your improvement.
▶ Exercise to music. Music makes the effort appear easier than it actually is.
▶ Set a definite time and place to exercise. This is particularly important during the early days of the program. Schedule exercise as you would any other activity of importance and then commit to the schedule.
▶ Participate in a variety of activities. Cross-training is excellent for the person who exercises for health or recreation.
▶ Do not become obsessive about exercise. Skipping exercise is not a good practice normally, but skipping is appropriate at times. Do not exercise when you are sick or overtired. Do not feel guilty about missing exercise for a day or two. Resume exercise as soon as you can.

sweat during the warm-up. This indicates that heart rate and body temperature have increased to some extent and the individual is ready for more vigorous activity.

Increasing the heart rate gradually during the warm-up period is most important. This allows the circulatory system to adjust to the load. If the heart rate elevates suddenly, circulation cannot adjust rapidly enough to meet the oxygen and nutrient demands of the heart muscle. The effects of this lag time are abolished in about 2 minutes, but this practice can be potentially hazardous, particularly for

Figure 3-7   Progress Chart

	Body Weight*		Exercise		Intensity		
Date	Pre	Post	Type	Duration†	RHR	THR	RPE

RHR, Resting heart rate; *THR*, training heart rate; *RPE*, rate of perceived exertion.
*Weigh yourself before and after exercise (dry, nude weight) for an indication of water loss and possible dehydration.
†Includes time, distance repetitions, and so on.

those with compromised circulation due to latent or subclinical heart disease. Even the healthy heart may be affected by eliminating this important phase of warm-up. One study showed that each of 44 healthy male subjects, ages 21 to 52 years, had normal electrocardiogram (ECG) responses to running on a treadmill when they were allowed a warm-up consisting of 2 minutes of easy jogging. However, 70% of the group developed abnormal ECG responses to the same exercise when they were not allowed to warm-up.[14]

Warm-up may be specifically tailored to the activity to be performed. For example, joggers may warm-up by slowly jogging the first ½ to ¾ mile, gradually speeding up to the desired pace. Cyclists, swimmers, cross-country skiers, and rope skippers may use the same approach.

Passive warm-up techniques such as massage, sauna baths, steam baths, hot showers, hot towels, and heating pads should not be used as a substitute for an active warm-up. These techniques may precede an active warm-up if you feel stiff and sore from the previous workout.

Cooling Down From Exercise

The cool-down is as important as the warm-up. Cool-down should last 8 to 10 minutes and consist of two phases. The first phase involves approximately 5 minutes of walking or other light activities to prevent blood from pooling in the muscles that have

been working. Light activity causes rhythmic contractions of the muscles, which in turn act as a stimulus to circulate blood from the muscles to the heart for redistribution throughout the body. This boost to circulation following exercise, often referred to as the *muscle pump*, is essential for recovery and shares some of the burden of circulation with the heart. The muscle pump effect does not occur if a period of inactivity follows exercise. An inactive cool-down forces the heart to work at a high rate to compensate for the reduced volume of blood returning to it because of blood pooling in the muscles. The exerciser runs the risk of dizziness, fainting, and more serious consequences associated with diminished blood flow to vital organs.

Light physical activity after exercise also speeds the removal of lactic acid that has accumulated in the muscles. *Lactic acid* is a fatiguing metabolite resulting from the incomplete breakdown of sugar. It is produced by exercise of high intensity or of long duration.

The second phase of cool-down should focus on the stretching exercises performed during the warm-up. Most participants find that stretching after exercise is more comfortable and possibly more effective because the muscles are heated and more elastic.

Type of Activity

Many activities contribute to one or more components of health-related physical fitness. Activity se-

TABLE 3-3 Rating 14 Sports and Exercises

Exercise	Cardio-respiratory Endurance (Stamina)	Muscular Endurance	Muscular Strength	Flexibility	Balance	General Well-Being				Total
						Weight Control	Muscle Definition	Digestion	Sleep	
Jogging	21	20	17	9	17	21	14	13	16	148
Bicycling	19	18	16	9	18	20	15	12	15	142
Swimming	21	20	14	15	12	15	14	13	16	140
Skating (ice or roller)	18	17	15	13	20	17	14	11	15	140
Handball/ squash	19	18	15	16	17	19	11	13	12	140
Skiing— nordic	19	19	15	14	16	17	12	12	15	139
Skiing— alpine	16	18	15	14	21	15	14	9	12	134
Basketball	19	17	15	13	16	19	13	10	12	134
Tennis	16	16	14	14	16	16	13	12	11	128
Calisthenics	10	13	16	19	15	12	18	11	12	126
Walking	13	14	11	7	8	13	11	11	14	102
Golf*	8	8	9	9	8	6	6	7	6	66*
Softball	6	8	7	9	7	7	5	8	7	64
Bowling	5	5	5	7	6	5	5	7	6	51

The ratings are on a scale of 0 to 3; thus a rating of 21 is the maximum score that can be achieved (a score of 3 by all 7 panelists). Ratings were made on the following basis: frequency, 4 times per week minimum; duration, 30 to 60 minutes per session.
*The rating was made on the basis of using a golf cart or caddy. If you walk the course and carry your clubs, the values improve.

lections should be based on objectives, skill level, availability of equipment, facilities, instruction, climate, and interest. The President's Council on Physical Fitness and Sports (PCPFS) enlisted the aid of seven experts to evaluate 14 popular physical activities for their contribution to physical fitness and general well-being. Although this assessment occurred several years ago, the ratings are as valid today as when they were originally conceived. A summary of these appears in Table 3-3.

Selected sports have been evaluated for their contribution to the health-related components of physical fitness. These appear in Table 3-4. Lifetime sports (such as tennis, badminton, and racquetball) are more conducive for fitness development than team sports (such as volleyball, soccer, softball, and basketball) because fewer players are needed. Ideally, fitness should be developed and maintained primarily through self-paced activities (for example,

jogging, cycling, walking, and swimming), but the challenge inherent in sports may be necessary to sustain the fitness program for some people. Lifetime sports are challenging and fun, and they inject variety into the program. However, fitness attained from these activities depends on skill level and a willingness to exert maximal effort in competition. The orthopedic demands of these activities may be greater than a sedentary beginner can tolerate. Quick stops and starts, bursts of high-intensity activity, sudden changes of direction, and rapid twists and turns place a great deal of stress on the musculoskeletal system. The physically fit can handle the aerobic and musculoskeletal requirements of active sports. Attempting to "play yourself into shape" is a mistake. With knowledge of the principles of exercise, warm-up, cool-down, and the contribution of various physical activities to physical fitness, you can design an exercise program using Assessment Activity 3-6.

TABLE 3-4 Rating of Selected Sports

| Sport | Cardiorespiratory Endurance | Muscular Strength/Endurance | | Flexibility | Body Composition |
		Upper	Lower		
Badminton	M-H	L	M-H	L	M-H
Football (touch)	L-M	L-M	M	L	L-M
Ice hockey	H	M	H	L	H
Racquetball	H	M	H	M	H
Rugby	H	M-H	H	M	H
Soccer	H	L	H	M	H
Volleyball	M	M	M	L-M	M
Wrestling	H	H	H	M-H	H

H, High; *M*, medium; *L*, low. The values in this table are estimates that vary according to the skill and motivation of the participants.

Environmental Conditions

Human beings work and exercise in a variety of environmental conditions. Hot and cold weather produce unique problems for people who function outdoors. Their safety and comfort depend on their knowledge of the ways the body reacts to physical activity in different climatic conditions.

Heat is produced in the body as a by-product of metabolism. Physical activities significantly increase metabolism, so more heat than normal is generated. Heat must be dissipated effectively, or heat build-up (hyperthermia) may result in illness and possible death. **Hyperthermia** is abnormally high body temperature. *Heat exhaustion* is a serious condition but not an imminent threat to life. It is characterized by dizziness, fainting, rapid pulse, and cool skin. Treatment includes immediate cessation of activity and moving to a cool, shady place. The victim is placed in a reclining position and given cool fluids to drink.

Heat stroke is a medical emergency and a threat to life. It is the most severe of the heat-induced illnesses. The symptoms include a high temperature (106° F or above) and dry skin caused by cessation of sweating. These symptoms are accompanied by some or all of the following: delirium, convulsions, and loss of consciousness. The early warning signs include chills, nausea, headache, and general weakness. Victims of heat stroke should be rushed immediately to the nearest hospital for treatment.

Mechanisms of Heat Loss

Heat is lost from the body by conduction, radiation, convection, and evaporation of sweat. Conduction, convection, and radiation are mechanisms responsible for heat loss and heat gain. These three depend on the difference between the temperature of the body and that of the environment. These mechanisms do not function alone to effect heat loss or gain.

Conduction occurs when direct physical contact occurs between objects as long as one of the objects is cooler than the other. The greater the difference in temperature between the objects, the greater the transfer of heat. If you enter an air-conditioned room from outdoors on a summer day and sit in a cool leather chair, you lose heat through contact with the cooler chair.

Conductive heat loss occurs even more rapidly in water.[15] Water is not an insulator but a conductor. It absorbs several thousand times more heat than air at the same temperature. This is the reason sitting at the poolside is more comfortable than sitting in the pool, even if the temperature of both air and water are equal.

Heat loss or gain by convection occurs when a gas or water moves across the skin. Heat is transferred from the body to the environment more effectively if a breeze is blowing. Convective heat loss in water is increased if you are swimming rather than floating because of the increased movement of the water across the body. The same principle applies to running outdoors because of the air flow over the body.

Heat is lost through radiation because humans, animals, and inanimate objects constantly emit heat by electromagnetic waves to cooler objects in the environment. This occurs without physical contact between objects. Heat is simply transferred on a temperature gradient from warmer objects to cooler ones.

Heat loss by radiation is very effective when the air temperature (ambient temperature) is well below skin temperature. This is one of the major reasons that outdoor exercise in cool weather is better tolerated than the same exercise in hot weather. Temperatures in the upper 80s and 90s will probably result in heat gain by radiation.

Evaporation of sweat is the major method of heat loss during exercise, and this process is most effective when the humidity is low. High humidity significantly impairs the evaporative process because the air is very saturated and cannot accept much moisture. If both temperature and humidity are high, losing heat is difficult by any of these processes. Under these conditions, adjusting the intensity and duration of exercise or moving indoors where the climate can be controlled may be beneficial.

Heat loss by evaporation occurs only when the sweat on the surface of the skin is vaporized, that is, converted to a gas. The conversion of liquid to a gas at the skin level requires heat supplied by the body. Beads of sweat that roll off the body do not contribute to the cooling process—only sweat that evaporates does.

Exercise in hot and humid conditions forces the body to divert more blood than usual from the working muscles to the skin in an effort to carry the heat accumulating in the deeper recesses to the outer shell. The net result is that the exercising muscles are deprived of a full complement of blood and cannot work as long or as hard. Exercise is therefore more difficult in hot and humid weather.

Heat loss by evaporation is seriously impeded when participants wear nonporous garments such as rubberized and plastic exercise suits. These garments encourage sweating, but their nonporous nature does not allow sweat to evaporate. This practice is dangerous because it may easily result in heat buildup and *dehydration* (excessive water loss), leading to heat-stress illnesses. You should dress for hot-weather exercise by wearing shorts and a porous top. A mesh, baseball-type cap is optional. It is effective in blocking the absorption of radiant heat if you exercise in the middle of the day because the sun's rays are vertical. You do not need to wear a cap when exercising in the cooler parts of the day or if the sun is not shining.

Guidelines for Exercise in the Heat

Guidelines for exercising in heat and humidity have been developed for road races, but these can be applied to any strenuous physical activity performed outdoors during warm weather. Ambient conditions are considered safe when the temperature is below 70° F and the humidity is below 45%. Caution should be used when the temperature is greater than 70° F or the humidity is over 45%. People who are sensitive to heat and humidity should reconsider exercising when the temperature is greater than 75° F or the humidity is more than 50%. People who are trained and heat acclimated can continue to exercise in these conditions, but they should be aware of the potential hazards and take precautions to prevent heat illness. Table 3-5 gives exercise guidelines when temperature and relative humidity are factors.

The keys to exercising without incident in hot weather are to acclimate to the heat and maintain the body's normal fluid level. The major consequence of dehydration (excessive fluid loss) is a reduction in blood volume.[16] This results in sluggish circulation that decreases the delivery of oxygen to the exercis-

TABLE 3-5 Guidelines for Exercise in Heat and Humidity

| Relative Humidity (%) | Temperature (°F) | | | | | Caution | | | Extreme Caution |
	60	65	70	75	80	85	90	95	100
20	59	62	65	68	70	73	76	79	82
40	59	63	66	69	73	76	79	83	86
60	60	63	67	71	75	79	83	87	91
80	60	64	69	73	78	82	86	91	95
100	60	65	70	75	80	85	90	95	100

In hot and humid conditions, drinking water and wearing loose clothing help prevent hyperthermia and heat stress illnesses.

ing muscles. Second, lowered blood volume results in less blood that can be sent to the skin to remove the heat generated by exercise. If too much of the blood volume is lost, sweating will stop and the body temperature will rise, leading to heat-stress illness. Heat illness is a serious problem that can be avoided by following a few guidelines designed to preserve the body's fluid level:

▶ Preexercise fluid ingestion—Drink 12 to 20 ounces of a salted liquid 15 to 30 minutes before exercising. You can purchase a commercially prepared sports drink such as Gatorade or mix a teaspoon of salt in a gallon of lemonade. Water is not the best liquid source because it stimulates the production of urine, leaving less liquid for sweating.

▶ Fluid replacement during exercise—Guidelines for replacing liquid during exercise are less clear. The primary reason for drinking during exercise is to maintain body water stores so that sweating can continue.

▶ Water is the preferred drink when exercise lasts less than 2 hours. Water exits the stomach rapidly and moves to the tissues that need it.

▶ Urine production is not a problem during exercise because fluid is used to produce sweat.

▶ A beverage containing salt and sugar is preferred if exercise lasts longer than 2 hours (for example, during marathons, long-distance cycling, and ultra-distance running events and triathalons).

▶ You should drink 6 to 8 ounces every 15 minutes during exercise.

▶ Postexercise fluid replacement

▶ Plain water is a poor drink during recovery from exercise because it suppresses the thirst drive, so fluid intake stops before rehydration is complete.

▶ You should avoid alcoholic beverages and caffeinated beverages because these stimulate urine production. All ingested fluids need to be retained for the purpose of rehydration.

▶ You should drink fluids that contain salt and sugar. Again commercial sports drinks are appropriate. In addition, they taste good, which encourages exercisers to drink more. This counteracts the tendency of most people to drink less than they need if water is the alternative.

▶ Estimating water loss

▶ Weigh yourself nude before and after exercise.

▶ Towel off sweat completely after exercise and then weigh yourself.

▶ Each pound of weight loss represents about 1 pint of fluid loss. Be sure to drink that and more after exercise.

▶ Modify the exercise program by (1) working out during cooler times of day, (2) choosing shady routes where water is available, (3) slowing the pace and/or shortening the duration of exercise on particularly oppressive days, and (4) wearing light, loose, porous clothing to facilitate the evaporation of sweat.

▶ Other considerations

▶ Never take salt tablets. They are stomach irritants, they attract fluid to the gut, they sometimes pass through the digestive system undissolved, and they may perforate the stomach lining.

▶ Exercise must be prolonged, produce profuse sweating, and occur over a number of consecutive days to reduce potassium stores. For the average bout of exercise, you do not need to worry about depleting potassium or make a special effort to replace it. The daily consumption of fresh fruits and vegetables, as suggested by the new food pyramid, is all that is needed (see Chapter 6).

Guidelines for Exercise in the Cold

Problems related to exercise in cold weather include frostbite and **hypothermia** (abnormally low body temperature). Frostbite can lead to permanent damage or loss of a body part from gangrene. This can be prevented by adequately protecting exposed areas such as fingers, the nose, ears, facial skin, and toes. Gloves, preferably mittens or thick socks, should be worn to protect the fingers, hands, and wrists. A stocking hat is preferable for two reasons: (1) blood vessels in the scalp do not constrict effectively, so a significant amount of heat is lost if a head covering is not worn, and (2) a stocking-type hat can be pulled down to protect the ears. In very cold or windy weather, you can use surgical or ski masks and scarves to keep facial skin warm and to moisten and warm inhaled air. All exposed or poorly protected flesh is vulnerable to frostbite when the temperature is low and the wind chill high. Table 3-6 can be used as a safety guide for working and exercising in cold, windy weather.

People often experience a hacking cough for a minute or two after physical exertion in cold weather. This is a normal response and should not cause alarm. Very cold, dry air may not be fully moistened when it is inhaled rapidly and in large volumes during exercise, so the lining of the throat dries out. When exercise is discontinued, the respiratory rate slows and the volume of inhaled air decreases, allowing enough time for the body to fully moisturize it. Coughing stops within a couple of minutes as the linings are remoistened.

Hypothermia is the most severe of the problems associated with outdoor activity in cold weather. Hypothermia occurs when body heat is lost faster than it can be produced. This can be a life-threatening situation.

Exercise in cold weather requires insulating layers of clothing to preserve normal body heat. Without this protection, body heat is quickly lost because of the large temperature gradient between the skin and environment. In addition to the insulating qualities of layers of clothing, a layer or two can be discarded if you get too hot.

Hypothermia can occur even if the air temperature is above freezing. For instance, the rate of heat loss for any temperature is influenced by wind ve-

TABLE 3-6 Wind Chill Index

Wind Speed (mph)	Actual Thermometer Reading (°F)											
	50	40	30	20	10	0	−10	−20	−30	−40	−50	−60
	Equivalent Temperature (°F)											
Calm	50	40	30	20	10	0	−10	−20	−30	−40	−50	−60
5	48	37	27	16	6	−5	−15	−26	−36	−47	−57	−68
10	40	28	16	4	−9	−21	−33	−46	−58	−70	−83	−95
15	36	22	9	−5	−18	−36	−45	−58	−72	−85	−99	−112
20	32	18	4	−10	−25	−39	−53	−67	−82	−96	−110	−124
25	30	16	0	−15	−29	−44	−59	−74	−88	−104	−118	−133
30	28	13	−2	−18	−33	−48	−63	−79	−94	−109	−125	−140
35	27	11	−4	−20	−35	−49	−67	−82	−98	−113	−129	−145
40*	26	10	−6	−21	−37	−53	−69	−85	−100	−116	−132	−148

| Little danger (for properly clothed person) | Increasing danger—cover up fully (hands, ears, face, head) | Great danger— exercise indoors |

*Wind speeds greater than 40 mph have little additional effect.

locity (see Table 3-6). Wind velocity increases the amount of cold air molecules that come in contact with the skin. The more cold molecules, the more effective the heat loss. The speed of walking, jogging, or cycling into the wind must be added to the speed of the wind to properly evaluate the impact of wind chill.

You should wear enough clothing to stay warm but not so much that you induce profuse sweating. The amount of clothing appropriate is based on experience that comes from exercising in different environmental conditions. Clothing that becomes wet with sweat loses its insulating qualities. It becomes a conductor of heat, moving it from the body quickly and potentially endangering the exerciser.

If you exercise or work outdoors in cold weather, you may want to wear polypropylene undergarments. Polypropylene is designed to wisk perspiration from the skin so that evaporative cooling will not rob heat from the body. You should wear a warm outer garment, preferably made of wool, over this material. If it is windy, you should wear a breathable windbreaker as the outer layer.

If you follow the guidelines for activity in hot and cold weather, you can usually participate quite comfortably all year long.

Summary

▶ Physical fitness is defined in terms of performance-related and health-related fitness.
▶ Cardiorespiratory endurance is the most important component of health-related fitness.
▶ The long-term effects of physical training include modifications in heart rate, stroke volume, cardiac output, blood volume, heart volume, respiration, and metabolism.
▶ Aerobic capacity is finite, improves by 15% to 30% with training, and decreases with aging; this decrease is slower in those who are physically fit.
▶ The training effect is lost in stages if exercise is interrupted or discontinued.

▶ Exercise affects cholesterol levels, blood pressure, triglyceride levels, diabetes mellitus, and stress and is an alternative method for quitting tobacco products.
▶ LDLs that are oxidized are involved in the development of atherosclerosis.
▶ The principles of exercise can be manipulated to meet any exercise objective.
▶ Exercising by varying the activities per exercise session or during exercise sessions is cross-training.
▶ The heat generated by exercise is lost from the body by conduction, convection, radiation, and evaporation.
▶ Evaporation of sweat is the major mechanism for ridding the body of heat that develops during exercise.
▶ Hypothermia is the most severe problem associated with exercise in cold weather.

Action Plan for Personal Wellness

Use the information presented in this chapter to answer the following questions and to formulate an action plan to enhance your personal wellness.

1 Based on the information presented in this chapter, along with what I know about my family's health history, the health problems and issues that I need to be concerned about are:_____

_____

_____

2 Of those health concerns listed in number 1, the one I most need to act on is:_____

_____

_____

3 The possible actions that I can take to improve my level of wellness are (be specific):_____

_____

_____

4 Of those actions listed in number 3, the one that I most need to include in an action plan is:_____

_____

_____

5 Factors I need to keep in mind to be successful in my action plan are:_____

_____

_____

Review Questions

1. What are the physiological changes that occur from regular participation in aerobic exercise?
2. What are the health benefits that occur from regular participation in aerobic training?
3. Name and define the physiological changes that occur with exercise training.
4. Identify and define the principles of physical conditioning.
5. Define and give some examples of cross-training.
6. Why should you warm-up before exercise?
7. Identify and define the mechanisms of heat loss. Which of these is most important during exercise and why?
8. Describe fluid replacement before, during, and after exercise.

References

1. Wilmore JH, Costill DL: *Training for sport and activity*, Dubuque, IA, 1988, Wm C Brown.
2. American College of Sports Medicine: *Guidelines for exercise testing and prescription*, Philadelphia, 1991, Lea & Febiger.
3. Kasch FW et al: The effect of physical activity and inactivity on aerobic power in older men (a longitudinal study), *Physician Sportsmed* 18:73-83, 1990.
4. Coyle EF et al: Time course of loss of adaptations after stopping prolonged intense endurance training, *J Appl Physiol* 57:1857-1864, 1984.
5. Coyle EF: Effects of detraining on responses to submaximal exercise, *J Appl Physiol* 59:853-859, 1985.
6. Siscovick DS et al: The incidence of primary cardiac arrest during vigorous exercise, *N Engl J Med* 311:874-877, 1984.
7. Move on triglycerides, *Harvard Heart Letter* 2:7-8, 1992.
8. Duncan JJ et al: The effects of aerobic exercise on plasma catecholamines and blood pressure in patients with mild essential hypertension, *JAMA* 254:2609-2613, 1985.
9. Nelson L et al: Effect of changing levels of physical activity on blood pressure and hemodynamics in essential hypertension, *Lancet* 8491:473-476, 1986.
10. Crews DJ, Landers DM: A meta-analytic review of aerobic fitness and reactivity to social stressors, *Med Sci Sports Exercise* 19(suppl):5114-5119, 1987.
11. Howard JH et al: Physical activity as a moderator of life events and somatic complaints: a longitudinal study, *Can J Appl Sports Sci* 9:194-201, 1984.
12. American College of Sports Medicine: The recommended quantity and quality of exercise for developing and maintaining cardiorespiratory and muscular fitness in healthy adults. *Med Sci Sports Exercise* 22(2):265-274, 1990.
13. Davis AJ et al: A comparison of heart rate methods for predicting endurance training intensity, *Med Sci Sports* 7:295-298, 1975.
14. Barnard RJ et al: Cardiovascular responses to sudden strenuous exercise—heart rate, blood pressure, and ECG, *J Appl Physiol* 34:833-837, 1973.
15. McArdle WS, Katch FI, Katch VL: *Exercise physiology—energy, nutrition and human performance*, Philadelphia, 1991, Lea & Febiger.
16. Stamford B: How to avoid dehydration, *Physician Sportsmed* 18:135-136, 1990.

Annotated Readings

Clark N: Fluid facts—what, when and how much to drink, *Physician Sportsmed* 20:33-34, 1992.

Discusses the principles of fluid replacement before, during, and after exercise for the recreational exerciser and the competitive athlete.

Pollock CL: Does exercise intensity matter? *Physician Sportsmed* 20:123-126, 1992.

Exercise intensity is not important for people who are exercising for the health-related benefits. For these people, exercise of low intensity is much better than being sedentary. For those who wish to significantly improve their fitness level, the intensity of exercise may very well be the most important of the fitness principles.

Winter: A great time for outdoor exercise, *Univ Calif Berkley Wellness Letter* 9:4-5, 1993.

Discusses the important concepts associated with outdoor exercise in the winter. Covers clothing, hypothermia, frostbite, liquid replacement, eye and skin protection, adaptation to the cold, and myths associated with exercise in cold weather.

Duncan JJ et al: Women walking for health and fitness, *JAMA* 266:3295-3299, 1991.

Compares three levels of exercise intensity for their effect on physical fitness and serum cholesterol. The highest intensity group attained the greatest level of fitness, but there was no difference among the groups on the change in serum cholesterol. All three groups had a similar increase in HDL cholesterol.

By the way, doctor. . .: *Harvard Health Letter* 17:8, 1992.

Discusses the concern that many people have regarding exercise in the morning. Heart attacks and sudden death appear to occur most regularly between 7:00 AM and 11:00 AM. The benefits of exercise outweigh the risk, even for those who participate during these hours.

ASSESSMENT ACTIVITY   3 - 1

The Rockport Fitness Walking Test

Directions: This walking test estimates aerobic capacity based on the variables of age, gender, time required to walk 1 mile, and the heart rate achieved at the end of the test. The guidelines for taking the test are as follows:

1. Heart rate is counted for 15 seconds and multiplied by 4 to get beats per minute.
2. The course should be flat and measured, preferably a 440-yard track.
3. Use a stop watch or a watch with a second hand.
4. Warm up for 5 to 10 minutes before taking the test. Preparation for the test should include a ¼ mile walk followed by the stretching exercises.
5. During the test the walk should be a brisk pace and 1 mile should be covered as rapidly as possible.
6. Take your pulse rate immediately after the test. This rate should then be marked on the chart on the following pages that is appropriate for your age and gender.
7. Draw a vertical line through your time and a horizontal line through your heart rate. The point where the lines intersect determines your fitness level (see the charts on the following pages).

Rockport provides a series of 20-week walking-for-fitness programs that are based on the results of the walking test. These may be obtained for a nominal fee ($1.00 at this writing) by sending a request to Rockport Fitness Walking Test, 72 Howe St., Marlboro, Massachusetts, 01752.

These charts are designed to tell you how fit you are compared with other individuals of your age and gender. For example, if your coordinates place you in the "above average" section of the chart, you are in better shape than the average person in your category.

The charts are based on weights of 170 lb for men and 125 lb for women. If you weigh substantially more, your relative cardiovascular fitness level will be slightly overestimated. If you weigh substantially less, your relative cardiovascular fitness level will be slightly underestimated.

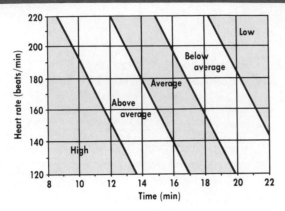

20- to 29-Year-Old Males

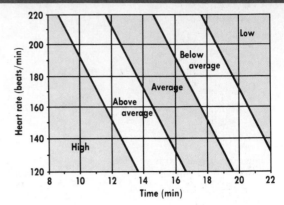

30- to 38-Year-Old Males

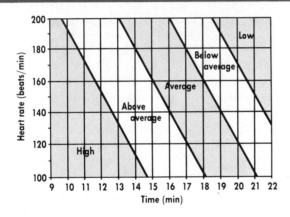

40- to 49-Year-Old Males

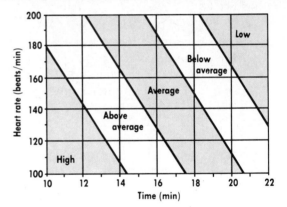

50- to 59-Year-Old Males

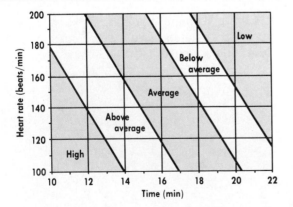

60-Year-Old and Older Males

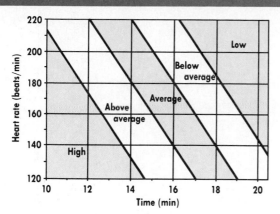
20- to 29-Year-Old Females

 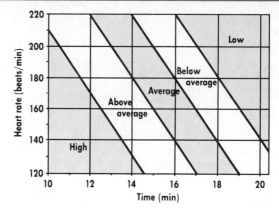
30- to 39-Year-Old Females

 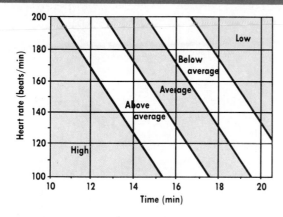
40- to 49-Year-Old Females

 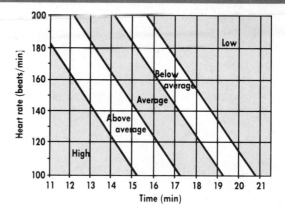
50- to 59-Year-Old Females

 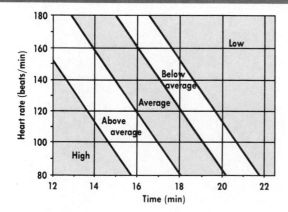
60-Year-Old and Older Females

ASSESSMENT ACTIVITY   3 - 2

The 3-Mile Walking Test

Directions: This is a 3-mile walking test to fatigue; no running is allowed. The length of this test and the fact that it demands a maximum effort (walking the distance as quickly as you can) requires you to train for at least 6 weeks before making the attempt. Students make their best scores when they are allowed two practive trials walking the distance. This experience enables them to find the pace that will result in the fastest time within their fitness capacity.

Suggestions for taking the test include the following:
1. Walk at an even pace, but attempt the fastest pace that you can maintain for the entire distance.
2. Avoid starting out too fast—if you do, you will run out of energy too soon.
3. Rest the day before and the day after the test.
4. Eat a predominantly carbohydrate meal (e.g., pasta, rice, potatoes, pancakes) that is low in fat. Select foods that have given you no digestive problems in the past. Eat approximately 2 to 3 hours before the test.
5. Be sure to drink plenty of liquids the day of the test. Water, Gatorade, and fruit juices diluted with half water are appropriate.
6. Warm up before the test. About 5 to 6 minutes of walking followed by stretching exercises will suffice.
7. Cool down after the test by walking at a slower pace for 5 to 6 minutes and do the same stretching excercises as you performed in the warm-up period.

The test is best administered on a running track that is ¼ mile long; 12 full laps around will complete the test. After completing the test, record your time and compare it with the numbers listed to determine your fitness level. For example, a 19-year-old female walks the 3 miles in 41 minutes and 28 seconds (41:28). Her fitness level is "Fair."

Complete the following data for the 3-mile walk test:

Name: _____ Age: _____

Date of test: _____ Gender: _____

Time to complete the test: _____

Fitness level from the chart below: _____

Fitness Categories for the 3-Mile Walking Test

Fitness Category	13-19 Yr		20-29 Yr		30-39 Yr	
	Male	Female	Male	Female	Male	Female
Excellent	<33:00	<35:00	<34:00	<36:00	<35:00	<37:30
Good	33-37:30	35-39:30	34-38:30	36-40:30	35-40:00	37:30-42:00
Fair	37:31-41:00	39:31-43:00	38:31-42:00	40:31-44:00	40:01-44:30	42:01-46:30
Poor	41:01-45:00	43:01-47:00	42:01-46:00	44:01-48:00	44:31-49:00	46:31-51:00
Very poor	>45:00	>47:00	>46:00	>48:00	>49:00	>51:00

<, Less than; >, greater than.

ASSESSMENT ACTIVITY 3 - 3

The 1.5-Mile Run/Walk Test

Directions: Select a measured course, preferably a running track, so that the starting and finishing points are at the same location for ease of timing and recording. Instruct the participants that they should cover the distance as rapidly as possible to attain a realistic estimate of their fitness level. The best performances occur when subjects are given an opportunity to practice running the course so that they can learn how to pace themselves. Subjects who cannot run the entire distance should be instructed to walk until they recover enough to continue running again. Allow a 5 to 10 minute warm-up before the test and an equal amount of time for cooling down after the test. Use the appropriate chart below for gender and age category to compare performance to the norm.

Aerobic Physical Fitness Classification

Males

Fitness Category	13-19 Yr	20-29 Yr	30-39 Yr	40-49 Yr
Very poor	>15:31	>16:01	>16:31	>17:31
Poor	12:11-15:30	14:01-16:00	14:44-16:30	15:36-17:30
Fair	10:49-12:10	12:01-14:00	12:31-14:45	13:01-15:35
Good	9:41-10:48	10:46-12:00	11:01-12:30	11:31-13:00
Excellent	8:37-9:40	9:45-10:45	10:00-11:00	10:30-11:30
Superior	<8:37	<9:45	<10:00	<10:30

>, Greater than; <, less than.

Females

Fitness Category	13-19 Yr	20-29 Yr	30-39 Yr	40-49 Yr
Very poor	>18:31	>19:01	>19:31	>20:01
Poor	16:55-18:30	18:31-19:00	19:01-19:30	19:31-20:00
Fair	14:31-16:54	15:55-18:30	16:31-19:00	17:31-19:30
Good	12:30-14:30	13:31-15:54	14:31-16:30	15:56-17:30
Excellent	11:50-12:29	12:30-13:30	13:00-14:30	13:45-15:55
Superior	<11:50	<12:30	<13:00	<13:45

ASSESSMENT ACTIVITY   3 - 4

The Bench Step Test

Directions: The equipment needed includes a sturdy, 12-inch high bench, a metronome, a stopwatch, and preferably a stethoscope. The metronome should be set at 96 beats per minute for a total fo 24 cycles. One cycle consists of four steps as follows: up left foot, up right foot, down left foot, down right foot.

The subject should step up and down in time with each beat of the metronome for 3 full minutes. At the end of the 3 miuntes, the subject sits down on the bench immediately. The pulse count must be started within the first 5 seconds and continued for 1 full minute. Do not count for 15 seconds and multiply by 4 because the heart rate will be higher than the actual minute heart rate. The 1-minute postexercise heart rate is the score for the test. Refer to the chart below for scoring.

Postexercise 1-Minute Heart Rate (beats/min)

	18-25 yr		26-35 yr		36-45 yr	
Fitness Category	**Male**	**Female**	**Male**	**Female**	**Male**	**Female**
Excellent	70-78	72-83	73-79	72-86	72-81	74-87
Good	82-88	88-97	83-88	91-97	86-94	93-101
Above average	91-97	100-106	91-97	103-110	98-102	104-109
Average	101-104	110-116	101-106	112-118	105-111	111-117
Below average	107-114	118-124	109-116	121-127	113-118	120-127
Poor	118-126	128-137	119-126	129-135	120-128	130-138
Very poor	131-164	141-155	130-164	141-154	132-168	143-152

Pulse is to be counted for 1 full minute after 3 minutes of stepping at 24 cycles/min on a 12-inch bench.

ASSESSMENT ACTIVITY   3 - 5

Calculating Your Target Heart Rate

Directions: Using the Karvonen Method of calculating heart rate described earlier in this chapter, fill in the blanks below.

THR = Target heart rate
MHR = Maximum heart rate
RHR = Resting heart rate (taken just after waking in the morning)
 TI% = Training intensity

1. 220 − _____ = _____
        (your age)   (your MHR)

2. THR = (MHR − RHR) × TI% + RHR

   THR = (_____ − _____) × _____ + _____
          (your MHR)   (your RHR)   (your desired TI%)   (your RHR)

   THR = _____ × _____ + _____
          (your MHR − your RHR)   (desired TI%)   (your RHR)

   THR = _____ beats/min

ASSESSMENT ACTIVITY   3 - 6

Design An Exercise Program

Directions: Design an exercise program for a 20-year-old male who wishes to (1) lose 25 lb, (2) develop greater strength, and (3) develop cardiorespiratory endurance.

1. Suggested activities:

2. Suggested frequency of exercise:

3. Suggested intensity of exercise:

4. Suggested duration of exercise:

5. Place the activity in the weekly calendar below with the suggested amount of time devoted to each activity:

Sunday	Monday	Tuesday	Wednesday	Thursday	Friday	Saturday

CHAPTER 4

Muscular Strength and Endurance

Key terms

anaerobic

circuit resistance training (CRT)

concentric contraction

eccentric contraction

isokinetic

isometric

isotonic

muscular endurance

muscular strength

variable resistance

Objectives

After completing this chapter, you will be able to:

▶ Explain the benefits of resistance training for older people.

▶ Define the different types of muscle contraction.

▶ Identify the various systems of dynamic and static exercise training.

▶ Describe the limitations of isometric exercise training.

▶ Explain the advantages and disadvantages of circuit resistance training.

▶ Define each of the principles of resistance training.

▶ Explain the differences in strength between men and women.

▶ Describe the short- and long-term effects of anabolic steroid use.

▶ Describe the health benefits of resistance training.

▶ Describe the progressive resistance technique that will increase muscle endurance.

Although muscular development is the focus of this chapter, cardiorespiratory development should be the focal point of a physical fitness program. However, it should not be the only component. Evidence has steadily mounted during the last decade regarding the growing importance of muscular development for fitness, health, and aesthetic purposes.

The body contains more than 600 muscles, and 65% of these are located above the waist. All muscles, regardless of location, respond to the physiological law of use and disuse. "Use it or lose it" is an axiom that applies to all human beings during every phase of the life cycle. Americans tend to become more sedentary as they age. The declining stimulation results in a progressive shrinking and weakening of the muscles.

With few exceptions, notably cross-country skiing, rowing, and swimming, aerobic activities provide limited stimulation of upper body musculature. Sedentary living neglects the muscular system entirely and accelerates the loss of muscle tissue and body strength. The need for resistance training was illustrated in a study of runners during a 10-year period. Runners who did no resistance training suffered muscle atrophy in their upper bodies while maintaining muscle size in their legs.[1] Their arms, which received little stimulation from jogging, decreased in circumference.

The loss of muscle tissue leads to a predictable loss in muscle strength. By the age of 74, 28% of American men and 65% of American women cannot lift objects that weigh more than 10 pounds.[2] Be-cause of this limitation, everyday functions taken for granted by the young become physical challenges, including opening bottle caps and jar lids, carrying groceries, and climbing stairs. If muscle atrophy progresses unabated, walking without assistance or an aid becomes very difficult if not impossible. The quality of life is severely compromised when one is unable to perform the ordinary tasks of everyday life.

Resistance training ideally begins during middle or late adolescence and continues throughout life, but starting at any age provides significant benefit if training is done properly. For example, 12 weeks of weight training increased the strength and size of the exercised muscles in men aged 60 to 72.[3] Strength training also improved the ability of the trained muscles to use oxygen. Even frail men and women with an average age of 90 years responded positively to 8 weeks of resistance training.[4] These very old subjects averaged a 174% increase in strength and a 9% increase in muscle size. After training, they walked a specified course 48% faster than they could previously. Two subjects discarded their walking canes and walked unassisted. Of three subjects who could not rise from a chair without using their arms before training, two of them were able to accomplish this feat after training.

These studies indicate that the muscular systems of older people are indeed trainable. Improving or maintaining muscle strength enhances mobility and independence during the later years. Cessation of training leads to physical decline at all age levels. The 90-year-old subjects experienced a 32% loss of maximum strength after 4 weeks of detraining.

Muscular Strength

Muscular strength is the maximum force that a muscle or muscle group can exert in a single contraction. It is best developed by some form of progressive resistance exercise, for example, weight training with free weights (barbells and dumbbells) or single multistation machine weights. Some of the exercises commonly used to develop the major muscle groups of the body are shown in Figures 4-1 to 4-16. The anatomical charts in Figures 4-17 and 4-18 provide the location of the muscles stressed in each exercise. These exercises are demonstrated on exercise machines and free weights; these methods are equivalent and work the same muscle groups.

Text continued on p. 99.

A   B

FIGURE 4-1 Biceps curl. **A,** Start with the arms extended, palms up. **B,** Flex both arms and slowly move the weight through a full range of motion and return to the starting position. The prime mover is the biceps brachii.

FIGURE 4-2 Biceps curl (free weights).

FIGURE 4-3 Overhead press. **A,** Sit upright with hands approximately shoulder width apart. **B,** Slowly press the bar upward until the arms are fully extended and lower to the starting position. Avoid an excessive arch in the lower back. The prime movers are the triceps and deltoid.

FIGURE 4-4 Overhead press (free weights).

A   B

FIGURE 4-5 Bench press. **A,** Lie on your back with the knees bent and your feet flat on the bench to prevent arching your back. **B,** Slowly press the bar overhead, fully extending your arms, and return to the starting position. The prime movers are the pectoralis major, triceps, and deltoid.

FIGURE 4-6 Bench press (free weights).

A   B

FIGURE 4-7 Abdominal crunch. **A,** Sit upright with the chest against the pads, hands folded across the stomach. **B,** Slowly press forward through a full range of motion and return to the starting position. The prime mover is the rectus abdominis.

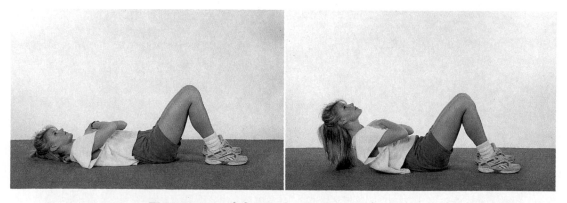

FIGURE 4-8 Abdominal crunch (mat exercise).

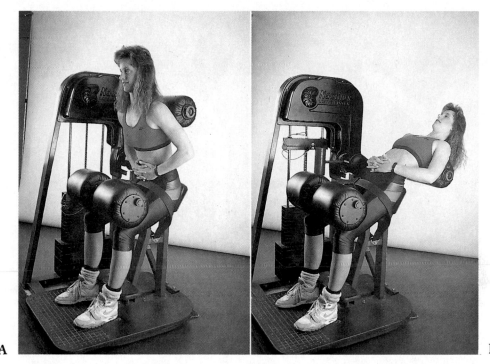

A   B

FIGURE 4-9 Lower back. **A,** Place your thighs and back against the pads. **B,** Slowly press backward until your back is fully extended and return to the starting position. The prime movers are the erector spine and gluteus maximus.

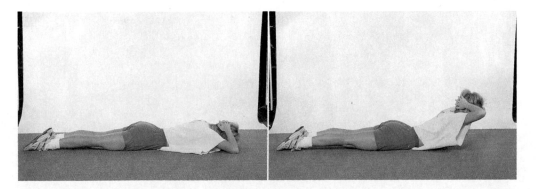

FIGURE 4-10 Back extension (mat exercise).

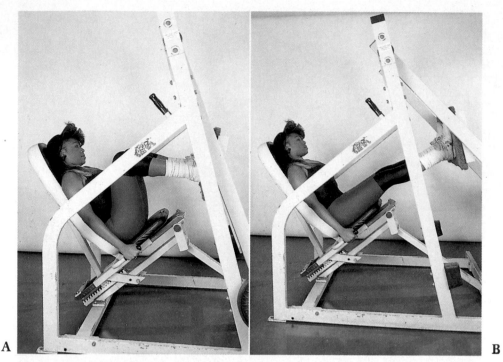

A   B

FIGURE 4-11 Leg press. **A,** Adjust the seat so that your legs are bent at approximately 90 degrees. **B,** Slowly extend your legs fully and return to the starting position. The prime moves are the quadriceps groups and the gluteus maximus.

FIGURE 4-12 Half-squat (free weights).

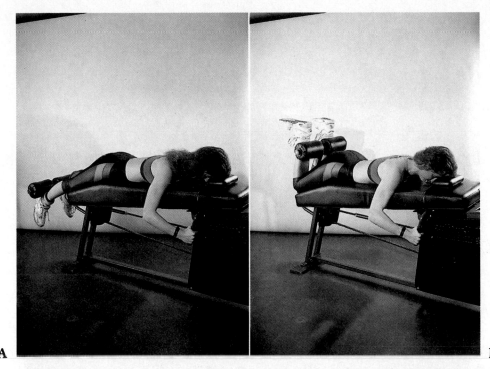

A   B

FIGURE 4-13 Hamstring curl. **A,** Lie face down with your lower legs under the pads. **B,** Curl the weight approximately 90 degrees and return to the starting position. The prime mover is the hamstring group.

FIGURE 4-14 Hamstring curl (free weights).

FIGURE 4-15 Chest press. **A,** Upper arms are parallel to the floor, elbows are bent at 90 degrees with your hands on the handles. **B,** Slowly push the bars until your elbows are pointing forward and return to the starting position. The prime movers are the pectoralis major and deltoid.

FIGURE 4-16 Lateral supine raises (free weights).

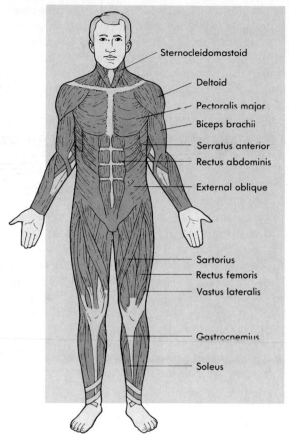

FIGURE 4-17 Anatomical chart. Selected muscles of the body—front view.

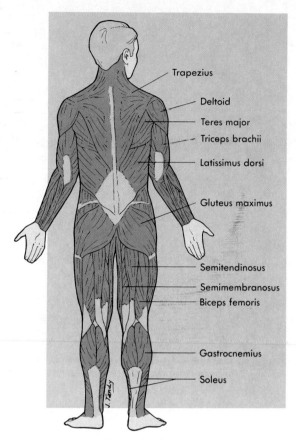

FIGURE 4-18 Anatomical chart. Selected muscles of the body—rear view.

A   B

FIGURE 4-19 A, A concentric contraction. **B,** An eccentric contraction.

The two types of muscular contractions are static and dynamic. Dynamic contractions occur when muscles shorten and move the bones to which they are attached, producing movement around a joint. Dynamic movements consist of concentric and eccentric muscle contractions (Figure 4-19). A **concentric contraction** occurs when a muscle shortens as it develops the tension to overcome an external resistance. An **eccentric contraction** occurs when the muscle lengthens and the weight or resistance is slowly returned to the starting position. In eccentric contractions the muscles are resisting the force of

FIGURE 4-20 Isometric contraction. A static contraction against an immovable object.

gravity as they lengthen, so the weight is not allowed to free-fall.

Static muscular contraction occurs when muscles exert force but do not shorten because the resistance is greater than the contractile force of the muscle. Static contractions are **isometric,** which literally means "equal length." Considerable force can be generated by contracting muscles isometrically (Figure 4-20).

See Assessment Activity 4-1 for a method of determining your strength based on body weight and gender.

Types of Resistance Training

Static Exercise

Isometric contractions are usually held for 6 to 10 seconds and require a minimum exertion of two-thirds maximum force. Maximum exertions produce greater results than submaximum efforts. A total contraction time of 30 seconds of applied force is desirable. This can be achieved by two or three contractions of long duration or more contractions of shorter duration for each muscle exercised.

Isometric exercises are effective for developing strength, but this approach has some important limitations. The most serious of these is a higher than

expected rise in exercise arterial blood pressure and an increased workload on the heart throughout the entire contraction. All-out straining isometric contractions should not be performed by individuals with heart and vascular disease. A second limitation is that strength developed isometrically is joint-angle specific. Maximum strength development occurs at the angle of contraction, with a training carryover of approximately 20 degrees in either direction from that angle. To develop strength throughout the muscle's range of motion, you must perform isometric contractions at several different points in the range of motion.

Because muscles cannot overcome the resistance in isometric training, measuring improvement is difficult, constituting another limitation of this system. Improvements in strength can be measured if exercisers have access to specialized equipment such as dynamometers and tensiometers that record the amount of force applied. Motivation for exercise is difficult to sustain without feedback.

Research indicates that isometric exercise systems are as effective as dynamic exercise systems for developing strength. The question is not which system is better but which system best satisfies the intended use for the newly acquired strength. The transferability of strength to occupational and leisure pursuits is very relevant.

Strength developed in the muscles is highly specific to the manner in which the muscles are trained. Muscles trained isometrically perform best when stressed isometrically; muscles trained dynamically perform best when stressed dynamically. There is some transfer of isometric training to everyday life. Carrying groceries, a baby, or any object in a fixed position or pushing and pulling objects require isometric strength, but most movements are dynamic, and transfer is more widely applicable from dynamic systems of training.

Dynamic Exercise

Dynamic exercises include **isotonic** (equal tension), variable resistance, free weights, and **isokinetic** (equal speed).

Isotonic training. Isotonic exercise training systems use both concentric and eccentric contractions as the exercising muscle shortens and lengthens about a joint. Both types of contractions contribute to the development of strength.

Isotonic exercises produce delayed muscle soreness 24 to 48 hours after a workout. Eccentric contractions cause microscopic damage to muscle fibers and their connective tissue.[5] Soreness occurs because the damaged tissues swell and apply pressure on the nerves. Delayed muscle soreness is more common among (1) beginning exercisers, (2) exercisers who attempt to overload too quickly, and (3) those who change from one activity to another.

Stretching exercises, light workouts, or complete rest may be required to alleviate muscle soreness. Prevention is the best treatment. Prevention involves allowing enough time to adjust to a new routine (at least 1 month), overloading the muscles in small increments (not trying to do too much too fast), and exercising within your capacity. Because muscle soreness may last 48 hours, those who use isotonic exercise systems are advised to exercise no more than every other day. This schedule ensures that the next bout of exercise will occur after soreness has abated.

Variable resistance training. Variable resistance exercise equipment was developed in response to isotonic exercises not maximally stressing muscles throughout their full range of motion. The maximum weight lifted isotonically is limited to the weakest point in the musculoskeletal leverage system. The weight appears lighter at some points in the joint movement and heavier at others. In reality, the weight itself is constant and the human bony leverage system changes.

Variable resistance equipment is designed to provide maximum resistance through the full range of motion. Universal Gym equipment accomplishes this by altering the lifter's leverage. Decreasing the leverage increases the resistance at points in the movement where the muscles are strongest. Nautilus equipment uses a system of cams to do the same. Variable resistance training challenges the individual to exert more force throughout the range of motion, which should result in greater returns. Whether variable resistance weight training is more effective than conventional weight training is yet to be resolved. Evidence indicates that it is as good and may be better.

Free-weight training. Isotonic training with free weights (dumbbells and barbells) continues to be an appropriate method for strength development. Free-weight training provides many advantages. For athletes, it yields some flexibility in strength development because the movements are not confined to a track. Exercises can be selected or improvised to simulate the movements required by specific sports, allowing the development of the muscles that will be used in competition. Concurrently, ancillary musculature that plays a supporting or stabilizing role

for the major muscles is also stimulated and developed.

For noncompetitors, free weights have several advantages. The equipment is inexpensive and versatile. A starter set of free weights typically costs less than $100. Free weights do not require much space, so the workout can occur in the home.

The major limitation of free-weight exercise is that this system does not provide maximum resistance throughout the full range of motion. A second limitation, one that is more of an inconvenience, is the constant changing of collars and plates as the exerciser adjusts the weight to perform the different exercises.

Isokinetic training. Isokinetic resistance training involves dynamic movements performed on exercise devices that produce maximum resistance throughout the full range of motion. The movement speed is preselected by the exerciser and remains constant throughout the movement. Isokinetic exercise theoretically improves on traditional and variable resistance dynamic systems.[6] Isokinetic devices adjust the resistance to accommodate the force applied by the exerciser. The greater the application of force, the greater the resistance to movement supplied by the device. Maximum force applied through the full range of motion is countered with maximum resistance at all joint angles. This activates the greatest number of motor units, producing greater gains in strength than other dynamic systems of exercise.

Circuit Resistance Training

Circuit resistance training (CRT) is very effective for individuals who wish to develop several fitness dimensions simultaneously. Muscular strength and endurance, changes in body composition, and improvement in cardiorespiratory endurance can be attained together.

A circuit usually comprises 8 to 15 exercise stations. The weight selected for each exercise station should equal 40% to 55% of the exerciser's capacity. The exerciser does as many repetitions as possible for 15 to 30 seconds at each station. The rest interval between exercise stations should equal the exercise time spent at each station. The circuit is repeated two to three times for a total elapsed time of 30 to 50 minutes per workout. As fitness improves, overload can be applied by (1) increasing the amount of weight at each station, (2) increasing the amount of exercise time at each station (up to 30 seconds), (3) decreasing the amount of rest between stations, or (4) any combination of these.

The CRT system is challenging, versatile, and

Figure 4-21   Circuit Resistance Training

The following is an example of a circuit. You should warm up before CRT and finish the workout with a cool down.

Station 1	Leg press or half-squat	15 to 30 sec
Station 2	Bench press	15 to 30 sec
Station 3	Back hyperextension	15 to 30 sec
Station 4	Biceps curl	15 to 30 sec
Station 5	Overhead press	15 to 30 sec
Station 6	Sit-up or abdominal crunches	15 to 30 sec
Station 7	Push-ups	15 to 30 sec
Station 8	Lateral raises	15 to 30 sec
Station 9	Hamstring curl	15 to 30 sec
Station 10	Pull-ups	15 to 30 sec

fun. Exercise stations can be rearranged, exercises that develop similar muscle groups can be substituted for each other, and the order in which the circuit is traversed can be changed. Because relatively light weights are used, the likelihood of injury is reduced. Circuits can be set up in relatively small spaces. Machine weights are ideal for CRT because of the speed that resistances can be changed, but free weights are adaptable to this system as well.

The major limitation is that optimal gains in strength cannot occur through the circuit approach. Strength development occurs best by lifting very heavy weights combined with a substantial rest period between sets. An example of a circuit is presented in Figure 4-21.

Principles of Resistance Training

The principles of exercise—intensity, duration, frequency, overload, progression, and specificity—apply to resistance training as well as aerobic training.

Intensity and Duration

For muscular development and health enhancement, the intensity of resistance training may be set by selecting a weight (through trial and error) that can be lifted at least 8 times but no more than 12 times. This weight probably represents 70% to 80% of a maximal effort.[7] Each of these lifts is called a *repetition*. The duration of resistance training is determined by the number of repetitions of each exercise and the number of sets completed; 8 to 12 repetitions of an

exercise constitutes one set of that exercise. If the development of strength is the primary goal, you may select the appropriate resistance for each exercise by determining, through trial and error, the amount of weight needed to perform 6 repetitions maximum (RM).[8] This means that you are strong enough to perform 6 repetitions but not 7. This is the basis of progressive resistance exercise. (The bench press exercise in Figures 4-5 and 4-6 is used to illustrate this system.) For example, if the 6 RM for the bench press is 120 lb, you should perform 3 sets of this exercise in the following manner:

Set 1: Perform 6 repetitions of 60% of 6 RM (0.60 × 120 = 72 lb)

Set 2: Perform 6 repetitions of 80% of 6 RM (0.80 × 120 = 96 lb)

Set 3: Perform 6 repetitions of 100% of 6 RM (120 lb)

The intensity level for resistance exercise varies according to the system used. The intensity level for isometric exercise usually ranges from a minimum of two-thirds maximum force to maximum force. The duration of exercise is the total of the time it takes to devote 30 seconds of muscle contraction to each of the exercises. The muscles should be stressed for 30 seconds at several joint angles in the range of motion.

Frequency

Isometrics can be performed every day because muscle soreness does not occur. However, for physiological and psychological reasons, you should designate 2 to 3 days of rest throughout the week.

The new ACSM guidelines for resistance training for healthy adults include the following: (1) the program should consist of 8 to 10 exercises designed to stress the major muscle groups, (2) the exercise program should be repeated a minimum of twice weekly, and (3) the exercise program should consist of a minimum of one set of 8 to 12 repetitions to near fatigue.[1] These must be regarded as minimum standards that will produce approximately 75% of the gain documented with resistance programs featuring three sets of each exercise 3 days per week. Resistance programs following the ACSM guidelines do not produce optimal results but are excellent adjuncts to the cardiorespiratory component and are appropriate when time is a limiting factor. Except for very advanced participants, resistance exercises should be performed no more than every other day.

Overload and Progression

The principle used to gain strength is straightforward—the muscles must be subjected periodically to greater resistance as they adapt to the previous resistance. This exemplifies the overload principle, which applies to all muscles regardless of the system of training.

Overload may be applied by progressively increasing the amount of weight lifted or the number of repetitions performed or by decreasing rest time between sets. An increase in the number of repetitions leads to increases in muscle endurance, an increase in the amount of weight lifted leads to an increase in muscle strength, and a decrease in rest time increases muscular and aerobic endurance.

Calisthenics are not as effective as weight training in the development of strength because overload is more difficult to apply. In calisthenic-type exercises the body weight is the resistance, and this cannot be conveniently changed as participants become stronger. Calisthenics lose their effectiveness in developing strength rather quickly and become more associated with promoting muscle endurance.

The principle of progression relates to the application of overload or, more precisely, how much and when an increase in resistance should occur. In a progressive resistance system of 6 RM, overload is applied by adding more weight when the exerciser can perform more than 6 repetitions on more than one occasion with the current weight. When 6 RM is surpassed with the new weight, it is time to add again.

Specificity

The principle of specificity reflects the body's response to exercise. The type of training dictates the type of muscle development. Training programs that emphasize high resistance and low repetitions increase muscle strength and size. The gains are the result of (1) muscle hypertrophy, which is an increase in the diameter of muscle fibers, and (2) the recruitment of more motor units.

Training programs that emphasize low resistance and a high number of repetitions develop muscle endurance. The high volume of work increases the blood and oxygen supply to the muscles by increasing capillary density and muscle myoglobin concentration. Myoglobin is similar to hemoglobin: It is an oxygen-carrying protein that makes oxygen available to the muscle for contraction.

Gender Differences in Strength Development

Resistance training increases strength by increasing muscle size and total muscle mass and by causing neural adaptations (recruitment of motor units). Is the difference in strength between men and women a true gender difference, or is it related to cultural expectations and constraints?

The difference in strength between males and females before puberty is inconsequential, but after puberty, it becomes significant: the average male can generate 30% to 50% more force than the average female. The difference is greatest in upper body strength and least for leg strength. When comparisons are made for the total amount of force that the muscles can generate, on average, males can produce more force than females for all muscle groups tested. Males are 50% stronger than females in upper body strength and 30% stronger in lower body strength.[6] These values persist regardless of the method used to measure strength. When researchers matched males and females on body size, body composition, and training status, males were still stronger.

When the genders are compared according to cross section of muscle, little difference is found if the muscle tested is of equal size in both genders. Human skeletal muscle can generate approximately 3 to 8 kilograms (kg) of force per centimeter squared (cm^2) of muscle cross section regardless of gender. Because the quality of muscle tissue is similar between the genders, the differences can be accounted for by the greater muscle mass of males. The greatest force is exhibited by individuals with the largest muscle cross section.

Another factor responsible for the strength differential after puberty is the increased production of testosterone in males. Testosterone stimulates the protein-synthesizing mechanisms and is responsible for the muscle hypertrophy that is unique to males. Females also produce testosterone but in much lower quantities, and this primarily accounts for their diminished capacity to develop muscle. However, research has shown that females can improve considerably in strength without developing large muscles.[9] For the average female the development of large muscles with resistance training is virtually impossible. The masculinizing effect of resistance training on women is a myth that continues to persist. To increase muscle size, some female body builders and other sports participants have resorted to using anabolic steroids.

Steroids

Anabolic steroid use by nonathletes is on the rise. This is particularly true for young males. A nationwide survey of 3403 male high school seniors indicated that 6.6% of this group were current users or had previously been users of steroids and that 25% of the current users showed signs of dependency.[10] According to this report, the improvement in phys-

TABLE 4-1 Anabolic Steroids in a Nutshell

Effects	Male	Female	Reversible
Increase in aggressive, hostile, and violent behavior	x	x	x
Dependence and potential addiction	x	x	x
Psychotic episodes	x	x	x
Hair growth on body and face		x	
Male pattern baldness		x	
Acne	x	x	x
Sexual dysfunction	x	x	x
Increased libido	x	x	x
Menstrual irregularities		x	x
Testicular atrophy and sterility	x		Unclear for long-term use
Deepening of the voice		x	
Decreased breast size		x	x
Increased breast size (gynecomastia)	x		Unclear for long-term use
Acceleration of atherosclerosis	x	x	x
High blood pressure	x	x	x
Decrease in high density lipoprotein cholesterol	x	x	x
Liver damage	x	x	Not all reversible
Prostate cancer	x		
Muscle growth	x	x	x
Ultimate height attained when use begins in adolescence affected	x	x	

ical appearance reputed to occur with steroid use, accompanied by peer approval of those physical changes, functioned as a powerful reinforcer for continued use.

Heavy steroid users were more likely than light users to take two or more steroids concomitantly and more apt to take these drugs by injection rather than in pill form. Injection as a method of delivery is highly characteristic of drugs that involve addiction. The steroid "hook" is insidious and powerful: 30% of the heavy users vowed that they would not discontinue steroid use if steroids were proved to cause liver cancer, 31% would not stop if they proved to cause heart attacks, and 39% would not stop if they proved to cause infertility.[10]

Although definitive evidence of the long-term effects of steroid use is not available, the potential for long-term harm is certainly real. Predicting how and when the effects of steroids will be manifested is impossible because people respond individually to those drugs as a result of differences in body chemistry. The steroid effect is complicated further because "black market" preparations contain additives, and some preparations are contaminated. The potential for harm is readily discernible; 80% to 90% of all steroids used are purchased through the black

market. Table 4-1 presents some of the known and possible effects of steroid use.

Anaerobic Exercise

Strength development exercises are **anaerobic.** Anaerobic literally means "without oxygen," and when applied to exercise, it refers to high-intensity physical activities whose oxygen demand is above the level that can be supplied during performance. Short-term supplies of fuel stored in the muscles provide the energy for anaerobic activities. As a result, these can only be sustained for several seconds. Sprinting 100 yards, lifting a heavy weight, and running up two or three flights of stairs are some examples of anaerobic activities.

The Health Benefits of Resistance Training

Evidence has been accumulating during the last decade that shows a positive relationship between dynamic resistance training and health enhancement. Weight training (exercising the major muscles of the body at an intensity level of 70% to 90% of maximum strength) rather than weight lifting (lifting

TABLE 4-2 The Health Benefits of Resistance Training

Training Effect	Outcomes
Increases muscle, decreases fat	More calories consumed at rest, results in improved body contour
Increases BMR	More calories required at rest, contributes to weight control
Develops antigravity muscles (abdominal, low back, hips, front and back of thighs, both calves)	Maintenance of or improvement in posture, results in less pressure on low back and less likelihood of back injuries
Strengthens and thickens ligaments, tendons, cartilage, and connective tissue	Stronger and more stable joints, results in less likelihood of injury
Thickens and strengthens bones	Maintenance of or increase in calcium density, prevents or delays osteoporosis
Increases HDL cholesterol	More healthful lipid profile, protects against cardiovascular disease
Reduces RBP	Decrease in effect of RBP as a major risk factor for cardiovascular disease, reduces risk for cardiovascular disease
Enhances body image and self-esteem	Healthful for mind-body connection, boosts mental health

BMR, Basal metabolic rate; *HDL*, high density lipoprotein; *RBP*, resting blood pressure.

maximum loads in power or Olympic style) has produced these changes.[7] Very recent studies have shown that cardiac patients can benefit from appropriately planned weight-training programs. Although weight training had always been considered too dangerous for cardiac patients, 25 cardiac patients participated in 3 years of circuit weight training. As a group, they had a 24% increase in strength and a 12% increase in cardiorespiratory endurance.[11] A summary of the wellness benefits of resistance training supported by research appears in Table 4-2.

Muscular Endurance

Muscular endurance is the application of repeated muscular force. Inflating a tire with a bicycle pump, walking up five flights of stairs, lifting a weight 20 times, and doing 50 situps are some examples of muscular endurance. It is developed by many repetitions against resistances that are considerably less than maximum. Absolute muscular endurance depends on muscle endurance.[12] On the basis of limited data, significant muscle endurance may be developed in most people with a weight-training program featuring 12 to 15 repetitions at 70% of maximal strength.[13]

A more systematic way to improve muscular endurance is to use a progressive resistance system similar to the one for strength development. You should select a weight for each exercise that you can lift 15 times (repetitions) but that you cannot lift 16 times. This weight becomes your 15 RM. You perform three sets, one each of 60%, 80%, and 100% of 15 RM. For example, if you can execute 15 repetitions of 80 lb for a particular exercise, you can proceed as follows:

Set 1: Do 15 repetitions at 60% of 15 RM (0.60 × 80 lb = 48 lb)

Set 2: Do 15 repetitions at 80% of 15 RM (0.80 × 80 lb = 64 lb)

Set 3: Do 15 repetitions at 100% of 15 RM (80 lb)

Muscular endurance exercises should be performed no more than every other day.

Assessment Activity 4-2 presents a method for determining your muscular endurance. Assessment Activity 4-3 measures abdominal muscle endurance, and Assessment Activity 4-4 measures muscular strength and endurance with calisthenics.

Keeping a Daily Training Log

Beginning weight trainers should keep a daily log of their training activities. The advantages of keeping such a record far outweigh the minimum amount of bother, time, and effort required to make the entries

Figure 4-22 Sample Training Log

Name Cathy Smith   Starting date Jan. 1, 1994
Program objectives To gain strength and muscle definition

Exercise	Jan. 1 Resis (lb)	Jan. 1 Reps	Jan. 1 Sets	Jan. 3 Resis (lb)	Jan. 3 Reps	Jan. 3 Sets	Jan. 5 Resis (lb)	Jan. 5 Reps	Jan. 5 Sets	Jan. 7 Resis (lb)	Jan. 7 Reps	Jan. 7 Sets	Jan. 9 Resis (lb)	Jan. 9 Reps	Jan. 9 Sets	Jan. 11 Resis (lb)	Jan. 11 Reps	Jan. 11 Sets	Jan. 13 Resis (lb)	Jan. 13 Reps	Jan. 13 Sets
Bench press	60	10	3																		
Biceps curl	25	10	3																		
Back extension	80	10	3																		
Leg press	150	10	3																		
Hamstring curl	30	10	3																		
Chest press	30	10	3																		
Abdominal crunch	—	25	3																		
Overhead	35	10	3																		

Resis, Resistance; *reps*, repetitions.

during the workout. Each entry should be recorded during the rest period between sets.

The advantages of maintaining a daily training log include the following:

▶ You will always know which exercises you performed and the amount of weight that was used for each.
▶ You will always know the number of repetitions and sets that you preformed of each exercise.
▶ The training log provides an objective account

of your improvement. You can compare the amount of weight you are currently lifting with the amount at the beginning of your training.
▶ The training log provides an accurate history.
▶ The training log is a motivating device that provides objective feedback of performance improvement.

A sample training log is shown in Figure 4-22. A blank training log is shown in Assessment Activity 4-5 for you to use to document your resistance training program.

Summary

▶ The physiological law of use and disuse applies to all human beings during all phases of the life cycle.
▶ The muscular systems of older adults are trainable and respond to resistance training with an increase in strength and muscle size.
▶ Muscular strength is the maximum force that a muscle or muscle group can exert in a single contraction.
▶ Dynamic exercises consist of concentric and eccentric muscle contractions.
▶ Isotonic exercises are dynamic in that muscles shorten and lengthen, producing movement around a joint.
▶ Variable resistance exercise equipment is designed to provide maximum resistance throughout the full range of motion.

▶ Circuit resistance training is a versatile system that allows an individual to develop several fitness dimensions simultaneously.
▶ The principles of exercise—intensity, frequency, duration, overload, progression, and specificity—apply to resistance training. These can be manipulated to meet all muscle development objectives.
▶ The average male can generate 30% to 50% more force than the average female.
▶ Anabolic steroids are performance-enhancing drugs that are harmful and illegal.
▶ Research in the last decade has shown that resistance training contributes to wellness in a variety of ways.
▶ Muscle endurance is the application of repeated muscular force.

Action Plan for Personal Wellness

Use the information presented in this chapter to answer the following questions and to formulate an action plan to enhance your personal wellness.

1 Based on the information presented in this chapter, along with what I know about my family's health history, the health problems and issues that I need to be concerned about are:_____

_____

_____

2 Of those health care issues listed in number 1, the one I most need to act on is:_____

_____

_____

3 The possible actions I can take to improve my level of wellness are (be specific):_____

_____

_____

4 Of those actions listed in number 3, the one that I most need to include in an action plan is:_____

_____

_____

5 Factors I need to keep in mind to be successful in my action plan are:_____

_____

_____

Review Questions

1. Define muscular strength and muscular endurance.
2. What are the differences among isometric, isotonic, isokinetic, and variable resistance exercises?
3. What are concentric and eccentric contractions?
4. What are the health benefits of participating in resistance exercise?
5. How do you account for the strength differences between males and females?
6. Name and define the principles of conditioning as they relate to resistance training.

References

1. American College of Sports Medicine: The recommended quantity and quality of exercise for developing and maintaining cardiorespiratory and muscular fitness in healthy adults, *Med Sci Sports Exerc* 22:265-274, 1990.
2. Strength training, *Mayo Clin Health Letter* 8:2-3, 1990.
3. Frontera WR et al: Strength training and determinants of $\dot{V}o_2$ max in older men, *J Appl Physiol* 68:329-333, 1990.
4. Fiatarone MA et al: High-intensity strength training in nonagenarians, *JAMA* 263:3029-3034, 1990.
5. Schwane JA et al: Effects of training on delayed muscle soreness and serum creatine kinase activity after running, *Med Sci Sports Exerc* 19:584-587, 1987.
6. McArdle WD, Katch FI, Katch VL: *Exercise, physiology, energy, nutrition and human performance*, Philadelphia, 1991, Lea & Febiger.
7. Fleck SJ, Kraemer WJ: Resistance training: basic principles (part 1 of 4), *Physician Sportsmed* 16(3):160-171, 1988.
8. Bartels RL: Weight training, *Physician Sportsmed* 20:233-234, 1992.
9. Cureton KJ et al: Muscle hypertrophy in men and women, *Med Sci Sports Exerc* 20:338-344, 1988.
10. Buckley WE et al: Estimated prevalence of anabolic steroid use among male high school seniors, *JAMA* 260:3441-3445, 1988.
11. Strong body, strong heart. *Johns Hopkins Med Letter* 2(4):1-2, 1990.
12. Kraemer WJ et al: A review: factors in exercise prescription of resistance training, *NSCA J* 10:36-41, 1988.
13. Pollock ML, Wilmore JH, Fox SM: *Exercise in health and disease*, Philadelphia, 1984, WB Saunders.

Annotated Readings

Bartels RL: Weight training, *Physician Sportsmed* 20:233-234, 1992.
Discusses several approaches to the development of strength and endurance. Presents guidelines for strength development and also discusses nutritional habits that will help to produce optimal strength gains.

The best workout: free weights vs. machines, *Univ Calif Berkeley Wellness Letter* 9:6, 1993.
Discusses the advantages and disadvantages of free weights versus machine weights in the development of strength and endurance. Both systems are effective. This article should help the reader to determine which of the two is most suitable.

Body building for the nineties, *Nutr Action Health Letter* 19:1, 5-7, 1992.
In an interview format, William Evans, chief of the human physiology laboratory at Tufts University, discusses the effect of strength training on the health of older Americans. As Americans age, they must avoid the "disability zone," and the best way to do this is through a program of strength training. Evans discusses his preference for strength training over aerobic training for older people.

Cobleigh B, Kaufer IJ: Circuit weight training—an answer to achieving physical fitness? *J Phys Educ Recreation Dance* 63:18-22, 1992.
Discusses the effectiveness of a high school circuit weight training program. Before and after measurements indicate that substantial improvements were achieved in resting heart rate, muscular endurance, upper and lower body strength, flexibility, and body composition.

Heinrich CH et al: Bone mineral content of cyclically menstruating female resistance and endurance trained athletes, *Med Sci Sports Exerc* 22:558-563, 1990.
Normally menstruating women who were classified as body builders had greater bone mineral content than swimmers, collegiate runners, recreational runners, and inactive control subjects. Bone is built slowly regardless of the type of exercise, but strength training appears to be more effective than other forms of exercise in developing bone.

ASSESSMENT ACTIVITY   4-1

Calculation of Strength (Selected Muscle Groups)

Directions: The calculation of strength by this method is expressed as the ratio of strength to body weight. The amount of weight accomplished for each lift is converted to a proportion of your body weight and is determined in the following manner.

1. Find your 1 RM for each of the following exercises: biceps curl (two arm), overhead press, bench press, half-squat or leg press, and hamstring curl.
2. Divide your 1 RM for each exercise by your body weight.
   EXAMPLE: A 130 lb woman performs a 1 RM bench press of 80 lb. Her score is $80 \div 130 = 0.61$. Turn to the chart for an interpretation of her score. Look under the "Bench press" column and you will note that her score of 0.61 is in the "Average" category. In this example, the female subject has the following results on the five lifts: biceps curl = 0.28 (fair), standing press = 0.26 (fair), bench press = 0.61 (average), half-squat or leg press = 1.35 (good), and hamstring curl = 0.52 (good). These data are plotted in the first strength profile chart.
3. When you have computed a score for each of your lifts, turn to the strength profile charts. Plot your data in the blank chart provided.
4. Refer to Figures 4-1 through 4-16 for a refresher on how to do these exercises.

Strength/Body Weight Ratio
Females

Biceps Curl	Standing Press	Bench Press	Half-Squat or Leg Press	Hamstring Curl	Strength Category
0.45 and above	0.50 and above	0.85 and above	1.45 and above	0.55 and above	Excellent
0.38-0.44	0.42-0.49	0.70-0.84	1.30-1.44	0.50-0.54	Good
0.32-0.37	0.32-0.41	0.60-0.69	1.0-1.29	0.40-0.49	Average
0.25-0.31	0.25-0.31	0.50-0.59	0.80-0.99	0.30-0.39	Fair
0.24 and below	0.24 and below	0.49 and below	0.79 and below	0.29 and below	Poor

Males

Biceps Curl	Standing Press	Bench Press	Half-Squat or Leg Press	Hamstring Curl	Strength Category
0.65 and above	1.0 and above	1.30 and above	1.85 and above	0.65 and above	Excellent
0.55-0.64	0.90-0.99	1.15-1.29	1.65-1.84	0.55-0.64	Good
0.45-0.54	0.75-0.89	1.0-1.14	1.30-1.64	0.45-0.54	Average
0.35-0.44	0.60-0.74	0.85-0.99	1.0-1.29	0.35-0.44	Fair
0.34 and below	0.59 and below	0.84 and below	Less than 1.0	0.34 and below	Poor

Strength Profile Charts

Example

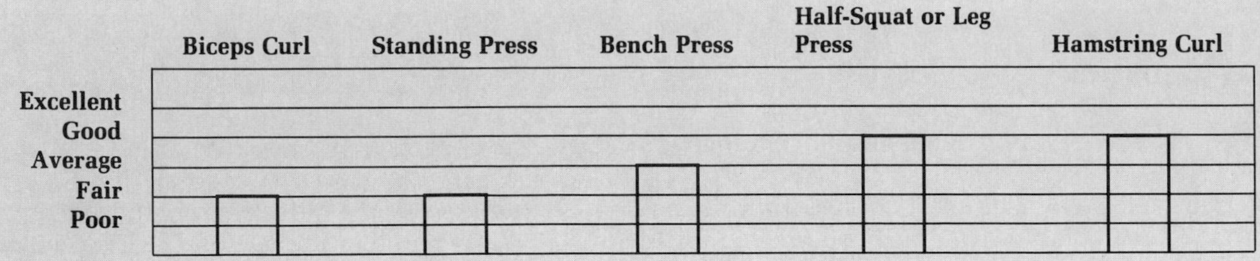

	Biceps Curl	Standing Press	Bench Press	Half-Squat or Leg Press	Hamstring Curl
Excellent					
Good					
Average					
Fair					
Poor					

Your Data

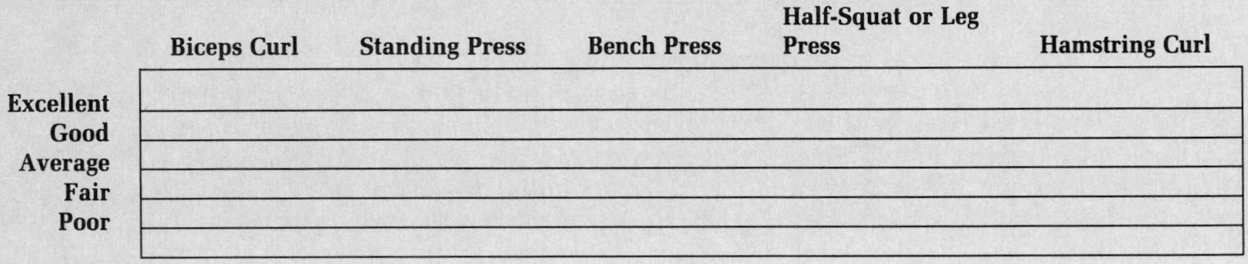

	Biceps Curl	Standing Press	Bench Press	Half-Squat or Leg Press	Hamstring Curl
Excellent					
Good					
Average					
Fair					
Poor					

ASSESSMENT ACTIVITY   **4 - 2**

Muscular Endurance

Directions: Through trial and error, select a weight that you can use while performing 20 RM for each of the following exercises: bench press, leg extension or half-squat, biceps curl, and hamstring curl.

EXAMPLE: A male subject weighing 150 lb can perform 20 RM of 100 lb in the bench press. The score for this exercise is computed as follows:

$$\frac{100 \text{ lb (20 RM)}}{150 \text{ lb}} = 0.67 \text{ or } 67\%$$

Now look at the chart under "Bench Press" and observe that a score of 67% is average. Perform each of the four exercises (20 RM) and calculate the muscle endurance scores following the example.

Muscle Endurance/Body Weight Ratio 20 RM

Males

Bench Press	Leg Extension or Half-Squat	Biceps Curl	Hamstring Curl	Strength Category
≥76%	≥166%	≥50%	≥40%	Excellent
70%-75%	150%-165%	43%-49%	33%-39%	Good
60%-69%	133%-149%	37%-42%	27%-32%	Average
50%-59%	116%-132%	30%-36%	20%-26%	Fair
<50%	<116%	<30%	<20%	Poor

Females

Bench Press	Leg Extension or Half-Squat	Biceps Curl	Hamstring Curl	Strength Category
≥50%	≥115%	≥32	≥38%	Excellent
42%-49%	100%-114%	23%-30%	31%-37%	Good
35%-41%	88%-99%	15%-22%	23%-31%	Average
27%-34%	77%-87%	12%-14%	15%-22%	Fair
≤27%	<77%	<12%	<15%	Poor

≥, Equal to or greater than; <, less than.

ASSESSMENT ACTIVITY 4 - 3

Abdominal Muscular Endurance—The Canadian Trunk Strength Test

Directions: The Canadian trunk strength test is used to measure abdominal endurance rather than the conventional sit-up test. It is not necessary or desirable to raise the trunk more than 30 degrees. Sit-ups beyond 30 degrees cause the abdomen to contract isometrically, so the hip flexors supply the power to raise the trunk above this level. The Canadian trunk strength test is performed in the following manner:

1. Lie on your back with knees bent 90 degrees.
2. Extend your arms so that the fingertips of both hands touch a strip of tape perpendicular to the body on each side.
3. Two additional strips of tape are located parallel to the first two strips, 8 cm apart.
4. Curl-up, sliding your finger tips along the mat until they touch the second set of tape strips, and then return to the starting position. The tester's hands are placed on the mat below the point where the back of the subject's head touches the tester's hands.
5. The curl-up is slow, controlled, and continuous, with a cadence of 20 curl-ups/min (3 sec/curl-up).
6. A metronome provides the speed of movement. It is set at 40 beats/min (curl-up on one beat, down on the second).
7. Subjects perform as many curl-ups as they can up to a maximum of 75 without missing a beat. See Figure 4-23 for a demonstration of the Canadian trunk strength test and then turn to the chart for an interpretation of your score.

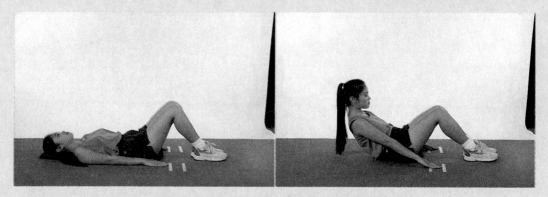

FIGURE 4-23 Canadian trunk strength test.

Standards for the Canadian Trunk Strength Test

	Number Completed					
	Men—Age			**Women—Age**		
Strength Category	**<35**	**35-44**	**>45**	**<35**	**35-44**	**>45**
Excellent	60	50	40	50	40	30
Good	45	50	25	40	25	15
Marginal	30	25	15	25	15	10
Needs work	15	10	5	10	6	4

ASSESSMENT ACTIVITY   4 - 4

Assessing Muscular Strength and Endurance with Selected Calisthenic Exercises

Directions: The tests making up this assessment require minimum equipment and are easy to administer.

▶ Chin-ups: Grasp an overhead horizontal bar, hands shoulder width apart, palms facing the body. On the upstroke, your chin must go above the bar and your arms must extend fully on the downstroke. Your legs must remain extended throughout the exercise and should not be used to thrust your body upward (Figure 4-24).

▶ Flexed-arm hang: Perform this exercise if you cannot do chin-ups. Have someone assist you to the exercise position with your chin above the bar, palms facing away from your body. A stop watch is started as soon as you assume this position and stopped if you tilt your head back to keep your chin above the bar, if your chin touches the bar, or if your chin drops below the bar. Record the time to the nearest whole second (Figure 4-25).

▶ Push-ups: Assume a prone position (face down) with your arms extended, hands on the floor under the shoulders. Keep your back and legs straight, with your feet together. The person counting the push-ups should place a fist under your chest. Bend your elbows, lowering your chest until contact is made with the counter's fist, and then return to the starting position by straightening your arms. Repeat as many times as possible without resting to a maximum score of 46 push-ups (Figure 4-26).

▶ Modified push-ups: Perform this exercise if you cannot do the standard push-up. The modified version is performed in the same manner as the standard push-up except that you support your body weight with your hands and knees. Do as many as you can without rest to a maximum of 24 (Figure 4-27).

When you have completed these tests, turn to the chart for an interpretation of your performance.

FIGURE 4-24 Chin-ups.

FIGURE 4-25 Flexed arm hang.

FIGURE 4-26 Push-ups.

FIGURE 4-27 Modified push-ups.

Muscular Strength and Endurance Standards

Chin-Ups	Flexed-Arm Hang (sec)	Push-Ups	Modified Push-Ups	Strength Category
20 or more	30 or more	40 or more	24 or more	Excellent
15-19	24-29	32-39	14-23	Good
10-14	15-23	26-31	8-13	Average
6-9	9-14	20-26	2-7	Fair
5 or less	8 or less	19 or less	1 or less	Poor

ASSESSMENT ACTIVITY

4 - 5

Resistance Training Log

Directions: Keep a record of your resistance fitness activities on the form provided.

Daily Training Log

Name _____ Starting date _____

Program objectives _____

Exercise	Resis (lb)	Reps	Sets	Resis (lb)	Reps	Sets	Resis (lb)	Reps	Sets	Resis (lb)	Reps	Sets	Resis (lb)	Reps	Sets	Resis (lb)	Reps	Sets

Resis, Resistance; *reps,* repetitions.

CHAPTER 5

Flexibility

Key terms	Objectives
ballistic stretching	After completing this chapter you will be able to:
flexibility	Define flexibility.
goniometer	Identify factors affecting flexibility.
proprioceptive neu-	Distinguish among static, ballistic, and proprioreceptive neuromuscular
romuscular facilita-	facilitation stretching.
tion (PNF)	Assess and prescribe a personal flexibility program.
static stretching	Discuss the problem of low back pain.
stretch reflex	Demonstrate proper lifting techniques for prevention of low back injury.

The term **flexibility** refers to the range of motion at a joint or series of joints such as the elbow, shoulder, and knee. Flexibility is specific to each joint; that is, a person may be quite flexible in the shoulders but inflexible in the lower back. The flexibility of one joint cannot be predicted by measuring another, so several measurements at different sites are necessary to assess this component of fitness. Flexibility is influenced by three factors: (1) the bony structure of the joint, (2) the amount of tissue around the joint, and (3) the elasticity of the muscles, tendons, and ligaments that cross over the joint. Improvement in flexibility is accomplished primarily by increasing the elasticity of muscles, tendons, and ligaments.[1]

Flexibility and Wellness

Flexibility is one of the most important components of health-related fitness. Several factors influence flexibility, including age, gender, and level and type of physical activity. Youngsters are more flexible than adults because tendons lose their elasticity with age. However, inactivity may play a greater role than the aging process in the loss of flexibility because muscles and other soft tissue lose elasticity when not used. Active individuals are usually more flexible than sedentary people.[2] Women tend to be more flexible than men because the hormones that permit women's tissue to stretch during the childbirth process facilitate all body stretching.[3] The range of motion for most movements begins to decline in the mid-twenties for males and at approximately 30 years of age for females. (Complete the Assessment Activities at the end of this chapter to determine your flexibility.)

Maintenance of flexibility is most important in the prevention of low back pain. For example, a sedentary lifestyle characterized by sitting for long pe-

riods leads to a loss of flexibility and increases the likelihood of low back injury. Flexibility of the hamstring muscles (a group of muscles in the back of the thighs) and the low back muscles, along with abdominal strength, good posture, and normal body weight, are essential for a healthy back.[4]

Developing a Flexibility Program

Flexibility can be improved by exercises that promote the elasticity of the soft tissues. (See Figures 5-1 through 5-8 for exercises that can maintain and improve the flexibility of the major body sites.) These 10-minute exercises can be done every day, both before and after exercise, and also during days of rest from exercise.

Flexibility is an important component of a fitness program designed to improve total fitness. Stretching exercises do improve flexibility but may not be effective in reducing injury from exercise. Muscle soreness and injury are possible when tight muscles are subjected to strenuous physical activity. Lack of stretching may appear to increase the potential for injury, but little evidence in the literature supports this idea.[4]

Types of Stretching

Muscles must contract for movement to occur. The contracting muscles are called *agonists* and are the prime movers. For an agonist to contract and shorten and produce movement, a reciprocal lengthening of its *antagonists* must occur. For example, when the biceps muscle of the upper arm contracts, its opposite, the triceps muscle, must relax and lengthen. In this case the biceps is the agonist and the triceps is the antagonist. The triceps becomes the agonist for movements that require it to contract, in which case the biceps becomes the antagonist. Understanding these concepts is necessary to understand stretching techniques.

Ballistic stretching uses dynamic movements to stretch muscles. Each time a muscle is stretched in this manner, the myotatic reflex **(stretch reflex)** located in that muscle is also stretched. It responds by sending a volley of signals to the central nervous system that orders the muscle to contract, thus resisting the stretch. This is not only counterproductive—the muscle is forced to pull against itself—but can lead to injury because the elastic limits of the muscle may be exceeded. Ballistic stretching is not recommended for flexibility development.

Static stretching involves slowly moving to desired positions that are held for 15 to 30 seconds and are then slowly released. This method of stretching does not activate the stretch reflex (automatic or reflexive contraction of a muscle being stretched), so the muscle is essentially stretched without opposition. These positions should produce a feeling of mild discomfort but not pain. Static stretching (Figures 5-1 to 5-8) results in little or no muscle soreness, has a low incidence of injury, and requires little energy.

These guidelines should be followed for safe and effective stretching:

▶ Warm-up for a few minutes before stretching by walking, slow jogging, and light calisthenics.
▶ Stretch to the point of discomfort.
▶ Do not stretch to the point of pain.
▶ Hold each stretch for 15 to 30 seconds.
▶ Move slowly from position to position.
▶ Perform each stretch at least twice.
▶ Stretch after the workout—this may actually produce the greatest benefit because the muscles are warm and more amenable to stretching.
▶ Perform stretching exercises daily if possible.

Proprioceptive neuromuscular facilitation (PNF) is another effective and acceptable stretching technique. It is more complex than most of the methods of stretching, but it is the most effective.[5,6] By combining slow passive movements (the force for passive movement is supplied by a partner) with maximum voluntary isometric contractions, you can bypass the myotatic reflex stimulation that accompanies changes in muscle and tendon length.

All variations of PNF stretching require a partner and some combination of passive stretching and isometric contractions. Two of the common PNF methods, contract-relax (CR) (Figure 5-9) and slow-reversal-hold-relax (SRHR) (Figure 5-10), are presented. For comparison, both figures exemplify

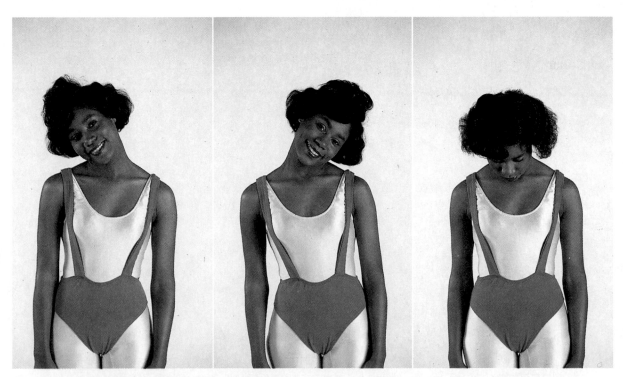

FIGURE 5-1 Neck stretches. Slowly bend your neck from side to side and front to back. Do not do head circles.

A B

FIGURE 5-2 Shoulder stretch. Gently pull your right arm behind your head **(A)** and hold for 15 to 30 seconds **(B)**. Repeat with the other arm.

FIGURE 5-3 Chest and shoulder stretch. Stretch your arms to full extension with both palms on the floor and press your chest down to the floor. Hold 15 to 30 seconds and slowly release.

FIGURE 5-4 Back stretch. Cross your legs and lean forward **(A),** extending your arms to the front **(B).** Hold for 15 to 30 seconds and slowly release.

A B

A   B

FIGURE 5-5 Groin stretch. **A,** Place the soles of your feet together and lean forward. Hold 15 to 30 seconds. **B,** Variation: Push down gently on both knees and hold for 15 to 30 seconds.

FIGURE 5-6 Quadriceps stretch. Lie on your side as shown. Bend the knee of your top leg, grasp your ankle with your free hand, and slowly pull your heel toward your buttocks until you feel the stretch in the muscles in the front of your thigh. Hold 15 to 30 seconds, roll over to the other side, and repeat with your other leg.

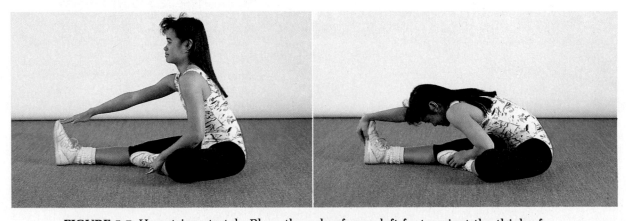

FIGURE 5-7 Hamstring stretch. Place the sole of your left foot against the thigh of your extended right leg. Lean forward without bending the knee of your extended leg. Hold for 15 to 30 seconds and repeat with your other leg.

FIGURE 5-8 Calf and Achilles tendon stretch. Assume the position shown. Be sure the heel of your extended leg remains in contact with the floor and both feet are pointed straight ahead. Slowly move your hips forward until you feel the stretch in the calf of your extended leg. Hold 15 to 30 seconds and repeat with your other leg.

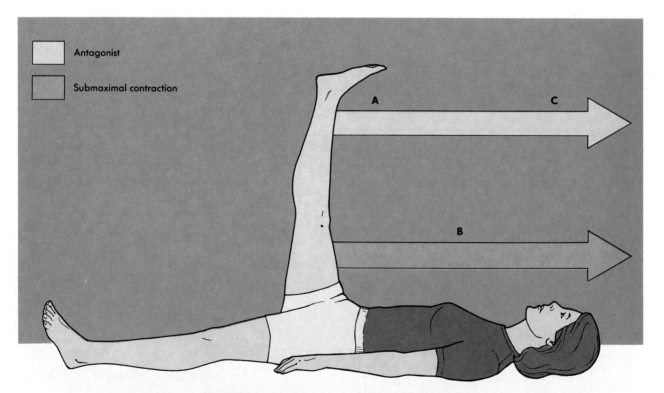

Antagonist

Submaximal contraction

A   C

B

FIGURE 5-9 Contract-relax (CR) technique.

stretching the hamstring group (muscles in the back of the thigh). The hamstrings are the antagonist muscle group and the quadriceps muscles (muscles in the front of the thigh) are the agonists. For example, the CR method is performed as follows (see Figure 5-9):

▶ A partner gently pushes the upraised leg in the direction of arrow a. This movement passively stretches the antagonist (hamstrings).

▶ The subject follows this with a 6-second submaximum contraction of the agonist (quadriceps).

▶ This is followed by another passive stretch of the hamstrings.

This is repeated twice with a few seconds rest between sequences.

The SRHR method is performed in the following manner (see Figure 5-10):

▶ A partner gently pushes the upraised leg in the direction of arrow a.

▶ The subject then performs a 6-second maximum voluntary isometric contraction (MVIC) of the antagonists (hamstrings) against resistance supplied by the partner.

▶ The subject follows this with a 6-second submaximum contraction of the agonists (quadriceps).

▶ This is followed by another passive stretch of the hamstrings.

This sequence is repeated twice with a few seconds of rest between exercises.

Although PNF appears to be the most effective of the stretching methods for enhancing flexibility, it has some limitations. It requires a partner, it produces more pain and muscle stiffness, it requires more time, and the risk of injury is increased, particularly when novices use this technique. Stretching statically is more convenient because this method does not require assistance or take much time.

Flexibility Assessment

Measuring flexibility is rather difficult, and several instruments have been developed. Probably the most widely used device is the **goniometer**. This device is a protractorlike device that measures the range of motion about a specific joint. This method is the

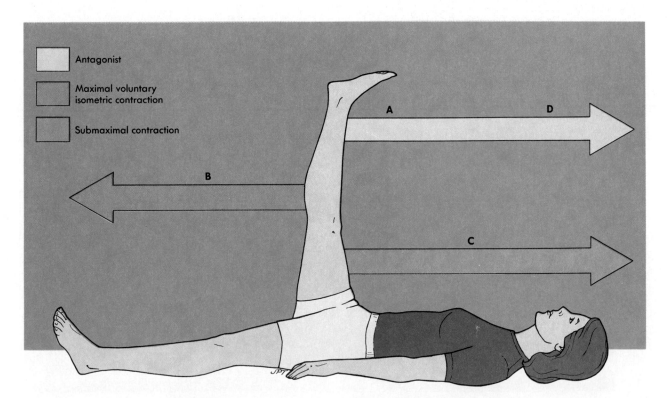

FIGURE 5-10 Slow-reversal-hold-relax (SRHR) technique.

most accurate means of assessing flexibility.[2] However, for the average person, assessing flexibility by using the goniometer is not practical.

Several tests are suitable for measuring flexibility when more sophisticated means cannot be used. (The directions and norms for these tests are provided in the assessment activities.) You should warm up and follow the rules for general stretching before taking the assessments.

Low Back Pain

An estimated 8 of every 10 Americans will suffer a back injury sometime during their lives.[7] It is the most common symptomatic complaint for both genders in the 25- to 60-year-old group who visit a physician's office.[8] The estimated annual cost of medical care for low back pain is approximately $13 billion.[9]

The high incidence of low back pain may be primarily attributed to mechanical factors.[7] These include overweight, poor posture, and lack of physical fitness. Most low back pain involves muscle and ligament strain and inflamed joints along the vertebral column. Some injuries involve disks that herniate or tear, resulting in the gel-like inner substance escaping and exerting pressure on the spinal nerves. Back pain also occurs as a result of injuries sustained from accidents, falls, incorrect lifting of objects, and participation in sports. Arthritis and osteoporosis also cause low back pain.

Approximately 90% of all back problems occur in the lumbar region (low back) of the spine. The spinal column consists of 33 bones (the vertebrae) and represents the only bony connection between the upper and lower halves of the body. Located between the bones of the spine are rings of tough fibrous tissue, the disks, which act as shock absorbers and keep the vertebrae from rubbing against each other. The spinal column is S shaped and consists of three naturally occurring curves. When these three curves are balanced, the body weight is evenly distributed and movement occurs fluidly. Because the bones are not stacked on each other in a straight line, susceptibility of injury increases, especially to the lower back, which must bear most of the weight of the torso. Misalignment in this region applies substantial stress to the concave, or inner side, of the exaggerated curve. The more pronounced the curve, the greater the stress because of the uneven distribution of weight on the bones and disks.

Overweight is a stressor of the low back because the excess weight pulls the spinal column forward, accentuating the lumbar curve and putting pressure on the disks. Research indicates that weak abdominal muscles and lack of flexibility in the lower back

FIGURE 5-11 Maintaining a healthy back.

and hamstring muscles promote fatigue and poor posture.[10] Fatigue causes the pelvis to tilt forward, increasing stress on the spinal column and its supporting structures. High-heeled shoes tilt the pelvis forward, and many wearers experience discomfort or pain in the low back at the end of the day.

Stress may be a factor in inducing or prolonging low back pain. Muscles that are under constant tension result in tightness and fatigue in the low back. Exercises that develop and strengthen the abdominal muscles and those that stretch the low back and hamstrings are invaluable in preventing low back pain. (Figure 5-11 illustrates commonly performed exercises for the maintenance of a healthy back.) Exercise also contributes to weight control, is an excel-

lent stress reducer generally and specifically for the muscles exercised, and develops the antigravity muscles—the calves, front and back of the thighs, hips, back, and abdominals, thereby contributing to correct posture. (Figure 5-12 illustrates correct lifting techniques that minimize the potential for injury.)

If a back problem occurs, you should consult a physician for treatment. If surgery is suggested, you should seek a second opinion and explore alternative treatments. Many back problems can be treated with Williams' flexion exercises[10] and McKenzie's extension exercises.[11] The selection depends on the type of problem being experienced and should be made by a health care professional.

FIGURE 5-12 How to lift properly.   *Continued.*

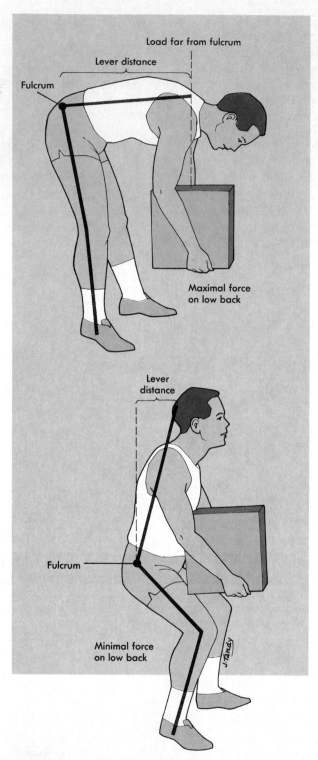

FIGURE 5-12—cont'd.

Summary

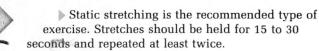

- Flexibility refers to the range of motion at a joint or series of joints and is specific to each joint.
- Factors that influence flexibility of a joint are the bony structure, the amount of tissue at the joint, and the elasticity of the muscles, tendons, and ligaments at the joint.
- Flexibility is influenced by age, gender, and physical activity.
- The maintenance of flexibility of the hamstrings and low back muscles is important in the prevention of low back pain.
- Normal body weight and good posture are also necessary for a healthy back.
- Ballistic stretching is counterproductive to improving joint elasticity and may contribute to injury.

- Static stretching is the recommended type of exercise. Stretches should be held for 15 to 30 seconds and repeated at least twice.
- Stretching should not be painful.
- Stretching exercises can be performed daily.
- Proprioceptive neuromuscular facilitation is the most effective but most difficult form of stretching.
- Proprioceptive neuromuscular facilitation combines passive movement with isometric contractions.
- The most accurate measurement of flexibility is obtained with a goniometer.
- Low back pain is the most common symptom for visits to a physician.
- Factors associated with low back pain include overweight, poor posture, inactivity, fatigue, weak abdominal muscles, high heels, and stress.

Action Plan for Personal Wellness

Use the information presented in this chapter to answer the following questions and to formulate an action plan to enhance your personal wellness.

1 Based on the information presented in this chapter, along with what I know about my family's health history, the health problems and issues that I need to be concerned about are:_____

_____

_____

2 Of those health care issues listed in number 1, the one I most need to act on is:_____

_____

_____

3 The possible actions I can take to improve my level of wellness are (be specific):_____

_____

4 Of those actions listed in number 3, the one that I most need to include in an action plan is:_____

_____

_____

5 Factors I need to keep in mind to be successful in my action plan are:_____

_____

_____

Review Questions

1. Explain why flexibility is such a important component of health-related fitness.
2. Discuss the steps to take when developing a flexibility program.
3. What concepts are necessary to understand the principles of stretching?
4. Distinguish among static, ballistic, and PNF stretching.
5. Discuss what guidelines should be followed for safe and effective stretching.
6. What factors are associated with low back problems?
7. Describe the proper lifting technique for preventing back injury.

References

1. Allsen PE, Harrison JM, Vance B: *Fitness for life—an individual approach*, Madison, Wis, 1993, Brown & Benchmark.
2. Prentice WE: *Fitness for college and life*, St Louis, 1994, Mosby.
3. Debruyne LK, Sizer FS, Whitney EN: *The fitness triad: motivation, training, and nutrition*, St Paul, Minn, 1991, West Publishing.
4. Rosato FD: *Fitness and wellness: the physical connection*, St Paul, Minn, 1994, West Publishing.
5. Neiman DC: *Fitness and sports medicine: an introduction*, Palo Alto, Calif, 1990, Bull Publishing.
6. Arnheim D, Prentice W: *Principles of athletic training*, St Louis, 1993, Mosby.
7. Low back pain, *Mayo Clin Health Letter* 7:4, 1989.
8. Mayer TG et al: A prospective two-year trial of functional restoration in testing industrial low back injuries, *JAMA* 258:1763-1767, 1987.
9. Low back pain: the scorecard, *Harvard Medical School Health Letter* 15:11, 1990.
10. Williams PC: *Low back and neck pain: causes and conservative treatment*, Springfield, Ill, 1974, Charles C Thomas.
11. McKenzie RA: *The lumbar spine: mechanical diagnosis and pain*, Waujjabae, New Zealand, 1981, Spinal Publications.

Annotated Readings

Alter J: *Stretch and strength*, Boston, 1986, Houghton Mifflin.
Provides recommendations for injury prevention by proper stretching. Discusses how stretching helps to strengthen.

Bennett WI, ed: Treatment for low-back pain, *Harvard Medical School Health Letter*, 15:3(3), 1990.
Examines the modalities available for treatment of low back pain. Discusses exercise, surgery, drugs, and prevention.

Eller D: Flextime, *Am Health* 12(3):68-73, 1993.
Discusses the various reasons why flexibility is an important factor in overall health and why it is important for people to maintain flexibility throughout life. Describes and illustrates major muscle group stretches.

Williams G: Pain: treating it and defeating it, *Am Health* 10:9, 1991.
Discusses chronic pain and devotes an entire section to back pain. Defines the extent and severity of the problem. Discusses the problem of weak muscles and ligaments as causative factors.

Zamula E: Back talk: advice for suffering spines, *FDA Consumer* 23(3):28-35, 1989.
Discusses the anatomy of the spinal column, causes of back problems, treatment modalities, and prevention techniques.

ASSESSMENT ACTIVITY   5 - 1

Sit-and-Reach Test

Directions: The sit-and-reach test is a frequently used field test to specifically measure hip, low back, and hamstring flexibility. Flexibility is a component specific to the muscle group or groups being measured. Therefore high achievement in performing the sit-and-reach does not ensure you will have equally high flexibility at other joints.

You should warm up 3 to 5 minutes before attempting this assessment. A box with a measurement scale of 23 cm is necessary to perform the test. After warming up, remove your shoes and place both feet flat against the back of the sit-and-reach box. Fully extend your legs and move your feet approximately shoulder width apart. Extend both your arms and place one hand exactly on top of the other on top of the measuring scale. The object of the test is to lean forward as far as possible while sliding the hands along the scale. A maximum stretch is reached when you can lean forward no farther but can hold your hands stationary for 1 second. A bounce cannot be used to increase the distance of the measure, and knees should remain straight throughout. The best of three trials is recorded as the final score.

   Trial one   _____inches

   Trial two   _____inches

Trial three   _____inches

Sit-and-Reach Test Standards*

Males	Females	Classification
17.5 or above	18 or above	Excellent
15.75-17.4	16.5-17.9	Good
13.5-15.74	14.5-16.4	Average
10.5-13.4	12.25-14.4	Fair
Less than 10.5	Less than 12.25	Poor

*Scores are in inches.

ACTIVITY ASSESSMENT 5 - 2

Shoulder Flexion Test

Directions: The objective of the shoulder flexion test is to measure the deltoids and shoulder girdle. A measuring scale and straight edge are needed to perform this assessment. Begin by assuming a prone position with your arms fully extended. Your chin should remain in contact with the floor throughout the exercise. Grasp the straight edge with both hands and raise it as high as possible from the floor. The distance from the floor to the straight edge is measured as the height in inches. Repeat this assessment three times and record the best number in inches as the final score. See the chart below for your classification.

Trial one _____inches

Trial two _____inches

Trial three _____inches

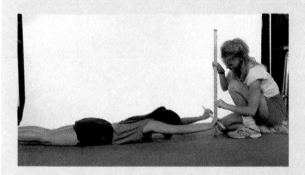

Shoulder Flexion Test Standard*

Males	Females	Classification
26 or above	27 or above	Excellent
23-25	24-26	Good
18-22	19-23	Average
13-17	14-18	Fair
12 or below	13 or below	Poor

*All scores are in inches. Use the best of three trials as the score.

ACTIVITY ASSESSMENT 5 - 3

Sling Test

Directions: The purpose of this test is to determine the length and flexibility of your sling muscles. If you have back problems or have had back surgery, consult a physician before attempting this test. This is a test and not an exercise, so it should not be used alone to increase flexibility.

Begin by lying on your back on the floor and bending both knees. Pull your right leg to your chest by tightly holding your knee with both hands. Straighten out your left leg and push it to the floor without letting your right leg move away from your chest. Use a scale to measure the distance of the back side of your left knee from the floor. Pull your left knee into your chest, releasing your right knee, and repeat the test on the other side. Refer to the chart below for your classification.

Sling Test Standards

Classification		Standard
Excellent		Able to hold one leg firmly against the chest with the other leg flat against the floor
Average		Able to hold one knee against the chest while the other knee is bent 2 to 4 in off the floor
Fair		Able to hold the knee firmly against the chest while the other leg is 4 to 8 in off the floor
Poor		Unable to pull one leg firmly against the chest without pain or discomfort and/or raising the other leg off the floor significantly (more than 8 in)

ACTIVITY ASSESSMENT   5 - 4

Trunk Extension

Directions: The purpose of this assessment is to measure the flexibility of the abdominal and hip flexor muscles. Begin the test by lying face down on the floor. Have a partner hold your legs as shown. Grasp your hands in the lower back area, breathe in, lift your upper body as high off the floor as possible, and hold. Repeat this two more times and record your best score. See the chart below for your classification.

Trunk Extension Assessment Standards*

Trial one _____inches

Trial two _____inches

Trial three _____inches

Males	Females	Classification
16	17	Poor
17-18	18-19	Average
19-21	20-23	Good
22	24	Excellent

*Scores are in inches.

Shoulder Rotation Test

Directions: This assessment is another test of shoulder flexibility. To do this test, you will need a tape measure or 48-in yard stick. The purpose of the test is to rotate your arms over your shoulders while keeping your hands as close together on the tape as possible. Grasp the tape measure as shown below (left). Arms should be kept locked throughout this assessment and fully extended. Place the tape over the top of your head and rotate backward, keeping your elbows locked. As resistance is felt, slide your hands along the tape but keep them as close together as you can and still keep your arms straight. Rotate your arms until the tape rests across the bottom of your back as shown below (right). Measure the distance between your hands. For example, if your left hand is at 4 inches and your right hand at 35 inches, the difference is 31 inches and the score that you record. Allow three trials and use the lowest score as your best.

How to Score the Test

Write down the figure that represents your best trial in the blank given below. Measure the width of your shoulders and record that number also. Subtract the shoulder width from your best trial and record it next to the score. Then check the chart below to learn your performance level.

Example

Best trial: __32__

Shoulder width: __19__

Score: __13__

Performance level: __Intermediate__

Your score

Best trial: _____

Shoulder width: _____

Score: _____

Performance level: _____

Performance Norms for Shoulder Rotation Test*

Performance Level	Males	Females
Advanced	7 or less	5 or less
Advanced intermediate	11.50-7.25	9.75-5.25
Intermediate	14.50-11.75	13-10
Advanced beginner	19.75-14.75	17.75-13.25
Beginner	20 and above	18 and above

*All scores are in inches.

Forming a Plan for Good Nutrition

Key terms

amino acids

calorie

complex carbohydrates

daily reference values (DRV)

essential nutrients

fiber

minerals

nutrient density

recommended dietary allowances (RDA)

reference daily intakes (RDI)

saturated fat

vitamin supplements

vitamins

Objectives

After completing this chapter, you will be able to:

▷ Discuss the dietary guidelines for Americans.

▷ Identify the major nutrition deficiencies and problems in the typical American diet.

▷ Describe the principles behind planning a nutritionally balanced diet.

N utrition has captured the interest of Americans more than perhaps any other topic related to fitness and wellness. Whether it is cholesterol or sodium, fat or fiber, or sugar or vitamins, nutrition issues make headlines in both scientific journals and popular magazines, and everybody seems to be an expert. So much is written by so many that it is difficult to know what and whom to believe.

In this chapter, basic concepts of the science of *nutrition*, the study of nutrients and the way the body processes them, are presented to guide you through the maze of nutrition information. The concepts presented here within the framework of *Dietary Guidelines for Americans* should provide you a basis for sound nutritional planning.

Dietary Guidelines for Americans

The relationship between nutrition and health has changed dramatically during the past 50 years. As recently as the 1940s, diseases such as rickets, pellagra, scurvy, beriberi, xerophthalmia, and goiter (caused by a lack of or deficiency in vitamin D, niacin, vitamin C, thiamin, vitamin A, and iodine, respectively) were common in the United States and throughout the world. Thanks to an abundant food supply, fortification of some foods with critical trace nutrients, and better methods of improving the quality of foods, such deficiency diseases have virtually been eliminated in developed countries. Nutrition deficiencies are rarely reported in the United States, and when they do occur, they are usually associated with poverty, high-risk conditions (such as premature birth or alcoholism), and conditions related to prolonged chronic illnesses.

The deficiency diseases of the past have been replaced by diseases of dietary excess and imbalance. For most Americans the problem is overeating—too many calories for the activity level and overconsumption of fat and sodium.[1] In the United States, 6 of the top 10 causes of death are associated with diet (heart disease, some types of cancer, stroke, non-insulin–dependent diabetes mellitus, atherosclerosis, and chronic liver disease).[2] The association between diet and health is so convincing that nutrition was designated as one of the target areas in the 1979 landmark publication *Healthy People: the Surgeon General's Report on Health Promotion and Disease Prevention*. In the late 1970s the US Senate commissioned a study on nutrition, which eventually concluded that overconsumption of certain dietary com-

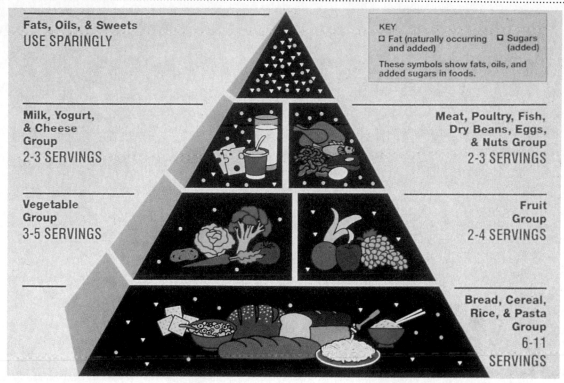

FIGURE 6-1 A guide to daily food choices. Children, teenagers, and adults under 25 years of age should choose three servings from the milk, yogurt, and cheese group.

ponents is a major concern for Americans. Chief among these concerns is the disproportionate consumption of foods high in fats, often at the expense of foods high in complex carbohydrates and fiber, which are healthier.[3] Also of concern are insufficient amounts of calcium, iron, zinc, and dietary fiber. In response to cricitism of the American diet, the US Department of Agriculture (USDA) and Department of Health and Human Services (DHHS) established recommendations that are the basis for the dietary guidelines for Americans[4]:

- ▶ Eat a variety of foods, and follow the guide to daily food choices.
- ▶ Maintain a healthy weight.
- ▶ Choose a diet low in fat and cholesterol. Reduce fat to 30% of calories and, specifically, saturated fat to 10% of calories.
- ▶ Choose a diet with plenty of vegetables, fruits, and grain products.
- ▶ Use sugars only in moderation.
- ▶ Use salt and sodium only in moderation.
- ▶ If you drink alcoholic beverages, do so in moderation.

Eat a Variety of Foods

The best way to plan a nutritionally balanced diet is to eat a variety of foods according to the guide to daily food choices (Figure 6-1). This helps to ensure that the **recommended dietary allowances (RDA)** of **essential nutrients**—substances that cannot be made by the body and must be supplied through the diet—are provided. RDAs represent the minimum intake of the more than 50 essential nutrients necessary to meet the needs of healthy people (Table 6-1). The guide to daily food choices is helpful for determining how many servings from each food group should be included. Table 6-2 gives some examples of what makes up a serving. Table 6-3 provides a sample diet plan that includes the recommended number of servings according to three calorie levels.

The foundations of good nutrition are variety and moderation. No one food or food group provides all essential nutrients in adequate amounts. Furthermore, you should consume a variety of foods within each food group. Potatoes are a good example of how foods within a group vary in nutrients and calories: 3 ounces of baked potato yield 98 calories, whereas 3 ounces of potato chips yield 470 calories. Similar examples within food groups include skim milk and ice cream, beans and bologna, olive oil and butter, and whole wheat bread and doughnuts.

Seek the right balance. Food is made up of six classes of nutrients: carbohydrates, fat, protein, vi-

TABLE 6-1 National Research Council Recommended Dietary Allowances, Revised 1989*

Category	Age (yr) or Condition	Weight† (kg)	Weight† (lb)	Height† (cm)	Height† (in)	Protein (g)	Vitamin A (μg RE)	Vitamin D (μg)‡	Vitamin E (mg α-TE)	Vitamin K (μg)
Males	15-18	66	145	176	69	59	1000	10	10	65
	19-24	72	160	177	70	58	1000	10	10	70
	25-50	79	174	176	70	63	1000	5	10	80
	51+	77	170	173	68	63	1000	5	10	80
Females	15-18	55	120	163	64	44	800	10	8	55
	19-24	58	128	164	65	48	800	10	8	60
	25-50	63	138	163	64	50	800	5	8	65
	51+	65	143	160	63	50	800	5	8	65
Pregnant						60	800	10	10	65
Lactating	1st 6 months					65	1300	10	12	65
	2nd 6 months					62	1200	10	11	65

RE, Retinol equivalents (1 RE = 1 μg retinol or 6 μg β-carotene); α- TE α-tocopherol equivalents (1 mg d-α tocopherol = 1 α-TE); NE, niacin equivalent (1 NE = 1 mg of niacin or 60 mg of dietary tryptophan). As cholecalciferol; 10 μg cholecalciferol = 400 IU of vitamin D.

*The allowances, expressed as average daily intakes over time, provide for individual variations among most normal persons as they live in the United States under usual environmental stresses. Diets should be based on a variety of common foods to provide other nutrients for which human requirements have been less well defined. See text for detailed discussion of allowances and nutrients not tabulated.

†Weights and heights of reference adults are actual medians for the US population of the designated age as reported by NHANES II. The use of these figures does not imply that the height-to-weight ratios are ideal.

‡As cholecalciferol; 10 μg cholecalciferol = 400 IU of vitamin D.

TABLE 6-2 What Counts as a Serving?

Food Group	Serving Size	Food Group	Serving Size
Bread, cereal, rice, and pasta group	1 ounce of ready-to-eat cereal ½ cup of cooked cereal, rice, or pasta 1 slice of bread ½ bagel or hamburger bun	Milk, yogurt, and cheese group	1 cup of milk, yogurt, ice cream, or custard pudding 1½ ounces of natural cheese 2 ounces of processed cheese
Vegetable group	1 cup of raw, leafy vegetables ½ cup of other vegetables, cooked or chopped raw ¾ cup of vegetable juice	Meat, poultry, fish, dry beans, eggs, and nut group	2-3 ounces of cooked lean meat, fish, or poultry ½ cup of cooked dry beans 1 egg 2 tablespoons of peanut butter (equal to 1 ounce of lean meat) 1 hot dog 2 slices of luncheon meat
Fruit group	1 whole piece of fruit or melon wedge ½ cup of chopped, cooked, or canned fruit ¾ cup of fruit juice		

Water-Soluble Vitamins							Minerals						
Vitamin C (mg)	Thiamin (mg)	Ribo-flavin (mg)	Niacin (mg NE)	Vitamin B$_6$ (mg)	Folate (µg)	Vitamin B$_{12}$ (µg)	Calcium (mg)	Phos-phorus (mg)	Magne-sium (mg)	Iron (mg)	Zinc (mg)	Iodine (µg)	Selenium (µg)
60	1.5	1.8	20	2.0	200	2.0	1200	1200	400	12	15	150	50
60	1.5	1.7	19	2.0	200	2.0	1200	1200	350	10	15	150	70
60	1.5	1.7	19	2.0	200	2.0	800	800	350	10	15	150	70
60	1.2	1.4	15	2.0	200	2.0	800	800	350	10	15	150	70
60	1.1	1.3	15	1.5	180	2.0	1200	1200	300	15	12	150	50
60	1.1	1.3	15	1.6	180	2.0	1200	1200	280	15	12	150	55
60	1.1	1.3	15	1.6	180	2.0	800	800	280	15	12	150	55
60	1.0	1.2	13	1.6	180	2.0	800	800	280	10	12	150	55
70	1.5	1.6	17	2.2	400	2.2	1200	1200	320	30	15	175	65
95	1.6	1.8	20	2.1	280	2.6	1200	1200	355	15	19	200	75
90	1.6	1.7	20	2.1	260	2.6	1200	1200	340	15	16	200	75

TABLE 6-3 Nutrition Plan for Three Calorie Levels

	Calorie Level*		
	1600	**2200**	**2800**
Grain group servings	6	9	11
Vegetable group servings	3	4	5
Fruit group servings	2	3	4
Milk group servings†	2-3	2-3	2-3
Meat group‡	5	6	7
Total fat (g)	53	73	93
Percent fat calories	30	30	30
Total added sugars (tsp)§	6	12	18

*1600 calories is appropriate for many sedentary women and some older adults. 2200 calories is appropriate for most children, teenage girls, active women, and sedentary men. Women who are pregnant or breastfeeding may need more. 2800 calories is appropriate for teenage boys, many active men, and some very active women.
†Women who are pregnant or breastfeeding, teenagers, and young adults to age 24 need 3 servings.
‡Meat group amounts are in total ounces.
§From candy, desserts, soft drinks, and other sweets.

You should eat a variety of foods from the guide to daily food choices.

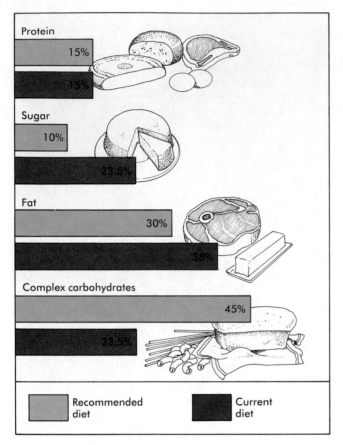

Protein

Sugar

Fat

Complex carbohydrates

Recommended diet

Current diet

FIGURE 6-2 Comparison of recommended diet and current diet of Americans.

tamins, minerals, and water. Some experts list fiber as a seventh nutrient, although it is technically a carbohydrate. The first three classes are called *energy nutrients* because they provide energy for the body. Food energy is expressed in the form of kilocalories. A **calorie** is the amount of heat required to raise the temperature of a gram of water 1° C. A kilocalorie equals 1000 calories of heat energy. Common reference to calories usually excludes the prefix "kilo," mainly for convenience. A gram of carbohydrates provides 4 calories (kilocalories) of energy, a gram of protein also provides 4 calories, a gram of fat provides 9 calories, and alcohol (which is in a separate category) provides 7 calories per gram.

The recommended diet for Americans emphasizes complex carbohydrates as the major source of energy. A total of 45% of calories should come from

complex carbohydrates. This percentage is almost double the present amount in the typical American diet, which consists of 38% fat, 15% protein, 24% sugar, and only 24% complex carbohydrates (Figure 6-2). Changing the diet to emphasize complex carbohydrates means eating significantly more fruits and vegetables, grain products, bread, spaghetti and other pasta, beans and peas, rice, and potatoes and significantly less fat and sugar.

The guide to daily food choices recommends a minimum of 11 servings from the vegetable, fruit, and grain groups. Although this is more than the average person consumes, many experts believe more servings are necessary. According to a survey of nutrition experts,[2] the recommended diet should include at least 7 servings of fruits and vegetables and 6 servings of grain products. For a person on a 2000-calorie diet, this meets the goal of 300 grams of carbohydrate recommended in the daily reference values (Table 6-4). **Daily reference values (DRV),** established in 1992 with new food label regulations (see p. 167), are guidelines for substances not included in the 1989 RDAs. These substances include carbohydrate, fat, saturated fat, cholesterol, sodium, potassium, and dietary fiber. DRV can be used to compare levels of these substances in planning diets and purchasing food. They also provide a reference point for substances thought to be highly related to many of the major chronic diseases in the United States.

Avoid protein excess. One of the main reasons Americans have trouble maintaining the right balance in their dietary habits is the mistaken notion that if a modest amount of protein is good for you, large amounts must be even better. Because protein is a "body builder," people believe that it makes them strong and that it is better for them than carbohydrates. However, protein consumed in excess of the body's requirement is not converted to muscle; rather, it is converted to energy or stored as fat just as surplus carbohydrates are.

Protein is different from carbohydrates and fats, the other nutrients that supply energy, in that it contains nitrogen as well as carbon, hydrogen, and oxygen. Because of their unique chemical structures, proteins contain the basic materials for cell growth and repair. They also help the body form antibodies to fight disease and produce substances such as insulin, enzymes, and hemoglobin.

Protein is made up of chemical structures called **amino acids.** Both animal and plant proteins are made up of approximately 20 amino acids: 11 can be produced in the body, and 9 must be supplied by the diet.[1] These 9 are called *essential amino acids.*

TABLE 6-4 Daily Reference Values*

Food Component	DRV	
	2000 calories	**2500 calories**
Total fat	65 g (maximum)	80 g (maximum)
Saturated fat	20 g (maximum)	25 g (maximum)
Unsaturated fat	45 g (maximum)	55 g (maximum)
Cholesterol	300 mg (maximum)	300 mg (maximum)
Sodium	2400 mg (maximum)	2400 mg (maximum)
Carbohydrate	300 g (goal)	375 g (goal)
Dietary fiber	25 g (goal)	30 g (goal)
Potassium	3500 mg (goal)	3500 mg (goal)

*For the general population.

A *complete protein* is one that contains all of the essential amino acids. A *high-quality protein* is a complete protein that contains the essential amino acids in amounts proportional to the body's need for them. Protein sources from animals, including meat, fish, poultry, eggs, milk, and cheese, are examples of high-quality, complete proteins.

A *low-quality protein,* or *incomplete protein,* does not contain all the essential amino acids in the proportions needed by the body. Examples include nuts, beans, seeds, wheat, rice, oats, and whole grains. Before a low-quality protein can be converted into a complete protein, it must be matched with another source of low-quality protein. The body cannot make partial proteins, only complete ones; protein synthesis operates by the "all-or-none law." If an amino acid is supplied by one source in a smaller amount than is needed, the total amount of protein made from the other amino acids will be limited. Therefore if a diet does not include sources of complete protein, which might occur in a *vegetarian* diet, the right mix of foods must be included. Some vegetarians *(lacto-ovo-vegetarians)* omit meat, fish, and poultry from their diets but eat eggs and dairy products. Others *(lactovegetarians)* exclude eggs and consume only dairy products. Both types consume high-quality proteins and do not need to worry about protein deficiency. *Strict vegetarians,* people who eat an all-plant diet, may need to be discriminating in their food selections because plant proteins are low-quality proteins. To obtain all essential amino acids from plant sources, strict vegetarians should eat a variety of foods from the legume groups, such as beans, peas, and peanuts, combined with foods from the cereal and whole-grain group, including pasta, wheat, rice, oats, and corn. Combining protein sources from cereal and grains with legumes is called *protein complement.* Deficiencies in essential amino acids in one group are compensated by the essential amino acid content of the other group.

Recommended protein intake. The recommended dietary allowance for protein is 0.8 grams per kilogram of body weight per day (see Assessment Activity 6-1). The average 19- to 22-year-old man weighs 154 pounds and requires 56 grams of protein per day (e.g., 2 cups of cottage cheese or one chicken breast). The average woman weighs 120 pounds and needs 44 grams of protein per day (e.g., two pork chops or two hamburger patties). Women who are pregnant or lactating require an additional 30 and 20 grams of protein, respectively.

For caloric intake, protein should make up 15% of the diet. Protein is one nutrient that most people consume in approximately the right amount. Average levels of protein consumption of 70 grams per day for women and 90 grams per day for men are slightly above the RDA.[1]

When more protein is consumed than is needed by the body, it is converted into energy or stored as fat. The body is less efficient at converting protein to energy than at converting carbohydrates to energy, regardless of the person's activity level. Exercise and other physical activities do not change the body's need for protein. Active people need food that is readily converted to energy, namely, carbohydrates. People who plan athletes' training meals emphasize large proportions of complex carbohydrates. Loading up on complex carbohydrates before a race is common practice among marathon runners.

A misconception among weight lifters and body

builders is that consumption of large quantities of *protein supplements*, usually commercially made protein powder, enhances muscle development. However, protein supplements are not needed to increase muscle mass during strength training. As stated previously, excess protein is converted to extra energy or stored as fat.

Some people may consume too much protein, which may cause the body to excrete calcium, the mineral that strengthens bones and teeth. High protein intake may also put excessive strain on the kidneys to excrete the excess nitrogen supplied by the protein into the urine. Although the kidneys of most healthy people can handle nitrogen excess with ease,[1] kidneys under strain have more difficulty. This is the reason people with kidney failure are placed on low-protein diets and the reason people who go on high-protein diets to lose weight (see Chapter 8) are encouraged to drink large quantities of water to flush out the kidneys.

Protein in food. The foods that supply enough complete proteins are those in the milk and meat groups. Most protein comes from animal foods. In 1990, beef, other red meat, chicken, and poultry consumption was 239 pounds per person per year in the United States. Fish consumption averaged 15 pounds per person. Over two thirds of protein comes from animal sources.[1]

Foods in the vegetable and bread groups contribute small amounts of protein to the diet, but these amounts are significant when several servings are consumed. The guide to daily food choices recommends two servings of plant protein per day. In addition to providing a good source of protein when consumed in proper combinations, plant and vegetable protein contain no cholesterol, are low in saturated fat, and are good sources of soluble fiber, vitamins, and minerals.

Vitamins. **Vitamins** are organic compounds that are necessary in small amounts for good health. Unlike carbohydrates, fats, and proteins, vitamins yield no energy. Instead, they serve as catalysts that enable energy nutrients to be digested, absorbed, and metabolized. Vitamins also interact with minerals. For example, vitamin C facilitates iron absorption, vitamin D improves calcium absorption, vitamin E aids in the absorption of vitamin A, and thiamin requires the mineral magnesium to function efficiently.

Diets deficient in the RDA of vitamins may impair the physiological processes of the body and lead to deficiency diseases. One major advantage of a varied diet is that it helps ensure consumption of the right amount and balance of vitamins.

Vitamins are grouped into two categories: water soluble and fat soluble. Water-soluble vitamins include vitamin B complex and vitamin C (Table 6-5). They are present in the watery components of food, distributed in the fluid components of the body, excreted in the urine, needed in frequent small doses, and unlikely to be toxic, except when taken in *megadoses* (very large quantities).

Fat-soluble vitamins include vitamins A, D, E, and K and are found in the fat and oily parts of food. Because they cannot be dissolved and absorbed in the bloodstream, these vitamins must be absorbed into the lymph with fat and transported by proteins. When consumed in excess of the body's need, fat-soluble vitamins are stored in the liver and fat cells. Their storage makes it possible to survive for months or years without consuming them. At least three of the fat-soluble vitamins (A, D, and K) may even accumulate to toxic levels. Megadoses of these vitamins should be avoided.

Vitamin supplements. Advertisements proclaim that vitamins provide energy and that taking more means more energy and better health. Consequently, 33% of all Americans take one or more **vitamin supplements** in multiple and single doses, in natural and synthetic formulations, and in amounts 10 or more times higher than recommended.[5] Vitamins do facilitate the release of energy from carbohydrates, fats, and proteins, but they do not provide energy. It is not possible to survive on water and vitamins.

Can vitamin supplements prevent diseases or reduce their severity? Until recently, the prevailing answer of many of the leading authorities was "no." Medical opinion is now divided depending on which vitamin, which disease, and which study are in question.

Vitamin C, which is the most widely consumed nutritional supplement and is taken by 9 out of 10 supplement users, is a good example of the conflicting reports from the medical community. Three major studies[6] were conducted at the University of Toronto School of Medicine to investigate the claim that megadoses (10 times the 60-milligram RDA or more) would prevent the common cold or reduce its severity. A placebo or vitamin C supplements were given to adolescent, adult, and elderly volunteers for several months. The supplements began at a level of 1000 milligrams while volunteers were well and increased to 4000 milligrams when sickness occurred. Researchers determined that there was no difference in the number of colds between groups. Vitamin C had no preventive effect, although cold sufferers in the vitamin C group did lose less time from work or

TABLE 6-5 Facts about Vitamins

Vitamin	Food Sources	Benefits to Wellness	Deficiency Signs and Symptoms
Water-Soluble Vitamins			
B complex	Meat products (beef, pork, poultry, eggs, fish), milk, cheese, grains, dried beans, nuts, starchy vegetables	Facilitates release of energy from other nutrients Aids in formation of red blood cells, growth and function of the nervous system, and formation of hormones Contributes to good vision and healthy skin Assists in the metabolism of proteins, fats, and carbohydrates	Fatigue, nausea, weakness, irritability, depression, weight loss, inflamed skin, cracked lips, muscle pain, cramps or twitching, low blood sugar, decreased resistance to disease, nerve dysfunction
C (ascorbic acid)	Citrus fruits, strawberries, cantaloupe, honeydew melons, broccoli, brussels sprouts, green peppers, cauliflower, spinach	Contributes to production of collagen Aids in protection against infection Contributes to tooth and bone formation and repair and as wound healing Aids in absorption of iron and calcium	Dry, rough, and scaly skin; bleeding gums; slowly healing wounds; listlessness; fatigue; low glucose tolerance
Fat-Soluble Vitamins			
A	Milk; cheese; butter; fat; eggs; liver; dark-green, leafy vegetables; carrots; cantaloupe; yellow squash; sweet potatoes	Is essential for growth of epithelial cells such as hair, skin, and mucous membranes Aids in vision in dim light Contributes to bone growth and tooth development Plays a role in reproduction (sperm production and estrogen synthesis) Increases resistance to infection	Decreased resistance to infection, skin changes, alteration of tooth enamel, night blindness, corneal deterioration
D*	Milk (fortified), butter, cheese, eggs, clams, fish, salmon, tuna	Is essential for bones and teeth Contributes to calcium and phosphorus absorption	Bone softening and fractures, muscle spasms, tooth malformation
E	Vegetable oils; green, leafy vegetables; liver; eggs; whole-grain cereals and breads	Assists in formation of red blood cells and muscle tissue Aids in absorption of vitamin A Serves as an antioxidant, which preserves vitamins and unsaturated fatty acids	Destruction of cell membrane of red blood cells
K	Green, leafy vegetables; liver; cabbage; cauliflower; eggs; tomatoes; peas; potatoes; milk	Aids in normal formation of the liver Contributes to normal blood clotting	Severe bleeding, prolonged coagulation, bruising

*Sunlight also stimulates vitamin D production.

The common cold is a contagious, infectious disease, not a nutritional disease.

school. The investigators concluded that vitamin C supplements did not help treat colds. They also warned that vitamin C taken in megadoses presents potential health risks including diarrhea, formation of kidney stones, and irritation of the digestive system.

In another report,[7] experts found that vitamin supplements help prevent atherosclerosis and heart attacks. Between 1971 and 1984, researchers conducted a survey involving 11,348 adults ages 25 to 74 years. They determined that for men with the highest vitamin C intake, the total number of deaths was 35% lower than predicted, mortality due to cardiovascular diseases was 42% lower, and cancer deaths were 22% less. Women also benefited but not as dramatically. Another conclusion was that vitamin C supplements may have a positive effect on survival even for people consuming the RDA of 60 milligrams. For example, the group of men whose diets provided the RDA of vitamin C showed a 7% reduction in cardiovascular mortality compared with 42% for those who took vitamin C supplements.

In a report of two studies conducted at the Harvard School of Public Health,[8] people who took vitamin E supplements were found to have a lower risk of heart disease over the next 5 to 8 years than those

who did not. The risk was 36% lower in women and 26% lower in men.

The changing opinions about vitamin supplements are related primarily to vitamins C, E, and A, or beta-carotene.[9] These vitamins are classified as *antioxidants*. (Technically, vitamin A is not an antioxidant, but the conversion of beta-carotene to vitamin A has an antioxidant effect.) Antioxidants are compounds that block the oxidation of substances in food or the body. Vitamins C and E and beta-carotene are believed to prevent the oxidation of cholesterol and other molecules linked to heart disease and cancer. (See Chapter 2 for more information on antioxidants and heart disease.)

A report[9] of two studies recently confirmed the relationship between heart disease risk and low blood levels of antioxidants. In the first study, which involved 6000 men ages 35 to 54 years, the risk of angina pectoris was more than double in those with the lowest antioxidant levels as compared with men who had the highest level. In the second study, blood samples from several thousand people were collected and stored. Several years later, after 125 of the people had suffered heart attacks, the researchers retrieved the blood samples and measured beta-carotene levels. People with the lowest beta-carotene levels had approximately twice the risk of having a heart attack as did those with the highest level.

Although forming any strong conclusions about vitamin supplements is still premature, the consensus among nutrition experts is that healthy adults who eat a variety of foods do not need them. More research is needed to evaluate the importance of the antioxidants properly, but your diet should include sufficient amounts of vitamin C and E and beta-carotene (Table 6-6). If the adequacy of daily intake of these antioxidants is in question, vitamin supplements are probably useful.[10] The conclusion of the *Harvard Health Letter* about this issue provides good advice: "While there is no reason to believe that judicious use of vitamin supplements is harmful, people who eat well-balanced diets cannot be confident that taking them will be beneficial."[7]

Vitamin supplements are sometimes needed by people with irregular diets or unusual lifestyles or by people following certain weight-reduction regimens or strict vegetarian diets. In addition, infants and pregnant and lactating women may need supplements. When taken as supplements, vitamins should be viewed as medicine and therefore recommended by a physician.

Natural versus synthetic vitamins. Many people mistakenly believe that vitamins in food are better than vitamins made in the laboratory. A vitamin

TABLE 6-6 Antioxidant Vitamin–Rich Foods

Vitamin	Food	Serving Size	mg
Vitamin C (RDI: 60 mg)	Broccoli, raw, boiled	1 cup	116
	Cabbage, white, raw	1 cup	44
	Sweet potato	1 cup	56
	Cauliflower, raw	1 cup	72
	Strawberries	1 cup	85
	Papayas	1 cup	87
	Orange juice	1 cup	86
	Lemon juice	1 cup	112
	Grapefruit juice	1 cup	94
	Tomato juice	1 cup	45
	Vegetable juice	1 cup	67
Beta carotene (RDI: 875 RE)	Broccoli, frozen, boiled	1 cup	350
	Carrot, boiled, sliced	1 cup	3830
	Cauliflower, boiled	1 cup	2584
	Collards, boiled	1 cup	1017
	Pumpkin pie mix	1 cup	2241
	Spinach, boiled	1 cup	1595
	Squash, baked	1 cup	1435
	Sweet potato, boiled, mashed	1 cup	5592
	Beef liver, fried	3 ounces	9216
	Chicken liver	1 cup	6886
	Apricots, dried	1 cup	941
Vitamin E (RDI: 30 mg [9.0 α-TE])	Nuts, mixed, dry roasted	1 cup	16
	Sunflower seeds	1 cup	70
	Pecans	1 cup	21
	Sweet potato, boiled, mashed	1 cup	15

RDI, Reference daily intake; *RE*, retinol equivalents; α- *TE*, α-tocopherol equivalents.

has the same chemical structure regardless of its source, and the body cannot distinguish between natural and synthetic vitamins. However, individuals who meet the RDA of vitamins through food sources probably enjoy better nutritional health.

Foods grown with natural, organic fertilizers are also not more nutritious or have more vitamins than food grown with chemical fertilizers. In fact, natural fertilizers cannot be used directly on plants. They must be broken down into the same compounds found in chemical fertilizers. Vitamins do not come from the soil but are manufactured by genetically controlled processes within the plants themselves. (This is not true for some minerals such as iron.)

Minerals. Minerals are simple but important nutrients. As inorganic compounds, they lack the complexity of vitamins, but they fulfill a variety of functions. For example, sodium and potassium affect shifts in body fluids, calcium and phosphorus contribute to the body's structure, iron is the core of hemoglobin (an oxygen-carrying compound in the blood), and iodine facilitates production of thyroxine (a hormone that influences metabolic rate).

There are 20 to 30 important nutritional minerals. Compared with other nutrients, minerals should be consumed in small amounts. Minerals that are present in the body and required in large amounts (more than 5 grams [1 teaspoon] per day) are called *major minerals* or *macrominerals.* They include, in descending order of prominence, calcium, phosphorus, potassium, sulfur, sodium, chloride, and magnesium. Major minerals contribute from 60% to 80% of all inorganic material in the human body.

Minerals that are required in small amounts (less than 5 grams per day) are called *trace minerals* or *microminerals.* There are more than a dozen trace minerals, with the best known being iron, zinc, and iodine (Figure 6-3).

Figure 6-3   Facts about Minerals

Major (macro) minerals

Calcium, phosphorus, potassium, sulfur, sodium chloride, and magnesium

Trace (micro) Minerals

Iron, iodine, zinc, selenium, manganese, copper, molybdenum, cobalt, chromium, fluorine, silicon, vanadium, nickel, tin, cadmium

Minerals of Special Concern*

Calcium

Wellness benefits: Contributes to bone and tooth formation, general body growth, maintenance of good muscle tone, nerve function, cell membrane function, and regulation of normal heart beat
Food sources: Dairy products, dark-green vegetables, dried beans, shellfish
Deficiency signs and symptoms: Bone pain and fractures, muscle cramps, osteoporosis

Iron

Wellness benefits: Facilitates oxygen and carbon dioxide transport, formation of red blood cells, production of antibodies, synthesis of collagen, and use of energy
Food sources: Red meat (lean), seafoods, eggs, dried beans, nuts, grains, green, leafy vegetables
Deficiency signs and symptoms: Fatigue, weakness

Sodium

Wellness benefits: Is essential for maintenance of proper acid-base balance and body fluid regulation, aids in formation of digestive secretions, assists in nerve transmission
Food sources: Processed foods, meats, table salt
Deficiency signs and symptoms: Rare

*Calcium and iron are of special concern because deficiencies are likely to exist, especially among women and children.

Some minerals are similar to water-soluble vitamins in that they are readily excreted by the kidneys, do not accumulate in the body, and rarely become toxic. Others are like fat-soluble vitamins in that they are stored and are toxic if taken in excess.

Minerals are different from vitamins; they are indestructible and require no special handling during food preparation. The only precautions are to avoid soaking minerals out of food and throwing them away in cooking water.

Major minerals are abundant in the diet; therefore deficiencies are highly unlikely, especially if a variety of foods is included. If a deficiency in major minerals does occur, it it most likely to be a calcium deficiency. About 80% of women over the age of 18 who were surveyed by the National Academy of Sciences reported having diets deficient in calcium.[11] The RDA for calcium for adults is 800 mg; for teenagers to 25-year-olds, the RDA is 1200 milligrams. The average calcium intake of women is 500 to 700 milligrams per day. Men average 800 to 900 milli-

grams. About 25% of women consume less than 300 milligrams per day. The National Institutes of Health recommends 1500 milligrams for postmenopausal women, an amount difficult to achieve without supplements.[2]

Of the various trace minerals, iron is the most abundant. It is also the one of most concern to nutritionists. Iron deficiency is the most common nutritional deficiency in the United States. It affects 9% of infants; 12% of adolescent boys, who need extra iron for growth spurts; and up to 14% of women aged 15 to 44 years, who lose iron in menstrual blood.[2]

Iron deficiency in the diet is responsible for the most prevalent form of anemia in the United States. Iron deficiency hampers the body's ability to produce *hemoglobin*, a substance needed to carry oxygen in the blood. A lack of hemoglobin can cause fatigue and weakness and can even affect behavior and intellectual function. Proper infant feeding through use of iron-fortified milk or breastfeeding is the best safeguard against iron deficiency in infants. Among

According to the Surgeon General, the majority of adolescent girls and adult women need to increase their consumption of high calcium foods.

adolescents and adults, iron intake can be improved by increasing consumption of iron-rich foods such as lean red meats, fish, certain kinds of beans, iron-enriched cereals and whole-grain products, and foods cooked in cast-iron skillet. In some individuals, especially premenopausal women with inconsistent diets, iron supplements may be justified. In addition, consuming foods that contain vitamin C enhances the body's ability to absorb iron.

Water. Next to air, water is the substance most necessary for survival. Everything in the body occurs in a water medium. Although people can live without vitamins and minerals for extended periods, death results in a few days without water.

Water makes up about 60% of the body's weight. Every cell in the body is bathed in water of the exact composition that is best for it. Even tissues that are not thought of as "watery" contain large amounts of water. For example, water makes up about 75% of brain and muscle tissues, and bone tissue is more than 20% water. As a rule the bodies of men con-

tain more water than the bodies of women. Men have more muscle tissue, and muscle tissue holds more water than fat tissue, which is more prominent in the bodies of women.

Water performs many functions. It is vital to digestion and metabolism because it acts as a medium for chemical reactions in the body. It carries oxygen and nutrients to the cells through blood, regulates body temperature through perspiration, and lubricates the joints. It also removes waste through sweat and urine, protects the fetus, and assists in respiration by moistening the lungs to facilitate intake of oxygen and excretion of carbon dioxide.

The average adult consumes and excretes about 96 ounces of water a day. People exposed to high temperatures, hot climates, or strenuous physical activity need considerably more water. Although most water intake comes from beverages, solid foods also make a significant contribution. Most fruits are more than 80% water, meats are 50% water, bread is 33% water, and butter is approximately 15% water.

Some beverages and foods can increase the need for water. Alcoholic beverages, tea, and coffee contain water but can have a contradictory effect on the body. An ounce of pure alcohol requires 8 ounces of water to be metabolized. Caffeinated beverages stimulate the adrenal glands and serve as *diuretics*, increasing water output and the need for water. The sugar and sodium found in many beverages and foods place an extra burden on the body because they require water to be dissolved, used, and excreted.

How much water should you drink? People are advised to drink six to eight 8-ounce glasses of fluids per day, regardless of thirst. Although thirst is usually a good indicator of the body's need to replenish its water supply, a person can drink just enough fluid to quench a thirst but not enough to satisfy the body's needs. One way to determine proper water consumption is to check the urine. A trickle of deep-yellow, cloudy urine that lasts only a few seconds indicates more water is needed. A flow of pale yellow or clear urine for 10 seconds means that a sufficient amount of water is being consumed.[12]

People on high-protein diets need more water than they thirst for to provide the kidneys with enough water to flush out the waste products of protein metabolism. Under normal circumstances, too much water cannot be consumed because the body is efficient at getting rid of what it does not need. However, water consumption should occur throughout the day. A sudden drinking binge in a short period early in the day will not satisfy the body's needs later; the excess will be excreted by the kidneys.

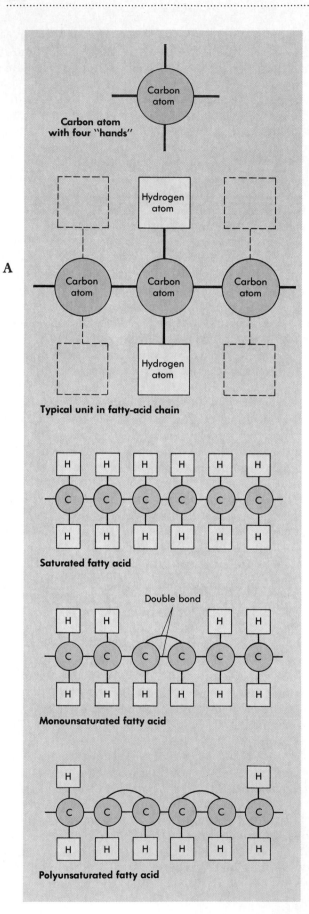

A

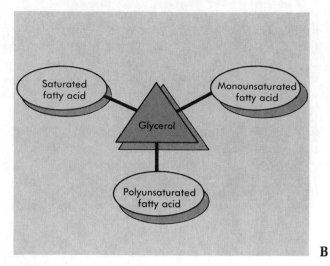

B

FIGURE 6-4 The basic fat facts. **A,** Fatty acids vary according to their chemical structure. Saturated fats have all carbon atoms occupied with hydrogen. Mononounsaturated fats have one point in the carbon chain unoccupied with hydrogen. Polyunsaturated fats have at least two points in the carbon chain unoccupied with hydrogen. **B,** Triglycerides are usually a mixture of different fatty acids.

Maintain Healthy Weight

The achievement and maintenance of a desirable weight are complex issues and are treated separately in this text. For a complete discussion of principles for maintaining desirable weight, refer to Chapter 8.

Choose a Diet Low in Fat and Cholesterol

Perhaps the greatest shortcoming of the American diet is the abundance of fat. The guide to daily food choices call for no more than 30% of total daily calories in the form of fat, of which no more than 10% comes from saturated fat. A good percentage ratio is 10:10:10 for saturated, monounsaturated, and polyunsaturated fat, respectively.

Basic facts on fats. *Fat,* also called *lipid,* is a compound made by chemically bonding fatty acids to glycerol to form *glycerides.* When three fatty acids are hooked to glycerol, the fat compound is a *triglyceride.* Almost 95% of fat stored in the body is triglyceride, with the remaining 5% consisting of other glycerides and cholesterol. Scientific literature usually refers to triglycerides when it discusses fat. The fatty acids that make up triglycerides can be saturated, monounsaturated, or polyunsaturated.

Chemically, fats are chains of carbon atoms

strung together with hydrogen atoms. If it is a **saturated fat,** the carbon chain carries all the hydrogen atoms it can (Figure 6-4). If it is *unsaturated*, there is room in the carbon chain for more hydrogen. If the chain is *monounsaturated*, there is room for one hydrogen atom. If it is *polyunsaturated*, there is room for more than one hydrogen atom. If it is *highly polyunsaturated,* there is room for many more hydrogen atoms.

The saturated/unsaturated ratio of food also may be affected by food-processing techniques. Because unsaturated fats are less stable, they are prone to spoilage. Consequently, for many foods, manufacturers use a chemical process called *hydrogenation*, in which hydrogen atoms are added to the unsaturated or polyunsaturated fats to make them more saturated and more resistant to spoilage. Many people mistakenly assume that the word "polyunsaturated" on a food label means that the fat in the food is not saturated. If the words "hydrogenated" or "partially hydrogenated" can be found on the food label, the food contains varying amounts of saturated fats.

Saturated and unsaturated fats can be differentiated by their appearance. Saturated fat is solid at room temperature. Lard, fat marbled in meat, and hardened grease from a skillet are good examples. Polyunsaturated fats are liquid at room temperature. Examples include safflower and corn oils. Solid vegetable shortenings are partially hydrogenated and have a soft consistency. Coconut oil, palm kernel oil, and palm oil are exceptions. They are vegetable oils and are liquid at room temperature, but they are among the most saturated of fats.

Fish oils are among the most unsaturated fats available. They are roughly twice as unsaturated as vegetable oils. They do not harden, even at low temperatures. Their unsaturation has created special interest in relation to heart disease. Fatty acids in cold-water seafood consist of *omega-3 fatty acids*, which are very effective at lowering cholesterol and triglyceride levels and reducing clot-forming rates, thereby reducing the risk of heart disease.

Cholesterol, a waxy substance that is technically a steroid alcohol found only in animal foods, is probably the most researched blood fat. High levels of cholesterol are usually discussed as one of the major risk factors of cardiovascular disease. (For information on cholesterol, see Chapter 2.)

Health effects of fat. Fats are an essential part of every cell. They maintain the health of the skin and hair; provide insulation and protection for body organs; help transport and absorb vitamins A, D, E, and K; and provide a concentrated source of energy.

Recommendations by the medical community to reduce fat have resulted in development of Simplesse, a fat substitute.

However, in excess, fats are associated with several health conditions.

Health studies usually report the health risks associated with dietary fat within the context of total intake of fat and saturated fat. Although a diet high in total fat is usually linked closely with a diet high in saturated fat and vice versa, a diet may be low in one type of fat and high in the other. This can then alter the risks of developing various health conditions.

Very little energy is used to transfer fat from foods to fat storage: the body requires only 3 calories to store 100 calories of fat as fat, but it takes 23 to 27 calories to digest 100 calories of carbohydrates and store it as fat. Fat also contributes more than twice as many calories as protein and carbohydrates. Therefore a high intake of total dietary fat is associated with obesity. Obesity increases the risk of developing high blood pressure and consequently the risk of stroke and non-insulin–dependent diabetes mellitus. In addition, a high intake of total dietary fat increases the risk of developing some types of cancer, especially cancer of the breast, colon and uterus. An association also exists between dietary fat and gallbladder disease.

TABLE 6-7 Fat Content of Representative Foods

Food	Fat/(g)	Percentage of total calories from fat†			
		Total*	Saturated	Monounsaturated	Polyunsaturated
Egg, whole, raw	5.01	64	19	25	8
Butter (pat)	11.4	100	67	31	4
Margarine, regular, hard (stick)	91.0	100	20	45	32
Cheese, cream (1 ounce)	9.9	90	57	25	3
Cheese, cheddar (1 cup)	37.5	74	47	20	2
Cheese, cottage (1 cup)	10.1	39	25	11	1
Milk, whole (1 cup)	8.2	49	30	14	2
Skim milk (1 cup)	1.0	6	4	1	Trace
Frankfurter (2 ounces)	16.6	82	33	40	3
Bologna, pork (slice)	4.6	72	26	36	8
Flounder, baked (0.8 ounce)	1.9	9	Trace	Trace	Trace
Fish sticks (1 ounce)	3.4	39	10	18	10
Tuna, canned, oil-packed (3 ounces)	6.9	38	8	10	17
Tuna, canned, water-packed (3 ounces)	2.1	7	Trace	Trace	Trace
Ground beef (3 ounces)	19.2	65	25	28	3
Steak, broiled, sirloin (2 ounces)	4.89	56	24	26	2
Pork chop, broiled (3 ounces)	22.3	62	23	29	7
Chicken breast, fried, flour-coated (7 ounces)	17.4	36	10	14	8
Beans, navy (1 cup)	2.1	4	Trace	Trace	3
Potato (baked)	0.06	1	Trace	Trace	4
Potato chips (1.5 ounces)	13.0	61	16	11	31
Ice cream, vanilla, regular (1 cup)	22.5	48	28	14	2
Apple (raw, unpeeled)	0.5	6	1	Trace	2
Danish pastry	13.6	50	14	29	4

Trace, Less than 0.9% of fat.
*Includes undifferentiated fats.
†Rounded off to the nearest whole number.

Consumption of high levels of saturated fat has been strongly and consistently associated with coronary disease. Saturated fat is the major dietary contributor to total blood-cholesterol levels. The consensus is that blood-cholesterol levels depend less on the intake of cholesterol from foods as on the total amount of saturated fat consumed. Only about 10% to 25% of people lower their blood cholesterol when they consume less cholesterol. Most people experience a minimal effect or no effect. However, almost all individuals who lower saturated-fat intake can lower cholesterol levels by 10% to 20%, especially if they are already eating many foods high in saturated fats. One explanation is that saturated fats in the diet affect the way the liver handles cholesterol. When saturated fat is low, the liver reacts by clearing cholesterol from the bloodstream.[1]

Dietary sources of fat. According to the National Research Council,[13] animal products, such as red meats, (beef, veal, pork, and lamb), fish and shellfish, separated animal fats (such as tallow and lard), milk and milk products, and eggs, contribute more than half of the total fat, three fourths of the saturated fat, and all the cholesterol to the diet of people in the United States. Of these, red meats provide the major source of fat for Americans in all age groups except infants, and ground beef is the greatest contributor of fat. Mayonnaise, salad dressings, and margarine are the chief sources of linoleic acid, an essential fatty acid. Eggs supply the most cholesterol.

Because the fat in food is a mixture of saturated and unsaturated, deciding which foods to eat and which to avoid is difficult. The amount of saturated, monounsaturated, and polyunsaturated fat in foods varies considerably. In addition, not all animal fats are more highly saturated than all vegetable fats, nor are all tropical oils, such as coconut oil, palm kernel oil, and palm oil, more saturated than animal oils and vegetable oils.

Table 6-7 presents the fat content of common foods. Some foods are naturally high in fat calories. For example, dairy products, such as cream cheese, cheddar cheese, and whole milk; beef products, such as hamburger and steak; pork products, such as pork chops, bologna, and frankfurters; and oils, such as butter and margarine, derive from 49% to 100% of their calories from fat (see Figure 6-5). Fish products, vegetables, and fruits are significantly lower in fat. The way food is processed, stored, and prepared can also have a dramatic effect on its fat content. For instance, whole milk has more than eight times the fat calories as skim milk, fish sticks fried in oil have four

times the fat calories as baked flounder, oil-packed tuna has five times more fat calories than water-packed tuna, and potato chips have 60 times more fat calories than a baked potato.

A food that is high in fat is not always high in saturated fat. For example, margarine is 100% fat, but only 20% of the fat is saturated. Most of the fat calories are monounsaturated or polyunsaturated. Butter is also 100% fat, but 67% of its fat content is saturated. In general, beef and pork products, foods made with butter fat and whole milk, and foods fried in oil are high in saturated fats. Consumption of fruits, vegetables, whole-grain cereals and other products, fish, poultry prepared without the skin, lean cuts of meat, and low-fat dairy products should be emphasized to help reduce consumption of total fat, especially saturated fat.

Hidden fat. To reduce the amount of saturated fat in their diets, many people choose foods and snacks whose labels say they are made with "100% pure vegetable oil" or "pure vegetable shortening." The assumption is that because it is a pure vegetable oil, it is free of saturated fat and healthier. Although snack foods do contribute to the high fat intake of Americans, cooking oils are the largest source of hidden fat in the American diet.[10]

Several vegetable oils are more highly saturated than lard and beef fat. Coconut oil and palm kernel oil are the worst: They contain 86% and 81% saturated fat, respectively, and they are widely used in snack items such as crackers, chips, cookies, cake mixes, and granola bars.[1] Figure 6-5 compares the

Beware of hidden fat.

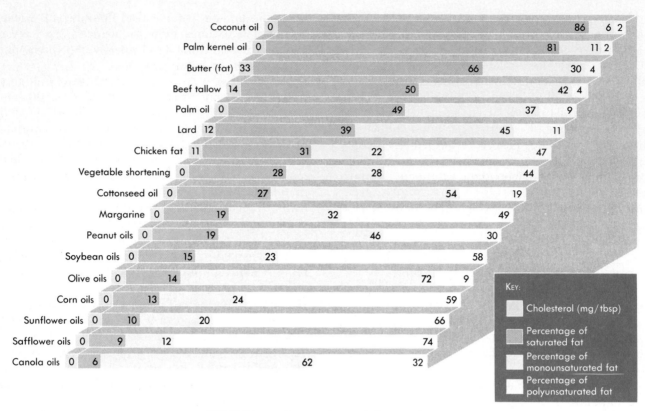

FIGURE 6-5 Comparison of dietary fats.

type and percentage of fat in various oils and foods. Individuals should look beyond the "vegetable oil" banner displayed prominently on many snack packages and scan the ingredients list for the words "coconut," "palm kernel," and "palm oil." Many items outside the snack aisle also contain palm or coconut oil. For instance, Cool Whip contains both palm kernel and coconut oils, making it more highly saturated than real whipped cream.

Another warning relates to "cholesterol-free" claims made on the labels of vegetable oils. Although vegetable oils do not contain cholesterol, they do contain varying amounts of saturated fat. Like all saturated fats, they tend to raise cholesterol levels in the blood. Therefore a steady diet of "cholesterol-free" baked goods can actually raise the cholesterol level if they contain one or more tropical oils.[14]

Dietary guidelines. Experts recommend a diet that achieves a total fat intake of 30% of total calories or less, with 10% coming from each type of fat (saturated, monounsaturated, and polyunsaturated), and a cholesterol intake below 300 milligrams per day. For a person on a 2000-calorie diet, 65 grams of fat are allowed (see Table 6-4). (Assessment Activities

6-2 and 6-3 provide an estimate of the maximum fat and saturated fat for your diet. See also Figure 6-6.)

Suggestions for meeting these recommendations are as follows:

▶ Limit meat, seafood, and poultry to no more than 5 to 7 ounces per day.
▶ Use chicken or turkey (without the skin) or fish in most meals.
▶ Choose lean cuts of meat, trim all the visible fat, and throw away the fat that cooks out of the meat.
▶ Substitute meatless or low-meat main dishes for regular entrees.
▶ Use no more than 5 to 8 teaspoons of fats and oils per day for cooking, baking, and preparing salads.
▶ Choose foods that contain less than 3 grams of fat per 100-calorie serving.
▶ Use low-fat dairy products.

To control cholesterol, the following can be used as guidelines:

▶ Use no more than four egg yolks per week, including those used in cooking.
▶ Limit consumption of shrimp, lobster, sardines, and organ meats.

Figure 6-6   How Much Fat is in Food?

The amount of fat in food depends on the way fat is measured. Measuring fat content by weight yields a completely different result than measuring fat by calories.

For example, 1 cup of whole milk weighs 244 grams (8.5 ounces). Because 8 of these grams come from fat, by weight, whole milk is 3.28% fat (8 ÷ 244 = 3.28%).

Calculating fat weight by calories provides a different picture. Most of the weight of milk (200 grams) comes from water, and water has no calories. This leaves 44 grams of calorie weight. Because 8 grams come from fat and because 1 gram of fat yields 9 calories, the fat content of 1 cup of whole milk provides 72 calories. The total percentage (72 ÷ 150 = 48%) of the calories is from fat, making it a fattier food than it seems at first glance. (By comparison, the fat weight by calories for 2%, 1%, and skim milk are 38%, 18%, and 0%, respectively.) In the case of milk, calculating fat content in relationship to calories rather than weight thus provides a more representative assessment.

Choose a Diet with Plenty of Vegetables, Fruits, and Grain Products

Starch and fiber belong to the carbohydrate family of nutrients. Carbohydrates are the primary energy source for all body functions and physical activity. They are also the preferred energy source; dietary guidelines recommend that complex carbohydrates make up at least 45% of the diet. A 2000-calorie diet that meets the DRV of 300 grams achieves the even higher level of 60% of carbohydrates (see Table 6-4).

Carbohydrates supply energy in the form of sugar, or *saccharides*. The simplest form of carbohydrates is the *monosaccharide*, which includes *glucose* and *fructose* (fruit sugar). Fructose is the sweetest of simple sugars. *Disaccharides* are double sugars, meaning that they are pairs of monosaccharides chemically linked. Included in this group of sugars are *sucrose*, or table sugar; *lactose*, or milk sugar; and *maltose*, or malt sugar. The last group of sugars are the *polysaccharides*, which are composed of many single monosaccharides. Polysaccharides are also called **complex carbohydrates.** They include starch and several forms of fiber.

Starch. Starch is the most significant polysaccharide in human nutrition. A diet high in starch is likely to be lower in fat, especially saturated fat and cholesterol; lower in calories; and higher in fiber. These factors are associated with lower rates of obesity, cardiovascular disease, diabetes, cancer, malnutrition, and tooth decay. An added benefit of starch is that it helps the body maintain a normal blood-sugar level through a slower, more even rate of digestion and glucose absorption. All starch is digested and circulates to the cells as glucose 1 to 4 hours after a meal. This is one reason athletes involved in endurance activities such as marathons load up on complex carbohydrates before competition.

All starchy foods are plant foods. Grains such as rice, wheat, corn, millet, rye, barley, and oats are the richest food source. The legume family (beans and peas), including peanuts and dried beans (butter beans, kidney beans, black-eyed peas, garbanzo beans, and soybeans), is another good source of starch. It also contains a significant amount of protein. A third source is the tubers, such as potatoes and yams.

Many weight-conscious people mistakenly avoid starches, thinking that they are high in calories. Starchy foods are often made fattening when they are prepared. For example, a baked potato contains 90 calories, compared with 285 calories in a hamburger of the same weight. Adding fat in the form of butter, sour cream, margarine, or cheese adds calories to the potato.

Fiber. One advantage of a high-starch diet is that it will almost automatically be high in fiber unless the foods are refined or highly processed.

Fiber (formerly called *roughage*) is a general term that refers to the substances in food resisting digestion. The amount of fiber in a food is determined by its plant source and the amount of processing it undergoes. In general, the more a food is processed, the more the fiber is broken down and the lower the fiber content.

The fiber content shown on food labels is usually listed as either dietary fiber or crude fiber. *Dietary fiber* is the actual residue of plant food that resists digestion in the human body. *Crude fiber* is the residue of plant food following a harsh chemical digestive procedure in the laboratory; 1 gram of crude fiber equals 2 to 3 grams of dietary fiber.

There are two kinds of fiber: *soluble fiber*, which dissolves in hot water, and *insoluble fiber*, which does not dissolve in water. Each plant food usually contains a mixture of fiber types.

Soluble fiber. Soluble fiber appears to have several favorable effects. Because it forms gels in water, it adds bulk and thickness to the contents of the stomach and may slow emptying, thus prolonging the sense of fullness and possibly helping dieters control their appetites. Studies have shown that soluble fiber lowers blood-cholesterol levels. The results of 10 studies reported in the *Journal of the American Medical Association*[15] showed that eating oat bran cereal or oatmeal every day can lower blood cholesterol by an average of 2% to 3%. Diets high in carbohydrate and fiber, especially soluble fiber, im-

prove blood glucose control, lower insulin requirements, and decrease blood cholesterol and blood pressure in people with diabetes.[16] Soluble fiber also slows the absorption of sugars from the small intestine, another benefit for those with diabetes.

Good sources of soluble fiber are fruits, vegetables, and grains. Specific foods include prunes, pears, oranges, apples, dried beans, cauliflower, zucchini, sweet potatoes, and oat and corn bran (Table 6-8).

Insoluble fiber. Insoluble fiber adds bulk to the contents of the intestine. This speeds the *transit time* (time of passage) of a meal's remnants through the small and large intestines. This in turn appears to offer several important health benefits:

▶ It helps prevent constipation because insoluble fiber attracts water into the digestive tract, thus softening the stool. Softer stools reduce the pressure in the lower intestine, creating less likelihood that rectal veins will swell and cause *hemorrhoids*.

▶ It helps prevent compaction of food in the intestines, which could obstruct the appendix and lead to appendicitis.

▶ It stimulates muscle tone in the intestinal wall, which helps to prevent *diverticulosis*, a condition that occurs when the intestine bulges out into pockets and that possibly leads to *diverticulitis*, in which the pockets become infected and sometimes rupture.

▶ It may reduce the chances of colon cancer. A shorter transit time reduces the exposure of the intestines to cancer-causing agents in the food. Insoluble fiber also stimulates the secretion of mucus in the colon. Mucus coats the colon wall and may provide a barrier that keeps cancer-causing agents from reaching the colon's cells.

The best source of insoluble fiber is wheat bran. Other good sources include whole grains, dried beans and peas, and most fruit and vegetables, especially those eaten with the skin.

If you are not used to eating fiber-rich foods, gradually add them to your diet over 4 to 6 weeks, using these suggestions[17]:

▶ Eat ¼ to ½ cup whole-grain cereal every day. Look for cereals that list wheat bran as their first ingredient and that contain at least 5 grams of dietary fiber per serving.

▶ Buy bread that lists "whole wheat" or "stone-ground wheat" as its first ingredient. Breads that do not list these ingredients first are made mostly from refined wheat flour that has been colored brown.

▶ To make whole-wheat breads, muffins, or other baked goods, substitute one of the following for

TABLE 6-8 Fiber Content of Selected Foods

Food	Fiber (g)
Fruits	
Apple, with peel	4.2
Banana	3.3
Blackberries (1 cup)	9.7
Dates, chopped (1 cup)	15.5
Grapes	1
Orange	2.9
Peach, peeled	2
Pear, with skin	4.9
Prunes, dried, pitted (10)	13.5
Raisins, seedless (1 cup)	9.6
Breads	
Oatmeal (1 slice)	0.86
Pumpernickel (1 slice)	1.33
Rye (1 slice)	1.65
Wheat (1 slice)	1.4
Whole wheat (1 slice)	3.17
White (1 slice)	0.68
Cereals	
Bran Chex (⅔ cup)	5
Bran flakes (⅔ cup)	5
Cheerios (1¼ cup)	2
Corn flakes (1 cup)	1
Grapenuts (1¼ cup)	2
Raisin Bran (½ cup)	4
Rice Krispies (1 cup)	Trace
Shredded Wheat (1 biscuit)	3
Life (⅔ cup)	3
Vegetables	
Lima beans (½ cup)	4.6
Green beans (1 cup)	3.1
Cauliflower (½ cup)	1.3
Corn, canned (½ cup)	6.3
Garbanzo beans (1 cup)	8.6
Greens (1 cup)	2.9
Navy beans (1 cup)	16.5
Baked potato, with skin	4.4
Tomato	2.2
Carrot	2.0

1 cup of white flour: 1 cup minus 2 tablespoons whole wheat flour, ½ cup white flour and ½ cup whole-wheat flour, or ¾ cup white flour and ¼ cup wheat germ or 100% bran.

▶ Add 2 to 3 tablespoons of 100% bran to low-fiber foods such as breakfast cereal, pudding, and applesauce.

▶ Substitute brown rice, millet, and bulgur for white rice and potatoes; add barley to soups and casseroles; and snack on popcorn instead of potato chips and pretzels.

How much fiber? Most Americans consume between 10 and 13 grams of dietary fiber per day. Some experts recommend that this level be raised to 20 to 35 grams.[15] Because the high meat content in American diets provides little or no residue, only vegetarians are likely to consume this amount of fiber. The DRV for fiber is 25 grams for a 2000-calorie diet.

As with most other nutrients, fiber can be consumed in excess. Indiscriminate consumption of fiber may interfere with the body's ability to absorb other essential nutrients. A person who eats bulky foods but has only a small capacity may not be able to take in enough food energy or nutrients. A high intake of dietary fiber, for example, 60 grams per day, also requires a high intake of water.[1]

Complex carbohydrates and cancer. Foods associated with decreased cancer risk are commonly found in the complex-carbohydrates group. The American Institute for Cancer Research[18] linked 35% of all cancers to diet. In a review of 156 studies, the *Journal of Nutrition and Cancer*[15] reported that in 128 of the studies, fruits and vegetables offered significant protection against cancers of the lung, colon, breast, cervix, esophagus, oral cavity, stomach, bladder, pancreas, and ovaries.

Figure 6-7 is a useful guide[19] for planning meals

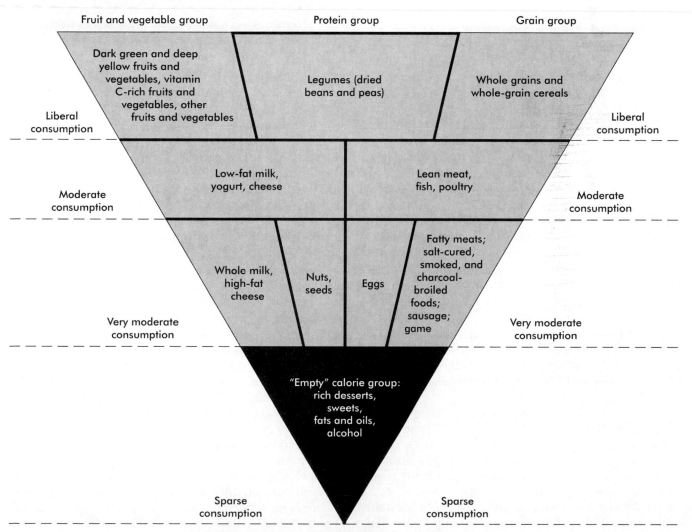

FIGURE 6-7 Eating guide to lower the risk for cancer.

to lower the risk for cancer. Consumption of cruciferous vegetables such as cabbage, broccoli, brussels sprouts, and cauliflower are thought to help prevent cancer of the gastrointestinal and respiratory tracts. Fruits and vegetables rich in vitamin A have been linked to a reduction in cancer of the ovaries, bladder, larynx, esophagus, and lung. Good sources of vitamin A are carrots, spinach, tomatoes, apricots, peaches, and cantaloupes. Cancer of the stomach and esophagus is less common among people whose diets are rich in ascorbic acid, or vitamin C. Green and yellow vegetables and citrus fruits are excellent sources of this vitamin.

Scientists often cannot provide firm evidence about the cancer-inhibiting qualities of a particular food. The interaction between food and disease is complex, and 20 to 40 years may be needed to determine a relationship between cancer and diet. People may mistakenly believe that if a little is good, a lot is much better. Some dietary practices that may help prevent cancer may lead to other toxic conditions if taken to the extreme. Therefore good judgment and moderation are important.

Use Sugar Only in Moderation

The *dietary guidelines for Americans* recommends that consumption of sugar be limited to 10%. For most people, this means cutting sugar consumption in half. The yearly consumption for the average American is 135 pounds, or 24% of total caloric intake.[1] This figure represents an increase of 11 pounds per person per year since 1976, two thirds of which has been hidden in common products by manufacturers. Much of the hidden sugar is not listed as table sugar but as high-fructose corn syrup, the chief sweetening agent used by the food industry.[13] Manufacturers often list the different forms of sugar separately, for example, corn starch, sucrose, and corn syrup. Although sugar may be the main ingredient, it does not appear first on the label.

Diets high in sugar are associated with obesity, malnutrition, heart disease, hypoglycemia, diabetes mellitus, hyperactivity, and tooth decay. Although experts debate the effect of sugar on the first six conditions, there is little doubt that sugar is guilty of contributing to tooth decay.

Dental caries are caused by acid buildup from bacteria that feed on carbohydrates. Brushing is recommended within the first 20 minutes after eating to negate the effects of sugar. If brushing is not practical, rinsing will help wash the sugar off the teeth. Flossing the teeth is even more effective. It takes 24 hours for the concentration of bacteria to accumulate on a tooth to produce enough acid to cause den-

Substituting artificial sweeteners for table sugar helps cut sugar consumption, but two thirds of the sugar consumed is "hidden" in other foods.

tal caries. Therefore flossing once a day can help offset the effect of a high-sugar diet.

Nutritive sweeteners. Sweeteners, which provide calories, or food energy, are considered nutritive sweeteners. Each one provides about the same number of calories per gram. Sugars occur naturally in fruits, vegetables, honey, and milk. They are the building blocks of complex carbohydrates such as starch. All carbohydrates must be broken down into usable energy—blood sugar—which is also called *glucose.*

Other common nutritive sweeteners. Included in this group of sweeteners are corn syrup, high-fructose corn syrup, sugar alcohols, and aspartame. *Corn syrup* is often used in foods as a partial or complete replacement for sucrose (table sugar) because it is less sweet and provides texture. *High-fructose corn syrup* is sweeter than sucrose and is the main nutritive sweetener in soft drinks. Because it is sweeter, it can be used in smaller quantities, which results in a slightly lower-calorie product. *Sugar alcohols* such as *sorbitol* are less sweet than sucrose and are used to add texture to hard candies and gums. *Aspartame*, which is marketed as Nutrasweet, has about the same number of calories as sucrose but is 180 to 220 times as sweet. Therefore only a small amount is needed to sweeten products. The taste of aspartame is similar to that of sucrose, and it leaves no aftertaste. Because aspartame is derived partially from the amino acid phenylalanine, products containing it must be labeled to warn individuals who have the inherited disease *phenylketonuria*.

Nonnutritive sweeteners. Nonnutritive sweeteners do not contribute any food energy to the diet. The most widely used nonnutritive sweetener is *saccharin*. It is approximately 300 times as sweet as sucrose and is colorless, odorless, and water soluble.

Cyclamate is another nonnutritive sweetener. It is 30 times sweeter than sucrose and has no aftertaste. The disadvantage of cyclamate is that it was linked with cancer and banned from the marketplace by the Food and Drug Administration (FDA) in the late 1960s. The FDA recently lifted its ban on cyclamate when studies could not prove that it causes cancer.

Acesulfame (Sunette) is the most recent sweetener to be introduced. It was approved by the FDA in 1988 for use in chewing gum, powdered drink mixes, puddings, and nondairy creamers. It is 200 times sweeter than sucrose; it contributes no calories because it is not broken down by the body.[20]

Does the use of artificial sweeteners lead to weight reduction? Scientific studies have not substantiated this claim. On the contrary, although sugar substitutes are low in calories, they may actually stimulate the appetite. Unlike sugar, which produces a feeling of *satiety*, or fullness, nonnutritive sweeteners do not ease the appetite and may encourage a craving for sweets by turning on sweet sensors on the tongue without putting sugar into the bloodstream. People who use artificial sweeteners may compensate by eating more fats.

Use Salt and Sodium Only in Moderation

Salt contains about 40% sodium by weight and is widely used in the preservation, processing, and preparation of foods. Although sodium is an essential mineral, it is consumed by adults in the United States at levels far beyond the RDA of 500 milligrams (one tenth of a teaspoon) per day[12] and more than double the 2400 milligrams considered adequate.[15] Most people average about 3 to 7 grams of sodium per day, which translates to 7.5 to 18 grams of salt. (A teaspoon of salt contains about 2 grams of sodium; a teaspoon of most dry substances equals approximately 5 grams.) The major health problem as-

sociated with consumption of too much sodium is hypertension (see Chapter 2). Approximately 20% of Americans are considered salt sensitive and risk contracting hypertension because of high salt intake.[21]

Two thirds of the salt consumed is in the form of hidden salt added during the processing of food. Just how much salt is in a processed food can be determined by reading the package label.

Taste buds cannot always judge salt content. Some foods that taste salty may be lower in salt content than those that do not. For example, peanuts taste salty because the salt is on the surface, where the taste buds immediately detect it. Cheese contains more salt than peanuts or potato chips, and chocolate pudding contains even more salt.

To cut down on salt consumption, you should do the following:
- ▶ Avoid adding salt before tasting food.
- ▶ Add little or no salt to food at the table.
- ▶ Season food with sodium-free spices such as pepper, allspice, onion powder, garlic, mustard powder, sage, thyme, and paprika.
- ▶ Avoid smoked meats and fish.
- ▶ Cut down on canned and instant soups.
- ▶ Read labels for sodium content, especially on processed food.

Drink Alcoholic Beverages In Moderation

Excessive use of alcohol is associated with liver disease, some types of cancer, high blood pressure, stroke, and disorders of the heart muscle. It is the principal cause of liver *cirrhosis* in the United States. Coupled with cigarette smoking, alcohol consumption increases the risk of developing cancer of the mouth, larynx, and esophagus. Alcohol also plays a causal role in deaths from accidents, homicide, and suicide and is associated with disrupted family functioning.

Dietary Guidelines for Americans recommends that alcoholic beverages be limited to one or two drinks per day. One drink means 12 ounces of beer, 5 ounces of wine, or 1½ ounces (one jigger) of distilled spirits (80 proof). A maximum level of alcohol consumption has not been set for women during pregnancy, so pregnant women and women who may become pregnant should not use alcohol.

Nutrient Density

A key strategy for eating well is to select foods that offer significant amounts of nutrients but a small number of calories. If a particular food has a high ratio of nutrients to calories, it is a nutritionally

TABLE 6-9 Nutrient Density

Pizza (Cheese)

Calories	354
Protein	28
Vitamin A	19
Vitamin C	20
Thiamin	25
Riboflavin	29
Niacin	19
Calcium	33
Iron	15
TOTAL	188
Nutrient density	53% (188 ÷ 354 × 100)

dense food. This ratio, called **nutrient density,** provides a quantitative basis for judging the nutritional quality of food. The procedure for determining the nutrient density of food consists of adding the percentage of the RDA for the eight essential nutrients listed on the package label for one serving and dividing by the number of calories per serving (Table 6-9). The higher the score, the higher the nutritional quality (nutrient density) of the food. If two foods have the same number of calories per serving but one has more nutrients, it is more nutritionally dense. The nutrient density of any food with a detailed label or any item listed in the food charts in Appendix A can be computed.

The concept of nutrient density can help the health-conscious and weight-conscious person make informed choices. With the number of foods avail-

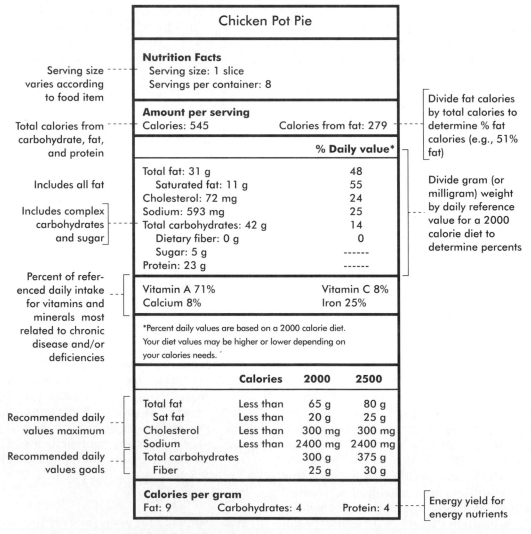

FIGURE 6-8 New food labels now provide information about those nutrients most associated with chronic disease risk factors. (For daily reference values, see p. 149. For referenced daily intake, see p. 168.)

able and the promises and claims that come with them, people need a way to evaluate foods. Nutrient density is one technique that consumers can use to select food.

Food Labels

The FDA oversees the labeling of food products other than meat and poultry. With the passage of new label laws in 1992, virtually all processed and packaged foods are required to have uniform labels. This includes processed meat and poultry, which are regulated by the USDA. Guidelines for voluntary labeling of raw vegetables and fruits and fish are also available and will likely be displayed in most supermarkets.

Labels must indicate the manufacturer and the packer or distributor, declare the quantity of contents either in net weight or by volume, and list the common name of each ingredient in descending order of prominence. Also included is information about those nutrients most closely associated with chronic disease risk factors, that is, the amount of total fat, saturated fat, cholesterol, sodium, sugar, dietary fiber, total carbohydrate, and protein.

Labels are divided into two parts (Figure 6-8). The top half lists nutrients both as an amount per serving and as a percentage of the 2000-calorie daily value. With these percentages it is possible to determine each food's contribution to the DRV. For example, a serving of chicken pot pie contains 31 grams of total fat, or 48% of the daily fat allowance of 65 grams for those consuming 2000 calories a day.

The bottom half contains the DRV for nutrients based on two diets: one for 2000 calories and one for 2500 calories. For example, total fat intake should be less than 65 grams for a 2000-calorie diet and less than 80 grams for a 2500-calorie diet.

In the past, manufacturers often used labeling ploys to deceive consumers. Currently, laws limit labels to the following six health claims[22]:

▶ High-calcium foods may reduce the risk of osteoporosis.
▶ A diet low in saturated fat and cholesterol may lower the risk for heart disease.
▶ A low-fat diet may reduce the risk of some cancers.
▶ A low-sodium diet has been linked with reduced incidence of hypertension.
▶ High-fiber foods may reduce the risk of heart disease and certain forms of cancer.
▶ Vitamins A and C in fruits and vegetables may reduce the risk of some types of cancer.

The FDA has defined commonly used words describing calories, sodium, sugar, fiber, fat, and cholesterol in food. For example, when the word "free" is highlighted on a package in reference to calories, it means that the product yields less than 5 calories per serving; in reference to sodium, it contains less than 5 milligrams; and in reference to fat, it contains less than 0.5 grams (Table 6-10).

Another important change in the 1992 revised food label regulations was the establishment of **Reference daily intakes (RDI)** for protein, minerals, and vitamins (Table 6-11). RDI values represent minimum standards for essential nutrients and replace the U.S. recommended daily allowance (USRDA) established in 1968. RDI figures are based on the average RDA value set for a nutrient that spans a particular age range. For example, the RDIs in Table 6-11 are for children over 4 years of age to adults. Food package labels contain RDI values as a basis for comparing the nutrient values in food.

Changes In American Eating Patterns

The stereotype of an American family with two parents and several children eating three meals a day appears to be a thing of the past. The increase in single-person households, single-parent families, and women in the labor force has had far-reaching effects on eating patterns. Three trends are particularly prominent: snacking, eating at fast-food restaurants, and consuming frozen dinners.

Snacking

Snacks are foods consumed between the three main meals of the day. Most Americans have at least one snack per day, and the sale of snack foods is growing at a rate of 10% a year.[23] College students have

Snacking is clearly a trend.

TABLE 6-10 Common Food Terms Defined

Food Term	Definition
More	Has 10% more of DRV or RDI in reference to protein, vitamins, minerals, dietary fiber, or potassium; has 4% more of DRV in reference to complex carbohydrate or unsaturated fat
Source of	Provides at least 10% to 19% of the amount of the nutrient in the RDI or DRV
Free	Contains less than 5 calories, less than 0.5 grams of sugar, less than 5 milligrams of sodium, less than 0.5 grams of fat, or less than 2 milligrams of cholesterol and 2 grams of saturated fat per serving
Low	Contains less than 140 milligrams of sodium, less than 40 calories, 3 grams or less of fat per serving size, 20 milligrams or less of cholesterol, or 1 gram or less of saturated fat; is not defined for sugar.
Reduced	Contains at least 50% less than the original product in sodium, fat, saturated fat, or cholesterol; has at least 33.3% less calories and a reduction of more than 40 calories per serving
Less	Contains at least 25% less than the original product in sodium, calories, fat, saturated fat, or cholesterol
Light/lite reduction	Contains 33.3% less calories and a minimum reduction of more than 40 calories per serving; if more than 50% of calories come from fat, fat must be reduced by at least 50%, with a minimum reduction of more than 3 grams of fat per serving; if less than 50% of calories are from fat, product can be either 50% reduced in fat or have 33.3% less calories; for sodium, content of original product is reduced 50%

RDI, Reference daily intake.

TABLE 6-11 Referenced Daily Intakes*

Nutrient	RDI	Nutrient	RDI
Protein	50 g	Biotin	60 µg
Vitamin A	875 RE	Pantothenic acid	5.5 mg
Vitamin C	60 mg	Phosphorus	900 mg
Calcium	900 mg	Magnesium	300 mg
Iron	12 mg	Zinc	13 mg
Vitamin D	6.5 µg	Iodine	150 µg
Vitamin E	9.0 α-TE	Selenium	55 µg
Vitamin K	65 µg	Copper	2.0 mg
Thiamin	1.2 mg	Manganese	3.5 mg
Riboflavin	1.4 mg	Fluoride	2.5 mg
Niacin	16 NE	Chromium	120 µg
Vitamin B_6	1.5 mg	Molybdenum	150 µg
Folate	180 µg	Chloride	3150 mg
Vitamin B_{12}	2.0 µg		

RE, Retinol equivalents; α = TE, α tocopherol equivalents; NE, niacin equivalents.

shown preferences for soft drinks, candies, gum, and fresh fruit as snacks, followed by bakery items, milk, and corn and potato chips.

Snacking, or "grazing," is clearly a trend, and it does not have to be an unhealthy one. The key issue is not the time or frequency of eating but what is eaten. Nutritionally dense foods eaten as snacks are just as good for health as when they are consumed as meals. The converse is also true: Foods low in nutrient density eaten at mealtime are just as worthless as they are when eaten as snacks. The problem occurs when a person's diet is dominated by foods low in nutrient density. With the exception of foods restricted for medical reasons, all foods can contribute to a healthful diet. Rather than to rule out snacking, snack foods that enhance wellness should be promoted.

Fast-Food Eating

Changes in the American family are mirrored in the trend toward eating in fast-food restaurants. Family meals at home are becoming the exception rather than the rule. Breakfasts and lunches are seldom eaten in a family setting by many American families, and as many as 25% of American households do not have a sit-down dinner as often as five nights a week.[23] Instead, more families plan mealtimes at fast-food restaurants. Every day an estimated 46 million Americans eat in fast-food restaurants, ordering, among other things, approximately 200 hamburgers every second.[24]

From a nutritional viewpoint the criticisms of fast-food eating are the same as those of the rest of the American diet: too much protein, fat, calories, and sodium and not enough complex carbohydrates and fiber. The average meal of a cheeseburger, milk shake, and fries supplies about 1500 calories, 43% of which comes from fat. Chicken and fish are just as fatty as other protein sources at fast-food restaurants because they are breaded and fried. Frying has the same effect on potatoes. Milk shakes get most of their calories from sugars. Table 6-12 gives the percentage of calories from fat, protein, and carbohydrates for selected fast-food items (see Appendix C for the nutritive values of fast-food items).

Eating at fast-food restaurants does not have to be nutritionally worthless. Many restaurants are now aware that Americans are becoming more knowledgeable about the nutrient content of food and are demanding wholesome, safe, and nutritious foods. Consequently, there has been a trend toward more nutritious menus, including salad, pasta, and potato

TABLE 6-12 Calorie Sources of Fast-Food Items

	Calories	Weight (g)	Percentage of Calories from Protein	Percentage of Calories from Carbohydrates	Percentage of Calories from Fat
Arby's roast beef	350	140	25	36	39
Burger King Whopper	630	261	17	32	51
McDonald's Big Mac	563	204	18	29	53
Wendy's double hamburger	670	285	26	20	54
Church's Fried Chicken (white)	327	100	26	11	63
Church's Fried Chicken (dark)	305	100	29	9	62
Kentucky Fried Chicken Original Recipe (dark)	643	346	22	29	49
Kentucky Fried Chicken extra crispy (dark)	765	376	20	28	52
Long John Silver's fish (2 piece)	366	136	24	23	52
Taco Bell Burrito Supreme	457	225	18	38	43

bars. With good judgment in the choice of foods, an occasional meal at a fast-food chain does not have to compromise a well-balanced diet.

Frozen Dinners

Frozen dinners have also become part of the American diet. Consumers spend $4 billion a year on them, and food manufacturers are constantly turning out new lines.[25] The challenge for health-conscious consumers is to determine which ones fit easily into a nutritious diet.

In a study[26] of frozen foods, strict criteria were used to identify entrees that are suitable for people wanting to limit their intake of fat, calories, and sodium while including essential vitamins and minerals. The results were encouraging. A total of 173 frozen dishes had less than 20% of calories from fat, 73 contained less than 200 milligrams of sodium per 100 calories, and 50 had at least 30% of the RDA for vitamins A and/or C. Frozen dinners can be evaluated by applying the following criteria:

- No more than 30% calories from fat, preferably less
- No more than 200 milligrams of sodium per 100 calories
- At least 40% of RDA for vitamins A and/or C

However, just because a dinner meets the above criteria, it does not necessarily provide every nutrient. Some meals are likely to be deficient in some nutrients, so foods that will compensate must be added.

Planning a Nutrition Strategy for Wellness

Fortunately, it is not necessary to be a nutritionist to form a nutrition strategy that works for you. A nutrition plan will work only if it is personalized. Several strategies should be helpful in personalizing your nutrition plan.

Assess Your Nutrition

You should take an honest look at your eating choices and analyze your nutrition profile (Assessment Activity 6-5) to determine whether you are doing the following:

- Eating a variety of foods every day from the guide to daily food choices
- Avoiding high-fat foods (more than the equivalent of 3 grams of fat per 100 calories)
- Including sufficient fiber in the form of whole

grains, dried beans, and fresh fruits and vegetables

- Consuming six to eight servings of water (8 ounces each)
- Limiting high-sugar desserts or sweets to no more than three or four each week
- Restricting the intake of high-salt foods such as processed meats
- Consuming no more than one or two alcoholic drinks a day or letting drinking interfere with your appetite

Make Small Adjustments

The principle of changing health behavior is that the smaller the change, the longer it lasts (see Chapter 1). For example, rather than vowing to abstain from eating ice cream, you can make one small change at a time. You can reduce the amount or number of servings at first and substitute a low-fat brand. If your diet is heavy in salt, you can gradually substitute sodium-free seasonings. If you have a sweet tooth, you can try low-sugar snacks. If you eat for fullness, you can prepare less food or leave food on your plate. You should plan an approach that builds on the cumulative effect of many small successes.

You should think of balancing your diet over a long period rather than in just a day or a meal. You should try to meet the dietary guidelines over several days or a week. For example, every meal does not need to contain less than 30% fat. Portions of favorite foods high in fat should be kept small, and other sources of fat should be limited. In addition, you should check labels to get an idea of what nutrients you are consuming, but you do not need to keep a calculator by your plate. If you eat foods from the guide to daily food choices, you will get all the vitamins, minerals, and protein you need.

Choose Foods for Wellness

Choosing foods for wellness means following the *Dietary Guidelines for Americans*. This means following a diet that meets the following criteria:

- Is low in highly saturated fat (maximum of 10%)
- Emphasizes complex carbohydrates such as bread, potatoes, and pasta
- Provides six to eight glasses of water throughout the day
- Provides iron and calcium
- Emphasizes fresh fruits and vegetables
- Is low in sugar, salt, alcohol, and caffeine

Summary

- The major nutritional problems of Americans are caused primarily by dietary excess and imbalance.
- A good nutritional plan is one that consists of a variety of foods from the basic food groups.
- The recommended diet for Americans calls for an emphasis on complex carbohydrates as the major source of energy.
- The greatest shortcoming of the American diet is the overconsumption of fat, especially saturated fat.
- The amount of saturated, monounsaturated, and polyunsaturated fat in foods varies considerably. Most foods contain a mixture of these fats.
- A diet high in starch is likely to be lower in fat (especially saturated fat and cholesterol), lower in calories, and higher in fiber.

- Fiber benefits the body by adding bulk to the contents of the intestines, thus increasing the transit of food through the body, which reduces the chance of developing colon cancer, and lowering blood-cholesterol levels.
- Consumption of fruits and cruciferous vegetables are associated with a decreased risk of cancer.
- Sugar and salt are consumed in the United States in excessive amounts. They are usually hidden in common products to which they have been added by food manufacturers.
- A food has a high index of nutritional quality when it has a high ratio of nutrients to calories.
- The criticisms of fast-food eating are the same as those of the rest of the American diet: too much protein, fat, calories, sodium, and sugar and not enough complex carbohydrates and fiber.

Action Plan for Personal Wellness

Use the information presented in this chapter to answer the following questions and to formulate an action plan to enhance your personal wellness.

1 Based on the information presented in this chapter, along what I know about my family's health history, the health problems and issues related to nutrition that I need to be concerned about are:____

_____

_____

2 Of those nutrition issues listed in number 1, the one I most need to act on is:_____

_____

_____

3 The possible actions that I can take to improve my ability to form a plan for good nutrition are (be specific):_____

_____

_____

4 Of the actions listed in number 3, the one that I most need to include in an action plan is:_____

_____

_____

5 Factors I need to keep in mind to be successful in my action plan are:_____

_____

_____

Review Questions

1. What is meant by the statement that nutritional diseases of the past have been replaced by diseases of dietary excess and imbalance?
2. What are the importance and implications of variety as related to planning a nutritionally balanced diet?
3. What is the difference between a high-quality, complete protein and a low-quality, incomplete protein?
4. What are the similarities and differences between water-soluble and fat-soluble vitamins?
5. Under what circumstances (if any) should vitamin and/or mineral supplements be added to a person's daily regimen?
6. What are the rules about water and the functions of it that make water an essential nutrient?
7. What is the difference between saturated and unsaturated fats? What are some food sources for each?
8. What are five dietary practices that will help lower consumption of fat, especially saturated fat?
9. How does a diet high in complex carbohydrates contribute to health and wellness?
10. What are the major benefits of soluble and insoluble fiber in the diet?
11. What is the relationship between cancer and diet?
12. What effects have snacking and fast-food eating had on the nutritional status of Americans?
13. What are six guidelines for planning a diet that satisfy the criteria presented in *Dietary Guidelines for Americans*?

References

1. Wardlaw G, Insel P: *Perspectives in nutrition*, ed 2, St Louis, 1993, Mosby.
2. Consumers' Union: Are you eating right? *Consumer Reports* 57(10):645-648, 1992.
3. US Department of Health and Human Services: *The surgeon general's report on nutrition and health*, Washington, DC, 1988, US Government Printing Office.
4. Perkin BB: Dietary guidelines for Americans, 1990 edition, *J Am Diet Assoc* 90:1725, 1990.
5. Long P: The power in vitamin, *Health* 6(6):67, 1992.
6. Thomas P: Which supplements should you take? *Am Health* 10(3):39, 1991.
7. High C—sounding better? *Harvard Health Letter* 17(11):8, 1992.
8. The supplement-taker's guide to the universe, *Nutr Action Health Letter* 20(1):4, 1993.
9. Antioxidant vitamins: preventive medicine for the 21st century? *Harvard Heart Letter* 3(7):2-3, 1993.
10. Can vitamins help prevent heart attacks? *Health Letter* 39(9):7-8, 1992.
11. Office of Disease Prevention and Health Promotion: *Disease prevention/health promotion: the facts*, Palo Alto, Calif, 1988, Bull Publishing.
12. Davis R: It's clearly healthful: Americans should drink lots of water, *Commercial Appeal* 153(190):C2, 1992.
13. National Research Council: *Recommended dietary allowances*, ed 10, Washington, DC, 1989, National Academy Press.
14. Consumers Union: What's your nutrition IQ? *Consumer Reports* 55(5):322, 1990.
15. Consumers Union: Are you eating right? *Consumer Reports* 57(10):648, 1992.
16. Thompson L: Potential health benefits of whole grains and their components, *Contemporary Nutr* 17(6):1, 1992.
17. How to add fiber to your diet, *Mayo Clin Health Letter* 8(5):2, 1990.
18. *Everything doesn't cause cancer*, Washington, DC, 1992, American Institute for Cancer Research.
19. American Cancer Society: *Learn to eat for better health*, New York, 1992, The Association.
20. Greely A: Not only sugar is sweet, *FDA Consumer* Apr 1991, p 17.
21. American's top ten food myths, *Health* 6(6):64, 1992.
22. Hermann M: At long last, here come food labels that are truly "new and improved," *Am Health* 12(2):89, 1993.
23. Williams SR: *Nutrition and diet therapy*, ed 7, St Louis, 1994, Mosby.
24. Mayer J: How fast food figures in, *Tufts Univ Diet Nutr Letter* 8(1):7, 1990.
25. Mayer J: Special report: more than 100 frozen dinners worth heating, *Tufts Univ Diet Nutr Letter* 8(2):3, 1990.
26. Hurley J, Schmidt S: The frozen food case, *Nutr Action Health Letter* 20(1):10, 1993.

Annotated Readings

Center for Science in the Public Interest: *Nutr Action Health Letter* 70(1):1-3, 1993.
   Features two articles on vitamin supplements: one recommends how to buy them, and one provides a shopper's guide to 36 major brands. Also features an article on frozen dinners and identifies 173 that are suitable for people trying to limit intake of fat, calories, and sodium.

Center for Science in the Public Interest: *Nutr Action Health Letter* 19(10):8-9, 1992.
   Introduces the center's healthy eating pyramid with specific suggestions of foods that are recommended anytime, sometimes, and seldom. Complete with a cut-out model of the food pyramid.

Harvard Medical School: Antioxidant vitamins: preventive medicine for the 21st century? *Harvard Heart Letter* 3(7):1-5, 1993.
   Provides an in-depth look at vitamins C, E, and beta carotene with discussion of theories on their preventive role regarding heart disease. Also presents findings of epidemiological studies involving people on antioxidant-vitamin supplements.

Hurley J, Schmidt S: The frozen food case, *Nutr Action Health Letter* 20(1):10, 1993.
   Identifies 173 frozen dinners that are suitable for people trying to limit intake of fat, calories, and sodium.

National Research Council: *Recommended dietary allowances*, ed 10, Washington, DC, 1989, National Academy Press.
   Widely regarded as the authoritative source on nutrient allowances for healthy people. Reviews the function of each nutrient in the human body, food sources, usual dietary intake, and effects of deficiencies and excessive intake.

Wardlaw G, Insel P: *Contemporary nutrition*, ed 2, St Louis, 1994, Mosby.
   Provides an in-depth, comprehensive presentation on all aspects of nutrition.

ASSESSMENT ACTIVITY   6 - 1

Assessing Your Protein RDA

Directions: Complete the following steps to determine your RDA for protein.

1. How much do you weigh?   _____ lb
2. Convert weight in pounds to kilograms by
   dividing pounds by 2.2.   _____ kg
3. Multiply kilograms by 0.8.   _____ g (your protein RDA)

EXAMPLE: Someone who weighs 150 pounds needs 54 g of protein:

$150 \div 2.2 = 68$ kg

68 kg $\times 0.8 = 54$ g of protein

ASSESSMENT ACTIVITY   6 - 2

Assessing Your Maximum Fat Intake

Directions: Complete the following steps to determine your estimated maximum fat intake in grams
to stay within the dietary guidelines of 30% of total calories in fat.

Enter your body weight: _____ lb

Multiply by 15: $\times 15$

The result equals caloric intake for body weight (approximate number of calories consumed daily assuming that you are not in a weight-loss or weight-
gain program):   _____ calories

Multiply by 30%: $\times 0.30$

The result equals maximum fat calories: _____ calories

Divide by 9: $\div 9$

The result equals maximum fat in grams: _____ g

EXAMPLE: For an individual weighing 185 lb:

1. Body weight   185 lb
2. $\times 15$ 15
3. Caloric intake   2775 calories
4. $\times 30\%$ 0.30
5. Maximum fat   822 calories
6. $\div 9$ $\div$ 9
7. Maximum fat   92 g

This amounts to approximately 3 ounces of saturated fat ($92 \div 28 = 3.3$ ounces).

Assessing Your Maximum Saturated Fat Intake

Directions: Complete the following steps to determine your estimated maximum saturated fat intake in grams to stay within the dietary guidelines of 10% of total calories in fat.

Enter your body weight: _____ lb

Multiply by 15: × 15

The result equals caloric intake for body weight (approximate number of calories consumed daily assuming that you are not in a weight-loss or weight-gain program): _____ calories

Multiply by 10%: _____ 0.10

The result equals maximum saturated fat calories: _____ calories

Divide by 9: _____ ÷ 9

The result equals maximum saturated fat in grams: _____ g

EXAMPLE: For an individual weighing 185 lb:
1. Body weight   185 lb
2. × 15   15
3. Caloric intake   2775 calories
4. × 10%   0.10
5. Maximum saturated fat 277.5 calories
6. ÷ 9   ÷ 9
7. Maximum saturated fat   30.8 g

This amounts to approximately 1 ounce of saturated fat (30.8 ÷ 28 = 1.1 ounces).

Assessing Your Carbohydrate Intake Goal

Directions: Complete the following steps to determine your estimated goal for carbohydrate intake in grams to meet the recommended dietary guidelines of 55% of total calories in carbohydrate (including sugar and complex carbohydrate).

Enter your body weight: _____ lb

Multiply by 15: × 15

The result equals caloric intake for body weight (approximate number of calories consumed daily assuming that you are not in a weight-loss or weight-gain program): _____ calories

Multiply by 55%: _____ 0.55

The result equals recommended carbohydrate calories: _____ calories

Divide by 4: ÷ 4

The result equals recommended carbohydrate in grams: _____ g

EXAMPLE: For an individual weighing 185 lb:
1. Body weight   185 lb
2. × 15   15
3. Caloric intake   2775 calories
4. × 58%   0.55
5. Recommended carbohydrates 1526 calories
6. Divide by 4   ÷ 4
7. Recommended carbohydrates 382 g

This amounts to approximately 14 ounces of carbohydrate (382 ÷ 28 = 14 ounces).

ASSESSMENT ACTIVITY

6 - 5

Nutrition Assessment

One way to determine if you are getting sufficient quantities of the proper nutrients is to keep a record of your diet. Ideally this covers a time span of at least a week. However, in this exercise you are asked to assess your dietary selections for only one day. Therefore choose a day that is most representative of your overall nutritional practices.

Directions: Your instructor may ask you to conduct a 2- or 3-day assessment. In this case, photocopy additional copies of the assessment forms as needed.

1. Use the following form to record your dietary selections. Include all foods and beverages, and specify the amount eaten, how cooked, and so on. List condiments and seasonings such as mustard, ketchup, butter, and dressings and trimmings such as lettuce, onions, marshmallows, and sugar. The more detailed your record, the more you will learn from this assessment and the more accurate your nutrition assessment will be.
2. Once foods have been listed, refer to the nutritive values of foods (see Appendix C) and record appropriate values in the spaces provided. If some foods are not included in the appendix, refer to package labels if available to determine nutritive values.
3. When you have finished with this assessment, proceed to Part II to determine your nutrition profile.

Part I: Nutrition Profile

| | Foods | | | | | | |
	Burger King Whopper						TOTAL*
Calories	630						
Protein (g)	26						
Carbohydrates (g)	50						
Fat (g)	36						
Cholesterol (mg)	75						
Saturated Fat (g)	7.5						
Sodium (mg)	990						
Potassium (mg)	520						
Iron (mg)	6						
Vitamin A (IU)	641						
Vitamin C (mg)	13						
Thiamin (mg)	0.02						
Riboflavin (mg)	0.03						
Niacin (mg)	5.2						
Calcium (mg)	37						
Fiber (g)	—						

*Transfer totals to Part II.

Part II: Are You Meeting the RDI?

Based on the results of your 1-day assessment, indicate how you are doing in meeting the RDI for the nutrients listed below.

▶ Transfer the totals from Part I to the appropriate column.
▶ Subtract the RDI from your totals and indicate your status in the appropriate column. A positive value means that you are meeting the RDI for that nutrient; a negative value means that you are deficient in that nutrient.
▶ For nutrients with a negative value, identify several specific foods that will eliminate the deficiency.

Nutrient	Total	RDI	Status	Food Prescription
Protein	_____	50 g*	_____	_____
Iron	_____	12 mg	_____	_____
Vitamin A	_____	875 RE	_____	_____
Vitamin C	_____	60 mg	_____	_____
Thiamin	_____	1.2 mg	_____	_____
Riboflavin	_____	1.4 mg	_____	_____
Niacin	_____	16 NE	_____	_____
Calcium	_____	900 mg	_____	_____

*Refer to Assessment Activity 6-1 for your personal RDI for protein and substitute it for the value above.

Part III: Are You Meeting the DRV?

Based on the results of your 1-day assessment, indicate how your diet compares with the DRV.
▶ Transfer the totals from Part I for the nutrients below to the appropriate column.
▶ Compare the DRV listed to your totals. Indicate your status. Note that some values are maximums and should not be exceeded; others are goals that serve as minimums.

Nutrient	Total	DRV*	Status
Total fat	_____	65 g (maximum)	_____
Saturated fat	_____	20 g (maximum)	_____
Cholesterol	_____	300 mg (maximum)	_____
Sodium	_____	2400 mg (maximum)	_____
Carbohydrate	_____	300 g (goal)	_____
Dietary fiber	_____	25 g (goal)	_____
Potassium	_____	3500 mg (goal)	_____

*DRV based on 2000-calorie diet. Refer to Assessment Activities 6-2, 6-3, and 6-4 for your personal DRV for total fat, saturated fat, and carbohydrate and substitute for the values above.

How Does Your Diet Compare with the Recommended Diet?

Directions: The recommended guidelines suggest that carbohydrate calories should make up at least 55% of the diet (including complex carbohydrates and sugar), fat calories should be less than 30%, and protein calories should be 15%. The purpose of this assessment is to compare your diet with these recommendations. First convert your caloric intake to percentages as follows.

Percent Carbohydrate Calories

Carbohydrate intake (refer to total carbohydrate intake from Part I, Assessment Activity 6-5): _____ g

Multiply by 4;   4

Carbohydrate calories: _____ calories

Total calories, all food (refer to Part I, Assessment Activity 6-5): _____ calories

Percent carbohydrate calories (divide carbohydrate calories by total calories and multiply by 100): _____ %

Draw a bar on the graph to indicate percentage of carbohydrate calories.

EXAMPLE: For an individual on a 2000-calorie diet who consumed 175 g of carbohydrate:

$$175 \times 4 = 700 \text{ carbohydrate calories}$$
$$700 \div 2000 = 0.35$$
$$0.35 \times 100 = 35\%$$

Percent Protein Calories

Protein intake (refer to total protein intake from Part I, Assessment Activity 6-5): _____ g

Multiply by 4:   × 4

Protein calories: _____ calories

Total calories, all food (refer to Part I, Assessment Activity 6-5): _____ calories

Percent protein calories (divide protein calories by total calories and multiply by 100): _____ %

Draw a bar on the graph to indicate percentage of protein calories.

EXAMPLE: For an individual on a 2000-calorie diet who consumed 100 g of protein:

$$100 \times 4 = 400 \text{ protein calories}$$
$$400 \div 2000 = 0.20$$
$$0.20 \times 100 = 20\%$$

Percent Fat Calories

Fat intake (refer to total fat intake from Part I, Assessment Activity 6-5): _____ g

Multiply by 9:   × 9

Fat calories: _____ calories

Total calories, all food (refer to Part I, Assessment Activity 6-5): _____ calories

% fat calories (divide fat calories by total calories and multiply by 100): _____ %

Draw a bar on the graph to indicate percentage of fat calories.

EXAMPLE: For an individual on a 2000-calorie diet who consumed 100 grams of fat:

$$100 \times 9 = 900 \text{ fat calories}$$
$$900 \div 2000 = 0.45$$
$$0.45 \times 100 = 45\%$$

Example Profile

The graph below shows the percentages of the example given in the assessment as the bar below the recommended amount.

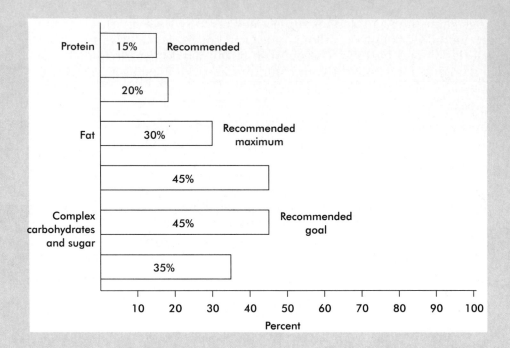

Your profile

Complete the bars with the amounts calculated for your diet.

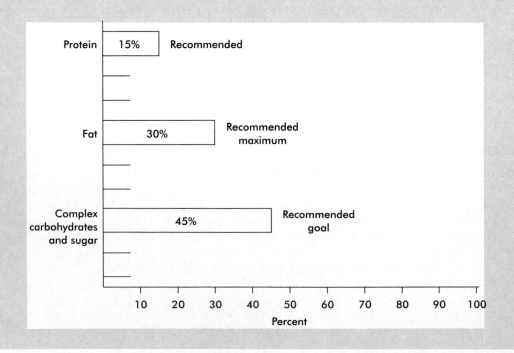

Fat Ratio of Foods

Directions: Select 10 foods and determine their percent fat (fat ratio) by completing the following table. (Two examples are provided.) You can select foods that were included in your 1-day assessment, your instructor may assign foods, or you may choose foods of interest.

1. Determine calories and fat grams per serving. (Refer to label or to food tables in the appendix.)
2. Determine fat calories by multiplying fat grams times 9. EXAMPLE: Star Kist Light Tuna = 0.5 g × 9 = 4.5 fat calories.
3. Determine fat ratio by dividing fat calories by total calories per serving and multiplying by 100. EXAMPLE: Star Kist Light Tuna = 4.5 ÷ 60 = 0.075 × 100 = 7.5%.
4. If fat percent (ratio) is less than 30%, indicate "yes" in the recommendation column; if more than 30%, indicate "no."

Product	Calories/Serving	Fat (g)	Fat Calories	Fat Ratio (%)	Recommendation (Yes or No)
Star Kist Light Tuna	60	0.5	4.5	7.5%	Yes
Nestle Sugar-Free Hot Cocoa Mix	70	4	36	51%	No

Eating Behaviors to Consider

Directions: Answer the following questions to reveal information about your eating habits, how you developed certain tastes, and your attitude about various foods.

1. When was the last time you tried a new food? What was the food? What were the circumstances?
2. What new foods have you learned to eat during the past year?
3. Name the foods that have been on your "will not try" list (that is, foods that you will not eat under any circumstances).
4. What special events do you celebrate in some way with food?
5. Where is your favorite place to eat?
6. If you were to go on an eating binge, what foods would you be most likely to eat?
7. Describe in detail your favorite meal.
8. Do you consider yourself a slow eater, moderately fast eater, or gulper? What do you think is responsible for your eating pattern?
9. To what extent, if any, are your eating habits related to stress? Emotions?
10. What do you consider to be your good eating habits? Poor eating habits?

Body Composition

Objectives

After completing this chapter, you will be able to:

▷ Define body composition.
▷ Define essential and storage fat.
▷ Define and differentiate between obesity and overweight.
▷ Discuss the health implications of regionally distributed fat.
▷ Discuss the limitations of height/weight tables for weight management.
▷ Calculate body mass index and interpret the results.
▷ Describe hydrostatic weighing, bioelectrical impedence, and skinfold measurements as methods for determining body composition.

B ody composition can be divided into two compartments: fat mass and fat-free mass. **Body composition** is the ratio of fat to fat-free mass. Fat-free weight includes all tissues—muscle, bone, blood, organs, fluids—exclusive of fat. Fat, which composes the other compartment, is found in the organs (e.g., brain, heart, liver, lungs) and adipose cells. Adipose cells are fat cells that are located subcutaneously (beneath the skin) and surrounding various body organs.

The majority of fat is found in adipose cells, where it acts as a vast storage depot for energy. A smaller amount of fat is classified as essential because it is a constituent of the nervous system, a component of cell membranes, an insulator against heat loss, and a protection for the internal organs against trauma. A certain amount of essential fat is required for normal biological function. The amount needed differs according to gender requirements. In males, 3% to 5% of their total weight is essential fat, whereas females require 11% to 14% of their total weight as essential fat.[1] The higher female requirement is directly related to fertility and childbearing. Women whose body fat drops below essential requirements, such as gymnasts, ballerinas, long-distance runners and anorexics, will probably become amenorrheic. The period of infertility will continue until weight is gained and essential fat is restored. In both genders, essential fat represents a minimum threshold or lower limit for the maintenance of health.

Obesity

Obesity, or overfatness, is gender specific. For males, **obesity** is defined as body fat equal to or greater than 25% of the total weight of the body, and for females, it is equal to or greater than 32% of the total body weight.[2] These values are arbitrary because an optimal definition of obesity is unknown. The point at which fat storage actually increases health risks has not been determined. Methods of assessing the amount of body fat are indirect, and each contains a degree of measurement error. Most authorities agree with the guidelines set by the American College of Sports Medicine, which state that obesity begins at 30% of total weight for females and between 20% and 25% of total weight for males.[2]

Body fat values of 26% to 31% for females and 19% to 24% for males probably negatively affect health. Table 7-1 presents accepted classifications of percent body fat for adult males and females.

Overweight

Overweight refers to excessive weight for height without regard for body composition. Because the term *overweight* makes no allowances for body composition, it is a poor criterion for deciding desirability of weight loss. For example, well-muscled individuals may be overweight but be lean in regard to

TABLE 7-1 Classification: Percent Body Fat

Males	Females	Classification
<8%	<13%	Lean
8%-15%	13%-20%	Optimal
16%-20%	21%-25%	Slightly overfat
21%-24%	26%-31%	Fat
≥25%	≥32%	Obese

<, Less than; ≥, equal to or greater than.

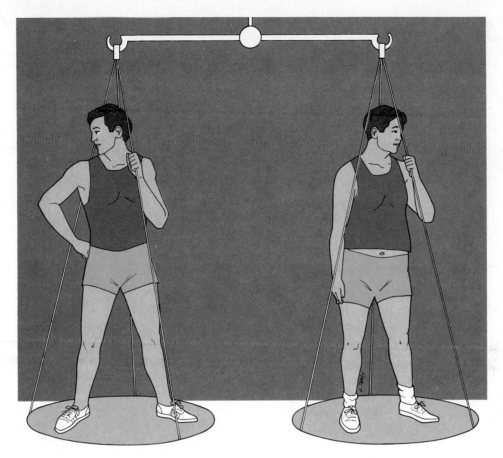

FIGURE 7-1 People who are the same age, height, and gender may weigh the same, but one can be overfat whereas the other is not.

body fat (Figure 7-1). By American social standards, this is healthy, aestheticly pleasing, and desirable. Other individuals may be well within the norms for total body weight but **overfat;** that is, they carry a large proportion of their body weight in the form of fat rather than lean tissue. This is unhealthy and unattractive according to American social standards.

Regional Fat Distribution

The deposition of fat varies among individuals. The amount of fat and the storage sites are influenced by heredity and gender (Figure 7-2). Females generally deposit fat in the buttocks, hips, breasts, and thighs. These preferential sites are largely dictated by the female hormone estrogen.[3] This is known as the *gynoid* or female pattern of fat deposition. Between 15 and 20 extra pounds stored does not seem to be related to the development of chronic disease. Gynoid fat deposition is not confined exclusively to females; a few men deposit fat in this configuration as well.

Because they produce very little estrogen, men deposit minimum amounts of fat in the female pattern. Instead, they primarily store fat in the abdomen, lower back, chest, and nape of the neck. Some females store fat this way as well. After menopause, estrogen production decreases and the prevalence of android fat deposition increases.

The masculine or android pattern of fat deposition is related to an increase in the risk for heart disease, stroke, type II diabetes, and some forms of cancer. There are several reasons for this increased risk. First, enzyme activity in abdominal adipose cells is very active, so fat moves in and out easily. For sedentary individuals, abdominal fat enters the bloodstream and is routed directly to the liver, where it becomes the raw material needed for the manufacture of cholesterol. As serum cholesterol level increases, so does the risk of cardiovascular disease. On the other hand, active people direct abdominal fat to the muscles where it is used as fuel for physical work. The second reason is that abdominal fat cells are large compared with other fat cells. Large fat cells are associated with blood glucose (sugar) in-

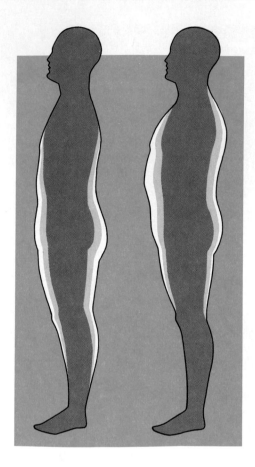

FIGURE 7-2 Feminine versus masculine deposition of fat.

ers. The information obtained from cadaver studies has been used to develop indirect methods for estimating fat content. Because these estimates are indirect, they contain some degree of measurement error and should be interpreted accordingly. These indirect methods are commonly used in exercise physiology laboratories and fitness and wellness centers.

Methods for Measuring Body Composition

Height/Weight Tables

Optimal body weight is not necessarily reflective of optimal body composition. This was illustrated by a comparison of young and middle-aged men who were within 5% of their ideal weight as determined by height, weight, and frame-size charts. Although both groups were within the ideal range, the middle-aged subjects had twice the amount of fat as the young subjects. Height/weight tables and scales are not indicators of body composition, nor are they reliable reference points to use for weight management.

Height/weight tables do not actually measure body composition. They simply act as a standard for total body weight based on height, body frame size, and gender without regard to the composition of weight. These tables are therefore poor criteria for the establishment of weight loss recommendations. The height/weight tables' other limitations include the following:

▶ Body frame sizes were never measured for the thousands of insurance policy holders on whom the charts were developed.

▶ The current tables are more liberal than the former tables with regard to the range of weight to height.

▶ The tables do not reflect the general population. The subjects were predominantly white, middle-class adults aged 25 to 59 who were able to afford private insurance.

▶ The major limitation of the height/weight tables was that no allowances were made for cigarette smoking. Cigarette smokers are lighter in body weight than nonsmokers but have a shorter life expectancy. When some leaner than average people in this analysis died sooner than expected, it was not because of leanness but because many of them were cigarette smokers. The developers of the ta-

tolerance and excessive amounts of insulin in the blood. Such an environment is conducive to the development of type II diabetes. Third, excessive insulin in the blood interferes with the removal of sodium by the kidneys, possibly leading to hypertension.[4]

Fat stored in a android pattern is more easily removed from the body than fat stored in the gynoid pattern. People who store fat in the masculine pattern can usually lose it through exercise. Dietary restriction, although helpful, is often not necessary. Fat stored in the female pattern is highly resistant to removal from its storage depots. Losing gynoid fat usually requires calorie restriction and exercise. Even the best effort may not result in the removal of enough fat from the lower half of the body to suit the dieter. Lower extremity fat is recalcitrant and much more difficult to lose than upper body fat. Complete Assessment Activity 7-1 to determine your fat distribution.

Measurement of Body Fat

The only direct means to measure the fat content of the human body is by chemical analysis of cadav-

bles erroneously concluded that leanness was a detriment to longevity. As a result, they increased the desirable range of weight to height, unwittingly contributing to the perception that mild to moderate overweight is not harmful to health or longevity.

▶ Another serious limitation concerns muscularity. Those who are muscular may be heavier than the recommendations for their height. People in this category should not follow the height/weight tables because they are not at risk. Muscularity is not a risk for premature death but obesity is.

▶ Conversely, sedentary people may be in the desirable weight range for height but carrying a higher than average percentage of fat. The height/weight tables provide a false sense of security for these people because overfat rather than overweight is the risk.

Determination of Body Frame Size

Some of the guesswork associated with using height/weight tables can be eliminated by measuring body frame size. This measurement, however, does not negate the limitations already listed. Measuring frame size is a simple procedure. You measure your ankle above the ankle bones at the smallest circumference with a cloth tape measure. Be sure the tape runs parallel to the floor and pull it tightly around the an-

TABLE 7-2 Determining Body Frame Size*

Frame Size	Male	Female
Small	<8	<7½
Medium	8-9¼	7½-8¾
Large	>9¼	>8¾

<, Less than; >, greater than.
*All measurements are in inches.

kle. Read the tape to the nearest ¼ inch and refer to Table 7-2 to determine your frame size.

Relative Weight

When frame size has been measured, you can refer to Table 7-3 to determine whether you fall in the desirable weight range. Relative weight has been used to define obesity and to make recommendations for weight loss. **Relative weight** is defined as the ratio of actual weight to desirable weight.[5] The desirable weight for height is represented by the midpoint of the range of weight for the individual's height. For example, the desirable weight for a medium-framed female who is 66 inches tall is 137 lb. This is calcu-

TABLE 7-3 Metropolitan Height/Weight Tables 1983 (In Pounds by Height and Frame in Indoor Clothing, Men—5 lb, 1-in Heel; Women—3 lb, 1-in Heel)

	Men				Women		
Height (in)	Small	Medium	Large	Height (in)	Small	Medium	Large
62	128-134	131-141	138-150	58	102-111	109-121	118-131
63	130-136	133-143	140-153	59	103-113	111-123	120-134
64	132-138	135-145	142-156	60	104-115	113-126	122-137
65	134-140	137-148	144-160	61	106-118	115-129	125-140
66	136-142	139-151	146-164	62	108-121	118-132	128-143
67	138-145	142-154	149-168	63	111-124	121-135	131-147
68	140-148	145-157	152-172	64	114-127	124-138	134-151
69	142-151	148-160	155-176	65	117-130	127-141	137-155
70	144-154	151-163	158-180	66	120-133	130-144	140-159
71	146-157	154-166	161-184	67	123-136	133-147	143-163
72	149-160	157-170	164-188	68	126-139	136-150	146-167
73	152-164	160-174	168-192	69	129-142	139-153	149-170
74	155-168	164-178	172-197	70	132-145	142-156	152-173
75	158-172	167-182	176-202	71	135-148	145-159	155-176
76	162-176	171-187	181-207	72	138-151	148-162	158-179

lated by locating the weight range in Table 7-3 for a 66-inch tall female of medium frame. The weight range for her is 130 to 144 lb. The midpoint is equal to the following:

$$144 - 130 = 14 \text{ lb}$$
$$\frac{14}{2} = 7 \text{ lb}$$
$$130 + 7 = 137 \text{ lb}$$
$$\text{(desirable weight)}$$

If the female subject weighed 152 lb for the same height, you need to calculate her relative weight (RW). You divide her body weight by the midpoint of the weight range for the height and frame size:

$$\frac{152 \text{ lb}}{137 \text{ lb}} = 1.109$$

Her relative weight is 110.9%, so she is 10.9% above desirable weight. This method defines obesity as 20% above desirable weight.[2] If this subject weighed only 130 lb, her relative weight would be the following:

$$RW = \frac{130 \text{ lb}}{137 \text{ lb}} = 0.948 \text{ or } 94.8\% \text{ of ideal weight}$$

Complete Assessment Activity 7-2 to determine your relative weight.

Body Mass Index

Another method for measuring body weight status is by **body mass index (BMI).** BMI is the ratio of body weight to height and is expressed in kilograms of weight divided by height in meters squared (kg/m^2). Although BMI does not provide an estimate of percent body fat, it is more useful than the height/weight tables.[6] BMI also uses height/weight data but is more relevant and can be used to compare population groups.[7] It also correlates fairly well (r = 0.70) with percent fat derived from hydrostatic (underwater) weighing.[8]

BMI is easily calculated. However, care should be taken in assessing weight and height. The following are minimal guidelines for determining body weight:

▶ Weigh yourself on a beam scale (physician's scale) that has been calibrated to zero.
▶ Weigh in the morning, after voiding and before eating, while wearing light clothing and no shoes.
▶ Make sure you are not dehydrated.

The following guidelines apply to the assessment of height:

▶ Create a ruler by marking a flat wall in ¼-inch increments starting at 4′6″ up from the floor.
▶ The wall should have no baseboard and the floor should have no carpeting.
▶ Subjects should stand erect, without shoes, and with their heels, buttocks, shoulders, and head against the wall.
▶ Place a right-angle object such as a framing square, a short piece of 2 × 4, or a clipboard on edge against the wall and on top of the subject's head. This should provide a straight edge from head to wall.
▶ Read the rule for height to the nearest ¼ inch.

For example, a 63-inch female weighs 136 lb. Her BMI is calculated as follows:

1. Body weight in pounds is converted to kilograms by dividing it by 2.2:

$$\frac{136 \text{ lb}}{2.2 \text{ lb/kg}} = 61.8 \text{ kg}$$

2. Height in inches is converted to height in meters by multiplying it by 0.0254:

$$63 \text{ in} \times 0.0254 \text{ m/in} = 1.6 \text{ m}$$

3. Enter these two values in the following formula:

$$BMI = \frac{Wt \text{ (kg)}}{Ht \text{ (m}^2)} = \frac{61.8 \text{ kg}}{1.6^2 \text{ m}}$$
$$= \frac{61.8 \text{ kg}}{2.56 \text{ m}^2} = 24.1 \text{ kg/m}^2$$

4. Now turn to Assessment Activity 7-3 to calculate your BMI.

The American College of Sports Medicine has suggested that a BMI of 21 to 23 kg/m^2 is desirable for women and 22 to 24 kg/m^2 is desirable for men.[5] The risk for cardiovascular disease increases significantly when a BMI surpasses 27.3 kg/m^2 for women and 27.8 kg/m^2 for men.[9] Tables 7-4 and 7-5 provide further information regarding BMI and weight classification.[10]

The early Framingham Heart Disease Study investigators found a consistently high relationship among a high BMI and hypertension, high total cholesterol, low high-density lipoprotein cholesterol, high serum triglycerides, and poor glucose intolerance. This is an excellent profile for the development of premature cardiovascular disease. A 26-year follow-up study of the Framingham subjects confirmed the original findings and reinforced the significant correlation between a high BMI and cardiovascular disease.[11]

TABLE 7-4 BMI and Weight Classification—Males

BMI	Classification
<20.7	Underweight
20.8-26.5	Acceptable weight
26.5-27.9	Marginal overweight
27.9-31.2	Overweight
31.2-45.5	Severe overweight
>45.5	Morbid obesity

<, Less than; >, greater than.

TABLE 7-5 BMI and Weight Classification—Females

BMI	Classification
<19.1	Underweight
19.2-25.9	Acceptable weight
25.9-27.4	Marginal overweight
27.4-32.3	Overweight
32.3-44.9	Severe overweight
>44.9	Morbid obesity

<, Less than; >, greater than.

Determining desirable body weight from BMI. If your BMI is high enough to be a risk to health, it should be lowered to an acceptable level. The problem is how much weight should be lost to achieve this value. This is easily determined by following this example. A woman who is 5′3″ tall weighs 160 lb. She has a BMI equal to 28.4 kg/m². Her current BMI poses a health risk and should be reduced to a more healthful 23 kg/m². How much weight does she need to lose to accomplish her goal? The problem is solved as follows:

1. Convert body weight in pounds to kilograms:

$$\frac{160 \text{ lb}}{2.2 \text{ lb/kg}} = 72.7 \text{ kg}$$

2. Convert height in inches to meters:

$$63 \text{ in.} \times 0.0254 \text{ m/in} = 1.6 \text{ m}$$

3. Square the answer to number 2:

$$(1.6 \text{ m})^2 = 2.56 \text{ m}^2$$

4. Desired body weight (DBW) in kg:

$$
\begin{aligned}
\text{DBW} &= \text{Desired BMI} \times \text{Height (m}^2) \\
&= 23 \text{ kg/m}^2 \times 2.56 \text{ m}^2 \\
&= 58.9 \text{ kg}
\end{aligned}
$$

5. Convert desired body weight in kg to lb:

$$58.9 \text{ kg} \times 2.2 \text{ lb/kg} = 129.6 \text{ lb}$$

6. Subtract desired body weight in lb from current body weight in lb to find out how much weight she should lose to reach her desired BMI:

$$160.0 \text{ lb} - 129.6 \text{ lb} = 30.4 \text{ lb}$$

7. Now turn to Assessment Activity 7-4 at the end of this chapter to compute your desired BMI level.

Hydrostatic Weighing

Hydrostatic weighing, one of the most accurate of the measurement techniques, involves weighing subjects while they are completely submerged in water (Figure 7-3). Subjects may contribute to optimal accuracy if they can exhale the maximum amount of air possible from the lungs and can sit still for a 6 to 10 seconds while completely submerged. Accuracy is further enhanced if the technician has the equipment to measure residual air (the amount of air remaining in the lungs after a maximum exhalation).[12]

The equipment required for hydrostatic weighing includes an autopsy scale with a capacity of approximately 8 kg. The scale is suspended over a tank of water that is at least 3 feet deep. The subject sits suspended chin-deep, exhales completely, and bends forward from the waist until entirely submerged. This position is maintained for 6 to 10 seconds to allow the scale to stabilize. From 5 to 10 trials are required, and the underwater weight is attained by averaging the three heaviest readings. The subject's net underwater weight is calculated by subtracting the weight of the seat, its supporting structure, and a weight belt (if needed) from the gross underwater weight.

Bioelectrical impedance. Bioelectrical impedance is a relatively new and simple method of determining body composition. The equipment is portable, computerized, and expensive, but it is safe, noninvasive, quick, and convenient to use (Figure 7-4). A

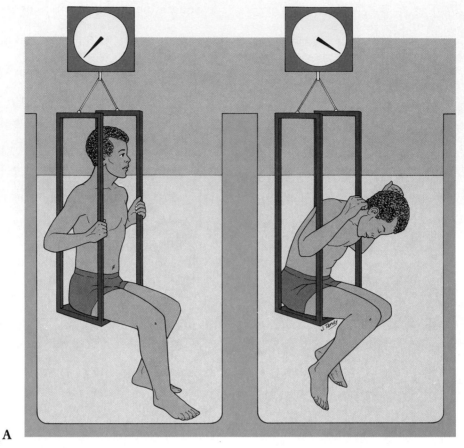

FIGURE 7-3 Underwater weighing apparatus. **A,** Subject in the ready position for underwater weighing. **B,** Subject being weighed.

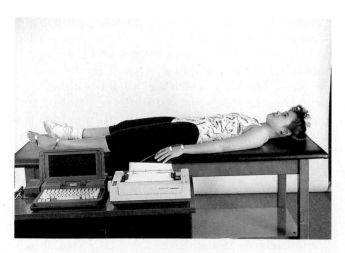

FIGURE 7-4 Bioelectrical impedance.

harmless electrical current is sent through the supine body via electrodes attached to the right hand and foot. Water is an excellent conductor of electricity, whereas fat, which is essentially anhydrous (lacking water), is a nonconductor. Lean body mass includes all tissues of the body except fat, so the two components can be separated. The measurement of electrical conductance or impedance is the tissue resistance to the transmission of an electrical current. The determination of total body water is used to calculate lean weight, fat weight, and percentage of body fat. This measurement correlates with hydrostatic weighing.

Skinfold Measurements

Skinfold measurements are one of the least expensive and most economical methods of measuring body composition. The cost of skinfold calipers ranges from $10 to as much as $450 for computerized models. The most accurate calipers maintain constant jaw pressure of 10 g/mm^2 of jaw surface area.

The thumb and index finger are used to pinch and lift the skin and the fat beneath it. The caliper is placed beneath the pinch (Figures 7-5 through 7-9). You can use Tables 7-6 and 7-7 to convert the sum of millimeters of skinfold thickness to percentage of body fat.

Determining desirable body weight from body fat. Calculating desirable body weight is a simple procedure when the percentage of body fat is known. The following example is for a 148-lb female whose body fat is equal to 30% of her total body weight, based on her skinfold measurements. She wishes to reduce her body fat to 17%. The following are the steps in calculating desirable body weight:

Find fat weight (FW) in pounds:

$$FW\ (lb) = \frac{Body\ weight\ (BW)\ (lb) \times \%\ fat}{100}$$

$$= \frac{148\ lb \times 30}{100}$$

$$= \frac{4440\ lb}{100}$$

$$= 44.4\ lb$$

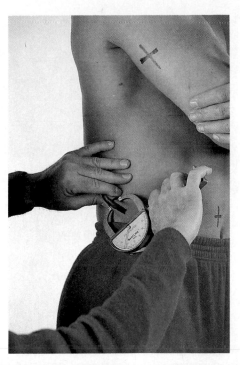

FIGURE 7-5 Suprailium skinfold measurement. Take a diagonal fold above the crest of the ilium directly below the midaxilla (armpit).

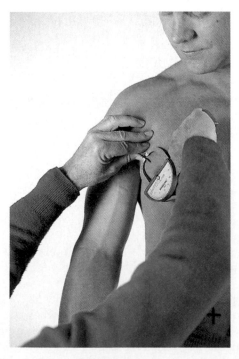

FIGURE 7-6 Chest skinfold measurement. Take a diagonal fold half the distance between the anterior axillary line and the nipple.

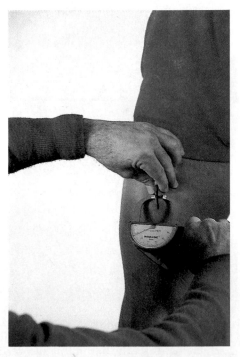

FIGURE 7-7 Thigh skinfold measurement. Take a vertical fold on the front of the thigh midway between the hip and the knee joint. The midpoint should be marked while the subject is seated.

FIGURE 7-8 Abdominal skinfold measurement. Take a vertical fold about 1 inch from the navel.

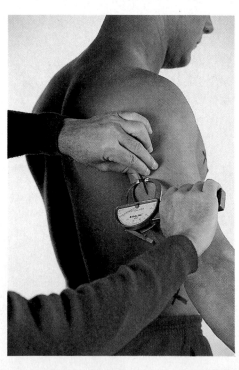

FIGURE 7-9 Triceps skinfold measurement. Take a vertical fold on the midline of the upper arm over the triceps, halfway between the acromion and olecranon processes (tip of the shoulder to the tip of the elbow). The arm should be extended and relaxed when the measurement is taken. All skinfold measurements should be taken on the right side.

Find lean weight (LW) in pounds:

$$LW \text{ (lb)} = BW - FW$$
$$= 148 \text{ lb} - 44.4$$
$$= 103.6 \text{ lb}$$

Find desirable body weight (DBW) in pounds:

$$DBW \text{ (lb)} = \frac{LW \text{ (lb)}}{1.0 - \% \text{ fat desired}}$$

Convert the percentage of fat desired (17%) to a decimal (0.17):

$$= \frac{103.6 \text{ lb}}{1.0 - 0.17}$$
$$= \frac{103.6}{0.83}$$
$$= 124.8 \text{ lb}$$

The method for calculating desirable body weight based on percent body fat is relatively effective if the subject does the following:

▶ Exercises to maintain muscle tissue
▶ Loses no more than 1½ lb per week
▶ Is evaluated for body fatness two to three times during the weight loss period
▶ Understands that indirect measurements of body fatness contain some error

Complete Assessment Activity 7-5 to determine your desirable body weight.

TABLE 7-6 Percentage of Fat Estimated for Men (Sum of Chest, Abdomen, and Thigh Skinfolds)

Sum of Skinfolds (mm)	Age to Last Year								
	Under 22	23-27	28-32	33-37	38-42	43-47	48-52	53-57	Over 57
8-10	1.3	1.8	2.3	2.9	3.4	3.9	4.5	5.0	5.5
11-13	2.2	2.8	3.3	3.9	4.4	4.9	5.5	6.0	6.5
14-16	3.2	3.8	4.3	4.8	5.4	5.9	6.4	7.0	7.5
17-19	4.2	4.7	5.3	5.8	6.3	6.9	7.4	8.0	8.5
20-22	5.1	5.7	6.2	6.8	7.3	7.9	8.4	8.9	9.5
23-25	6.1	6.6	7.2	7.7	8.3	8.8	9.4	9.9	10.5
26-28	7.0	7.6	8.1	8.7	9.2	9.8	10.3	10.9	11.4
29-31	8.0	8.5	9.1	9.6	10.2	10.7	11.3	11.8	12.4
32-34	8.9	9.4	10.0	10.5	11.1	11.6	12.2	12.8	13.3
35-37	9.8	10.4	10.9	11.5	12.0	12.6	13.1	13.7	14.3
38-40	10.7	11.3	11.8	12.4	12.9	13.5	14.1	14.6	15.2
41-43	11.6	12.2	12.7	13.3	13.8	14.4	15.0	15.5	16.1
44-46	12.5	13.1	13.6	14.2	14.7	15.3	15.9	16.4	17.0
47-49	13.4	13.9	14.5	15.1	15.6	16.2	16.8	17.3	17.9
50-52	14.3	14.8	15.4	15.9	16.5	17.1	17.6	18.2	18.8
53-55	15.1	15.7	16.2	16.8	17.4	17.9	18.5	19.1	19.7
56-58	16.0	16.5	17.1	17.7	18.2	18.8	19.4	20.0	20.5
59-61	16.9	17.4	17.9	18.5	19.1	19.7	20.2	20.8	21.4
62-64	17.6	18.2	18.8	19.4	19.9	20.5	21.1	21.7	22.2
65-67	18.5	19.0	19.6	20.2	20.8	21.3	21.9	22.5	23.1
68-70	19.3	19.9	20.4	21.0	21.6	22.2	22.7	23.3	23.9
71-73	20.1	20.7	21.2	21.8	22.4	23.0	23.6	24.1	24.7
74-76	20.9	21.5	22.0	22.6	23.2	23.8	24.4	25.0	25.5
77-79	21.7	22.2	22.8	23.4	24.0	24.6	25.2	25.8	26.3
80-82	22.4	23.0	23.6	24.2	24.8	25.4	25.9	26.5	27.1
83-85	23.2	23.8	24.4	25.0	25.5	26.1	26.7	27.3	27.9
86-88	24.0	24.5	25.1	25.7	26.3	26.9	27.5	28.1	28.7
89-91	24.7	25.3	25.9	26.5	27.1	27.6	28.2	28.8	29.4
92-94	25.4	26.0	26.6	27.2	27.8	28.4	29.0	29.6	30.2
95-97	26.1	26.7	27.3	27.9	28.5	29.1	29.7	30.3	30.9
98-100	26.9	27.4	28.0	28.6	29.2	29.8	30.4	31.0	31.6
101-103	27.5	28.1	28.7	29.3	29.9	30.5	31.1	31.7	32.3
104-106	28.2	28.8	29.4	30.0	30.6	31.2	31.8	32.4	33.0
107-109	28.9	29.5	30.1	30.7	31.3	31.9	32.5	33.1	33.7
110-112	29.6	30.2	30.8	31.4	32.0	32.6	33.2	33.8	34.4
113-115	30.2	30.8	31.4	32.0	32.6	33.2	33.8	34.5	35.1
116-118	30.9	31.5	32.1	32.7	33.3	33.9	34.5	35.1	35.7
119-121	31.5	32.1	32.7	33.3	33.9	34.5	35.1	35.7	36.4
122-124	32.1	32.7	33.3	33.9	34.5	35.1	35.8	36.4	37.0
125-127	32.7	33.3	33.9	34.5	35.1	35.8	36.4	37.0	37.6

TABLE 7-7 Percentage of Fat Estimated for Women (Sum of Triceps, Suprailium, and Thigh Skinfolds)

Sum of Skinfolds (mm)	Age to Last Year								
	Under 22	23-27	28-32	33-37	38-42	43-47	48-52	53-57	Over 57
23-25	9.7	9.9	10.2	10.4	10.7	10.9	11.2	11.4	11.7
26-28	11.0	11.2	11.5	11.7	12.0	12.3	12.5	12.7	13.0
29-31	12.3	12.5	12.8	13.0	13.3	13.5	13.8	14.0	14.3
32-34	13.6	13.8	14.0	14.3	14.5	14.8	15.0	15.3	15.5
35-37	14.8	15.0	15.3	15.5	15.8	16.0	16.3	16.5	16.8
38-40	16.0	16.3	16.5	16.7	17.0	17.2	17.5	17.7	18.0
41-43	17.2	17.4	17.7	17.9	18.2	18.4	18.7	18.9	19.2
44-46	18.3	18.6	18.8	19.1	19.3	19.6	19.8	20.1	20.3
47-49	19.5	19.7	20.0	20.2	20.5	20.7	21.0	21.2	21.5
50-52	20.6	20.8	21.1	21.3	21.6	21.8	22.1	22.3	22.6
53-55	21.7	21.9	22.1	22.4	22.6	22.9	23.1	23.4	23.6
56-58	22.7	23.0	23.2	23.4	23.7	23.9	24.2	24.4	24.7
59-61	23.7	24.0	24.2	24.5	24.7	25.0	25.2	25.5	25.7
62-64	24.7	25.0	25.2	25.5	25.7	26.0	26.7	26.4	26.7
65-67	25.7	25.9	26.2	26.4	26.7	26.9	27.2	27.4	27.7
68-70	26.6	26.9	27.1	27.4	27.6	27.9	28.1	28.4	28.6
71-73	27.5	27.8	28.0	28.3	28.5	28.8	29.0	29.3	29.5
74-76	28.4	28.7	28.9	29.2	29.4	29.7	29.9	30.2	30.4
77-79	29.3	29.5	29.8	30.0	30.3	30.5	30.8	31.0	31.3
80-82	30.1	30.4	30.6	30.9	31.1	31.4	31.6	31.9	32.1
83-85	30.9	31.2	31.4	31.7	31.9	32.2	32.4	32.7	32.9
86-88	31.7	32.0	32.2	32.5	32.7	32.9	33.2	33.4	33.7
89-91	32.5	32.7	33.0	33.2	33.5	33.7	33.9	34.2	34.4
92-94	33.2	33.4	33.7	33.9	34.2	34.4	34.7	34.9	35.2
95-97	33.9	34.1	34.4	34.6	34.9	35.1	35.4	35.6	35.9
98-100	34.6	34.8	35.1	35.3	35.5	35.8	36.0	36.3	36.5
101-103	35.3	35.4	35.7	35.9	36.2	36.4	36.7	36.9	37.2
104-106	35.8	36.1	36.3	36.6	36.8	37.1	37.3	37.5	37.8
107-109	36.4	36.7	36.9	37.1	37.4	37.6	37.9	38.1	38.4
110-112	37.0	37.2	37.5	37.7	38.0	38.2	38.5	38.7	38.9
113-115	37.5	37.8	38.0	38.2	38.5	38.7	39.0	39.2	39.5
116-118	38.0	38.3	38.5	38.8	39.0	39.3	39.5	39.7	40.0
119-121	38.5	38.7	39.0	39.2	39.5	39.7	40.0	40.2	40.5
122-124	39.0	39.2	39.4	39.7	39.9	40.2	40.4	40.7	40.9
125-127	39.4	39.6	39.9	40.1	40.4	40.6	40.9	41.1	41.4
128-130	39.8	40.0	40.3	40.5	40.8	41.0	41.3	41.5	41.8

Summary

- Essential fat is necessary for normal biological function.
- Males carry 3% to 5% of their weight in the form of essential fat; females carry 11% to 14% of their weight as essential fat.
- Obesity is defined as overfatness.
- Males are obese when fat constitutes 25% or more of the body's weight, and females are obese when fat constitutes 32% or more of the body's weight.
- The majority of females store fat in the hips, buttocks, thighs, and breasts (gynoid fat).
- The majority of males store fat in the abdomen, lower back, chest, and nape of the neck (android fat).
- Height/weight tables are limited and poor instruments for weight loss recommendations.

- Relative weight is the ratio of actual weight to desirable weight.
- Body mass index correlates fairly well with percent fat derived from hydrostatic weighing.
- A high body mass index correlates with hypertension, high total cholesterol, low high-density lipoprotein cholesterol, high serum triglycerides, and poor glucose intolerance.
- Bioelectrical impedance is a safe, quick, and relatively accurate method for assessing percent body fat.
- Skinfold measurements are one of the least expensive and most economical methods of measuring body composition in terms of the cost of equipment and the time required to determine percent body fat.

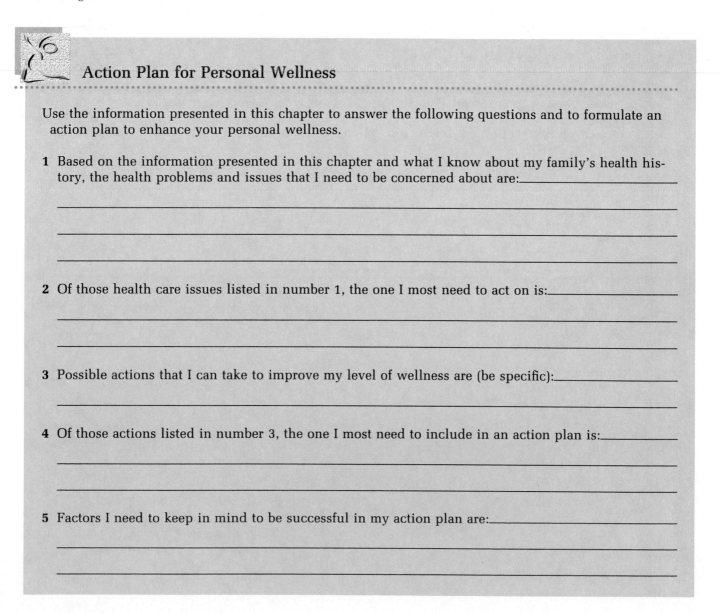

Action Plan for Personal Wellness

Use the information presented in this chapter to answer the following questions and to formulate an action plan to enhance your personal wellness.

1 Based on the information presented in this chapter and what I know about my family's health history, the health problems and issues that I need to be concerned about are:_____

_____

_____

_____

2 Of those health care issues listed in number 1, the one I most need to act on is:_____

_____

_____

3 Possible actions that I can take to improve my level of wellness are (be specific):_____

_____

4 Of those actions listed in number 3, the one I most need to include in an action plan is:_____

_____

_____

5 Factors I need to keep in mind to be successful in my action plan are:_____

_____

_____

Review Questions

1. What is essential fat and how is it distributed in males and females?
2. How would you define obesity and overweight?
3. At what level of fat deposition does obesity become a health hazard for males and females?
4. What are gynoid obesity and android obesity? Which is a greater health risk and why?
5. What are the limitations of height/weight tables for recommending weight loss?
6. What is relative weight and how is it determined?
7. What is body mass index, and how is it classified for men and women?
8. How are hydrostatic weighing, bioelectrical impedance, and skinfold measurements used to determine percent body fat?
9. How is desirable body weight determined when the percent body fat is known?

References

1. Howley ET, Franks BD: *Health fitness instructor's handbook,* Champaign, Ill, 1992, Human Kinetics Books.
2. American College of Sports Medicine: *Guidelines for exercise testing and prescription,* Philadelphia, 1991, Lea & Febiger.
3. Bjorntorp P: Regional patterns of fat distribution, *Ann Intern Med* 103:994-995, 1985.
4. Stamford B: Apples and pears, *Physician Sportsmed* 19:123-124, 1991.
5. National Institutes of Health: Consensus development conference statement: health implications of obesity, *Ann Intern Med* 103:981-1077, 1985.
6. Nieman DC: *Fitness and sports medicine,* Palo Alto, Calif, 1990, Bull Publishing.
7. Davies GJ: *A compendium of isokinetics in clinical usage and rehabilitation techniques,* Onalaska, Wis, 1987, S & S Publishers.
8. Revick DA, Israel RG: Relationship between body mass indices and measures of body adiposity, *Am J Pub Health* 76:992-997, 1986.
9. Wardlaw G, Insel P: *Perspectives in nutrition,* ed 2, St Louis, 1993, Mosby.
10. McArdle WD, Katch FI, Katch VL: *Exercise physiology,* Philadelphia, 1991, Lea & Febiger.

Annotated Readings

ACSM: *Guidelines for exercise testing and prescription,* Philadelphia, 1991, Lea & Febiger.
Discusses the rationale for measuring body composition, several methods for estimating body composition, and a rationale for interpreting body composition measures.

Pears to apples, *Nutr Action Health Letter,* 19(4):4, 1992.
Discusses "pear" shape and "apple" shape. Pear shape is the feminine pattern of fat deposition; apple shape is the masculine pattern. As women experience menopause, body fat increases and more fat is deposited in the masculine pattern. This increases the risk for cardiovascular disease, diabetes, and cancer.

Prentice W: *Fitness for college and life,* St Louis, 1994, Mosby.
Defines body composition and discusses several methods for determining body composition. Presents several laboratory exercises for measuring body composition.

A S S E S S M E N T   A C T I V I T Y   7 - 1

Your Body's Shape

Directions: Do you have an android or a gynoid pattern of fat distribution? This can be calculated quite easily by determining the waist/hip ratio. Measure the circumference of your waist about ½ inch above the navel and measure the circumference of your hips at the greatest protrusion of the buttocks. Divide the waist circumference by the hip circumference. If the number is less than 0.75, you are a gynoid. If it is more than 0.85, you are an android. Numbers between these two values are neutral. A waist/hip ratio above 1.0 for men and above 0.8 for women increases the risk of developing type II diabetes, high blood pressure, coronary heart disease, stroke, and gout. These data suggest that even mild obesity is a risk to health and longevity when fat is deposited in the male pattern.

1. Measure the circumference of your waist: _____.

2. Measure the circumference of your hips: _____

3. Divide the waist measurement by the hip measurement:

$$\frac{\text{Waist}}{\text{Hip}} = \underline{\hspace{1cm}}$$

4. Are you an android or a gynoid or are you in the neutral category?

A S S E S S M E N T   A C T I V I T Y   7 - 2

Calculating Relative Weight Using Height/Weight Tables

Directions: Calculate your relative weight with the following procedure:

1. Determine your body frame size by the following:
   ▶ Pull a measuring tape tightly around the smallest part of the ankle above the ankle bones.
   ▶ Refer to Table 7-2 for frame size.
2. Determine your height and weight following the procedures recommended in this chapter.
3. Refer to Table 7-3 for your frame size and height to find your desirable weight range.
4. Calculate relative weight (RW) by dividing your actual weight by the midpoint of the range in which your weight should fall:

$$RW = \frac{\text{Actual weight}}{\text{Midpoint weight}} = \underline{\hspace{1cm}}$$

5. Move the decimal point two places to the right to interpret your score.

   ▶ Are you underweight, overweight, or ideal weight? _____

   ▶ If you deviate from your ideal, what is the percent of deviation? _____%
   ▶ Are you more than 20% overweight?   Yes   No

Using BMI to Estimate Overweight

Directions: Calculate your BMI by the following procedure:

1. Convert your body weight (BW) in lb to kilograms (kg):

$$\frac{BW\ (lb)}{2.2\ lb/kg} = \underline{\hspace{1.5cm}}\ kg$$

2. Convert height (ht) in inches to meters (m):

$$Ht\ (in) \times 0.0254\ m/in = \underline{\hspace{1.5cm}}m$$

3. Insert the weight (wt) and height (ht) conversions into the following formula:

$$BMI = \frac{Wt\ (kg)}{Ht\ (m^2)} = \underline{\hspace{1.5cm}}\ kg/m^2$$

4. For an interpretation of the results, refer to Table 7-4 for males and Table 7-5 for females.

Using BMI to Estimate Desirable Body Weight

Directions: After completing Assessment Activity 7-3, use those data to determine your optimal body weight according to the BMI calculation. If your BMI is in the desirable range, 21 to 23 kg/m² for females and 22 to 24 kg/m² for males, it will not be necessary for you to make any change.

For you to gain experience in calculating desirable body weight with this method, assume that a friend of yours has asked you to help perform the calculations. Your friend is a male whose data are as follows: He is 5'9" tall, weighs 205 lb, and has a current BMI of 30 kg/m². He would like to find out how much weight he needs to lose to lower his BMI to 22 kg/m².

Anyone whose BMI is outside the desirable range should use their own data to determine the amount of weight to lose to lower their BMI to an optimal level. Follow the steps below to find your desirable body weight (DBW):

1. Your current BMI is $\underline{\hspace{1cm}}$ kg/m²
2. Your weight in kg is $\underline{\hspace{1cm}}$ kg
3. Your height in m² is $\underline{\hspace{1cm}}$ m²
4. Your desirable weight in kg is found by:

$$DBW = Desired\ BMI \times Height\ (m^2) = \underline{\hspace{1cm}} \times \underline{\hspace{1cm}} = \underline{\hspace{1cm}}\ kg$$

5. Convert DBW from kg to lbs:

$$\underset{\text{(DBW)}}{\underline{\hspace{1.5cm}}}\ kg \times 2.2\ lb/kg = \underset{\text{(DBW)}}{\underline{\hspace{1.5cm}}}\ lb$$

6. Subtract DBW (lb) from current body weight (lb) to find out how much weight must be lost to reach a BMI of 22 kg/m²:

Current body weight (lb) $\underline{\hspace{1cm}}$ − DBW (lb) $\underline{\hspace{1cm}}$ = Amount of weight to lose (lb) $\underline{\hspace{1cm}}$

ASSESSMENT ACTIVITY   7 - 5

Calculating Desirable Body Weight from Percent Body Fat

Directions: To find your desirable body weight, insert your current weight, percentage of fat, and the desirable body fat that you wish to attain in the appropriate spaces below. Then calculate fat weight, lean weight, and desirable body weight. Subtract desirable body weight from your current weight. This tells you how much weight you must lose to achieve your desirable percentage of body fat.

Current weight = _____ lb

Current percentage of body fat = _____ %

Desirable body fat = _____ %

1. Fat weight

$$= \frac{\text{Body weight} \times \text{Percentage of fat}}{100}$$

= _____

2. Lean weight
   = Body weight − Fat weight
   = _____

3. Desirable body weight

$$= \frac{\text{Lean weight}}{1.0 - \text{Percentage of fat desired}}$$

= _____ lb

4. Amount of weight to lose = _____ lb

Overcoming the Diet and Weight Obsession

Key terms

anorexia nervosa

basal metabolic rate (BMR)

bulimia

essential fat

hyperplasia

hypertrophy

setpoint

thermic effect of food (TEF)

weight cycling

Objectives

After completing this chapter, you will be able to:

▶ Define obesity and overweight.

▶ Describe the development of adipose cells.

▶ Discuss the role of genetics, diet, exercise, and behavior modification in weight management.

▶ Identify and discuss the health aspects of obesity.

▶ Define and identify eating disorders and their symptoms and treatment.

mericans are obsessed with body weight and dieting. Why are we so preoccupied, how have we gotten into such a predicament, and what are appropriate solutions to weight management? This chapter attempts to answer these and other important questions.

The Changing Ideal: Thinness on the Wane

American society is constantly changing. Just a few years ago the slogan was "thin is in." Today, the fit and muscular look is gaining momentum and the thin look is on the way out.[1] From a health and an aesthetic perspective, this represents a long overdue change. Many dieters starved themselves in an effort to attain an ultrathin silhouette, and many failed, harming their body image and ego. More women than men pursued the ultrathin ideal, which was unattainable for most, despite sacrificial efforts.

The thinness mania, pervasive since the 1960s, is finally relenting. Although ultrathinness was unachievable or unmaintainable for the majority of dieters, physical fitness is within the grasp of most if not all people. The pursuit of physical fitness develops large energy reserves and confers health benefits that reduce the risks associated with many chronic diseases. In addition, the processes leading to development of physical fitness naturally encourage leanness.

The fact that Americans are overweight and obsessed with dieting is reflected in the number of people trying to change their physical appearance. Approximately 24% of men and 27% of women between the ages of 20 and 74 years weigh at least 20% more than what is recommended by nutritionists.[2]

These people meet or exceed the definition of clinical obesity as determined by the National Institutes of Health (NIH). Nearly 90% of Americans judge their weight to be excessive, and approximately 35% want to lose at least 15 pounds. A total of 24% of American men and 40% of women are dieting at any given time; an average 2.3 diets are attempted per year. Many Americans attempting to achieve their perceived optimal size are using approaches guaranteed to fail. A total of 90% to 95% of all dieters regain all or most of the weight that was lost within 5 years.[3]

In the United States, between 15% to 25% of children are overweight, and approximately 15% of adolescents are obese.[4] These figures are 40% higher than 25 years ago.[5] This trend was also observed in the National Children and Youth Fitness Study (NCYFS).[6] Skinfold measures on elementary-school children were significantly higher in 1986 than they were 20 years ago. The obsession with weight control permeates all age groups. Of fourth-grade girls, 80% have had at least one experience with dieting.

Factors That Affect Body Weight

Diet, exercise, and heredity are the major factors associated with the loss or gain of body weight. Until recently, advice to overfat persons was imprecise. For example, the suggestion to "cut back on calories" does not provide information on the nutritional changes appropriate for successful weight management. The term *weight loss* is also too generic and implies that indiscriminate weight loss—liquid, fat, and protein—represents a successful program. Advice to weight watchers can be enhanced by including the following points:

▶ The success of a weight-management program should be measured by the amount of fat lost rather than by muscle or fluid loss.

▶ The term *weight loss* should be replaced by the more specific term *fat-weight loss*.

▶ Calories from fatty foods and calorically dense and nutritionally poor foods, such as alcohol and sugar-laden snacks, should be reduced. The proportion of calories derived from foods high in complex carbohydrates, such as potatoes and pasta, should be increased. The **thermic effect of food (TEF)** represents the amount of energy required by the body to digest, absorb, metabolize, and store nutrients. It is equivalent to 5% to 10% of total calories consumed.[4] The thermic effects of carbohydrate and protein are higher than fat (Figure 8-1). Therefore converting dietary fat into fat stores takes less energy than converting glucose into glycogen or amino acids into protein. (Examples of high-fat foods are given in Assessment Activity 8-1.)

▶ Exercise that meets the prescribed specifications for fat loss should be an integral component of the program.

▶ Behavior-modification strategies can positively supplement a successful program.

Figure 8-1 Dietary Fat Versus Dietary Carbohydrate

Dietary fat promotes fat storage in the body. The body expends only 3 calories to convert an extra 100 calories of dietary fat to storage fat.[7] Fat storage is accelerated if dietary fat is combined with simple sugar in the same meal, such as a hamburger with a sugared cola drink. Sugar triggers the release of extra insulin. Insulin activates fat cell enzymes that promote movement of fat from the blood to the fat cells. On the other hand, the ingestion of an extra 100 calories of complex carbohydrates requires that the body expend 25 calories to convert it to fat for storage. The conversion process for carbohydrates is more costly than that for fats and provides another reason for reducing fat consumption and increasing carbohydrate consumption.

▶ Successful, permanent weight loss is rarely the result of following a diet for a specific period; rather it is the result of healthy lifestyle changes that can be pursued throughout a lifetime.

Development of Obesity

Adipose cells (fat cells) grow by **hypertrophy** (an increase in size) and **hyperplasia** (an increase in number). Obesity occurs when fat cells increase excessively in size and/or number. Obesity that results from an increase in the size of fat cells is hypertrophic, obesity that results from an increase in the number of fat cells is hyperplastic, and obesity that results from an increase in both is hypertrophic/hyperplastic.

Adipose cells follow a normal pattern of growth and development. When obesity develops in infancy or childhood (juvenile-onset obesity), the person develops more adipose cells and each cell grows greatly, resulting in hypertrophic/hyperplastic obesity. When obesity develops in adulthood (adult-onset obesity), the person usually ends up with a normal number of adipose cells, but each cell contains a large amount of fat (Table 8-1). In extreme cases, adult-onset obesity can be both hyperplastic and hypertrophic.[4] Once filled with fat, fat cells do not disappear in the adult state.

Adipose cells have a long lifespan. If adult obesity is both hypertrophic and hyperplastic, is it more

Many people today are preoccupied with their weight.

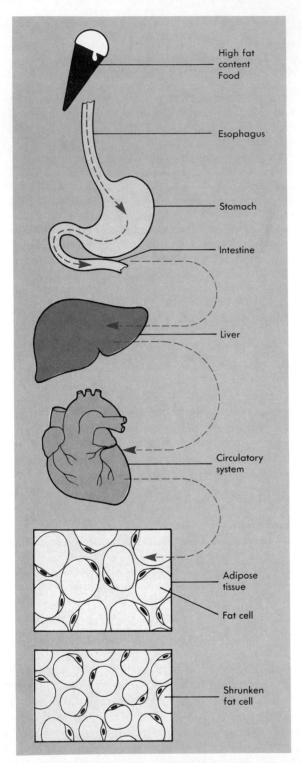

TABLE 8-1 Classification of Obesity

Type	Description
Juvenile-onset obesity	Caused by an increase in both the number (hyperplastic) and size (hypertrophic) of fat cells
Adult-onset obesity	Caused primarily by an increase in size of fat cells (hypertrophic)
Other types	Caused by endocrine and/or genetic disorders such as hypothyroidism, brain tumors, and Turner syndrome

FIGURE 8-2 Fat can be manufactured in the body from any food and stored when caloric intake exceeds expenditure. Fat droplets travel to the liver from the stomach and intestines and then enter the circulatory system where they are delivered to the cells and organs. Excess fats are stored in adipose tissue. When more energy is needed, fats are released from adipose cells. If the energy needs continue, the cells will shrink.

difficult to lose weight than if adult obesity is due to hypertrophy alone? Some evidence indicates that an increased number of fat cells increases the body's reluctance to reduce fat stores. The needs of adipose cells may require that they store at least nominal amounts of fat. More fat cells would then result in more fat storage, complicating efforts to lose weight. The longer a person remains obese, the more difficult it is to correct the problem (Figure 8-2).

Gender differences in depositing subcutaneous fat become noticeable during and after puberty. Males distribute fat primarily in the upper half of the body, and females tend to deposit it in the lower half. The percentage of fat in the body reaches peak values during early adolescence for males and then declines during the remainder of adolescent growth. Females experience a continuous increase in the percentage of fat from the onset of puberty to age 18.

From approximately 2 years of age, obese children develop a greater number of fat cells than children of normal weight. Some evidence had suggested that overfeeding during infancy stimulates development of excess fat cells and predisposes affected children to later obesity. However, more recent evidence refutes this idea. Most obese infants become normal-weight preschoolers. Although the majority of obese children do not become obese adults, 70% of obese adults were obese children. Approximately 80% to 90% of obesity is thought to be adult onset.[4]

Causes of Obesity

Obesity is a complex eating disorder with multiple causes, including heredity, diet, lack of exercise, and behavioral considerations. It was formally declared a disease by the National Institutes of Health Development Conference in 1985.

The laws of thermodynamics state that energy cannot be destroyed; it is used for work or converted into another form. Accordingly, the progressive accumulation of stored fat in the body is the result of consumption of more calories (energy) than are expended. Food energy in excess of the body's need is converted to fat and is stored in adipose cells. This relationship applies to almost all individuals. For the majority of people, excessive caloric intake and deficient energy expenditure are responsible for their obesity.

The Effects of Genetics

Studies of adoptees. The genetic influence on weight control is becoming more clearly established. Researchers at the University of Pennsylvania examined the relative obesity and the body type of adults who had been adopted during childhood.[8] They classified 540 adoptees in the following categories: thin, median weight, overweight, and obese. They found that the subjects resembled their biological parents rather than their adoptive parents even though they learned and practiced the lifestyle of their adoptive parents.

Studies of identical twins. The same research team from the University of Pennsylvania studied identical and fraternal male twins for more than 25 years.[9] Height, weight, and *body mass index (BMI)*, a measure of relative obesity, were measured when the subjects entered the military and 25 years later. *Identical twins* are excellent subjects for these studies because they have identical genetic makeups. Any physical differences that occur in one of a pair of identical twins can be attributed to environmental and/or lifestyle factors. The identical twins in this study were very similar in height, weight, and BMI when they entered the military and again 25 years later. Each member of the pair gained the same amount of weight at approximately the same time in life. The similarity in the identical twins was twice that observed in *fraternal twins* (twins who emanate from separate eggs and do not have identical genes). This supports the idea that obesity and fat deposition are significantly influenced by genetics. Another group of researchers fed identical twins 1000 calories per day more than they needed for 100 days.[10] Food consumption and physical activity were closely monitored. Each member of the set gained about the same amount of weight, and their weight was distributed in the same places. The amount and distribution of weight gain also seemed to be controlled by genetic factors. Studies indicate that at least 60% of the reason a person weighs a certain weight is related to inherited factors.[11]

The setpoint theory. The setpoint theory of weight control also reflects the role of genetics. Proponents of this theory suggest that the body works to maintain a certain weight. More specifically, each person has an internal **setpoint** for fatness that the body seems to regulate by adjusting hunger, appetite, food intake, and energy expenditure. Researchers have demonstrated that human and animal subjects who have been put on low-calorie and/or high-calorie diets lose and gain only to a certain level. When the diet ends, they spontaneously return to their approximate original weight.

Dieting denies the body, so it takes a conscious effort to ignore natural signals to eat. Interestingly, dieting does not seem to lower the setpoint. Americans are consuming about 10% fewer calories today than 20 years ago, yet they weigh about 4 to 5 pounds more.

Some proponents of the setpoint theory suggest that because some people are genetically programmed to have unwanted pounds, efforts to eliminate fat with diet, exercise, or both are doomed.[12] The body can shut down its calorie-losing mechanism by lowering metabolism and can stimulate appetite to the point that a person must have food.

Other proponents of the setpoint theory argue that vigorous regular exercise lowers the setpoint and thereby lowers the level of fat that the body will accept and defend. Exercise induces the body to stabilize at a lower body weight, which is precisely what dieters are trying to do. This is a classic case of a genetic inclination being modified through appropriate lifestyle behavior. It supports the idea that heredity is not destiny. Living a healthy life—through regular exercise, sound nutritional habits, and maintenance of normal weight—cannot negate heredity, but it can modify it.

The Effects of Diet

Statistics show that dieting is the method of choice for most Americans trying to lose weight. Although dieting usually works only temporarily, most people who have failed to maintain weight loss are willing to try again. Many people seek the miraculous diet that will transform them from fat to thin, preferably with minimal effort and in the shortest time possible.

The success rate of diet-only strategies is dismal.

Only 5% of all dieters are successful in reducing to a target weight and maintaining that weight for more than 1 year.[12] Maintaining postdiet weight is one of the major failures of weight loss through dieting because dieters do not learn the habits and behaviors needed to remain at the new weight. As a result they lose and regain weight many times in their lives. This pattern of repeated weight loss and gain, known as **weight cycling,** yo-yo, and seesaw approaches to weight loss, is potentially harmful and counterproductive.

In a review of the literature throughout 1991 on weight cycling, Wing[13] concluded that contrary to popular opinion, there did not appear to be any negative effects of cycle dieting on total body fat, the distribution of fat, or metabolism. Subsequent efforts to lose weight also appeared to be unaffected. However, evidence suggests that weight cycling increases the risk of death, especially from cardiovascular conditions.

Researchers at Harvard University[14] studied data on 11,703 subjects over 30 years to see whether weight cycling had any effect on longevity. As expected, those whose weight remained stable had a lower mortality rate. However, those who lost weight were more likely to die than those who gained weight. Men who gained more than 11 pounds were 36% more likely to die than those whose weight remained stable. The men who lost more than 11 pounds, however, had a 57% higher chance of dying. The explanation proposed was that those who had lost 11 pounds over the decade had actually gained and lost an average of 100 pounds over their lifetimes. The stress of yo-yo dieting contributed to the higher death rates. Ideally, it is better to lose weight and keep it off. However, with the high recidivism rate of dieters, the researchers concluded that it is probably better to remain slightly overweight than to weight cycle.

The goals of a weight-loss program are to lose fat weight and to retain or gain muscle weight. This cannot be accomplished by diet-only approaches to weight loss. This concept was exemplified almost 20 years ago in a study of young and middle-aged overweight women who were grouped into three weight-loss strategies, each configured to produce a conservative 1-pound loss per week.[15] Table 8-2 presents the results of this study.

All three groups lost essentially the same amount of body weight. The important outcome was that 2.4 pounds, or 21% of the total amount of weight lost by the diet-only group, was in the form of lean tissue. This occurred despite a nutritionally sound diet of modest caloric restriction. The other two groups lost fat and gained rather than lost lean tissue. Main-

TABLE 8-2 Average Weight Lost by Groups

Weight-loss Strategy	Fat Tissue Loss (lb)	Lean Tissue Change (lb)	Total Weight Loss (lb)
Diet only	−9.3	−2.4	−11.7
Exercise only	−12.6	+2.0	−10.6
Diet and exercise	−13.0	+1.0	−12.0

+, Gain; −, loss.

taining the strength of the muscular system and/or enhancing it while losing weight is crucial to success.

Diets very low in calories (800 calories per day or fewer), including those that have been promoted as having a "protein-sparing effect" (conserving lean tissue), have often been associated with serious medical complications, including *cardiac arrhythmias* (irregular heart rate that is sometimes intractable) and sudden death.[16] Diets very low in calories produce distinctive and abnormal *electrocardiographic (ECG)* rhythm patterns that are most likely caused by protein loss from the *myocardium* (heart muscle) and/or cell-membrane instability from rapid weight loss.[17]

Low-calorie diets (800 to 1000 calories per day) result in atrophy of the heart muscle. When low-calorie diets are accompanied by regular exercise, the muscle loss is minimized, but it still occurs.[18] However, regular exercise combined with a *moderate-calorie diet* (1300 to 1600 calories per day) results in loss of body weight and gain of cardiac muscle. Exercise-induced cardiac hypertrophy results in a stronger, more efficient heart.

Some obese people seem to be diet resistant in that their weight stays the same even when caloric intake is low. Several factors may be responsible, including an underactive thyroid, a slow metabolism, and a hereditary tendency toward obesity. Some studies suggest another reason: the underreporting of food consumption and overreporting of physical activity. In one study, researchers[19] found that subjects on a low-calorie diet underestimated their food intake by 47% and overestimated their physical activity by 51%.

A popular assumption is that obese people eat more than people of normal weight. However, evidence indicates that they usually eat no more and

TABLE 8-3 Food Substitutions That Reduce Fat, Cholesterol, and Calories

Instead of eating	Substitute	To save*
1 croissant	1 plain bagel	35 calories, 10 g fat, 13 mg cholesterol
1 cup cooked egg noodles	1 cup cooked macaroni	50 mg cholesterol
1 whole egg	1 egg white	65 calories, 6 g fat, 220 mg cholesterol
1 oz cheddar cheese	1 oz part-skim mozzarella	35 calories, 4 g fat, 15 mg cholesterol
1 oz cream cheese	1 oz cottage cheese (1% fat)	74 calories, 9 g fat, 29 mg cholesterol
1 teaspoon whipping cream	1 tablespoon evaporated skim milk, whipped	32 calories, 5 g fat
3.5 oz skinless roast duck	3.5 oz skinless roast chicken	46 calories, 7 g fat
3.5 oz beef tenderloin, choice, untrimmed, broiled	3.5 oz beef tenderloin, select, trimmed, broiled	75 calories, 10 g fat
3.5 oz lamb chop, untrimmed, broiled	3.5 oz lean leg of lamb, trimmed, broiled	219 calories, 28 g fat
3.5 oz pork spare ribs, cooked	3.5 oz lean pork loin, trimmed, broiled	157 calories, 17 g fat
1 oz regular bacon, cooked	1 oz Canadian bacon, cooked	111 calories, 12 g fat
1 oz hard salami	1 oz extra-lean roasted ham	75 calories, 8 g fat
1 beef frankfurter	1 chicken frankfurter	67 calories, 8 g fat
3 oz oil-packed tuna, light	3 oz water-packed tuna, light	60 calories, 6 g fat
1 regular-size serving french fries	1 medium-size baked potato	125 calories, 11 g fat
1 oz oil-roasted peanuts	1 oz roasted chestnuts	96 calories, 13 g fat
1 oz potato chips	1 oz thin pretzels	40 calories, 9 g fat
1 oz corn chips	1 oz plain, air-popped popcorn	125 calories, 9 g fat
1 tablespoon sour-cream dip	1 tablespoon bottled salsa	20 calories, 3 g fat
1 glazed doughnut	1 slice angel-food cake	110 calories, 13 g fat, 21 mg cholesterol
3 chocolate sandwich cookies	3 fig-bar cookies	4 g fat
1 oz unsweetened chocolate	3 tablespoons cocoa powder	73 calories, 13 g fat
1 cup ice cream (premium)	1 cup sorbet	320 calories, 34 g fat, 100 mg cholesterol

*The values listed are the most significant savings; smaller differences are not shown. Weight given for meats are edible portions.

sometimes eat less than normal-weight people.[20] Studies of obese people have shown that their weight gain began when a decrease in physical activity, not an increase in food consumption, occurred. This pattern is frequently observed in people who are establishing a career. Although appetite and food consumption are not increased, the time once devoted to physical activity decreases, resulting in an imperceptible yet relentless weight gain.

In general, dieting is an ineffective weight-management method. The expectation that temporary changes in eating habits will lead to permanent weight loss is unrealistic. Sensible and permanent dietary changes that depend on wise food choices are not only an excellent way to cut calories but also a healthy way to eat. (Table 8-3 demonstrates how to reduce calories that come from fat and cholesterol by making appropriate substitutions.)

A variety of diets. Many diets on the market are nutritionally sound, and many are not. Some are potentially hazardous, and many are based on faulty nutritional and physiological concepts. Some require that food be eaten in a certain order and severely restrict allowable foods. Diets like Jenny Craig come in premeasured servings. Some require medical supervision. Others impose unrealistic demands on caloric restrictions, and still others make promises based more on fantasy than facts (Table 8-4). The Food and Drug Administration (FDA)

TABLE 8-4 Popular Diets

Type	Description	Weight Loss	Health Drawbacks	Pros/Cons
Balanced (available in book stores)				
Weight Watchers Quick Success Program (Weight Watchers International) Jane Fonda's New Workout & Weight Loss Program I Don't Eat (But I Can't Lose Weight) Complete University Medical Diet Jane Brody's Nutrition Book Fit or Fat Target Diet Popcorn Plus Diet Getting Thin Setpoint Diet Nautilus Diet Take Off Pounds Sensibly (TOPS) Overeaters Anonymous	Recommends 1000 or more calories/day; provides at least 50% carbohydrate, less than 30% fat, 15% to 20% protein; includes variety of foods from all food groups; requires regular exercise and lifestyle changes	1 to 2 lb/week, promotion of permanent loss of fat, especially if combined with regular exercise	None (no side effects in healthy people); includes adequate amount of food in all major food groups; no specialized medical supervisions necessary in healthy people	Provides variety and good nutrition; combined with exercise, can be used as a basis of lifelong weight control; no vitamin supplementation necessary; weight lost is fat, not muscle
High carbohydrate				
Bloomingdale's Eat Healthy Diet Pritikin Permanent Weight Loss Manual	Involves varying calorie levels, encourages increasing carbohydrate intake to more than 60% of diet, can severely restrict protein and fat intake, often advocates exercise and positive lifestyle changes	Gradual or rapid, depending on caloric intake	May be too low in protein and require vitamin and mineral supplements	Are safe and effective if protein level and caloric intake are adequate; may be so restrictive that they are difficult to maintain
Formula/Rx*				
HMR (Health Management Resources) Medifast Optifast	Suggests only 800 calories or less/day; requires dieters to forgo food for about 12 weeks and eat only a protein supplement; after initial fast, gradually reintroduces food; may encourage exercise and lifestyle changes	Very rapid, 3 to 4 lb/week; protein supplements claimed to reduce loss of muscle tissue; unknown whether dieters keep weight off	Can produce severe metabolic disturbances, heart beat irregularities, hair loss, dehydration, kidney problems, and sense of feeling cold; vitamins and mineral supplements required	Are expensive, with costs as high as $500 per month; only for obese people (20% or more overweight), for those with a weight-related health problem, or for those who have failed on other diets; requires close medical supervision

Type of diet / Examples	Description	Weight loss	Disadvantages	Other effects
Formula/OTC (over the counter) Nutrament Slender Slim Fast	May advocate less than 1000 calories/day, replaces one or more meals with a low-calorie shake or food bar that contains some combination of protein, carbohydrates, fats, vitamins, minerals	Can be rapid, 3 or more lb/week if daily caloric level falls below 1000; possible promotion of water and muscle loss; weight often regained	May be low in protein, carbohydrates, vitamins, or minerals; can be dangerous if used for sole source of nutrition	Teaches reliance on patented products, not on sound, lifelong eating habits
Low carbohydrate/high protein Dr. Atkins' Diet Revolution Complete Scarsdale Medical Diet Doctor's Quick Weight Loss Diet (Stillman's "water diet") 35-Plus Diet for Women Calories Don't Count Wild Weekend Diet Drinking Man's Diet Four Day Wonder Diet	Involves varying calorie level, severely restricts carbohydrates such as bread, cereals, grains, starchy vegetables	Rapid, 3 or more lb/week; promotion of loss of water and muscle tissue; weight usually regained	Is usually unbalanced; may be very high in saturated fat and cholesterol, can cause fatigue, headaches, nausea, dehydration, and dizziness	Does not promote good eating habits, nutritional claims are unsound
Very low calorie Diet Principal Rotation Diet	Suggests less than 1000 calories/day for part of diet or for its entirety, is based on low-fat, high-carbohydrate foods	Rapid, 3 or more lb/week; initial loss of water and muscle, not fat; weight usually regained	May be unbalanced and require vitamin and mineral supplements	Usually does not teach long-term good eating habits
Novelty diets Beverly Hills Diet Fit for Life Rice Diet Report Dr. Berger's Immune Power Diet Dr. Debetz Champagne Diet The Rotation Diet The Junk Food Diet Sun Sign Diet The Ultrafit Diet The Diet Bible The Love Diet Eat to Succeed Eat to Win	Usually involves less than 1000 calories/day, often makes false claims that specific foods or combinations burn fat, suggests eating one type of food to exclusion of others	Can be rapid, depending on caloric intake; weight generally regained	Are unbalanced; may be dangerously low in protein; are often deficient in vitamins and minerals; can result in dizziness, diarrhea, gas, hair loss, brittle nails, and loss of vital muscle tissue	Are based on unsound nutritional guidelines, weight is lost because of reduction in calories, can be dangerous, may be extremely restrictive and monotonous, may lead to binging

*Available through a physician or hospital-run program.

does not investigate every new fad diet, and many diet plans are published without the FDA's endorsement. A diet that has been published usually means that a publisher sees potential profits from its sales. Publishers know that the advice "eat less fat and increase physical activity" will not sell books but fad diets with secret ingredients and/or magic formulas will.

Because fad diets are unlikely to disappear, identifying some of the characteristics and marketing strategies used by diet promoters to appeal to unwitting consumers is helpful[4]:

▶ They promote quick results.
▶ They stress eating one type of food to the exclusion of others.
▶ They emphasize gimmick approaches such as eating food in a particular order.
▶ They cite anecdotes and testimonials usually involving well-known people.
▶ They claim to be a panacea for everyone.
▶ They often promote a secret ingredient.
▶ They often recommend expensive supplements.
▶ They rarely emphasize permanent changes in eating habits.
▶ They usually show little concern for accepted principles of good nutrition (see Chapter 6).
▶ They are usually cynical of the evidence that comes from the scientific community.

The modern lifestyle fosters unfitness.

The Effects of Exercise

Exercise has been one of the most neglected aspects of weight management. Not long ago, exercise was often discouraged because of the mistaken belief that it would stimulate the dieter's appetite. A second unfounded idea was that the calories used during physical activity were too few to have a substantial effect on weight loss. The consensus was that the results were not worth the effort. Fortunately, most people realize that these assertions are erroneous. Today, research evidence regarding the effectiveness of exercise in weight management is extremely compelling. Most authorities agree that the prevalence of obesity in the United States is primarily due to physical inactivity—not overeating.

In the early 1900s, physical fitness was essential, and fit people were the rule rather than the exception. Physical activity was integrated into work, play, and home life. Tilling the soil, digging ditches, and working in factories were physically demanding jobs. Lumberjack contests and square dances were vigorous leisure pursuits. Taking care of home and family required long hours at strenuous tasks. One third of the energy for operating factories came from muscle power.

Today, most Americans live sedentary lives. Scientific and technological advances have led to labor-saving devices that decrease the need for physical activity. Less than 1% of the energy for operating factories comes from muscle power. Devices such as mechanized golf carts have made leisure activities less strenuous. Each new invention fosters a receptive attitude toward a life of ease. The mechanized way is generally the most expedient way, and in the time-oriented American society, this has become another reason to indulge in a sedentary lifestyle. Exercise for fitness is now separate from other parts of life. Although the basic need for physical activity has not changed, people must commit themselves to exercising regularly.

Exercise uses calories. One of the obvious benefits of exercise is that it burns calories. They are consumed according to body weight, so heavier people burn more calories per minute than lighter people for the same activity (Figure 8-3). Table 8-5 includes some physical fitness activities and a few common physical activities. To use it, multiply your body weight by the coefficient in the calories/min/lb column and then multiply this value by the number of minutes spent participating in the activity. For example, to determine the calories expended by a 170-pound person who walks at 4.5 mph for 30 minutes, do the following:

FIGURE 8-3 Physical activities are more difficult for the obese but, because of their size, they burn more calories per unit of exercise.

TABLE 8-5 Estimated Caloric Cost of Selected Activities

Activity	Calories/min/lb*
Aerobic dance (vigorous)	0.062
Basketball (vigorous, full-court)	0.097
Bathing, dressing, undressing	0.021
Bed-making (and stripping)	0.031
Bicycling (13 mph)	0.071
Canoeing (flat water, 4 mph)	0.045
Chopping wood	0.049
Cleaning windows	0.024
Cross-country skiing (8 mph)	0.104
Gardening	
Digging	0.062
Hedging	
Raking	0.034
Weeding	0.038
Golf (twosome carrying clubs)	0.045
Handball (skilled, singles)	0.078
Horseback riding (trot)	0.052
Ironing	0.029
Jogging (5 mph)	0.060
Laundry (taking out and hanging)	0.027
Mopping floors	0.024
Peeling potatoes	0.019
Piano playing	0.018
Rowing (vigorous)	0.097
Running (8 mph)	0.104
Sawing wood (crosscut saw)	0.058
Shining shoes	0.017
Shoveling snow	0.052
Snowshoeing (2.5 mph)	0.060
Soccer (vigorous)	0.097
Swimming (55 yd/min)	0.088
Table tennis (skilled)	0.045
Tennis (beginner)	0.032
Walking (4.5 mph)	0.048
Writing while seated	0.013

*Multiply calories/min/lb by your body weight in pounds and then multiply that product by the number of minutes spent in the activity.

1. Multiply body weight by calories/min/lb:

   170 lb × 0.048 calories/min/lb = 8.16 calories/min

2. Multiply calories/min by the exercise time in minutes:

   8.16 calories/min × 30 min = 244.8 calories

Body fat contains about 3500 calories per pound. Fat storage, however, which includes some lean support tissue—muscle, connective tissues, blood supply, and other body components—represents approximately 2700 calories per pound.[4] If this person performs this exercise daily, 1 pound will be lost in approximately 11 days or 33 pounds in 1 year, provided caloric intake is unchanged. The annual weight loss is calculated as follows:

$$\frac{2700 \text{ calories/lb}}{245 \text{ calories/day}} = 11.02 \text{ days/lb}$$

$$\frac{365 \text{ days/year}}{11.02 \text{ days/lb}} = 33.1 \text{ lb/year}$$

Follow the example in Assessment Activity 8-2 and

Technological advances have contributed to a sedentary lifestyle.

apply the directions to your situation or to a hypothetical situation.

Aerobic exercises such as walking, jogging, cycling, swimming, and rowing contribute significantly to weight loss. According to the American College of Sports Medicine (ACSM), optimal benefits are derived from activities that burn 300 to 500 calories per exercise session. Minimal guidelines for maintaining fitness and losing weight require 300 calories per exercise session performed at least three times per week or 200 calories per session performed at least four times per week.[21] Added weight loss can be accomplished by increasing the length of each exercise session and/or the number of sessions per week. High-intensity activities burn extra calories, but low-intensity exercises are recommended to prevent injury. Complete Assessment Activity 8-4 to determine the number of minutes that you should participate in your favorite activities to burn a minimum of 300 calories.

Deconditioned people should start slowly and gradually progress to using 300 to 500 calories per exercise session. For weight loss, all calories do not have to be expended in one exercise session. Three 15-minute walks in a day result in a substantial expenditure of energy. Any physical activity above the amount normally done in a day is a bonus for weight

control. The cumulative effect of activities such as walking upstairs, mowing the lawn, and mopping floors can be combined with a structured exercise program to produce steady, safe weight loss.

Exercise and appetite: eat more, weigh less.. Exercise either stabilizes or increases the appetite, depending to some extent on the individual's body weight at the start of the program. In studies at St. Luke's Hospital in New York,[22] obese women lost 15 pounds after 57 days of moderate-intensity exercise on a treadmill. Their voluntary food intake during the 2 months of exercise was essentially the same as before the start of the exercise program. On the other hand, women of normal weight for their height had an immediate surge in appetite. Their food consumption increased when they began exercising, but they neither gained nor lost weight during the 2-month period.

Wood[23] investigated the effect of a year of jogging on previously sedentary middle-aged men. The men were encouraged to not reduce their food intake or to lose weight during the time of the study. At the end of 1 year, the men who ran the most miles lost the most fat and also had the greatest increase in food intake. In addition, the more fat they lost, the more they increased their food intake. Often men and women joggers who consume more calories are slimmer than sedentary people of the same age and sex. Exercise is the only viable method for losing weight while eating more calories.

Exercise stimulates metabolism. Basal metabolic rate (BMR) is the energy required to sustain life when the body is in a rested and fasted state. BMR is measured in calories and represents the energy needed to keep the heart beating, the lungs moving air, and the liver, kidneys, and all other organs functioning. More calories are used to maintain BMR than to perform any other function. Approximately 70% of the energy liberated from food is expended to support BMR.[4]

Metabolism is affected by age, gender, secretions from endocrine glands, nutritional status, sleep, fever, climate, body surface area, and amount of muscle tissue. Because men have more muscle tissue than women, their BMRs average 5% to 10% higher. See Assessment Activity 8-3 to learn how to estimate your BMR.

BMR declines with age, primarily because of the physical inactivity and muscle loss that often accompany aging. The annual decrease in BMR beginning at 25 or 30 years of age, though imperceptible, has serious ramifications for weight management and ac-

Physical activity that develops muscle can also increase metabolism.

tissue, thus accelerating metabolism and using calories (Table 8-6).

The examples in Table 8-6 are hypothetical but based on fact. The lean-tissue values in the table apply to men. The process applies to women as well but to a lesser degree because they have less muscle tissue to lose.

Subject 1 is most representative of the typical American man who loses muscle, replaces it with fat, and then gains additional fat. Fat is less dense than muscle, so a pound of fat takes up 18% more room in the body than a pound of muscle. Subject 2 is inactive but manages to maintain his body weight while aging. However, an inactive lifestyle has resulted in muscle loss, and the accompanying reduction in BMR demands that he keep a tight reign on his appetite to prevent weight gain. He weighs the same at the age of 60 as he did at age 20, but his body composition has changed significantly (Figure 8-4). Subject 3 is inactive, but he compensates for the expected muscle loss by controlling food consumption, so he weighs 15 pounds less at age 60 than he did at age 20. His body composition has changed because the loss of muscle tissue means that he is smaller all over. This subject is perpetually dieting—a strategy that is virtually impossible for most people. Subject 4 has been physically active throughout life. Little muscle loss and no fat gain have occurred. Exercises and physical activities that develop and maintain muscle tissue will preserve and/or enhance BMR, resulting in improved quality of life and a youthful and healthy appearance for many decades.

Combining Dietary Modification and Exercise

In its simplest terms, weight management involves control of caloric intake versus caloric expenditure. Weight gain results when more calories are consumed than expended, weight loss occurs when less calories are consumed than expended, and weight maintenance occurs when calories consumed equals

counts for a significant amount of the weight gained with age. Authorities estimate that the loss of muscle tissue is equal to 3% to 5% every decade after age 25 to 30 years. The subsequent decline in BMR produces changes in body composition. Exercise and physical activities are the keys to weight management because they increase and/or sustain muscle

TABLE 8-6 Effects of Physical Inactivity on Body Composition

Subject	Body Weight at Age 20 (lb)	Body Weight at Age 60 (lb)	Activity Level	Lean Tissue	Fat	Body Composition
1	150	165	Inactive	Lost 12%-20%	Gain	Changed
2	150	150	Inactive	Lost 12%-20%	Gain	Changed
3	150	135	Inactive	Lost 12%-20%	Gain	Changed
4	150	150	Active	No loss	No gain	Unchanged

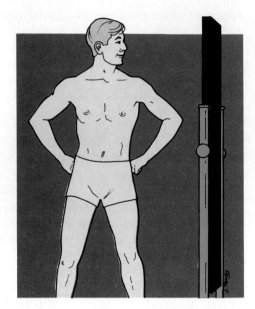 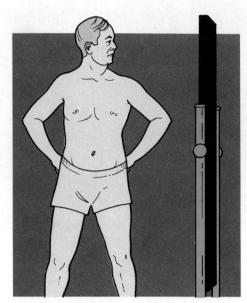

FIGURE 8-4 Joe at age 25. Joe at age 55.

calories expended. Because caloric consumption and expenditure are involved in weight management, both should be manipulated to be effective. Combining sensible exercise and sensible changes in eating habits that can be maintained for life is the most effective approach to permanent weight management. Table 8-2, which summarizes the results of the Zuti and Golding study,[15] shows the effectiveness of combining exercise and changed eating habits on total weight loss, fat loss, and lean-tissue gains of young and middle-aged women. Leon et al.[24] observed a similar effect in men. Subjects in this study walked for 90 minutes a day, 5 days a week, progressively increasing their speed and consequently their energy expenditure over 16 weeks. The average total loss was 12.5 pounds, fat loss was 13 pounds, and lean-tissue gain was 0.5 pounds. Combining nutritional changes with regular exercise meets the goals of weight management most effectively—it promotes weight loss, fat loss, and lean-tissue gain.

Behavioral Effects

Some evidence suggests that obese people are more likely than normal-weight people to eat in response to external cues. A clock that says it is suppertime, media messages advertising food and beverages, and the sight, sounds, and aroma of food are more apt to elicit eating behavior in the obese. This is the basis of the "externality" hypothesis: if people can learn to eat in response to external cues, they can also learn to recognize cues that stimulate eating behavior, substitute other behaviors for eating, and use techniques that decrease the amount of food eaten.

As a result of this training the response to external cues should be reduced and replaced by attention to internal hunger signals. Many techniques have been developed over the past 20 years that may assist people in resisting the tendency to eat indiscriminately or to overeat. (See Figure 1-11 for a brief list of some of the techniques that have been successful for some people.) Rarely have these techniques produced large weight losses (as much as 40 pounds), and rarely has the loss been maintained. However, these techniques may be useful as a supplement to sensible food choices and exercise.

Behavioral and psychological hypotheses have been developed to explain the development and perpetuation of obesity in population groups (Table 8-7). These hypotheses attempt to account for differ-

TABLE 8-7 Selected Behavioral and Psychological Hypotheses to Account for Obesity

▶ Abnormal eating styles
▶ External eating cues
▶ Response to appetizing food
▶ Taste perception
▶ Restrained eating—response to caloric restriction
▶ External locus of control
▶ Preference of immediate gratification
▶ Response to anxiety or depression

ences between normal-weight and obese persons. Although each of the hypotheses is supported by some research, none has been able to account consistently for group differences, and the behavioral and psychological determinants might be the result of obesity rather than the cause.[25]

Health Aspects of Obesity

In declaring obesity a disease almost 10 years ago the NIH confirmed what had been known for years: morbidity occurs more frequently and with greater severity and mortality occurs at an earlier age among obese people compared with those of normal weight. Obesity coexists with or is a precursor of the chronic diseases that kill Americans. It is highly correlated with coronary heart disease, stroke, atherosclerosis, some forms of cancer, and type II diabetes—5 of the top 10 causes of death.[12] Obesity contributes to the formation of gallstones, respiratory disorders, and degenerative changes in the joints, particularly those of the knees and hips. It predisposes men to cancer of the colon, rectum, and prostate and women to cancer of the ovaries, uterus, and breasts. Researchers at Harvard's School of Public Health[26] reviewed 25 studies regarding the relationship between body weight and health. They concluded that excess weight caused premature death and that each extra pound increased the death rate by 1% in men 30 to 49 years of age and 2% for men age 50 to 62 years.

The link between obesity and chronic diseases is well established, but evidence has emerged indicating that the distribution of fat is equally important (see Chapter 7).

In addition to the medical hazards, obese people suffer from economic and social discrimination, poor body image, and poor self-concept. They pay higher premiums for health insurance or are denied coverage, obese children are often ridiculed by their slim peers, and armed forces personnel are forced out of the military if they gain weight beyond an acceptable level.

Eating Disorders

Anorexia nervosa (anorexia) and bulimarexia nervosa (bulimia) are eating disorders familiar to most Americans. Although they are different eating disorders, they share a common factor: an intense fear of becoming overweight. However, the methods used by persons with the disorders to attain this goal differ. Starvation is the primary strategy of the anorectic, but the bulimic gorges and then purges by vomiting or using diuretics and laxatives. Bulimics seldom starve to the point of emaciation; instead they

are usually at or slightly above normal weight.[4] A person may exhibit characteristics of both diseases, severely limiting food intake, perhaps as low as 1000 calories a day, and also purging. This group is referred to as *anorexic-bulimic*.[4] Most bulimics do not become anorexic, but many anorectics practice bulimic behavior. Approximately 1% of girls between the ages of 12 and 18 years suffer from anorexia; 2% to 8% of adolescents and college-aged women suffer from bulimia.[4] Young females account for more than 90% of both disorders.[27] Fewer men are affected, partly because extra weight often reinforces their ideal image. However, a growing number of male athletes report bulimic practices, especially swimmers, track participants, and men in weight-control sports such as wrestling.[4]

Anorexia Nervosa

Anorexia nervosa is defined as a "serious illness of deliberate self-starvation with profound psychiatric and physical components."[28] Refusal to eat is the hallmark of the disease, regardless of whether other practices such as binge-purge cycles occur. Although specific causes of anorexia have not been identified, a combination of biological, social, and psychological factors contribute to the disorder. Support for an organic influence has centered on the hypothalamus (the portion of the brain reputed to house the appetite center) and the pituitary gland (the master gland of the body). Evidence supporting a genetic influence is weak, but the disease does occur more frequently among sisters. Psychodynamic causes take various forms, the most popular of which centers on the trauma experienced by young girls whose mothers are excessively domineering and unempathetic. This proposition is currently more theory than fact. Sociocultural theories focus on the compulsion of adolescent girls to become and remain lean. This exaggerated goal manifests itself at a time when girls are naturally depositing fat.

Anorexia is characterized by extreme weight loss, amenorrhea (absence of a menstrual period), and a variety of psychological disorders culminating in an obsessive preoccupation with the attainment of thinness. Fortunately, most anorectics recover fully after one experience with the disease. But for 5% to 10%, the disease becomes episodic and relentless, resulting in death from the consequences of starvation or related psychiatric problems.[26] Figure 8-5 gives the criteria that have been developed by the American Psychiatric Association for diagnosing anorexia.

When confronted, anorectics typically deny the existence of a problem and the weight-loss behaviors that have resulted in their emaciated physical ap-

Figure 8-5 Criteria for Diagnosing Anorexia Nervosa

▶ Weight change
  1. Unwilling to maintain minimal normal body weight for the person's age and height
  2. Weight loss that leads to the maintenance of a body weight that is 15% below normal
  3. Failure to gain the amount of weight expected during a period of growth, resulting in a body weight that is 15% below normal
▶ Inordinate fear of gaining weight and/or becoming fat despite being significantly underweight
▶ Disturbed and unrealistic perceptions of body weight, size, or shape; feeling of being "fat" although emaciated and possibly perceiving one specific part of the body as "too fat."
▶ Absence of at least three menstrual cycles for women when they would normally be expected to occur (amenorrheic women have a normal menstrual cycle only during administration of hormone therapy)
▶ Rigid dieting, maintenance of rigid control in lifestyle, security found in control and order
▶ Rituals involving food and excessive exercise

pearance. They also avoid medical treatment, refuse the well-intended advice of family and friends regarding professional assistance, and submit to treatment under protest. Anorexia is a subtle disease, and anorectics become secretive in their behaviors. They are evasive, and many hide their disease in deep denial even while undergoing treatment, making the diagnosis especially difficult.

The course of treatment for anorexia is complex, involving a coordinated effort by several health-care specialists. Hospitalization is often required because anorectics may have to be fed intravenously or by some other method if they cannot or will not eat. Medications that stimulate the appetite and medications that calm the patient are usually necessary. Nutritional counseling and psychological counseling—individual, group, and family—are integral components of treatment. Finally, behavior-modification techniques are used to help change the perceptions and lifestyle of the anorectic. At this point, no single treatment has proved to be unusually successful in the treatment of anorectic patients.

Bulimia (Bulimarexia Nervosa)

Bulimia is characterized by alternate cycles of binge eating and restrictive eating. Binges are usually fol-

lowed by purging, primarily by self-induced vomiting supplemented with laxatives and diuretics. The physical and psychological ramifications of such a struggle include esophageal inflammation, erosion of tooth enamel caused by repeated vomiting, the possibility of electrolyte imbalances, and altered mood states, particularly anxiety and depression.

The diagnostic criteria for bulimia are given in Figure 8-6. These criteria specify that to be diagnosed a bulimic, a person must vomit at least twice a week for 3 months. Binge-purge cycles may occur daily, weekly, or in other intervals.[28] Bulimic behaviors range from binge eating frequently or from time to time, binge eating with a feeling of being unable to control food intake, severely restricting the diet between binge periods, and binge eating followed by purging.[11] Because many people with bulimia engage in binge-purge practices in isolation, they cannot be diagnosed by their appearance.

Foods chosen for a binge are usually convenience foods—cakes, cookies, pies, ice cream, donuts, and pastries. As much as 20,000 or more calories may be eaten in a binge.[29] Purging in the form of laxatives, vomiting, diuretics, fasting, and excessive exercise follows in the hope that weight gain will be blunted. Approximately 60% of those with bulimia use laxatives, often in huge amounts.[11] Even when vomiting immediately follows the binge, 20% to 33% of the calories taken in are still absorbed.[4] Even more calories are absorbed when other purging methods are used.

Figure 8-6 Criteria for Diagnosing Bulimia

▶ Episodic secretive binge eating characterized by rapid consumption of large quantities of food in a short time, never overeating in front of others
▶ At least two eating binges per week for at least 3 months
▶ Loss of control over eating behavior while eating binges are in progress
▶ Frequent purging after eating; using techniques such as self-induced vomiting, laxatives, or diuretics; engaging in fasting or strict dieting; or engaging in vigorous exercise
▶ Constant and continual concern with body shape, size, and weight
▶ Erosion of teeth, swollen glands
▶ Purchase of syrup of ipecac

Bulimics are treated similar to anorectics except that hospitalization is usually not required. In addition to nutritional and psychological counseling, treatment often includes antidepressive medication, since bulimia is associated with clinical depression. Treatment focuses on correcting typical bulimic behaviors, such as the "all-or-none" thinking, "If I'm not perfect, I'm a failure, so one slip-up—one cookie—justifies a binge." Generally, psychotherapy aims primarily to help a person with self-acceptance and to be less concerned with body weight.[4]

Underweight

A small number of people who are not anorectic or bulimic are naturally thin, and some of them are dissatisfied with their appearance. Being underweight presents as much of a cosmetic problem for the affected individual as obesity does for the obese person. Many underweight people find it more difficult to gain a pound than obese people find losing one.

In their attempts to gain weight, many very lean people have consumed large quantities of food, particularly those that are rich in calories. Unfortunately, these foods are high in fat and sugar. This is an unhealthy eating pattern for anyone, regardless of body weight. The preferred approach is to combine muscle-building exercises with three well-balanced nutritious meals supplemented by two nutritious snacks. The amount and type of weight gain should be closely monitored. Fat stores should not be increased unless the individual is extremely thin and on the verge of dipping into stores of essential fat. **Essential fat,** found in organs, muscles, bone marrow, intestines, and the central nervous system, is necessary for individuals to function biologically and to support life processes. Essential fat in men constitutes about 3% to 5% of the total body weight, whereas in women it constitutes 11% to 14% of total weight. The difference between men and women is due to sex-specific essential fat that is vital for maintenance of fertility. Values for essential fat plus storage fat that are consistent with healthy leanness are 8% to 12% for men and 16% to 20% for women.

Putting It All Together

This chapter began by asking these questions: (1) Why are Americans preoccupied with their body weight? (2) How do we find ourselves in such a predicament? (3) What can we do about it?

Americans are preoccupied with body weight for several reasons. First, society emphasizes and deifies the youthful, lean body. This is the message of advertisers, clothing designers, models, and media, who reinforce the desirability of the slim silhouette. Fatness is not synonymous with aesthetics. Second, obese people have been the victims of social and economic discrimination. Third, most obese people suffer from poor self-esteem, poor body image, and social disapproval. Fourth, obesity is a health hazard; it is a disease that is also associated with other catastrophic diseases. Finally, obese people are often perceived as weak-willed, lazy people who eat too much.

We find ourselves in the predicament of having to make an effort to achieve and maintain a desirable appearance because lifestyles have changed significantly in the past 50 to 60 years. Muscle power has been replaced by machine power, and labor-saving devices pervade all segments of life. Refrigeration, freezing, dehydration, and other methods of preserving foods have provided Americans with the opportunity to have access to foods all year that were previously available only seasonally. Fast foods and processed foods are convenient, affordable, and time saving, but they are also high in calories, fat, and preservatives.

What Is the Solution to Weight Management?

The best solution to weight management is the most obvious: maintaining a moderate lifestyle so that excess weight is not gained. In summary, the basic principles of weight loss are the following:

▶ The most important factor in permanent weight loss is physical exercise. Even though Americans eat 10% less today than in 1970, they still weigh more.[30] Men and women between the ages of 25 and 34 years are likely to gain an average of 7 pounds over the next 10 years of life, and over 6% will gain nearly 30 pounds.[31] This increase in weight is because of decreased involvement in physical activity.

Successful dieters are typically those who incorporate physical activities in their lifestyles. Approximately 90% of successful dieters in a weight loss program at the University of California at Davis participated in regular exercise (at least 30 minutes three times a week).[7] Exercise burns calories, increases metabolism, and helps prevent loss of muscle tissue in the course of a diet. The key issue in exercising is consistency. Plan an activity program that can be sustained 1 year from now and 5 years from now.

▶ Avoid high-fat foods and stress consumption of complex carbohydrates. Calories from fat convert easily to fat, with only 3% being lost in the digestive process. By comparison, 25% of carbohydrate calories are lost in the process. A weight loss diet should include at least 150 grams of carbohydrate daily.[4]

▶ Set realistic goals. Weight loss per week should not exceed 1 to 2 pounds. The ideal approach is to lose pounds at the same rate at which they were gained.

▶ Make a gradual lifestyle change. This means a calm, deliberate approach rather than a frenetic "lose it now" attitude. A 200-pound person should exercise, reduce calories, and eat like a 180-pound person to become a 180-pound person. Once the weight is lost, the person cannot revert to the habits of a 200-pound person. A diet is only successful if the weight does not return.

▶ Anticipate a plateau. During the first week of a diet, weight loss comes primarily from loss of protein, glycogen, and water but very little fat. As the body adjusts to a diet, fat loss increases. This adjustment takes about a week on a moderate diet and still longer when the diet is severe.[7] Many dieters experience a plateau after about 3 to 4 weeks, not because they are cheating but because they have gained water weight while still losing body fat. After several months, the number of calories burned per pound of weight goes up steadily, making each pound progressively harder to lose. After losing 20 to 30 pounds, expect to reach a stable plateau.

▶ Avoid fad diets. In addition to imposing health risks, most fad diets result in temporary weight loss that leads to cycle dieting. The more extreme the diet, the less likely the weight loss will be permanent.

▶ Avoid low-calorie diets. Low-calorie diets decrease BMR 10% to 20%, making dieting success even harder. A dieter should not try to eat less than 1000 calories daily. A diet plan should minimize hunger and fatigue.

▶ Develop an eating plan that includes easily obtained foods.

▶ Develop a less rigid lifestyle, one that reduces the need to consciously control what is eaten. Maintaining weight loss is the antithesis of counting every calorie.

▶ Avoid meal skipping, fasting, and restrictive dieting. These practices often lead to a preoccupation with food, weight, and/or dieting. Dieting should allow people to attend parties, eat at restaurants, and participate in normal activities. Labeling some foods as "good" or "bad" often promotes a denial-guilt-preoccupation cycle in which one slight deviation of a diet or food choice is interpreted as a failure: A forbidden food is eaten (denial), a sense of relief from restraint leads to a binge, the binge leads to guilt and a feeling of failure, and both denial and guilt exacerbate the preoccupation. The preoccupation leads back to denial and the cycle continues. This exerts considerable pressure on the dieter. To avoid the dissonance that comes with failure, the dieter often abandons attempts to lose weight. Given moderation and discretion, almost any food can be enjoyed.

▶ Incorporate behavioral strategies such as those presented in Chapter 1 (see Figure 1-11).

▶ Form a buddy system or join a support group. The support and encouragement of a friend or relative are often the difference between success and failure.

▶ Finally, accept yourself. Before trying to lose weight, determine how great a risk your weight poses to your health. People at risk for chronic conditions such as hypertension and type II diabetes, for example, often improve dramatically with a weight loss of 10% or less.[30] Some people, however, are overweight despite their best efforts to reduce. For such people, striving to attain a certain weight may be futile and even damaging to health. Everyone cannot be skinny. Everyone can try to be healthy.

Summary

▶ The thin look is becoming passé and is being replaced by the fit and muscular look.

▶ Obesity is defined as body fat that is equal to or greater than 25% of the body weight of men and 30% or greater of the body weight of women.

▶ There are more overweight children today than there were 20 years ago.

▶ Obese children who are the progeny of obese parents have a greater chance of becoming obese adults than children of normal-weight parents.

▶ Diet, exercise, and heredity are the major factors associated with the loss or gain of body weight.

▶ Obesity has been declared a disease by the National Institutes of Health.

▶ The development and distribution of body fat is under substantial genetic control.

▶ Only 5% of all dieters are able to reach a target weight and maintain that weight for more than 1 year.

▶ Cycle dieting is ineffective as a weight-management strategy.

▶ Approximately 70% of the energy liberated from food is expended to support the BMR.

▶ Diet-only strategies result in the loss of lean body weight.

▶ Weight gain is caused more by physical inactivity than overeating.

▶ Exercise burns calories, stimulates metabolism, and brings appetite in line with energy expenditure.

▶ BMR declines because of muscle loss as people age and become inactive.

▶ Behavioral techniques may be a good supplement to exercise and dietary modification for weight management.

▶ Obesity is positively related to the chronic diseases that are the major killers and disablers of Americans.

▶ Anorexia and bulimia are two potentially destructive eating disorders with complex causes.

Action Plan for Personal Wellness

Use the information presented in this chapter to answer the following questions and to formulate an action plan to enhance your personal wellness.

1 Based on the information presented in this chapter, along with what I know about my family's health history, the health problems and issues that I need to be concerned about are:_____

_____

_____

2 Of the health concerns listed in number 1, the one I most need to act on is:_____

_____

_____

3 The possible actions that I can take to improve my level of wellness are (be specific):_____

_____

_____

4 Of the actions listed in number 3, the one that I most need to include in an action plan is:_____

_____

_____

5 Factors I need to keep in mind to be successful in my action plan are:_____

_____

_____

Review Questions

1. What are the definitions of obesity and overweight?
2. What evidence exists to support the idea that Americans are obsessed with weight control?
3. What is the pattern of growth of adipose cells from birth through puberty?
4. Do you agree or disagree with the idea that neonatal adiposity is not a good predictor of adult obesity? Defend your answer.
5. What evidence can you use to support the existence of an influential role of heredity in the development of obesity?
6. How effective are diet-only strategies in weight management?
7. What is weight cycling?
8. What is the role of exercise in weight management?
9. How effective are behavior-modification techniques in weight management?
10. Why does obesity increase morbidity and mortality?
11. What are the symptoms of anorexia and bulimia, and how is each treated?
12. What is essential fat, and why does it differ for each gender?

References

1. Briton AG: Thin is out, fit is in, *Am Health* 7(6):66-71, 1988.
2. US Department of Health and Human Services: *Healthy people 2000*, Washington, DC, 1990, US Government Printing Office.
3. Yo-yo dieting: the losing game, *Harvard Heart Letter* 3(1):1, 1993.
4. Wardlaw GM, Insel PM: Perspectives in nutrition, ed 2, St Louis, 1993, Mosby.
5. Gortmaker SL et al: Increasing pediatric obesity in the United States, *Am J Disabled Child* 141:535-539,1987.
6. Ross JG, Pate RR: The national children and youth fitness study, II, a summary of findings, *J Phys Educ Recreat Dance* 58:51-56, 1987.
7. Rubin R: Losers, weepers: why most diets fail, *Am Health* 10(6):46, 48, 1991.
8. Stunkard A et al: An adaption study of human obesity, *N Engl J Med* 314:193-198, 1986.
9. Stunkard A et al: A twin study of human obesity, *JAMA* 256:51-54, 1986.
10. Bouchard C et al: The response to long-term overfeeding in idential twins, *N Engl J Med* 322:1477, 1990.
11. Lamb L: Bulimia and anorexia nervosa update, *Health Letter* 36(11):1-3, 1990.
12. Lamb L: The Oprah Winfrey syndrome, *Health Letter* 37(7):1-2, 1991.
13. Wing RR: Weight cycling in humans: a review of the literature, *Ann Behav Med* 14:113, 1992.
14. Do yo-yo dieters die young? *Health* 7(2):10, 1993.
15. Zuti B, Golding L: Comparing diet and exercise as weight reducing tools, *Physician Sportsmed* 4:49-54, 1976.
16. Moss AJ: Caution: very-low calorie diets can be deadly, *Ann Intern Med* 102:121-123, 1985.
17. Munnings F: Exercise and estrogen in women's health: getting a clearer picture, *Physician Sportsmed* 16:152-161, 1988.
18. Lamb L: Exercise protects heart during dieting, *Health Letter* 31:3, 1988.
19. Lichtman SW et al: Discrepancy between self-reported and actual caloric intake and exercise in obese subjects, *N Engl J Med* 327:1893, 1992.
20. Myers RJ et al: Accuracy of self-reports of food intake in obese and normal-weight individuals: effects of obesity on self-reports of dieting intake in adult females, *Am J Clin Nutr* 48:1248-1251, 1988.
21. American College of Sports Medicine: The recommended quantity and quality of exercise for developing and maintaining cardiorespiratory and muscular fitness in healthy adults, *Med Sci Sports* 22:265, 1990.
22. Wood P: *California diet and exercise program*, Mountain View, Calif, 1983, Anderson World Books.
23. Wood PD: Increased exercise level and plasma lipoprotein concentrations: a one-year, randomized controlled study in sedentary middle-aged men, *Metabolism* 31:31, 1983.
24. Leon AS et al: Effects of a vigorous walking program on body composition and carbohydrate and lipid metabolism of obese young men, *Am J Clin Nutr* 32:1776-1787, 1979.
25. *The Surgeon General's report on nutrition and health*, Washington, DC, 1988, US Department of Health and Human Services.
26. Manson JE et al: Body weight and longevity: a reassessment, *JAMA* 257:353-357, 1987.
27. Hendricks J: Anorexia nervosa and bulimia: two serious eating disorders, *Alternatives Health Wellness* Aug 1991, p 2.
28. Greene GW et al: Dietary intake and dieting practices of bulimic and non-bulimic female college students, *JAMA* 90:576, 1990.
29. Farley: Eating disorders require medical attention, *FDA Consumer* Mar 1992, p 27.
30. Are you eating right? *Consumer Reports* 57(10):651, 1992.
31. Lamb L: Getting fat starts early, *Health Letter* 33(2):3, 1989.

Annotated Readings

Chinnici M: Picking the perfect diet, *Walking Magazine* 4:40-43, 46, 48, 1989.
Discusses the futility of rapid weight loss, describes 29 of the most popular diets, and presents the health implications and their positive and negative points.

Lamb L: Bulimia and anorexia nervosa update, *Health Letter* 36(1):1-3, 1990.
Presents characteristics of anorexia and bulimia and addresses common misconceptions.

Long P: What America eats, *Hippocrates* 3:38-45, 1989.
Shows how American eating patterns have changed in the last few decades and the reasons this has taken place. Convenience is replacing cooking, and sit-down meals in the home are rare.

Rubin R: Losers, weepers: why most diets fail, *Am Health* 10(6):46, 48, 1991.
Discusses why diets fail and gives advice for people wanting to lose weight.

To lose weight, walk, don't swim, *Tufts Univ Diet Nutr Letter* 7:2, 1989.
Presents a rationale for walking for weight loss and discusses the reasons swimming appears to be ineffective in promoting fat loss.

Wardlaw GM, Insel PM: Perspectives in nutrition, ed 2, St Louis, 1993, Mosby.
Comprehensive reference text on nutrition with separate chapters on dieting, weight control, and eating disorders.

A S S E S S M E N T   A C T I V I T Y   8 - 1

Where Is the Fat?

The major dietary recommendation for weight management is to eat less fat but more complex carbohydrates. The purpose of this assessment is to generate an awareness of foods that are high in fat.

Directions: To complete this assessment, refer to the food composition tables in the appendix and identify the 15 foods that have the highest fat content in grams per serving listed. Arrange them in rank order and supply the information for each column.

Food	Serving Size	Fat (g)
1.		
2.		
3.		
4.		
5.		
6.		
7.		
8.		
9.		
10.		
11.		
12.		
13.		
14.		
15.		

Complete the following:

After completing this assessment, I was surprised to learn that _____

_____

ASSESSMENT ACTIVITY   8-2

Calculating Caloric Expenditure Through Exercise

Directions: The following exercise illustrates the necessary calculations used for determining weight loss through exercise. In the example below a subject weighing 195 lb wishes to lose 12 lb by exercising 40 minutes per day five times per week. The form of exercise will be riding a bike at 13 mph. Table 8-5 gives the appropriate coefficient (0.071) for this activity, and as previously mentioned, there are 2700 calories in 1 lb of fat. Study this example and then apply it to the problem presented at the end of this assessment to answer the following questions:
1. How many calories are expended per exercise session?
2. How many pounds may be lost per week at this energy expenditure?
3. How long will it take to lose 12 lb?

1. Multiply body weight by the appropriate activity coefficient.
    a. 195 lb × 0.071 = 13.8 calories/min
    b. 13.8 calories/min × 40 min = 552 calories
2. Multiply the number of calories expended per workout by the number of workouts per week.
    a. 552 calories × 5 workouts/week = 2760 calories/week.
    b. $\dfrac{2760 \text{ calories/week}}{2700 \text{ calories/lb}}$ = 1.02 lb lost/week
3. Divide the total pounds you want to lose (12 lb) by the number of pounds lost per week.

$$\dfrac{12 \text{ lb}}{1.02 \text{ lb lost/week}} = 11.8 \text{ weeks}$$

  This subject would lose 12 lb in 12 weeks by riding a bike at 13 mph for 40 minutes per day five times per week. Your weight-loss goals can be achieved in the same way.
  Now apply your knowledge of energy expenditure through exercise by solving the following problem. Jim weighs 220 lb and wishes to lose 25 lb by jogging at 5 mph for 30 minutes per exercise session 5 days per week. Do the calculations to solve Jim's problem by following the steps below.
1. Multiply body weight by the appropriate activity coefficient from Table 8-5 for jogging 5 mph.
    a. 220 lb × _____coefficient = _____calories/min
    b. _____calories/min × 30 min = _____calories
2. Multiply the number of calories expended per workout by the number of workouts per week.
    a. _____calories × 5 workouts/week = _____calories/week
    b. _____calories/week ÷ 2700 calories/lb = _____lb lost/week
3. Divide the total pounds to be lost by the number of pounds lost per week.
    ___25 lb___ ÷ _____lb lost/week = _____weeks
4. a. How many calories would Jim expend per exercise session?_____
    b. How many pounds will he lose per week at this energy expenditure?_____
    c. How many weeks will it take Jim to lose 25 lb?_____

ASSESSMENT ACTIVITY	8 - 3

Estimating Your Basal Metabolic Rate

Directions: Study the example below and then calculate your personal total energy expenditure.

The calculations for estimating BMR use different constants for men and women. The constant for men is 1 calorie per kilogram (2.2 lb) per hour; for women 0.9 calories per kilogram per hour. These constants are referred to as the BMR factor. An example for a 125-lb woman follows:
1. Convert body weight in pounds to kilograms: 125 lb ÷ 2.2 lb = 56.8 kg
2. Multiply weight in kilograms by the BMR factor: 56.8 kg × 0.9 calories/kg/hr = 51.1 calories/hr
3. Multiply calories/hr by 24 hours: 51.1 calories/hr × 24 hr/day = 1226.4 calories/day
4. The BMR is 1226.4 calories/day.
   To determine the total daily calories expended, you need to estimate the number of calories used in muscular movement during a typical day. This is a rough approximation at best, but you should be within your range if you follow the guidelines below and select the category that fits you best.
1. Sedentary—Student, desk job, sitting during most of your work and leisure time: add 40% to 50% of the BMR.
2. Light activity—Teacher, assembly line worker, walk 2 miles regularly: add 55% to 65% of the BMR.
3. Moderate activity—Waitress, waiter, aerobic exercise at about 75% of maximum heart rate: add 65% to 70% of the BMR.
4. Heavy activity—Construction worker, aerobic exercise above 75% of maximum heat rate: add 75% to 100% of BMR.
   If our subject determines that her level of activity is in the light category, she will calculate the range of her daily total caloric expenditure as follows:
1. Multiply BMR by the level of activity:
   a. 1226.4 × 0.55 = 674.5
   b. 1226.4 × 0.65 = 797.2
2. Add BMR calories to level of activity calories to get total calories:
   a. 1226.4 + 674.5 = 1900.9 calories/day
   b. 1226.4 + 797.2 = 2023.6 calories/day
   This subject's total calorie expenditure in a day falls between 1904.5 and 2023.6 calories.

Calculate your BMR by doing the following:
I. Calculate BMR:
   1. Convert body weight (BW) in pounds to kilograms:

   _____ ÷ 2.2 = _____ kg
   BW in lb

   2. Multiply weight in kilograms by the BMR factor for your sex (male factor 1.0, female factor 0.9):

   _____ × _____ = _____ calories/hr
   BMR factor   weight in kg

   3. Multiply _____ × 24 hrs/day = _____ calories/day
                calories/hr

   4. BMR = _____ calories/day

II. Determine your level of physical activity:
  1. Multiply BMR by the level of activity factor:

  _____ × _____ = _____calories/day
  BMR   Level of activity
                   factor

  _____ × _____ = _____calories/day
  BMR   Level of activity
                   factor

  2. Add the number of BMR calories to the level of activity calories to get the range of total calories expended in a day:

  _____ + _____ = _____calories/day
  BMR calories   Level of activity
                   calories

  _____ + _____ = _____calories/day
  BMR calories   Level of activity
                   calories

  3. Total calories expended range from _____ to _____.

ASSESSMENT ACTIVITY   8 - 4

Assessing Caloric Costs of Activities

According to the American College of Sports Medicine, optimum weight loss benefits are derived from activities that burn from 300 to 500 calories per activity session. The purpose of this assessment is to determine the amount of time required to expend 300 calories.

Directions: The caloric costs for three activities are listed below (see Table 8-5). Add seven activities of your choice from Table 8-5 and complete the information required in each column to determine the amount of time required for you to burn 300 calories. An example is provided for a person weighing 180 lb who walks at a rate of 4.5 mph.

Activity	Caloric Cost	×	Weight	=	Calories/min	÷	$\frac{300}{}$	=	Recommended Workout (Time)
Example (180-lb person)									
1. Walking	0.048	×	180	=	8.64	÷	$\frac{300}{8.64}$	=	34.7 min
Personal Assessment:									
1. Walking	0.048	×	____	=	____	÷	$\frac{300}{}$	=	____
2. Aerobic dance	0.062	×	____	=	____	÷	$\frac{300}{}$	=	____
3. Raking	0.024	×	____	=	____	÷	$\frac{300}{}$	=	____
4. _____	____	×	____	=	____	÷	$\frac{300}{}$	=	____
5. _____	____	×	____	=	____	÷	$\frac{300}{}$	=	____
6. _____	____	×	____	=	____	÷	$\frac{300}{}$	=	____
7. _____	____	×	____	=	____	÷	$\frac{300}{}$	=	____
8. _____	____	×	____	=	____	÷	$\frac{300}{}$	=	____
9. _____	____	×	____	=	____	÷	$\frac{300}{}$	=	____
10. _____	____	×	____	=	____	÷	$\frac{300}{}$	=	____

Coping With and Managing Stress

Key terms	Objectives
coping	After completing this chapter, you will be able to:
distress	▷ Define stress and name different stressors.
eustress	▷ Describe types of stress and stages of the general adaptation syndrome (GAS).
general adaptation syndrome (GAS)	▷ Describe how stress can be beneficial.
relaxation techniques	▷ Identify sources of stress and recognize warning signs.
	▷ Explain the physiological response to stress.
stress	▷ List the short- and long-term health effects of stress.
stressor	▷ Identify strategies that effectively deal with stress.
	▷ Develop an action plan for coping with stress.

Stress profoundly affects people's lives. Everyone lives with stress—whether a student, business person, parent, or athlete. Stress is frequently viewed as an enemy. This is a misconception. Stress is neither positive nor negative. How people deal with or react to what they perceive as stress is what determines its effect on their lives. As has been stated, "It is often said that stress is one of the most destructive elements in people's daily lives, but that is only a half truth. The way we react to stress appears to be more important than the stress itself."[1] The effects of stress can be either positive or negative. Positively used, stress can be a motivator for an improved quality of life. Viewed negatively, it can be destructive to the development of wellness.

What is Stress?

Dr. Hans Selye was the first to define the term *stress* as the "nonspecific response of the body to any demands made upon it." It can be characterized by diverse reactions such as muscle tension, acute anxiety, increased heart rate, hypertension, shallow breathing, giddiness, and even joy. From a positive perspective, stress is a force that generates and initiates action. Using Selye's definition, stress can accompany pleasant or unpleasant events. Selye re-

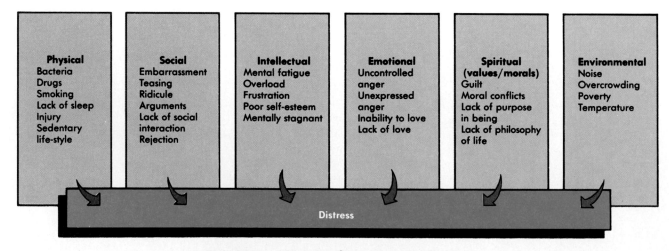

FIGURE 9-1 Stressors that can create distress.

ferred to stress judged as "good" as **eustress.** This form of stress is the force that serves to initiate emotional and psychological growth. Eustress provides the experience of pleasure, adds meaning to life, and fosters an attitude that tries to find positive solutions to even complex problems. Eustress can accompany a birth, graduation, a new car, a new friend, accomplishment of a difficult task, and success in an area that has previously produced anxiety. **Distress,** on the other hand, is stress that results in negative responses. Unchecked, negative stress can interfere with the physiological and psychological functioning of the body and may ultimately result in disease or disability.[2]

Stress also provides humans with the ability to respond to challenges or dangers. It is vital to self-protection and also serves as a motivator that enhances human ability.

A **stressor** is any physical, psychological, or environmental event or condition that initiates the stress response (Figure 9-1). What is considered a stressor for one person may not be a stressor for another. Speaking in front of a group may be stimulating for one person and terrifying for another. Some people may experience extreme test anxiety, whereas others do not. Fortunately, the stress response is not a genetic trait, and because it is a response to external conditions, it is subject to personal control. A person may not avoid taking a test, but techniques and precautions can be used to lessen the effects of the stress. For example, knowing the material thoroughly and engaging in deep breathing several minutes before a test will help dissipate anxiety. To maximize quality of life, people *can* find positive ways of coping with stress.

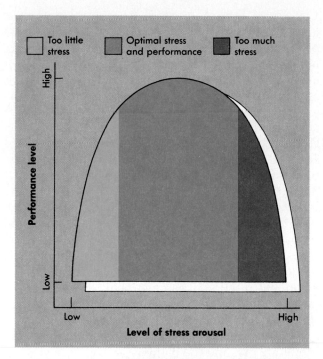

FIGURE 9-2 The inverted-U theory.

A stress response can serve to enhance and actually increase the level of either mental or physical performance. This response is referred to as the *inverted-U theory.*[3] Not enough stress may result in a poorer effort, but too much stress can inhibit effort. There appears to be an optimal level of stress that results in peak performance (Figure 9-2). An appropriate level of stress depends on the individual and the type of task. Table 9-1 lists some of the potentially positive outcomes that are associated with stress.

TABLE 9-1 Positive Outcomes of Stress

Mental	Emotional	Physical
Enhanced creativity	Sense of control	High energy level
Enhanced thinking ability	Responsiveness to environment	Increased stamina
Greater goal orientation	Improved interpersonal relationships	Flexibility of muscles and joints
Enhanced motivation	Improved morale	Freedom from stress-related disease

Your body is constantly attempting to maintain a physiological balance. This balance is referred to as *homeostasis*. Any event or circumstance that causes a disruption (a stressor) in your body's homeostasis requires some type of adaptive behavior. Physiologically, whether a stressor is conceived of as positive or negative, the body responds with the same three-stage process. This series of changes is known as the **general adaptation syndrome (GAS).**[4] The three phases are alarm, resistance, and exhaustion (Figure 9-3).

The *alarm* phase occurs when homeostasis is initially disrupted. The brain perceives a stressor and prepares the body to deal with it, a response sometimes referred to as the *fight-or-flight syndrome*. The subconscious appraisal of the stressor results in an emotional reaction. The emotional response stimulates a physical reaction that is associated with stress, such as the muscles becoming tense, the stomach tightening, the heart rate increasing, the mouth becoming dry, and the palms of the hands sweating.

The second stage is *resistance*. In this phase the body meets the perceived challenge through increased strength, endurance, sensory capacities, and sensory acuity. Hormonal secretions regulate the body's response to a stressor. Only after meeting and satisfying the demands of a stressful situation can the internal activities of the body return to normal. Girdano and Everly[5] state that individuals have different levels of energy to deal with stressors. With short-term stressors, only a superficial level of energy is required, allowing deeper energy levels to be protected. Superficial levels of energy are readily accessible and easily renewable. Unfortunately, all stress cannot be resolved with superficial energy levels. When long-term or deep levels of stress are experienced, the amount of energy available is limited. If sufficient stress is experienced for an extended period, loss of adaptation can result. Although some scientists believe that energy stores may be genetically programmed, all people can replenish their energy stores through exercise, good nutrition, adequate sleep, and other positive behaviors.

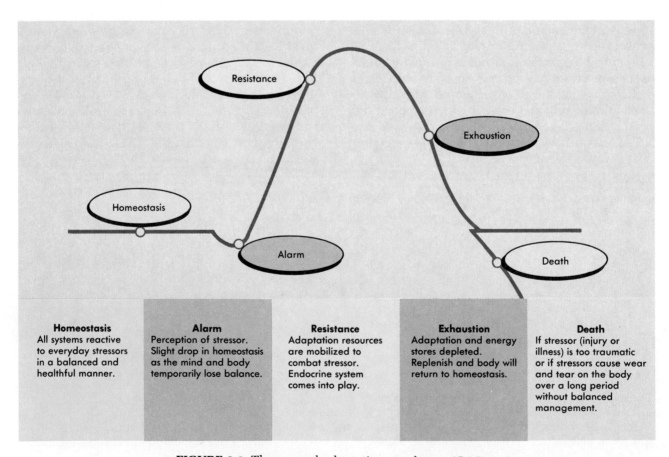

Homeostasis
All systems reactive to everyday stressors in a balanced and healthful manner.

Alarm
Perception of stressor. Slight drop in homeostasis as the mind and body temporarily lose balance.

Resistance
Adaptation resources are mobilized to combat stressor. Endocrine system comes into play.

Exhaustion
Adaptation and energy stores depleted. Replenish and body will return to homeostasis.

Death
If stressor (injury or illness) is too traumatic or if stressors cause wear and tear on the body over a long period without balanced management.

FIGURE 9-3 The general adaptation syndrome (GAS).

When stressors become chronic or pervasive, the third phase, *exhaustion*, is reached. In exhaustion, energy stores have been depleted and rest must occur. Although weeks to years may pass before the effects of long-term stressors occur, if a person does not learn how to adequately deal with stress, exhaustion will result. At this point, stress may affect the stomach, heart, blood pressure, muscles, and joints. Fortunately, the effects of stressors can be completely or partially reversed when adequate management techniques are initiated. The earlier these management techniques are learned and used, the fewer problems will be experienced.

Sources of Stress and Warning Signs

Most stressful situations fall into one of three categories. They include (1) harm-and-loss, (2) threat, and (3) challenge.[6] Examples of *harm-and-loss situations* are the death of a loved one, loss of personal property, physical assault, physical injury, and severe loss of self-esteem. *Threat situations* may be real or perceived as menacing and can range from being caught in traffic to being unable to perceive an event. Threatening events tax a person's ability to deal with everyday life. Threat stressors are any stressors that result in anger, hostility, frustration, or depression. *Challenge situations* are catalysts for either growth or pain. These stressors often involve major life changes and include such events as taking a new job, leaving home, graduating from college, and getting married. Challenge events are usually perceived as being good but involve stress because they disrupt homeostasis and require considerable psychological and physical adjustment.

Being aware of the mental and physical signals associated with stress is the beginning step in learning how to manage it. Assessment Activity 9-1 will aid you in identifying some of the major stressors. By using self-assessments to monitor for signs of stress, you can avoid excessive stress. The negative results of distress are shown in Table 9-2. Some indicators of excessive distress include the following:

▶ Chronic fatigue, migraine headaches, sweating, lower back pain, sleep disturbances, weakness, dizziness, diarrhea, and constipation

▶ Harder and/or longer work or study while accomplishing less, an inability to concentrate, general disorientation

▶ Denial that there is a problem or troubling event

▶ Increased incidence of illness, such as colds and flus, or constant worry about illness or becoming ill; overuse of over-the-counter drugs for the purpose of self-medication

▶ Depression, irritability, anxiety, apathy, an overwhelming urge to cry or run and hide, feelings of unreality

▶ Excessive behavior patterns, such as spending

TABLE 9-2 Negative Results of Distress

Mental	Physical	Emotional
Short-Term Effects		
Poor memory	Flushed face	Irritability
Inability to concentrate	Cold hands	Disorganization
Low creativity	Gas	Conflicts
Poor self-control	Rapid breathing	Mood swings
Low self-esteem	Shortness of breath	Chronic sleep problems
	Dry mouth	Acid stomach
		Overindulgence in alcohol, drugs, food
Long-Term Effects		
Bouts of depression	Hypertension	Overweight/underweight
Mild paranoia	Coronary disease	Drug abuse
Low tolerance for ambiguity	Ulcers	Excessive smoking
Forgetfulness	Migraine/tension headaches	Ineffective use of work/leisure
Inability to make decisions/ quick to make decisions	Strokes	Overreaction to mild work pressure
	Allergies	

too much money, drinking, breaking the law, and developing addictions
▶ Accident proneness
▶ Signs of reclusiveness and avoidance of other people
▶ Emotional tension, "key up" feeling, easily startled, nervous laughter, anxiety, hyperkinesia, and nervous tics

Physiological Responses to Stress

Stress abounds in life and can be experienced as the result of happy and unhappy events. Regardless of the stressor, each time a stressful event occurs, a series of neurological and hormonal messages are sent throughout the body (Figure 9-4).

The nervous system serves as a reciprocal network that sends messages between the awareness centers of the brain and the organs and muscles of the body. Part of this system is referred to as the *limbic system*. The limbic system contains centers for emotions, memory, learning relay, and hormone production and includes the pituitary gland, thalamus, and hypothalamus.

When a stressor is encountered, the body sends a message to the brain via the nervous system. The brain then synthesizes the message and determines whether it is valid or not. If a message is not verified by the brain as being particularly threatening, the limbic system overrides the initial response and the body continues to function normally. If the initial response is translated as accurate, the body responds with some emotion (fear, joy, terror), and the hypothalamus begins to act.

When a stressor is perceived, the *hypothalamus* sends a hormonal message to the pituitary gland. It

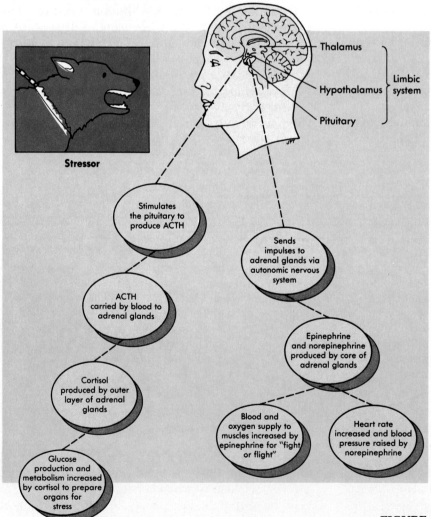

FIGURE 9-4 The physiological response to stress.

then releases a hormone *(ACTH)* that helps signal other glands in the endocrine system to secrete additional hormones, the primary one being *cortisol,* which provides fuel to respond with the fight-or-flight reaction.

As the result of another hormonal message the adrenal cortex increases blood pressure to facilitate the transportation of food and oxygen to the active parts of the body. Blood volume is augmented through a decrease in urine production and an increase in sodium retention, causing less fluid to be eliminated from the body. Systolic blood pressure may rise 15 to 20 mm Hg because of the presence of aldosterone.

The hypothalamus also sends a message to release the hormones *epinephrine* and *norepinephrine,* which initiate a variety of physiological changes. These changes include increased heart rate, increased metabolic rate, increased oxygen consumption, increased force in the pumping of the blood from the heart, and the release of other hormones called *endorphins,* which decrease sensations of pain.

The *autonomic nervous system* is responsible for a second major set of physiological responses. In reaction to a threat, the autonomic nervous system increases heart rate, the strength of the skeletal muscles, mental activity, and basal metabolic rate; dilates the coronary arteries, pupils, bronchial tubes, and arterioles; and constricts the abdominal arteries. This system also returns the body to a normal, relaxed state.

Health Effects of Stress

The mind and body act on each other in remarkable ways. Recent research indicates that nerves connect the thymus and spleen directly to the hypothalamus and that white blood cells respond directly to some of the same chemicals transmitting messages from one nerve cell to another. That is, the immune system is in direct contact with and under at least partial control of the part of the brain physiologically reactive to emotions. Thus there may be a biological link between emotions and disease and even death. Mortality is three times higher in individuals with few close relationships, whereas people with strong support groups have additional protection against life stressors. Death rates are higher for cancer patients with pessimistic attitudes. Illness is more common among people who feel locked into strife-ridden marriages. Conversely, AIDS patients with healthy psyches seem better able to withstand the disease.[7]

Any stressful situation takes its toll on the human body. Stress can be a primary enemy of overall health and a major contributor to disease. Because stress affects the immune system, the body becomes more susceptible to a multitude of ailments, from colds to cancer. Respiratory conditions, such as asthma, may become worse. The cardiovascular system reacts by constricting the blood vessels while increasing blood volume. The net result is a rise in blood pressure throughout a stress-ridden day. Multiple increases in blood pressure can eventually contribute to chronic high blood pressure. More forceful contraction of the heart elevates levels of free fatty acids, enhancing the development of clogged arteries leading to and including the heart itself. In extreme cases, sudden death can occur, especially if an individual has been experiencing high levels of uncontrolled stress for an extended period.

Headaches, including migraines, have long been associated with stress. Tension headaches are caused by involuntary contractions of the scalp, head, and neck muscles. Typical muscular reaction to stress is contracting or tensing. When chronic stress occurs, the body reacts by being constantly ready to respond and the muscles become *braced,* or always in a state of tension. More stress magnifies the tension the muscles are already undergoing. Increased muscular tension manifests itself in headaches, backaches, neck aches, and other pains. The smooth muscles that control internal organs also experience pains. More intense contractions can lead to stomach ache, diarrhea, hypertension, heartburn, gastritis, diarrhea, bloating, inflammation of the pancreas, and blockage of the bile ducts.

Stress decreases saliva in the mouth, often making speaking awkward. Swallowing may become difficult, and the increase in stomach acids contributes to ulcer pain. People tend to perspire more, and electrical currents are transmitted more quickly across the skin. Skin conditions such as acne, psoriasis, herpes, hives, and eczema are exacerbated.

Stress also seems to affect the body's nutritional status and immune response to disease. Individual nutritional patterns can also influence stress management efforts. For example, eating too much or too little, eating the wrong kinds of food, and overusing products such as caffeine or alcohol upset homeostasis. Diets high in fat, simple carbohydrates (sugar), and processed foods place a heavy burden on various body systems such as the cardiovascular and gastrointestinal systems. However, ingesting too few calories can lead to the breakdown of lean tissue to meet the nutritional demands of the body for normal functioning. To meet the demands of stress, you

Figure 9-5 Stress, Nutritional Status, and Immunity: an Interactive Effect

Although the mechanism is not completely understood, stress significantly affects nutritional status and therefore immunity. Several nutritional factors have implications for how your body responds to stress.

Energy

Stress can increase the body's basic caloric needs by as much as 200%. The stress hormones increase body heat production. When this heat is released, it is not available for cell metabolism. The caloric inefficiency induced by stress accounts for the increased need for energy intake.

Protein

Stress may increase the body's need for protein from 60% to as much as 500%. The integrity of the body's tissues, such as the skin and the tissue lining the mouth, lungs, and nose (called *mucosal tissue*), depends on adequate protein repair and maintenance of secretions of biochemicals that serve as protective agents. The formation of antibodies also requires protein.

Fats

Dietary fatty acids influence the synthesis of a group of fatty acid derivatives called *prostaglandins*. Prostaglandins stimulate or depress other cellular and immune functions in relation to stress.

Vitamins

Vitamin A functions to maintain healthy skin and mucous membranes. Individuals who are vitamin A–deficient have fewer mucus-secreting cells and those they do have produce less mucus—thus the protection provided by the mucus lining is diminished. Vitamin C has been shown to enhance the engulfing or "eating" actions of the immune cells called *macrophages*. If vitamin C is deficient, macrophages are less mobile and less able to consume disease-causing organisms. Deficiencies of vitamins A, B_{12}, and folate can impair production of the cells that enable antibody responses. Large doses of vitamin E have been associated with suppression of B cells, which are vital to the immune response. Finally, metabolic requirements for thiamin, riboflavin, and niacin are increased in response to a stressful situation.

Minerals

Deficiencies of zinc impair immune cell reproduction and responsiveness.

should maintain adequate nutrition through a balanced and varied diet. (Chapter 6 provides guidelines for developing a beneficial nutritional plan.) Figure 9-5 provides some insight into the interactive nature of stress, nutritional status, and immunity.

Ultimately, no body system escapes the effects of stress. Long-term presence of certain stress-associated hormones in the brain damages receptors and cells found in the hippocampus. (The hippocampus sends messages when stress is occurring.) Because brain cells do not regenerate, these cells are lost forever. The effects of this loss are unknown, but indications are that eventually humans become less able to respond to stress appropriately.[8] Assessment Activity 9-2 provides guidelines for identifying stress style and provides suggested relaxation activities for each style.

Self-Esteem and Stress

How people feel about themselves and others and their perceptions of the stressors in their lives are part of the psychology of stress. Ability to cope with stress often hinges on impressions of how detrimental a stressor is and how adequately resources can deal with the situation. How much stress people feel themselves experiencing is also closely associated with their own sense of self-esteem. Self-esteem includes beliefs and attitudes about changes, beliefs about personal talent and skills, and the ability to deal with the changes and challenges that inevitably occur in life. It is also the basis of self-efficacy and the locus of control (see Chapter 1). In fact, the most influential factor in determining response to stress may be people's own perceptions of themselves.

Personality and Stress

Two physicians, Friedman and Roseman,[9] have written extensively about personality, cardiovascular disease, and stress. These researchers have described two stress-related personality types—type A and type B. Most people are neither type exclusively but fall somewhere between the two.

Type A personality is characterized by an urgent sense of time, impatience, competitiveness, aggressiveness, insecurity over status, and inability to relax. People with type A behavior characteristics are likely to be highly stressed. Type B people have a more unhurried approach to their lives. The type B personality does not become as upset at losing or not attaining a goal. Type B people also tend to set more realistic goals.[10] Researchers have disagreed, however, whether there is a possible relationship between the stress-prone type A personality and cardiovascular disease.[11] Several studies have reported a correlation of type A behavior and cardiovascular disease, whereas other research literature has reported little association. In general, researchers believe that being a type A personality is not a problem if there is no underlying hostility. However, regardless of whether type A individuals are more susceptible to heart disease, they will experience more negative effects, such as tiredness and frustration, from short-term stress. Some type A people may actually be more resilient to stress and use their type A behaviors to resist stress. These people have been characterized as type C and seem to channel their energies into creative endeavors without suffering the effects of high stress.

"Stress survivors"—people who have been found to handle stress successfully or have successful coping abilities—have several common characteristics. Psychologist Suzanne Kobasa[12] has isolated these attributes and characterized the type person who exhibits them. A *hardy personality* tends to remain healthy even under extreme stress. Characteristics of a hardy personality or *hardiness* are challenge, commitment, and control (see Assessment Activity 9-3).

Challenge is the ability to see change for what it is—that is, not only inevitable but an opportunity for growth and development of unique individual abilities. *Commitment* is delineated by a strong sense of inner purpose. It is necessary to want to succeed for success to be achieved. Commitment is the ability to become really involved while maintaining the discernment to know when dedication and desire are harmful. *Control* is exhibited by the recognition that people have power over their lives and attitudes. People who have a sense of control act in situations rather than react to them.

Dealing with Stress

All events in life precipitate a reaction. How people react or respond to situations is individual. **Coping** is the effort made to manage or deal with stress. Coping is independent of outcome—it does not mean that an individual will experience success.

Dealing successfully with stress may require using a variety of techniques (Figure 9-6). Because stress-related responses are based primarily on mental perceptions, developing coping strategies that

Figure 9-6 Guidelines for Dealing with Stress

The following are guidelines for effectively dealing with potentially harmful stress:
Schedule time effectively: Practice good time management techniques by using time wisely. This means taking time out for yourself everyday and scheduling work when you are usually at peak ability (see Assessment Activity 9-5).
Set priorities: It is necessary to know what is important to *you*. Do not attempt to work on four or five projects simultaneously. Keep efforts focused on one or two major items.
Establish realistic goals: Goals must be achievable. Do not establish impossible expectations and then become frustrated when they are not accomplished as quickly as you would like. Write down long-range goals and then establish checks for keeping you on track and monitoring progress. Short-term goals help you see how you are moving toward your goal and provide rewards as you advance toward success.
See yourself as achieving the goals: Visualize yourself as being successful. Go over in your mind what it will look and feel like to accomplish the goal.
Give yourself a break: Take time every day to exercise and relax.

Figure 9-7 Michelle's Day—Approaching Stress

Event	Michelle's Stress Response	A Better Approach
7:00 AM: Late rising for first class. Stayed up late studying the night before.	Skips first class to study for exam; misses notes from that class and cannot contact friend to see if she can use her notes, skips breakfast.	Begin studying for a test a few days before the exam; do not attempt to cram everything into one night; get a good night's rest and get up early to review notes; eat breakfast and attend first class.
Late for test.	Stays home too long and gets caught in traffic; walks in late for the test; does not have a full hour to complete the test.	Leave early to allow for traffic and parking problems; be on time so can concentrate on test and have time to relax a few minutes.
Lunch	Skips lunch—has a soft drink and potato chips.	Have a nutritionally balanced meal in a relaxing atmosphere; go with friend to just chat.
Afternoon: Late for work because had to return library book.	Rushed to library; forgot to return overdue book; upset that had to pay fine, had to stand in line 15 minutes at the library.	Write down when books are due and return on time; use a daily calendar to plan activities and allot time to take care of personal business.
Evening: Watches TV until midnight; neglects to study for test the day after tomorrow.	Too tired and "stressed out" to study so just watches TV all evening; has a hamburger and soda for dinner.	Take a short nap after work and have a nutritious meal; plan the evening so that some time is spent watching TV and some is spent studying; go to bed early so can get to school on time and rested.
Next morning: Gets up late for class again.	Begins the same cycle of feeling tired and pressured and being late.	Analyze current time constraints to determine where more time needs to be alloted and how to develop a more efficient plan (see Assessment Activity 7-5).

achieve desirable results may need to originate with a change in attitude or outlook. If specific situations or people are perceived as disruptive, one solution is to avoid the situation or person.

Although there are no easy answers, there is always some kind of answer or solution. When dealing with a stressor reaches a point where it seems there are no solutions, the tension from the situation is also increasingly detrimental. It may then become necessary to consider changing attitudes, goals, and values. When an ideology or outlook on life becomes unlivable, something must change. This is probably the most difficult form of coping—when it seems the only way to cope is to change. If a long-held belief is creating stress, it may be time to alter that belief or replace it with a belief, attitude, or behavior that better promotes a sense of peace and personal harmony. Seeking the help of a professional counselor is frequently beneficial when attempting to resolve particularly stressful situations. Assessment Activity

9-4 provides ways to recognize some of the positive and negative behaviors that can be used to deal with stress.

Learning about and using relaxation techniques can help alleviate or even prevent detrimental effects associated with stress. Engaging in positive self-talk and relabeling negative experiences, for example, viewing difficulties as "challenges" rather than as problems, are positive steps in reducing stress-related disorders. Eating well, taking time to enjoy life, laughing, exercising, and living in the present all serve to reduce stress. Stress can be handled effectively when individuals work on developing all their abilities to the fullest, when they develop a lifestyle that is compatible with personal values, and when they develop realistic expectations for themselves. Working toward these goals is how a wellness lifestyle is established (Figure 9-7).

Successful coping is being aware of incidents and situations that are perceived as being stressful. Recognition of stressors includes awareness of how your body responds to stress. Recognition requires continuous monitoring of your body and mind for evidence of excessive stress.

Successful coping takes real effort. Assistance in successful coping may lie in the development of the quality of hardiness. Kobasa[12] has three suggestions to encourage the growth of this characteristic. One suggestion is to focus on the signals the body is sending when experiencing stress and then to think back to the event or situation that might have triggered those feelings. Another suggestion is to recreate a recent event that has been stressful. After visualizing the episode, you can write down six ways that the outcome could have been different—three with a worse outcome and three with a better outcome. The latter will increase awareness of how to better handle similar situations in the future. A last suggestion is to try something new. The idea is to be challenged and to meet that challenge successfully. Trying something new and meeting the challenge reinforces the sense of being able to deal with life successfully.

Relaxation Techniques

The ultimate goal in stress coping and management is to reduce the negative effects of stress. Different **relaxation techniques** have proved successful and should be used based on individual preference. Brief descriptions of various techniques follow.

Deep Breathing

Deep breathing is the most basic technique used in relaxation and is often the foundation for other methods. The primary benefit is that deep breathing can be done anywhere and anytime. It is beneficial to practice deep breathing several times a day. The methodology consists of completely filling the lungs when breathing so that the abdomen expands outward. You begin by taking a deep breath and then exhaling slowly through the mouth. When inhaling, you think to yourself "I am" and when exhaling, think "relaxed". A hand can be placed on the stomach to ensure that it is fully expanded. If the stomach does not rise, the breath is not deep enough or the abdomen is being held too tightly. You repeat this cycle several times and then rest quietly for 3 to 5 minutes.

Progressive Muscle Relaxation

Progressive muscle relaxation creates awareness of the difference between muscular tension and a relaxed state. Progressive muscle relaxation is a three-step process that begins by tensing a muscle group and noticing how the tension feels. Next, a conscious effort is made to relax the tension and notice that feeling. The third phase consists of concentrating on the differences between the two sensations. Beginning at either the head and working down or at the feet and working up, all major muscle groups should be tensed and relaxed (see Figure 9-8).

Autogenics

Autogenics uses self-suggestion to produce a relaxation response. Autogenics begins with a deep breath and a conscious effort to relax. This technique may follow a progression from head to feet or feet to head and also uses a phrase such as "my arm feels heavy and warm" repeated several times before moving on to the next muscle group. Other phrases that carry a message of calming, such as "I am completely calm and relaxed," can be used and repeated. The session can be ended by silently stating, "I am refreshed and alert." Autogenics takes practice, time, and commitment to achieve the relaxation response and should be practiced twice a day for about 10 minutes. Commercial tapes are available that are very beneficial.

Meditation

Meditation can be approached from a variety of perspectives. As a stress-reduction technique its purpose is to temporarily tune out the world and invoke relaxation. Meditation was first introduced to this country on a wide scale as transcendental meditation (TM) in the 1960s. With TM, each meditator is given a *mantra* (a particular word or sound to be used while meditating). During a meditation session the person meditating concentrates on that word or sound and attempts to eliminate all outside distractions. The mantra is kept secret to enhance attentiveness. Meditation as a method of stress reduction uses the same precepts. You begin by taking a comfortable position on a couch or in a chair. You take several deep breaths, slowly inhaling and exhaling. You can shut your eyes or softly focus them on an object so that the details are blurred. All thoughts should be concentrated on a word or phrase, such as one or peace or any other appropriate phrase while continuing to breathe slowly and deeply.[13] The relaxation response can also be initiated by using the same format and then counting breaths backward from 100 or by imagining a white light that slowly travels throughout the body, letting in light and energy while expelling tension and fear. Many commercial tapes are available.

Visualization

Visualization (imagery) is a form of relaxation that uses the imagination. Visualization begins when a

Figure 9-8 Progressive Muscle Relaxation

There are numerous progressive muscles relaxation activities. The exercises are frequently structured by a facilitator, with some exercises beginning with the feet or hands or face. Because of space constraints, only the relaxing of the face will be described here. You can add the other parts of the body by recording the entire process on audiotape and listening to the tape as often as desired—usually once a day or two to three times a week. Take your time (3 to 4 minutes) for each area of the body.

▶ Assume a comfortable position and concentrate on the instructions. You may find it beneficial to lay down or be seated in a comfortable chair.

▶ Close your eyes.

▶ Allow all your muscles to relax and feel loose and heavy. Take several deep breaths.

▶ Wrinkle your forehead and hold for 6 seconds.
  ▶ Notice the feelings.
  ▶ Relax, allow the forehead to become smooth.
  ▶ Notice the feeling of relaxation.

▶ Frown with your eyes, forehead, and scalp and hold for 6 seconds.
  ▶ Experience the sensation of tension.
  ▶ Relax the muscles.
  ▶ Notice the feelings of relaxation.

▶ Keeping your eyes closed, clench your jaw and push your teeth together.
  ▶ Hold for 6 seconds.
  ▶ Notice the tension.
  ▶ Relax the jaw and allow the lips to part slightly.

▶ Now press your tongue against the roof of your mouth and feel the tension.
  ▶ Hold for 6 seconds.
  ▶ Allow your tongue to return to its normal position, experiencing the sensation of relaxation.

▶ Now press your lips together as tightly as possible.
  ▶ Hold for 6 seconds.
  ▶ Relax and notice the feelings of relaxation over your lips.

▶ Using the same principles, gradually move through the body from the shoulders to the arms to the hands, fingers, back, chest, abdomen, hips, legs, ankles, feet, and toes.

person finds a comfortable position, shuts the eyes, and takes several deep breaths. Several variations of visualization can then be used. Individuals can imagine a tranquil scene, such as a beach on a sunny day or a valley with a stream or forest and then place themselves in the scene. All the sights, sounds, smells, and feelings can be imagined. People suffering from a terminal illness frequently imagine scenes such as their immune system attacking or destroying the disease, or they envision themselves as healthy and disease free with surprisingly good results. Individuals who want to make major life changes, such as losing weight or stopping smoking, can envision themselves slim or not smoking or imagine themselves in trouble situations and plan what to do to avoid eating or smoking in that situation. Visualization can also be used to improve ath-

letic performance. Tapes are available that can assist in learning how to develop this technique.

Biofeedback

Biofeedback is based on scientific principles and is designed to enhance awareness of body functions. Sensory equipment is used to demonstrate subtle body changes such as increases or decreases in skin temperature, muscle contraction, and brain wave variations. Biofeedback enables people to become aware of muscle tensions and learn how to control these tensions through awareness of the sensations that are relaxing. Biofeedback is an educational tool. After a few sessions, people should begin to recognize and thereby alter their typical bodily responses to those situations that serve as stressors for them.

Laughter is an excellent way to reduce stress.

Music

Quiet music soothes by causing people to breathe more deeply, stilling turbulent emotions, reducing metabolic response, and calming the autonomic nervous system.

Humor

Laughter is a powerful stress-reducing agent. A deep laugh temporarily raises pulse rate and blood pressure and tenses the muscles. After a good laugh, however, pulse rate and blood pressure actually go down, and the muscles become more relaxed. Laughter works in two ways. Being able to laugh at a situation reminds you that life is seldom perfect or predictable. Laughing helps keep events in perspective. Laughing also works to reinforce a positive attitude. Laughing or even smiling can actually improve a mood.

Time Management

A major contributor to stress is the pressure associated with time constraints. By effectively managing time, you can eliminate a great deal of stress. For the college student, effective use of time is crucial, especially when working and attending school at the same time. Procrastination can add to stress and undermine academic work, personal relationships, and work efforts. Assessment Activity 9-5 provides a log to help manage time more effectively. Depending on individual needs, the following are some suggestions:

1. Organize and write down realistic goals and priorities: Current activities should be as-sessed as to whether they are essential, important, or trivial. Ask yourself the question, "When does the task have to be completed?" Write down the priorities for the next day before going to sleep each night and rank them in order. This provides a night to "sleep on them." They can then be approached systematically, according to need the next day.

2. Develop a time framework: To help alleviate stress, establish the amount of time to be spent on each activity. Some tasks cannot be completed in a day's time. If this is the case, estimate the days or weeks required to complete the task. This is especially important in accomplishing long-term commitments. Allotting blocks of time each day of each week helps to alleviate the extreme pressure of completing a difficult task in a short time. For example, if a term paper is due at the end of a semester, you can spend a certain number of hours each week working on the paper. You can establish goals for the completion of the paper with a reward for yourself each time a goal is achieved. Another example is to study each course everyday by allotting a specific time to read and review the subject material covered in class.

3. Know where and when you can best complete a task: Know the circumstances under which you function best. Is it easier for you to concentrate if you work in the library or the dorm room? Where will you have the least interruptions? Do you concentrate best in the morning, afternoon, or evening?

4. Establish priorities for time: To find time for everything that must be done, you have to know your priorities. Tasks can be divided into those that must be done immediately, those that can wait a brief time, and those that are not essential to accomplish. Once priorities are established, start with the highest priority item and work through the list.

5. Ask for help if responsibilities become overwhelming: Say "no" when there are too many tasks to handle. Do not feel guilty over saying no, this only adds more stress. For example, if sorority or fraternity demands are too great, either ask others to share the workload or refuse the responsibility.

6. Take a break: Every day should provide for fun, leisure, time alone, and relaxation. Make the most of every day. Assessment Activity 9-5 will help you establish a better time management framework.

Exercise is an effective way to cope with stress.

Exercise

Because the fight-or-flight syndrome stimulates the body into action, exercise is a logical method of responding to that physiological command. Exercise has been found to directly affect the brain chemistry. Studies have shown an increase in endorphin levels after an easy or a strenuous run.[14] (Endorphins are natural pain killers and function to help alleviate sensations of pain and stimulate a positive response from the immune system.) Exercise is a positive stressor (eustress) and, when properly used, seems to offset the adverse effects of distress.[15] Studies have demonstrated that there is a relationship be-

tween exercise and stress. Exercise reduces the severity of the stress response, shortens the recovery time from the stressor, and diminishes vulnerability to stress-related disease. The higher the fitness level, the more beneficial the exercise is in reducing stress.[16] (The recommended types of exercise programs are discussed in Chapter 3.)

A correctly designed exercise program produces beneficial physiological responses and can induce psychological effects that serve to reduce anxiety, promote feelings of accomplishment, and help evoke muscle relaxation.

Selecting a Stress-Reducing Technique

No single stress-reduction technique automatically reduces stress for everyone. People are comfortable with and enjoy different activities and this is what determines long-term use. When dealing with your stress, two factors are of primary importance. First, awareness that a stress response is occuring is necessary. People are frequently unaware that the reason they are always tired or irritable or have body aches is because they are experiencing stress's negative effects. Second, everyone has to find the stress-reduction techniques that work best for them. This usually requires more than one approach, depending on the individual and the type of stress response each individual experiences. Any technique that helps create a sense of relaxation, provides personal time, and allows you to gain control can lead to a happier, healthier, more enjoyable life.

Summary

▶ Stress is the nonspecific response of the body to any demands made on it.

▶ Anything that creates stress is a stressor. Stressors may take the form of eustress (good) or distress (bad).

▶ The general adaptation syndrome (GAS) explains how the body responds to a stressor. The three stages are alarm, resistance, and exhaustion.

▶ The stress response can enhance physical and mental performance.

▶ Whether positive or negative, each time a stressful event occurs, a series of neurological and hormonal messages are sent throughout the body.

▶ People's perceptions of stress are associated with self-esteem, self-efficacy, and locus of control.

▶ People who deal effectively with stress seem to exhibit hardiness in their personality. Hardiness consists of a sense of challenge (viewing stressful situations as opportunities for growth), commitment (a sense of inner purpose), and control (power over your life).

▶ Coping is the effort made to manage or deal with stress.

▶ Many techniques can help to reduce stress. They include autogenics, deep breathing, visualization, muscle relaxation, meditation, massage, biofeedback, exercise, yoga, music, and humor.

Action Plan for Personal Wellness

Use the information presented in this chapter to answer the following questions and to formulate an action plan to enhance your personal wellness.

1 Based on the information presented in this chapter, along with what I know about my family's health history, the health problems and issues that I need to be concerned about are:_____

_____

_____

2 Of those health concerns listed in number 1, the one I most need to act on is:_____

_____

_____

3 Possible actions that I can take to improve my level of wellness are (be specific):_____

_____

_____

4 Of those actions listed in number 3, the one that I most need to include in an action plan is:_____

_____

_____

5 Factors I need to keep in mind to be successful in my action plan are:_____

_____

_____

Review Questions

1. What is stress? What are stressors?
2. What are the stages the mind and body go through when exposed to a stressor?
3. What are some potential signals that a person is experiencing chronic stress, and what are the possible effects?
4. What factors influence how an individual perceives and copes with stress?
5. Define hardiness and how it may help an individual effectively deal with stress.
6. What are some guidelines for handling stress positively?
7. Discuss various stress-reducing techniques.

References

1. Siegal BS: *Love, medicine and miracles*, New York, 1988, Perinnial Library.
2. Selye H: *Stress without distress*, New York, 1975, New American Library.
3. Hanson PG: *The joy of stress*, Kansas City, Kan, 1986, Andrews, McMeel & Parker.
4. Selye H: *The stress of life*, rev ed, New York, 1978, McGraw-Hill.
5. Girdano D, George E Jr: *Controlling stress and tension*, Englewood Cliffs, NJ, 1989, Prentice Hall.
6. Folkman S: Personal control and stress and coping processes: a theoretical analysis, *J Pers Soc Psychol* 46:839-852, 1984.
7. Gelman D, Hager M: Body and soul, *Newsweek*, Nov 7, 1988, pp 88-97.
8. Greenberg J: *Stress management*, Dubuque, Iowa, 1990, Wm C Brown.
9. Friedman M, Roseman R: *Type A behavior and your heart*, New York, 1984, Alfred A Knopf.
10. Flannery RB: Toward stress-resistant persons: a stress management approach to the treatment of anxiety, *Am J Prevent Med* 3(1):25-30, 1987.
11. Fischman J: Type A on trial, *Psychol Today* 21(2):42-64, 1987.
12. Kobasa S: How much stress can you survive? *Am Health* 5(7):64-77, 1984.
13. Benson H: *The relaxation response*, New York, 1985, Berkley.
14. Appenzeller D et al: Neurology of endurance training versus endorphins, *Neurol* 30:418, 1980 (abstract).
15. Lamb LE: Understanding stress, *Health Letter* 39(suppl):12, 1992.
16. Crews D, Landers D: A meta-analytic review of aerobic fitness and reactivity to psychosocial stressors. *Med Sci Sports Exerc* 19:5114-5120, 1987.

Annotated Readings

Allman WF: The mental edge, kept to peak performance in sports and life, *US News & World Report*, Aug 3, 1992, pp 50-56. *Discusses motivation, concentration, mental imagery, and stress control in creating optimal performance in sports and life.*

Gallagher W: The healing touch, *Am Health*, Oct 1988, pp 45-53. *Introduces the concept of "bodywork," which are techniques that change how people can experience their own bodies and perhaps their minds.*

Goldman D: "What's your stress style?" *Am Health*, Apr 1986, pp 41-45. *Most experts agree that there is tremendous variability in the way individuals respond to stress. Consequently, a stress management program should be personalized.*

Squires S: Visions to boost immunity, *Am Health*, Jul 1987, pp 56-61. *Discusses the relationship between emotional states and the immune system. This field of research is psychoneuroimmunology. Clinical findings indicate that imagery may serve as treatment for disease by involving the immune system.*

Stark E: Stress—It's all relative and relatively easy to manage, *Am Health*, Dec 1992, pp 41-48. *Describes how the body responds to stress and provides guidelines for coping.*

Tierney J: The heartbeat of America, *Hippocrates*, Jan/Feb 1989, pp 34-36. *A humorous look at things commonly considered stressors and the way they affect blood pressure.*

ASSESSMENT ACTIVITY 9-1

Stressors of Life

The stress scale below represents an adaptation of Holmes and Rahe's Life Event Scale. It has been modified to apply to college-age adults and is a rough indication of stress levels and health consequences for teaching purposes.

Directions: To determine your stress score, add the number of points corresponding to the events you have experienced in the past 12 months.

Death of a close family member	____100	Increase in workload at school	____ 37
Death of a close friend	____ 73	Outstanding personal achievement	36
Divorce between parents	____ 65	First quarter/semester in college	____ 36
Jail term	____ 63	Change in living conditions	____ 31
Major personal injury or illness	____ 63	Serious argument with instructor	____ 30
Marriage	____ 58	Lower grades than expected	____ 29
Firing from a job	____ 50	Change in sleeping habits	____ 29
Failure of an important course	____ 47	Change in social activities	____ 29
Change in health of family member	____ 45	Change in eating habits	____ 28
Pregnancy	____ 45	Chronic car trouble	____ 26
Sex problems	____ 44	Change in number of family get togethers	____ 26
Serious argument with close friend	____ 40	Too many missed classes	____ 25
Change in financial status	____ 39	Change of college	____ 24
Change of major	____ 39	Dropping of more than one class	____ 23
Trouble with parents	____ 39	Minor traffic violations	____ 20
New girl or boyfriend	____ 37		TOTAL ____

Here's how to interpret your score. If your score is 300 or higher, you are at high risk for developing a health problem. If your score is between 150 and 300, you have a 50/50 chance of experiencing a serious health change within 2 years. If your score is below 150, you have a one in three chance of a serious health change. Use of effective stress reduction techniques can reduce the chances of experiencing a serious health change.

Stress Style: Body, Mind, Mixed?

Directions: Imagine yourself in a stressful situation. When you are feeling anxious, what sensations do you typically experience? Check all that apply.

_____ 1. My heart beats faster.
_____ 2. I find it difficult to concentrate because of distracting thoughts.
_____ 3. I worry too much about things that don't really matter.
_____ 4. I feel jittery.
_____ 5. I get diarrhea.
_____ 6. I imagine terrifying scenes.
_____ 7. I cannot keep anxiety-provoking pictures and images out of my mind.
_____ 8. My stomach gets tense.
_____ 9. I pace up and down nervously.
_____ 10. I am bothered by unimportant thoughts running through my mind.
_____ 11. I become immobilized.
_____ 12. I feel I am losing out on things because I cannot make decisions fast enough.
_____ 13. I perspire.
_____ 14. I cannot stop thinking worrisome thoughts.

There are three basic ways of reacting to stress—primarily physical, mental, or mixed. Physical stress types feel tension in the body—jitters, butterflies, the sweats. Mental types experience stress mainly in the mind—worries and preoccupying thoughts. Mixed types react with both responses in about equal measure.

Give yourself a Mind point if you answered "yes" to each of the following questions: 2, 3, 6, 7, 10, 12, 14. Give yourself a Body point for each of these: 1, 4, 5, 8, 9, 11, 13. If you have more Mind than Body points, consider yourself a mental stress type. If you have more Body than Mind points, your stress style is physical. About the same number of each? You're a mixed reactor.

Choosing a Relaxer

Body: If stress registers mainly in your body, you will need a remedy that will break up the physical tension pattern. This may be a vigorous body workout, but a slow-paced, even lazy, muscle relaxer may be equally effective. Here are some suggestions to get you started:

Aerobics	Progressive relaxation
Swimming	Body scan
Biking	Rowing
Walking	Yoga
Massage	Soaking in a hot bath, sauna

Mind: If you experience stress as an invasion of worrisome thoughts, the most direct intervention is anything that will engage your mind completely and redirect it—meditation, for example. On the other hand, some people find the sheer exertion of heavy physical exercise unhooks the mind wonderfully and is very fine therapy. Suggestions:

Meditation	Autogenic suggestion
Reading	Crossword puzzles
TV, movies	Games like chess or cards
Any absorbing hobby	Vigorous exercise
Knitting, sewing, carpentry, or other handicrafts	

Mind/Body: If you are a mixed type, you may want to try a physical activity that also demands mental rigor:

Competitive sports (racquetball, tennis, squash, volleyball, etc.)
Meditation
Any combination from the Mind and Body Lists

How Hardy Are You?

Directions: Below are 12 items similar to those that appear on a hardiness questionnaire. Really evaluating an individual's hardiness requires more than one quick test, but this simple exercise can be a good indication of your own "hardiness." Write down how much you agree or disagree with the following statements, using this scale:

0 = Strongly disagree
1 = Mildly disagree
2 = Mildly agree
3 = Strongly agree

_____ A. Trying my best at work makes a difference.
_____ B. Trusting to fate is sometimes all I can do in a relationship.
_____ C. I often wake up eager to start on the day's projects.
_____ D. Thinking of myself as a free person leads to great frustration and difficulty.
_____ E. I would sacrifice financial security in my work if something really challenging came along.
_____ F. It bothers me when I have to deviate from the routine or schedule I have set for myself.
_____ G. An average citizen can have an impact on politics.
_____ H. Without the right breaks, it is hard to be successful in my field.
_____ I. I know why I am doing what I'm doing at work.
_____ J. Getting close to people puts me at risk of being obligated to them.
_____ K. Encountering new situations is an important priority in my life.
_____ L. I really don't mind when I have nothing to do.

To Score Yourself:

These questions measure control, commitment, and challenge. For half the questions, a high score (agreement) indicates hardiness; for the other half, a low score (disagreement) does.

To get your scores on control, commitment, and challenge, first write in the number of your answer—0, 1, 2, or 3—above the letter of each question on the score sheet. Then add and subtract as shown. (To get your score on control, for example, add your answers to questions A and G; add your answers to B and H; and then subtract the second number from the first.)

Add your scores on commitment, control, and challenge together to get a score for total hardiness. A total score of **10-18 = hardy personality; 0-9 = moderate hardiness; below 0 = low hardiness.**

$$(\underline{\quad} + \underline{\quad}) - (\underline{\quad} + \underline{\quad}) = \underline{\quad} = \text{Control score}$$
(A)　　(G)　　(B)　　(H)

$$(\underline{\quad} + \underline{\quad}) - (\underline{\quad} + \underline{\quad}) = \underline{\quad} = \text{Committment score}$$
(C)　　(I)　　(D)　　(J)

$$= \underline{\quad}$$
(Total hardiness score)

$$(\underline{\quad} + \underline{\quad}) - (\underline{\quad} + \underline{\quad}) = \underline{\quad} = \text{Challenge score}$$
(E)　　(K)　　(F)　　(L)

Paths to Hardiness

Three techniques are suggested to help become happier, healthier, and hardier. They are the following:

▶ **Focusing:** Recognize signals from the body that something is wrong. Focusing increases the sense of control over plans and puts individuals in a psychologically better position to change.

▶ **Reconstructing stressful situations:** Think about a stress episode and then write down three ways the situation could have gone better and three ways it could have gone worse. Doing this helps to recognize that things could have been worse and, even more important, that there are better ways to cope.

▶ **Compensating through self-improvement:** It is important to distinguish between what can be controlled and what cannot. A way to regain control is by taking on a new challenge or task to master.

ASSESSMENT ACTIVITY 9-4

Identification of Coping Styles

Directions: There are a variety of ways and methodologies to help us deal with stress. Consider each of the activities below and determine whether you are currently using any of them to deal with stress.

	Often	Rarely	Not at all
Listen to music			
Go shopping with a friend			
Watch television/go to a movie			
Read a newspaper, magazine, or a book			
Sit alone in peaceful outdoors			
Write prose or poetry			
Attend athletic event, play, lecture, symphony, etc.			
Go for a walk or drive			
Exercise (swim, bike, jog)			
Get deeply involved in some other activity			
Play with a pet			
Take a nap			
Get outdoors, enjoy nature			
Write in journal			
Practice deep breathing, meditation, autogenics, muscle relaxation			
Straighten up desk or work area			
Take a bath or shower			
Do physical labor (garden, paint)			
Make home repairs, refinish furniture			
Buy something—records, books			
Play a game (chess, backgammon, games, video games)			
Pray, go to church			
Discuss situations with spouse or close friend			
Others (list)			
_____			
_____			
_____			

Directions: Below is a list of negative coping behaviors. Mark them according to how much you currently use them.

	Often	Rarely	Not at all
Become aggressive			
Use negative self-talk			
Yell at spouse/kids/friends			
Drink a lot of coffee or tea			
Get drunk			
Swear			
Take a tranquilizing drug			
Avoid social contact with others			
Try to anticipate the worst possible outcome			
Think about the possibility of suicide			
Smoke tobacco			
Chew fingernails			
Overeat, undereat			
Become irritable, short tempered			
Cry excessively			
Kick something, throw something			
Drive fast in car			
Others (list)			
_____			
_____			
_____			

Scoring Instructions: Count the Number of Positive and Negative Coping Techniques You Use.

Number of negative techniques:_____

Number of positive techniques:_____

How often do you employ negative coping strategies?

Do you use more positive than negative strategies or is it the reverse?

Do you recognize a need to change some of the techniques you are now using? If so, which ones?

What are some ways in which you can maximize your positive coping behaviors? How can you minimize your negative ones?

ASSESSMENT ACTIVITY   9 - 5

Analyzing My Use of Time

Managing your time effectively can significantly contribute to the feelings of control you have over your life. A by-product of this is reduced stress and tension as you are able to meet daily demands with less effort. Since the basis of change is recognizing that there needs to be a change and then determining the areas in your life that need change, a good place to begin with time management needs is by analyzing how you are currently managing your time.

Directions: Make several copies of this log and keep track of your time for a week. Include all your activities—from classess to meals to driving time to conversations with friends. At the end of the day and week, rate each hour as to how important the activities that occurred during that time were. Taking time to relax, talk to friends, and be alone are considered important to total well-being and should not be discounted.

Daily Log

Time	Activities	Where	Essential, Important, or Trivial
6-7:00 AM			
7-8:00			
8-9:00			
9-10:00			
10-11:00			
11-12:00			
12-1:00 PM			
1-2:00			
2-3:00			
3-4:00			
4-5:00			
5-6:00			
6-7:00			
7-8:00			
8-9:00			
9-10:00			
10-11:00			
11:00 PM-6:00 AM			

Analyzing Your Log

1. Which activities did you find to be the most productive for you? Which were the least?
2. Where were your most productive activities performed? Your unproductive activities?
3. What time of day did you find to be the most productive for you—morning, afternoon, or evening?

The analysis should be based on the full week's activities. You are looking for patterns of behavior that provide the best effects for you. You may find that you work best at home or in the dormitory in the afternoons or at the library in the evenings. Using this assessment, try to find the best patterns of achievement for you.

Assuming Responsibility for Substance Use

Key terms	Objectives
alcohol	After completing this chapter, you will be able to:
caffeine	▷ Identify the reasons people use drugs
cocaine	▷ Define terms associated with drugs and drug usage
depressants	▷ List the various drug classifications
designer drugs	▷ Describe the effects of various drugs
drug	
inhalants	
marijuana	
narcotics	
nicotine	
psychoactives	
stimulants	

Quality of life is not necessarily concerned with doing "right" or "wrong" or being "good" or "bad." The ultimate determinant of quality of life are the decisions you make that affect your life positively or negatively. To have a high quality of life means to make intelligent choices that contribute to physical, mental, emotional, and spiritual well-being. You must have accurate information and recognize the consequences of actions to make the best possible choices. The decisions you make are cumulative. As time goes on and aging occurs, consequences of previous actions, habits, and modes of behavior increasingly affect the way your body functions. The emphasis of this book has been on personal behaviors such as exercising, weight maintenance, proper nutrition, and the prevention of cardiovascular disease. However, other vital areas influence your quality of life. This chapter deals with the subject of drugs. Drug use or nonuse can strongly affect health and quality of life. For example, when a drug is used for treatment, cure, prevention, or relief of pain, it is categorized as *medicine*. Many people are alive because of the therapeutic effect of drugs in preventing disease and maintaining health. However, not all drugs are used as medicines. When usage involves reasons other than medicinal, even if that behavior is considered "recreational," the potential still exists for tragic consequences.

Reasons for Drug Use

A **drug** is a chemical substance that can alter the structure and functioning of a living organism. (Other terms that may be important to understanding drugs are listed in Figure 10-1.) People use drugs for many reasons. Some individuals need drugs to maintain a normal life or to alleviate specific symptoms, whereas others indulge in drugs to alter their moods. Researchers have identified several reasons people use drugs[1]:

▶ Recreational/social facilitation: People frequently use drugs they feel will lessen the tension associated with social encounters. Marijuana and alcohol are particularly popular in social situations. Potential dangers in using drugs for this purpose include mental dependency on the drug and an inability to cope with social events without using the drug.

▶ Sensation seeking: Some people enjoy taking risks. For them, drugs fulfill the need for excitement and adventure. Others turn to drugs out of boredom or a sense of inadequacy in their lives. They are seeking sensations of pleasure that are artificially induced. Unfortunately, they frequently turn to increasingly dangerous drugs or to increased doses to provide equivalent or more exciting thrills.

▶ Religious/spiritual factors: Throughout history, people have used drugs to enhance their spirituality or become more godlike. Too often the drug becomes the object of worship rather than the god or spiritual essence being sought. Though many people have tried, the spiritual realm has not been achieved through mind-altering drugs.

▶ Altered states: Drugs are used to increase the intensity of a mood or create a state of euphoria.

Figure 10-1 Understanding Drug Terminology

Listed are terms that may be unfamiliar but are useful in understanding the effects of substances.

Antagonistic: Opposing or counteracting

Designer drugs: Illegally manufactured psychoactive drugs that are similar to controlled drugs on the FDA's schedule

Drug abuse: The excessive and pathological use of a drug that has dangerous side effects

Drug misuse: The use of a drug for purposes other than for what it is intended

Effective dose: The amount that produces the desired effect

Lethal dose: The amount capable of causing death

Medicines: Drugs used to prevent illness or to treat symptoms of an illness

Over-the-counter (OTC) drugs: A nonprescription drug

Physical dependence: A physiological need for a drug

Polyabuse: The use of multiple drugs

Potentiating: An exaggerated drug response obtained when two drugs are taken together; a much greater effect is obtained than when either drug is taken separately

Prescription drugs: Drugs obtained only by order of a physician or dentist

Psychoactive: Affecting mood and/or behavior

Psychological dependence: An emotional or mental need to use a drug

Synergistic: A combined effect that is greater than the sum of the individual effects when two or more drugs are used at the same time; the combination produces an exaggerated effect or a prolonged drug action

Toxic dose: The amount that produces a poisonous effect

Figure 10-2 Addiction and Personality

Addiction has been defined as a "pathological relationship with a mood-altering experience that has life-damaging consequences." Behaviors that result in addiction must initially provide some sense of pleasure or have a positive association, even though the long-term results are not pleasurable. The spectrum of addictions can range from drugs such as tobacco and alcohol to behaviors such as compulsive eating and working.

The causes of addiction are complex and interrelated, and a number of variables are required for development. Suggested factors contributing to addiction include genetics, family influences, life events, social and cultural mores, availability, and personality. Many studies have linked specific personality traits with addiction. Traits such as low self-esteem, anxiety, and antisocial behavior have been associated with the abuse of alcohol and drugs and other compulsive behaviors. This is enhanced by the fact that addicts often seem to trade one addiction for another (e.g., alcohol for cigarettes or cigarettes for food). Researchers have been unable to define a personality that has a predisposition toward addiction. The question still remains—Does addiction cause the development of low self-esteem, or does low self-esteem lead to addiction? Because innumerable circumstances and conditions influence personality, predestination to addiction, either chemically, genetically, or psychologically, has not been proved.[25,26]

Some people attempt to enhance physical performance or stimulate artistic creativity. Evidence indicates that perceptions of improvement are false.

▶ Rebellion and alienation: The use of drugs can be a deliberate act of rebellion against social values, especially the values of parents. Individuals who experience extreme pressures and who have difficulty coping frequently turn to drugs as an escape. This includes college-age students facing academic pressure and increased personal freedom.

▶ Peer pressure and group entry: People who have a great desire to feel accepted will often use drugs to demonstrate their sameness with other members in the group. Feeling accepted, modeling behavior after someone who is admired, and attempting to create an identity or specific image are reasons offered for engaging in drug use. Self-esteem seems to be a vital component. Individuals with high self-esteem see themselves as competent, successful, self-sufficient, accepting, outgoing, and well rounded. People with low self-esteem tend to feel isolated and unloved and lack the capacity for joy or self-fulfillment. In the attempt to magically overcome these sensations and perceptions, many people turn to drugs.

The reasons any individual uses drugs are usually not easily categorized. Most drug-use situations depend on personality, experience, perceptions of the environment, and expectations (Figure 10-2).

Drug Classification

Drugs are commonly classified according to the physiological effect they have. Categories include stimulants, depressants, hallucinogens, narcotics, and inhalants. Two other types are also important. First, designer drugs are those that mimic drugs found in the previously mentioned categories. The other drug, marijuana, is difficult to classify but is usually included as a hallucinogen. Depending on the dosage, marijuana can mimic a variety of substances found in other categories. The following is a list of drug categories and the effect they have on the body.

▶ **Stimulants:** Stimulants speed up the central nervous system, producing an increase in alertness and excitability.

▶ **Depressants:** Also known as *sedatives* and *tranquilizers,* depressants slow down the central nervous system, causing an individual to feel relaxed.

▶ **Psychoactives:** Psychoactives can alter feelings, moods, and/or perceptions. Marijuana is classified as a psychoactive drug but can exhibit effects similar to those of stimulants, depressants, and narcotics.

▶ **Narcotics:** Narcotics are powerful painkillers. They also produce pleasurable feelings and induce sleep.

▶ **Inhalants:** Inhalants are volatile nondrugs that cause druglike effects if inhaled. Examples include glue and gasoline. Some, such as nitrous oxide and amyl nitrate, have medical uses.

▶ **Designer drugs:** Designer drugs are drug analogs that have been manufactured in an illegal laboratory and mimic a controlled substance. They are often more powerful and less predictable than the drugs they imitate. The number and variations of designer drugs available are increasing rapidly.

Commonly Abused Substances

This section briefly examines caffeine, alcohol, nicotine, cocaine, marijuana, and designer drugs. In addition, a variety of other substances are potentially dangerous if misused or abused. The drugs listed in Table 10-1 have the most prevalent use.

Caffeine

Caffeine is probably the most used drug in American society. Each day millions of Americans drink, chew, or ingest caffeine in some form. It is a stimulant that speeds the heart rate, temporarily increases blood pressure, and disrupts sleep. It also relieves drowsiness, helps in the performance of repetitive tasks, and improves work ability. Negative effects include insomnia, anxiety, heart arrhythmias, gastrointestinal complaints, dizziness, and headaches.

In the past, caffeine consumption was thought to cause birth defects, breastfeeding problems, cardiovascular disease, cancer, and fibrocystic breast disease. Current research has found no substantial association with these conditions.[2,3] However, pregnant and nursing women should consume no more than two cups of coffee a day and should consume tea and caffeine-containing soft drinks in moderation.[3] Furthermore, women who suffer from premenstrual tension (PMS) should eliminate caffeine. Research has indicated that women who drink a half to four cups of caffeinated tea a day were twice as likely to suffer PMS symptoms as women who drank none at all.[3]

It is easy to consume a great deal of caffeine. Table 10-2 lists the amounts of caffeine found in various products. By becoming familiar with the amount of caffeine in a product and restricting consumption to less than 400 milligrams of caffeine per day, you can benefit from the effects of the drug without suffering any negative aspects.[4]

Alcohol

Alcohol use is pervasive. **Alcohol** is a drug that is deemed socially acceptable by many, but no other drug causes so much physical, social, and emotional damage to individuals and families. People drink alcoholic beverages in many situations and for many reasons. They drink when they are among friends and when they are upset or depressed. People drink to enhance a romantic mood, to put themselves at ease in social situations, and to celebrate special occasions. In addition, people drink because their role models drink and because the advertising industry has convinced them that alcohol contributes to self-enhancement. Unfortunately, the devastation associated with alcohol is often not mentioned. Table 10-3 summarizes the short- and long-term effects of the drug. Because society has labeled alcohol appropriate and even necessary for some occasions, abstinence may be unrealistic for most people. If alcohol is to be used, it must be used responsibly. Figure 10-3 provides suggestions for responsible drinking.

Although there are several types of alcohol, the intoxicating agent in all alcoholic drinks is *ethyl alcohol,* a colorless liquid with a sharp, burning taste. The percentage of alcohol in a beverage is measured by its *proof,* which is twice the percentage of alcohol. A beverage that is 40% alcohol has a proof of 80. The *blood alcohol concentration (BAC)* is the

TABLE 10-1 Commonly Used Substances

Type	Name	Appearance	Method of use
Stimulants			
Amphetamines	Speed, uppers, ups, black beauties, pep pills, copilots, bumblebees, hearts, benzedrine, dexedrine, footballs, biphetamine	Capsules, pills, tablets	Taken orally, injected, inhaled through nasal passages
Cocaine	Coke, snow, flake, white, blow, nose candy, big C, snowbirds, lady	White crystalline powder, often diluted with other ingredients	Inhaled through nasal passages, injected, smoked
Crack cocaine	Crack, freebase rocks, rock	Light brown or beige pellets or crystalline rocks that resemble coagulated soap, often packaged in small vials	Smoked
Methamphetamines	Crank, crystal meth, crystal, methedrine, speed, ice	White powder, pills, a rock that resembles a block of paraffin	Taken orally, injected, inhaled through nasal passages
Additional stimulants	Ritalin, Cylert, Preludin, Didrex, Prestate, Voranil, Tenuate, Tepanil, Pondimin, Sandrex, Plegine, Ionamin	Pills, capsules, tablets	Taken orally, injected
Depressants			
Barbiturates	Downers, barbs, blue devils, red devils, yellow jacket, yellows, Nembutal, Secanol amytal, Tuinals	Red, yellow, blue, or red and blue capsules	Taken orally, injected
Methaqualone	Quaaludes, ludes, sopors	Tablets	Taken orally
Tranquilizers	Valium, librium, equanil, miltown, serax, Tranxene	Tablets, capsules	Taken orally
Psychoactives			
Lysergic acid diethylamide	LSD, acid, green or red, dragon, white lightning, blue heaven, sugar cubes, microdot	Brightly colored tablets, impregnated blotter paper, thin squares of gelatin, clear liquid	Taken orally, licked off paper, inserted in the eyes (gelatin and liquid)
Mescaline and peyote	Mesc, buttons, cactus	Hard brown disk, tablets, capsules, tablets and capsules	Swallowed, chewed, or smoked (disks); taken orally
Phencyclidine	PCP, angel dust, loveboat, lovely, hog, killer weed	Liquid, capsules, white crystalline powder, pills	Taken orally, injected, smoked, sprayed on cigarettes, parsley, and marijuana
Psilocybin	Magic mushrooms, mushrooms	Fried or dried mushrooms	Chewed and swallowed

Continued.

TABLE 10-1 Commonly Used Substances—cont'd

Type	Name	Appearance	Method of use
Narcotics			
Codeine	Empirin compound with codeine, Tylenol with codeine, codeine, codeine in cough medicines	Dark liquid varying in thickness, capsules, tablets	Taken orally, injected
Heroin	Smack, horse, brown sugar, junk, mud, big H, black tar	Powder, white to dark brown; tarlike substance	Injected, inhaled through nasal passages, smoked
Meperidine	Pethidine, Demerol, Mepergan	White powder, solution, tablets	Taken orally, injected
Methadone	Dolophine, Methadose, Amidone	Solution	Taken orally, injected
Morphine	Pectoral syrup, hypodermic tablets	White crystals, injectable solutions	Injected, taken orally, smoked
Opium	Paregoric, Dover's powder, Parepectolin	Dark-brown chunks, powder	Smoked, eaten
Other narcotics	Percocet, Percodan, Tussionex, Fentanyl, Darvon, Talwin, Lomotil	Tablets, capsules, liquid	Taken orally, injected
Inhalants			
Amyl nitrite	Poppers, snappers	Clear or yellowish liquid in ampules	Vapors inhaled
Butyl nitrite	Rush, bolt, locker room, bullet, climax	Packaged in small bottles	Vapors inhaled
Chlorohydrocarbons	Aerosol sprays	Aerosol paint cans, containers of cleaning fluid	Vapors inhaled
Hydrocarbons	Solvents	Cans of aerosol propellants, gasoline, glue, paint thinner	Vapors inhaled
Nitrous oxide	Laughing gas, whippets	Propellant for whipped cream in aerosol spray can, small, 8-g metal cylinder sold with a balloon or pipe (buzz bomb)	Vapors inhaled

percentage of alcohol content in the blood. This percentage determines the alcohol's effect on the individual (Table 10-3). The more quickly the alcohol is absorbed, the quicker the BAC increases.

Alcohol enters the bloodstream quickly from the stomach and even more quickly from the small intestine. In the stomach, food inhibits absorption of alcohol. Food does not affect absorption in the small intestine.[5] Other factors that affect the rate of absorption are the following:

▶ Rate of consumption: How quickly the beverage is consumed affects the rate of absorption.
▶ Type of beverage: Beer and wine contain substances that slow the rate of absorption. Carbonated beverages added to liquor speed absorption because the carbon dioxide in carbonation allows the stomach contents to pass more rapidly to the small intestine.
▶ Body weight: More weight means more blood

TABLE 10-1 Commonly Used Substances—cont'd

Type	Name	Appearance	Method of use
Marijuana			
Hashish	Hash	Brown or black cakes or balls	Eaten, smoked
Hashish oil	Hash oil	Concentrated syrupy liquid varying from clear to black	Smoked—mixed with tobacco
Marijuana	Pot, grass, weed, reefer, dope, Mary Jane, sinsemilla, Acapulco gold, Thai sticks	Parsleylike substance mixed with stems that may include seeds	Eaten, smoked
Tetrahydrocannabinol	THC	Soft gelatin capsules	Taken orally, smoked
Designer drugs			
Analogs of amphetamines and methamphetamines (hallucinogens)	MDMA (ecstasy, XTC, Adam, essence), MDM, STP, PMA, 2,5-DMA, TMA, DOM, DOB	White powder, tablets, capsules	Taken orally, inhaled through nasal passages
Analogs of fentanyl (narcotic)	Synthetic heroin, China white	White powder resembling heroin	Inhaled through nasal passages, injected
Analogs of phencyclidine (hallucinogens)	PCPy, PCE, (PCP) TCP	White powder	Taken orally, injected, smoked

and body mass, which has a diluting effect on alcohol.

▶ Tolerance to alcohol: Some individuals seem to remain sober, whereas others react very quickly. One drink to a novice may have the same effect as three on a more-experienced drinker. This indicates that the experienced drinker's body is adapting to the alcohol at the cellular level.

Alcoholism is a disease in which an individual loses control over drinking. An *alcoholic* is any person who suffers from the disease of alcoholism. For an alcoholic, alcohol assumes more importance while family, social, and work or school responsibilities become less important and are eventually disrupted by the desire and need for alcohol. Some alcoholics make this transition very rapidly, whereas others maintain the appearance of being only a so-

Figure 10-3 Responsible Drinking

Following are suggestions to help each person be a responsible drinker and host:

▶ Drink slowly; never consume more than one drink per hour.

▶ Eat while drinking, but do not eat salty food.

▶ When mixing drinks, measure the amount of alcohol; never just pour.

▶ Serve and choose nonalcoholic drinks as an alternative.

▶ As host, always serve the guests or hire a bartender. Do not have an open bar or serve someone who is intoxicated.

▶ Stop using or serving alcohol 1 hour before a party is over.

▶ Don't drink and drive. Have either a nondrinker drive the car or call a cab.

TABLE 10-2 Caffeine Amounts in Selected Products (mg)

Product	Amount*	Product	Amount
Coffee (5 oz)		**Prescription drugs (per dose)**	
Brewed, drip method	60-180 (115)	Cafergot (for migraine headache)	100
Brewed, percolator	40-170 (80)	Darvon compound (for pain)	32.4
Instant	30-120 (65)		
Decaffeinated, brewed	2-5	**Nonprescription drugs**	
		No Doz (alertness tablets)	100
Tea (5 oz)		Vivarin (alertness tablets)	200
Brewed, major U.S. brands	20-90 (40)	Aqua-Ban (diuretic)	100
Brewed, imported brands	25-110 (60)	Aqua-Ban Plus	200
Iced (12 oz)	67-76 (70)	Anacin	32
Instant	25-50 (30)	Excedrin	65
		Midol	32.4
Soft drinks (12 oz)		Vanquish	33
Sugar-Free Mr. PIBB	58	Duradyne	15
Mountain Dew	54	Coryban-D capsules	30
Mello Yello	52	Triaminicin tablets	30
TAB	46	Duradyne	15
Coca-Cola (classic/new)	46		
Diet Coke	46	**Other**	
Shasta Cola	44	Cocoa (5 oz)	2-20(4)
Shasta Cherry Cola	44	Chocolate milk (8 oz)	2-7(5)
Shasta Diet Cola	44	Milk chocolate (1 oz)	1-15(6)
Mr. PIBB	40.8	Semisweet chocolate (1 oz)	5-35(26)
Dr. Pepper	40.8	Chocolate-flavored syrup (1 oz)	4
Diet Dr. Pepper	40.8		
Pepsi-Cola	38.4		
Big Red	38		
Diet Pepsi	36		
RC Cola	36		
Cherry RC	36		
Canada Dry Jamaica Cola	30		
Canada Dry Diet Cola	1.5		

*Averages shown in parentheses.

cial drinker for many years. Unfortunately, predetermining who will have trouble with alcohol is impossible. Alcoholism crosses all social and economic barriers and can include clergy, medical doctors, high school students, college students, and professors. Each year, more research seems to link alcoholism to an inherited susceptibility or predisposition for the disease.[6] Whether the causes of alcoholism are heredity or social or a combination of these and other variables, any consumption of alcohol places an alcoholic at risk.

Treatment for alcoholism is often long term. The course of treatment usually occurs in three stages: (1) detoxification—eliminating the alcohol from the body, (2) medical care—attending to any health-related problems, and (3) changing long-term behavior—helping the recovering alcoholic overcome long established drinking patterns and destructive behaviors. (See Figures 10-4 and 10-5 for treatment and aftercare programs and Figure 10-6 for resources.)

Alcoholics remain alcoholics for life, regardless of whether they drink. Recovering alcoholics must therefore be careful about any products they consume, including medicines and mouthwashes, many of which contain alcohol. Currently, an estimated 10 million adults and 3 million adolescents under the age of 18 are alcoholics.[6]

Alcohol use has also been demonstrated to have a strong association with crime and violence. Data

TABLE 10-3 Effects of Alcohol Use

Short term or immediate		Long term	
Blood alcohol concentration (BAC)	**Effect(s)**	**System/organ**	**Health risks**
0.00-0.05	Usually relaxation and euphoria, decrease in alertness	Breast	50% higher risk for cancer in women who drink any alcohol, 100% increase for women having three or more drinks per day
0.05-0.10	Exaggerated feelings and behavior, emotional instability, increased reaction time and diminished motor coordination, impaired driving, legally drunk in most states	Cardiovascular	High blood pressure, irregular heartbeat, chest pain/angina, myocardial infarctions, damage to coronary arteries
0.10-0.15	Loss of peripheral vision, extremely dangerous driving, unsteady walking/standing	General gastrointestinal	Risk of mouth, tongue, throat, esophageal, stomach, and liver cancer; pancreatitis; malnutrition; digestive impairment
0.15-0.30	Significant impairment of sensory perceptions, slurred speech, decreased sensitivity to pain, difficult and staggering walk	Immune	Lower resistance to infectious diseases
		Liver	Hepatitis, cirrhosis
		Pancreas	Interference with insulin production
>0.30	Stupor or unconsciousness, anesthetization, possible death at levels greater than 0.35	Small intestine	Interference with or prevention of absorption of proteins, iron, calcium, thiamine, and vitamin B_{12}
		Stomach	Bleeding from irritation, ulcers
		Muscular	Destruction of muscle fibers
		Nervous	Destruction of brain cells, interference with neurotransmitters, slowing of reaction time
		Reproductive	Impotence, decreased testosterone production, fetal alcohol syndrome, miscarriage

clearly indicate that homicide is more likely to occur in a situation in which drinking has occurred.[7] Assaults such as spouse and child abuse were all correlated with drinking. A Canadian study[7] found that at least 42% of violent crimes involved alcohol.[7] In addition, 75% of suicide attempts involved alcohol.[8]

Tobacco Products

All tobacco products, including cigarettes, cigars, pipes, and smokeless tobacco (snuff and chewing tobacco), contain the drug nicotine. **Nicotine** is an addictive substance and an alkaloid poison. It affects the body by increasing heart and respiratory rates, elevating blood pressure, increasing cardiac output and oxygen consumption, and constricting the bronchi (the two main branches of the trachea that lead to the lungs). Nicotine is inhaled when smoking a tobacco product. With smokeless tobacco, nicotine is absorbed through membranes of the mouth and cheek.

Smoking is directly or indirectly responsible for the conditions and diseases listed in Table 10-4. Some components of cigarette smoke are known

Figure 10-4 Approaches to Treatment and Aftercare of Alcoholism

There are several approaches to providing long-term medical and psychological support to recovering alcoholics. Several current trends are listed.

Alcoholics Anonymous (AA)

AA uses a group approach for individuals who have made a personal decision to stop drinking and want to have the support of others who have made the same decision and understand the emotions and thoughts associated with this decision. AA members view their condition as a *disease* that they must manage daily. A group support system and buddy system help each person through difficult times. AA also helps people with other types of drug problems or refers the individual to specific groups such as Narcotics Anonymous and Cocaine Anonymous. Groups such as Alateen, Alatot, and Al-Anon help the offspring and families of alcoholics.

Drug Therapy

Usually part of an aftercare program, the drug Antabuse (disulfiram) is used to create a severe reaction if alcohol is consumed. Reactions produced include headache, neck aches, nausea, vomiting, and other unpleasant symptoms. Disulfiram works by blocking the enzymes that metabolize alcohol.

Group Therapies

AA provides a model for many different group therapies. Another widely used approach is a behavioral model that teaches coping skills. Special attention is paid to developing self-esteem and to conducting intense self-analysis to modify attitudes, emotional states, and behavior.

Figure 10-5 The Twelve Steps of Alcoholics Anonymous

1. We admitted we were powerless over alcohol—that our lives had become unmanageable.
2. Came to believe that a Power greater than ourselves could restore us to sanity.
3. Made a decision to turn our will and our lives over to the care of God *as we understood Him.*
4. Made a searching and fearless moral inventory of ourselves.
5. Admitted to God, to ourselves, and to another human being the exact nature of our wrongs.
6. Were entirely ready to have God remove all these defects of character.
7. Humbly asked Him to remove our shortcomings.
8. Made a list of all persons we had harmed and became willing to make amends to them all.
9. Made direct amends to such people wherever possible except when to do so would injure them or others.
10. Continued to take personal inventory and when we were wrong promptly admitted it.
11. Sought through prayer and meditation to improve our conscious contact with God as *we understood Him,* praying only for knowledge of His will for us and the power to carry that out.
12. Having had a spiritual awakening as the result of these steps, we tried to carry this message to alcoholics and to practice these principles in all our affairs.

Figure 10-6 Where to Get Help

The telephone numbers listed can be used to find information and help. In addition, local agencies can usually provide information and help (for example, local chapters of Alcoholics Anonymous or Al-Anon).

▶ National Alcohol Hotline-24 hour Helpline
1-800-ALCOHOL

▶ Alcoholics Anonymous (New York, NY)
Contact the local chapter (listed in the phone book) or call for information throughout the United States.
(212)870-3400

▶ Al-Anon (New York, NY)
Provides help for families of alcoholics. Contact the local chapter or call for information throughout the United States.
(212) 254-7230

▶ BACCHUS (Boost Alcohol Consciousness Concerning the Health of University Students)
(303) 871-3068

▶ National Cocaine Hotline
1-800-COCAINE

▶ National Clearinghouse for Alcohol and Drug Information (Rockville, MD)
(301) 468-2600

▶ MADD (Mothers Against Drunk Driving [Irving, TX])
(214) 744-6233

▶ SADD (Students Against Drunk Driving).
P.O. Box 800
Marlboro, MA 01752
(508) 481-3568

TABLE 10-4 Risks of Smoking

Risks	Results
Coronary heart disease	An estimated 169,000 to 226,000 deaths from coronary heart disease can be attributed to cigarette smoking.
Peripheral arterial disease	Smokers are two to three times more likely to suffer from abdominal aortic aneurysm than nonsmokers. Smokers have more atherosclerotic occlusions.
Lung cancer	Smoking cigarettes is the major cause of lung cancers in men and women. Rates are currently increasing faster among women than men.
Cancer of the larynx	Laryngeal cancer in smokers is 2.0 to 27.4 times that of nonsmokers.
Oral cancers	Use of smokeless tobacco and snuff is associated with an increased risk of oral cancer, Pipes and cigars are also major risk factors. Use of alcohol seems to enhance the possibility of developing oral cancer.
Cancer of the esophagus	Smoking cigarettes, pipes, and cigars increases the risk of dying from esophageal cancer from two to nine times. Alcohol use in combination with smoking adds to that risk.
Bladder cancer	Percentage of bladder cancer attributed to smoking is estimated at 40% to 60% in males and 25% to 35% in females.
Cancer of the pancreas	Smokers have twice the risk of nonsmokers for cancer of the pancreas.
Chronic obstructive pulmonary (lung) disease (COPD)	Between 80% to 90% of more than 60,000 deaths per year from COPD are from smoking.
Peptic ulcers	Cigarette smokers develop peptic ulcers much more frequently than nonsmokers. Ulcers are also more difficult to cure in smokers.
Complications in pregnancy, illnesses in children	Smoking mothers have more stillbirths and babies with low birth weight. The hospital admission rates for pneumonia and bronchitis is 28% higher in children of smoking mothers. Asthma is more common among children of smoking mothers. Parental smoking is a risk factor associated with persistent middle-ear effusion in young children.

carcinogens (substances that cause cancer or enable the growth of cancer cells). Nicotine, tars, and carbon monoxide are all found in cigarette smoke. The *tar* in tobacco is a black, sticky, dark fluid composed of thousands of chemicals. Many of the chemicals found in tar are cancer causing. *Carbon monoxide* is a deadly gas emitted in the exhaust of cars and in burning tobacco. The carbon monoxide level in cigarette smoke is 400 times greater than what is considered safe in industrial settings. Carbon monoxide binds to hemoglobin more readily than oxygen, interfering with the ability of blood to transport oxygen to the body; impairs the nervous system; and increases the risk of heart attacks and strokes.

Effects of smoking on the nonsmoker. *Passive smoking* is the inhalation of cigarette smoke by a nonsmoker from the environment. The most common form of inhaled smoke is *sidestream smoke,* which results from burning tobacco products and the end of the lighted tip of a cigarette.[9] Sidestream smoke has higher concentrations of nicotine and other carcinogenic agents than the smoke inhaled by the smoker. Many studies have shown that passive smoking can cause cancer in nonsmokers. Nonsmokers married to smokers have a 30% greater risk of lung cancer and are more likely to experience heart attacks than nonsmoking spouses of nonsmokers.[12] There are no "safe" levels of exposure to cigarette smoke, and there are no "safe" tobacco products.

Advantages of quitting. Smoking is an extremely strong addiction. When individuals stop smoking, their risk of developing the listed diseases and conditions eventually decreases to that of nonsmokers; in other words, the effects of smoking are reversible. To quit completely, many people require the help of trained professionals. Although quitting is difficult, the health benefits gained far outweigh the problems. Suggestions on ways to stop smoking are shown in Figure 10-7. Figure 10-8 discusses the nicotine patch.

Cocaine

At one time **cocaine** was considered the drug of upper class America. Unfortunately, the use of cocaine and its derivative *crack* is epidemic. Estimates are that 25 to 30 million people have experimented with cocaine in the United States. Approximately 5 million use the drug regularly. Among young adults, 6.7% have tried crack, and 40% have tried cocaine. In a recent survey of high school seniors, 1 in 18 admitted trying crack and 14% used cocaine in other forms.[16]

Figure 10-7 Smoking Cessation

To quit smoking is not easy! For the person who chooses (and it is a choice) to quit, the Mayo Clinic Health Letter offers the following suggestions[13]:

▶ Set a date: Make the date reasonably soon. Make a list of reasons why you want to quit.
▶ Start stopping before you reach the date: Taper off the number of cigarettes you are currently smoking. Choose a milder brand.
▶ Make your plans known: Tell a friend, your family, and colleagues of your plans. Ask for their support.
▶ Take it one day at a time: Get up every morning and decide not to smoke that day. Focus your attention on that day only.
▶ Change your routine: Avoid or change situations where you have previously smoked.
▶ Alter your surroundings: Start new activities such as exercising or needlepoint.
▶ Time the urge: Identify when your urge to smoke is the strongest. Being prepared will help you resist.
▶ Use substitutes: Substitutes can include gum, celery, carrots, and pickles.
▶ Prepare a daydream: Have a pleasant daydream ready to help fight off the desire to smoke. This can be an image of yourself without a cigarette in a situation you find highly desirable.
▶ Use relaxation techniques: Deep breathing or progressive muscle relaxation can help.
▶ Practice positive thinking: Tell yourself, "I can make it." Remember that you *can* make it.

If you try these suggestions and continue to fail, you may benefit from contacting a physician for a prescription of nicorette gum. This gum contains small amounts of nicotine and helps some people overcome the nicotine addiction. Nicorette gum can be used whenever the urge to smoke occurs. Initially, you may need 12 to 24 pieces a day. The use of nicorette gum can cause mouth ulcers and nausea and should not be used by pregnant or nursing women.[14]

A powerful stimulant, cocaine is derived from the leaves of the South American coca shrub and ground into a crystalline powder. The most common methods of using the drug are *snorting* it or liquefying it and then *injecting* or *freebasing* (smoking). When snorted, the white powder is sniffed up through the nose. The most potent and expensive method of cocaine use is freebasing. The drug is usu-

Figure 10-8 The Transdermal System (The Patch)—Does it Work?

The latest attempt to help people stop smoking is the transdermal systems developed by several pharmaceutical companies. The "patch" is designed as an aid to smoking cessation by relieving nicotine withdrawal. The patch system is based on the concept of providing different levels of nicotine for various periods as an individual stops smoking. Initially, the patch contains 15 to 21 milligrams of nicotine a day. After 4 to 12 weeks the dosage is reduced to 10 to 14 milligrams a day. This patch is used for 2 to 4 weeks. The last set of patches is worn for 2 to 4 weeks and contains 5 to 7 milligrams of nicotine. Some transdermal patches are worn for 24 hours; other brands are worn for 16 hours each day. The transdermal systems include a patient support kit that may have items such as a guide booklet, a booklet for family and friends, a relaxation audiotape, and a certificate of commitment for quitting.

The transdermal system must be prescribed by a physician and is quite expensive ($300 to $500). The person must stop smoking completely before the first patch is applied. People who suffer from hypertension, have cardiovascular disease, are insulin users, are pregnant, or suffer from peptic ulcers should not use the patch. Success rates vary and seem to be related to motivation, cigarettes smoked per day, years smoked, and exposure to other smokers.[15]

The physical consequences of cocaine use are extreme and highly dangerous. Cocaine use can cause headaches, exhaustion, shaking, blurred vision, nausea, impaired judgment, hyperactivity, loss of appetite, loss of sexual desire, and paranoia that can lead to violence. Snorting cocaine can destroy the septum in the nose. Freebasing may damage the liver and the lungs; fluid buildup in the lungs has resulted in death for some individuals who freebase. Cocaine can initiate strokes, bleeding in the brain, heart attacks, irregular heartbeat, and sudden death.

Women who use cocaine while pregnant have newborns that suffer withdrawal and permanent disability. Fluctuations in blood pressure in the mother can deprive the baby's brain of oxygen, causing the blood vessels in the baby's brain to break down. Essentially, the baby suffers the equivalent of a stroke. Babies born of cocaine addicts have more respiratory, kidney, and visual problems; lack coordination; and are developmentally retarded.[17] Paternal cocaine use may result in the sperm carrying cocaine to the ovum, thus providing early cocaine exposure to the developing embryo. It seems unlikely that a significant amount of cocaine could result in any damage. However, rat studies indicate that exposure of the father to cocaine resulted in behavioral changes in baby rats sired by that father.[18]

Cocaine addiction is extremely difficult to overcome. Antidepressants seem to help reduce dependency. Tyrosine and tryptophan have also been used for treatment. These chemicals are amino acids that seem to block a cocaine high when taken with an antidepressant.[19]

Marijuana

Approximately 25 years ago, marijuana became a cultural phenomenon, the symbol of one generation's disregard for another. The marijuana found on the streets at that time, however, lacked the potency of current crops. Crossbreeding of more potent varieties, improved cultivation, and the part of the plant being used all contribute to increased levels of *delta-9-tetrahydrocannabinol (THC)*, the major psychoactive drug found in marijuana. Some marijuana currently grown in the United States rivals the previously stronger varieties of Mexico, Jamaica, and other areas. The THC percentage in *Cannabis sativa* (the Indian hemp plant from which marijuana is derived) in plants grown in the United States can range from 2% to as high as 7%.[20] The higher the percentage of THC, the more potent the drug. **Marijuana** is composed of the dried leaves and flowering tops of the cannabis plant. *Hashish*, which has stronger effects, is processed from the resin of the plant. The

ally smoked in a water pipe because this provides faster absorption into the bloodstream.

Crack is relatively easy to make and fairly inexpensive to buy. At $10 to $15 a dose, crack is the form of the drug that is most prevalent on the streets. When snorted, crack reaches the brain in about 5 minutes. When injected or smoked, it takes only a few seconds for the drug to take effect.

Use of cocaine produces feelings of well being, euphoria, and extreme exhilaration. Mental alertness seems to increase. Blood vessels constrict, causing heart rate and blood pressure to rise. Cocaine is rapidly metabolized by the liver. Snorting cocaine results in a 5 to 15 minute "high," whereas the effects of crack last 20 to 30 minutes. Psychological and physical dependency on crack develop rapidly because of the brief period of stimulation. The feelings of exhilaration experienced while under the influence of the drug are quickly followed by depression.

resin is either dried and pressed into cakes or sold in liquid form called *hash oil*. Marijuana is used more extensively than hashish in the United States.

Over 400 known chemicals constitute marijuana. More than 60 of these are *cannabinoids,* chemicals found only in cannabis. THC is the cannabinoid that appears most responsible for the sensations experienced by marijuana users. Cannabinoids are different from other drugs in that they are fat soluble rather than water soluble; they have a decided affinity for binding to fat in the human body. Although other drugs enter and then leave the body within relatively short periods, marijuana tends to attach to fatty organs such as the gonads and brain and remain.[21] A single ingestion of THC may require up to 30 days to be eliminated from the body.

Marijuana can be eaten in baked goods such as brownies, but the effects tend to be less predictable. Smoking is a more efficient and powerful technique. When inhaled, THC reaches the brain in as little as 14 seconds. Hashish is so concentrated that a single drop can equal the effects of an entire marijuana joint (cigarette). Cannabis products are difficult to classify but are considered hallucinogens.

Small doses or short-term use of marijuana creates sensations of euphoria and relaxation, often accompanied by hunger or sleepiness. Time seems to slow, and the senses appear heightened. Memory of recent events, physical coordination, and perceptions may be impaired. Even with small amounts of marijuana, driving ability can be affected. Physiologically, heart rate speeds up and certain blood vessels become dilated, which may create problems for individuals with any type of heart problem. Some users experience anxiety, panic, and paranoia. In rare cases or with stronger doses, individuals may suffer from a sense of depersonalization, image distortion, and hallucinations. Chronic use seems to lead to behavioral changes in some people that may be permanent. Lack of motivation or interest in activities unrelated to drug use is one result. For example, students may have difficulty remembering events that occurred when they were high. Use by teenagers leads to impairment of thinking, poor reading comprehension, and reduced verbal and mathematical skills.[4,9,20]

All the long-term effects of marijuana use have not been determined. This is partly because of the lesser potency of marijuana used previously. In addition, individuals vary greatly in their responses to the drug. Chronic users may experience psychological dependence, and increased doses are needed as tolerance develops. Very heavy users experience withdrawal symptoms of restlessness, irritability,

tremors, nausea, vomiting, diarrhea, and sleep disturbances.[22]

Physically, marijuana appears more carcinogenic than tobacco. Known carcinogens occur in larger amounts in marijuana, and when marijuana is smoked, the smoke is held in the lungs. Cannabis smoke contains more tars than tobacco smoke. Marijuana use quickly affects pulmonary function adversely, and long-term use causes cellular changes in the lungs. People who have angina pectoris (chest pains associated with heart disease) may be significantly at risk because more oxygen is required when using marijuana. Marijuana binds readily to hemoglobin, reducing the amount of oxygen carried to heart tissue.

Many individuals consider cannabis an aphrodisiac. Over time it actually has the opposite effect, depressing the sex drive and causing impotence. Regular male users show a decrease in sperm count and reduced motility of sperm. Proportionately, more sperm appear abnormally shaped, a phenomenon associated with lessened fertility. In females, TCH blocks ovulation. Pregnant women who smoke marijuana frequently use other drugs, all of which have a detrimental effect on the fetus. Marijuana also depresses the immune system.

Therapeutic use is still being explored. At this time the most promising application seems to be as an antinausea drug for cancer chemotherapy patients.

Marijuana is an illegal drug. Many people who use marijuana eventually experiment or use other, "harder" drugs. As with alcohol and all other drugs, the way a person will react or who will be most adversely affected cannot be predicted. People do not begin use with the intention of having a drug become the focus of their lives, but some ultimately allow a drug to control them. Marijuana is a drug that has that potential.

Other Drugs of Concern

Drugs discussed in the following sections have been abused for many years. Unfortunately, some that had become less popular seem to be reappearing, along with a dangerous new generation of illicit drugs.

Heroin

Heroin is a narcotic that is synthesized from morphine. This drug induces a strong sensation of euphoria but quickly leads to physical and psychological dependency. The physical tolerance for heroin develops rapidly. Because heroin is usually injected, addicts often share needles, which increases the risk

Crystal methamphetamine is more commonly called "ice" and is extremely addictive.

of contracting diseases such as AIDS and hepatitis. Experts fear the younger generation may become addicted to heroin through a substance called *moonrock*—a mixture of heroin and cocaine that can be injected, smoked, or snorted. Heroin is used in this way to reduce the paranoia and depression that follow a cocaine high.[23]

Methamphetamine (Crank)

Methamphetamine is a potent stimulant that can cause uncontrollable manic behavior or paranoid thinking. The most current use of this drug is as crystal methamphetamine or "ice." Although crystal methamphetamine has been touted as a safe alternative to cocaine, evidence indicates otherwise. Overdoses are often fatal, and the drug is extremely addictive. In many areas of the United States, use of ice is a widespread problem.

Lysergic Acid Diethylamide (LSD)

LSD is a hallucinogenic drug that has become more popular in recent years. The substance induces altered perceptions of shapes, images, time, self-image, and sound. Tolerance to the drug develops quickly with daily use.[9] Flashbacks can occur in some individuals.

Phencyclidine (PCP)

PCP was originally intended for use as a surgical anesthetic for humans. However, the drug was determined to be unsuitable for this purpose because of unusual and undesirable effects on patients.[9] Also called *angel dust*, PCP provokes a variety of unpredictable responses from users. These reactions include feelings of unreality, depersonalization, confusion, depression, anxiety, aggressive and violent behavior, acute or permanent psychosis, and coma. Users often fail to experience sensations of pain and report feeling uncoordinated in their movements. Classified as a hallucinogen, PCP has been used as an additive to cocaine, a combination that multiplies the toxic effects of both drugs.

Designer Drugs

Designer drugs resemble those that are controlled by the Federal Drug Administration (FDA); that is, they act like known drugs but have a different chemical composition. Probably the two best known-designer drugs that are currently being used are China white, an analog of heroin, and "ectasy." Ecstasy is an analog of the amphetamines and hallucinogens under FDA control since 1985. However, designer drugs appear so rapidly that it is difficult or impossible to restrict sales. Poor quality control of these drugs can result in neurological damage or death.[23, 24] Brain damage is often caused with a single dose.

A Final Thought

To develop a high level of wellness, you must address the issue of drug use. Drugs prescribed as medicine can promote quality of life, but unwise use severely diminishes quality of life. Some evidence indicates that the use of psychoactive drugs is meeting with disfavor among college students. The exception to decreasing drug use is widespread use of alcohol, which continues to be *the* most abused drug—particularly among college students. Perhaps as each person becomes more aware of the dangers associated with alcohol and drug use, a smaller percentage of college students will use them. Ideally, the general public, particularly young people of junior high and high school age, will begin to refrain from the most destructive behavioral patterns associated with drug abuse.

Preventing Sexually Transmitted Diseases

Key terms

acquired immuno-
deficiency syn-
drome (AIDS)

chlamydia

genital warts

gonorrhea

herpes

sexually transmitted
diseases (STDs)

syphilis

viral hepatitis

Objectives

After completing this chapter, you will be able to:

▷ Discuss the different sexually transmitted diseases.

▷ Evaluate the risks of having multiple sexual partners.

Sexuality is a lifelong aspect of each individual. It is involved in every facet of human existence, including relationships, anatomy, behaviors, thoughts, and values. Numerous vital decisions must be made about human sexuality. Sexual behaviors is only one aspect of sexuality.

Making decisions about sexual behaviors is not easy. If people choose to have several partners, they must realize that for each act of coitus, the sexual history of both people is brought to that union. Although it may be the first experience for one, if the other partner has had intercourse with three other people, the person for whom it is the first time is essentially having sex with four other individuals. Any of the diseases or infections any of those four people had may be brought to the present association.

Decisions concerning sexual behavior have many far-reaching consequences. These choices can enhance or severely diminish an individual's feelings of well-being. Sex can be wonderful and fulfilling but may also cause serious problems. This chapter examines some of the **sexually transmitted diseases (STDs)** that can result when people engage in behavior that puts them at risk and identifies how to prevent contacting and spreading STDs.

Genital Warts

Warts on the genitalia, around the anus, in the vagina, and on the cervix are called **genital warts,** or *condyloma.* These warts are caused by the *human papilloma virus (HPV).* Experts postulate that this condition is the third most prevalent STD after chlamydia and gonorrhea. Between 1966 and 1989, the Centers for Disease Control reported a 459% in-

crease in HPV patients. It is also estimated that 1.2 million people are infected annually.[2] Approximately 1 in 10 Americans may be carrying the virus.[3] Genital warts most commonly involve people between the ages of 15 and 24.

Genital warts are cauliflower-like. In moist areas, they are soft and either pink or red. On dry skin, they are usually yellow-gray and hard. The warts are transmitted sexually and generally appear 1 to 6 months after exposure. There are 56 distinct varieties of HPV, some of which have been specifically linked to cervical cancer[1] and cancers of the rectum, vulva, skin, and penis.[2] The warts appear most often on the shaft of the penis, the vulva, the vaginal wall, the cervix, and the perineum. They may also be found in the anal area of both sexes and are associated with anal intercourse with an infected partner. Cryosurgery (freezing), electrocautery (burning),

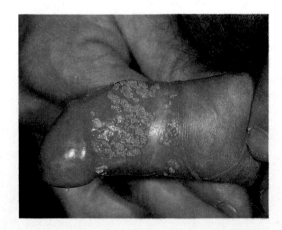

Genital warts are the result of human papilloma virus.

and use of the topical agent podophyllin are successful methods of treatment. Podophyllin should not be used during pregnancy or on warts in the cervical area. If the individual has had a variety of partners, the genitalia of all partners should be examined so that treatment can be initiated if appropriate.

Chlamydia

Chlamydia is the most common sexually transmitted disease in the United States, with an estimated 3 million new cases each year.[4] The causative agent is the bacteria *Chlamydia trachomatis*. Chlamydia is frequently found with other STDs such as gonorrhea, herpes, and syphilis, and it may be contracted through anal and vaginal intercourse.

In men, the infection is usually manifest by inflammation of the urethra (urethritis). Infected men generally experience a burning sensation during urination and possibly a mild discharge. One third of all men with chronic chlamydia infection develop no symptoms.

Symptoms in women include vaginal discharge, intermittent vaginal bleeding, and ill-defined discomfort or pain on urination. Infected mothers may pass the infection to their babies during the birth process. This may result in conjunctivitis in the child or a more serious condition known as *chlamydial pneumonia*. Over 30,000 newborns are affected by this condition each year.[5]

When left untreated, chlamydia can lead to arthritis and damage the heart valves, blood vessels, and heart muscle itself. In men the condition can also lead to sterility. In women, the disease can infect the uterus, fallopian tubes, and upper reproductive areas, producing the chronic condition pelvic inflammatory disease (PID). This scarring of the fallopian tubes by PID causes sterility and increased risk of ectopic pregnancy (a condition in which the embryo is implanted outside the uterus).

Tetracycline and erythromycin are the drugs used for treatment. They are taken orally for 1 to 3 weeks. Taking the full course of medication is extremely important because relapse can occur. All sexual partners should be treated or the disease can be passed among them.

Herpes

Herpes is caused by the virus herpes simplex virus (HSV). Five different strains of the herpes virus infect human beings. The most common are herpes simplex-1 (HSV-1) and herpes simplex-2 (HSV-2). Type 1 is usually confined to nongenital areas in the

form of cold sores or fever blisters. It is a very common form of herpes but is not categorized as an STD. Type 2 generally causes lesions on and around the genital areas and is an STD. However, through either direct or indirect contact, type 1 can affect the genital area and type 2 can produce sores in the mouth. The common sites for type 1 and type 2 can thus be reversed.

Type 2 herpes usually appears as a single blister or a series of very painful blisters on the penis or inside the vagina or cervix. The blisters may also be present on the buttocks and thighs and in the groin area. The infection usually lasts 2 to 4 weeks and then abates, but it does not leave the body. The virus retreats to the nerve endings where it remains dormant. Herpes can become active again without any warning; that is, the disease may be recurrent. Menstruation, stress, trauma to the skin (such as too much sunlight), lack of sleep, and poor nutrition seem to be triggers that stimulate recurrences. Recurrences are generally less severe and of shorter duration than the initial episode.[6]

Men do not seem to experience any major long-term complications. Women, however, may be faced with the possibility of cancer of the cervix and infection of their newborns during the birth process. Any woman with a history of herpes should have an annual pap smear test. Physicians attending the pregnancy of a woman with a history of herpes should be informed so that the course of the pregnancy can be monitored. If herpes becomes active or the physician feels the child is at risk in a vaginal birth, *caesarean section delivery* (surgical removal of the fetus through the abdominal wall) is often

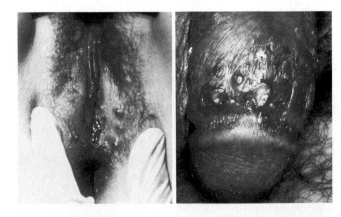

The sores associated with genital herpes are extremely painful.

used to prevent the possibility of infection. Additional hazards of herpes infection are herpes encephalitis, in which the virus invades the brain, and herpes keratitis, or eye infection. These two conditions are rare and can be effectively treated with antiviral drugs.

There is no cure for herpes. The prescription drug acyclovir, which comes in either ointment or capsule form, helps control and treat herpes. The drug does not kill the virus, but it does seem to help shorten the duration and severity of genital herpes. The capsule form appears best suited for treatment purposes but must be taken at the first sign of a flare-up to be effective.

Viral Hepatitis

Hepatitis is an inflammation of the liver caused by one or more viruses. There are currently four distinct known types of **viral hepatitis:** hepatitis A (formerly infectious hepatitis), hepatitis B (formerly serum hepatitis), Hepatitis C (non-A, non-B hepatitis), and the newest form called *hepatitis D,* or *delta.* Hepatitis A is the least serious form and tends to be self-limiting. The spread of hepatitis A is associated with overcrowding, poor hygiene, unsanitary conditions, contamination of food and water, and direct contact with the virus, including sexual contact. Type A is a common infection in the United States, with almost half the adult population having antibodies against the virus.[7] The incubation period is 2 to 6 weeks, and protection is provided if gamma globulin is administered within 10 days of exposure.

At one time, hepatitis B was spread primarily through tattoo needles, the sharing of needles by drug users, and transfusions of contaminated blood. Today, it is more commonly spread through body secretions, including sweat, breast milk, and semen. Hepatitis B is an STD that is found particularly among male homosexuals who have multiple sexual partners. The incubation period is 6 weeks to 6 months. A vaccine has been developed to immunize against the disease.

Hepatitis C is caused by one or more viruses that cannot be traced to A, B, or D. Hepatitis C is most often associated with posttransfusion patients, but there is a growing concern over possible sexual transmission.

The hepatitis D virus cannot initiate an infection alone but acts with the hepatitis B virus to create a more severe form of the disease. Hepatitis D is contracted the same way as B.

Symptoms for all forms of viral hepatitis are similar. They include fatigue, loss of appetite, mild fever, nausea, vomiting, diarrhea, aching muscles and joints, and tenderness in the upper right abdomen. A few people may have jaundiced (yellowed) skin and eyes, itching skin, darkened urine, and light-colored feces. Still others may exhibit no symptoms except those usually associated with the flu. This group does not usually seek treatment but still can transmit the infection to others.

Viral hepatitis is a type of liver injury. Most patients with hepatitis recover without serious problems. However, serious scarring of the liver or even death may occur. In some cases of hepatitis B and hepatitis C, the individual with the disease becomes a chronic carrier or can develop chronic progressive hepatitis that eventually leads to liver failure.

Gonorrhea

Nearly 2 million cases of **gonorrhea** are reported each year, making it the second most prevalent STD. Gonorrhea is caused by the bacterium *Neisseria gonorrheae,* which attacks the mucous membranes of the penis, vagina, rectum, throat, and eyes. The disease is spread by vaginal, oral, and rectal contact.

Gonorrhea produces symptoms in 80% of men. The symptoms appear 2 to 10 days (average 3 to 5 days) after contact with the bacteria and include a thick, yellowish discharge from the penis and a painful, burning sensation on urination. These signs should cause men to seek medical treatment immediately. Untreated, gonorrhea can result in sterility.

The symptoms in women are discharge and burning on urination, but they may be so mild that they are unnoticed. The bacteria can survive in the vagina and other areas of the female reproductive system for years. During this time, women can infect any sex partners and their fetus if they become pregnant. Contact by the child with the bacteria during childbirth can lead to an eye infection resulting in blindness. Untreated gonorrhea can lead to PID, the leading cause of sterility in women. In both men and women, rectal and oral gonorrhea may go unnoticed. The disease can develop into a serious infection, resulting in arthritis, meningitis, and skin lesions and liver, heart, brain, and spinal cord problems.

Gonorrhea is diagnosed by obtaining a smear from the penis or cervix. Penicillin is the drug of choice for treatment. If a person is allergic to penicillin, tetracycline is usually used. Physicians commonly treat for chlamydia when gonorrhea has been diagnosed. Gonorrhea can be completely cured, although there is no immunity to the disease. If a person has multiple sexual partners, medical help and advice must be sought regularly.

Syphilis

Syphilis is caused by a corkscrew-shaped bacterial spirochete called *Treponema pallidum*. Kissing, oral-genital contact, and intercourse are the most common forms of transmission. The spirochete dies quickly when exposed to air, so primary entry to the body is through a break in the skin. Once in the bloodstream, it exists in a variety of organs and mimics the symptoms of many major chronic diseases. Because of this ability to mimic other diseases, it is referred to as *the great imitator*. There are four stages of syphilis.

Primary Syphilis

The initial sign of primary syphilis is a lesion called a *chancre* located at the site of entry of the pathogen. The incubation period can range from 10 to 90 days (average 21 days) before symptoms appear. The chancre can vary from the size of a pinhead to the size of a dime. Even though the chancre may look painful, it is not and may go unnoticed. If the lesion occurs on the labia, vagina, or rectum, it can very easily remain undetected. The chancre disappears within 3 to 6 weeks.

Secondary Syphilis

From 1 month to a year after the chancre disappears, the symptoms of secondary syphilis may appear. Symptoms include headaches, swollen glands, low-grade fevers, skin rash, white patches on the mucous membranes of the mouth and throat, hair loss, arthritis pain, and large sores around the mouth and genitals. These sores contain the bacteria responsible for syphilis, and contact with them can spread the disease. Symptoms may be mild or severe, and in rare instances, no symptoms appear. Even if left untreated, symptoms usually run their course, lasting anywhere from a few days to several months. The pathogen remains active in the body even with the absence of symptoms and will reappear later—perhaps as long as 20 years after the initial infection.

Latent Syphilis

During latent syphilis there are few or no clinical signs that the disease exists, although the spirochetes are invading the various organs and systems of the body, including the brain, heart, and central nervous system. The spirochetes multiply relentlessly and begin to destroy the tissue, bones, and organs. At this stage a person is not contagious.

Late Syphilis

From 10 to 20 years after the onset of latent syphilis, the disease progresses to its most devastating stage. Late syphilis can cause heart damage, central nervous system damage, blindness, deafness, paralysis, and psychosis.

Penicillin is the preferred drug for treating syphilis. Individuals who are penicillin sensitive are placed on other antibiotics. Persons with syphilis commonly have other STDs such as gonorrhea and chlamydia, thereby requiring greater doses of antibiotics.

Human Immunodeficiency Virus and AIDS

Acquired immunodeficiency syndrome (AIDS) is characterized by a breakdown of the immune system that allows a variety of infections, cancers, and neurological disorders to develop. The causative agent is a virus called the *human immunodeficiency virus (HIV)*. AIDS has been recognized by the World Health Organization as a worldwide epidemic. First diagnosed in this country in New York in 1981, AIDS is found in Europe, Africa, Australia, South America, the Caribbean, Asia, and the Middle East. In many African nations the number of men and women infected is approximately equal, but in the United States, the vast majority of individuals with AIDS are promiscuous homosexual males, bisexual men, and IV drug users. This statistic is changing as more heterosexual individuals acquire the disease.

Two types of HIV have been identified.[8] The virus replicates inside human cells and is transmitted by blood, blood products, semen, vaginal secretions, and breast milk. HIV is an extremely fragile virus in that it does not survive in air and can be readily destroyed by soap and water, household bleach, and chlorine used in swimming pools. Figure 11-1 explains how HIV is and is not transmitted.

The HIV virus attacks the helper T-lymphocytes, specifically the T-4 cells, which are possibly the most critical element in the body's immune system.[9] HIV attaches to the part of the T-cell that recognizes viral infections and blocks its ability to react to them. Over time, HIV may even multiply and destroy T-cells, leaving the body more defenseless against the invasion of opportunistic organisms that can lead to illness and even death.

Not everyone who has been infected with HIV has developed AIDS. Many people who carry HIV are apparently healthy individuals with no indications of disease. However, even people with no obvious symptoms can transmit HIV to others, who may develop AIDS or *symptomatic HIV infections* while the carrier remains symptomless. Once infected, a person can transmit the virus from shortly

Figure 11-1 How HIV Is and Is Not Transmitted

How HIV Is Transmitted

Sexual activity

Homosexual, between men
Heterosexual, from men to women and women to men

Blood inoculation

Needle sharing among intravenous drug users
Transfusion of blood and blood products
Needle stick, open wound, and mucous membrane exposure in health-care workers
Injection with unsterilized needle (including needles used in acupuncture, medical injections, ear piercing, and tattooing)

Childbirth

Intrauterine (within the uterus)
Peripartum (during labor and delivery)

How HIV Is Not Transmitted

Food, water
Sharing of eating and drinking utensils
Shaking or holding hands
Use of the telephone
Toilet seat
Insects
Whirlpools or saunas
Coughing or sneezing
Domestic pets
Exchange of clothing
Swimming in a pool
Bed linens

after the time of infection to the end of life. Some people develop symptomatic HIV infections (see Table 11-1). These chronic conditions involve fever, weight loss, diarrhea, skin rash, fatigue, and swollen lymph glands. These infections are a result of HIV infection caused by immunodeficiency, but they are not AIDS.

The reason some people develop AIDS rapidly whereas others do not is not known. Factors that may contribute to the advancement of the condition are weakening of the immune system through other infections, alcohol or drug abuse, poor nutrition, and stress.[10] The longer the virus is in the system, the greater the chances of developing AIDS. In one study spanning 6 years, 30% of the participants with the virus developed AIDS, 49% displayed symptomatic HIV infections, and 21% remained free of symptoms.

All these individuals could continue to spread the disease.

HIV is spread through intimate sexual contact and the transfusion of blood from an infected individual and from an infected mother to her fetus during the prenatal period, birth process, or breastfeeding. In no cases has HIV been spread through casual contact—this includes family members or friends living in close contact with infected adults or children. Very few health-care professionals working with AIDS patients have contracted the disease in rare situations in which mishandling of blood occurred. The AIDS virus is not transmitted from toilet seats, foods, beverages, or social kissing. The virus is found in small amounts in tears and saliva, although transmission through these mediums is undocumented.[11]

Anal sexual intercourse is currently the most prevalent means of spreading AIDS, whether through homosexual or heterosexual contact. This may be because this activity increases the likelihood of making small tears that facilitate the spread of the virus from semen to blood. Vaginal and oral sex are also considered highly dangerous. Sharing of needles among drug users and having sex with an IV drug user are dangerous activities. Sex with a prostitute is a significant risk factor. Anyone who has had multiple sexual partners during the last 5 to 10 years is at risk because there is no way of knowing the sex partners these people had. People who are not sexually active are not at risk. Individuals in a monogamous relationship in which neither individual has an STD or used IV drugs are considered safe.

Current knowledge is that anyone who is HIV positive will eventually develop AIDS. Table 11-1 provides a list of the opportunistic diseases that appear when the immune system becomes severely disabled as a result of HIV. The diseases include bacterial, viral, fungal, parasitic, and tumorous disorders. In addition, some AIDS patients develop AIDS dementia complex, which involves hallucinations, incoherent speech, disorientation, and memory loss. AIDS victims do not die from the HIV infection but from the opportunistic diseases that develop as a result of the severely weakened immune system.[12]

Two tests are currently being used to detect HIV. The ELISA is the antibody test initially used. If the ELISA result is positive, another test—the Western blot assay—is administered for confirmation. A third test, the single-use diagnostic system (SUDS), is currently being readied. An individual may not test positive on the ELISA if the virus has not been present long enough for antibodies to develop. Antibodies may develop within 2 months or may take up to 36 months to develop.[13] Anyone who tests pos-

TABLE 11-1 Symptoms and Infections Associated with Symptomatic HIV Infection and AIDS

Symptoms	Infectious Agent	Type of Infection
Symptomatic HIV infection		
Night sweats	—	—
Swollen lymph nodes	Lymphoma	Malignancy
Loss of appetite and weight	—	—
Persistent diarrhea	Cryptosporidium	Parasite
White spots in mouth	*Candida albicans*	Fungus
Painful skin rash	Shingles	Virus
AIDS		
Persistent diarrhea	Cryptosporidium	Parasite
White spots in mouth	*Candida albicans*	Fungus
Pneumonia, including cough and difficult breathing	*Pneumocystis carinii*	Parasite
Pneumonia, blindness	Cytomegalovirus	Virus
Oral lesions	*Herpes simplex*	Virus
Cough	Turberculosis	Bacteria
Neuromuscular impairments	Mycobacterium	Bacteria
Blindness, mental disorder	Toxoplasmosis	Parasite
Blue or red skin rash	*Kaposi's sarcoma*	Malignancy

itive is infected with HIV and can transmit the infection.

There is no cure for AIDS. However, the drug AZT is beneficial in prolonging the lives of patients. Early use of AZT seems to help alter the replication of the virus. A new drug called *ddC* was approved in 1992 for treating HIV. Used in combination with AZT, this drug seems to cause an increase in white blood cells, which results in a more effective immune system. More recently, clinical trials are beginning on using a combination of three drugs that includes AZT, ddC, and the compound pyridinone. This group of drugs has stopped the HIV from reproducing in laboratory conditions.[14]

AIDS is a devastating disease. It took 8½ years for the first 100,000 cases of AIDS to be reported. The second 100,000 cases were reported in only 2½ years. The Centers for Disease Control has estimated that there are over 1 million HIV-positive persons in the United States. About 20% of that total have developed AIDS.[15] No one has ever recovered from AIDS, and over 50% of those diagnosed since 1981 have died. Individuals who may have been or currently are at risk should consult a physician or public health department for a screening to determine whether they are carrying the virus. AIDS is the most deadly of all STDs, but it is preventable. With education, wisdom, and reduction in high-risk behaviors, AIDS can be prevented (Figure 11-2). Informa-

Figure 11-2 Preventing the Spread of AIDS[7]

The spread of AIDS can be stopped by preventing the transmission of the AIDS virus from one person to another. This means eliminating direct sexual contact with infected people and not using contaminated needles. Recommendations to reduce the possibility of becoming infected include the following:

▶ Practice abstinence or mutual monogamy.
▶ Always use protection (that is, latex condom and spermicide such as nonoxynol-9) if having sex with multiple partners or with persons who have multiple partners.
▶ Do not have unprotected sex with individuals with AIDS, those who engage in high-risk behavior, or those who have had a positive test for the AIDS virus.
▶ Avoid sexual activities that might cut or tear the rectum, vagina, or penis, such as anal intercourse.
▶ Do not have sex with prostitutes.
▶ Do not use IV drugs or share needles. Refrain from sex with IV drug users

Figure 11-3 AIDS Information Sources

Any questions or concerns you may have about AIDS can be answered by the hotline listed. The hotline can also provide testing referral and locations of support groups. Your local health department also has valuable information.

AIDS Hotline: 1-800-342-2437

tion on AIDS can be obtained through various sources (Figure 11-3).

Safer Sex: An Individual Responsibility

The purpose of this book is to increase awareness of how modifying lifestyles can help individuals achieve optimal wellness. Prevention of STDs requires personal responsibility. Sexual abstinence and a monogamous relationship are the only situations in which STDs can be prevented. People who choose to engage in sexual contact with more than one partner place themselves at risk. If a choice is made to have sex with someone, questions about sexual history need to be asked. The integrity of the partner is vital. If the history places either partner at high risk, contact should be considered very carefully. A condom should always be used with any new partner.

Safer sex is difficult because few people want to discuss it. Having sex should be viewed as a major decision that may have lifelong consequences. If a decision is made to engage in sexual intercourse, a condom should be used—a practice that can help in preventing pregnancy and the transmission of STDs. The decision for safer sexual behavior rests with each person.

Summary

▶ Genital warts, or condyloma, are caused by the human papilloma virus (HPV) and have been linked to some cancers. Cryosurgery, electrocautery, and use of a topical agent are methods of treatment.

▶ Chlamydia is a bacteria that produces the most common STD in the United States. Left untreated, it can cause arthritis, damage the heart and blood vessels, and cause sterility. Pelvic inflammatory disease (PID), resulting in ectopic pregnancies, may develop from chlamydial infection. Treatment is available.

▶ Herpes is caused by the herpes simplex virus. In humans, lesions are usually located around the mouth or genital area. Herpes does not disappear; it remains dormant in the human body and can recur at any time. Although men do not experience major long-term complications, women may develop cancer of the cervix or infect newborns during the birth process. There is no cure for herpes.

▶ Viral hepatitis is an injury to the liver. Hepatitis has several types of viruses associated with it.

▶ The second leading STD is gonorrhea. Gonorrhea can lead to sterility in men and women and PID in women. Symptoms are often unnoticed by women but can cause serious problems if left untreated. Although there is no immunity to the disease, treatment is available.

▶ Syphilis is caused by a bacteria. There are four stages of syphilis, and the full effects may not be experienced for 10 to 20 years after infection occurs.

▶ AIDS is the result of the human immunodeficiency virus (HIV), which attacks the immune system. AIDS can be transmitted if an individual has symptoms or not. HIV is spread through intimate sexual contact and the sharing of needles and from mother to child. There is no cure for AIDS, and over 50% of the patients diagnosed since 1981 have died.

▶ The only way to avoid acquiring a STD is through abstinence or monogamy. Use of condoms is associated with decreased risk when a person has a number of sexual partners.

Action Plan for Personal Wellness

Use the information presented in this chapter to answer the following questions and to formulate an action plan to enhance your personal wellness.

1 Based on the information presented in this chapter, along with what I know about my family's health history, the health problems and issues that I need to be concerned about are:_____

_____

_____

2 Of those health concerns listed in number 1, the one I most need to act on is:_____

_____

_____

3 Possible actions (be specific) that I can take to improve my level of wellness are:_____

_____

_____

4 Of those actions listed in number 3, the one that I most need to include in an action plan is:_____

_____

_____

5 Factors I need to keep in mind to be successful in my action plan are:_____

_____

_____

Review Questions

1. How can people accept responsibility for their sexual behavior?
2. Why does chlamydia represent a serious problem?
3. Discuss why HPV is more dangerous for women than for men.
4. What are the various kinds of viral hepatitis, and how are they spread?
5. List and explain the four stages of syphilis.
6. What makes HIV an extremely dangerous infection?
7. What precautions can you take to protect against the spread of AIDS?
8. If one STD is present, why may it be necessary to get treatment for more than one?

References

1. Genital warts and cancer, *Health Letter* 32(8):4, 1988.
2. Symptoms of HPV commonly missed, *Commercial Appeal* Aug 20, 1989, p 5E.
3. Nuovo GJ et al: Human papillomavirus types and recurrent cervical warts, *JAMA* 263:1223-1226, 1990.
4. Chlamydia: cloak and dagger, *Harvard Med School Health Letter* 13(12):7, 1988.
5. *Chlamydia trachomatis* infection, *Mortal Morbid Weekly Rep* 33:805-807, 1985.
6. Braude AL, Davis CE, Fierer J, eds: *Infectious diseases and medical microbiology*, ed 2, Philadelphia, 1986, WB Saunders.
7. Crowly LV: *Introduction to human disease*, ed 2, Boston, 1988, Jones & Bartlett.
8. Stine GJ: *Acquired immune deficiency syndrome—biological, medical, social, and legal issues*, Englewood Cliffs, NJ, 1993, Prentice-Hall.
9. Haseltine WA, Wong-Staal F: The molecular biology of the AIDS virus, *Sci Am* 259(4):52-64, 1988.
10. Yarber WL: *AIDS: what young adults should know*, Reston, Va, 1987, AAHPERD.
11. The facts about AIDS, *NEA Higher Education Advocate* 4(13):1-14, 1987.
12. Jackson JK: *AIDS, STD, and other communicable diseases*, Guilford, Conn, 1992, Dushkin Publishing Group.
13. Creager JG, Black JG, Davison VE: *Microbiology: principles and application*, Englewood Cliffs, NJ, 1990, Prentice-Hall.
14. Brink S: Triple teaming the deadly AIDS virus, *US News and World Report* 114(8):60,1993.
15. The second 100,000 cases of acquired immunodeficiency syndrome, *Mortal Morbid Weekly Rep* 41(2):28-30, 1992.

Annotated Readings

Franklin D: AIDS file, *Health* May/Jun 1990, p. 17.
  Based on a study of 238 gay and bisexual men, brain damage has been found in individuals with the HIV virus.

Gallup G Jr, Gallup A: AIDS—we worry about the wrong things, *Am Health* Jun 1988, pp 50-52.
  A worldwide special report that seeks information about what people know and what the common fears are concerning the AIDS epidemic.

Hall SS: Gadfly in the ointment, *Hippocrates* Sept/Oct 1988, pp 76-82.
  Discusses molecular biologist Peter Duesberg's view that AIDS is not caused by the HIV virus. His views have generally won him the scorn of colleagues. Right or wrong, the article points out how little is actually known about the disease.

Japenga A: The secret, *Health* Sept 1992, pp 42-52.
  Questions whether doctors who are HIV positive should inform their patients.

Mason M: The AIDS file: a nonlethal strain of HIV, *Health* Jan/Feb 1993, p 17.
  HIV-positive individuals were remaining healthy, and researchers speculated that these individuals were infected with a strain of HIV that lacks the virulence of other strains of the virus. Only 5 of 118 subjects in this investigation remained healthy.

Shilts R: *And the band played on: politics, people, and the AIDS epidemic*, New York, 1987, St Martin's Press.
  This article was written by an AIDS victim expressing his views concerning the political aspects of AIDS and the difficulties in receiving treatment.

ASSESSMENT ACTIVITY   11-1

Are You at Risk for a Sexually Transmitted Disease?

Directions: Review each of the sexual behaviors listed below. If you engage in any of the activities, assess your personal risk for contracting a sexually transmitted disease by checking the appropriate line.

	Activity	Risk	Precautions
_____	No sex (1)	No risk: There is virtually no chance of getting an STD.	No precautions are necessary.
_____	Sex with only one partner (2)	Low risk: If both partners have no other sexual partners and no disease, there is almost no risk of getting an STD.	Remain monogamous.
_____	Sex with a variety of partners (3)	High risk: Each time there is another partner, the risk increases.	Choose partners carefully, use condoms and spermicides, wash after sex, do not douche, and urinate after sex.
_____	Sex partner who has sex with a variety of partners (4)	High risk: The more partners, the greater the risk an STD will be transmitted.	Be aware of symptoms.
_____	Sex with someone who is or has been an IV drug user (5)	High risk: If needles are shared, the risk is great, particularly of getting AIDS and hepatitis B.	Know social and sexual history of your partner.
_____	Oral sex (6)	No risk: There is no risk for Activity (1). Low risk: The risk is low for Activity (2). High risk: The risk is high for Activities (3), (4), and (5).	Know your partner, do not engage in oral sex if the history is not known.

After reviewing the different categories of activities, are there areas of concern for you?

ASSESSMENT ACTIVITY   11-2

Making a Decision

The decision to have sexual intercourse is a major one. Many factors affect this decision, and many factors will be affected by it. People engage in sexual activity for a variety of reasons that are often unrelated to love and often without regard to the consequences of that behavior.

Directions: Listed below are several factors that may influence your decision to engage in sexual activity. Rank each of these factors as to how they affect your behavior now and when you are in a situation in which you have to make a decision. This activity is not handed in, so answer as truthfully as possible.

Factor	Not Important	Slightly Important	Important	Very Important	Extremely Important
Risk of AIDS					
Risk of other STD					
Risk of pregnancy					
Sexual history of partner					
Partner not an IV drug user					
Biological gratification (physical sensations)					
Need for money					
Desire to be accepted by partner/ cultural group					
Dissipation of stress or to get mind off other problems					
Intense need to feel loved/cared for					
Sign of commitment in a relationship					
Expression of love for partner					
Monogamous relationship					
Desire for a variety of partners					
Evidence of desirability					
Proof of sexual prowess					

In examining your responses, consider asking your potential partner to also take this assessment as a basis for a discussion. As you assess your responses, note the factors that are important to you in making this decision.

What are the most important factors?_____

Does the person you are considering have sex with have any factors that you consider to be negative?

What are they?_____

How important are these factors to you?_____

How severe are the potential consequences of you or your partner's ideas and/or actions?_____

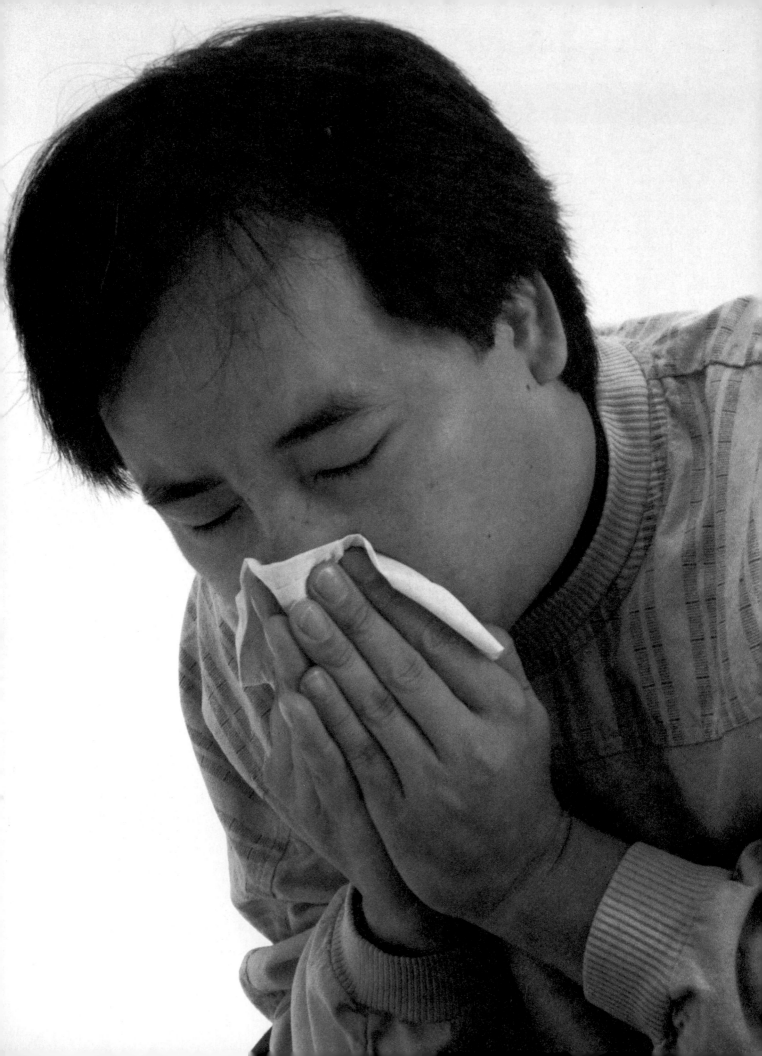

Impact of Lifestyle on Common Conditions

Objectives

After completing this chapter, you will be able to:

▷ Define cancer, identify the various types, state possible causes, and explain the precautions that can be taken to protect against cancer.

▷ Discuss the difference between malignant and benign neoplasms.

▷ Discuss diabetes.

▷ Identify the most common forms of arthritis.

▷ Discuss the common cold and influenza.

▷ Explain the difference between a tension and migraine headache.

▷ Describe the effects of exercise on the development of osteoporosis.

This chapter focuses on conditions that are detrimentally affected by lifestyle. If precautions are taken against the onset of these diseases, their impact on the body may be lessened or even avoided. Although every condition affected by lifestyle cannot be described, those that frequently occur and those in which lifestyle has the greatest impact are discussed. The diseases or conditions include cancer, diabetes, the common cold, headaches, influenza, arthritis, and osteoporosis. The effects of a positive lifestyle are primary in all of these, including the importance of early detection for optimal treatment.

Cancer

With the possible exception of AIDS, there is probably no disease that strikes more fear in people than cancer. The term **cancer** refers to a group of diseases characterized by uncontrolled disorderly cell growth. It is the second leading cause of death, accounting for 22% of all deaths.[1] Although it strikes more frequently with advancing age, cancer causes the death of more children than any other disease. Over 100 different kinds of cancers occur, and 3 out of 10 Americans will develop the disease. Although one of every five people with cancer will die, the American Cancer Society estimates that over 8 million Americans are alive today who have a history of cancer. About 4 million of these are considered cured because they have survived for 5 years or more with no further symptoms of the disease.[2] The chances of developing cancer can be reduced by assuming control of the things you do every day (see Figure 12-1).

Cell growth is controlled by DNA (deoxyribonucleic acid) and RNA (ribonucleic acid) in the nucleus of each cell in the body. If the nuclei lose the ability to regulate and control this growth, cellular metabolism and reproduction are disrupted and a mutant cell is produced that has a variation in form, quality, and function from the original. When a mass of these cells develop, it is a neoplasm, or tumor. It may be *malignant* (cancerous) or *benign* (noncancerous). A malignant neoplasm is the most dangerous and can become life threatening quickly if not treated rapidly. Cancer cells can crowd out normal cells, invade surrounding tissue, and move through the lymphatic or circulatory system to infiltrate other areas of the body. The process by which cancerous cells spread from the original location to another location is called **metastasis.** This ability of cancerous cells to metastasize makes early detection critical. Benign tumors, on the other hand, are enclosed by a membrane that prevents them from invading other tissue. A benign tumor is not life threatening unless it is in an area that interferes with normal functioning. Table 12-1 describes types of cancer and where they are most often found.

Causes of Cancer

The causes of cancer are not understood. Correlations have been found linking cancer to everything from genetic factors to exposure to the sun's radiation. Many **carcinogens** (cancer-causing agents) trigger development of cancer. (Table 12-2 contains a list of substances known to be carcinogenic.)

An inherited tendency for cancer has been theorized for years. Everyone seems to have genes that may cause cancer, but not everyone gets cancer. In most cases, environmental factors actually activate the cancer. A good example of the interplay between genetic and environmental factors is cigarette smoking. Approximately 80% of lung cancers occur in cig-

Figure 12-1 Tips for Cancer Prevention

What To Do

1. Eat more broccoli, cauliflower, and brussels sprouts. Eat more cabbage-type vegetables. All cabbages and kale are examples. These vegetables protect against cancers of the colon, rectum, stomach, and lung.
2. Add more high-fiber foods to your diet. Eat more peaches, strawberries, potatoes, spinach, tomatoes, wheat and bran cereals, rice, popcorn, and whole-wheat bread. Fiber protects against cancer of the colon.
3. Choose foods containing vitamin A. Eat more carrots, peaches, apricots, squash, and broccoli. Fresh foods are the best source and are far better than vitamin pills. Vitamin A protects against cancers of the esophagus, larynx, and lung.
4. Choose foods containing vitamin C. Eat more grapefruit, cantaloupe, oranges, strawberries, red peppers, green peppers, broccoli, and tomatoes. These help fight cancers of the esophagus and stomach.
5. Practice weight control. Exercise and eat foods low in calories. A good exercise for most people is walking. Obese people have a high chance of getting cancers of the uterus, gallbladder, breast, and colon. Check with your doctor before you start an exercise program or a special diet.

What To Avoid

1. Trim fat from your diet. Eat lean meat, fish, and low-fat dairy products. Cut extra fat off meats and skin poultry before cooking. Avoid pastries and candies. A high-fat diet increases the chance of getting cancer of the breast, colon, and prostate. Calories loaded with fat cause weight gain.
2. Avoid salty foods. Stay away from nitrite-cured and smoked foods. Bacon, ham, hot dogs, and salt-cured fish are examples. People who eat these foods have a greater chance of cancer of the esophagus and stomach.
3. Stop smoking cigarettes. Smoking is the main cause of lung cancer. It causes 3 of 10 cancers. Pregnant women who smoke harm their babies. Parents who smoke at home cause breathing and allergy problems for kids. Chewing tobacco can cause cancers of the mouth and throat. Pick a day to quit and call the American Cancer Society for help.
4. Drink alcohol in moderation. If you drink a lot, you may get cancer of the liver. It is worse to smoke and drink. This increases the chances of getting cancers of the mouth, throat, larynx, and esophagus.
5. Avoid too much sun. The sun causes skin cancer and other damage to skin. Use a sunscreen. Wear long sleeves and a hat between 11 AM and 3 PM. Do not use indoor sunlamps, tanning parlors, or pills. Be alert for changes in a mole or sore that does not heal. If these occur, go to a doctor.

arette smokers,[1] but only 10% of smokers develop lung cancer.[3] Why not the other 90%? The 10% who develop cancer are thought to be susceptible to the disease on the basis of their genes. If they had not activated the cancer genes by smoking, they probably would not have contracted the disease.

A gene that causes cancer is called an **oncogene.** Within a tiny segment of DNA is an area that can be activated to form an oncogene. This segment is called a *proto-oncogene*, and unless it is activated, it will never become an oncogene or cause cancer. If an oncogene is formed, it acts with other oncogenes to produce abnormal cells that can replicate and spread. The oncogene itself is not inherited, but the proto-oncogene is.[3]

Another explanation of cancer is an error in cell duplication on the basis of chance alone. Several trillion new cells are formed each year, and perfect duplication does not occur with each new cell formation. When an abnormal cell develops, the immune system recognizes it as a rogue cell and attacks it. Every cancer cell need to be killed because almost all cancers arise from a single cancer cell. Cancer develops as a result of the immune system's failure to

TABLE 12-1 Types of Cancer and Most Common Sites

Type	Most Common Site	Method of Spread
Carcinoma	Tissues covering body surfaces and lining the body cavities are the most common locations. Sites include the breast, lungs, intestines, skin, stomach, uterus, and testes.	Lymphatic and circulatory system
Sarcoma	The connective system is most commonly affected. Sites include bones, muscle, and other connective tissue.	Circulatory system
Lymphoma	Condition develops in the lymphatic system, the infectious regions of the neck, armpits, groin, and chest. Hodgkin's disease is an example.	Lymph system
Leukemia	The blood-forming areas, bone marrow and spleen, are particularly affected.	Circulatory system

TABLE 12-2 Factors That Can Cause Cancer[2]

Carcinogen	Site of Cancer	Comments
Alcohol	Liver, larynx, pharynx, breast, esophagus	Heavy drinking increases the risk of cancer, especially when accompanied by cigarette smoking or chewing tobacco.
Smoking	Lungs, mouth, pharynx, larynx, bladder, esophagus	Smoking accounts for about 30% of all cancer deaths. It is considered the number one carcinogen in the United States and the most preventable cause of death. It is responsible for 87% of lung cancer deaths.
Ultraviolet radiation	Skin	Almost all skin cancers are sun related.
Ionizing radiation	Blood-forming areas, lungs	Excessive exposure to radiation increases cancer risk. Excessive radon exposure increases risk of lung cancer.
Smokeless tobacco	Mouth, larynx, pharynx, esophagus	Oral cancer increases with the use of chewing tobacco and snuff.
Estrogen	Endometrium, liver, breast	Oral contraceptives increase the risk of liver cancer. Estrogen treatment to control menopausal symptoms increases risk of cancer. The risk is reduced with the inclusion of progesterone.
Industrial agents		Industrial chemicals and agents such as nickel, chromate, asbestos, and vinyl chloride increase the risk of various cancers.
Dietary fat		High consumption of dietary fat is related to cancer of the colon, prostate, and pancreas; replacing fat with complex carbohydrates provides protection against several cancers (see Chapter 6).

clear the body of cancer cells. This is one reason the immune system is receiving considerable attention among cancer researchers.

Much research appears to link psychological states with the prevalence of disease in individuals. People with positive, involved attitudes and who view life's challenges as opportunities for personal growth seem to have fewer diseases and recover from them more often. Individuals who feel lonely and depressed and lack appropriate social support are more cancer prone than their mentally healthy counterparts.

A 12-year Maryland study of 2264 persons discovered that depression combined with heavy smoking caused 18.5 times more cancers at sites associated with tobacco risk compared with nonsmokers with nondepressed mood.[1] However, a 1989 study from the National Institute on Aging found no relationship between attitude and development of can-

cer in 6403 individuals.[4] The relationship between depressed mood and cancer remains an unresolved question.

Although some of these concepts are controversial, it is generally accepted that substances such as tobacco, tobacco smoke, alcohol, asbestos, herbicides, and pesticides are carcinogens. Scientists believe more than 80% of all cancers are associated with lifestyle factors that are easily controlled: diet, smoking, and exposure to the sun.[5] Almost two thirds of cancer deaths are attributed to diet and tobacco. (Figure 12-2). (Chapter 6 provides guidelines for cancer prevention as related to diet—also see Figure 12-2.) One of the major carcinogens may be radiation from the sun. People who spend hours in the sun without protection have an increased risk for skin cancers (Figure 12-3). Using tanning devices to produce a tan also increases the risk for skin cancer[6] (Figure 12-4).

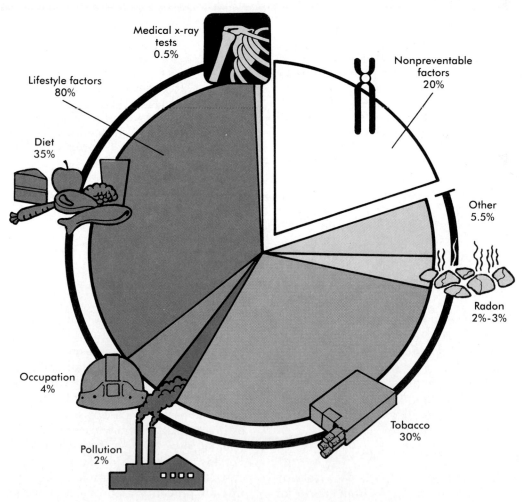

FIGURE 12-2 Percent of cancer deaths caused by preventable factors.[5]

Figure 12-3 Skin Cancer—The Case Against Too Much Sun

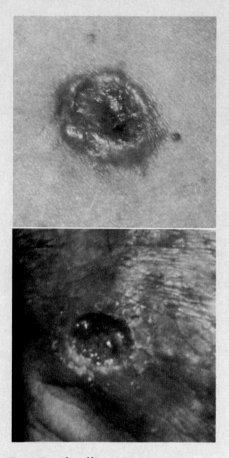

Every year more than 600,000 Americans are diagnosed with skin cancer. Fortunately this type of cancer is the easiest to detect, and most forms can be treated successfully. The most important risk factor for skin cancer is excessive exposure to the sun. The types of skin cancer are the following:

▶ **Basal cell carcinoma:** This type of skin cancer is the most common of the three types of skin cancer. Basal cell carcinoma grows slowly and usually does not spread to other areas of the body.

▶ **Squamous cell carcinoma:** This is the second most frequent type. Like basal cell cancer, squamous cell rarely spreads to distant organs but does grow faster than the basal cell kind.

▶ **Malignant melanoma:** A much less common form of skin cancer, melanoma can be very dangerous if not detected and treated early. Every year about 32,000 people develop melanoma, and approximately 6700 die from it. No one is immune, although darker skinned individuals who seldom sunburn are at less risk. Melanoma has a strong tendency to spread to other areas of the body. Melanoma may appear suddenly without warning or it may begin near a mole or other dark spot in the skin. Some birthmarks or congenital moles carry an increased risk and should be observed closely for changes. Excessive exposure to the sun increases the risk, especially for individuals who have been severely sunburned in their teens or twenties.

Top: Basal cell carcinoma.
Bottom: Squamous cell carcinoma.

Finally, the herpes viruses have been connected with cancer of the cervix (see Chapter 11). Viruses may be involved in the development of some forms of leukemia, Hodgkin's disease, and Burkett's lymphoma. The exact role of viruses in causing cancer is not known, but they may provide an opportunistic environment for cancer development. Other researchers have suggested that a combination of factors, of which the virus may play a part, rather than the virus itself causes a cancer.

Cancer Sites

The American Cancer Society reports each year on the incidence and number of deaths from cancer for a variety of sites (Figure 12-5). Skin cancer is the most common cancer. More than 600,000 people are diagnosed annually with basal and squamous cell skin cancer. Almost all of these are considered sun-related cases.[2] Fortunately, the vast majority of skin cancers are highly curable. For both genders the cancer that kills most often is lung cancer. Excluding basal cell and squamous cell carcinomas, the breasts are the most prevalent site for females and the prostate is the leading cancer site for males. In 1992 an estimated 132,000 new cases of prostate cancer and 180,000 new cases of breast cancer were reported. For any cancer, early detection is imperative. Figures 12-6, 12-7, and 12-8 provide suggestions for checkups for prevention and early detection of different types of cancer.

Figure 12-4 Are Tanning Devices Hazardous to Your Health?

Sunlight produces two types of ultraviolet radiation: ultraviolet A (UVA) and ultraviolet B (UVB). UVB is 1000 times more likely to cause burns than UVA. Because it penetrates the skin more deeply, UVA radiation causes the skin to tan or burn more slowly. A small amount of UVB radiation, however, can cause skin damage.

Most tanning devices (for example, sunlamps) give off either mostly UVA or UVB radiation. Newer UVA sunlamps give off as much as 10 times more UVA than is received from the sun or from older UVB sunlamps. Although exposure to UVA sunlamps is less likely to cause burns of the skin and eyes, UVA radiation in high dosages may increase the risks of skin cancer and premature skin aging. Studies also suggest that skin cancer is exacerbated when people combine tanning in the sun with tanning by sunlamps.

What Are the Hazards of Tanning Devices?

▶ *Skin cancer* risks increases each time the skin is exposed to UV radiation.
▶ *Burns* of the skin and eyes may occur.
▶ *Photosensitivity* means being extra sensitive to UV radiation as a result of using or consuming various substances that may cause allergic reactions, severe skin burn, itchy and scaly skin, and rash. Examples of photosensitizing products are soaps, shampoos, makeup, birth control pills, antibiotics, antihistamines, diuretics, and tranquilizers.
▶ *Cataracts,* an eye condition in which the lens becomes cloudy, may develop as a result of unprotected exposure to UVA and UVB radiation. For this reason, tanning devices are required to instruct users to wear protective eyewear.

▶ *Premature skin aging* in which the skin becomes dry, wrinkled, and leathery is one of the most noticeable signs of repeated UV exposure.
▶ *Blood vessel damage and reduced immunity* may be affected negatively by exposure to UV radiation.

Who Is At Highest Risk for Damage from UV Radiation?

Individuals who have red or blond hair and blue eyes, are fair-skinned, have freckles, and sunburn easily are at highest risk for skin damage. If you burn and do not tan in sunlight, you will probably burn and will not tan using sunlamps.

Does a Tan Protect the Skin?

A UVA tan offers some protection against further UV damage—about the same as sun protector factor (SPF) of 2 or 3. Even with a dark tan, UV damage continues to accumulate.

Will Sunscreen Prevent Skin Damage While Tanning Indoors?

Sunscreens are not recommended except to protect parts of your body you do not want to tan (for example, the lips) because they require longer tanning sessions. Sunscreens do not prevent UVA allergic-type reactions for people who are photosensitive.

How Can UV Radiation Exposure be Reduced When Using Tanning Devices?

Always wear special goggles that block UV radiation, avoid using photosensitizing products, avoid tanning if your skin never tans, and follow the manufacturer's recommended time exposure for your skin type.

Treatment

Cancer is often treated surgically. A surgeon removes the malignant tissue and some additional normal tissue. Today, the tendency is to remove less surrounding normal tissue and combine surgery with *chemotherapy* and/or *radiotherapy*. Radiotherapy is the use of radiation to destroy cancer cells or their reproductive mechanism so that they cannot replicate. This treatment can cause unpleasant side effects such as diarrhea, itching, and difficulty in swallowing. When cancer has spread throughout the body, chemotherapy is used. Chemotherapy is the use of drugs and hormones to treat such cancers as acute leukemia and testicular cancer. About 50 anticancer drugs are in use.

Another technique that offers hope for treating cancer is *immunotherapy*. This process involves stimulating the body's immune system to help destroy malignant growths. Interferon and interleukin-2 (proteins produced by the body to protect against

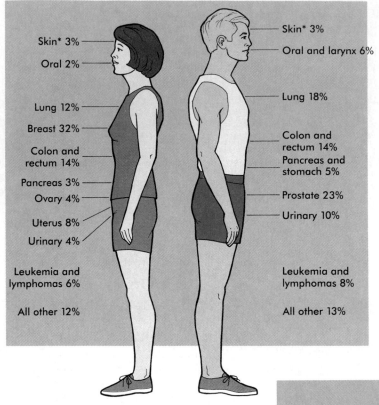

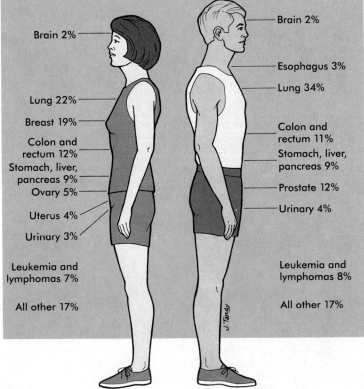

FIGURE 12-5 Cancer incidence **(A)** and death **(B)** by site and sex—1992 estimates.

Figure 12-6 Cancer-Related Checkup Guidelines

Listed below are the checkup guidelines for healthy people for early cancer detection. These are guidelines and not rules. They apply only if none of the seven warning signs are present. The seven warning signs are the following:

C hange in bowel or bladder habits
A sore throat that does not heal
U nusual bleeding or discharge
T hickening or lump in breast or elsewhere
I ndigestion or difficulty in swallowing
O bvious change in wart or moles
N agging cough or hoarseness

The *Health Letter*[3] adds two more signs:
▶ Weakness or fatigue that may be caused by an anemia resulting from cancer-causing bleeding or bone marrow failure
▶ Unexplained weight loss
These signs do not necessarily mean cancer, but they do mean cancer should be ruled out as a cause.

Checkups for Healthy People:

▶ A cancer-related checkup that includes the thyroids, testes, prostate, mouth, ovaries, skin, and lymph nodes should be done every 3 to 4 years for people ages 20 to 40 years and every year for people aged 40 and over.
▶ Breasts should be examined by a physician every 3 to 4 years for people ages 20 to 40 years, self-examination should be performed every month regardless of age, and baseline mammogram should be done for women ages 35 to 39, every 2 years for women up to age 50, and annually after age 50.
▶ The uterus should be checked with a pelvic examination every 3 years for people ages 20 to 40 and an annual pelvic examination after age 40.
▶ For cervical cancer, women who are or have been sexually active or have reached age 18 should have an annual pap test. After three consecutive, satisfactory, normal, annual examinations, the pap test may be performed less frequently at the discretion of her physician.
▶ Testes should be self-examined every month for men age 20 and over.
▶ Colon and rectum checkups require digital rectal examination every year for people of both genders age 40 and over, a stool blood test annually for people of both genders age 50 and over, and a proctology examination every 3 to 5 years after two negative annual examinations for people age 50 and over.
▶ The prostate is checked with a digital rectal examination after age 40 and a blood test for prostate-specific antigen (PSA) by the age of 50 for most men but earlier for African Americans and sons of men with prostate cancer.[7]

viral invasions of healthy cells) are undergoing research for this purpose. Interferon is used for treatment of a rare blood cancer called *hairy cell leukemia*. Interleukin-2 is under study in the treatment of kidney cancer and melanoma.[1]

Cancer and Exercise

Researchers are currently investigating the role of exercise in the prevention of some types of cancer, including colon cancer, breast cancer, and cancer of the reproductive organs. Since 1980 at least eight studies involving large numbers of people in America, Europe, and China have examined the relationship between physical activity and colon cancer; seven concluded that exercise reduces risk.[8] Other studies involving the risk of breast cancer among more than 5000 alumnae of 10 colleges and universities revealed 86% higher rates for nonathletes compared with their athletic peers. In another study of 25,000 women in Washington State, women who worked at physically demanding jobs were less

Figure 12-7 Breast Self-Examination

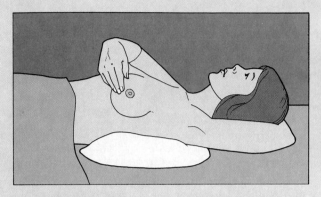

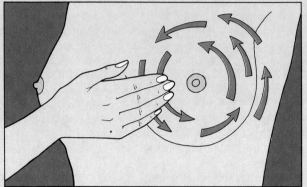

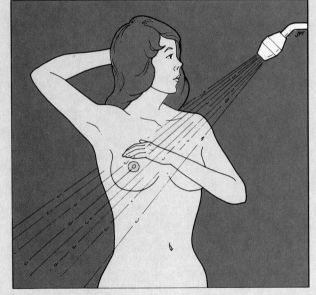

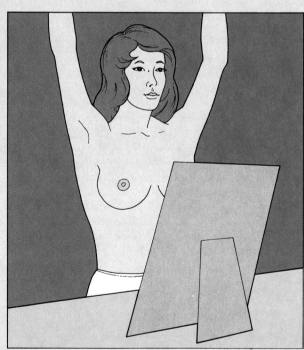

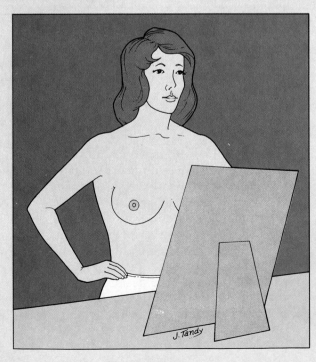

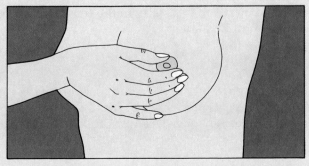

Figure 12-7 Breast Self-Examination—cont'd

1. Lying in bed, place a pillow under one shoulder to elevate and flatten the breast. Examine each breast using the opposite hand, first with the arm under the head and again with the arm at your side.
2. Make small rotary motions with flat pads (not tips) of your fingers.
3. Palpate breasts in concentric circles from rim inward toward the nipple. Feel for knots, lumps, thickenings indentations, and swellings. Be sure to include the armpit.
4. Wet, soapy skin makes it easier to feel lumps. Keep one hand overhead and examine each breast with the opposite hand.
5. In front of a large mirror, stand with your arms relaxed at sides. Examine the breasts for swelling, dimpling, bulges, retractions, irritations, and sores or changes in mole or nipple color, texture, or orientation. Repeat with the arms extended and again with your arms clasped behind your head.
6. Repeat the inspection in step 5 while contracting your chest muscles: first clasp your hands in front of your forehead, squeezing your palms together, then place your palms flat on the sides of your hips, pressing downward. This highlights the bulges and indentations, which may signal the growth of tumors.
7. Bend forward from the hips, resting your hands on your knees or two chair backs. Use a mirror to examine your breasts for normal irregularities and abnormal variances; both are pronounced in this position.
8. Squeeze your nipples to inspect for secretions and discharge.
9. Report any suspicious findings to your doctor without delay.
10. Supplement your self-examination with a breast examination by your doctor as part of a regular physical examination and cancer checkup.

Figure 12-8 Testicular Self-Examination

Cancer of the testes (the male reproductive glands) is one of the most common cancers in men 15 to 34 years of age. It accounts for 12% of cancer deaths in this group. The best hope for early detection of testicular cancer is a simple, 3 minute monthly self-examination. The best time is after a warm bath or shower when the scrotal skin is most relaxed.

Roll each testicle gently between the thumb and fingers of both hands. If you find any hard lumps or nodules, see your doctor promptly. It may not be malignant, but only a doctor can make the diagnosis.

After a thorough physical examination, your doctor may perform x-ray studies for the most accurate diagnosis.

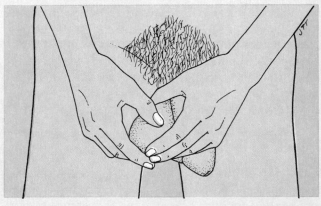

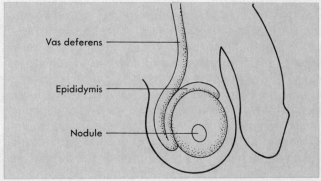

Vas deferens

Epididymis

Nodule

likely to have breast cancer than those with sedentary jobs. Cancers of the female reproductive system also seem to be related to exercise. In the Harvard alumnae study, women who played sports during their college years were 153% less likely to develop cervical, uterine, or ovarian cancer than nonathletes. The same relationship, however, has not been demonstrated in men. Prostate cancer is as common in active men as in those who lead sedentary lives.[8]

Although large-scale studies indicate that physical fitness appears to postpone the risks of dying from a variety of malignancies, the evidence falls short of cause and effect. Several hypotheses attempt to explain the reasons exercise may prevent cancer. One possible mechanism involves the effect of exercise in reducing body fat. The amount of body fat is positively correlated with the incidence of cancer. In the case of colon cancer, physical activity promotes bowel movements, thus reducing the exposure of the intestinal wall to potentially toxic fecal material. Some studies have also indicated that exercise may augment or stimulate the body's immune system in several ways, the end result being that cancerous cells are recognized and destroyed early in their development.[9]

How Much Exercise Is Enough?

If the results of a colon cancer study of 17,148 men is representative of other cancers, exercise that requires as little as 1000 calories per week lowers the risk of cancer by 50%. The study indicated, however, that active people were only protected against cancer if they continued to exercise for 11 to 15 years.[8] Exercise does not guard against every kind of tumor. Cancers are diverse in terms of their genetic, environmental, and biological characteristics. Nevertheless, in 1985 the American Cancer Society recommended exercise to protect against cancer.[10]

Diabetes Mellitus

Diabetes mellitus is a metabolic disorder involving the pancreas. The pancreas fails to produce an enzyme called *insulin*. (An enzyme is a complex protein that induces changes in other substances without undergoing changes itself.) A lack of insulin results in an inability to store or use glucose, the blood sugar the body uses as its primary energy source. As a result, diabetics cannot use the energy they consume, and high glucose levels build up in the blood and urine, a condition known as *hyperglycemia*. Large amounts of sugar in urine require additional water so that the sugar can be diluted for elimination. The increased need by the body for water leads to a depletion of the body water stores, causing excessive thirst and frequent urination. When the body becomes unable to completely break down glucose as a source of energy, fat must be used. Fat is metabolized differently than glucose, and its breakdown is incomplete when glucose is not available. Incomplete metabolism causes an excess amount of chemicals called *ketone bodies* to build up in the body. The buildup of ketones is used to perform the functions that glucose would perform under normal conditions (supplying energy), but the excess amounts of ketone bodies disrupt the body's chemical balance, altering the blood's chemistry and making it more acidic. Acidic conditions in the body are extremely hazardous.

Diabetes can be a serious disorder. Symptoms include excessive thirst, increased urination, hunger, a tendency to tire easily, wounds that heal slowly, blurred vision, and frequent skin, vaginal, and urinary tract infections. Dehydration and build-up of ketones can result in ketoacidosis (the accumulation of ketones) and can cause nausea, vomiting, abdominal pain, lethargy, and drowsiness. This often leads to severe sickness, coma, and even death. Of equal significance is that prolonged periods of elevated glucose levels disrupt normal enzyme and membrane functions. Chronic complications that may result include eye disease, kidney disorders, painful nerve and muscle symptoms, and decreased circulation. Diabetes is a leading cause of foot and leg amputations. Diabetes can also produce impotence in males, chronic diarrhea, and increased risk of heart disease and heart attacks in both genders. Of the 14 million people with diabetes in the United States, many are unaware they have it. By the time individuals realize they have this condition, they may have already suffered severe consequences.[11]

Type I Diabetes

Although there are varying degrees of diabetes, it is generally divided into two diagnostic categories. Type I diabetes is insulin-dependent diabetes. Initial onset of type I diabetes occurs most commonly in children and young adults, although it may develop at any age. Symptoms may be quite sudden and sometimes progress rapidly, requiring quick intervention to prevent death. Type I diabetics produce little or no insulin and require insulin injections to function. Before insulin was discovered, the average life span for a type I diabetic was 2 years after diagnosis. Properly treated, these people now live almost as long as the general population.

Type II Diabetes

Type II diabetes, also known as *noninsulin−dependent diabetes mellitus (NIDDM)*, is the most common type and is found primarily in individuals over the age of 40. Scientists believe that it is strongly linked to genetic factors.[11] If an identical twin develops NIDDM, the other most likely will as well. Type II diabetics either develop a resistance to insulin activity or experience insufficient insulin action. Their bodies are usuallly capable of producing adequate amounts of insulin—something a type I diabetic cannot do. The difficulty in type II diabetes is that body cells become resistant to insulin at the receptor sites (the place where insulin attaches to the cell). Type II diabetes is linked so strongly to obesity that it can be considered a symptom. Almost 80% of all type II diabetics are overweight at the time of diagnosis.[12] Primarily and often the only treatment necessary for type II diabetics is weight loss, although some individuals still require medication or injections of insulin to help control the condition.

Causes of Diabetes

The causes of diabetes are not known. A number of factors, including viral infections, heredity, chemical injury, and other environmental components, are associated with the development of diabetes.

There is no cure for diabetes. Many individuals with type II diabetes can control the disease through weight loss, exercise, and adequate nutrition. Losing weight helps to lower insulin resistance, enabling the body to make more efficient use of the insulin available. Evidence that links exercise to a decreased incidence of NIDDM is increasing. In an 8-year study, women who exercised once a week lowered their risk of type II diabetes by 33%. Another 6-year study of 22,271 male physicians showed a 42% reduction in risk for NIDDM.[12] It is estimated that 50% to 85% of all complications of diabetes are preventable or treatable, but diagnosis and proper treatment are necessary. Negligence of diabetes and its complications may result in early death.

Arthritis

Arthritis is an inflammatory disease of the joints. The over 100 varieties of arthritis include gout, ankylosing spondylitis, systemic lupus erythematosis, osteoarthritis, and rheumatoid arthritis. Osteoarthritis and rheumatoid arthritis are found most often. Both result in pain and deformed joints.

Osteoarthritis is the most common form of arthritis, afflicting nearly 16 million adults in the United States. X-ray studies show that about 97% of people over age 60 have osteoarthritis joint changes,[13] and 60% of them experience related pain.[14] Osteoarthritis is characterized by deterioration of the articular cartilage that covers the gliding surfaces of the bones

in certain joints. The cartilage develops small cracks, leading to erosion of the cartilage and causing localized inflammation and painful motion.[15] The deterioration associated with osteoarthritis seems related to the wear and tear of daily living, age, and injury. Other factors may include heredity, diet, abnormal use of joints (for example, throwing a curve ball year after year), and an impaired blood supply to affected joints. Disability most often afflicts the weight-bearing joints of the ankles, knees, hips, and spine. Treatment for osteoarthritis includes aspirin and cortisone drugs to relieve pain. Mild exercise, heat, cold, or a combination of heat and cold application accompanied by massage are used as treatment measures. Exercise is used for therapeutic purposes to help maintain range-of-motion and to strengthen the muscles that can help alleviate joint problems. Exercise is usually prescribed by a physical therapist. Occasionally, surgery is performed to replace joints or repair tendons and ligaments.

Should a person with osteoarthritis exercise to avoid deconditioning, or will the exercise cause further damage to the arthritic joints? The answer seems to be yes and no to both questions, depending on the individual. The results of some studies[13] have shown that exercise does not contribute to osteoarthritis, but other studies show the opposite. In addition, exercise of an arthritic joint may cause pain, and the pain may be relieved by rest. As osteoarthritis progresses, pain may also occur at rest.

An 8-week walking study of patients with osteoarthritis of the knee, one of the most common arthritic problems, provides a reason for optimism regarding exercise. Patients who walked 30 minutes three times a week reported a 27% decrease in pain

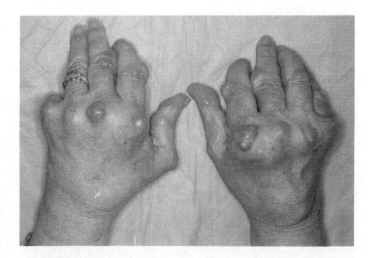

Rheumatoid arthritis can be very painful and disfiguring.

and improved their ability to walk longer distances compared with a nonwalking control group. The researchers concluded that supervised walking can be helpful in people with significant arthritis of the knee. Stretching exercises also help to relieve arthritis pain by lengthening tendons, which reduces muscle spasms, the source of much of the pain in osteoarthritis.

Rheumatoid arthritis is found three times more often in women than men. Onset of rheumatoid arthritis is usually between the ages of 20 and 50. Although the exact causes are unknown, this form of arthritis may be an *autoimmune disease* (one in which there is an immune response against the cells of a person's body). Symptoms of rheumatoid arthritis include joint swelling, redness, stiffness, pain, muscle atrophy, joint deformity, and limited mobility. The condition is unpredictable because it can suddenly flare up and just as suddenly go into remission. Emotional stress is often associated with an attack. The disease frequently results in disability. Treatment for rheumatoid arthritis is the same as for osteoarthritis. Emphasis is placed on relieving the pain and improving mobility.

Osteoporosis

Osteoporosis is a chronic disease in which the mineral content of the bones progressively decreases so that the bones become brittle and break. It is responsible for more than a million fractures annually, including 227,000 hip fractures.[16] Vertebral bones in the spine shrink and fracture, causing a deformed spine. One third of women over 65 years of age experience this condition. Bones in the wrist are also a common site of fractures from osteoporosis.

The primary risk factors for osteoporosis include female gender, white or Oriental race, slender body type, and early menopause. The secondary risks include alcohol and tobacco abuse, calcium deficiency, family history, sedentary lifestyle, anticonvulsant medication use, and thyroid hormone use.

Type I osteoporosis affects eight times as many women as men, and the effects are seen during the first 2 years after menopause.[17] In order of prevalence, the fractures in type I are vertebral crush fractures and fractures of the arm above the wrist. Accelerated bone loss after menopause because of estrogen deficiency contributes significantly to these fractures. Type II osteoporosis occurs later in life, about age 70, and affects twice as many women as men. Fractures of the hips are the most frequent events. Estrogen deficiency is one of many possible causes of type II osteoporosis. Other contributing causes include calcium deficiency, fluoride deficiency, and lack of exercise.

Bone is living organic tissue that responds to physical stress. It is continuously undergoing remodeling, but osteoporosis accelerates bone loss so that replacement cannot keep pace; this results in weakened and brittle bone. Inactivity and the absence of gravitational force (weightlessness) contribute to the process. Conversely, physical exercise forces bone to adapt to the stresses imposed on it and it hypertrophies in response. Bones atrophy when they are unstressed.

The development of the muscular system is essential to the development and maintenance of bone mass. Athletes have greater bone density than age-matched nonathletes. Unilateral athletes, those who use one limb extensively and vigorously such as tennis players and baseball pitchers, have larger and thicker muscles and bones in the dominant arm compared with their nondominant arm. Weight-bearing activities, such as jogging, racquetball, and weight training, are more effective activities for the development and maintenance of the skeletal system than nonweight-bearing activities such as swimming and cycling.

Mild to moderate exercises have been effective in promoting bone strength in the elderly. Studies whose subjects were 60 to 95 years of age suggest that exercise effectively arrests bone loss and/or increases bone mineral content well into old age.

People with osteoporosis can and should exercise, but the type of physical activity and the intensity of exercise must be carefully selected. Forceful contractions of muscles and high-impact activities should be avoided because they may stress the bones beyond their breaking point. Swimming, water aerobics, stationary cycling, walking, and light weight training are good starting activities for those with osteoporosis.

The Common Cold

Over 110 viruses, known as *rhinoviruses*, can cause the *common cold*. An individual may develop a temporary immunity to one or two viruses and still be infected by another. Any time people are together, viruses causing the common cold are present. Adults average 2 to 4 colds each year, and children experience 6 to 10.[18] Colds can be contracted by shaking hands, sneezing, and breathing. Evidence indicates that hand-to-hand contact is the main way a cold is spread. As infected individuals blow or touch their noses, the virus is transferred to their hands. When an uninfected person touches the infected person's hands, the virus is again transferred to the uninfected individual. Touching the face with hands that carry the virus leads directly to developing a cold. Frequent hand washing may prevent the spread of the virus.

The signs and symptoms of a cold are easily recognized. They include a feeling of listlessness, general aches and pains, watery eyes, and runny nasal passages. As the cold progresses, the nasal membranes swell, resulting in a stuffy nose. Infections affecting the throat can lead to sore throats and coughing. These symptoms tend to last 7 to 10 days. As an old axiom points out, if a cold is treated, it will go away in 7 days, and left alone, it will last a week. A cold may occasionally persist for several weeks, but complications are infrequent in adults and older children. When they do occur, it is most often a middle ear or sinus infection.

Antibiotics do not cure the common cold because they only fight bacterial infections. Over-the-counter nasal sprays may offer temporary relief but should be avoided because they can create additional swelling in the nasal passages when the effects of the spray wear off (a rebound effect). Nasal sprays can also become habit forming if used for prolonged periods. Research is being conducted with interferon and various drugs to study their effects on preventing colds or speeding relief.[19] Interferon is a protein manufactured by the immune system after a virus has invaded an organism. It prevents the spread of a virus to cells adjacent to infected cells. It is being used by people to whom a cold poses significant danger, such as patients receiving chemotherapy for cancer, the elderly, and transplant patients. Interferon has not been approved for sale. The best advice for treating a cold is still to take aspirin (or ibuprofen or acetaminophen), drink plenty of liquids, eat a nutritious diet, and get plenty of rest.

Cough syrups may offer temporary relief, but many physicians question the effectiveness of these products. Cough syrups fall into two groups: suppressants and expectorants. Suppressants turn off the brain's cough center, and an expectorant supposedly loosens phlegm. It is particularly important for people suffering from emphysema or other chronic lung condition to avoid using suppressants.

Influenza

Influenza, or "flu," is also caused by a virus. There are three primary strains of the influenza virus: A, B, and C. Most influenza develops from the A and B strains. These strains can change genetically, reappearing in an altered form every few years. Symptoms of all types of flu include chills, fever, weakness, headache, sore throat, dry cough, nausea, vomiting, and muscular aches and pains. All symptoms may not be present, and the severity varies greatly among people. Treatment for flu is the same as for the common cold. Aspirin should not be taken by children or teenagers because the potentially fatal Reye's syndrome can develop.

Vaccines are available that can prevent a particular type of influenza. Current recommendations are that priority should be given to children and adults with chronic cardiovascular and lung disorders, residents of nursing homes, medical personnel who may transmit the virus to high-risk patients, everyone over 65, and anyone with conditions such as diabetes, kidney disease, hereditary anemias, and impaired natural immunity.

Headaches

One of the conditions causing great discomfort to people is the headache. Some **headaches** may be the result of injury or brain disease, but most are caused by distress, tension, and anxiety. *Tension headaches* are the most common. Caused by involuntary contractions of the scalp, head, and neck muscles, tension headaches may be precipitated by anxiety, stress, and allergic reactions. Tension headaches can often be relieved by massaging the scalp and muscles in the neck. Aspirin or other pain relievers usually alleviate a tension headache.

The common cold is most often spread by hand-to-hand contact.

Migraine headaches are characterized by throbbing pain that can last for hours or even days. Nausea and vomiting occasionally occur. Migraines seem to be initiated by stress and range from mild to severe. The exact cause of migraines is unknown, but it is thought they originate from constriction and dilation in the arteries near the surface of the brain. People who experience migraines may have advance warning symptoms, such as dizziness, sensitivity to flashing lights, the appearance of a blind spot, and an indescribable feeling that a headache is coming. Techniques such as deep breathing, progressive relaxation, biofeedback, meditation, and visualization seem to help relieve the pain associated with migraines. People who have symptoms and know a migraine is coming may be able to avoid it by taking medications that contain ergot alkaloids. Beta blockers (used to treat angina) may also be helpful.

Cluster headaches usually cause a knife-like pain behind the eye that quickly spreads to the forehead. The pain can spread to the neck, back of the head, and even into the teeth. The nose often runs and the involved eye tears. The pain is often described as one of the worst a person can endure.

Cluster headaches get their name because they occur in clusters, at least one each day and sometimes several attacks daily. The attacks begin suddenly and may last from several minutes to several hours. The cluster may last a few weeks or several months. Individuals may be symptom free for weeks or months. The cause of cluster headaches is unknown, but they also appear to be related to arterial constriction and dilation.

Ergot alkaloids, which constrict arteries, are often used to treat cluster headaches. Victims are warned to avoid alcohol during a cluster attack because it can trigger an episode.[20]

Summary

▶ Cancer is a group of diseases characterized by uncontrolled, disorderly cell growth.

▶ When the DNA or RNA in the nucleus of a cell loses the ability to regulate and control cellular metabolism, mutant cells develop. A mass of mutant cells is a neoplasm and may be either malignant or benign.

▶ The process by which cancerous cells spread from their original location to another location is metastasis.

▶ Carcinogens are agents that trigger the development of cancer. The tendency to develop cancer has also been linked to genetics, stress, and psychological outlook.

▶ The cancer site that has the highest incidence of death in males and females is the lungs. This is followed by the prostate for males and breasts for women.

▶ Cancer may be treated surgically, often in combination with chemotherapy and radiotherapy. A relatively new technique involves immunotherapy.

▶ About 80% of all cancers are associated with lifestyle factors that include diet, smoking, and exposure to the sun.

▶ Ultraviolet radiation from tanning devices increases the risk of skin cancer and premature skin aging.

▶ Physical activity appears to reduce the risk of several types of cancer.

▶ Diabetes is a metabolic disorder in which the pancreas fails to produce sufficient insulin, resulting in a lack of glucose, or the receptor sites become less sensitive. This inability can lead to a number of conditions, including ketoacidosis, which may result in death.

▶ Hyperglycemia is a condition in which large amounts of sugar build up in the blood.

▶ There are two major categories of diabetes. Type I usually occurs early in life and requires insulin injections. Type II is found mainly in obese individuals over the age of 40. Most type II diabetics can control their condition without insulin injections.

▶ Physical activity decreases the incidence of type II diabetes.

▶ Arthritis is an inflammatory disease of the joints. The most common form of arthritis is osteoarthritis, which is characterized by deterioration of the cartilage covering the surfaces of the bones in certain joints.

▶ It is believed that rheumatoid arthritis is a disease of the immune system that results in joint swelling, pain, deformity, and decreased mobility.

▶ The common cold is caused by rhinoviruses, of which there are over 110 varieties. Antibiotics do not cure cold.

▶ Influenza is caused by only three strains of virus, but these agents have the ability to change and reappear in different forms. Because influenza can range widely in severity, certain high-risk groups are encouraged to have an annual flu vaccine.

▶ Osteoporosis is a chronic disease characterized by a loss of mineral content of the bones that makes them brittle and vulnerable to breakage.

▶ Mild to moderate exercises are effective in promoting bone strength in the elderly.

▶ Headaches are divided into three categories—tension, cluster, and migraine. People who experience migraines can use techniques such as deep breathing and meditation to alleviate or prevent onset of a headache.

Action Plan for Personal Wellness

Use the information presented in this chapter to answer the following questions and to formulate an action plan to enhance your personal wellness.

1 Based on the information presented in this chapter, along with what I know about my family's health history, the health problems and issues that I need to be concerned about are:_____

_____

_____

2 Of those health concerns listed in number 1, the one I most need to act on is:_____

_____

_____

3 The possible actions that I can take to improve my level of wellness are (be specific):_____

_____

_____

4 Of the actions listed in number 3, the one that I most need to include in an action plan is:_____

_____

_____

5 Factors I need to keep in mind to be successful in my action plan are:_____

_____

_____

Review Questions

1. Describe the process by which cancer cells develop. What characteristics differentiate cancer cells from other cells?
2. List and explain the factors that possibly contribute to development of cancer. What are the leading types and sites for cancer in males and females?
3. Explain how type I and type II diabetes differ and describe the symptoms of each. What can happen when these symptoms are ignored? What are some of the factors that contribute to type II diabetes?
4. What is arthritis? Explain the differences in the two most common forms of the condition, their causes, and the preferred methods of treatment.
5. What causes colds? What are some of the methods being used to treat colds?
6. Influenza viruses act somewhat differently than the viruses that cause colds. How many are there, and how do they differ from cold viruses? Why should children not be given aspirin when suffering from influenza?
7. Explain the difference between tension headaches and migraine headaches. How do the causes, symptoms, and treatments differ?
8. Define osteoporosis. Distinguish between type I and type II osteoporosis.
9. Discuss the relationship between physical activity and the conditions discussed in this chapter.

References

1. Williams G: Causes and prevention of cancer, *Stat Bull* 72(2):6, 1991.
2. American Cancer Society: *Cancer facts and figures—1992,* Atlanta, Ga, 1992, The Society.
3. Lamb L: Understanding cancer, *Health Letter* 38(9):1-8, 1991.
4. Is there a cancer personality?, *Johns Hopkins Medical Letter, Health After 50* 2:1, 1990.
5. American Institute for Cancer Research: *Everything doesn't cause cancer,* Washington, DC, 1992, The Institute.
6. US Department of Health and Human Services: *The darker side of indoor tanning,* Rockville, Md, 1992, FDA.
7. Prostate cancer: knowledge, hope, and camaraderie, *Harvard Health Letter* 18(4):2, 1993.
8. Can you run away from cancer, *Harvard Health Letter* 17(5):5-7, 1992.
9. Simopoulous AP: Obesity and carcinogenesis: historical perspective, *Am J Clin Nutr* 45:271-276, 1987.
10. Fauthier MM: Can exercise reduce the risk of cancer? *Physician Sportsmed* 14:170-178, 1986.
11. Collins C: Diabolical diabetes, *Am Health* 12(1):68-72, 1993.
12. Exercise and adult-onset diabetes, *Harvard Health Letter* 18(1):6-8, 1992.
13. Lamb L: Exercise helps osteoarthritis, *Health Letter* 39(11):4, 1992.
14. Osteoarthritis: a joint endeavor, *Harvard Health Letter* 17(6):1-4, 1992.
15. Krames communications: *Osteoarthritis,* Daly City, Calif, 1988, Patient Information Library.
16. Lamb L: News on osteoporosis, *Health Letter* 37(1):5-6, 1991.
17. Johnston CC, Slemeda C: Osteoporosis: an overview, *Physician Sportsmed* 15:64-68, 1987.
18. Colds, part I: common misery, *Harvard Health Letter* 17(1):6-8, 1991.
19. Common cold, part II, *Harvard Health Letter* 17(2):5-7, 1991.
20. Lamb L: Cluster headaches, *Health Letter* 39(12):2-3, 1992.

Annotated Readings

American Cancer Society: *Cancer facts and figures—1992,* Atlanta, Ga, 1992, The Society.
Provides a current, concise statistical update on cancer morbidity and mortality, describes the risks associated with selected cancers, and discusses trends in diagnosis and treatment.

Can you run away from cancer, *Harvard Health Letter* 17(5):5-7, 1992.
Presents the results of ongoing, longitudinal studies on the role and preventive effects of exercise on various cancers.

Exercise and adult-onset diabetes, *Harvard Health Letter* 18(1):6-8, 1992.
Highlights the results of longitudinal studies that demonstrate the effects of exercise on the development, prevention, and control of type II diabetes mellitus.

Lamb L: Understanding cancer, *Health Letter* 38(9):1-8, 1991.
Discusses the development of cancer cells, including genetic and extracellular factors, and general principles in diagnosis and treatment.

Osteoarthritis: A joint endeavor, *Harvard Health Letter* 17(6):1-4, 1992.
Describes characteristics of osteoarthritis and discusses nondrug, over-the-counter drugs, and prescription drug treatments.

Cancer Awareness Inventory

This inventory was developed to help with early detection and treatment of cancer. It presents common symptoms for various cancer sites. If you have symptoms, check with your physician. The chances are that you will not have cancer, but these symptoms do suggest a potential problem with your health. It is always wise to be safe and consult your physician when you are assuming responsibility for your health. Directions: For each cancer site, check any of the symptoms you experience.

Symptoms

Bladder

1. Blood in urine? _____
2. Unusual change in bladder habits? _____
3. Discomfort in urination? _____
4. Change in flow in urination? _____
5. An urge to urinate more frequently? _____

Bone

1. Pain in the bone or joint? _____
2. Swelling in the bone or joint? _____
3. Unusual warmth in the bone or joint? _____
4. Protruding veins along the bone or joint? _____

Breast

1. Thickening or lump in the breast? _____
2. Lump under the arm? _____
3. Thickening or reddening of the skin of the breast? _____
4. Puckering or dimpling of the skin of the breast? _____
5. Nipple discharge? _____
6. Inverted nipple, if nipple was previously erect? _____
7. Persistent pain and tenderness of the breast? _____
8. Unusual changes in the nipple and areolae? _____
9. Benign breast lumps? _____

Colon/Rectum

1. Continuous constipation or diarrhea? _____
2. Rectal bleeding? _____
3. Change in bowel habit? _____
4. An increase in intestinal gas? _____
5. Abdominal discomfort? _____

Lung

1. An unusual cough? _____
2. Shortness of breath? _____
3. Sputum streaked with blood? _____
4. Chest pain? _____
5. Recurring attacks of pneumonia or bronchitis? _____

Lymphomas

1. Painless enlargement of a lymph node or cluster of lymph nodes? _____
2. Profuse sweating and fever? _____
3. Weight loss? _____
4. Unexplained weakness? _____
5. Unusual itching? _____

Oral

1. A sore in the mouth that does not heal? _____
2. Lump or thickening that bleeds easily? _____
3. Difficulty in chewing or swallowing food? _____
4. The sensation of something in the throat? _____
5. Restricted movement of the tongue or jaw? _____
6. Poor oral hygiene? _____

Prostate

1. Weak or interrupted flow of urine? _____
2. Inability to urinate or difficulty in starting urination? _____
3. A need to urinate frequently, especially at night? _____
4. Blood in urine? _____
5. Urine flow that is not easily stopped? _____
6. Painful or burning urination? _____
7. Continuing pain in lower back, pelvis, or upper thighs? _____

Skin

1. Obvious change in wart or mole? _____
2. Unusual skin condition? _____
3. Chronic swelling, redness, or warmth of the skin? _____
4. Unexplained itching? _____
5. Overexposure to the ultraviolet rays of the sun? _____

Testes

1. An enlargement and change in the consistency of the testes? _____
2. A dull ache in the lower abdomen and groin? _____
3. Sensation of dragging and heaviness? _____
4. Difficulty with ejaculation? _____

Thyroid

1. A lump or mass in the neck? _____
2. Persistent hoarseness? _____
3. Difficulty in swallowing? _____
4. Overexposure to head and neck x-ray treatments? _____

Uterus/cervis

1. Irregular bleeding? _____
2. Unusual vaginal discharge? _____
3. Positive Pap smear, Class 2 to 5, some signs of abnormality? _____
4. Recurring herpes simplex virus? _____
5. Fibroid tumors of the uterus? _____

Application

Any statement you have checked should be carefully evaluated. If the symptom appears severe (for example, blood in the stool), see a physician immediately. However, pain in a joint may be observed for a short period to see if there is improvement. Never wait longer than 2 weeks to see a physician if the symptom persists.

1. How many symptoms have I checked?_____

2. How serious do these symptoms seem?_____

3. Should I see a physician now or wait?_____

ASSESSMENT ACTIVITY   12-2

Are You at Risk for Diabetes?

Directions: Check the appropriate column in response to the questions below to assess your probability of having diabetes. The more questions that are answered with a *yes*, the higher the probability you have of being diabetic.

	Yes	No
1. Is there a history of diabetes in your family?	____	____
2. Do you tire quickly or seem to always be fatigued?	____	____
3. Do you urinate frequently?	____	____
4. Are you constantly thirsty?	____	____
5. Is your vision blurry?	____	____
6. Have you suddenly lost weight?	____	____
7. Are you overweight?	____	____
8. Do you eat excessively?	____	____
9. Do wounds heal slowly?	____	____
10. Is your skin frequently itchy?	____	____

Taken alone, any *yes* answer does not necessarily indicate you are a diabetic. However, if you have answered *yes* more than five times, consult your physician for a urine test.

Self-Responsibility in the Health-Care Market

Key terms

contraindications

diagnostic labora-
tory tests

health insurance

health maintenance
organization (HMO)

immunizations

implied consent

informed consent

primary-care physi-
cian

reliability

selective health ex-
aminations

self-care

validity

Objectives

After completing this chapter, you will be able to:

▶ Explain how to evaluate the accuracy and validity of health information

▶ Discuss criteria in determining when, where, and how to choose health care

▶ Describe the functions and purposes of the three major components of a physical examination

Traditionally, Americans have had a rather passive attitude toward health care. Whether it was taking medicine, purchasing health-care products, undergoing surgery, or having a diagnostic test administered, the general attitude was simply to follow orders. Fortunately, this attitude is changing. People are viewing themselves as active participants in their health care. They are asking questions, placing demands on *health-care providers* (people and/or facilities that provide health-care services), getting second opinions, and sometimes even refusing treatments. People now realize that they must assume more responsibility for safeguarding their health. With this responsibility, however, comes the challenge of knowing what people can and should do for themselves. The purpose of this chapter is to lay the groundwork for becoming an informed, active participant in the health-care marketplace.

Understanding Health Information

The first and perhaps most difficult challenge for consumers is to make sense out of the health information explosion. Many popular magazines regularly print health articles, newspapers often devote entire sections to medicine, the publications of health newsletters abound, television programs feature numerous health stories, and a plethora of scientific health-related studies are published daily. Interest in health information appears to have reached an all-time high.

The availability of so much health information has drawbacks. The major one is that so much of the information is confusing, sometimes even contradictory (Figure 13-1). Even medical experts have trouble separating fact from fiction. It is not unusual to see some new finding headlined one day and completely refuted the next. For some people the ubiquity of refutations and contradictions leads to an attitude sometimes referred to as *health fatalism*, which maintains that nothing can be believed. People with a fatalistic view disregard health information because they believe that new findings will inevitably disagree with facts previously accepted as true.

Several examples illustrate this point. Cyclamate at one time was considered a safe sugar substitute. In 1969, however, an experiment seemed to show that rats in which cyclamate pellets had been surgically implanted were more likely to develop tumors. A health *hysteria cycle* followed. The cycle began with press releases suggesting that an artificial food ingredient was poisonous. These charges were based on data that could not be replicated but created a fear that forced the chemical off the market. After 17 years of research in which the National Cancer Institute fed a group of monkeys enough cyclamate to sweeten 150 cans of soda per animal per week, cyclamate was proved to be safe. Rather than develop-

Figure 13-1 Health Information Contradictions

Low fat? But what about fat and heart disease? And cancer? Rather than low fat, shouldn't that be polyunsaturated fat? Or should it be monounsaturated fat? People who eat omega-3 fatty acids found in cold water seafood have less heart attacks than people who eat low fat foods.

How can I make the right decision when the rules keep changing?

Example of an advertising strategy in which a health magazine highlights confusion about fat as a way to promote sales and cope with the health information explosion.

ing tumors, the monkeys flourished. Research proved that cyclamate is safe. The cycle ends when cyclamates return to the shelves of U.S. stores—years after it has been legally sold in other countries.

Cholesterol is another good example. Few if any risk factors related to heart disease have received so much publicity. At one time the evidence was so convincing that many people formed a simple cause-effect relationship between cholesterol and atherosclerosis. Later studies, however, proved that some people with high blood cholesterol did not have atherosclerosis. Conversely, some people with low blood cholesterol had advanced cases of atherosclerosis. The hysteria surrounding cholesterol finally gave way to the discovery of the high-density and low-density lipoprotein theory of heart disease.

The point of these examples is that an appropriate approach to health information is to adopt a skeptical and suspicious attitude, especially toward extreme and sensational health claims.

Guidelines for Evaluating Health Information

The guidelines that follow should help facilitate a discriminating search for correct health information.

Avoid Jumping to Conclusions

Most health misinformation is actually based on facts, not lies. The problem is that facts get exaggerated and sometimes lead people to wrong conclusions. Much health literature is based on research involving statistical *relationships* or associations among two or more events. Relationships are helpful clues to health but they cannot and do not establish *cause-and-effect* relationships. The mistake many people make is to read or hear about a new health finding and erroneously conclude that one event causes the other. One of the areas most commonly abused by reference to cause-and-effect relationships is cancer.

A good example is provided by Vickery[1] in the popular newsletter *Taking Care*. "The first physicians who investigated malaria concluded that it was caused by damp, stale air because it was more likely to occur in low-lying, swampy areas. It was several hundred years before it was demonstrated that it was a malaria parasite caused by mosquitoes which caused malaria. Malaria, mosquitoes, and bad air are all associated with each other, but these associations do not prove that any one factor caused any of the others.[11]

Relationships are based on statistical procedures. Although these relationships may provide a basis for better understanding health concerns, they usually fall short of supporting many of the sweeping generalizations and conclusions that make headlines.

Beware of Oversimplifications

In our desire to make sense out of health information, people often oversimplify the truth. For example, potato chips have long been reputed as a junk food. Actually, the quick cooking process of potato chips preserves its nutrients better than mashed, boiled, or baked potatoes. Ounce per ounce, potato chips provide more nutrients than other forms of potatoes. However, because potato chips are cooked in oil, they are high in fat and calories and not recommended for people trying to lose weight. By being aware that the truth is not simple for most health issues, the tendency to oversimplify and overgeneralize health information can be thwarted.

Health Discoveries Take Time

Health discoveries often mean media headlines, but a cardinal rule of science is that findings must be replicable. Health information based on a dramatic discovery is not usually valid unless it is confirmed in several follow-up studies or experiments.

Criteria of Valid, Reliable Health Information

Health information should be valid and reliable and based on scientifically controlled studies. In health research, **validity** means truthfulness. If a study is designed and conducted properly, its findings are likely to be valid. For example, it was found that adding vitamin E to human cells in the laboratory

Misleading words are often used to promote products.

stimulated cell division and growth. This was used to support the erroneous conclusion that vitamin E would delay the aging process. This was not a proper generalization because a simple laboratory experiment is not a valid procedure for demonstrating something as complex as aging.

Reliability is another key criterion for evaluating health information and refers to the extent that health claims can be consistently verified. If a claim is reliable, it can be demonstrated to occur consistently in study after study. Any health claim worth considering is based on several studies or experiments.

Health information must also pass scientifically controlled, *double-blind* studies. The classic study includes at least two groups in which one is an *experimental group* and receives some form of experimental treatment and the other is a *control group* and receives no treatment. The double-blind feature of a study means that neither the researcher nor the subjects knows who is receiving an experimental treatment. If a researcher wanted to prove, for example, that a particular brand of soap prevents athlete's foot, two groups would be needed. One would use the experimental soap, and the other would use a *placebo* or soap substitute. Researchers administering the soap treatment would not know which soap they were using, nor would the subjects in the experimental and control groups. Therefore if the experimental group has significantly fewer cases of athlete's foot, the results can be attributed to the treatment.

The experimental-control, double-blind requirement of scientific research is a difficult standard to pass. When evaluating new health claims, consumers should inquire about the nature and design of the study behind the claims.

Another consideration of a scientifically controlled study is characteristics of the study population. Scientific studies require random sampling of subjects that represent the racial, religious, gender, and cultural characteristics of the population at large. Medical breakthroughs should not be based on a small number of *homogenous*, or similar, subjects.

Sources of Information

Valid and reliable health information comes from respected journals, magazines, and newsletters. Such publications have health or medical editors and subject their articles to peer review and criticism by other scientists. A partial listing of reliable sources of health information published in newsletters that contain no advertisements is presented in Table 13-1.

Another source of health information and medical advice growing in popularity is the telephone.[2] Several telephone service businesses are now available that offer live interaction with health-care professionals (Figure 13-2). These services, which are available through toll-free 800 and/or moderately expensive 900 numbers, provide consumers with a private and convenient option for getting answers to questions ranging from the side effects of a medicine to the need for a second opinion regarding a particular diagnosis.

There are obvious limitations to what medical and pharmaceutical advice telephone services can do, since a telephone practitioner does not know a caller's medical history and cannot perform a physical examination. They are not a substitute for having a physician. Instead, they should be viewed as informational, advisory, and possibly helpful in deciding whether a medical procedure, test, or treatment is warranted.

You should be on guard for information that appears to be motivated by commercial interests and beware of the influence of advertising (Figure 13-3). Claims based on anecdotes, case studies, testimonials, and personal observations may reflect personal bias or serve a hidden agenda.

Managing Health Care

A major theme throughout this text is that you can control many factors that influence your health. An outgrowth of this attitude is the **self-care** movement, which is the trend toward individuals taking increased responsibility for prevention or management

TABLE 13-1 Health Newsletters: Reliable Sources of Information on General Health Topics

Title of Newsletter	Published	Address
Consumer Reports Health Letter	Monthly	Consumers Union 256 Washington St. Mount Vernon, NY 10553
Harvard Medical School Health Letter	Monthly	79 Garden St. Cambridge, MA 02138
The Health Letter	Biweekly	P.O. Box 19622 Irvine, CA 92713
The Johns Hopkins Medical Letter	Monthly	P.O. Box 420235 Palm Coast, FL 32142-0235
Mayo Clinic Health Letter	Monthly	200 First Street SW Rochester, MN 55905
Taking Care	Monthly	The Center for Corporate Health Promotion 1850 Centennial Park Drive Reston, Virginia 22091
University of California, Berkeley Wellness Letter	Monthly	Health Letter Associates P.O. Box 412 Prince Street Station New York, NY 10012-0007

Subscription rates vary according to newsletter; approximate range is $20 to $25 per year.

Figure 13-2 Medical Telephone Services

Name: Ask-A-Nurse
Telephone Number: 1-800-535-1111 (Available in 38 states. Call this toll-free number to find out whether this service operates in your calling area.)
Hours: 24 hours a day, 7 days a week
Type of Service: Calls on health problems, medical procedures, diagnostic tests, and treatments are answered by registered nurses with an average of 10 years of experience in emergency room, critical care, or occupational health settings.
Cost: None

Name: Doctors By Phone
Telephone Number: 1-900-77-DOCTOR
Hours: 8 AM to midnight EST, 7 days a week
Type of Service: Most physicians on duty are board certified, and many have newly established practices in internal medicine or are completing specialized fellowships and answer a wide range of general and/or specific medical questions.
Cost: $3.00 per minute; the average call lasts 5 to 6 minutes

---

Name: Pharmacy Question? Ask the Pharmacist
Telephone Number: 1-900-420-0275
Hours: 24 hours a day, 7 days a week
Type of Service: Questions about medicines are answered by pharmacists licensed in North Carolina who have been in practice an average of over 7 years.
Cost: $1.95 per minute; the average call lasts 5 minutes

Figure 13-3 Tobacco and Advertising

The tobacco industry claims that the purpose of their advertising is simply to obtain a larger share of the market of adults who smoke. In reality, the cigarette industry needs over 2 million children to start smoking each year, over 5000 per day, to replace the adult smokers who die or quit.

Under the banner of capitalism and profit, the tobacco industry has made a conscious effort to seduce people to take up smoking in large numbers. Massive sums of advertising dollars are spent to associate cigarettes and smoking with images of success, power, confidence, elegance, sex appeal, machismo, adventurousness, and maturity. The reasons these advertisements are so successful is that many individuals are quite likely to perceive they are lacking in those attributes that are the focus of industry advertising.

In 1987, Philip Morris Companies spent about $1.4 billion for advertising ($85 million just for Marlboro cigarettes, used by the vast majority of children and adolescents who smoke), and RJR-Nabisco spent almost $1.1 billion in advertising in magazines, billboards, and other print media. During this same period, tobacco companies spent another $1.4 billion on promotions such as concerts, sporting events, and free tobacco samples.

To dramatize the effects of tobacco advertising on African Americans, a study was carried out in which an informal survey of billboards was done using 150 junior high school students from seven junior high schools in Washington, D.C.. The students identified 181 different billboards around their homes and schools and discovered that 86 (48%) were for cigarettes. Nearly half the cigarette advertisements were located in the two poorest neighborhoods. In addition, 54% of the advertisements depicted African Americans, compared with 25% that depicted whites. Tobacco companies spent approximately $6 million in 1985 for advertisements on small billboards in African American communities, which accounted for 37% of total advertising for this medium.

Smoking prevalence is higher among adult African Americans than among whites. The smoking rates for adults are 46% for African American males (versus 35% for white males) and 35% for African American females (versus 31% for white females). This trend has been true since 1965 despite smoking being more prevalent among white high school students. The smoking rates for seniors in high school are 34% for white females, 30% for white males, 16% for African American males, and 13% for African American females. Smoking-attributable disease mortality is higher among African Americans than among whites.

of certain health conditions.[3] Armed with correct information, you can manage many aspects of your health care that were once thought possible only with the help of a physician.

Answers to the following questions provide clues to the use of health-care services, providers, and products and facilitate the self-care approach to wellness:

1. When should you seek health care?
2. What can you expect from a stay in the hospital?
3. How can you select a health-care professional?

When to Seek Health Care

People tend to fall into two groups regarding health care: those who seek health care for every ache and pain and those who avoid health care unless experiencing extreme pain. Both groups unwisely use the health-care establishment. Those in the first group fail to understand that too much health care can be ineffective or even harmful. They also fail to recog-

nize the powerful recuperative powers of the body. An estimated 80% of patients who seek medical care are unaffected by treatment, 10% get better, and 9% experience an *iatrogenic* condition in which they get worse because of the medical treatment. Those in the latter group fail to recognize the value of early diagnosis and detection of disease.

Perhaps the best way to find a balance between too much and too little health care is to establish a physician-patient relationship with a general practitioner. The general practitioner may be a family practice physician or an internist who specializes in internal medicine.

It is important to visit your doctor while in good health. This permits your doctor to serve as a facilitator of wellness and provides a benchmark for interpreting symptoms when they occur.

A second important way to balance health care is to trust your instincts. Nobody knows when something is wrong with your body better than you do. Health and illness are subject to a wide variation in interpretation. If you are attuned to your body, you are your own best expert for recognizing signs and symptoms of illness.

Several signs and symptoms warrant medical attention without question. Internal bleeding, such as blood in urine, bowel movement, sputum, or vomit or from any of the body's openings, requires immediate attention. Abdominal pain, especially when it is associated with nausea, may indicate a wide range of problems from appendicitis to pelvic inflammatory disease and requires the diagnostic expertise of a physician. A stiff neck when accompanied by a fever may suggest meningitis and justifies immediate medical intervention. Injuries, many first aid emergencies, and severe disabling symptoms require prompt medical care.

There is debate as to when medical care is needed in the case of fever. An elevated temperature may be a sign that the body's immune system is responding to an infection and working to destroy *pathogens* or disease-producing organisms. On the other hand, if left untreated for an extended time, a fever may cause harm to sensitive tissues in the body, such as connective tissue found in joints and tissues in the valves of the heart.

The normal body temperature of 98.6° F was studied at the University of Maryland.[4] Findings involving 700 temperature readings of 148 adults over a 3-day period suggests that the normal body temperature is 98.9° F. The study attributed the difference to less accurate techniques when the earlier standard of 98.6° F was established. Body temperature varies with exercise, rest, climate, and gender. Fever means a reading over 99° F. It is not usually necessary for an adult to seek medical care for a fever. Home treatment in the form of aspirin, acetaminophen, and sponge baths usually lowers fever. You should consult your physician if fever remains above 102° F despite your actions or, in the case of a low-grade fever (99° to 100° F), if there is no improvement in 72 hours. You should consult a physician if fever lasts more than 5 days, regardless of improvement. Symptoms such as sore throat, ear pain, diarrhea, urinary problems, and skin rash may be the cause of the fever and should be treated as such. Fever in young children should be discussed with a physician.

Entering a Hospital

A hospital is driven by the goal of saving lives. It may range in size and service from a small unit that provides general care and low-risk treatments to large, specialized centers offering dramatic and experimental therapies. You may be limited in your choice of a hospital by factors beyond your control, including insurance coverage, your physician's hospital affiliation, and type of care available.

Before entering a hospital, you should be aware of possible dangers. Well-known hospital hazards are unnecessary operations, unexpected drug reactions, harmful or even fatal blunders, and hospital-borne infections. Boston University researchers reported on a 5-month study of an unnamed teaching hospital in which 290 (36%) of 815 patients became ill and 15 died as a result of complications and mishaps. This was significantly worse than a similar study 20 years earlier when 20% suffered some ill effect as a result of an adverse reaction to a drug, test, or treatment.[5]

The greatest risk that the hospital presents is infection. "Some 40 million Americans enter hospitals every year, and about 2 million of them get infections that sometimes are fatal. The Centers for Disease Control estimates that 80,000 to 100,000 patients die each year as a direct or indirect result of hospital-incurred infection. At least a third of these infections are preventable."[6]

What can lay people do to ensure proper and safe care while in the hospital? The following guidelines should be considered:

▶ If you have a choice of hospitals, inquire about their accreditation status. Hospitals are subject to inspection to make sure they are in compliance with federal standards. Policies implemented in 1989 require the release of information on request to state health departments regarding a hospital's mortality rate, its accreditation status, and its major deficiencies.[7]

▶ Before checking into a hospital, you need to decide on your accomodations. Do you want to pay extra for a single room? Do you want a non-smoker for a roommate? Do you need a special diet? Do you need a place to store refrigerated medicine? If someone will be staying with you, will they need a cot? You should try to avoid going in on a weekend when few procedures are done. When you get to your room, you should speak up immediately if it's unacceptable.

▶ You need to be familiar with your rights as a patient. Hospitals should provide an information booklet that includes a Patients' Bill of Rights. The booklet will inform you that you have the right to considerate and respectful care; information about tests, drugs, and procedures; dignity; courtesy; respect; and the opportunity to make decisions, including when to leave the hospital.

Hospitals should provide you with a Patient's Bill of Rights.

▶ You should make informed decisions. Before authorizing any procedure, patients must be informed about their medical condition, treatment options, expected risks, prognosis of the condition, and the name of the person in charge of treatment. This is called **informed consent.** The only times hospitals are not required to obtain informed consent are cases involving life-threatening emergencies, unconscious patients when no relatives are present, and/or compliance with the law or a court order such as examination of sexually transmitted diseases. If you are asked to sign a consent form, you should read it first. If you want more information, you should ask before signing. If you are skeptical, you have the right to postpone the procedure and discuss it with your doctor.

▶ Authorization of a medical procedure may be given nonverbally, such as an appearance at a doctor's office for treatment, cooperation during the administration of tests, or failure to object when consent can be easily refused. This is called **implied consent.**

▶ You need to weigh the risks of drug therapy, x-ray examinations, and laboratory tests with their expected benefits. When tests or treatments are ordered, you should ask about their purpose, possible risks, and possible actions if a test finds something wrong. For example, the injection or ingestion of x-ray dyes makes body structures more visible and greatly facilitates a physician's ability to make a correct diagnosis. However, dyes can cause an allergic reaction that ranges from a skin rash to circulatory collapse and death. Finally, you should inquire about prescribed drugs. Studies suggest that almost one patient in five will suffer an adverse drug reaction.[8] You should avoid taking drugs, including pain and sleeping medication, unless you feel confident of their benefits and are aware of their hazards.

▶ You need to know who is in charge of your care and record the office number and when you can expect a visit. If your doctor is transferring your care to someone else, you need to know who it is. If your doctor is not available and you do not know what is happening, you can ask for the nurse in charge of your case.

▶ You should stay active within the limits of your medical problem. Many body functions begin to suffer from just a few days' inactivity. Moving about, walking, bending, and contracting muscles help clear body fluids, reduce the risk of infections (especially in the lungs), and help to cope with the stress of hospital procedures that add to the depression and malaise of hospitalization.

▶ You should be alert. Throughout your stay, you can keep asking questions until you know all you need to know. According to some experts, "the biggest improvement in health care in the last 15 years has not been technological advances. It's been patients asking questions. The more questions, the fewer mistakes, and the more power patients have in the doctor-patient relationship."[5]

Selecting a Health-Care Professional

Choosing a physician for your general health care is an important and necessary duty. Only physicians are discussed here, but this information applies to the selection of all health-care practitioners. You must select one who will listen carefully to your problems and diagnose them accurately. At the same time, you need a physician who can move you through the modern medical maze of technology (see Table 13-2).

For most people, good health care means having a **primary-care physician,** a professional who assists you as you assume responsibility for your overall health and directs you when specialized care is necessary. Your primary-care physician should be familiar with your complete medical history, as well as your home, work, and other environments. You are better understood in periods of sickness when

TABLE 13-2 Health-Care Specialists

Name of Specialist	Field of Specialty
Medical Specialists	
Allergist	Allergic conditions
Anesthesiologist	Administration of anesthesia (for example, during surgery)
Cardiologist	Coronary artery disease, heart disease
Dermatologist	Skin conditions
Endocrinologist	Diseases of the endocrine system
Epidemiologist	Cause and source of disease outbreaks
Family practice physician	General care physician
Gastroenterologist	Stomach, intestines, digestive system
Geriatrician	Diseases and conditions of the aged
Gynecologist	Female reproductive system
Hematologist	Study of blood
Immunologist	Diseases of the immune system
Internist	Treatment of diseases in adults
Neonatologist	Newborns
Nephrologist	Kidney disease
Neurologist	Nervous system
Neurosurgeon	Surgery of the brain and nervous system
Obstetrician	Pregnancy, labor, childbirth
Oncologist	Cancer, tumors
Ophthalmologist	Eyes
Orthopedist	Skeletal system
Otolaryngologist	Head, neck, ears, nose, throat
Otologist	Ears
Pathologist	Study of tissues and the essential nature of disease
Pediatrician	Childhood diseases and conditions
Plastic surgeon	Use of material to rebuild tissues
Primary-care physician	General health and medical care
Proctologist	Disorders of the rectum and anus
Psychiatrist	Mental illnesses
Radiologist	Use of x-rays
Rheumatologist	Diseases of connective tissues, joints, muscles, tendons
Rhinologist	Nose
Surgeon	Surgery
Urologist	Urinary tract of males and females and reproductive organs of males
Dental Specialists	
Dentist	General care of teeth and oral cavity
Endodontist	Diseases of tooth below the gum line (root canal therapy)
Orthodontist	Teeth alignment, malocclusion
Pedodontist	Dental care of children
Periodontist	Diseases of supporting structures
Prosthodontist	Construction of artificial appliances for the mouth

Continued.

your physician also sees you during periods of wellness.

For adults, primary-care physicians are usually *family practitioners*, once called "general practitioners," and *internists*, specialists in internal medicine. *Pediatricians* often serve as primary-care physicians for children. *Obstetricians* and *gynecologists*, who specialize in pregnancy, childbirth, and diseases of the female reproductive system, often serve as primary-care physicians to female patients. In

TABLE 13-2 Health-Care Specialists—cont'd

Name of Specialist	Field of Specialty
Other Specialists	
Chiropractor	Manipulation and adjustment of body structures
Dietician (registered)	Nutrition counseling
Naturopathic physician	Lifestyle and dietary therapies in the prevention and treatment of diseases
Nurse practitioner	Registered nurses trained in some states to serve as primary-care providers
Nurse (registered)	Board-certified nurse with training from an accredited nursing school
Occupational therapist	Physically and emotionally handicapped persons with vocational or recreational activities
Optometrist	Visual defects
Osteopath	Medical and surgical methods of diagnosis and therapy with an emphasis on body mechanics and manipulation methods
Pharmacist	Safe and efficacious distribution and use of medications, related substances, and appliances
Physical therapist	Rehabilition for those with temporary or permanent physical handicaps or other ailments
Podiatrist	Feet
Psychologist	Human behavior

some places, general surgeons may offer primary care in addition to the surgery they perform. Some *osteopathic* physicians also practice family medicine. A doctor of osteopathy (DO) emphasizes manipulation of the body to treat symptoms.

If you want a female physician, you will have a better chance to find one in the near future. In 1986, 13% of doctors were women. However, the numbers are growing. One third of medical students are now women.[9]

There are several sources of information for obtaining the names of physicians in your area:

▶ Local and state medical societies can identify doctors by specialty and tell you a doctor's basic credentials. You should check on the doctor's hospital affiliation and make sure the hospital is accredited. Another sign of standing is the type of societies in which the doctor has membership. The qualifications of a surgeon, for example, are enhanced by a fellowship in the American College of Surgeons (abbreviated as FACS after the surgeon's name). An internist fellowship in the American College of Physicians is abbreviated FACP. Membership in academies indicates a physician's special interest.

▶ All physicians board certified in the United States are listed in the American Medical Directory published by the American Medical Association and available in larger libraries.

▶ The American Board of Medical Specialists (ABMS) publishes the Compendium of Certified Medical Specialties, which lists physicians by name, specialty, and location.

▶ Pharmacists can be asked to recommend names.

▶ Hospitals can give you names of staff physicians who also practice in the community.

▶ Local medical schools can identify faculty members who also practice privately.

▶ Many colleges and universities have health centers that keep a list of physicians for student referral.

▶ Friends may have recommendations, but you should allow for the possibility that your opinion of the doctor may be different.

Once you have identified a leading candidate, you can make an appointment. You need to check with the office staff about office hours, availability of emergency care at night or weekends, backup doctors, procedures when you call for advice, hospital affiliation, and payment and insurance procedures. You should schedule your first visit while in good health. Once you have seen your doctor, reflect on the following: Did the doctor seem to be listening to you? Were your questions answered? Was a medical history taken? Were you informed of possible side effects of drugs or tests? Was respect shown for your need of privacy? Was the doctor open to the suggestion of a second opinion?

Patient-physician communication. Most doctors are not disinterested in you, but they are busy—so busy that many patients complain that their doctor cannot or will not listen to them. This is a problem because according to the American Society of Internal Medicine, 70% of correct diagnoses depend on what you tell your doctor. In a study of 74 visits to seven doctors, researchers found that only 16 patients were allowed to explain the problem fully. In 70% of the visits, doctors interrupted their patients before they completed their first statement. Usually the interruption occurred within 18 seconds. It was not surprising that an American Medical Association survey on public attitudes toward physicians indicated 37% of those surveyed did not believe doctors take a genuine interest in their patients. Only 45% believed doctors usually explain things well to their patients.[11] Fortunately, medical schools are beginning to emphasize communication skills. More physicians seem to realize that good medicine means establishing good rapport with patients. Patients can do much to facilitate the development of a physician-patient partnership. Understanding the meaning of commonly used medical words, abbreviations, suffixes, and prefixes can enhance this communication (Table 13-3). The following are some tips to ensure good communication:

▶ When you see your physician about a problem, you should state the most important problem first. Doctors tend to believe that the first thing a patient says is most important.

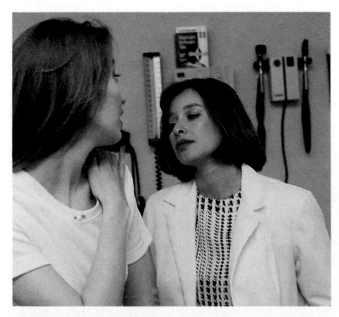

A correct diagnosis mostly depends on what the patient tells the doctor.

▶ You should be specific. If you have a headache, where does it hurt? How long does it last? How often does it occur?

▶ You should know your family history. Because many illnesses run in families, you may be at higher risk for certain diseases. Before your first visit, you should contact your parents and close relatives to learn of their health problems, especially heart disease, cancer, stroke, arthritis, diabetes, alcoholism, and tuberculosis.

▶ You need to list medications and treatments you are receiving, including over-the-counter drugs. You will also need to identify any allergies and drug reactions.

▶ You should ask questions. You can bring a written list of questions but try to make them brief and specific. You should ask about anything that is unclear and repeat the answers in your own words.

▶ Before leaving the doctor's office, you need to make certain you know the diagnosis or how to follow the recommended treatment. If drugs are prescribed, you should inquire about the possible **contraindications** (reason for not using a drug), side effects, and the possible substitution of generics.

Second opinions. Conditions involving elective surgery, chronic pain, and recurring illnesses often benefit from a second opinion. In many situations, a second opinion is appropriate and peace of mind is a sufficient reason for seeking it. A recent editorial in the *Harvard Medical School Health Letter* provides some helpful advice to the question, "When is a second opinion needed?" "As a general rule, patients should seek a second opinion whenever they are uncomfortable with the explanations offered by a physician, are not happy with the progress of recovery, question the proposed course of action, or simply feel the need for verification."[12] In some cases, such as elective surgery, your health insurer may require a second or third opinion before authorizing payment for certain treatments. (See Figure 13-4 for advice on getting a second opinion.)

If you decide to ask for a second opinion, common courtesy dictates that you discuss it with your physician. Your physician may suggest bringing in a consultant who will assess your situation and discuss it with you and your physician. You can also ask your physician for the name of someone to see separately.

A physician may feel that a second opinion is a waste of time or money. Regardless, your wish for more information should be respected. Reputable physicians do not feel threatened by another opin-

TABLE 13-3 Communicating with Health-Care Professionals

Term	Meaning
Here are some words, abbreviations, suffixes, and prefixes that are often used in health and medical care.	
a (prefix)	Without
Aberration	Different from normal action
Acute	A condition that occurs suddenly
Adult	Developed fully
Affinity	Attraction
Algia (suffix)	Pain in
Arrest	Stopping, restraining
Asymptomatic	Without symptoms
Bowel	Intestine
BP	Blood pressure
Cardiac (cardio)	Relating to the heart
CAT	Computerized assisted x-ray
CCU	Coronary care unit
Chronic	A condition that occurs for a long time
Coma	Complete loss of consciousness
Congenital	Existing at or before birth
Contraindication	A reason for not prescribing a drug, procedure, or treatment
Coronary	Relating to the heart
Degenerative	Deterioration of a part of the body
Diagnosis	Determination of a disease
Dilation	Stretching, increase in size
Distention	Widening or enlargement
DO	Doctor of osteopathy
Dose	Amount of medication to be given at one time
Dysfunction	Impairment of function
Edema	Swelling from accumulation of fluid
EEG	Electroencephalogram
EKG, ECG	Electrocardiogram
Embolus	Blood clot floating free in the bloodstream
Endemic	Disease prevalent in a particular area
ER	Emergency room
Etiology	Reference to the cause of a disease
Extra (prefix)	Outside of
Gastr (prefix)	Stomach
GP	General practitioner
Hem (prefix)	Blood
Hemorrhage	Bleeding
Hyper (prefix)	Excessive
Hypo (prefix)	Insufficient
Indication	Condition that leads to a prescribed drug, procedure, or treatment
ICU	Intensive care unit
Innate	Hereditary, congenital
Innocuous	Harmless
Insidious	Refers to a disease that does not show early symptoms of its advent
Ism (suffix)	Condition, theory, method
Itis (suffix)	Inflammation
IV	Intravenous (within a vein)
Jaundiced	Yellow
Malady	Illness

Continued.

TABLE 13-3 Communicating with Health-Care Professionals—cont'd

Term	Meaning
Malaise	Uneasiness
MD	Medical doctor
MI	Myocardial infarction
MRI	Magnetic resonance imaging
Myo (prefix)	Muscle
Opothy (suffix)	Cause unknown
Pernicious	Severe, fatal
Primary	Principal, most important
Prognosis	Medical outlook of a disease
Pulmo (prefix)	Lung
Renal	Kidney
Sign	Something tangible that can be observed
Stenosis	Constricted, decreasing in size
Symptom	Intangible evidence of a disease
Symptomatic	Relating to symptoms
Syndrome	Set of symptoms that occur together for unknown causes
Systemic	Affecting all systems of the body
Thrombus	Solid blood clot
TIA	Transient ischemic attack
TPR	Temperature, pulse, respiration
Trauma	Injury from external force
Tumor	Growth

Figure 13-4 How to Get A Second Opinion

If you are considering elective surgery and want a second opinion, the following are sources for referral:

▶ Ask your primary-care physician for the names of two or three experts in the field.
▶ Call a medical center or hospital and ask to talk to the chief of surgery for a surgical opinion or to the chief of medicine for a nonsurgical question.
▶ Call the county medical society.
▶ Call the Second Surgical Opinion Hotline (800-638-6833) for medical organizations, which provides referrals on surgical questions.
▶ Call Health Benefits Research Corporation, which offers a Second Opinion Hotline (800-522-0036, 800-631-1220 in New York) and referral service. Consultation with a board-certified specialist is available for a fee.

ion; to the contrary, they may welcome another perspective on a difficult case. If your physician expresses displeasure for or resists your wish to have a second opinion, you may want to consider looking for another doctor.

Assessing Your Health

Many tests, procedures, gadgets, and machines assess various aspects of health and wellness. They range from the hands-on physical examination to the use of sophisticated diagnostic tests. There is some debate, however, as to when and how often they are to be administered and how effective they are.

The Physical Examination

Until recently the annual physical examination was viewed as a normal and necessary part of health care. Now, considerable debate exists among medical experts as to who needs a physical examination, how often it is needed, and what it should include.

A controversial report[13] concluded that many of

the routine procedures doctors use in a physical examination on healthy adults are virtually useless. The report asserted that much of the touching, probing, thumping, and listening serves little purpose except to reassure patients.

Although many physicians are reluctant to eliminate the annual physical, the emphasis today is in the use of **selective health examinations,** that is, the practice of using specific tests for specific problems. The assumption is that tests are more useful if they are matched to specific complaints.

Criticisms of the comprehensive annual physical examination for a healthy adult are not meant to undermine the doctor-patient relationship. They simply cast doubt about the efficacy of the physical examination. However, this does not nullify the value of regular visits to the doctor. To the contrary, seeing a physician for a limited examination at regular intervals can be good preventive medicine.

How Often Is a Physical Examination Needed?

Healthy adults between the ages of 20 and 60 years should get a complete physical every 5 years.[14] Yearly physicals are advisable for children under 6 and adults over 60 years of age, even if they do not have symptoms.[15] No group suggests a complete annual physical examination for adults in good health.[16]

Regardless of age, individuals with a family history of heart disease, strokes, high blood pressure, cancer, and diabetes can benefit by periodic checkups, even if they are in good health. The same is true for individuals whose health habits or occupation put them at higher than normal risk for chronic diseases and disabling conditions. Even in these cases, good judgment and discretion should rule the choice of tests to be included in the physical examination.

Components of a Physical Examination

The three basic tools for completing a physical examination are medical history, hands-on examination, and diagnostic/laboratory tests.

A *medical history* is probably the most important part of the physical examination, especially during the first visit with your physician. It includes a history of habits, lifestyle, family history, and symptoms. Many physicians use *health-risk appraisals,* detailed questionnaires that provide information about health habits.

This is one area of the physical examination for which a patient can prepare. By following the guidelines for communicating with your physician presented earlier in this chapter, you can help their physician obtain an accurate health profile. This is important because a diagnosis can be made 80% to 90% of the time with only a thorough history and hands-on examination.[17]

The *hands-on examination* is the second part of the physical examination. It consists of an examination by touching, looking, and listening.

Physicians can feel or palpate for enlarged glands, growths, and tumors with procedures such as the breast examination, pelvic examination, rectal examination, and hernia examination. Thumping the back and chest lets the physician know whether any fluid has built up in or around the lungs. Tapping a knee for reflexes may reveal nervous system damage. A stethoscope is the physician's basic listening device and is used to listen to the heart, lungs, abdomen, and glands located near the surface of the skin. Possible problems that can be detected with the stethoscope range from a heart murmur to such conditions as poor circulation, lung infection, intestinal blockage, and an overactive thyroid gland.

Physicians have access to a number of instruments to visually inspect for problems. An *ophthalmoscope* is used to view the brain by looking into the eye. The first sign of some brain diseases is an unhealthy looking optic nerve. Leakage in the blood vessels of the eye may be a sign of diabetes or hypertension. An *otoscope* is used to inspect the ear, particularly the tympanic membrane. The *proctoscope* and *sigmoidoscope* are used to examine the rectum and colon. The *laryngoscope* and *bronchoscope* provide a look at the larynx and bronchial tubes.

The last part of the physical examination includes **diagnostic laboratory tests,** which may vary from a simple urinalysis to invasive dye tests. The effectiveness of these tests receives mixed reviews. Tests conducted for specific symptoms may be invaluable in pinpointing disabling conditions. They may be just as valuable for what they do not reveal as they are for what they do reveal. This can be reassuring to the patient and physician.

On the negative side, many physicians rely too heavily on laboratory tests. Patients often demand or acquiesce to more tests than necessary, sometimes more than is good for them. In one report,[17] a suggested 25% of all medical tests contribute little to health. For example, when researchers at the University of California, San Francisco, studied 2000 patients hospitalized for surgery, they found that 60% of the blood tests routinely ordered were unnecessary. Only 1 in about 450 revealed abnormalities, and they were ignored because they were either not noticed or dismissed as not significant. The researchers concluded that if a thorough history turns up no hint of a medical problem, routine testing is a waste.

Thus when you go for a physical examination,

you can help determine which tests you are willing to be subjected to by asking the right questions:

▶ What do you expect to find? You should start by asking why you need the test. How will it help facilitate a diagnosis? You need to ask about alternatives and the disadvantage of waiting and not testing. Sometimes the best test is the test of time. Agreeing to a test because it is routine procedure is not a satisfactory explanation.

▶ What risks are associated with the test? No test is risk free; therefore you should compare potential benefits and risks.

One problem with tests is that they are not 100% accurate. For example, the accuracy of such common tests as community screening for cholesterol levels has been the subject of considerable debate.[18] An inaccurate result can lead to a wrong diagnosis. A *false positive* may occur in which a test incorrectly reveals an abnormality and consequently provokes needless anxiety. Some people begin feeling and even acting sick. Conversely, normal results do not necessarily indicate good health. *False negatives* may occur in which test results indicate normality even though a person is sick. These results may lead to a false sense of health and may delay much needed treatment at critical stages of a disease.

Statistically, test results are accurate for about 95% of the population. Thus 5% of patients can be expected to have a false positive or false negative on any laboratory test. Other factors that may cause test errors include certain medications, exercise, stress, eating, time of day, and mistakes in handling or processing specimens.

Another problem with tests is that they may be associated with physical risks. Some of the more common risks are infection, bleeding, damage to vital structures, and reactions to anesthetics, drugs, and dye-contrast materials. A California study[17] of 303 patients found that as many as 14% who had invasive diagnostic procedures develop one or more complications.

▶ What are the options after the test? If a test is positive, then what? If none of the options is plausible to you, why have the test administered? If it is impossible to treat a disease that a test reveals, the test is not justified. The diagnosis of treatable diseases, on the other hand, usually justifies the test.

▶ Asking your physician about the value of a test need not be perceived as a confrontation. Instead, it should be viewed as time for questions and answers. If approached with sincerity and courtesy, discussions about the physical examination in general and laboratory tests in par-

ticular can serve as a basis for forming an active partnership with your physician in making decisions about your health care.

Common Diagnostic Laboratory Tests

Americans are having more diagnostic tests performed (Figure 13-5). Home medical tests are available in most pharmacies and allow you to monitor a growing list of medical conditions (Table 13-4). The tests should not be viewed as a substitute for your doctor. The accuracy rates and reliability of over-the-counter medical kits vary considerably, and their instructions do not always explain how to interpret the results. Test procedures are also subject to human error, but they provide a useful way to get involved in your own health care.

Regardless of the number and types of self-care medical kits you may want to use, some other inexpensive items should be included in your medicine cabinet (Figure 13-6). These items should help you cope with most common minor aches and pains.

Depending on your health status, gender, age, symptoms, and risk for a disease, some of the more common tests listed may be recommended when you go to your physician for a checkup.

Multiple blood screening tests check for high blood sugar, which indicates diabetes; blood urea nitrogen, an indicator of kidney function; calcium, for signs of an overactive parathyroid gland; and blood count, a screen for anemia.

Blood cholesterol screening is recommended for

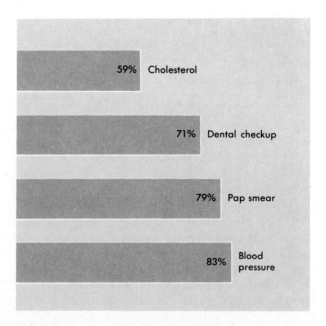

FIGURE 13-5 Percentage of adults having four common diagnostic tests.

TABLE 13-4 Self-Care Home Medical Test Kits*

Name of Test	Purpose
Lead test kit	To detect the presence of lead in dishes and cookware
Blood pressure monitor	To assess blood pressure
Peak flow meters	To measure how forcefully a person can exhale; useful as a warning for an impending asthmatic attack
Urinary tract infection kit	To detect nitrites and white blood cells in the urine, both of which indicate an infection, useful for people with recurrent urinary tract infection
Pregnancy test kit	To detect the level of HCG (human chorionic gonadotropin) hormone, which indicates pregnancy, in the first urine of the morning
Blood glucose monitor	To measure blood glucose; useful for diabetics
Thermometer	To measure body temperature; available in many forms
Sulfite test	To indicate the presence and quantity of sulfites in food and wine; useful for preventing headaches, allergies, nausea, and asthma attacks in sulfite-sensitive people
Ovulation predictor	To look for the luteinizing hormone that increases dramatically in a woman's urine just before ovulation
Fecal occult blood test	To screen stools for hidden blood that can indicate colorectal cancer
Mail-away home pollutant test kits	To measure radon in the house and to identify pollutants in tap water—lead, radon, minerals, bacteria, and pesticides; results usually have to be sent to laboratories

*Most of the medical kits are available without prescriptions in pharmacies.

everyone over 20 years of age. According to the National Heart, Lung, and Blood Institute, 25% of the population have cholesterol levels in the high range (240 mg/dl or above). If cholesterol is high, retesting is recommended. If it is still high, it is important to check *high-density lipoproteins* (HDLs), *low-density lipoproteins* (LDLs), and triglyceride levels. (See Chapter 2 for a more thorough discussion of cholesterol.)

Hemoccult tests are used to detect hidden blood in the bowel movement. If the test is positive, it may indicate signs of an early cancer of the colon. Individuals over 50 years of age should either test themselves (home screening kits are available in most pharmacies) or have their stools tested for blood every year.[19]

Pulse rate may be an indicator of a health problem. The normal resting heart rate is between 60 and 80 beats a minute. Resting heart rates above 80 per minute put a person in a higher risk category for heart attacks and sudden death.[19] The high heart rate does not increase the risk but is an indicator of basic problems such as cigarette smoking, too much caffeine, stress, anxiety, hyperthyroidism, and most commonly, a poor level of physical fitness.

Slow heart rates are normally found in physically fit individuals; in these cases, it is a sign of good health. Very slow rates below 50 per minute can occur in people who are not fit and who have a possible heart problem. These individuals should seek medical advice.

Blood pressure measurements should be monitored regularly, especially for individuals who have had a previously high reading or a family history of hypertension (high blood pressure). Inexpensive, accurate home blood pressure kits can be purchased at most drug stores. Because all kits are not equally reliable, you should ask your pharmacist for a recommendation. Individuals who have measurements higher than 140 over 90 mm Hg or lower than 100 over 60 mm Hg should keep a record of their blood pressure and present it to their physician during periodic checkups.

Mammography, an x-ray examination of the breast, detects early signs of breast cancer. The American Cancer Society advises women to get their first mammogram between ages 35 and 39, every 1 to 2 years between 40 and 49, and annually after age 50. High-risk women may be advised to have mammograms more often and at an earlier age.[14]

Pelvic examination and *pap smear* detect abnormalities of the ovaries, uterus, and cervix. The American Cancer Society recommends an annual Pap test starting at age 18 or when sexual activity begins, whichever comes first. Pap smears should not be done during the menstrual period. The test is more accurate during the first half of the cycle if oral contraceptives are taken. Midcycle is preferred in most other menstruating women. Regardless of when the test is done, the technician reading the smear must know whether you are taking oral contraceptives or estrogen replacement therapy and when the last menstrual period began. Only with this information can the smear be accurately interpreted.[20]

A complete *eye examination* includes a test for visual acuity; *tonometry*, a painless test for glaucoma; and cataract check. The American Academy of Ophthalmology recommends a complete eye examination from puberty to age 40 only if eye discomfort or vision problems occur. After age 40 a glaucoma test and cataract (a clouding over the lens) check should be done every 2 to 3 years.

Electrocardiograms (ECGs) are used to detect irregularities of the heart. Although there is some debate about its use as a routine screening procedure for *asymptomatic* (without symptoms) low-risk individuals, an ECG reading by age 35 provides a point for subsequent comparisons. Chest pain, hyperten-sion, and symptoms of cardiovascular disease justify earlier ECGs. *Stress tests* use ECG to assess how the heart functions under the stress of exercise and are routine when symptoms are present.

Chest x-ray examinations are valuable diagnostic tools for people with chest symptoms, respiratory diseases, and heart problems. For people without symptoms, their routine use is questionable. Several groups of experts, including those associated with the Food and Drug Administration, recommend discontinuation of chest x-ray examinations in most cases. However, if you go to a hospital or often your doctor's office, you can anticipate a chest x-ray study more out of the need to comply with business policy than for diagnostic potential. You will want to avoid a chest x-ray test if you may be pregnant.

Prostate cancer tests detect prostate cancer, the most common cancer among men. Men 40 years of age and older should have an annual digital rectal examination. Combined with a blood test that looks for prostate specific antigens (PSA), the digital examination significantly improves the chances of detecting early signs of cancer.

HIV test is recommended for people who think they may have been infected with the AIDS virus. This includes people who have had unprotected sex or a blood transfusion, have used IV drugs, or have participated in high-risk behaviors. After the blood test, these people should avoid high-risk behavior for 6 months to a year and then retest.

Immunizations for Adults

Many people believe that **immunizations** (administration of a preparation or vaccine, usually in the form of injections, for providing immunity or preventing a disease) are only for children. Consequently, many thousands of adults die every year of diseases they would not have acquired if they had received standard vaccines. For example, 91% of tetanus cases and 87% of hepatitis B cases in the United States affect adults over the age of 20 years.[21,22] Half the rubella cases are among adults. Although deaths from measles, rubella, mumps, tetanus, and diphtheria have been reduced to about 12 a year, most of these are among older people—a complete reversal of 30 years ago. In addition, 40,000 people die a year from pneumococcal infections; influenza viruses kill 20,000 more. Of the 300,000 people who contract hepatitis B, 10,000 are admitted to a hospital, and about 5000 die.

Adult immunization is recommended to prevent or ameliorate influenza, pneumonia, hepatitis B, measles, rubella (German measles), tetanus, and diphtheria. Table 13-5 provides immunization information for each of these diseases.

Figure 13-6 Essentials for Your Medicine Cabinet

With the exception of personal items and prescription medicines, what should you keep in your medicine chest? The following are the essentials according to experts:

1. *Thermometer* to assess body temperature (oral, rectal, and tympanic ear) and electronic models available)
2. *Ipecac* to induce vomiting
3. *Acetaminophen* to reduce fever and pain (In liquid form for children; not given to children under 15 years because of its link to Reye's syndrome)
4. An *antiseptic* such as hydrogen peroxide for cleaning open wounds
5. *Gauze and tape* to treat minor wounds
6. An *ice bag* to reduce swelling
7. *Ace bandage* to wrap pulled muscles or twisted ankles or to bind a splint
8. *Benadryl* or a similar antihistamine to reduce allergic reactions
9. An *antibiotic ointment* or *cream* to prevent infections from cuts
10. *Pepto-bismol* or another antidiarrheal medication

TABLE 13-5 Immunization Schedule for Adults

Immunization	Who	Shots	Precautions	Side effects
Tetanus and diphtheria	All adults	Three in initial series, boosters every 10 years	Pregnancy, previous reactions	Reddening of the skin, joint pain
Measles	All adults	One, no boosters	Pregnancy, allergy to eggs, reactions to antibiotics	Occasional fever and mild rashes
Rubella (German measles)	All adults, especially women of childbearing age	One, no boosters	Same as for measles, women should avoid conception within 3 months of vaccination	Joint pain
Mumps	All adults, especially males	One, no boosters	Same as for rubella	Allergic reactions and swelling of the salivary glands
Pneumonia and flu	All adults over 65 and chronically ill adults	One for pneumonia with revaccination every 6 years for some people, flu shots yearly	Pregnancy	Mild pain or redness
Hepatitis B	Adults at risk because of job, travel, or exposure to infected people	Three, no boosters	None	Some soreness

Paying for Health Care

The cost of health care in the United States is expensive and is escalating (Figure 13-7). In 1990, the annual cost of medical care plans to employers and/or employees averaged $3161, a 21.6% increase over the 1989 cost of $2600 and 46.3% higher than the $2160 average in 1983.[23]

A large majority of Americans cannot afford the cost of medicines, physicians' fees, or hospitalization without some form of health insurance. **Health insurance** is a contract between an insurance company and an individual or group for the payment of medical care costs. After the individual or group pays a premium to an insurance company, the insurance company pays for part or all of the medical costs depending on the type of insurance and benefits provided. The type of insurance policy purchased greatly influences where you go for health care, who provides the health care, and what medical procedures can be performed. The three basic health insurance plans include a private, fee-for-service plan; a prepaid group plan; and a government-financed public plan.

Private, Fee-For-Service Insurance Plan

Until recently, private, fee-for-service insurance was the principal form of health insurance coverage. In this plan an individual pays a monthly premium, usually through an employer, which ensures health care on a fee-for-service basis. On incurring medical costs, the patient files a claim to have a portion of these costs paid by the insurance company. There is usually a *deductible*, an amount paid by the patient before being eligible for benefits from the insurance company. For example, if your expenses are $1000, you may have to pay $200 before the insurance company will pay the other $800. Usually, the lower the deductible, the higher the premiums will be.

Typically, there are *fixed indemnity benefits*, specified amounts that are paid for particular procedures. If your policy pays $500 for a tonsilectomy and the actual cost was $1000, you owe the health-care provider $500. There are often *exclusions*, certain services that are not covered by the policy. Common examples include elective surgery, dental care, vision care, and coverage for preexisting illnesses and injuries. Some insurance plans provide options for adding dental and vision care. Other common options include *life insurance*, which pays a death benefit, and *disability insurance*, which pays for income lost because of the inability to work due to an illness or injury. The more options added to the insurance plan, the more expensive the insurance will be.

One strategy insurance companies are using to lower insurance premiums and out-of-pocket costs to the consumer is the formation of *preferred providers organization* (PPO). A PPO is a group of private practitioners who sell their services at reduced rates to insurance companies. When a patient chooses a provider that is in that company's PPO, the insurance company pays a higher percentage of the fee. When a non-PPO provider is used, a much lower portion of the fee is paid.

A major advantage of a fee-for-service plan is that the patient has options in selecting health-care providers. Several disadvantages are that patients may not routinely receive comprehensive, preventive health care; health-care costs to the patient may be high if unexpected illnesses or injuries occur; and it may place heavy demands on time in keeping track of medical records, invoices, and insurance reimbursement forms.

Prepaid Group Insurance

In prepaid group insurance, health care is provided by a group of physicians organized into a **health maintenance organization (HMO).** HMOs are health-care plans that provide a full range of medical services for a prepaid amount of money. For a fixed monthly fee, usually paid through payroll deductions by an employer, and often a small deductible, enrollees receive care from physicians, specialists, allied health professionals, and educators who are hired or contractually retained by the HMO.

There are about 550 HMOs.[24] Some have been formed by hospitals, some by physician groups, and some by entrepreneurs. All offer medical services for a fixed monthly premium, but the depth of health care varies. These services may range from the restrictive arrangements of traditional prepaid group plans to a loose confederation of doctors whose practices are similar to fee-for-service medicine.

HMOs provide an advantage in that they provide comprehensive care including preventive care at a lower cost than private insurance over a long period of coverage. One drawback is that patients are limited in their choice of providers to those who belong to an HMO.

Government Insurance

In a government insurance plan the government at the federal, state, or local level pays for the health-care costs of elgible participants. Two prominent examples of this plan are Medicare and Medicaid. Medicare is financed by social security taxes and is

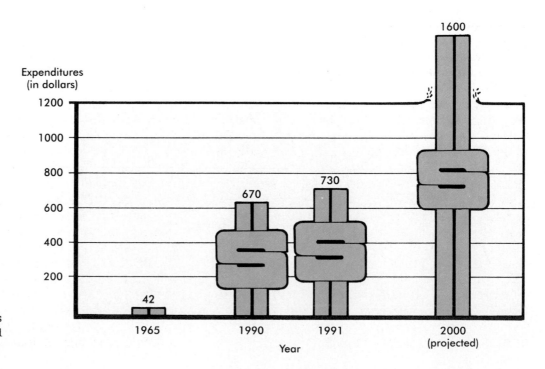

FIGURE 13-7 National health care expenditures for 1965, 1990, and 1991 and projection for 2000.

designed to provide health care for individuals 65 years of age and older, the blind, the severely disabled, and those requiring certain treatments such as kidney dialysis. Medicaid is subsidized by federal and state taxes. It provides limited health care, generally for individuals who are elgible for benefits and assistance from two programs: Aid to Families with Dependent Children and Supplementary Security Income.

Summary

▶ Health information that can be trusted is based on scientifically controlled studies that yield consistent results over time.

▶ Signs and symptoms that warrant immediate medical attention are signs of internal bleeding, abdominal pain associated with nausea, a stiff neck accompanied by fever, and serious first aid emergencies and injuries.

▶ People can help to ensure proper and safe care while in a hospital by checking on the hospital's accreditation status, deciding on accomodations before admission, knowing their rights as a patient, discussing treatments and procedures with their physician, asking questions, and staying active.

▶ Good health care means establishing a doctor-patient relationship while in good health.

▶ When telling a physician about a problem, you can enhance good communication by presenting the most important problem first, being as specific as possible, being familiar with your family medical history, knowing the names of medicines you are taking, and asking questions.

▶ The three major components of a physical examination are medical history, hands-on examination, and diagnostic laboratory tests.

▶ The seven diseases for which adults need to maintain immunization are influenza, pneumonia, hepatitis B, measles, rubella, tetanus, and diphtheria.

▶ The three basic options for paying for health care include private, fee-for-service insurance; prepaid group insurance; and government insurance.

Action Plan for Personal Wellness

Use the information presented in this chapter to answer the following questions and to formulate an action plan to enhance your personal wellness.

1 Based on the information presented in this chapter, along with what I know about my family's health history, the health issues and problems that I need to be concerned about are:_____

_____

_____

2 Of the health care issues listed in number 1, the one I most need to act on is:_____

_____

_____

3 The possible actions that I can take to improve my ability to understand health information and to make better use of the health care market are (be specific):_____

_____

_____

4 Of the actions listed in number 3, the one that I most need to include in an action plan is:_____

_____

_____

5 Factors I need to keep in mind to be successful in my action plan are:_____

_____

_____

Review Questions

1. How do the concepts of health fatalism and health hysteria cycle present a negative influence on the understanding of health information?
2. What criteria must a research study satisfy before its claims can be trusted?
3. What are some techniques and strategies that manufacturers and producers of health products use to mislead and deceive the public?
4. Why is it important to see a physician while in good health?
5. What can lay people do while in a hospital to ensure that they receive safe and proper care?

6. What is the major role and function of a primary-care physician?
7. List four sources of information for identifying physicians and specialists in your geographical area.
8. Identify four techniques that will facilitate communication between patient and physician.
9. Discuss the purpose and potential value and risks of the three major components of a physical examination.
10. Compare and contrast the three basic plans of health insurance.

References

1. Vickery D: Viewpoint—understanding health information, *Taking Care* 8(1):7, 1986.
2. Harvard Medical School: Medical advice lines, *Harvard Health Letter* 18(2):1-3, 1992.
3. Hahn D, Payne W: *Focus on health*, ed 2, St Louis, 1994, Mosby.
4. Associated Press: Body temperature of 98.6° F may not be normal for humans, *Commercial Appeal* 153(267):A2, 1992.
5. Cohn V: How to survive the hospital, *Am Health* 7(3):99, 108, 1987.
6. United Press International: Hospitals infect patients; threat grows, CDC says, *Commercial Appeal* 146(311):C3, 1985.
7. Mayer D: Accreditation panel to release hospital information to health care financing administration, *Med Benefits* 6(11):12, 1989.
8. Vickery D: The terrible I's: the hidden hazards of hospitalization, *Taking Care* 7(9):5, 1985.
9. Kiplinger Washington Editors: Shopping for a new doctor, *Changing Times* 40(6):51, 1986.
10. Shell E: How to talk to your doctor in 18 seconds, *Am Health* 6(1):82, 1987.
11. Gibbs N: Sick and tired, *Time* 134(5):49, 1989.
12. Second opinions, *Harvard Med School Health Letter* 14(4):1, 1989.
13. Browne M: Analysis discovers wasted motion in routine physical examinations, *Commercial Appeal* 150(43):C3, 1989.
14. Turk M: The tests that matter, *Am Health* 12(4):53, 1993.
15. Carey B: Do you need a physical? *In Health* 4(5):80-82, 1990.
16. The 10 best medical tests, *Am Health* 99(3):100, 1992.
17. Sobel D: When not to take medical tests, *Am Health* 5(9):54, 59, 1986.
18. Moore T: The cholesterol myth, *Atlantic Monthly* 264(3):37-70, 1989.
19. Lamb L: Do it yourself medical testing, *Health Letter* 29(12):2, 3, 1987.
20. Annual pap smears, *Consumer Rep Health Letter* 1(2):15, 1989.
21. Norton C: Not just for kids, *Hippocrates* 3(5):75, 1989.
22. Shots for grownups, *Harvard Med School Health Letter* 13(10):1, 1988.
23. Impact of fraudulent claims on health care costs, *Stat Bull* 17(4):14, 1991.
24. Are HMOs the answer? *Consumer Rep* 57(8):519, 1992.

Annotated Readings

ABC's of the human body, Pleasantville, NY, 1987, The Readers Digest Association.
Full-color presentation on the systems of the body with many health tips and advice. Contains a comprehensive index.

Bennett W, Goldfinger S, Johnson G: *Your good health*, Cambridge, Mass, 1987, Harvard University Press.
Published by the editors of the Harvard Medical School Health Letter, this book presents information and advice on a variety of health topics.

Editors of Consumer Reports books: *The new medicine show*, Mount Vernon, NY, 1989, Consumer's Union of the United States.
Gotcha! The traps in long-term care insurance: an empty promise to the elderly? *Consumer Rep* 56(6):425-442, 1991.
Exhaustively reviews insurance and ratings of nearly 100 long-term care policies.
Practical guide to some everyday health problems and health products including but not limited to pain relievers, cold remedies, indigestion and antacids, constipation and diarrhea medicines, diet and nutrition aids, skin and hair care, teeth and gums, and generic and brand-name drugs.

Sobel D, Ferguson T: *The people's book of medical tests*, New York, 1985, Summitt Publishers.
Presents information on 200 medical procedures including purpose of tests, how tests are performed, how long tests take, risks, and costs.

ASSESSMENT ACTIVITY   13-1

Are You Communicating with Your Physician?

Directions: Using the scale below, circle the appropriate number for each question. Total your responses and find your score at the bottom of the activity.

When I go to my physician for a health problem	Almost Always	Very Frequently	Frequently	Occasionally	Never
I plan ahead of time how I am going to describe my problem.	5	4	3	2	1
I describe my most important problem first.	5	4	3	2	1
I check with my immediate family to determine if my problem runs in the family	5	4	3	2	1
I take a list of medications, over-the-counter drugs, and treatments I am receiving.	5	4	3	2	1
Before the visit, I prepare a written list of questions to ask.	5	4	3	2	1
I ask about anything that is unclear to me.	5	4	3	2	1
I repeat in my own words the physician's answers to my questions.	5	4	3	2	1
I understand the doctor's diagnosis of my problem.	5	4	3	2	1
I make sure I know the benefits and risks of prescribed treatments.	5	4	3	2	1
I know if and when to return for a follow-up visit.	5	4	3	2	1

Scoring

46–50 = Excellent communication
41–45 = Good
36–40 = Average
31–35 = Fair
Less than 30 = Poor

ASSESSMENT ACTIVITY 13-2

Are Your Immunizations Working for You?

Directions: For each of the adult immunizations listed below, indicate the dates of your initial immunization and most recent booster shot. Check the immunization schedule in Table 12-5 and determine whether your immunizations are current. If it is, write "yes" in the last column. If it is not, write "no" in the last column. A "no" means you need to discuss your immunizations with your health-care provider.

	Dates		
Immunization	**Initial Shot**	**Booster Shot**	**Yes/No**
Tetanus and diphtheria			
Measles			
Rubella			
Mumps			
Pneumonia			
Influenza			
Hepatitis B			

ASSESSMENT ACTIVITY   13-3

Assessing Results of Diagnostic Tests

Directions: Use this assessment to record the dates and results of commonly administered diagnostic medical tests. The blank spaces at the bottom can be used to list additional tests. Refer to information in this chapter to review the purposes of these tests.

Diagnostic Test	Date	Results
Blood sugar		
Blood urea nitrogen		
Calcium		
Blood count		
Cholesterol		
High-density lipoprotein		
Low-density lipoprotein		
Triglyceride		
Hemoccult		
Pulse rate		
Blood pressure		
Mammography*		
Pap smear* and pelvic examination		
Prostate†		
Eye examination and tonometry		
Electrocardiogram (ECG)		
Stress ECG		
HIV text		
Chest x-ray		
Dental check-up		

*Women
†Men

ASSESSMENT ACTIVITY   13 - 4

Self-Care Inventory

Directions: Using the scale below, circle the appropriate number for each question. Total your responses and find your score at the bottom of the activity.

	Never	Occasionally	Most of the Time	Almost All of the Time
1. I read health-related advertisements in a critical and careful manner.	1	2	3	4
2. I maintain a suspicious attitude about health claims.	1	2	3	4
3. I have a primary-care physician.	1	2	3	4
4. I know which hospitals my physician recommends.	1	2	3	4
5. I ask about fees before using health-care services.	1	2	3	4
6. I ask about the risks and benefits of a medical test before its use.	1	2	3	4
7. I seek second opinions when I feel uncertain or uncomfortable with a recommended treatment.	1	2	3	4
8. I maintain adequate health insurance coverage.	1	2	3	4
9. I ask about the contraindications and side effects of prescription drugs before taking them.	1	2	3	4
10. I thoroughly read labels before taking a nonprescription drug.	1	2	3	4
11. I look for evidence of scientifically controlled studies when reading sensational health claims.	1	2	3	4
12. I am familiar with the medical history of close relatives.	1	2	3	4
13. I follow directions when taking medicines, including continuing their use for the prescribed duration.	1	2	3	4
14. I keep a supply of essential items in my medicine cabinet.	1	2	3	4
15. I keep records of the time, date, and results of medical tests.	1	2	3	4
16. I keep a record of my immunizations.	1	2	3	4
17. I engage in appropriate medical self-care screening procedures.	1	2	3	4
18. I understand which health conditions are covered in my health insurance policy and which are not.	1	2	3	4
19. I know the deductible amount of my health insurance policy.	1	2	3	4
20. I go for selective health examinations according to recommended schedule.	1	2	3	4

Scoring

70-80 = A highly skilled, discriminating, and assertive health consumer
60-69 = An adequately skilled health consumer
50-59 = Possibility for improvement
0-49 = Passive consumer

Lifestyle Assessment
Inventory

Section _____ Term _____ Date _____ Name _____

Directions: Wellness involves a variety of components that work together to build the total concept. Below are some questions concerning the different aspects of wellness. Using the scale, respond to each question by circling the number that most closely corresponds with your feelings and lifestyle. Remember to complete the Lifestyle Assessment Inventory at the completion of the course to compare the results.

Physical

	Yes/always	Often	Once	Rarely	No/never
1. I exercise aerobically at least three times per week for 20 minutes or more.	10	7	5	3	1
2. When participating in physical activities, I include stretching and flexibility exercises.	10	7	5	3	1
3. I include warm-up and cool-down periods when participating in vigorous activities.	10	7	5	3	1
4. I engage in resistance-type exercises at least two times per week.	10	7	5	3	1
5. My physical fitness level is excellent for my age.	10	7	5	3	1
6. My body composition is appropriate for my gender (men, 10%-18% body fat; women, 18%-25%).	10	7	5	3	1
7. I have appropriate medical check-ups regularly and am able talk to my doctor and ask questions that concern me.	10	7	5	3	1
8. I keep my immunizations up-to-date.	10	7	5	3	1
9. I keep up with the medical history of close relatives.	10	7	5	3	1
10. I keep records of the time, date, and results of medical tests.	10	7	5	3	1

Physical Assessment Score _____

Alcohol and Drugs Assessment

	Yes/always	Often	Once	Rarely	No/never
1. I avoid smoking.	10	7	5	3	1
2. I avoid using smokeless tobacco products.	10	7	5	3	1
3. I avoid drinking alcohol or restrict my consumption to two drinks or less.	10	7	5	3	1
4. I avoid drinking alcohol to the point of intoxication.	10	7	5	3	1
5. I do not drive when drinking alcoholic beverages or talking medicines that make me sleepy	10	7	5	3	1
6. I avoid using mood-altering substances.	10	7	5	3	1
7. I follow directions when taking medications.	10	7	5	3	1
8. I thoroughly read labels before taking a nonprescription drug.	10	7	5	3	1
9. I ask about contraindications and side effects of prescription drugs before taking them.	10	7	5	3	1
10. I keep a record of drugs to which I am allergic in my wallet or purse.	10	7	5	3	1

Alcohol and Drugs Assessment Score _____

Nutritional Assessment

	Yes/always	Often	Once	Rarely	No/never
1. I eat at least 3 to 5 servings of vegetables and 2 to 4 servings of fruits each day.	10	7	5	3	1

	Yes/always	Often	Once	Rarely	No/never
2. My daily diet includes at least 6 to 11 servings from the bread, cereal, rice, and pasta food group.	10	7	5	3	1
3. I limit my daily intake of dairy products to 2 to 3 servings.	10	7	5	3	1
4. My daily intake of meats, eggs, and nuts is 2 to 3 servings.	10	7	5	3	1
5. I make a conscious effort to choose or prepare foods low in saturated fat.	10	7	5	3	1
6. When purchasing a food item, I read the labels to identify foods high in salt, hidden sugars, tropical oils, and saturated fat.	10	7	5	3	1
7. I avoid adding salt to my food without first tasting it.	10	7	5	3	1
8. I avoid eating unless I'm hungry.	10	7	5	3	1
9. I stop eating before feeling completely full.	10	7	5	3	1
10. I avoid binge eating.	10	7	5	3	1

Nutritional Assessment Score _____

Social Wellness Assessment

	Yes/always	Often	Once	Rarely	No/never
1. I have at least one person in whom I can confide.	10	7	5	3	1
2. I have a good relationship with my family.	10	7	5	3	1
3. I have friends at work or school with whom I gain support and talk with regularly.	10	7	5	3	1
4. I am involved in school activities.	10	7	5	3	1
5. I am involved in my community.	10	7	5	3	1
6. I do something for fun and just for myself at least once a week.	10	7	5	3	1
7. I am able to develop close, intimate relationships.	10	7	5	3	1
8. I engage in activities that contribute to the environment.	10	7	5	3	1
9. I am interested in the views, opinions, activities, and accomplishments of others.	10	7	5	3	1

Social Wellness Score _____

Spiritual Wellness Assessment

	Yes/always	Often	Once	Rarely	No/never
1. I know what my values and beliefs are.	10	7	5	3	1
2. I live by my convictions.	10	7	5	3	1
3. My life has meaning and direction.	10	7	5	3	1
4. I derive strength from my spiritual life daily.	10	7	5	3	1
5. I have life goals that I strive to achieve every day.	10	7	5	3	1
6. I view life as a learning experience and look forward to the future.	10	7	5	3	1
7. I am satisfied with my spiritual life.	10	7	5	3	1
8. I am tolerant of the values and beliefs of others.	10	7	5	3	1
9. I am satisfied with the degree that my campus activities are consistent with my values.	10	7	5	3	1
10. Personal reflection is an important part of my life.	10	7	5	3	1

Spiritual Wellness Assessment Score _____

Emotional Wellness Assessment

	Yes/always	Often	Once	Rarely	No/never
1. I feel positive about myself and my life.	10	7	5	3	1
2. I am able to be the person I choose to be.	10	7	5	3	1
3. I am satisfied that I am performing to the best of my ability.	10	7	5	3	1
4. I can cope with life's ups and downs effectively and in a healthy manner.	10	7	5	3	1
5. I am nonjudgmental in my approach to others and take responsibility for my own decisions and actions.	10	7	5	3	1
6. I feel there is appropriate amount of excitement in my life.	10	7	5	3	1
7. When I make mistakes, I learn from them.	10	7	5	3	1
8. I can say "no" without feeling guilty.	10	7	5	3	1
9. I find it easy to laugh.	10	7	5	3	1

Emotional Wellness Assessment Score _____

Stress Control Assessment

	Yes/always	Often	Once	Rarely	No/never
1. I am easily distracted.	1	3	5	7	10
2. I tend to be nervous and impatient.	1	3	5	7	10
3. I prepare ahead of time for events/situations that cause stress.	10	7	5	3	1
4. I schedule enough time to accomplish what I need to do.	10	7	5	3	1
5. I set realistic goals for myself.	10	7	5	3	1
6. I can express my feelings of anger.	10	7	5	3	1
7. I avoid putting off important tasks to the last minute.	10	7	5	3	1
8. When working on tasks, I stay focused on what I'm doing and usually concentrate on them through completion.	10	7	5	3	1
9. When working under pressure, I stay calm and patient.	10	7	5	3	1
10. I can make decisions with a minimum of stress and worry.	10	7	5	3	1

Stress Control Assessment Score _____

Intellectual Wellness Assessment

	Yes/always	Often	Once	Rarely	No/never
1. I believe my education is preparing me for what I would like to accomplish in life.	10	7	5	3	1
2. I am interested in learning just for the sake of learning.	10	7	5	3	1
3. I like to be aware of current social and political issues.	10	7	5	3	1
4. I have interests other than those directly related to my vocation.	10	7	5	3	1
5. I am able to apply what I know to real life situations.	10	7	5	3	1
6. I am interested in the viewpoint of others, even if it is very different from my own.	10	7	5	3	1
7. I seek advice when I am uncertain or uncomfortable with a recommended health or medical treatment.	10	7	5	3	1
8. I ask about the risks and benefits of a medical test before its use.	10	7	5	3	1
9. When seeking medical care, I plan ahead how to describe my problem and what questions I should ask.	10	7	5	3	1
10. I keep abreast of the latest trends and information regarding health matters.	10	7	5	3	1

Intellectual Wellness Assessment Score _____

Wellness Assessment Summary

Transfer the total score for each section to the spaces below. Add the scores and divide by eight to determine your average wellness score.

Physical Assessment Score .... ＿＿

Alcohol and Drugs Assessment .... ＿＿

Nutritional Assessment .... ＿＿

Social Wellness Assessment .... ＿＿

Spiritual Wellness Assessment .... ＿＿

Emotional Wellness Assessment .... ＿＿

Stress Control Assessment .... ＿＿

Intellectual Wellness Assessment .... ＿＿

TOTAL ＿＿

Average Wellness Score ＿＿
(Divide total score by 8)

86-100—Excellent. You are engaging in behaviors and attitudes than can significantly contribute to a healthy lifestyle and a higher quality of life. If you scored in this range, you are an example to many.

70-85—Good. You engage in many health-promoting attitudes and behaviors that should contribute to good health and a more satisfying quality of life. However, there are some areas that could use some upgrading to provide optimal benefits. If you are at this level, you are showing how much you care about yourself and your life.

50-69—Average. You are typical of the average American who tends to act without really considering the consequences of your behaviors. Now is the time to consider your lifestyle and what ramifications it is having on you now and in the future. Maybe there are some positive actions that you can consider taking to improve your quality of life.

30-49—Below average. Perhaps you lack current information about behaviors and attitudes that can enhance your health and quality of life. Now is the time to begin to learn about positive changes that can improve your life.

Less than 30—Needs improvement. It's good that you are concerned enough about your health to take this test, but indications are that your behaviors and attitudes may be having detrimental effects on your health. You can easily begin to take action now to improve your prospects for the future.

Assessment Activity
Scoresheet

Directions: Listed below are the titles of the various assessments found in the text. Space is provided for your first assessment score and then for the assessment to be repeated at a later time. Retaking the various assessments at the end of the course or even at a later time will help to form a

comprehensive picture of where you are in moving toward a higher quality of life. Finally, it will help you identify what you are doing well. Not all assessment activities are listed because some are not appropriate for numerical scoring.

Assessment Activity 1-1 Barriers to Change

Score/date   Score/date
_____ _____

Comments: _____

Assessment Activity 1-2 Health Locus of Control

Subscale 1 ____ ____ ____
Subscale 2 ____ ____ ____
Subscale 3 ____ ____ ____
TOTAL ____ ____ ____

Assessment Activity 1-3 Assessing Your Health Behavior

Reconsider this activity to determine which health-promoting/health-inhibiting behaviors you are now experiencing. What has changed?
Comments: _____
_____

Assessment Activity 1-4 Assessment of Readiness for Lifestyle Change

Have your answers changed since last completing this activity?

Yes ____ No ____
Comments: _____

Assessment Activity 2-1 Arizona Heart Institute Cardiovascular Risk Factor Analysis

Score/date   Score/date
_____ _____

If you are in the medium or high-risk category, make appropriate lifestyle changes (start exercising, stop smoking, eat a low-fat diet) and take the test again in 6 months.

Assessment Activity 2-2 A Case Study on Bill M.
Assessment Activity 2-3 A Case Study on Bill M. Jr.

Score/date   Score/date
_____ _____

If you were unable to answer the questions asked about these two case studies, reexamine the section that cover the risk factors for cardiovascular disease.

Assessment Activity 3-1 The Rockport Fitness Walking Test

Score/date   Score/date
_____ _____

Assessment Activity 3-2 The 3-Mile Walking Test

Score/date   Score/date
_____

Assessment Activity 3-3 The 1.5-Mile Run/Walk Test

Score/date   Score/date
_____ _____

Assessment Activity 3-4 The Bench Step Test

Score/date   Score/date
_____ _____

Assessment Activity 3-5 Calculating Your Target Heart Rate

Pretraining THR   Posttraining THR
_____   _____

Assessment Activity 3-6 Design an Exercise Program Date _____

Your subject follows the training program that you have designed for 4 months. Would you reexamine the program at that time? If so, would you make any changes? What would the changes be? _____
_____

Assessment Activity 4-1 Calculation of Strength (Selected Muscle Groups)

		Score/date	Score/date
1 RM	Biceps curl	_____	_____
1 RM	Overhead press	_____	_____
1 RM	Bench press	_____	_____
1 RM	Half squat or leg press	_____	_____
1 RM	Hamstring curl	_____	_____

Assessment Activity 4-2 Muscle Endurance

		Score/date	Score/date
20 RM	Bench press	_____	_____
20 RM	Half squat	_____	_____
20 RM	Biceps curl	_____	_____
20 RM	Hamstring curl	_____	_____

Assessment Activity 4-3 Abdominal Muscle Endurance—The Canadian Trunk Strength Test

Score/date   Score/date

_____   _____

Assessment Activity 4-4 Assessing Muscle Strength and Endurance with Selected Calisthenic Exercises

Score/date   Score/date

Chin-ups   _____   _____
Flexed-arm hang   _____   _____
Push-ups   _____   _____
Modified push-ups   _____   _____

Assessment Activity 4-5 Resistance Training Log

Starting date _____

How has your program changed since you started, and what kind of improvement have you made? _____

_____

Assessment Activity 5-1 Sit-and-Reach Test

Score/date   Score/date

_____   _____

Comments: _____

Assessment Activity 5-2 Shoulder Flexion Test

Score/date   Score/date

_____   _____

Comments: _____

Assessment Activity 5-3 Sling Test

Score/date   Score/date

_____   _____

Comments: _____

Assessment Activity 5-4 Trunk Extension

Score/date   Score/date

_____   _____

Classfication   _____   _____
Comments: _____

Assessment Activity 5-5 Shoulder Rotation Test

Score/date   Score/date

_____   _____

Performance level   _____   _____
Comments: _____

Assessment Activity 6-1 Assessing Your Protein RDA

Score/date   Score/date

_____   _____

Assessment Activity 6-2 Assessing Your Maximum Fat Intake

Score/date   Score/date

_____   _____

Assessment Activity 6-3 Assessing Your Maximum Saturated Fat Intake

Score/date   Score/date

_____   _____

Assessment Activity 6-4 Assessing Your Carbohydrate Intake Goal

Score/date   Score/date

_____   _____

Assessment Activity 6-5 Nutrition Assessment

Reference daily intakes   Score/date   Score/date
Protein   _____   _____
Iron   _____   _____
Vitamin A   _____   _____
Vitamin C   _____   _____
Thiamine   _____   _____
Riboflavin   _____   _____
Niacin   _____   _____
Calcium   _____   _____
Daily reference values
Total fat   _____   _____
Saturated fat   _____   _____
Cholesterol   _____   _____
Sodium   _____   _____
Carbohydrate   _____   _____
Dietary fiber   _____   _____
Potassium   _____   _____

Comment on dietary strengths and weaknesses and formulate a nutrition prescription: _____

Assessment Activity 6-6 How Does Your Diet Compare with the Recommended Diet?

Score/date   Score/date

Percent carbohydrate
calories   _____   _____
Percent protein calories   _____   _____
Percent fat calories   _____   _____

How does your diet compare with the recommended diet? _____

_____

Assessment Activity 6-7 Fat Ratio of Foods

What generalizations can you formulate about foods that have a high fat ratio? _____

_____

Assessment Activity 6-8 Eating Behaviors to Consider
Based on your answers to the questions in this assessment, write a general statement about your eating habits in terms of attitude toward various foods and how you developed certain tastes and food preferences: _____
_____
_____

Assessment Activity 7-1 Your Body's Shape
                                    Score/date   Score/date
Waist/hip ratio: _____   _____
Are you an android or a gynoid? _____

Assessment Activity 7-2 Calculating Relative Weight Using Height/Weight Tables
                                    Score/date   Score/date
                                    _____   _____
Are you overweight, underweight or ideal weight? _____
If you deviate from the ideal, what is the percent of deviation? _____
Are you more than 20% overweight?
                        Yes _____   No _____

Assessment Activity 7-3 Using BMI to Estimate Overweight
                                    Score/date   Score/date
                                    _____   _____

Assessment Activity 7-4 Using BMI to Estimate Desirable Body Weight
Based on BMI, what is your desirable body weight? _____

Assessment Activity 7-5 Calculating Desirable Body Weight From Percent Body Fat
How much weight do you need to lose to reach your desired body weight? _____

Assessment Activity 8-1 Where Is the Fat?
Identify 5 foods that are high in fat grams in relationship to serving size. _____
_____

Assessment Activity 8-2 Calculating Caloric Expenditure Through Exercise
Calculate the number of weeks it would take you to lose 10 lb by riding a bike at 13 mph, 5 times a week, 40 minutes each exercise session: _____
_____

Assessment Activity 8-3 Estimating Your Basal Metabolic Rate
                        Date _____   Date _____
Basal metabolic rate   _____   _____
level of physical activity   _____   _____
Total calories expended   _____   _____

Assessment Activity 8-4 Assessing Caloric Costs of Activities
Select three of your favorite activities and determine the amount of participation time (in minutes) required to expend 300 calories. _____
_____

Assessment Activity 9-1 Stressors of Life
                                    Score/date   Score/date
                                    _____   _____
Retake the stress scale to determine whether your stress level has changed since the initial assessment.
Comments: _____

Assessment Activity 9-2 Stress Style: Body, Mind, Mixed?
                                    Stress style _____
Review this activity to determine whether you are using stress-reduction techniques appropriate for your stress style.
Comments: _____

Assessment Activity 9-3 How Hardy Are You?
                                    Score/date   Score/date
                                    _____   _____
Has your hardiness score changed? What can you do to increase your score? _____

Assessment Activity 9-4 Identification of Coping Styles
Date _____
Number of negative coping techniques
                                    _____   _____
Number of positive coping techniques
                                    _____   _____
Comments: _____

Assessment Activity 9-5 Analyzing My Use of Time
Redo the time-schedule assessment to determine whether you are using time most effectively.
Comments: _____

Assessment Activity 10-1 How Can You Tell Whether You Have a Drinking Problem?

Reassess the drinking scale to determine whether changes have occurred.

Comments: _____

Assessment Activity 10-2 Drugs in My Life

Take this assessment a second time to determine whether usage of any of the drugs listed has changed.

Comments: _____
_____

Assessment Activity 11-1 Are You at Risk for a Sexually Transmitted Disease?

Review this activity to determine your present risk for contracting an STD. _____
_____

Assessment Activity 11-2 Making a Decision

Review this activity to determine whether any of the listed factors have changed. _____
_____

Assessment Activity 12-1 Cancer Awareness Inventory

Review this activity to determine whether any of the listed factors have changed. _____
_____

Assessment Activity 12-2 Are You at Risk for Diabetes?

Review this activity to determine whether any of the listed factors have changed. _____
_____

Assessment Activity 13-1 Are You Communicating with Your Physician?

Score/date   Score/date
_____   _____

Assessment Activity 13-2 Are Your Immunizations Working for You?

Check the immunizations that are current

	Date _____	Date _____
Tetanus and diphtheria	_____	_____
Measles	_____	_____
Rubella	_____	_____
Pneumonia	_____	_____
Influenza	_____	_____
Hepatitis B	_____	_____

Assessment Activity 13-3 Assessing Results of Diagnostic Tests

Record the results to the following diagnostic tests

	Date _____	Date _____
Blood sugar	_____	_____
Blood urea nitrogen	_____	_____
Calcium	_____	_____
Blood count	_____	_____
Cholesterol	_____	_____
HDL	_____	_____
LDL	_____	_____
Triglyceride	_____	_____
Hemoccult	_____	_____
Pulse rate	_____	_____
Blood pressure	_____	_____
Mammography	_____	_____
Pap smear/pelvic exam	_____	_____
Prostate	_____	_____
Eye exam/tonometry	_____	_____
Electrocardiogram	_____	_____
Stress ECG	_____	_____
Chest x-ray	_____	_____
Dental check-up	_____	_____
HIV test	_____	_____

Assessment Activity 13-4 Self-Care Inventory

Score/date   Score/date
_____   _____

Nutritive Components

Food Name	Serving	Gram wt	Kcal	Prot (g)	Carb (g)	Fat (g)	Chol (mg)	Safa (g)	Sod (mg)	Pot (mg)
Beverages										
Beer-light	1 fl oz	29.5	8.000	0.100	0.400	0.000	0.000	0.000	1.000	5.000
Beer-regular	1 fl oz	29.7	12.00	0.100	1.100	0.000	0.000	0.000	2.000	7.000
Champagne-domestic-glass	1 item	120.0	84.00	0.200	3.000	—	—	—	—	—
Club soda	1 fl oz	29.6	0.000	0.000	0.000	0.000	0.000	0.000	6.000	0.000
Coffee-brewed	1 fl oz	30.0	1.000	0.000	0.100	0.000	0.000	0.000	1.000	16.00
Cola	1 fl oz	30.8	13.30	0.000	3.200	0.000	0.000	0.000	1.000	0.000
Diet soft drink	1 fl oz	29.6	0.000	0.000	0.000	0.000	0.000	0.000	2.000	0.000
Lemon lime soda-7Up	1 fl oz	30.7	12.00	0.000	3.200	0.000	0.000	0.000	3.000	0.000
Tea-brewed	1 fl oz	29.6	0.000	0.000	0.100	0.000	0.000	0.000	1.000	11.00
Water	1 cup	237.0	0.000	0.000	0.000	0.000	0.000	0.000	7.000	1.000
Whis/gin/rum/vod-80 proof	1 fl oz	27.8	64.00	0.000	0.000	0.000	0.000	0.000	0.000	1.000
Wine-white-table	1 fl oz	29.5	20.00	0.000	0.200	0.000	0.000	0.000	18.00	33.30
Wine cooler-white wine/7Up	1 srvg	102.0	54.90	0.050	5.720	0.000	0.000	0.000	7.480	41.00
Gatorade-Thirst Quencher	1 fl oz	30.1	7.000	0.000	1.900	0.000	0.000	0.000	12.00	3.000
Breads										
Bagel-egg	1 item	55.0	163.0	6.020	30.90	1.410	8.000	0.500	198.0	40.70
Biscuits-prepared/mix	1 item	28.0	93.20	2.070	13.60	3.320	—	0.600	262.0	56.00
Bread-French-enriched	1 slice	35.0	98.00	3.330	17.70	1.360	0.000	0.200	193.0	30.10
Bread-white-firm	1 slice	23.0	61.40	1.900	11.20	0.902	0.000	0.200	118.0	25.80
Bread-whole wheat-firm	1 slice	25.0	61.30	2.410	11.30	1.090	0.000	0.100	159.0	44.00
Crackers-Ry Krisp-natural	1 item	2.1	7.5	0.25	1.67	0.033	0	0	18.5	10.2
Muffin-English-plain	1 item	56.0	133.0	4.430	25.70	1.090	—	—	358.0	314.0
Roll-Brown & Serve-enr	1 item	26.0	85.00	2.000	14.00	2.000	—	0.400	144.0	25.00
Croissant–Sara lee	1 item	26.0	109.0	2.300	11.20	6.100	—	—	140.0	40.00
Roll-hamburger/hotdog	1 item	40.0	114.0	3.430	20.10	2.090	—	0.500	241.0	36.80
Breakfast Cereals										
100% Bran	1 cup	66	178	8.25	48.1	3.3	0	0.587	457	824
All Bran	1 cup	85.2	212	12.2	63.4	1.53	0	—	961	1051
Alpha Bits	1 cup	28.4	111	2.2	24.6	0.6	0	—	219	110
Bran Buds	1 cup	85.2	220	11.8	64.8	2.04	0	—	523	1425
Bran Chex	1 cup	49	156	5.05	39	1.37	0	—	455	394

Composition key: *Kcal*, Calories; *Prot*, protein; *Carb*, carbohydrates; *Chol*, cholesterol; *Safa*, saturated fats; *Sod*, sodium; *Pot*, potassium.

Nutritive Components—cont'd

Mag (mg)	Iron (mg)	Zinc (mg)	V-A (IU)	V-E (mg)	V-C (mg)	Thia (mg)	Ribo (mg)	Niac (mg)	V-B$_6$ (mg)	Fol (µg)	V-B$_{12}$ (µg)	Calc (mg)	Phos (mg)	Sel (mg)	Fibd (g)
Beverages															
1.000	0.010	0.010	0.000	—	0.000	0.003	0.009	0.116	0.010	1.200	0.000	1.000	4.000	0.000	—
2.000	0.010	0.000	0.000	—	0.000	0.002	0.008	0.135	0.015	1.800	0.010	1.000	4.000	—	—
—	—	—	—	—	—	—	—	—	—	—	—	—	—	—	—
0.000	—	0.030	0.000	—	0.000	0.000	0.000	0.000	0.000	0.000	0.000	1.000	0.000	—	0.000
2.000	0.120	0.000	0.000	—	0.000	0.000	0.000	0.066	0.000	0.000	0.000	1.000	0.000	0.000	0.000
0.000	0.010	0.000	0.000	—	0.000	0.000	0.000	0.000	0.000	0.000	0.000	1.000	4.000	—	0.000
0.000	0.010	0.020	0.000	—	0.000	0.001	0.007	0.000	0.000	0.000	0.000	1.000	3.000	—	0.000
0.000	0.020	0.020	0.000	0.000	0.000	0.000	0.000	0.005	0.000	0.000	0.000	1.000	0.000	—	0.000
1.000	0.010	0.010	0.000	—	0.000	0.000	0.004	0.000	0.000	1.500	0.000	0.000	0.000	0.000	0.000
2.000	0.010	0.060	0.000	—	0.000	0.000	0.000	0.000	0.000	0.000	0.000	5.000	0.000	—	0.000
0.000	0.030	0.020	0.000	0.000	0.000	0.002	0.000	0.000	0.000	0.000	0.000	0.000	1.000	0.000	0.000
3.000	0.090	0.020	0.000	—	0.000	0.001	0.001	0.020	0.004	0.100	0.000	3.000	4.000	—	0.000
5.000	0.193	0.063	—	—	—	0.002	0.043	0.003	0.007	0.100	0.000	6.110	6.950	—	—
0.000	0.020	0.010	0.000	0.000	0.000	0.002	0.000	0.000	0.000	0.000	0.000	0.000	3.000	—	0.000
Breads															
11.00	1.460	0.286	17.60	—	0.000	0.209	0.160	1.940	0.024	13.20	0.052	23.10	36.90	—	0.506
6.720	0.574	0.176	15.70	0.694	0.000	0.120	0.106	0.840	0.013	1.680	0.045	58.20	128.0	—	—
7.000	1.080	0.221	0.000	0.417	0.000	0.161	0.123	1.400	0.019	13.00	0.000	38.50	28.40	0.010	0.546
4.830	0.653	0.143	0.000	0.274	0.000	0.108	0.071	0.863	0.008	8.050	0.000	29.00	24.80	0.006	0.621
23.30	0.855	0.420	0.000	0.225	0.000	0.088	0.053	0.958	0.047	13.80	0.000	18.00	65.00	0.011	2.830
2.5	0.092	0.057	—	0.038	—	0.006	0.005	0.033	0.007	0.833	—	0.833	6.83	0.001	0.34
10.60	1.580	0.403	0.000	—	0.000	0.258	0.179	2.100	0.022	17.90	0.000	90.70	62.70	0.015	—
5.460	0.800	0.190	0.000	1.730	0.000	0.100	0.060	0.900	0.016	9.880	—	20.00	23.00	0.008	—
7.000	1.040	—	41.00	—	0.000	0.280	0.100	1.200	—	—	—	12.00	32.00	—	—
7.600	1.190	0.248	0.000	0.212	0.000	0.196	0.132	1.580	0.014	14.80	—	53.60	32.80	0.012	—
Breakfast Cereals															
312	8.12	5.74	0	—	62.7	1.58	1.78	20.9	2.11	46.9	6.27	46.2	801	0.02	19.5
318	13.5	11.2	1125	7.78	45.2	1.11	1.28	15	1.53	301	0	69	794	0.025	25.5
17	1.8	1.5	375	—	0	0.4	0.4	5	0.5	100	1.5	8	51	0.01	0.3
271	13.5	11.2	1125	3.45	45.2	1.11	1.28	15	1.53	301	0	57.1	740	0.025	23.6
126	7.8	2.14	11	—	26	0.6	0.26	8.6	0.9	173	2.6	29	327	0.01	7.9

Mag, Magnesium; *V-A*, vitamin A; *V-E*, vitamin E; *V-C*, vitamin C; *Thia*, thiamin; *Ribo*, riboflavin; *Niac*, niacin; *V-B$_6$*, vitamin B$_6$; *Fol*, folic acid; *V-B$_{12}$*, vitamin B$_{12}$; *Calc*, calcium; *Phos*, phosphorus; *Sel*, selenium; *Fibd*, dietary fiber; g, gram; mg, milligram; IU, international units; µg, microgram.

Nutritive Components—cont'd

Food Name	Serving	Gram wt	Kcal	Prot (g)	Carb (g)	Fat (g)	Chol (mg)	Safa (g)	Sod (mg)	Pot (mg)
Breakfast Cereals—cont'd										
Bran Flakes-Kellogg	1 cup	39	127	4.91	30.5	0.741	0	0	303	248
C.W. Post-plain	1 cup	97	432	8.7	69.4	15.2	0.184	11.3	167	198
Cheerios	1 cup	22.7	88.8	3.42	15.7	1.45	0	0.27	246	81
Corn Bran	1 cup	36	125	2.45	30.3	1.26	0	—	310	70.2
Corn Chex	1 cup	28.4	111	2.02	24.9	0.114	0	0	271	23
Corn Flakes-Kellogg	1 cup	22.7	88.3	1.84	19.5	0.068	0	0	232	20.9
Corn grits-enriched	1 cup	242	145	3.39	31.5	0.484	0	0.073	0	53.2
Corn-shredded-sugar	1 cup	25	95	2	22	0	0	0	247	—
Cracklin Bran	1 cup	60	229	5.52	41.2	8.76	0	—	487	355
Cream/wheat-instant	1 cup	241	153	4.4	31.6	0.6	8	0	6	48
Cream/wheat-packet	1 item	150	132	2.5	28.9	0.4	0	0	241	55
Cream/wheat-reg-hot	1 cup	251	133	3.8	27.7	0.5	0	0	2	43
Crispy Rice	1 cup	28.4	112	1.82	25.2	0.114	0	0	208	43
Farina-cook-enr	1 cup	233	117	3.26	24.7	0.233	0	0.023	0	30.3
Fortified Oat Flake	1 cup	48	177	8.98	34.8	0.72	0	0	429	343
Frost Flake-Kellogg	1 cup	35	133	1.75	31.7	0.07	0	0	284	22.4
Frosted Mini Wheats	1 item	7.1	25.5	0.731	5.86	0.071	0	0	2.06	24.2
Granola-homemade	1 cup	122	594	15	67.3	33.2	0	5.84	12.2	612
Granola-Nature Val	1 cup	113	503	11.5	75.5	19.6	0	13	232	389
Grape Nuts	1 cup	114	407	13.3	93.5	0.456	0	0	792	381
Grape Nuts Flakes	1 cup	32.5	116	3.48	26.6	0.358	0	0	792	381
Heartland Natural	1 cup	115	499	11.6	78.5	17.7	0	—	293	385
Honey Bran	1 cup	35	119	3.08	28.6	0.735	0	0	202	151
Honey Nut Cher-rios	1 cup	33	125	3.63	26.5	0.759	0	0.132	299	115
Life-plain/cinnamon	1 cup	44	162	8.1	31.5	0.836	0	0	229	197
Lucky Charms	1 cup	32	125	2.91	26.1	1.22	0	0.224	227	66.2
Malt O Meal-cook	1 cup	240	122	3.6	25.9	0.24	0	0	2.4	31.2
Maypo-cook-hot	1 cup	240	170	5.8	31.8	2.4	0	—	9.6	211
Nutri Grain-Barley	1 cup	41	153	4.47	33.9	0.328	0	0	277	108
Nutri Grain-corn	1 cup	42	160	3.36	35.4	0.966	0	—	276	98
Nutri Grain-rye	1 cup	40	144	3.48	33.9	0.28	0	0	272	71.6
Nutri Grain-wheat	1 cup	44	158	3.83	37.2	0.44	0	0	299	120
Oatmeal-inst-packet	1 item	177	104	4.4	18.1	1.7	0	0.289	286	100
Oatmeal-raw	1 cup	81	311	13	54.2	5.1	0	0.9	3	284
Oats-puffed-sugar	1 cup	25	100	3	19	1	0	0.185	294	—
Product 19	1 cup	33	126	3.23	27.4	0.231	0	0	378	51.5
Raisin Bran-Kellogg	1 cup	49.2	154	5.31	37.1	0.984	0	—	359	256
Ralston-cooked	1 cup	253	134	5.57	28.2	0.8	0	0	4	153
Rice Chex	1 cup	25.2	99.5	1.34	22.5	0.101	0	0	211	29.2
Rice Krispies	1 cup	28.4	112	1.93	24.8	0.199	0	0	340	29.5
Rice-puffed-plain	1 cup	14	56.3	0.882	12.6	0.07	0	0	0.42	15.8
Rice-puffed-sugar	1 cup	28.4	115	1	26	0	0	0	21	43

Nutritive Components—cont'd

Mag (mg)	Iron (mg)	Zinc (mg)	V-A (IU)	V-E (mg)	V-C (mg)	Thia (mg)	Ribo (mg)	Niac (mg)	V-B$_6$ (mg)	Fol (μg)	V-B$_{12}$ (μg)	Calc (mg)	Phos (mg)	Sel (mg)	Fibd (g)
Breakfast Cereals—cont'd															
71	24.8	5.15	516	0.823	0	0.507	0.585	6.86	0.702	138	2.1	19.1	192	0.004	5.5
67	15.4	1.64	1284	—	0	1.3	1.5	17.1	1.7	342	5.1	47	224	—	2.2
31.3	3.61	0.629	300	—	12	0.295	0.341	4	0.409	4.99	1.2	38.8	107	0.01	0.863
18.4	12.2	4	7.56	—	0	0.374	0.698	10.9	0.858	232	1.39	41.4	51.8	0.002	6.84
3.98	1.79	0.1	14	—	15.1	0.369	0.068	5	0.511	100	1.51	3.12	11.1	0.002	0.5
2.72	1.43	0.064	300	—	12	0.295	0.341	4	0.409	80.1	0	0.681	14.3	0.001	0.454
9.68	1.55	0.169	—	3.34	—	0.242	0.145	1.96	0.058	2.42	0	0	29	0.024	0.6
3.5	0.6	0.088	0	0.538	13	0.33	0.05	4.4	0.45	88.3	1.33	1	10	0.002	1.54
116	3.78	3.18	794	—	31.8	0.78	0.9	10.6	1.1	212	0	39.6	241	0.01	9.1
14	12	0.41	0	—	0	0.2	0.1	1.8	0.029	11	0	59	43	—	2.21
9	8.1	0.23	1250	1.41	0	0.4	0.2	5	0.5	100	0	40	20	—	2.02
10	10.3	0.33	0	—	0	0.251	0	1.51	0.035	10	0	50.2	42	—	1.94
11.9	0.71	0.471	0	—	1.14	0.114	0.028	2.02	0.044	3.12	0.083	5.11	31	0.004	1
4.66	1.17	0.163	—	2.19	—	0.186	0.117	1.28	0.023	4.66	0	4.66	28	—	3.26
57.6	13.7	1.5	636	—	0	0.624	0.72	8.45	0.864	169	2.54	68.2	176	0.01	1.2
2.8	2.21	0.049	463	—	18.6	0.455	0.525	6.16	0.63	124	0	1.4	25.9	—	0.77
5.82	0.447	0.376	94	0.153	3.76	0.092	0.107	1.25	0.128	25.1	0	2.34	18.5	—	0.54
141	4.84	4.47	10	—	1.22	0.732	0.305	2.14	0.428	98.8	0	75.6	494	0.023	12.8
116	3.78	2.19	—	—	—	0.39	0.19	0.83	—	85	—	71	354	0.037	4.2
76.4	4.95	2.51	1500	—	0	1.48	1.71	20.1	2.05	402	6.04	10.8	286	0.034	5.47
35.8	9.3	0.65	430	0.686	0	0.423	0.488	5.72	0.585	115	1.72	13	96.9	0.01	2.08
147	4.33	3.04	—	—	1.15	0.36	0.161	1.61	0.194	64.4	0	74.8	416	—	5.4
45.9	5.6	0.903	463	—	16.6	0.455	0.525	6.16	0.63	23.5	1.86	16.1	132	—	3.9
38.6	5.25	0.865	437	—	17.5	0.429	0.495	5.81	0.594	21.5	1.75	23.1	122	—	1.3
14.1	11.6	1.45	—	—	—	0.955	0.999	11.6	0.084	37	0	154	238	—	1.4
26.9	5.09	0.563	424	—	17	0.416	0.48	5.63	0.576	6.4	1.7	36.2	88.6	—	0.6
4.8	9.6	0.168	0	—	0	0.48	0.24	5.76	0.019	4.8	0	4.8	24	—	0.6
51	8.4	1.49	702	—	28.8	0.72	0.72	9.36	0.96	9.6	2.88	125	248	—	1.2
32.4	1.45	5.41	543	—	21.7	0.533	0.615	7.22	0.738	145	2.17	11.1	126	0.027	2.4
27	0.89	5.54	556	—	22.3	0.546	0.63	7.39	0.756	148	2.23	1.26	121	0.003	2.6
30.4	1.13	5.28	530	—	21.2	0.52	0.6	7.04	0.72	141	2.12	8.4	104	—	2.56
34.3	1.24	5.81	583	—	23.3	0.572	0.66	7.74	0.792	155	2.33	12.3	165	0.007	2.8
42.5	6.32	0.867	455	2.71	0	0.531	0.283	5.47	0.74	150	0	163	133	0.015	1.62
120	3.41	2.48	8.2	—	0	0.59	0.11	0.63	0.097	26	0	42	384	0.022	4.6
28	4	0.693	275	—	13	0.33	0.38	4.4	0.45	5.5	1.33	44	102	0.006	2.65
12.2	21	0.495	1748	—	70	1.75	1.98	23.3	2.34	466	7	3.96	46.5	—	0.4
63.5	22.3	5.02	500	—	0	0.492	0.59	6.69	0.689	133	2.02	17.2	183	0.005	5.31
59	1.64	1.42	0	2.38	0	0.2	0.18	2.05	0.114	17.7	0.19	12.7	148	—	4.2
6.3	1.59	0.348	1.85	0.071	13.4	0.328	0.008	4.44	0.454	89	1.34	3.53	24.7	0.004	0.151
10.2	1.79	0.48	375	0.08	15.1	0.369	0.426	5	0.511	100	0	3.98	34.4	0.004	0.1
3.5	0.148	0.144	0	—	0	0.015	0.014	0.42	0.011	2.66	0	0.84	13.7	0.001	0.1
7.56	0	1.48	300	—	15	0	0	0	0.504	98.8	1.48	3	14	0.002	0.2

Nutritive Components—cont'd

Food Name	Serving	Gram wt	Kcal	Prot (g)	Carb (g)	Fat (g)	Chol (mg)	Safa (g)	Sod (mg)	Pot (mg)
Breakfast Cereals—cont'd										
Roman Meal-cooked	1 cup	241	147	6.51	33	0.964	0	—	3	302
Special K	1 cup	21.3	83.1	4.2	16	0.085	0.028	0	199	36.8
Sugar Corn Pops	1 cup	28.4	108	1.42	25.7	0.085	0	0	104	17.3
Sugar Smacks	1 cup	37.9	141	2.65	33	0.72	0	0	100	56.1
Team	1 cup	42	164	2.69	36	0.756	0	0	259	71
Toasties	1 cup	22.7	87.8	1.84	19.5	0.045	0	0	238	26.3
Total	1 cup	33	116	3.3	26	0.693	0	0.099	409	123
Trix	1 cup	28.4	109	1.53	25.2	0.398	0	0	181	26.7
Wheat Chex	1 cup	46	169	4.55	37.8	1.15	0	—	308	173
Wheat flakes-sugar	1 cup	30	105	3	24	0	0	0	368	81
Wheat germ-sugar	1 cup	113	426	24.6	68.7	9.04	0	1.57	3.39	802
Wheat germ-toasted	1 cup	113	432	32.9	56.1	12.1	0	2.07	4.52	1070
Wheat-puffed-plain	1 cup	12	43.7	1.76	9.55	0.144	0	0	0.48	41.8
Wheat-puffed-sugar	1 srvg	38	138	5.59	30.2	0.456	0	—	1.52	132
Wheat-rolled-cooked	1 cup	240	180	5	41	1	0	0.182	535	202
Wheat-shred-biscuit	1 item	23.6	83	2.6	18.8	0.3	0	0	0.472	77
Wheat-whole meal	1 cup	245	110	4	23	1	0	0.182	535	118
Wheatena-cooked	1 cup	243	136	4.86	28.7	1.22	0	—	4.86	187
Wheaties	1 cup	29	101	2.8	23.1	0.5	0	0.07	276	108
Whole Wheat Natural	1 cup	242	150	4.84	33.2	0.968	0	—	1	171
Combination Foods										
Beans/pork/frankfurter-can	1 cup	257	365	17.3	39.6	16.9	15.4	6.05	1105	604
Beans/pork/sweet sauce-can	1 cup	253	281	13.4	53.1	3.69	17.7	1.42	850	673
Beans/pork/tom sauce-can	1 cup	253	248	13.1	49.1	2.61	17	0.999	1113	759
Beef and vegetable stew	1 cup	245	220	16	15	11	72	4.9	1006	613
Beef potpie-home recipe	1 slice	210	515	21	39	30	44	7.9	596	334
Beef-Raviolios-canned	1 oz	28.4	27.5	1.14	4.26	0.568	—	0.11	131	45.7
Chicken a la king-home rec	1 cup	245	470	27	12	34	186	12.9	759	404
Chicken Chow Mein-canned	1 cup	250	95	7	18	0	98	0	722	418
Chicken potpie-baked-home	1 slice	232	545	23	42	31	72	11	593	343
Chili con carne/beans-can	1 cup	255	340	19	31	16	38	7.5	1354	594
Chili with beans-canned	1 cup	255	286	14.6	30.4	14	43.4	6	1331	931
Macaroni and cheese-enr-can	1 cup	240	230	9	26	10	42	4.2	729	139
Macaroni and cheese-enr-home	1 cup	200	430	17	40	22	42	8.9	1086	240

Nutritive Components—cont'd

Mag (mg)	Iron (mg)	Zinc (mg)	V-A (IU)	V-E (mg)	V-C (mg)	Thia (mg)	Ribo (mg)	Niac (mg)	V-B$_6$ (mg)	Fol (μg)	V-B$_{12}$ (μg)	Calc (mg)	Phos (mg)	Sel (mg)	Fibd (g)
Breakfast Cereals—cont'd															
109	2.12	1.78	0	—	0	0.241	0.12	3.08	0.113	24.1	0	28.9	215	—	2.31
11.7	3.39	2.81	280	—	11.3	0.277	0.32	3.75	0.383	75.2	0.011	6.18	41.3	0.013	0.17
1.99	1.79	1.51	375	—	15.1	0.369	0.426	5	0.511	100	0	1.14	28.1	—	0.2
18.2	2.39	0.379	500	—	20.1	0.493	0.569	6.67	0.682	134	0	4.17	41.3	—	0.531
18.5	2.57	0.584	556	—	22.3	0.546	0.63	7.39	0.756	6.72	2.23	6.3	65.1	0.007	0.7
3.41	0.597	0.066	300	—	—	0.295	0.341	4	0.409	80.1	1.2	0.908	10	—	0.386
37	21	0.78	1748	—	70	1.75	1.98	23.3	2.34	466	7	282	137	—	2.4
6.25	4.52	0.13	371	—	15.1	0.369	0.426	5	0.511	2.56	1.51	5.68	19	—	0.32
58.4	7.31	1.23	—	0.971	24.4	0.598	0.166	8.1	0.828	162	2.44	17.9	182	—	3.4
32.7	4.8	0.669	330	0.633	16	0.4	0.45	5.3	0.54	9	1.59	12	83	0.003	2.7
271	7.71	14.1	0	—	—	1.41	0.7	4.73	0.829	298	0	37.3	971	—	5.7
362	10.3	18.8	50	31.1	7	1.89	0.93	6.31	1.11	398	0	50.9	1295	—	14.6
17.4	0.568	0.283	0	—	0	0.024	0.028	1.3	0.02	3.84	0	3.36	42.6	—	0.4
55.1	1.8	0.897	0	—	0	0.076	0.087	4.1	0.065	12.2	0	10.6	135	—	2.11
52.8	1.7	1.15	0	9.72	0	0.17	0.07	2.2	—	26.4	—	19	182	—	2.87
40.1	0.74	0.59	0	0.508	0	0.07	0.06	1.08	0.06	12	0	9.68	86	—	2.2
53.9	1.2	1.18	0	9.92	0	0.15	0.05	1.5	—	27	—	17	127	—	1.61
48.6	1.36	1.68	0	—	0	0.024	0.049	1.34	0.046	17	0	9.72	146	0.058	2.6
31.6	4.61	0.65	384	0.612	15.4	0.377	0.435	5.1	0.522	102	1.54	43.8	100	0.003	2
54	1.5	1.16	0	9.8	0	0.17	0.12	2.15	0.177	26.6	0	16.9	167	0.058	2.7
Combination Foods															
72	4.45	4.81	38.6	2.75	5.91	0.149	0.144	2.32	0.118	77.1	0	123	267	—	12.8
86	4.2	3.8	27.8	2.75	7.59	0.119	0.154	0.888	0.215	94.6	0	154	266	—	14
88	8.3	14.8	62	2.75	7.8	0.132	0.116	1.26	0.175	56.9	0	141	297	—	13.8
—	2.9	—	480	1.35	17	0.15	0.17	4.7	—	—	0.002	29	184	—	3.19
—	3.8	—	344	—	6	0.3	0.3	5.5	—	—	—	29	149	—	3.9
—	0.312	—	50	0.136	0.426	0.026	0.023	0.398	—	—	—	4.54	—	—	0.23
—	2.5	—	226	—	12	0.1	0.42	5.4	—	—	—	127	358	—	1.2
—	1.3	—	30	0.125	13	0.05	0.1	1	—	—	—	45	85	—	0.9
—	3	—	618	—	5	0.34	0.31	5.5	—	—	—	70	232	0.032	4.2
—	4.3	—	30	—	—	0.08	0.18	3.3	0.263	—	—	82	321	—	5
115	8.75	5.1	86.7	—	4.34	0.122	0.268	0.913	0.337	57.9	0.03	120	393	—	6.93
—	1	—	52	—	0	0.12	0.24	1	—	—	—	199	182	—	1.44
52	1.8	—	172	—	0	0.2	0.4	1.8	—	—	—	362	322	0.028	1.2

Nutritive Components—cont'd

Food Name	Serving	Gram wt	Kcal	Prot (g)	Carb (g)	Fat (g)	Chol (mg)	Safa (g)	Sod (mg)	Pot (mg)
Combination Foods—cont'd										
Meat loaf-celery/onions	1 srvg	87.6	213	15.8	5.23	13.9	107	5.29	103	182
Pizza-cheese-baked	1 slice	63	140	7.68	20.5	3.21	9	1.54	336	110
Pizza-pepperoni-baked	1 slice	71	181	10.1	19.9	6.96	14	2.24	267	153
Salad-carrot raisin-home	1 cup	268	306	3.8	55.8	11.6	—	—	—	—
Salad-chef salad-ham/cheese	1 srvg	200	196	13.4	7.42	12.7	46	6.98	567	415
Salad-chicken	1 cup	205	502	26	17.4	36.2	—	—	1395	521
Salad-coleslaw	1 tbsp	8	5.52	0.103	0.993	0.209	1	0.031	1.84	14.5
Salad-fruit-can/juice	1 cup	249	125	1.27	32.5	0.075	0	0.01	12.5	289
Salad-green salad-tossed	1 srvg	207	32	2.6	6.67	0.16	0	0.021	53	356
Salad-macaroni	1 srvg	28.4	50.7	0.7	5.3	3	—	—	148	21
Salad-mandarin orange gel	1 srvg	28.4	22.7	0.4	5.7	0	0	0	14	9
Salad-potato	1 cup	250	358	6.7	27.9	20.5	170	3.57	1323	635
Salad-three bean-Del Monte	1 oz	28.4	22.4	0.71	5.06	0.056	0	0	101	38.3
Salad-tuna	1 cup	205	350	30	7	22	68	4.3	434	—
Sand-bac/let/tom/mayo	1 item	148	282	6.8	28.8	15.6	—	—	—	—
Sandwich-club	1 item	315	590	35.6	41.7	20.8	—	—	—	—
Spaghetti/tom/che-can	1 cup	250	190	6	39	2	4	0.5	955	303
Spaghetti/tom/che-home rec	1 cup	250	260	9	37	9	4	2	955	408
Spaghetti/tom/meat-can	1 cup	250	260	12	29	10	39	2.2	1220	245
Spaghetti/tom/meat-home	1 cup	248	330	19	39	12	75	3.3	1009	665
Taco	1 item	171	370	20.7	26.7	20.6	57	11.4	802	473
Vegetables-mixed-froz-boil	1 cup	182	107	5.21	23.8	0.273	0	0.056	63.7	308
Dairy Products										
Cheese-American-processed	1 piece	28.0	106.0	6.280	0.450	8.860	27.00	5.580	406.0	46.00
Cheese-cheddar-shredded	1 cup	113.0	455.0	28.10	1.450	37.50	119.0	23.80	701.0	111.0
Cheese-cottage-4% lar curd	1 cup	225.0	232.0	28.10	6.030	10.10	33.80	6.410	911.0	189.0
Cheese-cream	1 srvg	28.0	99.00	2.140	0.750	9.890	31.00	6.230	84.00	34.00
Cheese-Swiss	1 piece	28.0	107.0	8.060	0.960	7.780	26.00	5.040	74.00	31.00
Cheese food-American-proc	1 srvg	28.0	93.00	5.560	2.070	6.970	18.00	4.380	337.0	79.00
Cream-Half & Half-fluid	1 cup	242.0	315.0	7.160	10.40	27.80	89.00	17.30	98.00	314.0

Nutritive Components—cont'd

Mag (mg)	Iron (mg)	Zinc (mg)	V-A (IU)	V-E (mg)	V-C (mg)	Thia (mg)	Ribo (mg)	Niac (mg)	V-B$_6$ (mg)	Fol (µg)	V-B$_{12}$ (µg)	Calc (mg)	Phos (mg)	Sel (mg)	Fibd (g)
Combination Foods—cont'd															
13.6	1.91	3.08	12.3	0.068	0.725	0.052	0.148	3.16	0.162	10.9	1.52	22.8	112	0.001	0.11
16	0.58	0.82	74	—	1.3	0.18	0.16	2.48	0.04	59	0.33	116	113	—	1.59
8	0.94	0.52	54	—	1.7	0.14	0.23	3.05	0.05	53	0.19	65	75	—	1.48
—	3	—	1100	—	12	0.16	0.16	1	—	—	—	96	130	—	16.7
28.4	1.17	1.73	740	0.995	24	0.337	0.24	2.21	0.206	46	0.474	227	251	0.019	2.39
—	—	—	—	—	—	—	—	—	—	—	—	—	—	—	—
0.8	0.047	0.016	6.56	—	2.62	0.005	0.005	0.022	0.01	2.12	0	3.6	2.56	—	0.297
21	0.62	0.349	149	—	8.22	0.027	0.035	0.886	0.067	6.47	0	27.4	34.9	0.001	1.64
22	1.3	0.43	235	—	48	0.06	0.1	1.15	0.16	77	0	26	80	0.001	2.11
—	—	—	—	—	—	—	—	—	—	—	—	—	—	—	0.29
—	—	—	—	—	—	—	—	—	—	—	—	—	—	—	0.57
37.5	1.63	0.775	82.5	—	25	0.193	0.15	2.23	0.353	16.8	0.385	47.5	130	—	5.25
6.25	0.284	0.093	8	—	0.852	0.014	0.014	0.085	—	—	—	9.66	16.2	—	1.52
—	2.7	—	118	3.05	2	0.08	0.23	10.3	—	—	—	41	291	—	1.03
—	1.5	—	174	—	13	0.16	0.14	1.6	—	—	—	53	89	—	2.88
—	4.3	—	350	—	27	0.38	0.41	10.2	—	—	—	103	394	—	4.17
28	2.8	—	186	—	10	0.35	0.28	4.5	—	—	—	40	88	0.025	2.5
—	2.3	—	216	—	13	0.25	0.18	2.3	—	—	—	80	135	—	2.5
28	3.3	—	200	—	5	0.15	0.18	2.3	—	—	—	53	113	—	2.75
—	3.7	—	—	—	22	0.25	0.3	4	—	—	—	124	236	0.022	2.73
71	2.42	3.93	147	—	2.2	0.15	0.45	3.22	0.24	23	1.04	221	203	—	2.67
40	1.49	0.892	778	—	5.82	0.129	0.218	1.55	0.135	34.6	0	45.5	92.8	0.001	6.92
Dairy Products															
6.000	0.110	0.850	343.0	0.280	0.000	0.008	0.100	0.020	0.020	2.000	0.197	174.0	211.0	0.003	0.000
31.00	0.770	3.510	1197	—	0.000	0.031	0.424	0.090	0.084	21.00	0.935	815.0	579.0	0.018	0.000
11.30	0.315	0.833	367.0	—	0.000	0.047	0.367	0.284	0.151	27.00	1.400	135.0	297.0	0.052	0.000
2.000	0.340	0.150	405.0	—	0.000	0.005	0.056	0.029	0.013	4.000	0.120	23.00	30.00	0.001	0.000
10.10	0.050	1.110	240.0	0.200	0.000	0.006	0.103	0.026	0.024	2.000	0.475	272.0	171.0	0.003	0.000
9.000	0.240	0.850	259.0	—	0.000	0.008	0.125	0.040	—	—	0.317	163.0	130.0	0.006	0.000
25.00	0.170	1.230	1050	1.520	2.080	0.085	0.361	0.189	0.094	6.000	0.796	254.0	230.0	0.001	0.000

Nutritive Components—cont'd

Food Name	Serving	Gram wt	Kcal	Prot (g)	Carb (g)	Fat (g)	Chol (mg)	Safa (g)	Sod (mg)	Pot (mg)
Dairy Products—cont'd										
Cream-sour-cultured	1 cup	230.0	493.0	7.270	9.820	48.20	102.0	30.00	123.0	331.0
Cream-whip-imit-froz	1 cup	75.0	239.0	0.940	17.30	19.00	0.000	16.30	19.00	14.00
Milk-chocolate-whole	1 cup	250.0	208.0	7.920	25.90	8.480	30.00	5.260	149.0	417.0
Milk-human-whole-mature	1 cup	246.0	171.0	2.530	17.00	10.80	34.00	4.940	42.00	126.0
Milk-2% fat-lowfat-fluid	1 cup	244.0	121.0	8.120	11.70	4.680	18.00	2.920	122.0	377.0
Milk-nonfat-instant-dried	1 cup	68.0	244.0	23.90	33.50	0.490	12.00	0.320	373.0	1160
Milk-nonfat-skim	1 cup	245	86	8.35	11.9	0.44	4	0.287	126	406
Milkshake-chocolate-thick	1 item	300.0	356.0	9.150	63.50	8.100	32.00	5.040	333.0	672.0
Yogurt-fruit flavor-lowfat	1 cup	227.0	231.0	9.920	43.20	2.450	10.00	1.580	133.0	442.0
Yogurt-plain-lowfat	1 cup	227.0	144.0	11.90	16.00	3.520	14.00	2.270	159.0	531.0
Desserts										
Brownies/nuts-mix/prep	1 item	20.0	85.00	1.000	13.00	4.000	0.000	0.900	50.00	34.00
Cake-yellow/icing-home rec	1 slice	69.0	268.0	2.900	40.30	11.40	36.00	3.000	191.0	72.50
Cookie-choc chip-home rec	1 item	10.0	46.30	0.500	6.410	2.680	5.250	0.600	20.60	20.50
Cookie-oatmeal/raisin/mix	1 item	13.0	61.50	0.732	8.930	2.600	0.000	0.500	37.10	22.60
Doughnuts-yeast-glazed	1 item	50.0	205.0	3.000	22.00	11.20	13.00	3.000	117.0	34.00
Froz yogurt-fruit variety	1 cup	226.0	216.0	7.000	41.80	2.000	—	—	—	—
Granola bar	1 item	24.0	109.0	2.350	16.00	4.230	—	—	66.70	78.20
Ice cream-van-soft serve	1 cup	173.0	377.0	7.040	38.30	22.50	153.0	13.50	153.0	338.0
Ice cream sundae-hot fudge	1 item	165.0	312.0	7.260	46.50	10.90	18.20	—	177.0	413.0
Pie-apple-home rec	1 slice	135.0	323.0	2.750	49.10	13.60	0.000	3.900	207.0	115.0
Pudd-choc-cooked-mix/milk	1 cup	260.0	320.0	9.000	59.00	8.000	32.00	4.300	335.0	354.0
Toaster pastries	1 item	50.0	196.0	1.930	35.20	5.750	0.000	—	230.0	84.50
Twinkie-Hostess	1 item	42.0	143.0	1.250	25.60	4.200	21.00	—	189.0	—
Eggs										
Egg-fried in butter-large	1 item	46.0	83.00	5.370	0.530	6.410	246.0	2.410	144.0	58.00
Egg-hard-large-no shell	1 item	50.0	79.00	6.070	0.600	5.580	274.0	1.670	69.00	65.00
Egg-scrambled-milk/butter	1 item	64.0	95.00	5.960	1.370	7.080	248.0	2.820	155.0	85.00
Egg-substitute-liquid	1 cup	251.0	211.0	30.10	1.610	8.310	3.000	1.660	444.0	828.0

Nutritive Components—cont'd

Mag (mg)	Iron (mg)	Zinc (mg)	V-A (IU)	V-E (mg)	V-C (mg)	Thia (mg)	Ribo (mg)	Niac (mg)	V-B$_6$ (mg)	Fol (µg)	V-B$_{12}$ (µg)	Calc (mg)	Phos (mg)	Sel (mg)	Fibd (g)
Dairy Products—cont'd															
26.00	0.140	0.620	1817	—	1.980	0.081	0.343	0.154	0.037	25.00	0.690	268.0	195.0	—	0.000
1.000	0.090	0.020	646.0	—	0.000	0.000	0.000	0.000	0.000	0.000	0.000	5.000	6.000	—	0.000
33.00	0.600	1.020	302.0	—	2.280	0.092	0.405	0.313	0.100	12.00	0.835	280.0	251.0	0.003	0.300
8.000	0.070	0.420	593.0	2.440	12.30	0.034	0.089	0.435	0.027	13.00	0.111	79.00	34.00	0.004	0.000
33.00	0.120	0.950	500.0	0.220	2.320	0.095	0.403	0.210	0.105	12.00	0.888	297.0	232.0	0.003	0.000
80.00	0.210	3.000	1612	—	3.790	0.281	1.190	0.606	0.235	34.00	2.720	837.0	670.0	—	0.000
8	0.07	0.42	178	2.16	12.3	0.034	0.089	0.435	0.027	13	0.111	79	34	0.004	0
48.00	0.930	1.440	258.0	—	0.000	0.141	0.666	0.372	0.075	15.00	0.945	306.0	378.0	0.005	0.900
33.00	0.160	1.680	104.0	—	1.500	0.084	0.404	0.216	0.091	21.00	1.060	345.0	271.0	—	0.800
40.00	0.180	2.020	150.0	—	1.820	0.100	0.486	0.259	0.111	25.00	1.280	415.0	326.0	—	0.000
Desserts															
—	0.400	—	20.00	1.090	0.000	0.030	0.020	0.200	—	—	—	9.000	27.00	0.001	—
13.10	0.787	0.338	47.60	5.860	0.000	0.076	0.097	0.656	0.023	5.520	0.123	57.30	60.70	0.004	—
3.500	0.249	0.044	4.300	0.545	0.000	0.015	0.015	0.146	0.002	0.900	0.010	3.300	8.400	0.001	0.080
3.640	0.285	0.085	10.40	0.708	0.000	0.022	0.021	0.241	0.006	1.560	—	4.420	14.40	0.001	—
9.500	0.600	—	25.00	2.030	0.000	0.100	0.100	0.800	—	11.00	—	16.00	33.00	—	0.300
24.00	0.000	—	0.000	—	0.000	0.010	0.260	0.000	—	—	—	200.0	200.0	—	—
—	0.763	—	—	—	—	0.067	0.026	—	—	—	0.000	14.40	66.50	—	—
25.00	0.430	1.990	794.0	0.606	0.920	0.080	0.448	0.178	0.095	9.000	0.996	236.0	199.0	0.003	0.000
34.70	0.611	0.990	231.0	0.577	3.300	0.066	0.314	1.120	0.132	9.900	0.660	216.0	238.0	—	—
10.80	1.220	0.230	25.70	9.840	2.000	0.149	0.108	1.240	0.035	6.750	0.000	12.20	31.10	0.015	—
—	0.800	—	340.0	—	2.000	0.050	0.390	0.300	—	—	—	265.0	247.0	—	0.000
9.000	2.000	0.290	482.0	—	0.000	0.160	0.170	2.100	0.190	40.00	0.000	96.50	96.50	—	—
—	0.545	—	40.50	—	0.000	0.055	0.060	0.500	—	—	—	19.00	—	—	—
Eggs															
5.000	0.920	0.640	286.0	—	0.000	0.033	0.126	0.026	0.050	22.00	0.581	26.00	80.00	—	0.000
6.000	1.040	0.720	260.0	—	0.000	0.037	0.143	0.030	0.057	24.00	0.657	28.00	90.00	—	0.000
8.000	0.930	0.700	311.0	—	0.130	0.039	0.156	0.042	0.058	22.00	0.638	47.00	97.00	—	0.000
—	5.270	3.260	5422	—	0.000	0.276	0.753	0.276	—	—	0.748	133.0	304.0	—	0.000

Nutritive Components—cont'd

Food Name	Serving	Gram wt	Kcal	Prot (g)	Carb (g)	Fat (g)	Chol (mg)	Safa (g)	Sod (mg)	Pot (mg)
Fast Foods										
Arthur Treacher-chick sand	1 item	156	413	16.2	44	19.2	—	—	708	279
Burger King-Whop hamburger	1 item	261	630	26	50	36	104	16.5	990	520
Churchs Chick-white meat	1 item	100	327	21	10	23	—	—	498	186
Dairy Queen-banana split	1 item	383	540	10	91	15	30	—	—	—
Dairy Queen-cone-regular	1 item	142	226	5.37	33.2	8.43	38.3	4.87	126	233
Dairy Queen-dip cone-reg	1 item	156	300	7	40	13	20	—	—	—
Dairy Queen-float	1 item	397	330	6	59	8	20	—	—	—
Dairy Queen-malt-regular	1 item	418	600	15	89	20	50	—	—	—
Dairy Queen-sundae-regular	1 item	177	319	6.31	53.4	9.66	23	5.63	204	443
Jack/Box-Break Jack Sand	1 item	121	301	18	28	13	182	—	1037	190
Jack/Box-Jumbo Jack Hambur	1 item	246	551	28	45	29	80	11.4	1134	492
Jack/Box-Jumbo Jack/cheese	1 item	272	628	32	45	35	110	15	1666	449
Jack/Box-Moby Jack	1 item	141	455	17	38	26	56	—	837	246
Jack/Box-onion rings-bag	1 item	83	275	3.7	31.3	15.5	14	6.95	430	129
McDonalds-Big Mac hamburger	1 item	215	560	25.2	42.5	32.4	103	10.1	950	237
McDonalds-QP Hamburger with cheese	1 item	194	520	28.5	35.1	29.2	118	11.2	1150	341
McDonalds-Cheeseburger	1 item	116	310	15	31.2	13.8	53	5.17	750	223
McDonalds-Egg McMuffin	1 item	138	290	18.2	28.1	11.2	226	3.82	740	213
McDonalds-Filet O Fish	1 item	142	440	13.8	37.9	26.1	50	5.16	1030	150
McDonalds-Hamburger	1 item	102	260	12.3	30.6	9.5	37	3.63	500	215
McDonalds-QP Hamburger	1 item	166	410	23.1	34	20.7	86	8.09	660	322
Taco Bell-Bean Burrito	1 item	168	332	16.7	42.6	11.5	79	5.6	1030	405
Taco Bell-Beef Burrito	1 item	110	262	13.3	29.3	10.4	32.5	5.23	746	370
Taco Bell-Beefy Tostada	1 item	225	334	16.1	29.7	16.9	75	11.5	870	490
Taco Bell-Burrito Supreme	1 item	225	457	21	43	22	126	7.7	367	350

Nutritive Components—cont'd

Mag (mg)	Iron (mg)	Zinc (mg)	V-A (IU)	V-E (mg)	V-C (mg)	Thia (mg)	Ribo (mg)	Niac (mg)	V-B$_6$ (mg)	Fol (μg)	V-B$_{12}$ (μg)	Calc (mg)	Phos (mg)	Sel (mg)	Fibd (g)
Fast Foods															
27	1.7	—	36.9	—	19	0.17	0.24	8.1	—	—	—	59	147	—	—
50	6	5.25	192	—	13	0.02	0.03	5.2	0.312	31.2	2.81	104	312	—	—
—	1		48	—	1	0.1	0.18	7.2	—	—	—	94	—	—	—
—	1.8	—	225	—	18	0.6	0.6	0.8	—	—	0.9	350	250	—	—
21.3	0.213	0.781	87.4	—	1.56	0.071	0.355	0.426	0.085	7.1	0.284	212	192	—	—
—	0.4	—	90.1	—	0	0.09	0.34	0	—	—	0.6	200	150	—	—
—	0	—	30	—	0	0.12	0.17	0	—	—	0.6	200	200	—	—
—	3.6	—	225	—	3.6	0.12	0.6	0.8	—	—	1.0	500	400	—	—
37.2	0.655	1.06	74.5	—	2.66	0.071	0.336	1.2	0.142	10.6	0.726	232	255	—	—
24	2.5	1.8	133	—	3	0.41	0.47	5.1	0.14	—	1.1	177	310	—	—
44	4.5	4.2	73.9	—	3.7	0.47	0.34	11.6	0.3	—	2.68	134	261	—	—
49	4.6	4.8	220	—	4.9	0.52	0.38	11.3	0.31	—	3.05	273	411	—	—
30	1.7	1.1	72.1	—	1	0.3	0.21	4.5	0.12	—	1.1	167	263	—	—
15	0.85	0.35	2.4	5.36	0.6	0.09	0.1	0.92	0.06	11	0.12	73	86	—	—
38	4	4.7	106	—	1.68	0.48	0.41	6.81	0.27	21	1.8	256	314	—	—
41	3.72	5.7	211	—	3.24	0.37	0.39	6.73	0.23	23	2.15	295	382	—	—
21	2.3	2.09	118	—	2.15	0.29	0.21	3.86	0.12	18	0.94	199	177	—	—
33	2.77	1.8	150	—	1.38	0.47	0.33	3.71	0.16	44	0.8	256	319	—	—
27	1.83	0.9	43.8	—	0.06	0.3	0.15	2.68	0.1	20	0.82	165	229	—	1.11
23	2.29	2.05	45.6	—	2.15	0.28	0.16	3.84	0.12	17	0.84	122	110	—	—
37	3.68	5.1	67	—	3.24	0.36	0.29	6.7	0.27	23	1.88	142	249	—	—
0.407	3.84	3.04	240	—	3.3	0.275	0.6	3.86	0.205	73	0.995	144	143	—	—
40.5	3.05	2.37	41.7	—	0.55	0.115	0.46	3.23	0.16	19.5	0.985	42	87.5	—	—
68	2.45	3.18	383	—	3.9	0.09	0.5	2.85	0.26	0.26	1.13	190	173	—	—
51.8	3.8	5.85	216	—	8	0.45	0.923	6.17	0.27	42.8	1.53	146	245	—	—

Nutritive Components—cont'd

Food Name	Serving	Gram wt	Kcal	Prot (g)	Carb (g)	Fat (g)	Chol (mg)	Safa (g)	Sod (mg)	Pot (mg)
Fast Foods—cont'd										
Taco Bell-Taco-regular	1 item	171	370	20.7	26.7	20.6	57	11.4	802	473
Taco Bell-Tostada-regular	1 item	144	223	9.6	26.5	9.86	30	5.37	543	403
Wendys-Double Hamburger	1 item	226	540	34.3	40.3	26.6	122	10.5	791	569
Wendys-Single Hamburger	1 item	218	511	25.7	40.1	27.4	86	10.4	825	479
Wendys-Triple Hamburger	1 item	259	693	50	28.6	41.5	142	15.9	713	785
Fats and Oils										
Butter-regular	1 tbsp	14.0	100.0	0.119	0.008	11.40	30.70	7.070	116.0	3.640
Margarine-diet-Mazola	1 tbsp	14.0	50.00	0.000	0.000	5.700	0.000	1.000	130.0	—
Margarine-corn-reg-soft	1 tsp	4.7	33.70	0.000	0.000	3.800	0.000	0.700	50.70	1.770
Margarine-reg-hard-stick	1 item	113.0	815.0	1.000	1.000	91.30	0.000	17.90	1070	48.10
Mayonnaise-light-low cal	1 tbsp	14.0	40.00	0.000	1.000	4.000	5.000	—	—	—
Sal dress-blue cheese	1 tbsp	15.3	77.10	0.700	1.100	8.000	9.000	1.500	167.0	6.120
Sal dress-French	1 tbsp	15.6	67.00	0.100	2.700	6.400	1.950	1.500	214.0	12.30
Sal dress-Italian	1 tbsp	14.7	68.70	0.000	1.500	7.100	0.000	1.000	116.0	2.000
Sal dress-Italian-low cal	1 tbsp	15.0	15.80	0.000	0.700	1.500	1.000	0.200	118.0	2.000
Sal dress-mayonnaise	1 tbsp	14.7	57.30	0.000	3.500	4.900	4.000	0.700	104.0	1.000
Sal dress-ranch	1 tbsp	15.0	54.00	0.400	0.600	5.700	—	—	97.00	—
Sal dress-Thousand Island	1 tbsp	15.6	58.90	0.000	2.400	5.600	4.900	0.900	109.0	18.00
Shortening-vegetable-soy	1 cup	205.0	1812	0.000	0.000	205.0	0.000	51.20	—	—
Vegetable oil-Corn	1 cup	218.0	1927	0.000	0.000	218.0	0.000	27.70	0.000	0.000
Fish										
Clams-breaded-fried	1 srvg	85.0	171.0	12.10	8.780	9.480	52.00	2.280	309.0	277.0
Cod-cooked-dry heat	1 piece	180.0	189.0	41.10	0.000	1.550	99.00	0.302	141.0	440.0
Crab-steamed-pieces	1 cup	155.0	150.0	30.00	0.000	2.390	82.20	0.206	1662	406.0
Stick-bread-froz-cook	1 item	28.0	76.00	4.380	6.650	3.420	31.00	0.882	163.0	73.00
Lobster-ckd-moist	1 cup	145.0	142.0	29.70	1.860	0.860	104.0	1.155	551.0	510.0
Oysters-raw-meat only	1 cup	248.0	170.0	17.50	9.700	6.140	136.0	1.570	277.0	568.0
Scallops-steamed	1 srvg	28.4	31.80	6.590	0.511	0.398	15.10	—	75.20	135.0
Shrimp-ckd-moist heat	1 srvg	85.0	84.00	17.80	0.000	0.920	166.0	0.246	190.0	154.0

Nutritive Components—cont'd

Mag (mg)	Iron (mg)	Zinc (mg)	V-A (IU)	V-E (mg)	V-C (mg)	Thia (mg)	Ribo (mg)	Niac (mg)	V-B$_6$ (mg)	Fol (µg)	V-B$_{12}$ (µg)	Calc (mg)	Phos (mg)	Sel (mg)	Fibd (g)
Fast Foods—cont'd															
71	2.42	3.93	257	—	2.2	0.15	0.45	3.22	0.24	23	1.04	221	203	—	—
59	1.88	1.9	187	—	1.3	0.1	0.33	1.33	0.17	75	0.68	211	116	—	—
49	5.95	5.68	30.6	—	1.2	0.36	0.39	7.57	0.54	27	4.07	102	314	—	—
43	4.92	4.87	93.4	—	2.5	0.42	0.38	7.28	0.33	36	2.38	96	233	—	—
55	8.33	10.8	47.4	—	1.4	0.31	0.56	11	0.62	31	4.92	65	393	—	—
Fats and Oils															
0.280	0.022	0.007	428.0	0.221	0.000	0.001	0.005	0.006	0.000	0.420	—	3.360	3.220	—	0.000
—	0.000	—	500.0	1.350	0.000	0.000	0.000	0.000		—	—	0.000	—	—	0.000
0.110	—	—	155.0	2.000	0.007	0.000	0.002	0.001	0.000	0.050	0.004	1.250	0.950	—	0.000
2.950	0.070	—	3750	65.10	0.181	0.011	0.042	0.026	0.010	1.340	0.108	33.90	26.00	—	0.000
—	—	—	—	8.120	—	—	—	—	—	—	—	—	—	—	9,999
—	0.000	—	32.10	7.260	0.300	0.000	0.020	0.000	—	—	—	12.40	11.30	—	0.050
—	0.100	0.010	—	7.410	—	—	—	—	—	—	—	1.700	2.200	—	0.000
—	0.000	0.020	—	6.990	—	0.000	0.000	0.000	—	—	—	1.000	1.000	—	0.050
—	0.000	—	—	7.130	—	0.000	0.000	0.000	—	—	—	0.000	1.000	—	0.090
0.290	0.000	—	32.00	4.400	—	0.000	0.000	0.000	—	—	—	2.000	4.000	—	0.000
—	—	—	—	4.500	—	—	—	—	—	—	—	—	—	—	0.000
—	0.100	0.020	50.00	7.450	0.000	0.000	0.000	0.000	—	—	—	2.000	3.000	—	0.600
—	—	—	—	197.0	—	—	—	—	—	—	—	—	—	—	0.000
0.000	0.000	0.000	—	181.0	0.000	0.000	0.000	0.000	0.000	0.000	0.000	0.000	0.000	—	0.000
Fish															
12.00	11.80	1.240	257.0	—	—	—	0.207	1.750	—	—	34.20	54.00	160.0	—	0.320
76.00	0.880	1.040	83.00	—	1.800	0.158	0.142	4.520	0.509	—	1.890	25.00	248.0	—	—
52.70	1.180	11.80	45.00	1.890	—	0.082	0.085	2.080	—	—	—	91.50	434.0	0.076	0.000
7.000	0.210	0.190	30.00	—	—	0.036	0.050	0.596	0.017	5.100	0.503	6.000	51.00	0.003	0.300
51.00	0.570	4.230	126.0	—	—	0.010	0.096	1.550	0.112	16.10	4.510	88.00	268.0	—	0.000
135.0	16.60	226.0	740.0	—	—	0.340	0.412	3.250	0.124	24.60	47.50	111.0	344.0	0.156	0.000
—	0.852	—	—	—	—	—	—	—	—	—	—	32.70	96.00	0.015	0.000
29.00	2.620	1.330	—	—	—	0.026	0.027	2.200	0.108	2.900	1.270	33.00	116.0	—	0.000

Nutritive Components—cont'd

Food Name	Serving	Gram wt	Kcal	Prot (g)	Carb (g)	Fat (g)	Chol (mg)	Safa (g)	Sod (mg)	Pot (mg)
Fish—cont'd										
Shrimp-french fried	1 srvg	85.0	206.0	18.20	9.750	10.40	150.0	1.770	292.0	191.0
Sole/flounder-baked	1 srvg	127.0	148.0	30.70	0.000	1.940	86.00	0.461	133.0	436.0
Trout-rainbow-ckd-dry	1 srvg	85.0	129.0	22.40	0.000	3.660	62.00	0.707	29.00	539.0
Tuna-can/oil-drained	1 srvg	85.0	169.0	24.80	0.000	6.980	15.00	1.300	301.0	176.0
Frozen Dinners										
Beef dinner-Swanson	1 item	326.0	320.0	25.00	34.00	9.000	—	—	1085	—
Che Cannelloni-Lean Cuisine	1 item	259.0	270.0	22.00	24.00	10.00	45.00	—	900.0	270.0
Fettucini alfredo-Stouffer	1 item	142.0	270.0	8.000	19.00	18.00	—	—	1195	240.0
Fish divan-Lean Cuisine	1 item	351.0	270.0	31.00	16.00	10.00	85.00	—	780.0	850.0
Salisbury steak din-Banq	1 item	312.0	390.0	18.10	24.00	24.60	—	—	2059	387.0
Lasagna-Stouffer	1 item	298.0	385.0	28.00	36.00	14.00	—	—	1200	580.0
Chicken Kiev-Le Menu	1 item	234.0	500.0	21.00	35.00	30.00	—	—	745.0	—
Veal parmigiana-froz din	1 item	213.0	296.0	24.00	17.00	14.00	—	—	973.0	466.0
Fruits										
Apples-raw-unpeeled	1 item	138.0	81.00	0.270	21.10	0.490	0.000	0.080	1.000	159.0
Apple juice-canned/bottled	1 cup	248.0	116.0	0.150	29.00	0.280	0.000	0.047	7.000	296.0
Applesauce-can-sweetened	1 cup	255.0	194.0	0.470	50.80	0.470	0.000	0.077	8.000	156.0
Apricot-raw-without pit	1 item	35.3	16.90	0.494	3.930	0.138	0.000	0.010	0.353	104.0
Avocado-raw-California	1 item	173.0	306.0	3.640	12.00	30.00	0.000	4.480	21.00	1097
Bananas-raw-peeled	1 item	114.0	105.0	1.180	26.70	0.550	0.000	0.211	1.000	451.0
Blueberries-raw	1 cup	145.0	82.00	0.970	20.50	0.550	0.000	0.000	9.000	129.0
Cherries-sweet-raw	1 item	6.8	4.900	0.082	1.130	0.065	0.000	0.015	0.000	15.20
Fruit Roll Up-cherry	1 item	14.4	50.00	0.000	12.00	1.000	—	—	5.000	45.00
Grapefruit-raw-white	1 item	236.0	78.00	1.620	19.80	0.240	0.000	0.034	0.000	350.0
Grapefruit juice-can-sweet	1 cup	250.0	116.0	1.450	27.80	0.230	0.000	0.030	4.000	405.0
Grapes-raw-American type	1 cup	92.0	58.00	0.580	15.80	0.320	0.000	0.027	2.000	176.0
Grape juice-froz-diluted	1 cup	250.0	128.0	0.470	31.90	0.230	0.000	0.073	5.000	53.00

Nutritive Components—cont'd

Mag (mg)	Iron (mg)	Zinc (mg)	V-A (IU)	V-E (mg)	V-C (mg)	Thia (mg)	Ribo (mg)	Niac (mg)	V-B$_6$ (mg)	Fol (µg)	V-B$_{12}$ (µg)	Calc (mg)	Phos (mg)	Sel (mg)	Fibd (g)
Fish—cont'd															
34.00	1.070	1.170	—	—	—	0.110	0.116	2.610	0.083	6.900	1.590	57.00	185.0	0.027	0.480
74.00	0.430	0.800	48.00	—	—	0.102	0.145	2.770	0.305	—	3.190	23.00	368.0	—	0.000
33.00	2.070	1.180	63.00	—	3.100	0.072	0.191	—	—	—	—	73.00	272.0	—	0.000
26.00	1.180	0.770	66.00	—	—	0.032	—	—	0.094	4.500	—	11.00	265.0	—	0.000
Frozen Dinners															
—	—	—	—	—	—	—	—	—	—	—	—	—	—	—	—
—	—	—	—	—	—	—	—	—	—	—	—	—	—	—	—
—	—	—	—	—	—	—	—	—	—	—	—	—	—	—	—
—	—	—	—	—	—	—	—	—	—	—	—	—	—	—	—
—	3.500	—	3956	—	7.000	0.160	0.190	3.600	—	—	—	90.00	206.0	—	—
—	3.150	—	1239	—	0.000	0.210	0.420	4.200	—	—	—	410.0		—	—
—	—	—	—	—	—	—	—	—	—	—	—	—	—	—	—
—	2.300	—	617.0	—	6.400	0.300	0.380	6.800	—	—	—	97.00		—	—
Fruits															
6.000	0.250	0.050	74.00	0.911	7.800	0.023	0.019	0.106	0.066	3.900	0.000	10.00	10.00	0.001	3.200
8.000	0.920	0.070	2.000	—	2.300	0.052	0.042	0.248	0.074	0.200	0.000	16.00	18.00	0.002	0.520
7.000	0.890	0.100	28.00	—	4.400	0.033	0.071	0.479	0.066	1.500	0.000	9.000	17.00	0.001	4.340
2.820	0.191	0.092	922.0	—	3.530	0.011	0.014	0.212	0.019	3.040	0.000	4.940	6.710	—	0.670
70.00	2.040	0.730	1059	—	13.70	0.187	0.211	3.320	0.484	113.0	0.000	19.00	73.00	—	6.130
33.00	0.350	0.190	92.00	0.365	10.30	0.051	0.114	0.616	0.659	21.80	0.000	7.000	22.00	0.001	2.650
7.000	0.240	0.160	145.0	—	18.90	0.070	0.073	0.521	0.052	9.300	0.000	9.000	15.00	0.001	3.920
0.800	0.026	0.004	14.60	—	0.480	0.003	0.004	0.027	0.002	0.286	0.000	1.000	1.300	0.000	0.100
—	—	—	—	—	—	—	—	—	—	—	—	—	—	—	—
22.00	0.070	0.160	24.00	0.614	78.60	0.088	0.048	0.634	0.102	23.60	0.000	28.00	18.00	0.001	2.500
24.00	0.890	0.150	0.000	0.450	67.30	0.100	0.058	0.798	0.050	25.90	0.000	20.00	27.00	0.001	0.000
5.000	0.270	0.040	92.00	—	3.700	0.085	0.052	0.276	0.101	3.600	0.000	13.00	9.000	0.001	1.500
11.00	0.260	0.100	19.00	—	59.70	0.038	0.065	0.310	0.105	3.100	0.000	9.000	11.00	0.001	0.000

Nutritive Components—cont'd

Food Name	Serving	Gram wt	Kcal	Prot (g)	Carb (g)	Fat (g)	Chol (mg)	Safa (g)	Sod (mg)	Pot (mg)
Fruit—cont'd										
Melons-cantaloupe-raw	1 cup	160.0	57.00	1.400	13.40	0.440	0.000	0.000	14.00	494.0
Melons-honeydew-raw	1 cup	170.0	60.00	0.770	15.60	0.170	0.000	0.000	17.00	461.0
Nectarines-raw	1 item	136.0	67.00	1.280	16.00	0.620	0.000	—	0.000	288.0
Oranges-raw-all varieties	1 item	131.0	62.00	1.230	15.40	0.160	0.000	0.020	0.000	237.0
Orange juice-froz-diluted	1 cup	249.0	112.0	1.680	26.80	0.140	0.000	0.017	2.000	474.0
Peaches-raw-whole	1 item	87.0	37.00	0.610	9.650	0.080	0.000	0.009	0.000	171.0
Pears-raw-Bartlett-unpeeled	1 item	166.0	98.00	0.650	25.10	0.660	0.000	0.037	1.000	208.0
Pineapple-raw-diced	1 cup	155.0	77.00	0.600	19.20	0.660	0.000	0.050	1.000	175.0
Raisins-seedless	1 cup	145.0	434.0	4.670	115.0	0.670	0.000	0.218	17.00	1089
Strawberries-raw-whole	1 cup	149.0	45.00	0.910	10.50	0.550	0.000	0.030	2.000	247.0
Watermelon-raw	1 cup	160.0	50.00	0.990	11.50	0.680	0.000	0.000	3.000	186.0
Plums-raw-prune type	1 item	28.0	20.00	0.000	6.000	0.000	0.000	0.000	0.000	48.00
Grains										
Corn chips	1 srvg	28.4	155.0	1.700	16.90	9.140	0.000	1.500	164.0	43.30
Crackers-graham-plain	1 item	7.0	27.50	0.500	5.000	0.500	0.000	0.100	33.00	27.50
Crackers-saltines	1 item	2.8	12.50	0.250	2.000	0.250	0.750	0.100	36.80	3.250
Crackers-Triscuits	1 item	4.5	21.00	0.400	3.100	0.750	—	—	—	—
Croutons-herb sea-soned	1 cup	30.0	100.0	4.290	20.00	0.000	—	0.000	372.0	38.60
Macaroni-cooked-firm-hot	1 cup	130.0	190.0	7.000	39.00	1.000	0.000	—	1.000	103.0
Noodles-egg-enr-cooked	1 cup	160.0	200.0	7.000	37.00	2.000	50.00	—	3.000	70.00
Pancakes-plain-mix	1 item	27.0	58.90	1.850	19.00	2.170	20.00	0.700	160.0	43.20
Popcorn-popped-plain	1 cup	6.0	25.00	1.000	5.000	0.000	0.000	0.000	0.000	—
Pretzel-thin-stick	1 item	0.3	1.190	0.028	0.242	0.011	0.000	—	4.830	0.303
Rice-white-instant-hot	1 cup	165.0	180.0	4.000	40.00	0.000	0.000	0.000	13.00	—
Rice-white-parboil-cooked	1 cup	175.0	185.0	4.000	41.00	0.000	0.000	0.000	4.000	75.00
Spaghetti-cook-tender-hot	1 cup	140.0	155.0	5.000	32.00	1.000	0.000	—	1.000	85.00
Tortilla chips-Doritos	1 srvg	28.4	139.0	2.000	18.60	6.600	0.000	1.430	180.0	51.00
Waffles-frozen	1 item	37.0	103.0	2.150	15.90	3.520	—	—	256.0	77.70

Nutritive Components—cont'd

Mag (mg)	Iron (mg)	Zinc (mg)	V-A (IU)	V-E (mg)	V-C (mg)	Thia (mg)	Ribo (mg)	Niac (mg)	V-B$_6$ (mg)	Fol (µg)	V-B$_{12}$ (µg)	Calc (mg)	Phos (mg)	Sel (mg)	Fibd (g)
Fruits—cont'd															
17.00	0.340	0.250	5158	0.496	67.50	0.058	0.034	0.918	0.184	27.30	0.000	17.00	27.00	0.001	1.400
12.00	0.120	—	68.00	0.527	42.10	0.131	0.031	1.020	0.100	—	0.000	10.00	17.00	0.001	1.530
11.00	0.210	0.120	1001	—	7.300	0.023	0.056	1.350	0.034	5.100	0.000	6.000	22.00	0.001	2.990
13.00	0.130	0.090	269.0	0.314	69.70	0.114	0.052	0.369	0.079	39.70	0.000	52.00	18.00	0.002	2.620
24.00	0.240	0.130	194.0	0.498	96.90	0.197	0.045	0.503	0.110	109.0	0.000	22.00	40.00	0.001	0.700
6.000	0.100	0.120	465.0	—	5.700	0.015	0.036	0.861	0.016	3.000	0.000	5.000	11.00	0.001	2.000
9.000	0.410	0.200	33.00	—	6.600	0.033	0.066	0.166	0.030	12.10	0.000	19.00	18.00	0.001	4.650
21.00	0.570	0.120	35.00	0.155	23.90	0.143	0.056	0.651	0.135	16.40	0.000	11.00	11.00	0.001	2.390
48.00	3.020	0.380	11.00	—	4.800	0.226	0.128	1.190	0.361	4.800	0.000	71.00	140.0	0.001	12.60
16.00	0.570	0.190	41.00	0.387	84.50	0.030	0.098	0.343	0.088	26.40	0.000	21.00	28.00	0.001	3.200
17.00	0.280	0.110	585.0	—	15.40	0.138	0.032	0.320	0.230	3.400	0.000	13.00	14.00	0.001	0.300
1.960	0.100	0.028	80.00	—	1.000	0.010	0.010	0.100	0.023	0.161	0.000	3.000	5.000	0.000	0.588
Grains															
21.90	0.376	0.435	—	—	—	0.048	0.026	0.554	0.054	—	0.000	37.10	54.60	—	1.660
3.570	0.250	0.053	0.000	0.128	0.000	0.010	0.040	0.250	0.006	0.910	0.000	3.000	10.50	0.001	0.200
0.770	0.125	0.017	0.000	0.050	0.000	0.125	0.013	0.100	0.001	0.495	0.000	0.500	2.500	0.004	0.039
—	—	—	—	0.082	—	—	—	—	—	—	—	—	—	0.001	—
11.40	1.540	0.300	0.000	—	—	0.129	0.200	1.720	0.000	0.000	—	—	—	—	—
26.00	1.400	0.700	0.000	0.351	0.000	0.230	0.130	1.800	0.083	15.60	0.000	14.00	85.00	0.032	1.040
43.20	1.400	—	110.0	—	0.000	0.220	0.130	1.900	0.141	19.20	0.000	16.00	94.00	0.094	1.440
51.30	0.265	0.192	38.30	—	0.000	0.038	0.059	0.254	0.057	2.970	0.355	35.60	70.70	0.003	—
—	0.200	0.500	—	—	0.000	—	0.010	0.100	0.012	—	0.000	1.000	17.00	0.001	0.400
0.072	0.006	0.003	0.000	0.002	0.000	0.001	0.001	0.013	0.000	0.048	0.000	0.078	0.273	—	—
13.20	1.300	0.700	0.000	0.644	0.000	0.210	0.000	1.700	0.056	16.50	0.000	5.000	31.00	0.033	1.710
—	1.400	0.700	0.000	0.683	0.000	0.190	0.020	2.100	0.744	19.30	0.000	33.00	100.0	0.035	1.820
23.80	1.300	0.700	0.000	1.680	0.000	0.200	0.110	1.500	0.090	16.80	0.000	11.00	70.00	0.085	0.980
21.00	0.500	0.240	52.00	—	0.000	0.030	0.030	0.040	0.100	4.000	—	30.00	59.00	—	1.850
7.770	1.800	0.303	474.0	—	0.000	0.167	0.200	1.930	0.098	0.740	—	30.00	141.0	—	—

Nutritive Components—cont'd

Food Name	Serving	Gram wt	Kcal	Prot (g)	Carb (g)	Fat (g)	Chol (mg)	Safa (g)	Sod (mg)	Pot (mg)
Meats										
Bacon-pork-broiled/fried	1 slice	6.3	36.30	1.930	0.036	3.120	5.330	1.100	101.0	30.70
Beef-liver-fried/marg	1 slice	85.0	184.0	22.70	6.680	6.800	410.0	2.400	90.00	309.0
Bologna-pork	1 slice	23.0	57.00	3.520	0.170	4.570	14.00	1.580	272.0	65.00
Frankfurter-hot dog-no bun	1 item	57.0	183.0	6.430	1.460	16.60	29.00	6.130	639.0	95.00
Ham-reg-roasted-pork	1 cup	140.0	249.0	31.70	0.000	12.60	83.00	4.360	2100	573.0
Hamburger-ground-reg-fried	1 srvg	85.0	260.0	20.30	0.000	19.20	75.00	7.530	71.00	255.0
Hamb patty-beef-21% fat	1 item	85.0	231.0	21.00	0.000	15.70	74.00	6.160	65.00	256.0
Italian sausage-pork-link	1 item	67.0	217.0	13.40	1.010	17.20	52.00	6.050	618.0	204.0
Pork-chop-lean/fat-broiled	1 item	82.0	284.0	19.30	0.000	22.30	77.00	8.060	54.00	287.0
Pot roast-arm-beef-cooked	1 slice	100.0	231.0	33.00	0.000	9.980	101.0	3.790	66.00	289.0
Roast beef-rib-lean/fat	1 slice	85.0	308.0	18.30	0.000	25.50	73.00	10.80	52.00	257.0
Salami-cooked-beef	1 slice	23.0	58.00	3.380	0.570	4.620	14.00	1.940	266.0	52.00
Sausage-link-pork-cooked	1 item	13.0	48.00	2.550	0.130	4.050	11.00	1.400	168.0	47.00
Spareribs-pork-braised	1 srvg	28.4	113.0	8.230	0.000	8.580	34.30	3.330	26.30	90.70
Steak-round-lean/fat	1 srvg	85.0	179.0	26.20	0.000	7.490	72.00	2.800	51.00	365.0
Steak-sirloin-lean/fat	1 item	85.0	271.0	22.70	0.000	19.40	77.00	8.070	52.00	297.0
Veal-rib-roasted-no bone	1 srvg	85.0	230.0	23.00	0.000	14.00	87.00	6.100	68.00	259.0
Miscellaneous										
Baking powder-home use	1 tsp	3.0	5.000	0.000	1.000	0.000	0.000	0.000	339.0	5.000
Baking soda	1 tsp	3.0	0.000	0.000	0.000	0.000	0.000	0.000	821.0	—
Chewing gum-Wrigleys	1 item	3.0	10.00	0.000	2.300	—	0.000	—	0.000	0.000
Gelatin dessert-prep	1 cup	240.0	140.0	4.000	34.00	0.000	0.000	0.000	0.000	—
Olives-green-pickled-can	1 item	4.0	3.750	0.100	0.100	0.500	0.000	0.050	80.80	1.750
Pickle-dill-cucumber-med	1 item	65.0	5.000	0.000	1.000	0.000	0.000	0.000	928.0	130.0
Vinegar-cider	1 tbsp	15.0	0.000	0.000	1.000	0.000	0.000	0.000	0.125	15.00

Nutritive Components—cont'd

Mag (mg)	Iron (mg)	Zinc (mg)	V-A (IU)	V-E (mg)	V-C (mg)	Thia (mg)	Ribo (mg)	Niac (mg)	V-B$_6$ (mg)	Fol (μg)	V-B$_{12}$ (μg)	Calc (mg)	Phos (mg)	Sel (mg)	Fibd (g)
Meats															
1.670	0.103	0.206	0.000	0.037	2.130	0.044	0.018	0.464	0.017	0.333	0.110	0.667	21.30	0.002	0.000
20.00	5.340	4.630	30690	1.380	19.40	0.179	3.520	12.30	1.220	187.0	95.00	9.000	392.0	0.042	0.000
3.000	0.180	0.470	—	0.112	8.100	0.120	0.036	0.897	0.060	1.000	0.210	3.000	32.00	0.003	0.000
6.000	0.660	1.050	—	0.080	15.00	0.113	0.068	1.500	0.080	2.000	0.740	6.000	49.00	0.013	0.000
30.00	1.880	3.460	0.000	0.728	31.70	1.020	0.462	8.610	0.430	—	0.980	12.00	393.0	0.066	0.000
17.00	2.080	4.310	—	—	0.000	0.026	0.170	4.960	0.200	8.000	2.300	10.00	145.0	—	0.000
18.00	1.790	4.560	30.00	0.517	0.000	0.043	0.179	4.390	0.220	8.000	2.000	9.000	134.0	0.020	0.000
12.00	1.010	1.590	—	—	1.300	0.417	0.156	2.790	0.220	—	0.870	16.00	111.0	0.022	0.000
20.00	0.660	2.010	7.000	0.492	0.200	0.690	0.294	4.320	0.310	4.000	0.810	5.000	193.0	0.014	0.000
24.00	3.790	8.660	—	—	0.000	0.081	0.289	3.720	0.330	11.00	3.400	9.000	268.0	0.006	0.000
17.00	1.770	4.270	69.90	—	0.000	0.065	0.146	2.650	0.250	5.000	2.370	10.00	140.0	0.020	0.000
3.000	0.460	0.490	—	0.156	3.000	0.029	0.059	0.785	0.050	0.000	1.110	2.000	23.00	0.004	0.000
2.000	0.160	0.330	—	0.042	0.000	0.096	0.033	0.587	0.040	—	0.220	4.000	24.00	0.004	0.000
7.000	0.527	1.300	3.000	0.170	—	0.116	0.108	1.550	0.100	1.330	0.307	13.30	74.00	0.005	0.000
26.00	2.390	4.590	20.00	0.468	0.000	0.097	0.221	4.980	0.460	10.00	2.080	5.000	203.0	0.029	0.000
23.00	2.490	4.730	50.00	0.468	0.000	0.092	0.218	3.210	0.330	7.000	2.220	9.000	180.0	0.029	0.000
17.00	2.900	3.500	—	0.204	—	0.110	0.260	6.600	—	—	1.400	10.00	211.0	—	0.000
Miscellaneous															
—	—	—	0.000	—	0.000	0.000	0.000	0.000	—	—	—	58.00	87.00	0.000	0.000
—	—	—	—	0.000	0.000	0.000	0.000	0.000	0.000	0.000	0.000	—	—	—	0.000
0.000	0.000	0.000	0.000	—	0.000	0.000	0.000	0.000	0.000	0.000	0.000	3.000	0.000	—	—
—	—	—	—	—	—	—	—	—	—	—	—	—	—	—	0.000
—	0.050	—	10.00	—	—	—	—	—	—	0.040	0.000	2.000	0.500	0.000	0.080
7.800	0.700	0.176	70.00	—	4.000	0.000	0.010	0.000	0.005	0.650	0.000	17.00	14.00	0.000	—
—	0.100	0.020	—	—	—	—	—	—	0.000	—	—	1.000	1.000	—	0.000

Nutritive Components—cont'd

Food Name	Serving	Gram wt	Kcal	Prot (g)	Carb (g)	Fat (g)	Chol (mg)	Safa (g)	Sod (mg)	Pot (mg)
Nuts and Seeds										
Cashews-dry roasted	1 cup	137.0	787.0	21.00	44.80	63.50	0.000	12.50	21.00	774.0
Coconut-dried-shred	1 cup	93.0	466.0	2.680	44.30	33.00	0.000	29.30	244.0	313.0
Nuts-mixed-dry roasted	1 cup	137.0	814.0	23.70	34.70	70.50	0.000	9.450	16.00	817.0
Peanuts-oil roasted	1 cup	145.0	840.0	38.80	26.70	71.30	0.000	9.900	22.00	1020
Pecans-dried-halves	1 cup	108.0	721.0	8.370	19.70	73.10	0.000	5.850	1.000	423.0
Pistachio-dry roasted	1 cup	128.0	776.0	19.10	35.20	67.60	0.000	8.560	8.000	1242
Peanut butter-chunk style	1 cup	258.0	1520	62.00	55.70	129.0	0.000	24.70	1255	1928
Peanut butter-smooth	1 tbsp	16.0	95.00	4.560	2.530	8.180	0.000	1.360	75.00	110.0
Pumpkin/squash-roast	1 cup	64.0	285.0	11.90	34.40	12.40	0.000	2.350	12.00	588.0
Sunflower-oil roast	1 cup	135.0	830.0	28.80	19.90	77.60	0.000	8.130	4.000	652.0
Poultry										
Chicken-breast-fried/batter	1 item	280.0	728.0	69.60	25.20	36.90	238.0	9.860	770.0	564.0
Chicken-breast-fried/flour	1 item	196.0	436.0	62.40	3.220	17.40	176.0	4.800	150.0	506.0
Chicken-breast-roasted	1 item	196.0	386.0	58.40	0.000	15.30	166.0	4.300	138.0	480.0
Chicken-breast-no skin-fried	1 item	172.0	322.0	57.50	0.880	8.100	156.0	2.220	136.0	474.0
Chicken-breast-no skin-roast	1 item	172.0	284.0	53.40	0.000	6.140	146.0	1.740	126.0	440.0
Chicken-drumstick-fried	1 item	49.0	120.0	13.20	0.800	6.720	44.00	1.790	44.00	112.0
Chicken-leg-roasted	1 item	114.0	265.0	29.60	0.000	15.40	105.0	4.240	99.00	256.0
Chicken-thigh-fried/flour	1 item	62.0	162.0	16.60	1.970	9.290	60.00	2.540	55.00	147.0
Chicken-wing-fried/flour	1 item	32.0	103.0	8.360	0.760	7.090	26.00	1.940	25.00	57.00
Duck-flesh and skin-roasted	1 item	764.0	2574	145.0	0.000	217.0	640.0	73.90	454.0	1560
Turkey-breast-no skin-roast	1 item	612.0	826.0	184.0	0.000	4.500	510.0	1.440	318.0	1784
Sauces and Dips										
Dip-French onion-Kraft	1 tbsp	15.0	30.00	0.500	1.500	2.000	0.000	—	120.0	—
Dip-guacamole-Kraft	1 tbsp	15.0	25.00	0.500	1.500	2.000	0.000	—	108.0	—
Mustard-yellow-prepared	1 tsp	5.0	5.000	0.100	0.100	0.100	0.000	0.000	65.00	7.000
Sauce-barbecue	1 cup	250.0	188.0	4.500	32.00	4.500	0.000	0.670	2032	435.0
Sauce-salsa/chilies-canned	1 fl oz	16.0	10.00	0.400	2.000	0.700	0.000	0.000	111.0	87.00

Nutritive Components—cont'd

Mag (mg)	Iron (mg)	Zinc (mg)	V-A (IU)	V-E (mg)	V-C (mg)	Thia (mg)	Ribo (mg)	Niac (mg)	V-B$_6$ (mg)	Fol (μg)	V-B$_{12}$ (μg)	Calc (mg)	Phos (mg)	Sel (mg)	Fibd (g)
Nuts and Seeds															
356.0	8.220	7.670	0.000	15.00	0.000	0.274	0.274	1.920	0.351	94.80	0.000	62.00	671.0	0.007	10.00
47.00	1.780	1.690	0.000	—	0.600	0.029	0.019	0.441	—	—	0.000	14.00	99.00	0.016	3.900
308.0	5.070	5.210	21.00	16.40	0.600	0.274	0.274	6.440	0.406	69.00	0.000	96.00	596.0	0.007	11.60
273.0	2.780	9.600	0.000	16.70	0.000	0.425	0.146	21.50	0.576	153.0	0.000	125.0	733.0	0.055	11.10
138.0	2.300	5.910	138.0	21.40	2.100	0.916	0.138	0.958	0.203	42.30	0.000	39.00	314.0	0.003	8.300
166.0	4.060	1.740	—	—	—	0.541	0.315	1.800	—	—	0.000	90.00	609.0	0.007	9.900
409.0	4.900	7.170	0.000	—	0.000	0.323	0.289	35.30	1.160	237.0	0.000	105.0	817.0	—	9.800
28.00	0.290	0.470	—	3.200	0.000	0.024	0.017	2.150	0.062	13.10	0.000	5.000	60.00	0.002	1.400
168.0	2.120	6.590	—	—	—	—	—	—	—	—	0.000	35.00	59.00	—	—
171.0	9.050	7.040	—	70.40	1.900	0.432	0.378	5.580	—	316.0	0.000	76.00	1538	—	—
Poultry															
68.00	3.500	2.660	188.0	1.540	0.000	0.322	0.408	29.50	1.200	16.00	0.820	56.00	516.0	0.030	—
58.00	2.340	2.140	98.00	1.080	0.000	0.160	0.256	26.90	1.140	8.000	0.680	32.00	456.0	0.021	—
54.00	2.080	2.000	182.0	1.080	0.000	0.130	0.234	24.90	1.080	6.000	0.640	28.00	420.0	0.053	0.000
54.00	1.960	1.860	40.00	0.946	0.000	0.136	0.216	25.40	1.100	8.000	0.620	28.00	424.0	0.031	0.000
50.00	1.780	1.720	36.00	0.946	0.000	0.120	0.196	23.60	1.020	6.000	0.580	26.00	392.0	0.046	0.000
11.00	0.660	1.420	41.00	0.270	0.000	0.040	0.110	2.960	0.170	4.000	0.160	6.000	86.00	0.005	—
26.00	1.520	2.960	154.0	0.627	0.000	0.078	0.243	7.060	0.370	8.000	0.350	14.00	199.0	0.016	0.000
15.00	0.930	1.560	61.00	0.341	0.000	0.058	0.151	4.310	0.210	5.000	0.190	8.000	116.0	0.011	0.040
6.000	0.400	0.560	40.00	0.176	0.000	0.019	0.044	2.140	0.130	1.000	0.090	5.000	48.00	0.006	0.000
124.0	20.60	14.20	1608	5.350	0.000	1.330	2.060	36.90	1.400	50.00	2.260	86.00	1190	—	0.000
178.0	9.360	10.60	0.000	—	0.000	0.264	0.802	45.90	3.420	38.00	2.360	76.00	1370	—	0.000
Sauces and Dips															
—	—	—	—	—	—	—	—	—	—	—	—	—	—	—	—
—	—	—	—	—	—	—	—	—	—	—	—	—	—	—	—
2.000	0.100	—	—	0.208	—	—	—	—	—	—	—	4.000	4.000	0.000	0.060
—	2.250	—	2170	—	17.50	0.075	0.050	2.250	0.188	—	0.000	48.00	50.00	—	2.300
—	0.280	—	395.0	—	9.100	0.020	0.010	0.290	—	—	—	4.200	9.300	—	—

Nutritive Components—cont'd

Food Name	Serving	Gram wt	Kcal	Prot (g)	Carb (g)	Fat (g)	Chol (mg)	Safa (g)	Sod (mg)	Pot (mg)
Sauces and Dips—cont'd										
Sauce-spaghetti-canned	1 cup	249.0	272.0	4.530	39.70	11.90	0.000	1.700	1236	957.0
Sauce-soy	1 tbsp	18.0	11.00	1.560	1.500	0.000	0.000	0.000	1029	64.00
Sauce-Worchestershire	1 tbsp	15.0	12.00	0.300	2.700	0.000	—	0.000	147.0	120.0
Tomato catsup	1 tbsp	15.0	15.00	0.000	4.000	0.000	0.000	0.000	156.0	54.00
Soups										
Vegetable beef-can	1 cup	245.0	79.00	5.580	10.20	1.900	5.000	0.850	957.0	173.0
Chicken noodle-can	1 cup	241.0	75.00	4.040	9.350	2.450	7.000	0.650	1107	55.00
Clam-New England-milk	1 cup	248.0	163.0	9.460	16.60	6.600	22.00	2.950	992.0	300.0
Onion-dehy-packet	1 srvg	39.0	115.0	4.520	20.90	2.330	2.000	0.540	3493	260.0
Cream/mushroom-milk	1 cup	248.0	203.0	6.050	15.00	13.60	20.00	5.120	1076	270.0
Vegetarian-can-water	1 cup	241.0	72.00	2.100	12.00	1.930	0.000	0.290	823.0	209.0
Sugar and Sweets										
Milk chocolate-plain	1 srvg	28.0	145.0	2.000	16.00	9.000	0.000	5.500	28.00	109.0
Jelly beans	1 item	2.8	6.600	0.000	1.670	0.000	—	0.000	0.300	0.000
Kit Kat Bar	1 item	43.0	210.0	3.000	25.00	11.00	—	—	38.00	129.0
M & M's-package	1 item	45.0	220.0	3.000	31.00	10.00	—	—	—	—
Milky Way Bar	1 item	60.0	260.0	3.000	43.00	9.000	—	—	—	—
Peanut Butter Cup	1 piece	17.0	92.00	2.200	8.700	5.350	2.500	3.000	54.50	68.00
Snickers Bar	1 item	57.0	270.0	6.000	33.00	13.00	—	—	—	—
Icing-cake-white-uncooked	1 cup	319.0	1200	2.000	260.0	21.00	0.000	12.70	156.0	57.00
Jams/preserves-regular	1 tbsp	20.0	55.00	0.000	14.00	0.000	0.000	0.000	2.000	18.00
Syrup-choc flavored-fudge	1 fl oz	38.0	125.0	2.000	20.00	5.000	0.000	3.100	26.60	107.0
Syrup-pancake-Karo	1 tbsp	20.5	60.00	0.000	14.90	0.000	—	0.000	35.00	1.000
Sugar-brown-pressed down	1 cup	220.0	820.0	0.000	212.0	0.000	0.000	0.000	66.00	757.0
Sugar-white-granulated	1 tbsp	12.0	45.00	0.000	12.00	0.000	0.000	0.000	0.120	0.000
Sugar-white-powder-sifted	1 cup	100.0	385.0	0.000	100.0	0.000	0.000	0.000	0.830	3.000
Vegetables										
Artichokes-boil-drain	1 item	120.0	53.00	2.760	12.40	0.200	0.000	0.048	79.00	316.0
Asparagus-froz-boil-spears	1 cup	180.0	50.40	5.310	8.770	0.756	0.000	0.171	7.200	392.0
Beans-baked canned	1 cup	254.0	235.0	12.20	52.10	1.140	0.000	0.295	1008	752.0
Beans-refried	1 cup	253.0	270.0	15.80	46.80	2.700	—	1.040	1071	994.0
Beans snap green-can-cuts	1 cup	135.0	27.00	1.550	6.000	0.135	0.000	0.030	339.0	147.0

Nutritive Components—cont'd

Mag (mg)	Iron (mg)	Zinc (mg)	V-A (IU)	V-E (mg)	V-C (mg)	Thia (mg)	Ribo (mg)	Niac (mg)	V-B$_6$ (mg)	Fol (µg)	V-B$_{12}$ (µg)	Calc (mg)	Phos (mg)	Sel (mg)	Fibd (g)
Sauces and Dips—cont'd															
60.00	1.620	0.530	3055	—	27.90	0.137	0.147	3.750	—	—	0.000	70.00	90.00	—	—
8.000	0.490	0.036	0.000	—	0.000	0.009	0.023	0.605	0.031	1.900	0.000	3.000	38.00	—	—
—	0.900	—	51.00	—	27.00	0.000	0.030	0.000	—	—	—	15.00	9.000	—	—
3.600	0.100	0.034	210.0	—	2.000	0.010	0.010	0.200	0.016	0.750	0.000	3.000	8.000	0.000	—
Soups															
6.000	1.110	1.550	1891	—	2.400	0.037	0.049	1.030	0.076	10.60	0.310	17.00	40.00	0.008	0.980
5.000	0.780	0.395	711.0	—	0.200	0.053	0.060	1.390	0.027	2.200	—	17.00	36.00	0.008	—
23.00	1.480	0.799	164.0	—	3.500	0.067	0.236	1.030	0.126	9.700	10.30	187.0	157.0	0.008	—
25.00	0.580	0.231	8.000	—	0.900	0.111	0.238	1.990	—	6.300	—	55.00	126.0	0.000	2.200
20.00	0.590	0.640	154.0	—	2.300	0.077	0.280	0.913	0.064	—	—	178.0	156.0	0.008	—
7.000	1.080	0.460	3005	—	1.400	0.053	0.046	0.916	0.055	10.60	0.000	21.00	35.00	0.008	1.210
Sugar and Sweets															
16.00	0.300	—	80.00	1.570	0.000	0.020	0.100	0.100	—	1.960	—	65.00	65.00	0.001	—
—	0.030	—	0.000	—	0.000	0.000	—	—	—	—	—	0.300	0.100	0.000	0.000
19.00	0.560	0.430	30.00	—	—	0.030	0.110	0.100	—	—	—	65.00	78.00	0.002	—
—	—	—	—	1.890	—	—	—	—	—	—	—	—	—	0.002	—
—	—	—	—	2.520	—	—	—	—	—	—	—	—	—	0.002	—
14.50	0.240	0.240	3.500	0.714	—	0.050	0.030	0.800	—	—	—	14.50	41.00	0.001	—
—	—	—	—	2.390	—	—	—	—	—	—	—	—	—	0.002	—
—	0.000	—	860.0	—	0.000	0.000	0.060	0.000	—	—	—	48.00	38.00	0.003	0.000
—	0.200	—	0.000	—	0.000	0.000	0.010	0.000	0.004	1.600	0.000	4.000	2.000	0.000	—
—	0.500	0.300	60.00	—	0.000	0.020	0.080	0.200	—	—	—	48.00	60.00	—	—
—	0.800	—	0.000	—	0.000	0.000	0.000	0.000	—	—	—	9.000	3.000	0.000	0.000
—	7.500	—	0.000	—	0.000	0.020	0.070	0.400	—	—	—	187.0	42.00	0.003	0.000
—	0.000	0.006	0.000	—	0.000	0.000	0.000	0.000	—	—	—	0.000	0.000	0.000	0.000
—	0.100	—	0.000	—	0.000	0.000	0.000	0.000	—	—	—	0.000	0.000	0.001	0.000
Vegetables															
47.00	1.620	0.430	172.0	—	8.900	0.068	0.059	0.709	0.104	53.40	0.000	47.00	72.00	—	4.000
23.40	1.150	1.000	1472	2.860	43.90	0.117	0.185	1.870	0.036	242.0	0.000	41.40	99.00	0.007	2.160
82.00	0.740	3.550	434.0	—	—	0.389	0.152	1.090	0.340	60.70	0.000	128.0	264.0	—	6.600
99.00	4.470	3.450	—	—	15.20	0.124	0.139	1.230	—	—	—	118.0	214.0	—	—
17.50	1.200	0.390	471.0	0.068	6.500	0.020	0.075	0.270	0.054	43.00	0.000	35.00	34.00	0.001	1.760

Nutritive Components—cont'd

Food Name	Serving	Gram wt	Kcal	Prot (g)	Carb (g)	Fat (g)	Chol (mg)	Safa (g)	Sod (mg)	Pot (mg)
Vegetables—cont'd										
Beets-can-sliced-drain	1cup	170.0	54.00	1.560	12.20	0.240	0.000	0.040	479.0	284.0
Broccoli-raw-boil-drain	1 cup	155.0	46.00	4.640	8.680	0.440	0.000	0.068	16.00	254.0
Brussel sprouts-raw-boil	1 cup	156.0	60.00	3.980	13.50	0.800	0.000	0.164	34.00	494.0
Cabbage common-raw-shred	1 cup	90.0	21.60	1.090	4.830	0.162	0.000	0.021	16.20	221.0
Carrots-boil-drain-sliced	1 cup	156.0	70.00	1.700	16.30	0.280	0.000	0.054	104.0	354.0
Cauliflower-raw-boil-drain	1 cup	124.0	30.00	2.320	5.740	0.220	0.000	0.046	8.000	400.0
Celery-Pascal-raw-stalk	1 item	40.0	6.000	0.260	1.450	0.050	0.000	0.013	35.00	114.0
Corn-kernels from 1 ear	1 item	77.0	83.00	2.560	19.30	0.980	0.000	0.152	13.00	192.0
Corn-sweet-can-drained	1 cup	165.0	132.0	4.300	30.50	1.640	0.000	0.254	470.0	160.0
Cucumber-raw-sliced	1 cup	104.0	14.00	0.560	3.020	0.140	0.000	0.034	2.000	156.0
Lettuce-iceberg-raw-chop	1 cup	55.0	7.150	0.556	1.150	0.105	0.000	0.014	4.950	86.90
Lettuce-Romaine-raw-shred	1 cup	56.0	8.000	0.900	1.320	0.120	0.000	0.014	4.000	162.0
Mushrooms-raw-chopped	1 cup	70.0	18.00	1.460	3.260	0.300	0.000	0.040	2.000	260.0
Onions-mature-raw-chopped	1 cup	160.0	54.00	1.880	11.70	0.420	0.000	0.070	4.000	248.0
Peas-green-froz-boil-drain	1 cup	160.0	126.0	8.240	22.80	0.440	0.000	0.078	140.0	268.0
Potato-flesh and skin-bake	1 item	202.0	220.0	4.650	51.00	0.200	0.000	0.052	16.00	844.0
Potato-french fried-froz	1 item	5.0	11.10	0.173	1.700	0.438	0.000	0.208	1.500	22.90
Potato-mashed-milk/butter	1 cup	210.0	222.0	3.950	35.10	8.870	4.000	2.170	619.0	607.0
Potato chips-salt added	1 item	2.0	10.50	0.128	1.040	0.708	0.000	0.181	9.400	26.00
Spinach-raw-chopped	1 cup	56.0	12.00	1.600	1.960	0.200	0.000	0.032	44.00	312.0
Squash-acorn-baked	1 cup	205.0	115.0	2.290	29.90	0.290	0.000	0.059	9.000	896.0
Squash-zucchini-raw-boil	1 cup	180.0	28.00	1.140	7.080	0.100	0.000	0.018	4.000	456.0
Sweet potato-candied	1 piece	105.0	144.0	0.910	29.30	3.410	0.000	1.420	73.00	198.0
Tofu-soybean curd	1 piece	120.0	86.00	9.400	2.900	5.000	0.000	—	8.000	50.00
Tomato-raw-red-ripe	1 item	135.0	24.00	1.090	5.340	0.260	0.000	0.037	10.00	254.0
Tomato juice-can	1 cup	244.0	42.00	1.860	10.30	0.140	0.000	0.020	882.0	536.0
Tomato paste-can-salt added	1 cup	262.0	220.0	9.900	49.30	2.330	0.000	0.332	2070	2442
Vegetable juice-can	1 cup	242.0	44.00	1.520	11.00	0.220	0.000	0.032	884.0	468.0

Nutritive Components—cont'd

Mag (mg)	Iron (mg)	Zinc (mg)	V-A (IU)	V-E (mg)	V-C (mg)	Thia (mg)	Ribo (mg)	Niac (mg)	V-B$_6$ (mg)	Fol (µg)	V-B$_{12}$ (µg)	Calc (mg)	Phos (mg)	Sel (mg)	Fibd (g)
Vegetables—cont'd															
22.10	3.100	0.360	30.00	—	5.000	0.020	0.050	0.200	0.085	40.80	0.000	32.00	31.00	0.001	3.200
94.00	1.780	0.240	2198	0.992	98.00	0.128	0.322	1.180	0.308	107.0	0.000	178.0	74.00	—	6.400
32.00	1.880	0.500	1122	1.320	96.80	0.166	0.124	0.946	0.278	93.60	0.000	56.00	88.00	0.001	4.520
13.50	0.504	0.162	113.0	1.500	42.60	0.045	0.027	0.270	0.086	51.00	0.000	42.30	20.70	0.002	1.800
20.00	0.960	0.460	38300	0.713	3.600	0.054	0.088	0.790	0.384	21.60	0.000	48.00	48.00	0.002	5.770
14.00	0.520	0.300	18.00	0.113	68.60	0.078	0.064	0.684	0.250	63.40	0.000	34.00	44.00	0.001	2.230
5.000	0.190	0.070	51.00	0.292	2.500	0.012	0.012	0.120	0.012	3.600	0.000	14.00	10.00	0.000	0.400
24.00	0.470	0.370	167.0	0.868	4.800	0.166	0.055	1.240	0.046	35.70	0.000	2.000	79.00	0.001	6.600
28.00	1.400	0.640	256.0	1.020	7.000	0.050	0.080	1.500	0.330	59.40	0.000	8.000	81.00	0.001	2.150
12.00	0.280	0.240	46.00	0.322	4.800	0.032	0.020	0.312	0.054	14.40	0.000	14.00	18.00	0.001	1.460
4.950	0.275	0.121	182.0	0.413	2.150	0.025	0.017	0.103	0.022	30.80	0.000	10.50	11.00	0.000	0.600
4.000	0.620	—	1456	0.420	13.40	0.056	0.056	0.280	—	76.00	0.000	20.00	26.00	0.000	0.773
8.000	0.860	0.344	0.000	0.203	2.400	0.072	0.314	2.880	0.068	14.80	0.000	4.000	72.00	0.009	1.260
16.00	0.580	0.280	0.000	0.496	13.40	0.096	0.016	0.160	0.252	31.80	0.000	40.00	46.00	0.003	2.640
46.00	2.520	1.500	1068	1.040	15.80	0.452	0.160	2.370	0.180	93.80	0.000	38.00	144.0	0.001	6.080
55.00	2.750	0.650	—	0.121	26.10	0.216	0.067	3.320	0.701	22.20	0.000	20.00	115.0	0.001	4.850
1.100	0.067	0.021	0.000	—	0.550	0.006	0.002	0.115	0.012	0.830	0.000	0.400	4.300	0.000	0.160
37.00	0.550	0.580	355.0	0.126	12.90	0.176	0.084	2.270	0.470	16.70	0.000	54.00	97.00	0.001	—
1.200	0.024	0.021	0.000	0.146	0.830	0.003	0.000	0.084	0.010	0.900	0.000	0.500	3.100	0.000	0.029
44.00	1.520	0.300	3760	1.650	15.80	0.044	0.106	0.406	0.110	108.0	0.000	56.00	28.00	0.001	1.760
87.00	1.910	0.350	878.0	—	22.10	0.342	0.027	1.810	0.398	38.40	0.000	90.00	93.00	0.002	4.300
38.00	0.640	0.320	432.0	—	8.400	0.074	0.074	0.770	0.140	30.20	0.000	24.00	72.00	0.006	2.300
12.00	1.190	0.160	4399	—	7.000	0.019	0.044	0.414	0.043	12.00	0.032	27.00	27.00	0.001	1.100
—	2.300	—	0.000	—	0.000	0.070	0.040	0.100	—	—	—	154.0	151.0	—	—
14.00	0.590	0.130	1394	0.603	21.60	0.074	0.062	0.738	0.059	11.50	0.000	8.000	29.00	0.001	2.100
28.00	1.420	0.360	1356	1.730	44.60	0.114	0.076	1.640	0.270	48.40	0.000	20.00	46.00	0.001	2.900
134.0	7.830	2.100	6468	—	111.0	0.406	0.498	8.440	0.996	—	0.000	91.70	207.0	0.003	—
26.00	1.020	0.480	2832	—	67.00	0.104	0.068	1.760	0.339	—	0.000	26.00	40.00	0.001	2.700

Glossary

abstinence to refrain completely from engaging in a particular behavior. (p. 260)

acesulfame nonnutritive sweetener that is 200 times sweeter than sucrose and marketed as "sunette" in many food products. (p. 165)

Acquired Immunodeficiency Syndrome (AIDS) viral destruction of the immune system, causing loss of ability to fight infections. (p. 283)

adipose cells fat cells. (p. 205)

adrenocorticotropic hormone (ACTH) hormone released by the hypothalamus during periods of stress that initiates various physiological responses. (p. 237)

aerobic literally "with oxygen"; when applied to exercise, refers to activities in which oxygen demand can be supplied continuously by individuals during performance. (p. 59)

aerobic capacity maximum oxygen consumption. (p. 59)

alcohol socially acceptable drug. (p. 260)

alcoholism disease in which an individual loses control over drinking; inability to refrain from drinking. (p. 263)

amino acid chemical structures that form protein. (p. 148)

anabolic steroids drugs closely related to testosterone that increase muscle mass in humans. (p. 103)

anaerobic literally "without oxygen"; when applied to exercise, refers to high-intensity physical activities in which oxygen demand is greater than the amount that can be supplied during performance. (p. 104)

android deposition of fat that is characteristic of males; fat tends to accumulate in the abdomen and upper body. (p. 197)

aneurysm weak spot in an artery that forms a balloonlike pouch that can rupture (p. 32)

angina chest pain that is the result of ischemia (see **ischemic**). (p. 30)

anorexia nervosa serious illness of deliberate self-starvation with profound psychiatric and physical components. (p. 217)

antioxidants compounds that block the oxidation of substances in food or the body (vitamins C and E and beta-carotene are examples). (p. 36)

arthritis inflammatory disease of the joints. (p. 305)

asymptomatic without symptoms. (p. 331)

atherosclerosis slow, progressive disease of the arteries characterized by the deposition of plaque on the inner lining of arterial walls. (p. 31)

ATP adenosine triphosphate, the actual unit of energy used for muscular contraction. (p. 61)

autogenics form of suggestion that precipitates relaxation. (p. 241)

autoimmune disease disease in which the immune system fails to recognize its own body parts and produces antibodies against them to the point of causing injury. (p. 306)

autonomic nervous system part of the nervous system that is concerned with control of involuntary bodily functions. (p. 237)

ballistic stretching repetitive contractions of agonist muscles to produce very quick, rapid stretches of antagonist muscles. (p. 123)

balloon angioplasty surgical procedure that involves the insertion of a catheter with a balloon at the tip used to compress fatty deposits and plaque against the walls of the artery. (p. 46)

basal metabolic rate (BMR) number of calories needed to sustain life. (p. 214)

behavior assessment process of counting, recording, observing, measuring, and describing behavior. (p. 11)

behavior substitution lifestyle change technique in which an incompatible behavior is substituted for a behavior being altered. (p. 14)

behavioral contract a written agreement in a lifestyle-change program. (p. 13)

benign noncancerous. (p. 294)

biofeedback educational tool used to provide information about an individual's physiological actions. (p. 242)

blood alcohol concentration (BAC) percentage of alcohol content in the blood. (p. 260)

body composition amount of lean versus fat tissue in the body, (p. 184)

body mass index (BMI) measure of relative fatness. (p. 188)

bulimia eating disorder characterized by episodes of secretive binge eating and purging. (p. 218)

caffeine a stimulant that increases the heart rate. (p. 260)

calorie short for *kilocalorie*, which is the unit of measurement for food energy. A calorie is the amount of heat required to raise the temperature of 1 gram of water 1 degree Centigrade. (p. 148)

cancer group of diseases characterized by uncontrolled, disorderly cell growth. (p. 294)

cannabinoids chemicals found only in marijuana. (p. 270)

cannabis sativa Indian hemp plant from which marijuana and hashish are derived. (p. 269)

carbon monoxide deadly gas emitted in the exhaust of cars and in burning tobacco. (p. 268)

carcinogens substances that cause cancer or enable the growth of cancer cells; cancer-causing agents. (p. 294)

cardiac arrhythmia irregular heart rate that is sometimes intractable. (p. 208)

cardiac output amount of blood ejected by the heart in 1 minute. (p. 60)

cardiorespiratory endurance ability to take in, deliver, and extract oxygen for physical work. (p. 59)

catheterization in relation to heart disease, the passage of a catheter (slender plastic tube) into the heart through an arm vein and blood vessels leading into the heart to obtain cardiac blood samples, detect abnormalities, and determine intracardiac pressure. (p. 46)

cause and effect in medical research, the type of relationship in which one variable is scientifically proved to cause a certain effect. (p. 317)

cerebral hemorrhage bursting of a blood vessel in the brain. (p. 32)

Caesarean section delivery surgical removal of the fetus through the abdominal wall. (p. 281)

chemotherapy use of drugs and hormones to treat various cancers. (p. 299)

chlamydia one of the most common sexually transmitted diseases. (p. 281)

cholesterol steroid that is an essential structural component of neural tissue and cell walls and is required for the manufacture of hormones and bile. (p. 63)

chronic effects of exercise the physiological changes that result from cardiorespiratory training. (p. 59)

circuit resistance training a total of 8 to 15 exercises are usually used in a circuit. The exerciser goes through the circuit three times with minimum rest between exercise stations. (p. 100)

cocaine a stimulant used in powdered form. (p. 268)

concentric contraction shortening of the muscle as it develops the tension to overcome an external resistance. (p. 99)

complete protein protein that contains all the essential amino acids. (p. 149)

complex carbohydrates polysacchrides, including starch and fiber. (p. 161)

condyloma warts on the genitalia. (p. 280)

contraindication reason for not prescribing a drug or treatment. (p. 325)

control group in health research, the group receiving no treatment. (p. 318)

coping effort(s) made to manage or deal with stress. (p. 239)

coronary artery bypass surgery procedure involving the removal of a leg vein that is used as a shunt around the blocked area in the coronary artery. (p. 46)

cortisol primary hormone that provides fuel to respond with the fight-or-flight reaction. (p. 237)

crack smokable form of cocaine that is extremely dangerous and very addictive. (p. 268)

cross-training the attainment of physical fitness by participating in a variety of activities regularly. (p. 67)

crude fiber residue of plant food following chemical treatment in the laboratory. (p. 161)

daily reference values (DRV) provides nutritional guidelines for ingestion of carbohydrate, fat, saturated fat, cholesterol, sodium, potassium, and dietary fiber. (p. 148)

deceptive advertising advertising that misleads consumers by overstating or exaggerating the performance of a product. (p. 317)

deductible amount paid by a patient before being eligible for benefits from an insurance company. (p. 332)

delta-9-tetrahydrocannabinol (THC) major psychoactive drug found in marijuana. (p. 269)

depressants known as sedatives and tranquilizers; these agents slow the central nervous system. (p. 260)

designer drugs illegally manufactured drugs that mimic controlled substances. (p. 271)

diabetes mellitus metabolic disorder involving the pancreas and the failure to produce insulin; a risk factor for cardiovascular disease. (p. 304)

diagnostic laboratory tests tests conducted for specific symptoms during a physical examination. (p. 328)

dietary fiber residue of plant food after digestion in the human body. One gram of crude fiber equals 2 to 3 grams of dietary fiber. (p. 161)

disability insurance insurance that pays for income lost because of the inability to work due to an illness or injury. (p. 333)

distress form of stress that results in negative responses. (p. 233)

diverticulitis infection of the diverticula of the intestines. (p. 162)

diverticulosis condition of having saclike swellings (diverticula) in the walls of the intestines. (p. 162)

double-blind study type of health research in which neither the researcher nor the subjects know who is receiving an experimental treatment. (p. 318)

drug chemical substance that has the potential to alter the structure and functioning of a living organism. (p. 258)

eccentric contraction the lengthening of a muscle as the weight or resistance is returned to the starting position. (p. 99)

echocardiography noninvasive technique that uses sound waves to determine the shape, texture, and movement of the valves of the heart. (p. 46)

electrocardiograph (ECG) device for recording electrical variations in action of the heart muscle. (p. 208)

embolus mass of undissolved matter in the blood or lymphatic vessels that detaches from the vessel walls. (p. 32)

endorphins mood-elevating, pain-killing substances produced by the brain. (p. 237)

energy nutrients nutrients such as carbohydrates, fat, and protein that provide a source of energy for the body. (p. 148)

epinephrine hormone produced by the adrenal medulla that speeds up body processes. (p. 237)

essential fat fat that is indispensable for individuals to function biologically and necessary to support life. (p. 219)

essential hypertension high blood pressure due to unknown reasons. (p. 39)

essential nutrients nutrients that cannot be made by the body and must be supplied in the diet. (p. 145)

ethyl alcohol intoxicating agent in alcoholic drinks; colorless liquid with a sharp, burning taste. (p. 260)

eustress stress judged as "good"; positive stress or stress that contributes to positive outcomes. (p. 233)

exclusion medical services that are not covered by an insurance policy. (p. 332)

experimental group in health research, the group receiving some form of experimental treatment. (p. 318)

false negative test results that incorrectly show a person is healthy when an abnormality actually exists. (p. 329)

false positive test results that incorrectly show an abnormality when a person is actually healthy. (p. 329)

family practitioner medical doctor who serves as a general practitioner for an individual or a family. (p. 323)

fat mixture of triglycerides. (p. 156)

fiber substances in food that resist digestion; formerly called *roughage*. (p. 161)

fight-or-flight syndrome initial phase of the general adaptation syndrome (GAS); when a stressor is encountered, the body responds by preparing to stand and fight or run away depending on the situation; also called the *alarm phase* of the GAS. (p. 234)

fixed indemnity benefits specified amounts that are paid by an insurance company for particular medical procedures. (p. 332)

flexibility range of motion at a joint. (p. 122)

fraternal twins twins who emanate from separate eggs and do not have identical genes. (p. 207)

freebasing smoking liquefied cocaine. (p. 268)

fructose fruit sugar. (p. 161)

general adaptation syndrome (GAS) series of physiological changes that occur when a stressor is encountered; the GAS is conceived of as having three phases: alarm, resistance, and exhaustion. (p. 234)

genital warts warts on the genitalia. (p. 280)

glucose primary source of energy used by the body; blood sugar. (p. 161)

glyceride general term for fat compounds, including triglyceride, monoglyceride, and diglyceride. (p. 156)

goniometer a protractorlike instrument used to measure the flexibility of various joints. (p. 127)

gonorrhea bacterial disease that is sexually transmitted and can lead to serious complications if left untreated, including sterility and scarring of the heart valves. (p. 282)

gynoid fat deposition characteristic of females, in whom fat tends to accumulate on the hips and thighs. (p. 197)

hardiness label used in describing a particular type of personality that tends to remain healthy even under extreme stress; the three components of hardiness are challenge, commitment, and control. (p. 239)

hashish resin from the *cannabis sativa* plant that can be smoked to alter mood; a frequently abused drug. (p. 269)

headache a common discomfort that is often caused by distress, tension, and anxiety; may be the result of injury or brain disease. (p. 307)

health balancing of the physical, emotional, social, and spiritual components of personality in a manner that is conducive to optimal well-being and a higher quality of existence. (p. 2)

health behavior gap discrepancy between what people know and what they actually do regarding their health. (p. 8)

health-care providers people and facilities such as physicians and hospitals that provide health-care services. (p. 316)

health fatalism in health information the view that new information cannot be believed or trusted because it will inevitably be refuted. (p. 316)

health hysteria a reactionary cycle in which new health findings suggest a cause-and-effect relationship between some variable and health that leads to publicity, notoriety, fear, and sometimes legislation. (p. 316)

health insurance a contract between an insurance company and an individual or a group for the payment of medical care costs. (p. 332)

health maintenance organization (HMO) prepaid group insurance program that provides a full range of medical services. (p. 333)

health-promoting behaviors things done to maintain and improve one's level of wellness. (p. 9)

health promotion art and science of helping people change their lifestyle to move toward a higher state of wellness. (p. 2)

health-related fitness components of fitness that include cardiorespiratory endurance, muscular strength, muscular endurance, flexibility, and body composition. (p. 58)

health risk appraisals questionnaires used to provide information about health habits, lifestyle, and medical history. (p. 328)

heat exhaustion serious heat-related condition characterized by dizziness, fainting, rapid pulse, and cool skin. (p. 70)

heat stroke heat-related medical emergency characterized by high temperature (106° F or higher) and dry skin and accompanied by some or all of the following: delirium, convulsions, and loss of consciousness. (p. 70)

herpes simplex virus (HSV) virus responsible for herpes genitalis, a sexually transmitted disease. (p. 281)

highly polyunsaturated fat fatty acid composed of triglycerides in which the carbon chain has room for many hydrogen atoms. (p. 157)

homeostasis state of balance or constancy; the body is continually attempting to maintain homeostasis. (p. 234)

homogeneous group group of subjects with similar characteristics. (p. 318)

human immunodeficiency virus (HIV) virus that is the source of AIDS. (p. 283)

human papilloma virus (HPV) causative agent of condyloma (genital warts). (p. 280)

hydrogenation process of adding hydrogen to unsaturated fatty acid to make it more saturated. (p. 157)

hyperglycemia high blood sugar. (p. 304)

hyperplasia increase in the number of cells. (p. 205)

hypertension high blood pressure. (p. 38)

hyperthermia excessive buildup of heat in the body. (p. 70)

hypertrophy increase in the size of a cell. (p. 205)

hypokinesis physical inactivity. (p. 41)

hypothalamus part of the limbic system that contains the center for many bodily functions; in stressful situations the hypothalamus releases specific hormones to elicit appropriate bodily responses. (p. 236)

hypothermia cold weather-related condition that results in abnormally low body temperature. (p. 73)

iatrogenic disease condition caused as a result of receiving medical care. (p. 320)

identical twins twins who emanate from the same egg. (p. 207)

immunization a vaccine or other preparation administered to prevent disease. (p. 331)

implied consent nonverbal authorization of a medical procedure such as cooperation during the administration of tests. (p. 322)

incomplete protein protein that does not contain all the essential amino acids in the proportions needed by the body. (p. 149)

influenza commonly called *flu*; caused by a virus. (p. 307)

informed consent legal provision requiring patient's authorization of any medical procedure, therapy, or treatment. (p. 322)

inhalants substances that cause druglike effects when inhaled. (p. 260)

insoluble fiber fiber that does not dissolve in water; comes from wheat bran and vegetables. (p. 161)

insulin hormone secreted by the pancreas that increases the use of glucose by the tissues of the body. (p. 304)

intensity degree of vigorousness of a single bout of exercise. (p. 64)

internist medical doctor specializing in internal medicine and sometimes serving as a primary care physician. (p. 323)

ischemic diminished supply of blood to the heart muscle. (p. 32)

isokinetic method for developing muscular strength that involves a constant rate of speed and changes in the amount of weight resistance. (p. 100)

isometric use of static contractions to develop strength. (p. 100)

isotonic method for developing muscular strength that involves a variable rate of speed and a constant weight resistance. (p. 100)

lactic acid metabolite formed in muscles as a result of incomplete breakdown of sugar. (p. 68)

lactose simple sugar; milk sugar. (p. 161)

life insurance insurance that pays a death benefit. (p. 333)

limbic system large, C-shaped area that contains the centers for emotions, memory storage, learning relay, and hormone production (the pituitary gland, thalamus, and hypothalamus). (p. 236)

lipid class of nutrients more commonly referred to as *fat*. (p. 156)

locus-of-control perspective from which an individual views life. Individuals with an *internal* locus-of-control believe that their decisions make a difference and that they have control over their lives. People with *external* locus-of-control see themselves as "victims" and consider other people, situations, and conditions as being the controlling factors in their lives. (p. 8)

low-calorie diet diet that limits intake to 800 to 1000 calories a day; results in atrophy of heart muscle. (p. 208)

major minerals those minerals required in large amounts (more than 5 grams a day). (p. 153)

malignant cancerous; harmful. (p. 294)

mammography x-ray examination of the breast to detect cancer. (p. 330)

marijuana comes from the cannabis plant. (p. 269)

megadose large doses, usually in the form of supplements. (p. 150)

metabolism all chemical reactions that occur within the cells of the body. (p. 214)

metastasis process by which cancerous cells spread from their original location to another location in the body. (p. 294)

migraine headaches headaches characterized by throbbing pain that can last for hours or days, sometimes accompanied by nausea and vomiting. Migraines are thought to be the result of dilation of blood vessels in the head. (p. 308)

minerals inorganic compounds in food necessary for good health. (p. 153)

mitochondria the cell's "powerhouse." (p. 61)

moderate calorie diet diet that limits caloric intake to 1300 to 1600 calories a day. (p. 208)

monounsaturated fat fatty acid composed of triglycerides in which the carbon chain has room for one more hydrogen atom. (p. 157)

morbidity incidence of disease and/or sickness. (p. 9)

mortality incidence of death. (p. 9)

muscular endurance application of repeated muscular force developed by many repetitions against resistances considerably less than maximum. (p. 105)

muscular strength maximal force that a muscle or muscle group can exert in a single contraction. (p. 91)

myocardial infarction heart attack; death of heart muscle tissue. (p. 31)

narcotics powerful painkillers. (p. 260)

negative reinforcers penalties incurred in a lifestyle-change program when goals are not achieved. (p. 13)

neoplasm abnormal mass of cells; also called a *tumor* and can be benign or malignant. (p. 294)

nicotine addictive substance and alkaloid poison found in tobacco. (p. 265)

nutrient substance found in food that is required by the body. (p. 144)

nutrient density ratio of nutrients to calories; also called the *index of nutritional quality*. (p. 166)

nutrition science that deals with the study of nutrients and the way the body ingests, digests, absorbs, transports, metabolizes, and excretes these nutrients. (p. 144)

obesity excessive amount of storage fat. (p. 184)

omega-3 fatty acids type of fatty acid found in cold-water seafood and thought to lower the risks of heart disease. (p. 157)

oncogene cancer-causing gene. (p. 295)

osteoarthritis most common form of arthritis characterized by the deterioration of articular cartilage that covers the gliding surfaces of the bones in certain joints. (p. 305)

osteoporosis progressive decrease in the mineral content of bone, making bones brittle. (p. 306)

overfat may or may not be within normal guidelines for weight but with an excessive ratio of fat compared with lean tissue. (p. 185)

overweight excessive weight for one's height without regard for body composition. (p. 184)

pathogen disease-producing organism. (p. 321)

pelvic inflammatory disease (PID) chronic condition of infection in the uterus, fallopian tubes, and upper reproductive areas; the leading cause of infertility in women. (p. 281)

performance-related fitness sports fitness; composed of speed, power, balance, coordination, agility, and reaction time. (p. 58)

placebo inactive substance, such as a fake drug. (p. 318)

polyunsaturated fat fatty acid composed of triglycerides in which the carbon chain has room for two or more hydrogen atoms. (p. 157)

positive reinforcers rewards earned for achieving goals in a lifestyle-change program. (p. 13)

preferred providers organization (PPO) a group of private practitioners who sell their services at reduced rates to insurance companies. (p. 333)

preventive health behaviors health practices associated with the promotion of wellness and the prevention of sickness and death. (p. 9).

primary care physician medical doctor who is responsible for an individual's overall health. (p. 322)

proprioceptive neuromuscular facilitation (PNF) consists of several stretching techniques that involve some combination of contraction and static stretching and holding agonist and antagonist muscle groups. (p. 123)

psychoactives drugs that can alter feelings, moods, and/or perceptions. (p. 260)

radiotherapy use of radiation to either destroy cancer cells or destroy their reproductive mechanism so they cannot replicate. (p. 299)

RDA acronym for recommended dietary allowances. (p. 145)

recommended dietary allowances (RDA) daily recommended intakes of nutrients for normal, healthy people in the United States. (p. 145)

reference daily intakes (RDI) represents minimum standards for essential nutrients and replace the US recommended daily allowance established in 1968. (p. 167)

relative weight the ratio of actual weight to desirable weight. (p. 187)

relaxation techniques techniques used in coping with and managing stress. (p. 241)

reliability extent to which health studies yield consistent results. (p. 318)

residual volume amount of air remaining in the lungs after expiration. (p. 61)

rheumatoid arthritis most crippling form of arthritis, characterized by inflammation of the joints, pain, swelling, and deformity. (p. 306)

saccharides refers to sugars (general term). (p. 161)

saturated fat fatty acid composed of triglycerides in which all the fatty acids contain the maximum number of hydrogen atoms. (p. 157)

selective health examination specific test used in response to specific symptoms or for diagnosing a specific problem. (p. 328)

self-care movement toward individuals taking increased responsibility to prevent or manage certain health conditions. (p. 318)

self-efficacy people's belief in their ability to accomplish a specific task or behavior; that belief then affects the outcome of the task or behavior; the theory that individuals who expect to succeed tend to succeed and those who expect to fail tend to fail. (p. 8)

self-help approach to lifestyle change that assumes individuals can plan and execute their own plans. (p. 9)

setpoint theory theory that the body has a preference for maintaining a certain amount of weight and defends that weight quite vigorously. (p. 207)

sexually transmitted diseases (STDs) diseases spread through sexual contact, such as AIDS, chlamydia, gonorrhea, and herpes. (p. 280)

sidestream smoke smoke inhaled by nonsmokers when they are around people who smoke. (p. 268)

skinfold measures method for determining the amount of body fat by using skin calipers. (p. 190)

soluble fiber fiber that dissolves in water; comes from fruit pectins and oat bran. (p. 161)

starch plant polysacchrides composed of glucose and digestible by humans. (p. 161)

static stretching passive stretching of antagonist muscles by slowly stretching and holding a position for 15 to 30 seconds. (p. 123)

stimulants drugs that speed up the central nervous system. (p. 260)

stimulus control technique in lifestyle management involving the elimination and/or manipulation of stimuli related to a specific behavior. (p. 13)

stress nonspecific response of the body to any demands made on it. (p. 232)

stressor any physical, psychological, or environmental event or condition that initiates the stress response. (p. 233)

stretch reflex the myotatic reflex. (p. 123)

stroke volume amount of blood that the heart can eject in one beat. (p. 60)

sucrose table sugar. (p. 161)

syphilis a sexually transmitted disease. (p. 283)

tar black, sticky, dark fluid composed of thousands of chemicals and found in tobacco. (p. 268)

tension headaches most common kind of headache; caused by involuntary contractions of the scalp, head, and neck muscles and may be precipitated by anxiety, stress, and allergic reactions. (p. 307)

thermic effect of food the amount of energy required by the body to digest, absorb, metabolize, and store nutrients. (p. 205)

thrombus stationary blood clot; can occlude an artery supplying the brain. (p. 32)

trace minerals those minerals required in small amounts. (p. 153)

transit time the time it takes food to move through the body. (p. 162)

triglyceride compound composed of carbon, hydrogen, and oxygen with three fatty acids. (p. 156)

tropical oils oils that come from the fruit of coconut and palm trees. (p. 160)

unsaturated fat fatty acid composed of triglycerides in which the carbon chain has room for more hydrogen atoms. (p. 157)

validity extent to which the research design of a health study permits the assertion of certain health claims. (p. 317)

variable resistance provides increasing resistance as a weight is lifted through the full range of motion. (p. 100)

viral hepatitis inflammation of the liver caused by one or more viruses. (p. 282)

visualization a form of meditation that makes use of the imagination. (p. 241)

vital capacity amount of air that can be expired after a maximum inspiration. (p. 61)

vitamin supplements natural and synthetic compounds taken orally to supplement the vitamins consumed in food. (p. 150)

vitamins organic compounds in food necessary for good health. (p. 150)

Index

Credits

Chapter 1: p. 3 (Fig. 1-1), Modified from Travis JW and Ryan RS: Wellness workbook, second edition, Berkeley, Calif, Tenspeed Press, 1988; **p. 5 (Table 1-1),** Data from the National Center for Health Statistics, US Public Health Service, Department of Health and Human Services, Washington, DC, 1990; **p. 6 (Fig. 1-4),** Source: *Healthy People 2000: National Health Promotion and Disease Prevention Objectives*, Department of Health and Human Services, Washington, DC, 1991; **p. 8 (Fig. 1-6),** From Survey highlights, the prevention index '89, summary report: a report card on the nation's health, Emmaus, Penn, Rodale Press, Inc, 1989; **p. 11 (Fig. 1-8),** Source: Louis Harris survey for *Prevention* magazine; **pp. 19-20,** Adapted from Noland MP: The efficacy of a new model to explain leisure exercise behavior, PhD dissertation, University of Maryland, 1981, reprinted by permission of the author; **p. 21,** From Development of the multidimensional health locus of control (MHLC) scales in *Health Education Monographs*, copyright 1978, reprinted by permission of John Wiley & Sons, Inc.

Chapter 2: pp. 35, 37 (Tables 2-2, 2-3), Adapted from Report of the national cholesterol education program expert panel in detection, evaluation, and treatment of high blood cholesterol in adults, *Archives of Internal Medicine* 148:36, January 1988; **p. 36 (Fig. 2-8),** Source: Swain JF et al: Comparison of the effects of oat bran and low-fiber wheat on serum lipoprotein levels and blood pressure, *New England Journal of Medicine* 322:147-152, 1990; **p. 38 (Table 2-4),** Adapted from National Institutes of Health Consensus Development Conference statement: Lowering blood cholesterol, *JAMA* 253:2080, 1985; **p. 39 (Table 2-5),** From National Institutes of Health: The fifth report of the joint national committee on

detection, evaluation, and treatment of high blood pressure, US Department of Health and Human Services: NIH Publication No. 93:1088, January 1993; **p. 125 (Fig. 2-11),** Source: Trying to quit smoking? Drink less coffee, *Tufts University Diet and Nutrition Letter* 7(9):1, November 1989; **p. 42 (Fig. 2-12),** Data from Paffenbarger RS et al: Physical activity, all-cause mortality, and longevity of college alumni, *New England Journal of Medicine* 314:605-613, 1986; **p. 43 (Fig. 2-13),** Adapted from Blair SN et al: Physical fitness and all-cause mortality—a prospective study of healthy men and women, *JAMA* 262:2395-2401, 1989; **p. 45 (Fig. 2-14),** Source: Salonen JT et al: High stored iron levels are associated with excess risk of myocardial infarction in eastern Finnish men, *Circulation* 86:803-881, September 1992; **p. 47 (Fig. 2-16),** Source: Aspirin: low cost, low dose, big benefits, *Harvard Heart Letter* 2:1-5, June 1992; **pp. 51-52,** Arizona Heart Institute.

Chapter 3: p. 69 (Table 3-3), From Conrad CC: How different sports rate in promoting physical fitness, *Medical Times* (reprint), May 1976, p. 4, used by permission; **p. 70 (Table 3-4),** Adapted from Rosato FD: Fitness and wellness: the physical connection, St. Paul, West Publishing Company, 1986; **p. 71 (Table 3-5),** Adapted from Franklin BR et al: On the ball, Carmel Ind, Benchmark Press, 1990; **p. 73 (Table 3-6),** Adapted from Sharkey BJ: Physiology of fitness, Champaign, Ill, 1979, Human Kinetics Publishers, p. 226; **pp. 77-79,** Reprinted by permission of the Rockport Company (1990), The Rockport Company, all rights reserved; **p. 81 (chart),** Adapted from Cooper KH: The aerobics program for total well-being, NY, M. Evans and Company, Inc, 1982; **p. 83 (charts),** Adapted from Cooper KH: The aerobics way, NY, Bantam Books, 1988; **p. 85**

(chart), Adapted from Golding LA et al: The Y's way to fitness, Champaign, Ill, Human Kinetics, 1989.

Chapter 4: p. 111 (charts), Values adapted from Johnson BL and Nelson JK: Practical measurement in physical education, Macmillan Publishing Company, 1986; **p. 115 (standards),** Adapted from Faulkner RA et al: Partial curl-up research project final report. Report submitted to the Canadian Fitness and Lifestyle Research Institute, 1988.

Chapter 5: p. 133 (standards), Adapted from Pate RR: Norms for college students: health related physical fitness test, American Alliance for Health, Physical Education, Recreation, and Dance, 1985; **p. 135 (standards),** Adapted from Prentice WE: Fitness for college and life, St. Louis, Mosby, 1994; and Rosato, FD: Fitness and wellness: The physical connection, St. Paul, West Publishing Company, 1994; **p. 137 (standards),** From Thygerson A: Fitness and health: lifestyle strategies, Boston, Jones and Bartlett Publishers, 1989; **p. 141 (chart),** Reprinted with permission of Macmillan Publishing Company from Practical measurements for evaluation in physical education, fourth edition by Barry L. Johnson and Jack K. Nelson. Copyright 1986 by Macmillan Publishing Company.

Chapter 6: p. 145 (Fig. 6-1), US Department of Agriculture/US Department of Health and Human Services, August 1992; **pp. 146-147 (Table 6-1),** Recommended dietary allowances, edition 10, 1989 by the National Academy of Sciences, National Academy Press, Washington, DC, reprinted by permission; **pp. 146, 149, 166, 168 (Tables 6-2, 6-4, Fig. 6-8, Table 6-11),** Source: Food and Drug Administration; **p. 148 (Fig. 6-2),** From US Department of Health and Human Services:

The Surgeon General's report on nutrition and health: summary and recommendations, Washington, DC, US Government Printing Office, 1988; **pp. 158, 160, 162 (Table 6-7, Fig. 6-5, Table 6-8)**, Data from US Department of Agriculture: Home and garden bulletin no. 72, nutritive value of foods, Washington, DC, US Government Printing Office, 1988; **p. 161 (Fig. 6-6)**, Source: Mayer J: What is a gram of fat and how much should you eat? *Tufts University Diet and Nutrition Letter* 7(8):3, 1989; **p. 163 (Fig. 6-7)**, Source: American Cancer Society: Learn to eat for better health, NY, The Association, 1992; p. 169 (Table 6-12), Data from Williams SR: Nutrition and diet therapy, edition 7, St. Louis, Mosby, 1993.

Chapter 7: p. 187 (Table 7-3), Reprinted with permission from the Metropolitan Life Insurance Company, New York; **p. 189 (Tables 7-4, 7-5)**, Adapted from Wardlaw GM and Insel PM: Perspectives in nutrition, edition 2, St. Louis, Mosby, 1993; **pp. 193-194 (Tables 7-6, 7-7)**, From Jackson, AS, Pollack ML: Practical assessment of body composition, *The Physician and Sportsmedicine* 13(5):86, 1985. Reproduced with permission of McGraw-Hill, Inc.

Chapter 8: p. 208 (Table 8-2), Data from Zuti B and Golding L: Comparing diet and exercise as weight reduction tools, *The Physician and Sportsmedicine* 4:49-54, 1976; **pp. 210-211 (Table 8-4)**, Modified from *The Walking Magazine*, June 1989, copyright 1989, Walking, Inc, 9-11 Harcourt Street, Boston, Mass, 02116, reprinted with permission; **p. 213 (Table 8-5)**, Source: Physical fitness for practically everybody: the Consumers Union report on exercise, Mount Vernon, NY, The Consumers Union of the United States, 1983; **p. 216 (Table 8-7)**, Adapted from the Surgeon General's Report on Nutrition and Health, Washington, DC, US Department of Health and Human Services, 1988; **p. 218 (Figs. 8-5, 8-6)**, Adapted from the American Psychiatric Association, Diagnostic and statistical manual of mental disorders, Washington, DC, 1987.

Chapter 9: p. 234 (Fig. 9-3), From Selye H: Stress without distress, Philadelphia, JB Lippincott Co, 1974; **p. 238 (Fig. 9-5)**, Adapted from Williams SR: Nutrition and

diet therapy, edition 7, St. Louis, Mosby, 1993; **p. 247**, From Holmes TH and Rahe RH: The social adjustment rating scale, *Journal of Psychosomatic Research*, reprinted with permission of Pergamon Press, copyright 1967; **p. 249**, From What's your stress style? *American Health* April 1986, pp. 41-45, reprinted with permission of *The New York Times*; **p. 251**, *American Health Magazine*, Copyright, September 1984, pp. 64-77.

Chapter 10: pp. 258-259, From Schlaadt RG and Shannon PT: Drugs of choice, edition 2, Englewood Cliffs, NJ, Prentice Hall, 1986; **pp. 261-263 (Table 10-1)**, From What works: schools without drugs, US Department of Education, 1988; **p. 264 (Table 10-2)**, From the National Center for Drugs and Biologics, Food and Drug Administration, Washington, DC; **p. 266 (Fig. 10-5)**, Source: Alcoholics Anonymous World Services, Inc; **p. 268 (Fig. 10-7)**, Adapted from the *Mayo Clinic Health Letter*; **p. 275**, Quiz from Is AA for you? Reprinted with permission of Alcoholics Anonymous World Services, Inc.

Chapter 11: p. 285 (Table 11-1), From Health psychology: an introduction to behavior and health, edition 2, by Linda Brannon and Jess Feist. Copyright 1992 by Wadsworth, Inc, reprinted by permission of Brooks/Cole Publishing Company, Pacific Grove, Calif, 93950.

Chapter 12: p. 295 (Fig. 12-1), Adapted from Take control of your health: five do's and five don'ts. American Cancer Society; **p. 300 (Fig. 12-5), pp. 311-312**, Adapted from the American Cancer Society.

Chapter 13: p. 320 (Fig 13-3), Source: Price J, Telljohann S, Roberts S, and Smit D: Effects of incentives in an inner city junior high school smoking prevention program, *Journal of Health Education* 23(7):388-296, 1992; **p. 327 (Fig. 13-4)**, Source: Lipman M: Office visit, *Consumers Reports Health Letter* 1(2):14, 1989; **p. 329 (Fig. 13-5)**, Data source: Editors: The prevention index '89, summary report: a report card on the nation's health, Emmaus, Penn, 1989, Rodale Press, Inc, pp. 8-9; **p. 331 (Fig. 13-6)**, Source: Newman J: Things to keep in your

medicine cabinet, *American Health* 11(2):104, 1992; **p. 333 (Fig. 13-7)**, Source: Impact of fraudulent claims on health care costs, *Statistical Bulletin* 17(4):14, 1991.

Photo Credits

Chapter 1: pp. 0, 7, 9, 14, CLG Photographics, Inc.

Chapter 2: pp. 26, 38, 39, 46, CLG Photographics, Inc.

Chapter 3: pp. 56, 61, 72, CLG Photographics, Inc; **p. 65,** Sheri Seiser.

Chapter 4: p. 88, CLG Photographics, Inc; **pp. 91-100, 115, 117, 118,** Sheri Seiser.

Chapter 5: pp. 120, 123-126, 128, 129, 133, 135, 137, 139, 141, Sheri Seiser.

Chapter 6: pp. 142, 147, 155, CLG Photographics, Inc; **pp. 152, 159, 164, 167,** Linsley Photographics; **p. 157,** NutraSweet, Courtesy Monsanto Corporation.

Chapter 7: pp. 182, 190-192, Sheri Seiser.

Chapter 8: p. 203, Sheri Seiser; **p. 205,** Linsley Photographics; **pp. 212, 214, 215,** CLG Photographics, Inc.

Chapter 9: pp. 230, 243, 244, CLG Photographics, Inc.

Chapter 10: pp. 256, 271, CLG Photographics, Inc.

Chapter 11: p. 278, CLG Photographics, Inc; **p. 280,** Habif: Clinical Dermatology, ed 2, 1990, Mosby; **p. 281,** Centers for Disease Control, Atlanta.

Chapter 12: pp. 292, 307, CLG Photographics, Inc; **p. 298,** Courtesy American Academy of Dermatology; **p. 305,** Tate, Seeley, Stephens: Understanding the Human Body, 1994, Mosby, photo by Paul Manske.

Chapter 13: pp. 314, 325, CLG Photographics, Inc; **pp. 318, 322,** Linsley Photographics.